FAMILY LAW

Cavendish
Publishing
Limited

London • Sydney • Portland, Oregon

FAMILY LAW

Frances Burton, LLB, LLM, MA, Barrister
Principal Lecturer, University of the West of England
Director, BVC Open Learning
Bristol Institute of Legal Practice, University of the West of England

Cavendish
Publishing
Limited

London • Sydney • Portland, Oregon

First published in Great Britain 2003 by
Cavendish Publishing Limited, The Glass House,
Wharton Street, London WC1X 9PX, United Kingdom
Telephone: + 44 (0)20 7278 8000   Facsimile: + 44 (0)20 7278 8080
Email: info@cavendishpublishing.com
Website: www.cavendishpublishing.com

Published in the United States by Cavendish Publishing
c/o International Specialized Book Services,
5824 NE Hassalo Street, Portland,
Oregon 97213-3644, USA

Published in Australia by Cavendish Publishing (Australia) Pty Ltd
3/303 Barrenjoey Road, Newport, NSW 2106, Australia

British Library Cataloguing in Publication Data
Burton, Frances
Family law
1 Domestic relations – Great Britain
I Title
346.4'1'015

Library of Congress Cataloguing in Publication Data
Data available

ISBN 1-85941-471-0

1 3 5 7 9 10 8 6 4 2

Printed and bound in Great Britain

To my family law students (who told me what they wanted included)

PREFACE

This book aims to bridge the gap between the traditional academic texts and the vocational course manuals used on the Legal Practice and Bar Vocational Courses, and also to act as an introduction to a specialist subject for practitioners seeking a working knowledge of family law.

It also aims to address the increasing impossibility of understanding the academic issues in family law without some grasp of the procedural impact upon the substantive law.

Such a comparatively short book can only scratch the surface of some topics which are not included in all academic syllabuses, but which are worth flagging for a comprehensive overview of the widening subject area of family law. This may be particularly useful for vocational course students who will encounter in practice a wide variety of situations which will require them to think laterally as much as any academic student. For all readers seeking a wider and deeper understanding than can be imparted by an account of the principles of law and practice, the suggested further reading has some more detailed literature. For distance learning students, some of these can be accessed electronically from the publishers or the well known electronic library sources.

Frances Burton
University of the West of England
January 2003

CONTENTS

Contents

Contents

TABLE OF CASES

TABLE OF STATUTES

TABLE OF STATUTORY INSTRUMENTS

Treaties and Conventions

Regulations

Directions

PART I

MARRIAGE AND COHABITATION

CHAPTER 1

INTRODUCTION

1.1 WHAT IS FAMILY LAW?

Family law is of fairly recent invention, especially as an academic subject, credit for this achievement usually going to Professor Peter Bromley, who published the first edition of his now well known textbook in 1957. In the same decade, a practical text on 'Divorce', as the general subject of family law was then called, was published by Dmitri Tolstoy. Tolstoy was an ex-patriate Russian aristocrat practising at the common law end of the English Bar, and the father of the then equally unknown historian Nikolai Tolstoy, later famously sued by Lord Aldington for defamation in relation to the West's alleged post-Second World War betrayal of the Cossacks. At this time, only 50 years ago, Sir John Mortimer had not elevated to literary fame, nor into the realm of classic television entertainment, the career of his father, the blind divorce lawyer Clifford Mortimer, and neither family law in general nor divorce (its best known feature) in particular featured in serious academic programmes.

Indeed, Lord Shawcross (then Sir Hartley Shawcross, the post-war Labour Attorney General) commented that this was a 'very simple branch of the law' which required 'no study or thought at all'. Its precise scope has, therefore, over the years been by no means as settled as the province of other mainstream core or optional subjects of the qualifying law degree, either in terms of the perceived extent of the subject area for academic or vocational purposes, or within the undergraduate curriculum, where it is now usually a popular second or third year optional subject, although specific coverage varies enormously from law school to law school.

It is thus difficult in modern times to define 'family law'. First, one must define 'the family', a task hard enough in itself, since contemporary human rights law has accepted that a mere two persons who have never met but are linked by blood – such as the unmarried father and his child found to be a *de facto* family in the case of *Keegan v Ireland* (1994) 18 EHRR 342 – may comprise 'a family' sufficient to enable a breach of the right to 'family life'. Moreover, family law now operates in an international dimension, bringing into the ever widening concept of family law norms and traditions different from those which in the UK, and more specifically the jurisdiction of England and Wales, we take for granted. Article 8(1) of the European Convention on Human Rights and Fundamental Freedoms (ECHR) does not define the family life for which it guarantees a right to respect, although *Keegan* makes clear that 'the notion of "the family" ... is not confined solely to marriage based relationships and may encompass other *de facto* "family" where the parties are living together outside of marriage'.

Family law is therefore a law of relationships, between adults *inter se*, between adults and children, and between both adults and children and the State, as continually influenced by social and demographic changes. It is a body of rules of different types (some rules being so loose that they are basically discretions, a distinguishing feature of family law) and it defines and alters status, provides specific machinery for regulating property, protects both individuals and groups and attempts in so doing to support the family structure of our society. The current edition of Bromley's *Family Law* suggests that the family is almost impossible to define. Cretney, on the other hand, thinks that the 'key factor' running through family law is parentage, with a consequent focus on the child. Eekelaar and Maclean approach family law as a socio-legal study, and Barton and Hibbs examine the various family members (primary, secondary and tertiary) in order to define whether family law is 'interested' in them or not. Diduck and Kaganas look at the American feminist perspective, which seems to centre on the mother and child, although it is apparently accepted that a man could perform the 'mother' parenting role. After a canter along the philosophy corridor, they conclude sensibly that, as there is no statutory or common law definition of 'the family', then 'a family is what the ordinary man on the street thinks it is', and cite a series of cases in support, beginning with the housing case of *Sefton Holdings and Cairns* [1988] 2 FLR 109, *per* Lloyd LJ, and ending with the more recent *Fitzpatrick v Sterling Housing Association Ltd* [1999] 3 WLR 115 (HL); [1998] 1 FLR 6 (CA). The former was a tenancy succession case in which it was necessary to decide whether two unrelated unmarried women (not apparently in any form of lesbian relationship) were 'a family' so that the survivor could succeed to the deceased's statutory tenancy. The latter was an overt same sex couple case in which in the Court of Appeal Ward LJ, dissenting, wanted to find that the cohabitants were either the equivalent of persons living together as husband and wife or alternatively were simply 'a family', a view which was upheld in the House of Lords and has subsequently been developed in the case of *Mendoza v Gheidon* [2002] EWCA Civ 1533 to accept same sex couples as the equivalent of husband and wife.

Some university courses approach the scope of family law in a literal sense and offer a study of 'family life' from the cradle to the grave, including the law of inheritance, on the basis that many more marriages and other partnerships end by death than by divorce. The truth of the matter is that family law in modern times can be whatever a course designer wants it to be. Moreover, to spend much time wondering what is the precise extent of family law will only waste time which will already be pressing if any family course is to encompass a fraction of the peripheral influences which now impact upon the core topics, without some coverage of which those parts of the family course studied in detail will be somewhat sparse and dry. This is because of the fast changing nature of those influences, and of the finite nature of the time available to study any topic. Each year, parts of courses must be removed to accommodate new material or the course becomes unmanageable.

Contemporary academic family courses tend to include some sociological, political and procedural background to the law because of the impact of those peripheral areas of study on the way in which the black letter law operates. What the student of a modern family law course is therefore likely to gain from study is an understanding of how the modern family, however that is composed, works in law and practice. This is also the approach of this book, directing the reader to further sources where greater depth may be plumbed once the principles have been discovered.

1.1.1 The changing face of family law

Family law, in both academic and practical contexts, is an especially fast moving subject because it reflects life as it exists rather than making abstract rules for observance by society – a trend first identified in Maine's classic text, *Ancient Law*. Thus, any family law student or teacher must have a sound grasp of the basic *principles* of law and practice. The design and delivery of a well balanced family law course will usually benefit from a good deal of planning and skillful execution, within which the course leader's own subjective views and preferences will naturally play a part. Yet there is a basic common core of black letter law that every student family lawyer will need to acquire before any of the now extensive interdisciplinary influences, such as socio-legal studies and the wealth of empirical research around family law concepts, can be understood. One reason for this is that while family law is necessarily a human subject – because of its subject matter, and all students therefore bring human experience to its study which should help them in applying the discretionary rules that family law consists of – they do need to develop the new skill of looking at family law in a different way from the way they regard more traditional subjects such as contract or land law. It is the development of this practical as well as academic approach which this book aims to impart, by explaining how the law works in practice and, where possible, why it is as it is. The concept is not new: Professor Cretney, himself a solicitor, has been looking at the practical impact of the black letter law in his textbooks through several editions. It was doubtless this approach which rendered so successful his critical guides to the Family Law Act 1996, which were instrumental in flagging the impractical features of that Act and the extreme likelihood that they would simply not work in practice (see Chapter 22).

The new student of family law should therefore first be encouraged not to fall for the general assertion that family law is not really law at all, but to look at it in a different light from other law modules. Family law is definitely 'law', but there is no doubt that it is 'different', and not only in academic terms. Among practitioners, even dedicated litigators have discovered that the practice of family law demands a different approach (although in the context of the Woolf reforms in civil litigation generally, which require alternatives to litigation to be sought first before issuing proceedings, and then again at the earliest case management stage, the formerly exclusive family law approach will no longer be unique).

Secondly, those new to family law should be encouraged to absorb the culture of this distinct breed of law so as to see themselves from first base as family lawyers who must constantly remind themselves of its difference from other substantive law, and must continually hone their practice of its culture. Some undergraduates find this difficult, instinctively clinging to the black letter law of statute and precedent alone. Indeed, it is not so long since family law was approached in a much more legalistic way than is the fashion today. The watershed for this sea-change was when the Divorce Reform Act 1969 was passed, replacing the former entirely fault based divorce law with a system more attuned to modern life – still partially fault based but also recognising the complex nature of marriage and the interaction with it of other family relationships. From within this statutory watershed also emerged the multidisciplinary influences that generated the idea that family law was in a different category from other litigation.

Students who have difficulty grasping the nature of modern family law can often profit from a study of some of the early 1970s cases from which it is obvious that the older judges of the period also had difficulty in making the necessary conceptual changes. Some examples may be seen in Chapter 8, where there are several instances of judicial wrestling with the new concept of adultery as being a symptom, and not a cause, of marriage breakdown. Similar problems have been experienced with relating the new basis of 'behaviour' (in that it may be 'unreasonable' for the spouse to tolerate by continuing to cohabit with the offender) to the pre-1969 ground of 'cruelty', an altogether simpler concept which most people had little difficulty understanding. So students need not be alone in growing into the concepts of modern family law and the culture of their application in the round.

Nor are undergraduate students the only ones who may find difficulty in getting to grips with the profound impact that the reformed law of divorce and children has had on the law in practice. It is unusual today to find any generalist practitioner, even one who does not practise much in family law, still displaying that old fashioned pre-1969 approach which under the umbrella of the unreformed law of divorce treated marriage breakdown as a contest which had to be won by an 'innocent' party and 'lost' by the guilty. Such a practitioner, usually of a certain age, may occasionally still be found fighting a case brought under the Inheritance (Provision for Family and Dependants) Act 1975 where a divorced wife who has not remarried, and receives ongoing periodical payments which usually die with a former husband, seeks the provision she might have had had there been a clean break on her divorce. This type of practitioner usually relies, albeit apparently under the modern law, on all the old pre-1969 ideas: often the fossilised view of guilt and innocence that an older practitioner retains provides the stark contrast which the student needs to understand how family law has achieved its 'different' character when compared with the approach of the younger practitioner who, having studied and worked under the reformed law, knows no other. Similar stark contrasts arise in child cases, where in an era of joint parental responsibility any mud-slinging against each other by the parents is now actively discouraged: the pre-1969 lawyer, academic and practitioner alike, knew no other way to obtain an order but by character assassination of the child's other parent. Now the academic student is often confused by the apparently mutually exclusive nature of the law as read in the statute, and the practice, which the good lecturer or tutor will explain is not at all as it sounds in the books.

For this reason, some older cases, even those decided by distinguished judges, may need to be treated with caution, because on top of the changes in the law there has inevitably been significant social change in the intervening years, so that the norms on the basis of which such decisions were made will also have changed. Further, the student should also be cautioned that precedent often has a limited use in family law, either because a statute expressly says so, or because, as family law has a highly discretionary element, it is rare that a case will ever be precisely on all fours with an apparent precedent, which may therefore only offer useful guidance for consistency rather than a rule. It follows that this constant honing of modern themes means that while there is a place in the study of family law for the latest cases, the basic underlying principles are really what matters, because any recent decisions, unless in the House of Lords (and even there their Lordships can rapidly change their mind), may only indicate how some judges are thinking, or were at the time they decided the cases in question. All this may indicate why, nearly a decade after the Divorce Reform Act 1969 had been consolidated in the Matrimonial Causes Act 1973, a group of family solicitors decided that the time had come to recognise the way in which family law had grown away from other litigation, and to lay down some principles of practice.

1.2 HOW FAMILY LAW DIFFERS FROM OTHER CIVIL LITIGATION

It is now two decades since it was realised by practitioners that family law in general, and paradoxically divorce law in particular, could not be regarded as just another aspect of civil litigation, although for the first 130 years since the initial Matrimonial Causes Act was passed in 1857 there were few lawyers who realised this and fewer still who adopted an approach to family law work which reflected such a view. The Solicitors Family Law Association (SFLA), a well known group of specialist practitioners founded in 1982, must be credited with taking the significant step of introducing a constructive and civilised approach to the resolution of legal matters following matrimonial breakdown.

Innovative as this was at the time, it is now universally accepted that the legal resolution of family problems is not conveniently achieved by a predominantly litigious approach, even where a firm has no specialist family department. The SFLA was initially established to take family matters, as far as possible, out of the atmosphere of contentious litigation, with the aim of achieving agreed solutions which, while not substantially different from what the court would order if the matter were acrimoniously contested, might with co-operation be achieved at less cost, emotionally as well as financially.

As time has passed, this philosophy has become much more important since, for example, the passing of the Children Act 1989, which established the relatively innovative concept of parental responsibility and encouraged divorcing parents to continue good parenting regardless of the end of their marriage. However, whether or not a solicitor joins the 3,000 strong membership, the Law Society recommends that all solicitors practising family law observe the SFLA's principles and Code of Practice, adherence to which is made clear not to be a sign of weakness and not in any way to place the client at a disadvantage.

Of course, there are still solicitors who do not observe the Code, and who still insist on conducting matters in an aggressive and acrimonious manner, but the SFLA philosophy is now so well established that the majority do stick firmly to its principles even when encountering an aggressive opponent of the old fashioned disposition, and do not give in to the obvious temptation to retaliate in kind. There are in fact now few such aggressive solicitors; where they do still exist their identities are well known in the profession, and their approach well recognised for one unfortunately still rooted in the pre-1969 divorce and child law which was entirely adversarial and fault based. Experience has shown the bulk of the profession that the best response to the few diehards is one of increased politeness and courtesy backed up where necessary by immediate and decisive court action, which is in no way precluded or inhibited by the Code. The SFLA's principles merely require that litigation should not be the first resort where matters may instead be conveniently negotiated to start with and then formalised procedurally afterwards. This approach necessarily influences judges at every level and is to be easily identified in contemporary Court of Appeal judgments. It should also influence the approach of academic students to the interpretation of black letter family law.

1.3 THE FUNCTION OF FAMILY LAW

With the change in the philosophy of family practitioners has come a widening of the range of sub-divisions of family law, so now the modern family lawyer has an increasingly unwieldy portfolio of topics to service. In academic terms, as a survey for the National Centre for Legal Education's manual *Teaching Family Law* showed, this has meant that undergraduate courses now either embrace one (so called 'long thin') family course spread over one academic year, or two or more (so called 'short fat') modules studied over two semesters. The long thin course usually covers marriage, divorce and other decrees, including financial relief and increasingly mediation, plus child law and the unmarried family. The short fat modules course usually consists of one module covering marriage, divorce and allied topics, while child law – including children's rights, child abduction, adoption, human assisted reproduction and termination of pregnancy – makes up a separate course. However, as mentioned above, some courses look at the family in a wider context, including a study of the termination of marriage, and give greater space to the study of the consequences of cohabitation, and of the wider concepts of the family, such as in homosexual and extended family relationships. Some universities actually identify this imaginative type of course quite separately with labels such as 'the law of relationships'.

Inevitably, in this way the function of family law comes under scrutiny, and the influence of the socio-legal dimension increases in direct proportion to the introduction of such innovative topics depending on the space and weight given to them. This is, in practice, not only inevitable, but probably pragmatic and desirable. Even the President of the Family Division, Dame Elizabeth Butler-Sloss, upon taking office as Head of Division in the late summer of 1999, expressly commented in her first statements to the media on the changing shape and nature of the family which could be noted during the 40 years since she had commenced practice at the Bar. Shortly afterwards, the House of Lords, in the context of succession to a tenancy by a member of a deceased tenant's family, accepted that the definition of 'the family' was now to be construed in a contemporary light (*Fitzpatrick v Sterling Housing Association*, above). However, the House did stop short of recognising such a family member as a 'spouse', despite the claim of the survivor of the homosexual relationship, which had given rise to his recognition as a member of the deceased's family, that they were non-married partners in all other respects on the same footing as married persons. Addressing this point, Lord Slynn said that a 'spouse' was not to be interpreted at the present time as including two persons of the same sex who were intimately linked in a settled relationship, having all the characteristics of a marriage except for the fact that the parties could not have children. He based this view on the fact that in that particular case, the successful claim of the appellant to be a 'family member' depended on a 1988 amendment of the Rent Act 1977, into which could not, in his view, be read the words 'same sex partner' in lieu of 'spouse'. This was no doubt a convenient peg on which to hang this particular decision, since same sex partners are of course (without resorting to adoption) able to have their own genetic children in the same way as heterosexual couples, by means of human assisted reproduction, as well publicised surrogacy arrangements have recently shown in which sperm from both male partners was used in artificial insemination (a case only reported in the popular press), but see the further development of this evolving concept of the family in the *Mendoza* case (CA) above at 1.1.

It seems, therefore, that it is accepted that in the law of adult relationships marriage alone no longer defines the family, and nor does heterosexual cohabitation. Precisely how wide the family extends is uncertain, as the contemporary concept has spread through both blood and marriage *and* cohabitational (and perhaps *formerly* cohabitational) relationships. Certainly the concept of 'associated persons' envisaged by Pt IV of the Family Law Act 1996 has thrown the net very wide: in the practitioner context the concept of 'elder abuse', and the relatively new idea that there should be some protection for the elder relative akin to that afforded to children by the Children Act 1989, suggests that the family has an existence under the umbrella of the law that now regulates relationships from cradle to grave. In this context, the statement of Neuberger J in *Re The Estate of John Watson (Decd)* (1998) *The Times*, 31 December, that the court 'should not ignore the multifarious nature of marital relations', would appear to be more in tune with current social trends than the approach of the Crown (in that case claiming the whole estate as *bona vacantia*) for whom the Treasury Solicitor said that the relationship of a couple in their 50s, who had given up sexual relations but otherwise shared financial and domestic responsibilities, was merely a house sharing arrangement at arm's length. Such an approach certainly seems legalistic at a time when all cohabitants are constantly being urged to make clear financial arrangements, precisely because in the absence of a marriage certificate (giving rights on divorce under ss 23 and 24 of the Matrimonial Causes Act 1973) cohabitants who have provided the 'sweat capital' in a relationship are at risk of having few or no rights if a separation occurs during their joint lives (although the position is usually a little better on the death of a partner in such circumstances). The Inheritance (Provision for Families and Dependants) Act 1975 provides for persons living 'as the wife' of the deceased, as Mr Watson's partner was held by Neuberger J to be doing.

The student should nevertheless not be discouraged by the wider spread of topics potentially to be covered as a result of this expansion of the subject, nor be suspicious of the validity of the interdisciplinary dimension. Family law has come a long way since the first Matrimonial Causes Act 1857 (as the historical background explained in Chapter 6 shows). The concept of unity in the arts, developed not long after that Act by the philosopher and reformer William Morris, is now taken for granted: perhaps when a future President of the Family Division (now probably still at law school) takes office in the 2040s, the unity of sources of family law will not only be taken for granted, but will be seen in the same informative light as the crucial developments of the past 40 years commented upon by Dame Elizabeth Butler-Sloss in 1999.

Since family law is so wide and diffuse in scope, it is in the interests of students to keep abreast of changing trends and of trends within trends. The journal *Family Law* is useful for this, since it summarises and comments on cases in each issue and offers articles on currently controversial topics and points of interest. It guides critical thinking in a way which may be useful to the student who does not have time to seek out and read all the potentially interesting or impacting peripheral texts.

1.4 FAMILY LAW AND HUMAN RIGHTS

The greatest changes to family law are probably yet to come. The Human Rights Act 1998 came into force in October 2000, enabling the ECHR to be enforced directly against the State as part of English law. The articles of the Convention most likely to impact upon family law are as follows:

- Article 6 (right to a fair trial).
- Article 8 (right to respect for private and family life).
- Article 9 (right to freedom of thought).
- Article 12 (right to marry).
- Article 14 (prohibition of discrimination).

It will be clear from 1.3, above, that Art 8 does not refer solely to marriage based relationships, and the existing Strasbourg case law already indicates that a very slight relationship between a father and his child will be enough to invoke the concept of 'family'. Those whose sole contact has been to provide sperm for artificial insemination will clearly not be able to show a sufficient connection to establish a familial relationship, but (especially as the Convention is a living, legal organism and not a static body of rules) anything more, however temporary, may well be sufficient to create the necessary relationship. It should be noted that the Court of Appeal has already sounded a warning about using common sense in invoking human rights arguments: in *Daniels v Walker* (2000) *The Times*, 17 May, the Master of the Rolls called for a 'responsible attitude' from lawyers raising such arguments, so as not to clog the courts with an unnecessary workload generated by meretricious points. Lord Woolf expressed the hope that judges would take a robust attitude with inappropriate arguments, which he categorised as any which take 'the court down blind alleys'. There has already been some practitioner consideration of whether this might lead to adverse costs orders.

INTRODUCTION

WHAT IS FAMILY LAW?

Family law is a young academic subject, having been recognised as such since the 1950s. There is no statutory or common law definition of 'the family', nor any clear boundaries to the topics and issues to be studied on a family law course. The subject area divides naturally into, first, a law of adult relationships and, secondly, child law: the former tends to cover marriage, nullity, divorce and judicial separation (and financial relief following or without decree), and some introduction to the law of unmarried relationships, and the latter a study of the Children Act 1989, and of wardship, children's rights, child abduction, adoption, and human assisted reproduction.

Family law defines and alters status, protects individuals and groups, provides machinery to divide and manage property, and attempts to support the family as a desirable social unit.

THE CHANGING FACE OF FAMILY LAW

Family law is a relatively 'new' subject area of law, both in the academic and vocational fields. The first Matrimonial Causes Act was in 1857 and the first academic textbook, establishing family law as a recognised subject in the academy, Bromley's *Family Law*, was first published in 1957. Family law is often claimed not to contain much 'law' but is interdisciplinary and supplemented by socio-legal studies. The nature of family law either side of the Divorce Reform Act 1969 is significantly different, and its practical application even more so.

HOW FAMILY LAW DIFFERS FROM OTHER CIVIL LITIGATION

Family law litigation is not conducted adversarially except by a few old fashioned practitioners. The contemporary approach is co-operative, putting the overall welfare of the family first, and seeking alternatives to litigation before resorting to court proceedings. This was an initiative generated by the establishment of the SFLA in 1982. It is not seen as a weak approach, but as one which facilitates the resolution of family disputes in a timely and constructive manner, particularly since the Children Act 1989 promoted the concept of parental responsibility, enduring on the part of both parents in relation to their children even after divorce.

THE FUNCTION OF FAMILY LAW

The academic study of family law is no longer confined to one type of family law course, as the potential field of study is so wide that individual law schools often now assemble their own menu of preferred topics, usually in one family law course over an academic year, or two or more shorter single semester courses, roughly divided into marriage, divorce, cohabitation (and the attendant topics such as financial relief) in one module and child law in a second. Some courses are actually identified as a study of the law of relationships. Academic writers increasingly accept that family law is either what the ordinary person thinks it is, or (since teaching time and resources are finite) what the course leader has selected to teach.

The concept of the family has changed over time and is now recognised as not being restricted to married families or heterosexual cohabitation, but to include the extended family, possibly even after divorce and dissolution of cohabitational relationships, and even to include a law of 'elder abuse' requiring statutory protection. Thus, family law in practice now effectively equates to a law of relationships. The Human Rights Act 1998 is likely to impact significantly on family law.

CHAPTER 2

MARRIAGE

2.1 MARRIAGE: A STATUS

Despite the fact that neither marriage nor heterosexual cohabitation now alone defines the family, it is still usually important to establish whether there is a marriage or other partnering relationship, since such status is at present still crucial to most statutory family law. This may change in the foreseeable future, as increasing claims are made with regard to parentage as the core status relationship (see Chapter 1). The government is at present still explicitly supporting the institution of marriage as the best environment in which to bring up children. Nevertheless, confusing messages are coming out from this source, which also espouses the principle that children's interests should be paramount and identifies this as the 'first principle' of modern family law (see the Home Office's consultation document, *Supporting Families*, 1998). Thus, has Tolstoy's *Divorce,* which alone constituted the family law of 50 years ago, been overtaken by a wider view?

2.1.1 The essential validity of a marriage: 'valid', 'void' and 'voidable'

No 'marriage' can either be dissolved by divorce or annulled pursuant to the law of nullity if no valid marriage has been contracted in the first place. See, for example, *Hall v Jagger* (1999), unreported, 13 September, where the 'divorce' suit of the model and actress Jerry Hall against rock star Mick Jagger was nevertheless settled on the basis that Ms Hall received a financial package such as might have been ordered on decree of divorce or nullity. However, the court appears not to have actually pronounced either decree since the 'marriage', celebrated on a beach in Bali, but without the necessary formalities even in that jurisdiction, appears not to have been valid and moreover to have been *void* (as opposed to *voidable*) from the start. Mr Jagger may have been inspired by the earlier case of *Gereis v Yacoub* [1997] 1 FLR 854 (a Coptic marriage in a Coptic church in London which was not registered for marriages) where the husband robustly argued that as the church was unregistered there was no marriage, but as the ceremony appeared to be merely an ordinary Christian marriage in an unregistered building, this defence failed.

It is important to understand the difference of status, depending on whether a marriage is 'valid', 'void' or 'voidable':

(1) A 'valid' marriage is one which complies with the relevant law and practice in all respects: the parties will be man and wife, it can be ended only by divorce or death and on death the survivor will be a widow or widower.

(2) A 'void' marriage is one which has some incurable defect, so that it could never be valid, whatever the parties wished. This type of defective marriage requires the parties who wish to maintain the relationship to start again from scratch, with a new

effective ceremony, this time complying with the law and practice of any jurisdiction which has a matrimonial regime, and if in the meantime one of the parties dies, it will be too late to achieve the status of marriage, as the deceased will have died single and the surviving party is a single person.

(3) A 'voidable' marriage is one which is valid for all purposes until 'avoided', a process which can only be effected by the parties to the marriage who may affirm it instead if they wish (and no other person may attack its status). Such a marriage will usually be ended if the parties wish by an 'annulment' on a nullity decree, but might subsist until death, after which it is too late for a nullity decree, in which case it will be ended by death and the surviving party will be a widow or widower.

Marriage is, therefore, a definable status which requires to be established by proof of the marriage in due form before the court can entertain a suit for divorce in order to dissolve it, and in the case of apparently void marriages where a declaration of nullity is sought, whether there *is* actually a marriage to *annul* or not will depend on whether the marriage is in fact void or merely voidable. In the former, while a declaration may be sought for any necessary purpose, in truth the marriage may be treated as void from the start and the declaration *is* only evidence of that fact; in the case of the latter, a decree is actually required to annul the union, which will otherwise be treated as valid until any decree of nullity is obtained. See Chapter 3.

Marriage is also a contract and has been defined as 'a voluntary union for life of one man and one woman to the exclusion of all others' (*per* Lord Penzance in *Hyde v Hyde* (1866) LR 1 P & D 130, at p 133). It is a contract which creates a legal relationship with mutual rights and duties. This is particularly important in the era of European and human rights law, as the approach to marriage in English law has always been that marriage is voluntary, for life, heterosexual and monogamous: since English law continues not to embrace the contemporary amendments to those traditional qualities of Christian marriage which are accepted in some other jurisdictions, the European Court of Human Rights has until recently always upheld our right to sustain this stance and treated our core beliefs that these concepts are central to our understanding of marriage in English law as part of our margin of appreciation (see further at 2.2.3, below).

2.1.2   Essential formalities of marriage

In view of the practical consequences described above, formalities are important, and this includes demonstrable capacity to marry. Until Lord Hardwicke's Act (also called the Clandestine Marriages Act) of 1753, there were few formalities for marriage, which could be effected *inter alia* by simple declaration. The background to this Act is rooted in one of the above four central concepts, namely that marriage must be voluntary.

Prior to 1753, marriage in effect was left to the canon law of the church and the common law recognised such marriages as proceeding from consent of the parties and their declaration that they took each other as husband and wife, a situation which subsisted in Scotland until 1940 and is still recognised in some American States (eg, the Carolinas where spouses spending the 'honeymoon' in that State might still cure any ceremonial defect elsewhere – a fact obviously not known to Jerry Hall). In Scotland it is still possible to establish marriage by 'cohabitation with habit and repute' unless the parties have specifically rejected the institution of marriage, of which Ms Hall was perhaps similarly unaware since none of the numerous Hall/Jagger homes was located in Scotland.

In the Middle Ages, the emphasis was on the contract of marriage, which was therefore the origin of the requirement that marriages needed to be demonstrably consensual. The custom was to agree a marriage contract and then to have the ceremony blessed in church, although before the Council of Trent in 1563 no religious ceremony as such was required: there was a simple declaration *per verba de praesenti* or *de futuro* ('I take you' – or I 'shall take you' – 'as my wife/husband') and the marriage was binding as soon as consummated. It was even common for the religious ceremony to take place only when the bride had proved that she could become pregnant, because marriages were often important for providing an heir to property. In due course, however, a custom developed of exchanging the vows before a priest or (after the Reformation) a clerk in holy orders, and eventually there were three ways of contracting a marriage, either as above, or 'clandestinely' (ie, speaking the words in private without the presence of the priest or clerk and subsequently consummating the marriage by sexual intercourse) or in church after publication of banns or with a licence (and after obtaining any necessary consents for minors).

The clandestine marriage option, which was sufficiently valid as to make any subsequent marriage void, was a problem because it meant that no one could safely marry without fear that there might be already in existence an earlier clandestine marriage which made the subsequent union void. Moreover, as women's property passed under even a clandestine marriage to her husband, there were predictable abuses, especially as the consent of a parent was not required for a minor to contract a clandestine marriage, although a priest was sometimes used to conduct the ceremony – for example, in the Fleet prison marriages where priests incarcerated there would preside over a ceremony for a fee, so that the parties could say that they had made their vows before a priest.

To tackle this abuse, Lord Hardwicke's Act therefore required that all marriages should be in church according to the rites of the Church of England, in a parish where one of the parties resided and following publication of banns there and in the other party's parish. Moreover, the marriage had to be performed by a clergyman in the presence of two witnesses. If either party was under the age of 21, parental consent was required, or dispensation of parental consent had to be sought elsewhere, at first from the Lord Chancellor and later by application to the court.

The result was the growth of a marriage trade at Gretna Green in Scotland, where some parties fled in order to avoid the new stringent requirements, particularly that of parental consent. The Act was subsequently amended and then replaced by later 19th century statutes which enabled those who were not members of the Church of England (and therefore unwilling to use its rites) to marry in other ceremonies: from 1836, the Marriage Act and Births and Deaths Registration Act enabled other religious buildings to be registered for marriages and also enabled civil marriage to take place on a Registrar's certificate as an alternative to banns. By 1898, ministers of all religions could perform marriages and there was a civil alternative. These Acts, which had become somewhat diffuse, were all consolidated in 1949.

In short, marriage is now regulated by the modern Marriage Acts, most recently that of 1949 as amended, including in 1970 and 1994: the latter Act now permits civil marriage in a wide range of licensed venues, although many couples still opt for a religious ceremony, whether or not they are themselves religious observers. Failure to observe proper formalities can, but does not necessarily, make a marriage void. The law has twice been reviewed in the past 30 years, first by the Law Commission Working Party in 1973 and by Green and White Papers in 1988, 1990 and 2002 none of which have so far achieved a thorough overhaul.

2.2 GROUNDS ON WHICH A MARRIAGE WILL BE VOID

Both capacity and formalities are at the root of this. There are various distinct situations to be considered here.

2.2.1 Where the marriage is not valid under the Marriage Act 1949 as amended

Pursuant to s 11(a) of the Matrimonial Causes Act (MCA) 1973, this would be because:

(1) The parties are within prohibited degrees (of blood relations and relations by marriage pursuant to the traditional tables of 'kindred and affinity' as established by the medieval Christian churches).

(2) Either party is under age 16: two cases illustrate the operation of this rule.

In *Alhaji Mohamed v Knott* [1968] 2 WLR 1446; [1968] 2 All ER 563, the parties were both domiciled Nigerians. The wife was only 13 years old; however, as the marriage was recognised in Nigeria it was still valid when they came to this country.

In *Pugh v Pugh* [1951] 2 All ER 680, the marriage was between a 15 year old Hungarian girl and a British domiciled soldier. The marriage took place in Austria and was recognised both there and in Hungary, but not in England, and as this was the law of the husband's domicile it was fatal to the validity of the marriage.

(3) The formalities are defective, which may occur because the marriage is:

- not by the rites of the Church of England (ie, after banns duly called, by common licence from the bishop, by special licence from the Archbishop of Canterbury);
- not by Superintendent Registrar's certificate;
- not in a Quaker or Jewish ceremony;
- not conducted by a proper clergyman or without the presence of the Registrar;
- in a civil ceremony not in a registered building; or
- not in the building specified in the certificate.

These defects will only render a marriage *void* if the marriage is entered into *knowingly and wilfully* by both parties (Marriage Act 1949).

Under (3), above, false information to obtain a Superintendent Registrar's certificate does not make the marriage void, but the opposite is true in the case of banns. The reason is that the banns procedure is to obtain *publicity* for the proposed marriage – a procedure developed due to the historical incidence of forced marriages in earlier centuries as explained above – but the Register Office procedure is not, so misdescription in that situation does not invalidate the marriage. Three cases illustrate this point.

Puttick v Attorney General [1979] 3 WLR 542; [1979] 3 All ER 463 involved the terrorist Astrid Proll, who had married while on the run in England, using the name of another

German and a false passport, as her visa was about to expire. It was held that the marriage was not void in spite of the false particulars she gave.

Small v Small (1923) 67 SJ 277 concerned a deserter from the British Army who had taken a false name to conceal his identity. It was held that the banns were not duly published because the false name was given with fraudulent intent.

Dancer v Dancer [1948] 2 All ER 731 was a case of a bride's innocent use of an incorrect name in publication of the banns where the banns were held duly published. The reason was that she had always been known by the name of Jessamine Roberts, Roberts being her mother's cohabitant with whom the mother had had five further children, then having assumed his name for herself and the three year old Jessamine whom she had taken into the relationship. The real name of Jessamine and her mother was actually Knight. The truth was discovered on the death of the mother but the daughter continued to use the name Jessamine Roberts. Clearly there had been no intention to deceive in this case.

Some foreign marriages can be valid despite defective formalities, even though they do not comply with either local law or English law. An example of this is marriages in wartime, as in the case of *Taczanowska v Taczanowska* [1957] 2 All ER 563, which was a marriage between a Polish soldier serving in Italy and a Polish civilian refugee which was conducted in Rome by a Roman Catholic priest. As both parties were theoretically domiciled in Poland and the marriage was void by that law, the *lex patriae*, and also by Italian law as it had not complied with the local regulations, the Court of Appeal held its validity could be saved by common law on the grounds that it was a marriage celebrated by exchange of words before an episcopally ordained priest, and as a member of the conquering allied army the husband could not be expected to submit to the *lex loci celebrationis*. Moreover the marriage did not need to comply with the *lex domicilii* as that was relevant only to capacity to marry.

2.2.2 Where the marriage is not valid because either party is already lawfully married (MCA 1973, s 11(b))

What this means is illustrated by the following cases.

Baindall v Baindall [1946] 1 All ER 342 was a case of a valid (albeit potentially polygamous) first marriage in India of a Hindu man who subsequently purported to marry an English domiciled wife in England. As the first marriage was clearly valid in India and therefore had to be recognised, and in England we do not practise polygamy, the second marriage had to be void.

Padolecchia v Padolecchia [1967] 3 All ER 863 was a case of a first marriage by an Italian which was from the point of view of Italian law ineffectively dissolved in Mexico, thus making his second marriage in London necessarily void.

Maples v Maples [1987] 3 All ER 188 was a case of a Jewish divorce obtained in a religious ceremony not recognised in England by Israelis who had settled here. The wife's second marriage was thus void as she was still married to the first husband.

The second marriage may not be a criminal offence, for example, as in *R v Gould* [1968] 2 WLR 643, where the accused honestly and reasonably believed that there was no subsisting first marriage, and *R v Sagoo* [1975] 2 All ER 926, where the first polygamous marriage was a potential defence to criminal liability.

2.2.3 Where the marriage is not valid because parties are not respectively male and female (MCA 1973, s 11(c))

Corbett v Corbett [1970] 2 WLR 1306 is the leading case on this point in English law, where the court concluded that in England and Wales a person's biological sex is fixed at birth according to his or her chromosomes and cannot subsequently be changed by the artificial intervention of surgery to change the external appearance. This, however, is not the case in other jurisdictions such as some States of the USA, and subsequent cases in the European Court of Human Rights have indicated a growing trend among European judges to regard the UK stance on sex and gender as a potential breach of the European Convention on Human Rights and Fundamental Freedoms. This is because a transsexual is unable to marry at all under English law unless marrying a person of the (originally) opposite sex, which such a transsexual would be unlikely to want to do.

It has long been thought that there would in due course be scope for a realignment of the law in this respect to create a valid status for transsexuals, following successive judgments in the Court of Human Rights. It was always recognised that there would be problems in the short term because of the consequential legislation which would be required. The cases of *Rees v UK* (1986) 9 EHRR 56; *Cossey v UK* [1993] 2 FCR 97; (1991) 13 EHRR 622; and *Sheffield and Horsham v UK* [1998] 2 FLR 928; (1998) 27 EHRR 163 indicated that in most post-operative transsexual cases the Court supported the English view that sexual identity is not thus changed, and that the detriment suffered was not sufficient to override the State's margin of appreciation, despite the guarantee of respect for private and family life under Art 8 of the Convention which has been imported into English law by the Human Rights Act 1998. Similarly, the above cases did not establish a right pursuant to Art 12 for transsexuals to marry, as it was accepted that in English law that meant traditional marriage between parties of the opposite sex. However, recent ECHR and English decisions have gone further than the strong dissenting judgments in the earlier cases, and the UK will now be obliged to enable transsexuals to be recognised in their new gender for the purpose of contracting a valid marriage under English law.

The traditional stance of English law ignores the fact that transsexuals usually regard themselves as 'philosophically, psychologically and socially' aligned to their new sexual attribution, have been living in that state since the pressure for sexual reorientation resulted in their change of sex, and as a result of surgery and often extensive other treatment have lost all or most of the external attributes of their former sex. This theme, which was identified as long ago as the *Corbett* case (where it was held to be irrelevant), has resurfaced in every succeeding attempt to secure acceptance of regendering as well as of practical reorientation, and is recognised as sometimes producing anomalous results (see, eg, *R v Tan* [1983] QB 1053, where the issue was whether a transsexual was a 'man' for the purposes of ss 5 and 30 of the Sexual Offences Act 1967, ie, living off immoral earnings, and the Court of Appeal accepted that 'both common sense and the desirability of certainty and consistency' required the *Corbett* approach to be followed).

The crux of the matter in English law seems to be registration (see *Re P and G (Transsexuals)* [1996] 2 FLR 90, where two transsexuals lost their judicial review applications of the Registrar General's refusal to alter the sex on their birth certificates). While the European Court found in *B v France* (1993) 116 EHRR 1 that re-registration of civil papers to reflect a change of sex could be done in France without changing the law, and basically was essential to any quality of life for the applicant due to French bureaucracy, failure to do this in the UK (where such re-registration is not possible) was found not to be a breach of Art 8 in *X, Y and Z v UK* (1997) 24 EHRR 143 (where the female to male transsexual 'father' of a child conceived by artificial insemination by donor (AID) was refused registration as the father of his partner's child because that could be allowed only to a 'man', although the court did point out that the father could act as such in a social sense and could apply for a joint residence order with his partner so as to acquire parental responsibility: for this parental responsibility lifeline, see Chapter 24). Further it was made clear that there was no protection of family life for a relationship with a transsexual partner.

Curiously, although the applicant's case in *Rees* (in 1986) was mainly about the inability of a transsexual to marry (because of the inability to marry a person of the transsexual's post-operative sex, and obvious lack of desire to marry a person legally considered to be of the opposite sex), the embarrassment caused by the mismatch between the original birth certificate and apparent post-operative gender was also an issue, and raised exactly the same principles as those found to warrant re-registration in *B v France*. Although the European Court of Human Rights said that English law should clearly remain under review because of ongoing scientific developments, this has not only not happened, but in the subsequent case of *Cossey* (in 1991) little significant progress appears to have been made, despite a strong dissenting judgment by three members of the Court. Moreover, even seven years later, in 1998, the *Sheffield and Horsham* case appears to be similarly trapped in a time warp, since the issue was still basically re-registration – Miss Horsham wanted to marry a male partner in the Netherlands but realised that her valid marriage there would not be recognised in the UK. In the era of harmonisation of law in Europe, as well as of EU co-operation on many fronts and of ease of travel and the right to relocation between the countries involved, this was clearly an area of law which required urgent holistic reappraisal and which surely could not shelter any longer behind a margin of appreciation which, in common sense terms, belongs to a much earlier period of European integration, especially now the Human Rights Act 1998 is in force. That moment of truth has now finally arrived.

The traditional view within English law that, despite the guarantee of respect for privacy and family life under Art 8 of the Convention, marriage was only reserved to individuals as their biological sex must now be reconsidered following the decision of the European Court of Human Rights in *Goodwin v UK* No 28957/95 (11 July 2002). Here the Court stated that the margin of appreciation held by individual States in relation to their national law is not available to reduce the Convention rights 'so as to impair the very essence of the right'. The Court found that the traditional approach, and the claim that a transsexual, after full reassignment surgery, marry as their birth gender, was 'artificial' since 'The applicant lives as a woman, is in a relationship with a man and would only wish to marry a man. She has no possibility of doing so … [H]er right to marry has been infringed'. The Court also criticised the UK government for not progressing further on this issue, and for failing to take action on the Report of the Interdepartmental Working Group on Transsexual People (2000).

As this is a constantly developing area in medical and sociological terms, change was inevitable although by no means straightforward (see, eg, *Bellinger v Bellinger* [2002] Fam Law 150; [2002] 2 WLR 411, where a majority of the Court of Appeal once again adhered to the party line by pointing as ever to the accumulation of existing authority and tradition even in the light of medical advances where the status of transsexual is certainly a recognised medical condition, although Thorpe LJ gave a powerful dissenting judgment and the President, Butler-Sloss LJ, led unanimous criticism of government inaction for failing to implement the Working Group's recommendations). It has been suggested that the simple speedy solution is a 'recognition' certificate, to be kept alongside the birth certificate, noting the sex realignment, although a Bill to effect this limited change of status failed in Parliament some years ago.

Curiously, not all cases of void marriages under this head concern transsexuals. In *J v S-T (Formerly J)* [1997] FCR 349; [1997] 1 FLR 402, CA, the marriage was void because the 'husband' was in fact a woman who managed to conceal from the wife during a lengthy marriage where children were adopted that she was in fact female. The deception was found by the court to be sufficiently cruel as to bar the 'husband' from ancillary relief since it must have been obvious that the marriage could not be valid.

2.2.4 Where the marriage is not valid because polygamous and either party is domiciled in England and Wales (MCA 1973, s 11(d))

This rule does not always apply, however, if the parties are not necessarily intending to live in England at the time of the marriage. In *Radwan v Radwan (No 2)* [1972] 3 WLR 939; [1972] 3 All ER 1026, the husband was Egyptian and already married to an Egyptian woman when he contracted a second marriage to a domiciled English woman at the Egyptian Consulate in Paris, intending to live with her in Egypt. Eventually when they returned to England the marriage was still held to be valid as it was so by the law of the intended matrimonial domicile at the time of the ceremony. *Hussain v Hussain* [1982] 3 All ER 369 was similar.

Thus, if there is a potentially polygamous marriage which would not in fact ever have the chance of becoming actually polygamous (eg, because the husband was an English domiciled man who would not be able while subject to English law to take a second wife), the marriage will not be void.

2.3 THE EFFECT OF A VOID MARRIAGE

Lack of capacity or defective formalities to the knowledge of the parties will make the marriage incurably void: such a union can never be valid regardless of the parties' wishes, and none of the defences or bars which apply to voidable marriages will have any effect on a void marriage.

2.4 GROUNDS ON WHICH A MARRIAGE WILL BE VOIDABLE

Where a marriage is voidable it will, on the other hand, be valid until annulled according to the law of nullity which is contained in ss 12 and 13 of the MCA 1973 (see Chapter 3).

MARRIAGE

MARRIAGE AS A STATUS

Traditionally, English marriage has been regarded as voluntary, for life, heterosexual and monogamous. The spouses must have capacity to marry and observe the necessary formalities in the Marriage Act 1949, as amended. Faulty formalities are not necessarily fatal if the parties did not knowingly and wilfully disregard them, but normally marriages must be conducted in compliance with the law in order to be valid and to achieve the status of marriage. There is no longer any common law marriage in England and Wales, although it is possible to establish marriage retrospectively in Scotland – provided the status of marriage has not been expressly rejected – by means of 'cohabitation, habit and repute'.

VOID MARRIAGES

A marriage is void if the formalities of the Marriage Act 1949 are knowingly and wilfully not observed, or if the parties are within the prohibited degrees of relationship, under the age of 16 at which marriage may be contracted, not respectively male and female, already validly married or if the marriage is polygamous and either party is domiciled in the UK (MCA 1973, s 11). The UK approach to post-operative transsexual marriage has long remained unaltered by modern scientific and medical developments in this area; it appears that the European Court of Human Rights no longer continues to respect the margin of appreciation in English law in this matter: *Goodwin v UK* No 28957/95 (11 July 2002).

EFFECT OF A VOID MARRIAGE

A void marriage can never be valid regardless of the parties' wishes and third parties can seek such a declaration. Voidable marriages, however, remain valid until avoided and no third party can seek to avoid them.

CHAPTER 3

NULLITY

3.1 ANNULLING VOIDABLE MARRIAGES

Unlike void marriages, which can never be valid whatever the parties wish (see Chapter 2), voidable marriages present a practical alternative to divorce (ie, of 'annulment' under the law of nullity, pursuant to ss 12 and 13 of the Matrimonial Causes Act (MCA) 1973). This remedy has not been much used of late since the categories of persons whose religious objections to divorce used to favour nullity seem to have shrunk in recent years. Moreover, nullity has never been obtainable via the Special Procedure, under which divorces are granted without a hearing (see 11.6, below). This is a likely discouragement to seeking an annulment instead of divorce in many cases.

However, there is potentially a powerful new market for nullity, due to the increasing incidence of marriage breakdown in ethnic communities of arranged marriages which turn out to have been forced. This has been combined with the increasing willingness of Westernised women of Asian origin to resist unacceptable pressure from families to forego a Western style marriage to a person of their own choice so as to marry the family's choice of partner within their race and religion, and to encourage their older, formerly less assertive sisters finally to leave marriages to which they never truly consented. For such women the remedy of nullity is preferable since they have never regarded themselves as genuinely married: since they seek a decree of nullity of a voidable marriage, such a decree enables their children always to be and remain legitimate while they themselves can start a new life on the basis that, despite their belief that they were obliged to do what their families wanted at the time of the ceremony, they have never been validly married.

The Foreign and Commonwealth Office is currently exploring ways in which to prevent the continued abuse of imposing forced marriages on young women and girls in the ethnic minority communities, and consideration has even been given to whether there should be a new crime of arranging or assisting such a marriage, although it should be noted that an *arranged* marriage will not necessarily be *forced*. Meanwhile, some solicitors are raising awareness of the remedy of nullity for those for whom prevention has come too late.

The range of situations which give rise to voidable marriages includes (besides lack of consent and duress) incapacity or wilful refusal to consummate the marriage, mistake, unsoundness of mind and pregnancy by another man at the time of the marriage (see 3.3, below).

A voidable marriage can thus be annulled pursuant to ss 12 and 13 of the MCA 1973 with little more delay or difficulty than obtaining a decree of divorce, albeit that there will have to be a hearing, and as with divorce an undefended case will be easier to conclude than one that is defended.

3.2 NULLITY (MCA 1973, ss 11–13)

The historical background to nullity is in ecclesiastical law before divorce was developed (see Chapter 6).

3.2.1 Two categories of null marriages: void and voidable

Unlike in the case of void marriages, the validity of which anyone may challenge, annulment of a voidable marriage requires action on the part of one of the parties, as the marriage remains valid for all purposes until annulled.

De Reneville v De Reneville [1948] 1 All ER 56, *per* Lord Greene MR, famously expresses the distinction:

> A void marriage is one that will be regarded by every court in any case in which the existence of the marriage is in issue as never having taken place and can be so treated by both parties to it without the necessity of any decree annulling it; a voidable marriage is one that will be regarded by every court as a valid subsisting marriage until a decree annulling it has been pronounced by a court of competent jurisdiction.

3.2.2 Void and voidable marriages compared

Voidable marriages require a decree which may only be obtained by the parties and during the lifetime of both of them: however, any third party can challenge the validity of a void marriage, for example, a trustee of a marriage settlement. Void marriages do not require a decree, though this may be required for ancillary relief.

Children of voidable marriages are legitimate, as are the children of void marriages, provided both or either parents believed the marriage was valid at the time of conception, artificial insemination or marriage, whichever was the later, and the father was domiciled in England and Wales at the date of the birth, or if he died beforehand at the date of his death (Legitimacy Act 1976, s 1 as amended by the Family Law Reform Act 1987).

In the case of void marriages, it is presumed that one of the parties reasonably believed the marriage was valid unless the contrary is shown.

3.2.3 Effect of a nullity decree on a voidable marriage

The marriage is valid until the decree is granted (MCA 1973, s 16). This is not always very convenient to the parties: the practical importance is shown by two cases, *Re Roberts* and *Ward v Secretary of State for Social Services*.

In *Re Roberts (Decd)* [1978] 3 All ER 225, a husband made a will giving property to a woman, whom he then married, in apparent ignorance of the fact that the marriage revoked the gift to the woman in the will. The husband then died and the wife wanted to argue that the marriage was voidable because of the husband's insanity within the meaning of s 12(c) of the MCA 1973 so that she could still receive the property left to her. Unfortunately for her, the court held that this was irrelevant as even if she were correct about the insanity, by s 16 of the same Act the marriage remained valid for all purposes until a decree absolute was obtained so that the gift had been revoked by the marriage and remained revoked.

Ward v Secretary of State for Social Services [1990] Fam Law 58 was a similar case where the wife married a Royal Naval officer who died, so that she obtained a Navy pension which ceased if she remarried. Some years later she did remarry, but then discovered that her new husband was a manic-depressive. As the marriage was never consummated and had only lasted a week, she was able to obtain a s 12(a) decree and attempted to retain her Navy pension on the ground that her second marriage had been avoided. However, again the court held that by s 16 the marriage was valid until it was avoided and so the regulation depriving her of the pension had come into effect during that period and operated to end the right to the pension.

It should be noted that there are possible defences under s 13 of the MCA 1973 to a petition for a decree annulling a voidable marriage (see 3.4, below). A petition to obtain a nullity decree is the same as for divorce and the two decrees can be petitioned for in the alternative. The same ancillary relief is obtainable after nullity as after divorce.

3.3 GROUNDS ON WHICH A MARRIAGE WILL BE VOIDABLE

Broadly, these strike at the concept of the marriage relationship, as a consensual contract creating the relationship of husband and wife so that the marriage should be freely entered into by persons with the mental capacity to appreciate its obligations and should be consummated. There are several distinct situations to consider here.

3.3.1 If the marriage is not consummated owing to incapacity of either party to consummate it (MCA 1973, s 12(a))

A party can petition on his or her own incapacity (but see *Harthan v Harthan* [1948] 2 All ER 639, where the husband actually tried to petition both on his own incapacity and on his wife's wilful refusal to consummate, which the court not surprisingly found mutually exclusive grounds).

3.3.1.1 'Incapacity'

This has a precise meaning:

- the defect must be incurable;
- it must be incapable of remedy, or only so with danger or little chance of success; or
- the respondent must refuse treatment.

Incapacity must be in existence at the date of the marriage and there must be no practical possibility of consummation at the date of the hearing. In *Napier v Napier* [1915] P 184 it was necessary to seek an adjournment because the wife had an operation six days before the hearing, and the petition was eventually dismissed as the incapacity was curable.

Medical inspection may be required in defended cases.

3.3.2 If the marriage is not consummated owing to wilful refusal of the respondent (MCA 1973, s 12(b))

A party cannot petition on that party's own refusal under this section. The meaning of consummation is important. It must be:

- after marriage, not before; and
- ordinary complete intercourse.

The following should be noted:

(a) sterility or inability to ejaculate is irrelevant;

(b) lack of satisfaction is irrelevant;

(c) the birth of a child by *fecundia ab extra* (fertilisation outside the body due to incomplete or attempted intercourse) is not consummation;

(d) contraceptives do not prevent consummation and neither does *coitus interruptus*.

Baxter v Baxter [1947] 2 All ER 197 is the leading case on non-consummation. The decision suggests that tact and persuasion must be employed to attempt to reverse a refusal or the petition on this ground might fail.

3.3.2.1 Meaning of 'wilful refusal'

The meaning of 'wilful refusal' is that there is a 'settled and definite decision come to without just excuse' (*per* Lord Jowitt in *Horton v Horton* [1947] 2 All ER 871). A failure to undergo medical treatment to cure an incapacity to consummate, where that treatment is not 'dangerous', may be 'wilful refusal'. An examination of some of the leading cases shows what this means and how it works in practice.

Jodla v Jodla [1960] 1 All ER 625 established that a just excuse may include religious reasons. In that case, two Roman Catholics married in a Register Office but it was expressly understood that they would not live together until there had been a religious ceremony. The husband refused to go through with the religious service and this was held to amount to refusal to consummate.

Kaur v Singh [1972] 1 All ER 292 was a similar case, where the parties were Sikhs. It was intended according to the religious and social custom of their people that a religious ceremony would have to follow, but the husband who had the obligation of arranging that ceremony refused to do so and this too was held to amount to refusal to consummate.

Morgan v Morgan [1959] 2 WLR 487; [1959] 1 All ER 539; and *Scott v Scott* [1959] 2 WLR 447; [1959] 1 All ER 531 show that just excuse may include an agreement that the marriage is for companionship only and that there would therefore not be intercourse. In the case of *Morgan* the parties were respectively aged 72 and 59, and the agreement was therefore held to be reasonable having regard to their ages, but in the case of *Scott* there was initially some doubt since the parties were only 43 and 40. Nevertheless, it was held that the parties had accepted the condition because the wife found intercourse distasteful and the husband was not allowed to petition so as to remarry when he met another woman without the same aversion.

Potter v Potter [1975] 5 Fam Law 161 makes it clear that mere loss of sexual ardour is not sufficient. The husband tried to consummate the marriage immediately after the wife had had an operation to cure a physical defect, but failed, after which he refused to try again. However, the wife did not succeed with her petition because his failure on the sole occasion on which he had attempted consummation had been natural and not a deliberate refusal.

Ford v Ford [1987] Fam Law 232 clarifies a common misconception that a pre-marriage relationship including intercourse obviates the necessity for specific consummation after the celebration of the marriage. In that case, the husband was in prison for five years and the marriage actually took place in prison where there was no opportunity for consummation. When he was eventually released on a visit prior to the end of his sentence he did not go home but stayed with a former girlfriend. When the wife eventually petitioned, it was held that he had not refused consummation in prison as there were no facilities, but he *had* done so as soon as he had the opportunity on a visit out of prison prior to his release, so that his conduct then had demonstrated wilful refusal to consummate the marriage either at that time or in the future.

A v J (Nullity) [1989] Fam Law 63 highlights the fact that there may be *indirect* refusal to consummate. In that case there appear to have been tantrums on both sides: the marriage was an arranged one between two Indians and there was to be a civil ceremony followed by a religious one some four months later. Between the two ceremonies the husband was abroad on business, which the wife seemed to seize on as an excuse not to go ahead with the religious ceremony, as she said he had been offhand with her in going abroad. She declined the husband's apologies, and the court held that *she* was the one who was wilfully refusing to consummate the marriage due to her adamant refusal to go ahead with the religious ceremony which was essential for them to cohabit.

3.3.3 If the marriage is not valid owing to lack of proper consent due to mistake, duress, unsoundness of mind or otherwise (MCA 1973, s 12(c))

These grounds also strike at the essential concept of consent to the marriage.

3.3.3.1 Mistake

This must be as to the identity of a party or as to the nature of the ceremony, not as to the quality or fortune of a party, or other mistake of fact, such as pregnancy by another man. The scope of mistake in this context is best illustrated by the cases since it is a situation in which the nature of the mistake and its consequences are often misunderstood.

Mehta v Mehta [1945] 2 All ER 690 was a case of sufficient mistake to avoid the marriage where the ceremony was thought to be one of conversion to the Hindu religion – clearly a fundamentally different matter from marriage.

Valier v Valier (1925) 133 LT 830 was a similar case where an Italian who did not speak English thought a Register Office wedding was merely one of many formalities preceding marriage (as is common in Italy) rather than the ceremony itself – clearly also a different situation from the binding ceremony of marriage.

Mistakes as to the *effect* of the ceremony, rather than its *nature*, are in a different category. *Kassim v Kassim* [1962] 3 WLR 865; [1962] 3 All ER 426 was a case where the mistake was insufficient, being that the marriage was polygamous instead of monogamous (an obvious example of a mistake only as to the *effect* of the ceremony rather than the nature of it). In *Way v Way* [1949] 2 All ER 959, the husband thought that the Russian wife would be allowed to leave Russia to live with him in England – another mistake only as to the *effect* of the ceremony, and therefore of course insufficient, however important her departure with him might have been to that husband.

Vervaeke v Smith [1982] 2 All ER 144 was a case of a similar mistake about the effect of the ceremony, in this instance an inaccurate belief in a resulting protection from deportation.

Puttick v Attorney General [1979] 3 WLR 542; [1979] 3 All ER 463 (see 2.2.1, above) illustrates the point that where a party gives a false name, this is insufficient to avoid the marriage, any mistake on the part of the other spouse being only as to the *quality* of the party giving the false name, since the intention is usually to marry the person actually present for the ceremony.

3.3.3.2 Unsoundness of mind

The decision in *In re Estate of Park* [1953] 3 WLR 1012; [1953] 2 All ER 1411 established the point that no high degree of understanding is required for capacity to enter into a marriage. The test is whether the party in question was capable of understanding the nature of the marriage contract and the duties and obligations that imports. There is a presumption of valid consent when a marriage is contracted. *Re Roberts* (see 3.2.3, above) is a more recent case on similar facts.

3.3.3.3 Duress

This means a fear so great that there is no reality of consent. However, the party claiming duress must not himself be responsible for being put in fear.

It is now established that the fear in question need not literally be of life, limb or liberty. The leading case in modern times is *Szechter v Szechter* [1971] 2 WLR 170; [1970] 3 All ER 905, where it was said that the 'will of one of the parties must be so overborne by genuine and reasonably held fear that the constraint destroys the reality of consent'. The case was one of a Polish woman in prison in Poland following arrest by the security forces, who married so that she could leave both prison and Poland itself. It was accepted that she was in poor health and that her life was in danger if she remained, and this was accepted as sufficient duress for a decree to be granted.

Parojcic v Parojcic [1958] 1 WLR 1280; [1959] 1 All ER 1 was a similar case of a refugee from Yugoslavia who was forced by her father to marry a man on her arrival in England on pain of being sent back to Yugoslavia.

Hussein v Hussein [1938] 2 All ER 344 was a case of marriage entered into under threat of being killed by the husband, again sufficient for a decree.

Singh v Singh [1971] 2 WLR 963; [1971] 2 All ER 828, on the other hand, was a case where the only duress compelling the marriage was the young Sikh bride's respect for her parents, and this was held to be insufficient. This case can be compared with that of

Hirani v Hirani (1982) 4 FLR 232, where again there was no physical duress but the Hindu parents threatened to withdraw all support from their 19 year old daughter and eject her from the family home if she did not comply with their wishes for her marriage. The judge said that threat to actual life, limb or liberty is not essential to establish duress, provided that what is done is extreme enough that it 'overbears the will of the individual'. This sort of duress is at the root of many marriages now being annulled in the wake of the initiatives against forced marriages.

Buckland v Buckland [1967] 2 WLR 1506; [1967] 2 All ER 300 shows that false accusations of crime and threats of unjustified exposure will be sufficient, provided the accusations are unjust as otherwise the situation will not meet the requirement that the party coerced should not himself be responsible for the duress applied to him.

There is some doubt over whether the test of fear should be objective or subjective. What is established is that there must be some fear or coercion, not merely an ulterior motive imposed by the party alleging he is coerced, such as in *Silver v Silver* [1955] 2 All ER 614 where the only coercion was the German petitioner's own desire to come to England to live with an Englishman other than the one whom she married in order to gain entry to the UK.

3.3.4 If the marriage is not valid owing to mental disorder, etc (MCA 1973, s 12(d))

The marriage may not be valid because at the time of the marriage either party, though capable of giving a valid consent, was suffering (whether continuously or intermittently) from mental disorder within the meaning of the Mental Health Act 1983 of such a kind or to such an extent as to be unfitted for marriage.

Bennett v Bennett [1969] 1 WLR 430; [1969] 1 All ER 539 is a case which illustrates what this means. The wife was not clinically ill, but suffered from a temporary hysterical neurosis which meant that she was likely to be difficult on a short term basis, but this was insufficient to invalidate the marriage.

3.3.5 If the marriage is not valid due to venereal disease (MCA 1973, s 12(e))

The marriage may not be valid due to a party to the marriage suffering at the time of the ceremony from venereal disease in a communicable form.

3.3.6 If the marriage is not valid due to pregnancy *per alium* (MCA 1973, s 12(f))

This means pregnancy of the respondent at the date of the ceremony by someone other than the petitioner. Due to the decision in *Moss v Moss* [1897] P 263, pregnancy *per alium* at the time of the ceremony concealed from the petitioner did not nullify consent to the marriage, so the statutory ground had to be enacted to remedy the situation in an appropriate case.

3.4 BARS TO A NULLITY SUIT

These only apply in the case of a voidable marriage. There are two only:

- approbation (MCA 1973, s 13(1)); and
- other statutory bars (MCA 1973, s 13(2) and (3)).

3.4.1 The bar of approbation (MCA 1973, s 13(1))

The section has enacted the pre-existing bar of approbation, so that a decree of nullity will not be granted if the petitioner, with knowledge that it was open to him or her to have the marriage avoided, so conducted him or herself in relation to the respondent as to lead the respondent reasonably to believe that he or she would not seek to do so, and it would be unjust to the respondent to grant the decree.

For this bar to operate, the court must be satisfied on three points:

(1) That there is evidence of the petitioner's actual knowledge that he or she had a legal right to a decree of nullity.

(2) That there is evidence that despite this knowledge he or she behaved towards the respondent in such a way as to lead the respondent to believe that he or she would not seek a decree. What this means is best illustrated through the cases.

   Aldridge v Aldridge (1888) 13 PD 210 establishes that an express agreement between the parties not to have the marriage annulled is an absolute bar. Institution of other proceedings as in *W v W* [1952] 1 All ER 858 (adoption of a child) and *Tindall v Tindall* [1953] 2 WLR 158; [1953] 1 All ER 139 (proceedings for maintenance) suggests that the petitioner has treated the marriage as valid and might be a bar to a nullity decree, although the court reached a different conclusion on similar facts to *W v W* in *D v D* [1979] 3 All ER 337.

(3) That there is evidence that it would be unjust to the respondent to grant the decree.

   Pettit v Pettit [1962] 3 WLR 919; [1962] 3 All ER 37 illustrates what this means. The husband had always been impotent, but the wife had had their child by artificial insemination and had been a particularly loyal wife, including taking responsibility for the outgoings of the matrimonial home during the war by paying bills and the mortgage. When after 20 years the husband wanted a decree of nullity so as to marry another woman, the court was not minded to give him one on the grounds that it would be unjust to the wife.

Practitioners therefore realise that care should be taken with the wording of any alleged agreement putting the respondent on notice that the petitioner reserves the right to petition notwithstanding, for example, an adoption or artificial insemination. If consent to either of these courses is given and the petitioner makes it clear that he or she would still petition if the marriage is never consummated, then he or she will obviously not be debarred from doing so, perhaps with catastrophic emotional consequences for the respondent to such a petition. Similarly, since approbation or lack of it clearly depends on knowledge and, where appropriate, notice there will be no approbation if an adoption or artificial insemination takes place in ignorance of one of the parties' rights to have the marriage avoided for non-consummation, as happened in *Slater v Slater* [1953] 2 WLR 170; [1953] 1 All ER 246.

3.4.2 Matrimonial Causes Act 1973, s 13(2)

This section provides a bar against a nullity decree on any of the statutory grounds in s 12(c), (d), (e) or (f) (ie, all s 12 grounds but non-consummation) unless proceedings are begun within three years of the date of the ceremony, except where leave for later institution of proceedings is granted under s 13(4) (which allows an extension of time if the petitioner has at some time been suffering from mental disorder within the meaning of the Mental Health Act 1983, and it would be just to grant leave for such an extension).

3.4.3 Matrimonial Causes Act 1973, s 13(3)

This section provides a bar against a nullity decree on the s 12(c)–(f) grounds unless the court is satisfied on the basis of the facts alleged that the petitioner was ignorant of the true situation at the time of the marriage.

3.5 RELATIONSHIP BETWEEN NULLITY AND DIVORCE

There may be overlap in the following areas.

Pregnancy *per alium* or venereal disease in a communicable form at the time of the marriage (nullity) may be an alternative to establishing a case of adultery if the pregnancy arose or the venereal disease was contracted after the ceremony (when divorce would be appropriate) provided of course the marriage has been consummated: if it has not, nullity may be an alternative available in lieu of divorce.

Mental disorder at the time of the marriage (nullity) may be an alternative to establishing a case of behaviour under Fact B sufficient for divorce (for which see Chapter 8) where the mental and/or physical illness may not qualify under that head.

Invalidity of marriage sufficient to make it voidable (nullity) may be an alternative where there is only a weak basis for divorce or where the first year is not up (see Chapter 7 for these situations).

NULLITY

NULLITY (MCA 1973, ss 11–13)

Nullity has its origins in ecclesiastical law and approaches the marriage on the basis that it is an imperfect marriage and should therefore be annulled rather than dissolved. Voidable marriages are ended by a decree under the law of nullity (ss 11–13 of the MCA 1973). Nullity may be used either to secure a freestanding nullity decree or in the alternative in a divorce petition in cases of factual overlap. Voidable marriages (which are valid until avoided) must be distinguished from void marriages, which are void from the start and need no decree, though one may be desirable for various reasons. A voidable marriage will always need a decree to annul it.

GROUNDS FOR A NULLITY DECREE

A marriage may be voidable for incapacity or wilful refusal to consummate, for lack of consent due to mistake, unsoundness of mind, duress, or other vitiating factor, and also on the statutory grounds of mental disorder, venereal disease or pregnancy by another man at the time of the ceremony. There are, however, bars to the grant of a decree: approbation (where it would be unfair for a decree to be granted), or where proceedings on one of the statutory grounds have not been instituted within three years, although there might be an extension of time if the petitioner was suffering from mental disorder within the meaning of the Mental Health Act 1983.

OVERLAP WITH DIVORCE

There is some overlap with adultery and behaviour in the law of divorce. Nullity is not, however, available via the Special Procedure for obtaining divorces and a hearing is therefore always necessary. Nullity may still appeal to persons with religious objections to divorce, and those who wish to leave forced marriages to which they considered they never validly consented.

CHAPTER 4

LEGAL CONSEQUENCES OF MARRIAGE AND COHABITATION

4.1 THE MARRIAGE RELATIONSHIP

Traditionally, marriage created a single person and that person was the husband: see Blackstone's *Commentaries*, which states:

> By marriage, the husband and wife are one person in law ... the very being or legal existence of the woman is suspended in law ... or at least is incorporated into that of the husband.

The separate legal personality of the wife began to emerge in the late 19th century with such statutes as the Married Women's Property Act 1882 (although cynics always regarded this as a vehicle for protecting the family of the numerous and newly prosperous Victorian entrepreneurs against the bankruptcy of their *paterfamilias* rather than advancing the property interests of women as such) and developed throughout the 20th century, as women gained more and more independence. This ultimately took their uninhibited decision making even as far as interference in what was originally seen as the core purpose of marriage, the provision of children, in the recognition of the wife's right to take unilateral decisions in abortion, including to abort the husband's child against his express opposition (see *Paton v British Pregnancy Advisory Service* [1979] QB 276, where a husband was refused an injunction to stop such an operation).

This concept has been superseded by the social and political reality of the equality of the sexes, including since 1990 long awaited separate taxation of husbands and wives, which now (2002) looks as though it is stealthily being reversed in the introduction by the government of the various new tax credits for working families and children which require disclosure of a married or unmarried partner's incomes.

However, the previously dependent position of wives is a useful piece of historical background for the analytical student of family law, because it explains the approach to many family law concepts, such as the differing access to divorce when it finally became available to both parties (see Chapters 6 and 7) and the continuing rejection of equality of assets in the approach of the jurisdiction of England and Wales to ancillary relief following divorce and nullity. This latter point means that at present the UK cannot implement Protocol 7, Art 5 of the European Convention on Human Rights and Fundamental Freedoms since this requires equality of rights and obligations on the part of both spouses in relation to their property and their children. The recent case of *White v White* [2000] 2 FLR 981, HL has so far done nothing (beyond flagging the issue) to bring such equality into practical focus, although it has created a good deal of work, introspection and grief for the legal profession in its attempts to advise clients on the concept of overall 'fairness' which that decision now requires in applying the existing law of ancillary relief (see Chapter 12).

4.2 CONSORTIUM

Marriage also traditionally created the elusive state of consortium, the technical term for the practical aspects of living together in marriage, which broadly connotes the wife taking the husband's surname, the existence of a matrimonial home (absence from which may constitute desertion, though interestingly even the breadwinner does not appear to have the right to dictate where that should be (see Chapter 9)), sexual intercourse (without which the marriage is not consummated and may be annulled (see Chapter 3)) and respect for marital confidences (see generally *Argyll v Argyll* [1967] Ch 302; [1965] 1 All ER 611). As a result of the doctrine, the spouses have 'matrimonial home rights' (Family Law Act (FLA) 1996, s 30) which can be protected by means of an occupation order under s 33 of that Act.

Further, while husband and wife have for some time been competent and compellable witnesses against each other in most criminal cases, until the case of *R v R* [1992] 1 AC 599, the state of consortium meant that sexual intercourse within marriage could never be rape, regardless of the wife's consent on a particular occasion, or lack of it. This was the case in which the House of Lords officially recognised that marriage was 'in modern times regarded as a partnership of equals and no longer one in which the wife must be the subservient chattel of the husband'. For those interested in this discrete topic, the Law Commission Paper No 116, *Rape Within Marriage* (1990), provides an excellent review of marital rape in UK and non-UK jurisdictions.

Traditionally, a husband was responsible for the maintenance of his wife and children, but after the Second World War this gradually gave way to a mutual responsibility of both husband and wife to maintain one another and their children and not to throw this burden onto the State unless no other means were available of discharging the spouses' responsibilities (see the National Assistance Act 1948 and *Barnes v Barnes* [1972] 1 WLR 1381; [1972] 3 All ER 872). However, the primary obligation of the husband survived into the Divorce Reform Act 1969, subsequently consolidated into the Matrimonial Causes Act (MCA) 1973, and it remained the practice, until the law was amended by the Matrimonial and Family Proceedings Act 1984 to create the potential of a clean break after which wives could be self-supporting, that wives expected to be maintained after divorce.

4.3 COHABITATION

More recently, cohabitation has developed as a strong alternative to traditional marriage, yet unlike other common law jurisdictions (eg, Australia, which has had a De Facto Relationships Act since 1985) cohabitation is little recognised as a status in law in the UK. Common law countries have not been alone in such innovation since recently in Europe France has introduced a status of civil partnership in its PACS Law (see further at 5.9 below), under which cohabitants can enter into a formal agreement as an alternative to marriage, and for a long time previously has recognised cohabitation in the institution of *concubinage* which could be registered at the Town Hall.

Nevertheless, in England, stable cohabitation remains largely unrecognised in law, although there are some legal remedies available to cohabitants and their children which may alleviate the disadvantages that can otherwise sometimes accrue. It is true that some statutes (eg, the domestic violence protection of Pt IV of the FLA 1996) provide broadly similar but distinct remedies under different regimes for married and unmarried partners (see Chapters 5 and 23) and the unmarried father of a child born out of wedlock is recognised as a father for many purposes, including for example, child support, and if he is likely to apply for parental responsibility (and smart enough to make his intentions clear in sufficient time), to refuse to give consent to a child being freed for adoption (see Chapter 24 *et seq*). However, there is no holistic legal approach to cohabitation as a viable alternative to marriage, although the government has in the last year or so been equivocal in its wholehearted support for marriage for fear, it is said, of losing the votes of the increasing numbers of the population who prefer to cohabit than to marry and of offending the children of such relationships. This suggests further anecdotal support for the change of emphasis in family law from the marriage to parentage as the core relationship, as already flagged in Chapter 1.

It must be asked whether this formal disregard of the incidence of cohabitation is wise, given the alarming lack of knowledge of the sharply different legal consequences of marriage and cohabitation constantly revealed in research, most recently in a joint article, 'Why marry? – Perceptions of the affianced' [2001] Fam Law 197, by Mary Hibbs, Chris Barton and Joanne Beswick of the Centre for the Study of the Family, Law and Social Policy at Staffordshire University (see 4.5, below).

4.3.1   What is cohabitation?

It should be emphasised that 'cohabitation' is a term which in the marriage versus cohabitation context in English law traditionally only applies to heterosexuals, whatever may pertain in other jurisdictions, although this may change following the *Mendoza* case, see above at 1.1.

The definition is normally only examined when it is necessary to apply a statute, such as Pt IV of the FLA 1996, under which in *G v G (Non-Molestation Order: Jurisdiction)* [2000] 2 FLR 533 the court had to decide whether the parties were 'cohabitants' within the meaning of s 62 of the Act, as otherwise they had no remedy under s 36 or 38, which are designed to provide the occupation order element of domestic violence protection to (heterosexual) cohabitants and former cohabitants: same sex parties living together are catered for under different provisions, and only obtain the lesser protection of a non-molestation order if they qualify under s 62 as 'associated persons' for the purpose. The court in *G v G* decided that there was cohabitation by adopting the practical social security yardsticks, where a man and a woman are living together but are not married, of sexual relationship and financial support.

Similarly, cohabitation is relevant in divorce under s 1(2) of the MCA 1973 (see Chapters 7–10), where it may preclude divorce, or end the basis on which a decree might have been obtained, and/or preclude maintenance or even some capital provision. The test of whether the relevant parties are cohabiting is whether they are living together in the same household, as in *Mouncer v Mouncer* [1972] 1 All ER 289 (where they were held to be living together, albeit on bad terms, as they shared a common life, including meals, although not a bedroom); and *Hopes v Hopes* [1948] 2 All ER 920 (where Lord Denning commented the situation was one of 'gross neglect and chronic discord in one unhappy household'). On the other hand, in *Fuller v Fuller* [1973] 2 All ER 650, a sick and formerly separated husband who returned to live in his wife's house with her new lover was understandably not cohabiting with her when he occupied a separate room as a lodger, and nor was the wife in *Bartram v Bartram* [1949] 2 All ER 270, who was obliged to share the house with her husband (without sharing any household tasks) because she had nowhere else to go and considered the best solution was to treat him as a lodger whom she cordially disliked.

With the exception of social security legislation, which largely treats those living together as husband and wife *as if* they were married, legal rights in a cohabitants' household are entirely based on whatever legal provisions relate to the single persons involved. Financial responsibility for the other partner extends only to a liability to pay council tax, and not to ordinary financial support (a point made forcefully by Millett LJ in *Windeler v Whitehall* [1990] 2 FLR 505), although there is an obligation on both parties to support their children.

An unmarried father will therefore have expressly to obtain parental responsibility for his children, although this is due to change pursuant to the Adoption and Children Act 2002, and a cohabiting wife will usually be unable to obtain any maintenance for herself on separation or death of her partner (though there is a small provision for childcare in the child support rates where applicable, and the Inheritance (Provision for Family and Dependants) Act 1975 may provide ongoing provision for a partner who was being supported at the deceased's death). Property rights depend on the ordinary law of property, and there is no presumption of shared ownership outside the ordinary law of resulting and constructive trusts, nor any of the tax breaks available to married couples, such as favourable capital gains and inheritance tax treatment. Immigration is not nearly as simple for a cohabiting partner as for a spouse, in the case of whom there will usually be difficulty enough. Moreover, a child born to cohabitants in the UK will only be British if the mother is British, even if the father has parental responsibility, and cohabitants cannot jointly adopt (and have instead to resort to one applying for the adoption order and then obtaining parental responsibility for the other by means of a joint residence order: see Chapters 24 *et seq*).

The law is sometimes criticised for not giving to cohabitants the same rights as married people, especially in cases where the length and commitment of the relationship exceed those in many a marriage. A classic example is *Burns v Burns* [1984] Ch 317, where 'Mrs' Burns, who had changed her name by deed poll, had two children with Mr Burns and contributed in practical and financial terms to the household for 19 years, received nothing on the breakdown of the relationship as she could not bring herself within the law of constructive trusts so as to do so, whereas had she been a wife she would on divorce, after what would have counted as a 'long' marriage, have received probably half or more of the value of the property, or at least the right to live in it until her children were independent and then substantial capital provision.

However, cohabitants have usually chosen not to marry for reasons of their own so that it is an equally valid argument that they should not be compelled to live under a matrimonial regime which they have not chosen. Some cohabitants choose to deal with this by means of cohabitation contracts. For more detail on these points, see Chapter 5.

4.3.2   Same sex relationships

If the law of heterosexual cohabitants is still somewhat neglected, that applying to same sex relationships has mostly not yet achieved separate attention in the average family law syllabus, and tends therefore to be dealt with as necessary, where different demographics demand, within the traditional heads of academic and practical family law. For the impact of same sex relationships in these areas, see particularly 1.1 above and Chapters 24 *et seq* in relation to child law.

4.4 MARRIAGE AND COHABITATION

It is not easy to build an up to date picture of the incidence of marriage versus cohabitation as there is only a census every 10 years, although more frequent figures for marriage are revealed in *Social Trends* and the *General Household Survey*. As identified by Parker and Dewar in the fourth edition of their useful text, *Cohabitants* (1995), there is first a definitional problem in what one is measuring and then another in making that definition effective when collecting data, plus the added problem of assessing the truth of the answers given to researchers. They conclude that cohabitation is best assessed as 'an integral part of family organisation' (ie, pre-marriage, followed by marriage and divorce, new partner cohabitation and remarriage) 'rather than as a straight alternative to marriage', although they accept that some cohabitants will have made the choice to cohabit rather than to marry. They add that the most significant figure is the explosion over the last quarter of the 20th century of births outside marriage from one in 20 to one in three.

Numbers of marriages were certainly down 40% between 1972 and 1998, while cohabitation quadrupled to nearly one third of all single women between 1979 and 1998. Up to date figures are confused by lack of identification of the precise marital status of cohabitants but it would appear that about half of couples living together are not married to each other. While the government is said in its consultation paper *Supporting Families* (Home Office, 1998) to 'share the belief of the majority of people that marriage provides the most reliable framework for raising children' and states that 'marriage remains the choice of the majority of people in Britain', the same document refers to an informed guide to the rights and responsibilities of marriage to be made available through churches and Register Offices to those considering marriage, while there is a similar guide for intending cohabitants obtainable from Citizens Advice Bureaux and libraries. It would seem more appropriate to try to educate the public about the distinctions between marriage and cohabitation before they have selected one option or the other.

The public unfortunately does not appear to realise the differences between marriage and cohabitation and seems to think that there is still an institution called 'common law marriage'. This was the experience of the JUSTICE Family Law Committee some years ago when they designed and distributed an information leaflet to draw attention to the potential perils of adhering to this view, and attempted to generate an initiative on the part of solicitors to encourage cohabitants to consider their legal position in relation to property when they gave instructions for conveyancing. The Solicitors Family Law Association (SFLA) has now recommended that the law should be reformed expressly to protect cohabitants. While *Supporting Families* makes it clear that the government is considering making prenuptial contracts legally binding, there is no indication that any official thought has been given to the position of cohabitants, although there were two Private Members' Bills before Parliament in 2001/02.

4.5 THE STAFFORDSHIRE RESEARCH

The research behind the Hibbs, Barton and Beswick article mentioned at 4.3, above, attempted to establish why the parties in their sample were marrying at all and whether they appreciated the legal consequences. Ruth Deech has been well known for some years for widespread comment, in the course of her opposition to the reform of divorce law, that there are now virtually no duties attached to marriage. It is her view that this should be supported rather than divorce made easier. Nevertheless, there are still some fiscal advantages under the inheritance and capital gains tax regimes, together with rights to financial support during and after marriage, financial rights on intestacy and registrable matrimonial home rights, which are not enjoyed by cohabitants. Yet the reasons given in the Staffordshire research for getting married appear either mundane or frivolous in the extreme (eg, because it was the social norm, to have a party or because it was on the spur of the moment) and were accompanied by a depressing lack of legal knowledge. Of respondents, 41% thought marriage would not change their legal relationships and 37% thought it would not have any consequences in the future either for themselves or for their children. There was also a much greater weighting towards preparations for the wedding and honeymoon than any indication of practical or fiscal preparation, let alone consideration of why the election for marriage had been made at all.

4.6 THE FUTURE?

It would appear that some attention needs to be given to the respective legal consequences of marriage and cohabitation. The Law Commission's *Consultation Paper on Reform of the Law of Homesharers,* which was expected to shed some light on this issue, has now been overtaken by a new discussion paper *Sharing Homes: A Discussion Paper* (Law Commission, 2002) outlining the evolution and eventual abandonment of the original Law Commission scheme, and comparing it with a scheme proposed in 1999 by Anne Barlow and Craig Lind in their article 'A matter of trust: the allocation of rights in the family home' (1999) 19 LS 468 and with some overseas regimes recently recommended by the Law Society in their paper *Cohabitation: The Case for a Clear Law* (Law Society, 2002). This latest development in the already long running homesharing saga suggests that the discussion is now going to run for some time to come. A wider remit was included in the Civil Partnerships Bill 2002, and in the Relationships (Civil Registration) Bill 2002, both of which addressed property, financial and other rights of cohabitants (both heterosexual and same sex). On 6 December 2002, Barbara Roche MP announced that the Government was planning to bring these issues forward for discussion in 2003.

LEGAL CONSEQUENCES OF MARRIAGE AND COHABITATION

THE MARRIAGE RELATIONSHIP

Husband and wife are now regarded in law as separate persons, although there is still a concept of consortium which assumes a certain element of joint enterprise in the marriage partnership (eg, the wife still usually takes the husband's surname, there is a matrimonial home, an expectation of sexual intercourse and a concept of marital confidence). Marriage creates financial rights and responsibilities – a mutual obligation of maintenance of the other spouse and children and the concept of not shedding this burden onto the State if the spouses are able to discharge it themselves.

COHABITATION

The rise of stable cohabitation as an alternative to marriage has raised concerns due to the ignorance of the average member of the public of the difference in legal consequences. Cohabitation does not receive the same recognition as a status as has been effected in other common law countries and in France. The government is considering making premarital contracts legally binding and the SFLA has proposed that the law be reformed to protect cohabitants. Two bills introduced into Parliament in the 2001/02 sessions both failed to reach the statute book.

THE STAFFORDSHIRE RESEARCH

The Centre for the Family, Law and Social Policy at Staffordshire University has looked at why people in their catchment area decide to get married and discovered that in their sampling more preparation went into the wedding than into fiscal or practical planning for the marriage, or personal evaluation of the respective states of marriage or cohabitation.

CHAPTER 5

THE UNMARRIED FAMILY

5.1 INTRODUCTION

As has been made clear in earlier chapters, the prevalence of cohabitation and of births outside wedlock has led to the necessity to reconsider what precisely is now understood by 'the family'. The Rowntree Foundation has long been engaged in research on the contemporary concept of the family, which has in recent times experienced such changes that inevitably practitioners now encounter significant numbers of unmarried clients and need to be aware of their separate problems which require a distinct approach: thus the unmarried family has also become a routine study in academic terms and attracts its share of attention of law reformers. Already some steps have been taken to minimise the effect for children of the fact that their parents are not married (eg, in the application of the Child Support Acts, which catch both married and unmarried absent parents who are not maintaining their children in exactly the same way regardless of their marital status). Gradually the position has been reached that there are as many similarities as differences between the two types of family.

5.2 CURRENT INITIATIVES

Both the academic and vocational student will be familiar, through study of the core subjects, with the range of property problems which arise where cohabitants buy and occupy property together. Later chapters of this book deal with the existence of remedies available to cohabitants for domestic violence, the operation of the Child Support Agency in obtaining maintenance for children from their absent parents, and the provision made (under the Children Act (CA) 1989) for unmarried fathers to obtain both parental responsibility and other orders in respect of their children (for which see further Chapters 24 *et seq*). Unfortunately, there is very little else apart from this small portfolio of remedies which is available to unmarried parties when a relationship breaks down. However, two other useful possibilities should be stressed:

- a Children Act Capital (Transfer of Property) Order, which may be obtained under the CA 1989 to enable an unmarried carer parent to secure the occupation of the former cohabitational home for that parent and the child or children (although this is normally only until the child or youngest child attains majority (see *T v S* [1994] 2 FLR 883), thus normally leaving the carer parent without a home in middle age); and

- the Law Reform (Succession) Act 1995, which has improved the rights of cohabitants on the death of their partners.

Nevertheless, the law reform society JUSTICE has in recent years embarked on a campaign to inform cohabitants (especially women, who appear to suffer most from informal arrangements about property, particularly in respect of jointly acquired homes) of the possibility of entering into cohabitation contracts or at the very least of securing recognition of the respective property rights of the parties at the initial conveyancing stage, rather than later when the parties are separating. The importance of this initiative cannot be sufficiently stressed, since there is no statutory provision similar to that under s 24 of the Matrimonial Causes Act (MCA) 1973, to facilitate division of the cohabiting couple's assets on relationship breakdown, as is available to wives in such a position on *marriage* breakdown, although this is likely to be addressed before long, following the government's planned discussion of the entire area of cohabitation law in 2003.

5.3 PROPERTY DISPUTES

Where cohabitants or former cohabitants cannot agree on property rights, a declaration of ownership can always be sought whether of real or personal property. This will of course not be under the Married Women's Property Act (MWPA) 1882, except in the case of formerly engaged couples, as the parties are by definition not married, but is still obtainable under the strict rules of property rights applied under the ordinary law of property. Similarly, a cohabitant may also seek an order for sale under ss 14 and 15 of the Trusts of Land and Appointment of Trustees Act (TOLATA) 1996 (which have replaced s 30 of the Law of Property Act (LPA) 1925 for this purpose). If these remedies are adopted, the law is basically the same for married or unmarried couples (see Chapter 21, especially 21.3.1 and 21.3.2 for resulting and constructive trusts).

5.3.1 Declarations of ownership

To assess the rights of a cohabitant to a declaration of ownership it will therefore be necessary (as in the case of married parties):

- to check the deeds for any express legal or equitable title; and
- if the cohabitant was ever engaged to be married to the other party, to apply for a declaration of ownership under s 17 of the MWPA 1882 together with a consequential order for sale, exactly as in the case of a married person, except that in the case of a former fiancé(e) it is necessary to make the application within three years of the termination of the engagement.

It should be noted that if the cohabitant has made any substantial improvements to the property, this may provide a share or an increased share under s 37 of the Matrimonial Proceedings and Property Act 1970, which former fiancé(e)s – but not other cohabitants – may use pursuant to the right given to them by s 2(1) and (2) of the Law Reform (Miscellaneous Provisions) Act 1970. If the cohabitant was *not* ever engaged to be married then it is only possible to apply to the court for a declaration under s 53(2) of the LPA 1925.

5.3.2 Trusts of Land and Appointment of Trustees Act 1996, ss 14 and 15

Sections 14 and 15 of the TOLATA 1996 are the normal jurisdiction for an order for sale where land is held on trust for the parties jointly and cohabitants may use this where the position is clear that the land is held jointly, as in that case it is automatically held on trust of land, or where a declaration has been successfully sought. The court will then have the same discretion over whether to order a sale as in the case of married people, and the decision will depend on whether the terms of trust of land *have* or *have not* in fact come to an end (see Chapter 21, particularly the case of *Re Evers' Trust* [1980] 1 WLR 1327; [1980] 3 All ER 399, which is fairly typical of the cohabitational situation to which these remedies may apply).

5.3.3 Occupation to the exclusion of the other

The cohabitant has no rights similar to those of a spouse under the Matrimonial Homes Act 1983. There are, however, four ways of achieving sole occupation of the home for a cohabitant, either:

(a) under the domestic violence rules, currently Pt IV of the Family Law Act (FLA) 1996, which now applies specifically to cohabitants, which section depending on whether they or their partners are entitled or not (see Chapter 23), or by establishing the new statutory tort of *harassment* under the Protection from Harassment Act 1997, which enables an injunction to be granted ancillary to those proceedings in tort (ie, under the inherent jurisdiction of the court: see Chapter 23); or

(b) by establishing a licence to occupy, either as a *contractual licence* or under the rules of *proprietary estoppel* (see 21.4, below); or

(c) by establishing an interest in the proceeds of sale which carries with it a right to occupy (see *Bull v Bull* [1955] 1 QB 234); or

(d) by obtaining a Transfer of Property Order under Sched 1 to the CA 1989 whereby the property is held for the benefit of the minor child of the relationship.

It should be noted that it may also be possible to obtain a domestic violence injunction, for a short period only, ancillary to a s 8 order under the CA 1989.

Otherwise neither party can occupy the property to the exclusion of the other; thus, if it would be essential to obtain an occupation order under the inherent jurisdiction, such an application must be in support of some recognised legal or equitable right (see *Ainsbury v Millington* [1986] 1 All ER 73, where the order could not be made ancillary to an order for custody, care and control of children since the joint owner mother seeking it could not assert a superior title to that of the co-owner father). For this reason most cohabitants will now rely on Pt IV of the FLA 1996, pending a longer term resolution of the property problem, by transfer of ownership or of tenancy (see Chapter 23 for transfer of tenancies under s 53 of and Sched 7 to the FLA 1996). The provisions cover transfer by one cohabitant joint tenant of his or her interest to the other (see *Gay v Sheeran* [1999] 2 FLR 519; Bridge, 'Transferring tenancies of the family home' [1998] Fam Law 26; and Woelke, 'Transfer of tenancies' [1999] Fam Law 72). The Sched 7 criteria generally favour the financially weaker party, with a child or children, who will find it difficult to find alternative accommodation.

5.3.4 Trusts

All the usual rules of resulting and constructive trusts apply in determining cohabitants' interests. There will usually be a rebuttable presumption of a resulting trust where money has changed hands, as in any joint purchase, but cases may sometimes be complicated where a cohabitant is also involved with other members of the family – the precise status of payments made must be determined and the payee often claims that the payments in question were not made with an intention or agreement to share in the property. Useful cases to look at which may provide arguments by analogy are the wider family cases of *Sekhon v Alissa* [1989] 2 FLR 94, where there was a complex mother and daughter investment in a property, which the daughter tried to pass off as a gift, and *Passee v Passee* [1988] 2 FLR 263, which concerned an even more complex extended family arrangement of a man, his aunt and her daughter, where he (unsuccessfully) claimed the payments made towards the mortgage were either loans or rent.

5.3.5 Hazards

The cohabitant often has to contend with specious arguments intended to rebut what is otherwise a fairly obvious case of a resulting trust, for example, a claim that money spent was a 'loan' as in *Risch v McFee* [1991] 1 FLR 105 (where there was a loan, but as it had been interest free and was never repaid this was treated as a part payment towards the purchase); and *Stokes v Anderson* [1980] Fam Law 310; [1991] 1 FLR 391 (where two unmarried people lived together, the woman gave the man money to buy out his ex-wife's share and when they fell out the man claimed – again unsuccessfully – that this had been a loan).

The cohabitant's situation will often share similarities in this situation as with the cases of other family members whose financial affairs have become entangled, such as in *Re Sharpe* [1980] 1 WLR 219; [1980] 1 All ER 198 (where the loan was in fact from an aunt to a nephew). Such extended 'family' cases are often of assistance in arguing for recognition of financial contributions which were not intended to be made by way of non-proprietorial payments such as loans, rent, etc.

The simplest cohabitational situation is where (as in the case of married couples) a 'joint venture' can be established, as happened in *Bernard v Josephs* [1984] FLR 126, where both parties contributed and pooled their earnings, but had made unequal contributions to the deposit to buy their home. The court (in a 'broad brush' exercise similar to that adopted in *Midland Bank v Cooke* [1995] 4 All ER 562, CA) deduced that there had been a joint venture and, on separating, the parties were held to own the house in equal shares. On the other hand, in a similar case, *Walker v Hall* [1984] FLR 126, no joint venture was discernible and the woman received a quarter share.

It should be noted, however, that the broad brush approach of *Midland Bank v Cooke* is not to be relied on in cohabitational cases, since in that case Waite LJ had the assistance of a long marriage relationship on which to rely in reviewing the entire history of the financial relationship. Thus he ultimately decided the case on the basis that 'equality is equity', but that the court only resorts to such measures if genuinely unable to discern the amount of the respective contributions: in a marriage, the very marriage may be regarded as a joint enterprise, whereas in a cohabitational relationship the reverse is often the case, with independently maintained bank accounts and financial profiles.

The problem cases in cohabitational property terms are always those such as *Windeler v Whitehall, Burns v Burns* and *Richards v Dove* (see Chapter 21) where no trust can be established according to strict property rules. However, in the later *Burns*-type case of *Hammond v Mitchell* [1991] 1 WLR 1127, the woman did manage to gain a half share of the family home on the basis of a long past and brief conversation with her former partner which was taken by Waite LJ to evidence the vital common intention to share the property which Mrs Burns could not show. This perhaps indicates that practitioners are now becoming more adept at preparing cohabitational property cases, by requiring their clients to search their memories for the essential evidence of the 'agreement, arrangement or understanding' which Lord Bridge required in *Lloyds Bank v Rosset* [1991] 1 AC 107, 'however imprecise or imperfectly remembered'. This will establish the existence of the necessary common intention (although Waite LJ also said of the parties in *Hammond v Mitchell* that they were both 'prone to exaggeration'). Clearly this is an area of the law that needs reform and precision.

5.4 MAINTENANCE OF THE PARTNER IN LIFE

There is no direct obligation on a partner to maintain a cohabitant when the parties are not married unless there is some contractual arrangement between them, although indirect support may be obtained if there is a child support assessment where a percentage of the amount paid over is in fact a payment towards the expenses of the child's carer. Thus the only possible claim for support for a cohabitant is usually to make an ordinary application to the Benefits Agency for income support or other benefits, when there will nevertheless be only one claim per household. If the parties are still *cohabiting*, as is often the case when a relationship is breaking up, and the client is without funds, either the partner who is in work must provide support voluntarily, or if both parties are out of work, one or other of them must make an application for benefits on behalf of both (see Chapter 18). Once they separate, each partner may make separate applications, and the whole range of benefits will be available (see Chapter 18).

It should be noted that a female cohabitant with children will usually have child benefit including the single parent rate, where appropriate, and will make an independent claim for child support in respect of *her* children.

5.5 MAINTENANCE OF THE PARTNER AFTER DEATH

This is provided for by s 1(1)(c) of the Inheritance (Provision for Families and Dependants) Act (I(PFD)A) 1975 if the cohabitant can show that he or she 'immediately before the death was being maintained, either wholly or partly, by the deceased'. To use this section, the cohabitant must show that the deceased, 'otherwise than for full valuable consideration, was making a substantial contribution in money or money's worth towards the reasonable needs of that person' (I(PFD)A 1975, s 1(3)). If these conditions are proved, the court may make an order under s 2.

The court has wide powers to grant periodical payments, lump sums, transfers or settlements of property and even acquisition of property for the benefit of the surviving cohabitant, using assets from the estate to do so.

However, many cohabitants are unable to show the necessary dependence, for example, where the reason that the parties did not marry was because the surviving cohabitant had independent means, such as a pension which would be forfeited on remarriage. Section 2 of the Law Reform (Succession) Act 1995 now provides for them, amending the I(PFD)A 1975 to enable non-dependent cohabitants to apply, but at the same time requiring the court to have regard to a different set of guidelines from those applying to spouses. In particular, the court must have regard to:

(a) the applicant's age and the length of time he or she lived as husband and wife with the deceased in the same household; and

(b) the contribution made by the applicant to the welfare of the family, including any contribution made by looking after the home and caring for the family.

The cohabitant applicant can only receive such provision as would be reasonable for maintenance, whereas spouses receive such provision as would be reasonable, whether or not it is required for maintenance.

5.6 MAINTENANCE OF CHILDREN

Children of cohabitants are, however, in a much more advantageous position. They may obtain both maintenance from their natural parent, through the Child Support Agency (see Chapter 15), and orders for capital provision. These are of two types:

(1) Lump sums up to £1,000 from the family proceedings court.

(2) Lump sums of any amount and orders for transfer or settlement of property for their benefit from the county court or High Court (CA 1989, s 15 and Sched 1).

A parent who is not married to the child's other parent and who is able to secure such an order for the benefit of the child is thus able indirectly to obtain financial assistance with the upbringing of the child beyond mere maintenance, even including obtaining the right to remain in the family home, which may be transferred for the benefit of the child.

5.6.1 Establishing paternity for maintenance

If it is necessary to establish paternity in order to invoke the maintenance provisions of the Child Support Acts (CSA) 1991 and 1995, as amended, or the relief obtainable under the CA 1989, it will be necessary to apply to the court for a declaration to establish relationship to the child (CSA 1991, s 27). The application for declaration of parentage may be made by the carer parent, the Secretary of State (on behalf of the carer parent, who must authorise the Secretary of State to act if the carer is receiving a specified welfare benefit), or the alleged non-resident parent.

There are certain situations, as set out in the CSA 1991, s 26, where parentage will be assumed, and these include:

- where the parents were married at some time in the period between the conception of the child and the child's birth and the child has not subsequently been adopted;
- where the father has been registered as the child's father on the child's birth certificate;
- where the non-resident parent has refused to take a scientific test to prove parentage, or has taken such a test and been proven to be the parent;
- where the non-resident parent has adopted the child;
- where the parent has been declared as such under the provisions of the Human Fertilisation and Embryology Act 1990;
- where there has been a declaration of parentage in other proceedings, and the child has not subsequently been adopted.

Scientific tests can be provided at a reduced cost under the CSA 1991. If the carer parent (normally the mother) refuses to undergo scientific testing herself, or refuses permission for the child to be so tested, the assumption can be made that the alleged non resident parent is not in fact the parent. If there is a refusal, and it is deemed to be in the child's best interests to know who his or her parents are, then the court can order blood tests despite the mother's refusal (Family Law Reform Act 1969, s 21, as amended).

If, exceptionally, there is some good reason why this information should not be divulged, or scientific tests undertaken, the carer may explain this position to the child support officer, for example if there is a risk of violence or other undue harm or distress which is likely to be suffered. If this is not accepted by the child support officer then the benefits received by the carer parent may be reduced by 40% for anything up to three years, with a continuation of deductions after that period if the carer parent still refuses to co-operate.

5.6.2 Establishing paternity for other purposes

For the purposes of s 8 of the CA 1989, the natural father is treated as a 'parent', and therefore does not require leave to apply for a s 8 order, whether or not he has parental responsibility, which is a separate issue. If, however, the mother steadfastly refuses to recognise that the natural father is the child's father, and there is no proof one way or the other, then the father will probably have to obtain a declaration using scientific tests and an application to the court using the Family Law Reform Acts 1969 and 1987. If the parties have lived together, and hence with the child, for at least 3 years, the father would have the right to apply for a residence order or contact order without the leave of the court (CA 1989, s 10(7)), although this will not answer the question of paternity. Otherwise s 1 of the Family Law Reform Act 1987 gives the unmarried father status as a parent in all cases where paternity is accepted or proved, including in all statutes where the word 'parent' would otherwise include him if he were married to the mother.

5.7 PARENTAL RESPONSIBILITY

The default position has always been that the mother of a child has sole parental rights if not married to the father. However, the father could acquire parental responsibility rights in a number of ways provided by s 4 of the CA 1989 (see Chapter 24). This was not very satisfactory, despite the Lord Chancellor's long declared intention to introduce legislation to give parental responsibility to all unmarried fathers who registered the birth with the mother (about 75% of whom have been in the habit of doing so). It has also always been a further discrimination against the unmarried father that parental responsibility could later be removed from unmarried fathers for bad behaviour, whereas nothing a mother or married father does could result in such a penalty. It appears that the European Court of Human Rights accepts this on the basis that there are reasons to distinguish the two types of father (see *Smallwood v UK* [1992] EHRLR 221, where the court considered that parental responsibility should be removed in case the father used it to disrupt the children). This had always been regarded as a strange anomaly, given the disruption caused by some mothers and married fathers. However, the Adoption and Children Act 2002 effects the long awaited change: in future the unmarried father will be more closely aligned with the married father in respect of rights and duties towards his children.

5.8 COHABITATION CONTRACTS

As a result of the above, there is now a modest growth rate in the provision of cohabitation contracts, which can provide for the parties whatever terms they wish to regulate their relationship, both while they are cohabiting happily and when the relationship breaks down. They have a similar role to play for unmarried parties as separation and maintenance agreements do for married parties who separate, save that cohabitation agreements can sometimes hold the relationship together in the first place, while separation and maintenance agreements (see Chapter 19) usually provide a *modus vivendi* for those who know that they can no longer live together. In either case, this is an opportunity for imaginative advice and creative drafting, usually on the part of the solicitor of one of the parties, although both parties should have independent legal advice before entering into them. Thus, usually one party or the other will have to take the initiative in producing a working draft. Cohabitation contracts are contracts like any other and are perfectly legal.

Many firms of solicitors now keep precedents on the word processor and suitable forms will also be found in some drafting encyclopaedias, besides which there is at least one specialist collection commercially available. In view of the high incidence of cohabitation and of births in families who do not fit the marital template, yet which are at least semi-permanent (or at least as permanent as some marriages), further formalisation of cohabitational relationships is likely. Meanwhile, practitioners have become increasingly prepared to use such law as is available to assist their unmarried clients by providing such remedies as can be accessed when relationships break down, or better, by attempting to obviate problems by recommending a cohabitation contract and explaining to their clients what will happen if one is not entered into.

5.9 PROPOSALS FOR REFORM

A paper on the reform of property law for sharers, within and outside families, was yearly expected from the Law Commission over a long period and was finally issued in late July 2002, but was a great disappointment as it did not address the fundamental cohabitational property problems: see further 4.6 above. The last Labour Government on coming into power in 1997 promised that it would work across departments to support the family, but although it quickly published a consultation paper, *Supporting Families* (Home Office, 1998), the White Paper we supposed would follow is still awaited. The Solicitors Family Law Association (SFLA) has, however, proposed detailed statutory reform. The SFLA's Cohabitation Committee has published a report entitled *Fairness for Families*, making the following proposals:

(1) Cohabitational relationships should be defined to recognise that they are different from marriage, but offer commitment, in both heterosexual and same sex couples.

(2) A new statute should enable cohabitants to apply to the courts for financial relief on relationship breakdown.

(3) A qualifying period for this should be two years unless there are children, when no minimum period should apply.

(4) There should be a discretionary jurisdiction taking account of all the circumstances of the case, as in the case of married persons who separate and divorce.

(5) Similar relief should be available on cohabitation breakdown to that on marriage breakdown, but maintenance should be limited to three years after separation, unless there is severe financial hardship. (This is similar to the Family Law (Scotland) Act 1985 provisions for divorced wives in Scotland.)

(6) The CA 1989 should be amended so as in an appropriate case to obviate the hardship to women in a *T v S* [1994] 2 FLR 883 situation (where a home transferred to a mother for the benefit of a child of an unmarried relationship normally reverts to the settlor father when the child achieves majority, thus depriving the carer mother of her home).

The SFLA also recommends extended use of cohabitation contracts, which should:

• be by deed;

• state that they are intended to be legally binding (see *Layton v Martin* [1986] 2 FLR 227);

• be comprehensive, dealing with all (and only) property and financial issues;

• be made with legal advice; and

• be effected when the parties are already living together or intending to do so shortly.

The Cohabitation Committee has produced a set of precedents.

There is much to be said for these proposals. Occasionally in England and Wales a former cohabitant wins a case which makes it clear that morally the merits in the claim were with that person and that this would have been recognised if the parties had been married (see, eg, *Fitzpatrick v Sterling Housing Association Ltd* [2000] 1 FLR 271, which recognised that same sex couples are members of the same family and should be entitled to equal rights as those of married couples under the Rent Acts; *Rowe v Prance* [1999] 2 FLR 787, where a half share of her lover's yacht was achieved by the claimant due to his express declaration of trust, even though she had not contributed financially to the purchase; and *Haywood v Haywood* (2000) *Lawtel*, 2 August, where there was a similar trust of chattels).

The Law Society has also published proposals with some differences from the SFLA's, for example, suggesting that there should be no minimum qualifying period, that qualification for benefits should be the same as for the DSS, and that public acknowledgment of the relationship as well as stability should be a key ingredient (similar to the former status of common law marriage which ended in 1753 with the passage of Lord Hardwicke's Clandestine Marriage Act). Meanwhile, the Scots are proposing abolition of their courts' existing power to regularise marriages by recognition of cohabitation with 'habit and repute', due to proposals of the Scottish Law Commission to improve the position of cohabitants there by bringing them largely into line with that of spouses under the Family Law (Scotland) Act 1985, which aims to compensate spouses on divorce by sharing wealth accumulated during the period of marriage and, as mentioned above, therefore to restrict spousal maintenance to three years from separation.

In France, there is now the possibility of a *Pacte Civile de la Solidarité* (PACS) which enables opposite and same sex couples to enter into a form of civil agreement for a common life. This is regularised by sending the agreement to the local magistrates' court, and the content is up to the parties – similar to an English cohabitation agreement.

In Australia, where New South Wales has had a De Facto Relationships Act since 1985, most States, including the Capital Territory, now have statutory rights for cohabitants, and New South Wales, the pioneer, has recently amended its Act to cover same sex couples, thus placing Australia well ahead of England and Wales, and indeed of most other jurisdictions. In New Zealand there is also a new Property Relationships Act which came into force on 1 February 2002.

5.10 OTHER DISCRIMINATION

While various irritating differences still distinguish married and cohabiting status, none is perhaps as irritating as tax treatment, although the results are not quite as bad in the UK as in France. In the former, there is the lack of the married persons' advantages on death (whereby married couples may plan their estates in a beneficial way so that assets pass between the spouses at nil inheritance tax rate). This is hardly support for the unmarried family if it is recognised as such at all. The only consolation is that in France there is an extra penalty for being unmarried, in the form of an expressly much higher inheritance tax rate for a non-spouse beneficiary, which suggests that in that jurisdiction while the wages of sin are not necessarily death as such, they are certainly payable on death!

Basically, a comprehensive approach needs to be taken to the concept of the family and the law adjusted accordingly, rather than relying on piecemeal amendments. This should not be difficult since the difference between married and cohabitant status, if really necessary to preserve, has already been addressed in Pt IV of the FLA 1996. To meet the criticism of those who say that cohabiting rather than marrying indicates that the parties expressly chose an alternative to marriage, new legislation, such as that proposed by the SFLA, can quite well address any desirable differences in consequences to reflect the distinct status of the two types of relationship.

THE UNMARRIED FAMILY

COHABITANTS' PROPERTY

There is no regime of cohabitants' property, which needs therefore to be specifically conveyed to reflect the parties' interests. If this is not done they are reliant on the ordinary law of resulting and constructive trusts to unravel and establish their respective interests. Orders for sale may be obtained under ss 14 and 15 of the TOLATA 1996. Orders under the CA 1989 may protect the home for the female cohabitant and children. Pt IV of the FLA 1996 can secure occupation of the home for a cohabitant in case of violence by the partner, but not usually long term, although a transfer of tenancy of a rented property may be possible. The Law Reform (Succession) Act 1995 gives some recognition to cohabitants' rights in the family home. Cohabitation contracts can address these and other financial and non-financial issues.

MAINTENANCE OF COHABITANTS IN LIFE AND AFTER DEATH

There is no right to maintenance for cohabitants, although the children may be maintained either under the CSAs 1991–95, as amended, the CA 1989 or under the I(PFD)A 1975, and a cohabitant who has been dependent in life may be maintained under that Act after the partner's death.

PARENTAL RESPONSIBILITY

Only married fathers have parental responsibility unless the mother gives it to an unmarried father by agreement or he obtains it from the court. There is reform proposed to give parental responsibility to those (75%) who register the birth with their partners.

REFORM

Clearly the situation is unsatisfactory given the numbers of families now involved. The SFLA and the Law Society have proposed detailed reforms, and a consultation paper from the Law Commission on home sharing was published in 2002. Australia (the pioneer since 1985), New Zealand, Scotland and France are all ahead of England and Wales in recognising *de facto* relationships, although two Private Members' Bills have sought to introduce greater rights for cohabitants who register their partnerships.

PART II

DIVORCE

CHAPTER 6

HISTORICAL INTRODUCTION TO DIVORCE

6.1 ORIGINS OF ENGLISH DIVORCE LAW

English divorce law originated in the ecclesiastical courts. In the early middle ages remarriage was not uncommon since among the landed classes marriage was undertaken both for the purpose of obtaining, consolidating and protecting property and in particular for the personal protection of women in a violent society. In early times both Church and State recognised that marriages could be dissolved by what was known as divorce *a vinculo matrimonii* (literally from the chains of marriage). This was probably a relic of the influence of the Roman Empire in which serial marriages and divorces were common and politically acceptable – it was regarded as essential to preserve both property and personal relationships. It was only after the Church of Rome, basing its view of marriage on the Gospels, adopted the concept of the indissolubility of the marriage bond that the English ecclesiastical courts, in order to preserve some dissolution facility, began to distinguish between validly contracted marriages and those which had an impediment. The valid marriage they considered they could dissolve only *a mensa et thoro* – literally severing the physical links based on the common table and home shared by the spouses, and relieving them of a duty to live together, but *not* breaking the spiritual marriage tie, a result similar to a modern decree of judicial separation, but the concept of the invalid marriage offered the opportunity of complete annulment.

The Church (at this stage still the Church of Rome in England as elsewhere in Christendom) then developed the concept and separate remedy of nullity, in identifying marriages which had *not* been validly contracted and/or consummated as a Christian marriage should be, and which might therefore be declared void from the start, thus permitting the parties to remarry since they had technically never been married before.

One method of finding marriages invalid was to narrow the table of kindred and affinity so that only those less closely related than third cousins could marry. Any closer relationship was an impediment, as were spiritual relationships of religious rather than matrimonial affinity, through standing as godparents to children, which would place the godparent in a close family relationship with the child's parents.

During the Reformation, demand grew for a more effective method of divorce than that of the decree *a mensa et thoro* which was a hopelessly limited remedy for those who wished to remarry: this demand came not least from the King, Henry VIII, who wished to put away his first wife, Catherine of Aragon, in order to marry her maid of honour, Anne Boleyn, subsequently the mother of Queen Elizabeth I. However, the difficulties he endured in order to achieve the marriage before Elizabeth was born were such that he was obliged to secede from the Church of Rome and to set himself up as the Head of the new (at that stage still largely Catholic, if reformed) Church of England.

Yet the King was the only beneficiary of this move, since divorce was made no easier for lesser mortals, including the great landowners who were still obliged to rely on annulment or remain married. Despite the increased absorption of Protestant doctrines from the Reformation on the continent, the Church of England was not only not minded to extend divorce, but rather also to restrict access to the former ecclesiastical remedy of nullity.

In the 17th and early 18th centuries, therefore, a parliamentary method of divorce *a vinculo matrimonii* by private Act of Parliament was developed which enabled the aristocracy, which needed heirs to their estates, to end marriages which were infertile or otherwise inconvenient. In practice, at least at first, this was available only to men. For example, the Duke of Norfolk obtained such a divorce, petitioning the House of Lords for a Bill of divorce in 1701 on the grounds of his wife's adultery, and his lack of an heir. Later Parliament allowed wealthy business and professional men (including clergymen) to avail themselves of this remedy for their domestic problems. The method (which was expensive) was to obtain a divorce *a mensa et thoro* from the ecclesiastical courts, then to sue the wife's co-adulterer for 'criminal conversation', prior to petitioning and attending the House for cross-examination over whether the petitioner had connived at or colluded with the adultery, or partially or wholly caused it by living apart from his wife. It was hardly a popular service: only 317 divorces were thus obtained between 1714 and 1857.

Later in the period of the parliamentary divorce, which came to a head in the early 1800s and lasted only until 1857 when the first Matrimonial Causes Act was passed, four women succeeded in obtaining divorces: Mrs Addison in 1801, Mrs Turton in 1830, Mrs Battersby in 1840 and Mrs Hall in 1850. This advance was not secured on equal terms with men as, unlike their husbands, wives were obliged to allege some other matrimonial offence as well as adultery: the husband's adultery in Mrs Turton's case was incestuous, in Mrs Battersby's case aggravated by cruelty and in Mrs Hall's by bigamy.

Mrs Addison's case was argued in the House of Lords by Lord Thurlow, to the effect that it would be wrong if she were unable to obtain a divorce against her husband who had been engaged in an affair with Mrs Addison's sister, and had been duly sued by the sister's husband for the requisite 'criminal conversation'. While arguing that it would be unjust to reject Mrs Addison's petition, Lord Thurlow nevertheless did not accept that women should have the same general right to divorce as a husband, relying for this on the concept that marriage made the husband and wife one, and that therefore any damage to the wife – as where a third party engaged in intercourse with the wife outside marriage – was damage to the husband himself, so that he was entitled to sue on it, as much as in respect of damage to any other item of his property. Lord Thurlow's further argument was based on the old medieval concepts of kindred and affinity, for since Mrs Addison's husband had had intercourse with her sister, a resumption of cohabitation with his wife would be incest, thus making any reconciliation impossible.

While Lord Thurlow's arguments dissuaded Lord Eldon from opposing Mrs Addison's Bill, it was still regarded as much more important that a man should obtain a divorce by this means than that there should be equality between the sexes. As Lord Cranworth explained, 'A wife might ... condone an act of adultery on the part of a husband' but not *vice versa*, giving as his reason 'the adultery of the wife might be the means of palming off spurious offspring upon the husband', while the reverse would not be true. It is clear that one of the few advantages of women at this time was that they at least knew their children were their own.

Nevertheless, reform was needed even for men, as was shown by the case of *R v Hall* (1845) 1 Cox 231, in which Mr Hall, a poor working man, was indicted for bigamy, which he had committed since he could not afford to obtain a divorce prior to remarrying. His original wife had both committed adultery and deserted him, after having made their married life a misery with her drunkenness and dissipation – mitigation which the judge dismissed as 'irrational excuses', adding that the fact that Hall was a poor working man who could not afford the parliamentary procedure was 'not the fault of the law' which was 'impartial', making 'no difference between rich and poor'! Happily, the sentence was no more than Hall had already passed in jail, so he was released immediately.

6.2 MATRIMONIAL CAUSES ACT 1857

Following Lord Campbell's Royal Commission of 1850, the Matrimonial Causes Act 1857 transferred the existing divorce and matrimonial jurisdictions from Parliament and the ecclesiastical courts to a new court, the Court for Divorce and Matrimonial Causes, which assumed responsibility for all decrees of divorce and nullity and renamed the decree *a mensa et thoro* as 'judicial separation'.

The grounds were not much changed: a husband could still present a petition on the basis of adultery only, whereas a wife required some aggravating factor as well, such as incestuous adultery, cruelty, sodomy, bestiality or desertion for two years. Gladstone, who agreed in principle with the Act, was strongly against this distinction between the sexes.

The Act made the process more accessible but did not vastly increase the numbers of petitions compared to the previous processes (the period 1857–61 saw 781 divorce petitions and 248 for judicial separation). However, the magistrates entertained increasing business in applications for matrimonial maintenance and separation orders by poorer people (of which there were 87,000 between 1897 and 1906).

6.3 EARLY 20TH CENTURY REFORM

In 1909 there was another Royal Commission, chaired by Lord Gorell. The Gorell Commission recommended that the sexes should be placed on the same footing (implemented in Lord Buckmaster's Act in 1923), a decentralisation of divorce so that local registries could provide cheaper access to justice for people of small means (implemented in 1946) and extending the grounds to include cruelty, habitual drunkenness and incurable insanity (implemented in the Matrimonial Causes Act 1937).

The watershed in divorce reform appears to have been the Second World War. Wives who had been left behind to stand on their own feet became unwilling to remain in marriages where they were undervalued, but it was not until legal aid became available that they were able to consider divorce as a serious alternative, since most women had no independent access to money: most matrimonial homes and investments were in the husband's name owing to the culture at the time. A Private Member's Bill in 1951 first proposed divorce after a period of separation (seven years) instead of reliance on allegations of a matrimonial offence – a radical change which obviously scared the government sufficiently, especially when viewed in conjunction with the new access to legal aid, that the Bill was withdrawn on the promise of another Royal Commission. This was the Morton Commission of 1956 which, although divided, recommended against change, largely ignoring the perjury that was frequently occasioned by the existing law, and the concerns about illicit unions and illegitimate children. This was backed up by the Church of England, which said that the doctrine of the matrimonial offence was in accordance with the New Testament and that any change would threaten society and the stability and structure of the family.

Nevertheless, there was a further reconsideration by the Church. The Archbishop of Canterbury's research group published a report in 1966 entitled *Putting Asunder – A Divorce Law for Contemporary Society* (Society for the Promotion of Christian Knowledge, 1966) which drew three main conclusions:

(1) that the Church should co-operate with the State in recognising a secular divorce law, subject to protection of the weak and strengthening the law to support Christian marriage;

(2) that the existing mix of fault based and non-fault based grounds (such as insanity) was inept; and

(3) that the courts should inquire thoroughly into whether a marriage had broken down and, if so, dissolve it.

They also recommended that the basic ground for divorce should be irretrievable breakdown.

6.4 DIVORCE REFORM ACT 1969

Following the Archbishop's Group Report, the Law Commission undertook a thorough inquiry into divorce law. Their report was entitled *Reform of the Grounds of Divorce – The Field of Choice* (Cmnd 3123, 1966) with a twin goal: to support marriages which had a chance of survival and to bury with decency and expedition those which were already dead 'with the minimum of embarrassment, humiliation and bitterness'. They were against the inquest into the marriage suggested by the Archbishop's Group, but accepted the concept of divorce after separation, two years with consent of the other party, and five or seven years, subject to safeguards, without.

The report was backed up by some assumptions about public opinion which have never been scientifically substantiated. They were apparently the results of contemporary research, and appear to have some foundation in contemporary experience of divorce, for example, the lack of connection between the matrimonial fault relied on for the divorce and the actual breakdown of the marriage, such as in the treatment of adultery as a symptom rather than a cause of divorce, which may confidently be said to have generated Sir Roger Ormrod's approach to civilised divorce about which he wrote in the jointly authored text *Divorce Matters* (1987) (see further Chapter 8).

The resulting cocktail of reforms – one sole ground for divorce of irretrievable breakdown evidenced by one of five facts, three fault based and two based on simple separation, which was for the first time to be a basis of divorce – was enacted in the

Divorce Reform Act 1969. This was subsequently consolidated with the Matrimonial Proceedings and Property Act 1970 into the Matrimonial Causes Act 1973 which, as amended, still comprises the English law of divorce. The subsequent Pt II of the Family Law Act 1996, which was radically to reform the law again by removing virtually the entire 1973 system, was never implemented. The Lord Chancellor has now confirmed that those parts of the Act dealing with the ground for divorce and the controversial procedure for implementing the reforms (ie, Pt II) have been abandoned. It is anticipated that in due course some other reforms will be brought forward but there are at present no signs of any progress in this direction, and it would seem that reform of the law of ancillary relief is more urgent (see further Chapters 12 *et seq*).

HISTORICAL INTRODUCTION TO DIVORCE

ORIGINS OF ENGLISH DIVORCE LAW

Early English divorces were not uncommon, probably a relic of the Roman Law influence where divorce and remarriage was a normality of life. Subsequently, the ecclesiastical courts, believing in the indissolubility of Christian marriage, would only grant the equivalent of judicial separation, or an annulment where the marriage could be categorised as having an initial impediment so that it was no true marriage. After the Reformation, when Henry VIII seceded from the Church of Rome in order to obtain a divorce himself, the position paradoxically became more restrictive rather than easier, as the new Protestant influence reacted against the Church's extensive grounds for annulments, and a parliamentary method of divorce by private Act had to be developed. This lasted until 1857 by which time only about 300 divorces had been granted to wealthy people, including, however, only four women.

The sole ground on which men could obtain a divorce in this way was simple adultery, which enabled them to obtain an ecclesiastical decree, the equivalent of judicial separation. They were then obliged to sue the alleged co-adulterer in the courts for 'criminal conversation', only finally petitioning Parliament for a private divorce Bill. Women were obliged to allege some aggravating factor, such as cruelty or incest, and had no equivalent right as such to divorce as their husbands did. Lord Cranworth justified this on the basis that women's adultery could foist a bastard onto an unsuspecting husband, whereas wives were not subject to this risk.

MATRIMONIAL CAUSES ACT 1857

This statute created a new divorce court which had jurisdiction in matrimonial cases previously enjoyed by Parliament or the ecclesiastical courts. The basis for divorce was gradually widened in the recommendations of Royal Commissions until, by 1937, much of the present law of divorce was recognisable in successive Matrimonial Causes Acts. Men and women received equal access to remedies from 1923. The real watershed in this respect was the creation of legal aid in 1949, which enabled women to afford to bring petitions.

DIVORCE REFORM ACT 1969

This followed a Royal Commission, the Archbishop of Canterbury's Group Report in 1966, and a report by the Law Commission. It was subsequently consolidated with the

Matrimonial Proceedings and Property Act 1970 to become the Matrimonial Causes Act 1973, the source of contemporary divorce law.

CONTEMPORARY REFORM INITIATIVES

Part II of the Family Law Act 1996 (which has not been implemented) has now been abandoned and no further reform initiatives have so far been proposed.

CHAPTER 7

THE MODERN LAW OF DIVORCE

7.1 MATRIMONIAL CAUSES ACT 1973

Since the great watershed of 1969, and the consolidation of the 1969 and 1970 Acts in the Matrimonial Causes Act (MCA) 1973, there have been ongoing initiatives to continue the reform of contemporary divorce law, the last culminating in the Family Law Act (FLA) 1996, most of which has never been brought into force. Thus for the time being the existing law, now largely contained in the MCA 1973, as amended, continues in force, since the Lord Chancellor has now finally indicated that the crucial reforms of substantive law and process in Pt II of the FLA 1996 will not be implemented in their present form (for the background to these key 1973 and 1996 Acts, see Chapter 6).

7.2 MATRIMONIAL CAUSES ACT 1973 IN PRACTICE

Both the existing law and attempts to reform it are now firmly based on an acceptance by academics and practitioners alike that the legal resolution of marital problems is not conveniently achieved by a predominantly litigious approach. Even where a firm of solicitors consulted by a client initiating or already involved in a divorce has no specialist family department, and the work is probably therefore undertaken by a non-specialist litigator, the Law Society's recommendation that all solicitors should observe the spirit of the Code of Practice of the Solicitors Family Law Association (SFLA) – whether they are themselves personally members or not – should secure, for the conduct of the divorce and its ancillary issues, the contemporary non-litigious approach. In the contemporary climate of mediation (which now also influences funding for divorce) it is curious to reflect that it is in fact only 20 years since the SFLA was founded for the precise purpose of encouraging a conscious change of gear from the usual approach of the civil litigator. Many family law practitioners do now join the SFLA automatically upon commencing a family practice and some become further recognised as specialists under the Association's Specialist Accreditation Scheme. Moreover, it is impossible not to recognise the SFLA's contribution to the tailoring of the provisions of the MCA 1973 to the need for co-operation in shared parenting generated by the Children Act 1989, which has been a major catalyst in promoting the current trend towards greater co-operation between the parties to the actual divorce.

The Association was established in 1982 with the object of taking family matters as far as possible out of the atmosphere of contentious litigation and with the aim of achieving agreed solutions which, while not substantially different from what the court would order if the matter were acrimoniously contested, might with co-operation be achieved at less cost, emotionally as well as financially. The Children Act gloss came later, since in the early 1980s the Children Act 1989 was still only a gleam in the eye of the then Family Law Commissioner, Professor Brenda Hoggett, now Hale LJ. Indeed, the research that generated the legislation which, in families with children, would permit the continued parenting role envisaged by the Children Act concept of parental responsibility was only beginning. This infrastructure has been built upon in reforms to divorce procedure, such as the Ancillary Relief Pilot Scheme, which has been adopted nationally since June 2000. This scheme seeks to end the previously very long drawn out and costly ancillary proceedings for financial relief which sometimes followed and much soured a relatively quick and easy divorce decree. The scheme also aims to preclude the inevitable tactical moves resorted to in the past, by setting down a clear, precise system, under the control of the court, and making it difficult for the parties to manipulate it. These initiatives have been further assisted by the enactment of s 1 of the FLA 1996 which helpfully sets out in statutory form the objectives of contemporary divorce law:

PART I

PRINCIPLES OF PARTS II and III

1   **The general principles underlying Parts II and III**

The court and any person, in exercising functions under or in consequence of Parts II and III, shall have regard to the following general principles –

(a) that the institution of marriage is to be supported;

(b) that the parties to a marriage which may have broken down are to be encouraged to take all practicable steps, whether by marriage counselling or otherwise, to save the marriage;

(c) that a marriage which has irretrievably broken down and is being brought to an end should be brought to an end –

  (i)   with minimum distress to the parties and to the children affected;

  (ii) with questions dealt with in a manner designed to promote as good a continuing relationship between the parties and any children affected as is possible in the circumstances; and

  (iii) without costs being unreasonably incurred in connection with the procedures to be followed in bringing the marriage to an end; and

(d) that any risk to one of the parties to a marriage, and to any children, of violence from the other party should, so far as reasonably practicable, be removed or diminished.

There is no new philosophy in this section, but its inclusion in a statute for the first time is an innovation (since no such provision was included in the MCA 1973, although that Act was informed by much the same principles).

Thus the current divorce law to be found in the MCA 1973, as amended, and the practice which facilitates its contemporary application are not quite the same as what was envisaged when the Act was brought onto the statute book nearly 30 years ago. Practitioners have nevertheless 'made do' with the existing law by interpreting the provisions of the 1973 Act literally so as to serve the demands of contemporary society, as a comparison of current case law with its earlier equivalents will show. The academic student will sometimes make the point that this must be an abuse of the system: however, as procedure and practice is as valid an element of the law as the legislation which it administers, the better view is that the experienced practitioners who have made the MCA 1973 serve the purposes of the late 20th and early 21st century have followed faithfully in the tradition of English legal history in making do with an existing remedy, with a useful twist here and there where necessary, rather than clamouring to create a new one.

7.3 TERMINOLOGY IN DIVORCE SUITS

By way of emphasising the difference between the law of divorce and the course of ordinary litigation, it should be noted that the procedural terminology is distinct. This is partly due to the origins of divorce in ecclesiastical law (and the FLA 1996 would have changed the familiar vocabulary on the grounds that in modern times it is inappropriate and sends the wrong messages, possibly another mistake that added to that Act's unpopularity). Under the MCA 1973:

(a) the parties have always been known as the petitioner and the respondent (not plaintiff and defendant, nor – following the reform of civil justice in the Civil Procedure Rules – claimant and defendant);

(b) the parties proceed by petition (not statement of claim, particulars of claim or even simply claim as under the CPR); and

(c) a party defending files an 'answer' and, where appropriate, cross-petition (not a defence and counterclaim).

The marriage is then ended by 'decree', which comes in two parts: first 'decree *nisi*' (which decides in effect that the petitioner is entitled to the decree) and then (from six weeks after decree *nisi*) 'decree absolute', which finally ends the status of marriage. The courts having jurisdiction in divorce are also quite distinct. All divorces commence in a Divorce County Court (ie, a county court designated to deal with such work, which all county courts are not) and are then tried there unless transferred to the High Court (Matrimonial and Family Proceedings Act 1984, ss 33 and 39).

The primary source of the law of divorce is the MCA 1973, as amended – the statute which consolidated the Divorce Reform Act 1969 and the Matrimonial Proceedings and Property Act 1970 to form the main Act from which the contemporary 'reformed' law of divorce derives – and the main procedural source is the Family Proceedings Rules (FPR) 1991, as amended (which has produced many subsequent issues of Family Proceedings (Amendment) Rules).

There are other primary sources – in particular those dealing with other aspects of family and divorce practice and procedure, and with special topics such as jurisdiction, occupation of the home, financial provision without dissolution of the marriage and child matters – but the basic working knowledge of divorce law and procedure which both the academic and vocational student requires in order to understand how the substantive law works may be obtained from the MCA 1973 and the FPR 1991. The relevant parts of the

Act are conveniently reproduced in the standard family law statute books and in the leading practitioner text, *Rayden and Jackson* (a large looseleaf work often simply referred to as '*Rayden*'). In *Rayden* will be found all the statutory material referred to (including the various rules of court).

7.4 JURISDICTION

Jurisdiction in divorce in England and Wales is governed by s 5 of the Domicile and Matrimonial Proceedings Act 1973, subject from 1 March 2001 to 'Brussels II' (ie, the new EU requirements of the Brussels Convention of 1998 on Jurisdiction and the Recognition and Enforcement of Judgments in Matrimonial Matters (No 1347/2000): Art 2(1) of the Council Regulation is designed to harmonise Member States' courts' jurisdiction for divorce, regulation of forum proceedings and international child arrangements across 14 EU States). It must be read in conjunction with the European Communities (Matrimonial Jurisdiction and Judgments) Regulations 2001 SI 2001/310 and the Family Proceedings (Amendment) Rules 2001 SI 2001/821. This means that for divorce, judicial separation, and presumption of death and dissolution of the marriage, the court has jurisdiction under the Act if either of the parties is domiciled in England and Wales on the date when the proceedings are begun, or was habitually resident in England and Wales throughout the period of one year ending with that date (s 5(2)). But if another EU State is involved, at least six months' residence in England and Wales will now be required and, if proceedings are also started in another State, the first in date will establish the forum for the suit. This may be of some importance since the approach to ancillary relief is markedly different in the various States of the EU, both from that in England and Wales and also often from one another. In general terms, most States use the approach of 'community of property' which is unknown to English law. Thus the selection of a sympathetic jurisdiction will be uppermost in the minds of any couples with cross-border affiliations.

In practice there has in the past been rarely any difficulty if a petitioner wishes to obtain a divorce in England and Wales, and we may perhaps expect to see much more forum shopping in the future – as was demonstrated to achieve advantage to the husband in *Dart v Dart* [1996] 2 FLR 286, CA, where the husband expressly moved the family to England to establish sufficient residence, in order to evade the 'wife friendly' community property jurisdiction of the US State of Michigan. The basic concept of the Domicile and Matrimonial Proceedings Act 1973 is that jurisdiction should be based on domicile (of origin, choice or dependence). A detailed study of domicile is beyond the scope of this book, but the basic concept, which must be grasped in order to understand the alternative roles of domicile and habitual residence, is that to establish domicile requires the existence of a physical presence in a country together with a degree of settlement and without looking forward to any alternative permanent home (*Plummer v IRC* [1988] 1 All ER 27 – although once this is established the country in question may be left for visits elsewhere provided there is an intention to return). Residence, on the other hand, which also requires a physical presence (although visits elsewhere may still be made), only requires a more limited settled purpose such as for education (*Kapur v Kapur* [1985] 15 Fam Law 22), although the House of Lords has confirmed that for residence to become 'habitual' it must last for an appreciable period (and in the case of the MCA 1973 that is expressly stated to be for one year).

Domicile must be distinguished from nationality, which is irrelevant to divorce law. If domicile is relied on for jurisdiction, that may be domicile of origin, domicile of choice or domicile of dependence. Domicile of origin means that the party to the divorce was born to a parent or parents having domicile in England and Wales and has not changed that domicile since attaining majority: it should be noted that the *place* of birth is irrelevant if a person was born to such parents with domicile in England and Wales. Domicile of choice may be acquired by an adult deciding to change a domicile of origin by leaving that jurisdiction and taking up a domicile elsewhere. Domicile of dependence means that the party is a person under the age of majority who will automatically have the same domicile as the parent or parents on whom dependence is presumed until the age of majority. Thus, if the father of a legitimate child or the mother of a child born outside wedlock changes their domicile of origin, and acquires a domicile of choice, that domicile of choice will at the same time change the domicile of dependence of the child. At majority the child will take the domicile of dependence as a domicile of choice until he or she changes it again by moving elsewhere.

7.5 FIRST YEAR OF MARRIAGE: THE ABSOLUTE BAR ON DIVORCE

It is not possible to *petition for divorce* during the first year after the celebration of the marriage (MCA 1973, s 3(1), inserted by the Matrimonial and Family Proceedings Act 1984, s 1).

This is now an absolute bar to which there are no exceptions, although when the Act was passed in 1973 there was originally an absolute bar of one year and a further discretionary bar of three years which could be displaced on the facts by suitable circumstances. The remaining absolute bar still applies even where early presentation of the petition is inadvertent. In *Butler v Butler* [1990] Fam Law 21, the contravention of the rule occurred where the petition was originally presented (quite properly within the first year of marriage) for judicial separation, not divorce, and only later amended for divorce. This proved fatal, since the date of *presentation* of the amended petition was technically that of the original petition for judicial separation, and there was no remedy but to present a new one. The absolute bar during the first year is intended to encourage the newly married who regret the step to give the marriage a chance before seeking dissolution.

7.6 ALTERNATIVES DURING THE FIRST YEAR

There are, however, a number of other options open to the petitioner who dislikes s 3, although with the exception of obtaining a nullity decree none will permit remarriage, which realistically is what the would-be petitioner probably wants at the time of considering divorce, even though there may be no potential new spouse yet in view. Often, though, a potential petitioner merely wants a finite dissolution of the existing marriage so that new attachments may be formed with a clear conscience and with the bad experience firmly in the past. In these circumstances the law provides various possibilities that can utilise what scope there is for putting the reluctant spouse's affairs in order in a sensible manner while waiting to petition for divorce.

Because it would probably be foolish for most spouses with one failed marriage behind them to be in a position to contract another before the first anniversary has been reached, the year's wait is not in practice much of a drawback. Practitioners therefore tend to concentrate on pointing out to their clients the various alternatives available, some of which may apply in a particular case, and on either taking emergency or temporary action where appropriate or else in disposing in the intervening year of the 'baggage' which it will be undesirable to take into any new relationship (particularly as statistics show that many second and subsequent marriages fail because of unfinished business of one sort or another left over from the previous one). If, however, some legal step, rather than a temporary practical solution, is insisted upon by the disappointed spouse, the law can assist in the ways set out at 7.6.1–7.6.8, below.

7.6.1 Judicial separation or nullity

It often comes as a surprise to non-lawyers to learn that divorce is not the only decree available, and that the alternatives of judicial separation (under the MCA 1973, s 17) or nullity (under the MCA 1973, ss 11 and 12, for which see Chapter 3) may be applicable. Either of these decrees may be applied for if appropriate within days of the marriage ceremony, and in the case of nullity a lengthy delay in presenting a petition can even be fatal.

A detailed knowledge of these alternative decrees is often outside the scope of the average family law undergraduate syllabus, but all students should be aware of their usefulness for those who oppose divorce on religious grounds, or for whom it is important to achieve a formal break with a spouse where dissolution of the marriage by divorce is temporarily either:

- not possible (due to s 3); or
- not advisable even when the initial year is up, for example, due to an unresolved property dispute affected by the termination of the status of marriage, such as where steps must be taken to retain the spouse's rights under a pension scheme.

A student should therefore be aware of the existence and basic principles of the law of nullity and judicial separation so as to be able to judge whether either of these alternative decrees might be suitable in an appropriate situation. Recent concern about the continued practice of forced as opposed to consensual arranged marriages in some ethnic communities has expressly highlighted the contemporary relevance of nullity (which had recently suffered a drop in popularity due to the decline of religious objection to divorce and ease of obtaining a divorce decree under the MCA 1973).

7.6.2 Judicial separation

A decree of *judicial separation* can be obtained on the same facts as divorce save that it is not necessary to prove irretrievable breakdown of the marriage (see Chapters 8–11).

This may in particular satisfy the new spouse who wants to achieve a formal break in a situation where the marriage has obviously ended for all practical purposes but divorce is not yet possible. A further advantage is that such a decree records the separation which can later be used for a divorce decree when the year is up (ie, it preserves the evidence). However, judicial separation is not to be recommended where the client's real objective is to remarry, since the decree will inevitably cost money to obtain and by the time it is obtained it is likely to be time to petition for divorce.

Judicial separation used to be popular in cases where it was desired to preserve the status of marriage while permitting the parties officially to abandon the state of consortium which usually defines the 'normal' marriage. This might be, for example, where it was not possible fairly to compensate for the loss of pension rights by 'earmarking' under the Pensions Act 1995, or by variation of settlement on the lines of that adopted in *Brooks v Brooks* [1996] AC 375; [1995] 3 All ER 257, HL, and no other form of compensation (eg, a lump sum or increased share of the matrimonial home) was possible. However, now that pensions can be shared by pension attachment pursuant to the Welfare Reform and Pension Act 1999, also known as 'splitting', this use of judicial separation is likely to decline.

7.6.3 Nullity

A decree of *nullity* can be obtained where the marriage is either *void* or *voidable* (see Chapter 3). A decree of nullity in respect of a *void* marriage can always be obtained on proof of the relevant fact on the basis of:

- defective formalities;
- one of the parties already being married;
- the parties not being respectively male and female; or
- its polygamous nature, provided one of the parties is domiciled in England and Wales.

There is no time limit for petitioning on any of these grounds since the marriage is void anyway and strictly no declaration to that effect is actually necessary for it to be regarded as void. A void marriage can *never* be valid *whatever* the parties wish. Sometimes, however, an actual declaration is required, for example, by trustees of a settlement, who may wish to know whether to treat a marriage as void or voidable. Therefore, if any of the grounds apply which make a marriage void, the sooner a petition is presented the better, so that the true status of the marriage may be formally recognised.

Where the marriage is *voidable,* a petition sometimes needs to be presented within three years of the marriage, and even if that time limit does not apply, a delay in petitioning might give rise to the defence of approbation of the marriage – that is, that the petitioner acted as though he or she were willing to honour the marriage regardless of the fact that it could be annulled.

Where a marriage is voidable it is too late to dissolve it after the death of one of the parties. The marriage will have subsisted as a valid marriage until death and will therefore at that stage have been dissolved by death, upon which the surviving partner will have the status of a widow or widower in the normal way.

7.6.4 Separation agreements

Some non-lawyers are surprised to discover that a decree is not essential to effect a formal separation and that a separation agreement can deal formally with all matters over which a court has jurisdiction without the necessity of going to court, save only for ultimately dissolving the marriage when the parties are finally ready and able to seek a decree of divorce.

Separation agreements have the added advantage over court proceedings that it is possible with very few limits to insert into them virtually any provisions which the parties desire, although care needs to be taken to remember that financial arrangements may have a subsequent influence on provision which the court may order on dissolution of marriage.

It is of course open to the parties merely to separate, by informal mutual agreement or by the unilateral decision of one of them, without either decree or formal separation agreement, save only that if one leaves the other without just cause they will technically be in desertion and might ultimately be divorced for it (see Chapter 9).

7.6.5 Sources of funds

If the real reason behind the would be petitioner seeking advice is because the breakdown of the marriage has caused financial problems, there are three possible sources of funds without the need to petition for any decree whatsoever (four if the parties have children):

- ss 2, 6 and 7 of the Domestic Proceedings and Magistrates' Courts Act 1978 (see Chapter 19);
- s 27 of the MCA 1973 (see Chapter 19);
- welfare benefit advice (see Chapter 18);

and, if the parties have children,

- the Child Support Agency (see Chapter 15).

Alternatively, it might be possible to negotiate voluntary payments from the other spouse. Much will depend on the reason for the marital breakdown and on whether the separation was consensual.

7.6.6 Children Act proceedings

Very often the catalyst bringing the prospective petitioner to a consideration of divorce is a problem about the children. In this case a freestanding application can and should be brought under the Children Act 1989 to resolve such problems without taking any proceedings in relation to the *marriage* as such. The whole concept of the Children Act was to take child matters out of the realm of divorce, to treat the children of married and unmarried parents in substantially the same way, and to underline the separation between the Children Act (dealing with children) and the MCA 1973 (dealing with divorce) with a view to preserving the concept of parental responsibility for all parents regardless of their marital status. For example, a residence order may be obtained if there is a sufficient dispute as to where a child should live, or a contact order if contact is being denied, or a specific issue order or prohibited steps order in relation to urgent decisions about important matters such as medical treatment, education or religion (see Chapters 24 and 25).

7.6.7 Injunction orders and declarations

Similarly an act of violence or a dispute over occupation may be the immediate reason a prospective petitioner has thought of divorce.

The law in this area has now been consolidated in Pt IV of the FLA 1996, which provides for a simple regime of non-molestation and occupation orders to replace the formerly variegated terminology and substance of the preceding law (see Chapter 23). The courts (both High Court and county courts) also have inherent powers to grant injunction orders ancillary to any suit before them so that such orders can be granted ancillary to divorce proceedings, wardship or Children Act 1989 proceedings, and if such proceedings are already on foot it would be expected that any injunction would be ancillary to the proceedings in question.

7.6.8 The practical impact of the Matrimonial Causes Act 1973, s 3

As the absolute bar imposed by s 3 only affects presentation of a divorce petition for the relatively short period of one year from the celebration of the marriage, practitioners tend to consider that it is probably more cost-effective to prepare such a petition to file as soon as possible rather than to waste time and money obtaining a temporary decree of judicial separation which will ultimately need to be superseded by one for divorce in order to leave the client free to remarry. They therefore tend to suggest:

- making use of any of the remedies described at 7.6.1–7.6.7 which suit their client's circumstances; and to concentrate on such practical matters as:
  - ○ money to live on;
  - ○ somewhere suitable to live; and
  - ○ absence of any harassment, interference or violence from the other spouse.

It should be noted that a petition for divorce on the basis of either adultery or behaviour (see Chapter 8) can be presented one year and a day after the ceremony, regardless of how early in the marriage the matters relied upon occurred, as the statute places the ban on *petitioning*, not on reliance on the actual conduct which needs to be shown in order to obtain a decree, which is in no way limited by s 1(2). Moreover, the statute makes it explicit that the ban is on actually petitioning during the first year of marriage, and that any matters occurring during that year may still be relied on as the substance of the petition (see MCA 1973, s 3(2)).

7.7 THE RELATIONSHIP BETWEEN DIVORCE, FINANCIAL AND CHILD PROCEEDINGS

It will be clear from the above overview of the modern law of divorce that in the past 30 years the post-Divorce Reform Act 1969 regime has been developed to provide a framework of divorce and related law which can dissolve or annul marriages, or issue decrees of judicial separation as appropriate, and decide or formalise all consequent financial matters. The related statutes – the Children Act 1989 and the Pt IV of the FLA 1996 – can deal on an entirely freestanding basis with matters concerning the children of a marriage and/or with domestic violence and occupational rights problems. It is important that students understand at an early stage that these jurisdictions are separate, and that although there are special provisions within both the 1989 and the 1996 Acts relating to the married as distinguished from the unmarried, these two latter statutes are designed to cater overall for both the married and the unmarried in a comprehensive framework. Thus, family law seems to be moving consciously away from the concept of the married family as the core unit of society. In effect, we now have a law of divorce (for the married), a law of children (with parents of either status) and a law of domestic violence (applying not only to the married and the unmarried but to a much wider class of 'associated persons' whose original connection with one another is through a concept of extended family of the most informal type). The next chapters in this section, Chapters 8–11, examine the law of divorce as such and the financial matters ancillary to divorce or where divorce has not yet been initiated: child law and domestic violence topics are covered separately in later discrete sections.

THE MODERN LAW OF DIVORCE

MATRIMONIAL CAUSES ACT 1973 AND FAMILY PROCEEDINGS RULES 1991 AS AMENDED

These are the basic statutory sources of modern divorce law and practice.

MATRIMONIAL CAUSES ACT 1973 IN PRACTICE

The Act is in practice interpreted in a non-litigious manner, largely due to the influence of the SFLA. A co-operative approach to the resolution of all aspects of contemporary divorce cases is reinforced by the philosophy of the Children Act 1989, by procedural reforms such as the Ancillary Relief Pilot Scheme, adopted nationwide since June 2000, and by the enactment of this co-operative spirit in s 1 of the FLA 1996.

TERMINOLOGY IN DIVORCE SUITS

Terminology differs from that of civil litigation as a whole. Family courts are also distinct.

The MCA 1973 and FPR 1991 are reproduced in the leading practitioners' work, *Rayden and Jackson* ('*Rayden*').

JURISDICTION

This is governed by s 5 of the Domicile and Matrimonial Proceedings Act 1973, though it is rarely a problem in practice (see, eg, *Dart v Dart* [1996] 2 FLR 286, CA).

FIRST YEAR OF MARRIAGE: THE ABSOLUTE BAR ON DIVORCE

There is an absolute bar on *petitioning* during the first year after the celebration of the marriage (MCA 1973, s 3(1)). The bar is absolute even when contravention is inadvertent (*Butler v Butler* [1990] Fam Law 21).

ALTERNATIVES DURING THE FIRST YEAR

There are several alternative options, which are probably beneficial to the proposed petitioner, none of which permit remarriage: judicial separation or nullity, a separation agreement, sources of funds if early divorce is financially motivated, and injunctions and declarations to address domestic violence and disputed occupation of the home.

THE RELATIONSHIP BETWEEN DIVORCE, FINANCIAL AND CHILD PROCEEDINGS

Divorce (or nullity or judicial separation) and related financial matters ('ancillary relief') are both obtained under the MCA 1973, but the divorce suit and the consequential ancillary relief are completely separate sets of proceedings. Any proceedings in relation to children are similarly separate from the divorce and are dealt with under the Children Act 1989. Proceedings in relation to domestic violence or occupation of the home are separate again, and are governed by Pt IV of the FLA 1996. These two latter Acts provide remedies whether the adult parties are married or unmarried, again emphasising their discrete existence and operation independently of any divorce. This separation underlines the contemporary withdrawal from the concept of the family as the core unit of society.

CHAPTER 8

THE GROUND FOR DIVORCE, ADULTERY AND BEHAVIOUR

8.1 THE GROUND FOR DIVORCE AND THE FIVE FACTS

Theoretically, there is only one ground for divorce – irretrievable breakdown of the marriage (Matrimonial Causes Act (MCA) 1973, s 1(1)). As this is the sole ground, it is technically incorrect to speak of 'the grounds' for divorce. However, in order to prove the ground in s 1(1) it is necessary to prove one (or more) of the five facts which evidence that irretrievable breakdown. These are specified in s 1(2)(a)–(e). Thus, while academics usually appreciate the distinction, both practitioners and clients often speak of 'the grounds for divorce' by which they mean the s 1(1) 'ground' of irretrievable breakdown *and* the fact or facts by which the technical ground will be proved. It should be noted that 'Facts' in this sense are often written with a capital F to distinguish them from the factual scenario of the case, and are referred to as Facts A–E to correspond with the five facts detailed in s 1(2)(a)–(e).

The facts are:

- Fact A: adultery;
- Fact B: behaviour;
- Fact C: desertion;
- Fact D: two years' separation with consent of the respondent; and
- Fact E: five years' separation.

All statutory references in this chapter are to the MCA 1973 unless otherwise stated.

This chapter deals with adultery and behaviour, the two most commonly used Facts for which separation prior to the presentation of a petition is strictly unnecessary. The other Facts, for which separation is an essential prerequisite, are covered in Chapters 9 and 10.

8.2 PROOF OF THE GROUND

Sub-sections (1) and (2) are separate requirements which must be individually satisfied; one without the other will be insufficient (see *Buffery v Buffery* [1980] 2 FLR 365; and *Richards v Richards* [1972] 1 WLR 1073; [1972] 3 All ER 695, in both of which there was irretrievable breakdown but no Fact proved; and *Biggs v Biggs* [1977] 1 All ER 20, where there was a suitable Fact but no irretrievable breakdown). No link is, however, necessary between the two requirements (*Stevens v Stevens* [1979] 1 WLR 885).

Inability to satisfy both sub-ss (1) and (2) occurs more often than might at first be thought. It is common for marriages made in haste to be repented fairly quickly also, but undoing the status of marriage is more difficult. If a couple separate early in the marriage, for example, out of boredom with each other, and when neither has committed adultery nor could be said to have been guilty of sufficient 'behaviour' for a successful Fact B petition, they will need to wait for two years before being able to use Fact D for a successful separation petition. Although both may be quite sure that the marriage has irretrievably broken down, it will not be possible to prove any Fact, so no decree will be possible until such proof is possible.

If tactful enquiries do not reveal the slightest chance of a case of behaviour that the other spouse would not defend, and the parties are unwilling to wait, the practitioner's advice may be that someone should go and commit adultery as soon as possible! It is immaterial which party petitions as no tactical advantages are to be gained by petitioning or being petitioned against where both parties want a divorce.

The academic student may be surprised by this, since research relied on when the Family Law Act 1996 was going through Parliament indicated that the practical application of the law in this respect was little understood by the general public. It was clear from the Hansard reports of the debates in both Houses that ordinary people still appear to believe that divorce under the MCA 1973 is genuinely fault based and firmly rooted in traditional ideas of morality, so that divorce should not be possible unless an 'innocent' party divorces a 'guilty' one. The reality, as explained in earlier chapters, is that the Act is more often than not manipulated by both parties to a marriage and their advisers to obtain the result which they personally want, and the strict interpretation of the statute permits this result without any abuse of the law.

This, of course, is the difference between the lawyer's interpretation of the letter as well as the spirit of the law and that of the untutored layperson, not used to the interpretation of statutes (a common and widely understood illustration of this would be the famous court scene in Shakespeare's *Merchant of Venice*, where Shylock's mistake in assuming that he could with impunity cut off a pound of Antonio's flesh is revealed – his loan agreement with Antonio did not permit him also to take the blood which would inevitably accompany the severance of the flesh to which he was entitled).

Despite this now well established manipulation of contemporary divorce law, the court still has a duty to enquire, so far as it reasonably can, into the facts alleged by the petition. This, however, is balanced by a philosophy of avoiding pointless enquiries into conduct and fault which post-1969 divorce law is designed to escape (*Grenfell v Grenfell* [1977] 3 WLR 738; [1978] 1 All ER 561).

Therefore, if the court is satisfied that one of the Facts has been proved, it has a duty, subject to the restrictions of the s 5 defence to divorce after five years' separation (see Chapter 10), to grant the decree of divorce (s 1(4)) unless it is satisfied on all the evidence that the marriage has not broken down irretrievably. In other words, proving a Fact leads to a presumption of irretrievable breakdown.

8.3 ADULTERY: FACT A

The requirement to establish this Fact is that the respondent has committed adultery and the petitioner finds it intolerable to live with the respondent (s 1(2)(a)). Note that there are two separate elements to this Fact:

- the act of adultery; and
- that the petitioner also finds it intolerable to live with the respondent, *not necessarily because of the adultery.*

This is another example of the necessity to read the statute closely, without importing into it any vernacular gloss derived from the layperson's belief in what the law ought to be according to traditional morality. The elements of adultery must be examined in detail.

8.3.1 The act of adultery

'Adultery' means voluntary sexual intercourse between a married person and a person of the opposite sex, whether married or not, who is not that married person's spouse. It is necessary to consider the meaning of the individual words of the section in this definition.

8.3.1.1 'Voluntary'

A wife who has been raped does not commit adultery (*S v S* [1962] 2 All ER 816); neither does a child who cannot consent voluntarily to intercourse, but this will not stop the adult party being guilty of adultery (*Barnett v Barnett and Brown* [1970] 2 All ER 33). However, once intercourse is established it is for the respondent to show that it was not voluntary (*Redpath v Redpath* [1950] 1 All ER 600). Being intoxicated is generally not an excuse for adultery (*Goshawk v Goshawk* (1965) 109 SJ 290).

8.3.1.2 'Sexual intercourse'

There must be some penetration although a complete act of intercourse is not required (*Dennis v Dennis* [1955] 2 WLR 187; [1955] 2 All ER 51, where an impotent respondent spent a night in bed with a woman, giving rise to an inference of adultery which was nevertheless rebutted because he could prove he was incapable of penetration). Sexual familiarities short of intercourse, such as might have applied in the last case, are not enough (*Saps-Ford v Saps-Ford* [1954] 2 All ER 373). However, such an association might be a basis for a Fact B behaviour petition (see 8.5, below).

It should be noted that traditionally in the UK adultery is probably still not possible with a person who has changed sex, because in English law a person's biological sex is regarded as established at birth by chromosomes which cannot be artificially changed by a later sex change operation. A different view pertains in some American jurisdictions (*Corbett v Corbett* [1970] 2 All ER 33). However, following the recent ECHR ruling in *Goodwin v UK* No 28957/95 (11 July 2002) (mentioned at 2.2.3, above) there may now be room for prolific academic debate about whether adultery does result from intercourse with a transsexual who has undergone full gender reassignment surgery (the answer probably remains in the negative until consequential amendments are made to English law for the reasons given above).

8.3.2 Proof of the act of adultery

Proof of adultery may be something of a mechanical exercise in contemporary divorce suits since it is unusual for divorces to be defended, and the most common way of proving adultery is therefore by the respondent's admission, for which provision is made on the Acknowledgment of Service form (which is sent out to the respondent by the court with the petition) (see Chapter 11).

However, should the facts of a case indicate that it would be necessary to *prove* adultery, in the absence of clear evidence it would be necessary to consider whether there is any other Fact which could be relied upon instead. This is because the standard of proof required (which would certainly apply in a contested case) is not the general civil standard of proof but a higher (not precisely specified) standard based on the lingering historical background which has always regarded adultery as a serious accusation which used to be, at best, a grave offence and, at worst, a crime. This is curious as adultery is now generally regarded as a *symptom* rather than a *cause* of marriage breakdown, although in the past the standard of proof was agonised over (for example, in *Blyth v Blyth* [1966] 1 All ER 524, where the House of Lords was divided in its opinion, which was in any case *obiter*). Nevertheless, it means that, where adultery may not be admitted, it is neither sufficient nor wise merely to allege it without some seriously credible evidence: see *Bastable v Bastable* [1968] 3 All ER 701, where the husband petitioned on the basis of a mere suspicion of adultery due to the wife's persistent association with another man. His petition was dismissed.

8.3.3 Methods of proof

Possible methods of proof are as follows:

(1) *Circumstantial evidence* – in other words inclination and opportunity to gratify it (*Farnham v Farnham* (1925) 153 LT 320). A rebuttable presumption will be raised by the parties spending the night in the same room (*Woolf v Woolf* [1931] P 134), but this may be rebutted by evidence such as in *Dennis*, above.

(2) *Confession statement* – a method once much used, and still useful if adultery is not admitted on the Acknowledgment of Service form, but strong suspicions of adultery are confirmed, for example, by a private detective sent to watch the parties. The detective may also invite the parties to volunteer a formal written confession. Respondents will often give a confession statement when they realise that if they do not the private detective will give acceptable evidence anyway, and this is especially so if by giving the confession the respondent is able to keep the name of the third party involved out of the suit, as is now the norm (see 8.5 and 8.6, below, and Chapter 11).

(3) *Birth of a child* as a result of the adultery, which may be proved by entry on the birth register if the third party has signed the Register of Births in place of the father (*Jackson v Jackson and Pavan* [1961] 2 WLR 58; [1960] 3 All ER 621) or even by the absence of an entry in the space for the father's name (*Mayo v Mayo* [1948] 2 All ER 869).

(4) *Living with another partner* – one of the easiest methods of all since, whether or not the new partner is named in the petition (see 8.5 and 8.6, below, and 11.4.1), if the court sees that the respondent has set up house away from the petitioner with a new partner, adultery will be presumed, especially if a child has also been born.

(5) *Findings in other proceedings,* for example, where the respondent is named as co-respondent or is cited as a party in other divorce proceedings and adultery is proved, or where there are successful proceedings against the respondent spouse under Sched 1 to the Children Act 1989 for property transfer or a lump sum (see Chapter 15), or a conviction of rape against a respondent husband, or where adultery has already been used to obtain a decree of judicial separation, which by s 4(2) enables the judicial separation decree to be treated as proof of adultery.

(6) *DNA or blood tests,* both of which have always been possible if directed by the court. However, the court's power has until recently been limited to giving a *direction* rather than *ordering* a test against the will of the parties to be tested, since in the absence of some authority this would have amounted to an assault. A person with care of a child must usually consent on behalf of the child whose blood or genetic sample is required (FLRA 1969, s 20(1)), although ways round this have been found. For example, Hale LJ's solution was for the Official Solicitor to consent on behalf of the child to whom he was made guardian *ad litem*, though this was criticised as inappropriate. Also, the court can consent for a child who is a ward of court. However, the Child Support, Pensions and Social Security Act 2000 has now addressed the former problems: tucked away in s 82(3) is an amendment to s 20 of the FLRA 1969 enabling the court to consent if it 'considers that it would be in [the child's] best interests' for the samples to be taken. This will now address the court's previous lack of jurisdiction to compel a mother who has sole care and control of a child to consent to samples being taken (see *Re O and J (Children)* [2000] 2 All ER 29). Late in 2001, Bodey J granted one of the first applications for testing under the new provisions, overturning the previous adverse decision of the family proceedings court.

Neither of these tests may be directed to *establish* adultery (*Hodgkiss v Hodgkiss* [1985] Fam Law 87), but only to discover true parentage where that is in the interests of the child, which it usually is (*S v S* [1972] AC 24; [1970] 3 All ER 107, HL). In *S v S*, Lord Hodson said this was rarely not the case in modern times, as there is some psychiatric evidence that children need to know their true origins. If, however, a test is directed to establish parentage and it shows adultery must have been committed, *then* the results may be used to *prove* that adultery. Tests may be directed on the application of any party or on the court's own motion, but if the application is contested the direction may only be given by the judge.

Inferences may be drawn if a test is not taken (FLRA 1969, s 23(1)). In particular, an applicant for financial relief is likely to have the application dismissed if a test is refused (FLRA 1969, s 23(2)). In *McVeigh v Beattie* [1988] 2 All ER 500, a man's refusal to take a test was held to amount to the necessary corroboration of the woman's assertion that the child was his to obtain an affiliation order. However, sometimes there are good grounds for refusing a test: in *B v B and E* [1969] 3 All ER 1106, for example, the mother did not raise the question of the child's parentage until he was three years old and the father established that it was reasonable for him to rely on the presumption of legitimacy after such a long period of believing the child was his. Unfortunately, only the DNA fingerprinting test is virtually 100% reliable; blood tests can only exclude (and not identify) any party as a parent of the child. Generally, the result of the latter test, unless a rare blood group is involved, will only indicate whether a person could or could not be a parent of the child, and indicate within what percentage of the population such a person falls as a potential parent.

There is, however, a *strong presumption of legitimacy* and, in the absence of proof of adultery, a child born in wedlock or within nine months of the last possible date for married intercourse is presumed legitimate, although this may still be rebutted by proof of non-access. Rebuttal of the presumption is on a balance of probabilities (Family Law Reform Act (FLRA) 1969, s 26), but the standard of proof in such a case is a heavy one (*Serio v Serio* (1983) 4 FLR 756; and *W v K* [1988] 4 FLR 756 (a wife-swapping case)).

However, this presumption will not always operate in favour of a respondent accused of adultery against whom adultery cannot be *proved* in one of the usual ways. In *Preston-Jones v Preston-Jones* [1951] AC 391; [1951] 1 All ER 124 – still the classic case on non-access – the wife was of a serious and sober disposition and there was no evidence of any associations or loose behaviour on her part. Adultery was still established, however, as her husband had gone abroad between six and 12 months before the birth. Thus the period of gestation was entirely incredible and adultery was held to be established.

If adultery cannot be proved, because there has apparently been no sexual intercourse, the non-adulterous association might be sufficient for a behaviour petition presented on the basis of Fact B (see 8.5, below). This is because it has been accepted by the Court of Appeal that such a relationship may be more destructive of marriage than an act of adultery, since adultery is now seen as a symptom rather than a cause of marital breakdown (*Wachtel v Wachtel* [1973] 2 WLR 366; [1973] 1 All ER 829, CA).

8.4 PROOF OF THE INTOLERABILITY ELEMENT OF FACT A

The petitioner must also find it intolerable to live with the respondent. The actual act of adultery and the fact that the petitioner finds it intolerable to live with the respondent are construed independently, although it is doubtful if this is what Parliament intended when the Divorce Reform Act 1969 was passed. The matter was raised in *Goodrich v Goodrich* [1971] 1 WLR 1142; [1971] 2 All ER 1340, where it was held that the two requirements were independent of each other, and also that whether it was intolerable for the petitioner to be obliged to continue to live with the respondent was a subjective test for that particular petitioner. As a result, if the actual adultery alleged is proved and the petitioner states that further cohabitation with the respondent is intolerable, the court has no option but to grant the decree.

The independence of these two elements of Fact A has since been confirmed in *Cleary v Cleary* [1974] 1 WLR 73; [1974] 1 All ER 498, CA; and *Carr v Carr* [1974] 1 WLR 1534;

[1974] 1 All ER 1193, CA. In the former case the intolerability sprang from the wife's going out, leaving the husband to baby-sit and by corresponding with another man, although neither of these actions was linked to the adultery, and in the latter by the wife's treatment of the children, which similarly had no connection with the adultery.

8.4.1   Time within which adultery petitions must be presented

An act of adultery only remains a valid basis on which to petition for divorce for six months after it is discovered by the potential petitioner. Thus, if the parties continue to cohabit after an act or acts of adultery is or are *discovered*, then after a *total period of six months* of such continued cohabitation after the last act relied on, a petition will not be possible on the basis of that adultery – some renewal of the adulterous association, or some fresh act of adultery with another person, will be required (s 2(1)). This is designed as a reconciliation provision, so that the parties may attempt to overlook such incidents of adultery, even possibly separating and then resuming cohabitation, following the initial discovery that adultery has been committed. Many couples do this because they are not sure if the marriage is really over.

This ambivalence is *completely irrelevant* – it does not matter how many times they separate and then change their minds and decide to try again until there has been six months' *actual* cohabitation since the adultery in question was discovered. Periods of *separation* are not counted in the total six months which finally bar a petition under s 2(1).

It should be remembered that it is the discovery of the adultery, not the date of its commission, which is relevant to the continued ability to petition, so it is still possible to petition on the basis of an act of adultery which took place many years before, provided discovery was more recent and the s 2(1) bar does not apply.

8.5 BEHAVIOUR: FACT B

The requirement to establish this Fact is that the respondent has behaved in such a way that the petitioner cannot reasonably be expected to live with him or her (s 1(2)(b)).

There is no finite list of conduct which does or does not constitute sufficient 'behaviour' for this Fact, so that it is a less straightforward Fact to use than that of adultery. On the other hand, like adultery, behaviour does provide an opportunity for an immediate divorce on the basis of the petitioner's complaints against the respondent. Indeed, given that the marriage will have broken down for some reason or reasons which have given the petitioner (and possibly the respondent also) cause for dissatisfaction, and given that there is such a low incidence of defended divorces, it may still be possible to obtain a divorce on the basis of quite slight behaviour, provided the allegations are not too trivial for the court to allow and provided the respondent does not defend. It is not therefore surprising that behaviour and adultery usually between them account for the largest number of decrees.

If it is suspected that a petition might be defended, greater care will need to be taken in advising a spouse to petition on Fact B than if it is likely to go undefended. In this case the drafting of the particulars of behaviour may be crucial (see 8.6, below, and Chapter 11).

The academic student will need to acquire a good grasp of what is and what is not behaviour within the meaning of s 1(2)(b), so as to gain a working knowledge of the main groupings of behaviour where case law has established that such behaviour qualifies, and also to appreciate the role of *intention* in such qualifying behaviour, as it is now established that behaviour for Fact B does not have to be either deliberate or positive. In practice, it is very unlikely that cases practitioners encounter will be on all fours with those which have appeared in the law reports, and much the same may be said of those appearing in tutorial and examination scenarios. It is therefore essential to be able to distinguish between what is worth a little effort in the drafting of a petition and what is really too feeble an allegation to succeed, especially if the petition were to be defended. While drafting is not usually within the academic law syllabus, it is in fact very difficult to understand whether any given behaviour might be sufficient for a Fact B petition without appreciating that drafting skills (to make the most of such material as is available for the petition) may tip the balance in a borderline case. Provided the suit is undefended, good drafting can obtain a decree on the basis of initially quite unpromising material, as consultation of a good collection of precedents will indicate! A classic case was that of *Richards v Richards,* mentioned in 8.2, above. This was a case of a depressive husband, whose depression was not clinical but was still causing a great deal of discomfort to his wife and family. The circumstances of this case, which would certainly be sufficient to obtain a decree today, indicate that in 1972 neither practitioners nor the judiciary had really grasped the potential of the new Fact of behaviour to succeed in cases where the old matrimonial offence of cruelty would not have been made out.

8.5.1 The test for behaviour

The test by which the court will decide whether any conduct is or is not behaviour is a hybrid one, partly subjective and partly objective. It should always be remembered that the Fact is *not* one of 'unreasonable behaviour' – and it is incorrect to speak of Fact B in this way – because, as the Court of Appeal stated in *Bannister v Bannister* [1980] 10 Fam Law 240, CA, the behaviour contemplated by the working of the section is significantly different from 'behaving unreasonably'. In *Carew-Hunt v Carew-Hunt* (1972) *The Times*, 28 June, Ormrod J confirmed this view and added that it was not up to the court to pass moral judgments and to say whether a person's behaviour was 'right or wrong, good or bad'.

The proper test for this Fact is generally regarded as that stated in *Buffery v Buffery,* namely (to paraphrase the judgment):

> Can this petitioner (looking at the petitioner's own behaviour) be expected to live with this respondent (looking at the respondent's behaviour), taking into account the kind of people they are and also whether there has been any provocation, deliberate or otherwise, eg, through anti-social conduct or even illness.

This test builds on the much earlier judgment of Bagnall J in *Ash v Ash* [1972] 2 WLR 347; [1972] 1 All ER 582, a case of violence and alcoholism, where the judge suggested that like can always be expected to live with like, for example, the violent/alcoholic/sport addicted petitioner with the like respondent, so the situation where each party is as bad as the other might result in neither being able to obtain a divorce as, logically, there ought to be some disparity in the parties' conduct. However, in practice this situation does not arise very often, because most petitions are not defended and go through to decree *nisi* without a hearing, so that the court will not know that the petitioner's behaviour is just as bad as that complained of in the respondent. If the allegations are *objectively* of the type that a petitioner might reasonably complain of, a decree will be granted especially if the case is undefended, as it usually is. This is a classic example of the impact of procedure on substantive law in divorce, and a most important pointer to the academic student's understanding of the subject.

Dunn J put this practical approach in a nutshell in *Livingstone-Stallard v Livingstone-Stallard* [1974] 3 WLR 302; [1974] 2 All ER 776 when he suggested a 'jury approach', as in 'what would the right thinking man conclude' about the behaviour complained of. The case also established that, although the behaviour relied on should not be absolutely trivial overall, a weight of trivia taken together may be sufficient. In *Livingstone-Stallard*, the husband, a much older man, had basically nagged, bullied, criticised and irritated his younger, rather nervous wife to the point where she lacked all confidence and could no longer stand living with him, and her petition succeeded. This case is therefore a useful precedent where, as in the majority of contemporary marriages, the conduct complained of is not far off what in other jurisdictions would simply be called 'incompatibility', which is not, however, a basis for divorce in English law. *O'Neill v O'Neill* [1975] 1 WLR 118; [1975] 3 All ER 289 (as to which see further below) affirmed this approach and also stressed that no other extraneous concepts should be imported into the test, such as that the behaviour should be 'grave and weighty' (as it used to have to be under the pre-1969 law, which involved the completely different concept of cruelty).

The modern approach, therefore, is primarily concerned with assessing any conduct which is not utterly trivial and in looking at that conduct objectively in the light of its effects on the particular petitioner (thereby importing the subjective element of the hybrid test). A good, relatively recent example of this approach is *Birch v Birch* [1992] 1 FLR 564, where the petitioner insisted that the behaviour complained of affected her particularly badly and her assertion was accepted.

8.5.2 The role of intention

From these developments it can be seen that intention has progressively assumed a more minor role than either in the early days of the post-1969 reformed divorce law or under the old pre-1969 concept of cruelty. In the early 1970s there was a discernible backward looking tendency in decisions which adhered to the philosophy of the former, entirely fault based law and which seemed to insist that intention must play a major part in any 'behaviour'. However, when *Katz v Katz* [1972] 1 WLR 955; [1972] 3 All ER 219 and *Thurlow v Thurlow* [1975] 3 WLR 161; [1975] 3 All ER 979 (both cases of physical and mental deterioration) came before the court, the approach changed significantly. Previously, it seemed that the court had always been influenced by the concept of marriage being 'for better for worse, for richer for poorer, [and particularly] in sickness and in health', so that obtaining a decree based on the respondent's involuntary behaviour due to mental and/or physical illness was problematic.

Thus, *Katz* established that mental illness of even a relatively minor sort could be sufficient to obtain a decree if, after making full allowances for the respondent's disabilities, the temperament of both parties and the obligations of marriage, the type and seriousness of the behaviour was such that the petitioner should not really be called upon to endure it. *Thurlow*, however, was really the watershed in establishing a sufficient degree of mental or physical illness combined: in that case, a depressing degree of deterioration was regarded as 'behaviour' within the terms of Fact B. In particular, *Thurlow* established that such 'behaviour' was nevertheless acceptable for Fact B, despite its being *involuntary*, and despite the ordinary connotation of the word 'behaviour' suggesting something positive and active, rather than unavoidable and passive. The judge decided that it was for the court to say in each case whether despite the obligations of marriage the petitioner could be called upon to withstand the stress imposed by the respondent's condition, considering in particular the length of time the condition had existed and the effect on the petitioner's health.

8.5.3 Some types of Fact B behaviour

Each case turns on its own facts, but it is helpful to look at cases where sufficient behaviour has been found to establish the Fact (eg, violence (physical and verbal), including false accusations (especially if combined with alcoholism), insensitivity, lack of communication, excessive unsociability, general neglect, bullying, constant criticism, financial irresponsibility, excessive financial restrictions, and obsessive DIY).

Examples of all the above classes of generally unpleasant behaviour appear in the cases below, and may be expected to recur with some regularity: so if a potential petitioner's complaints do not seem to disclose enough material to petition (since people are sometimes extraordinarily reticent in providing detail, though others will give a blow-by-blow account), it is always worth considering whether any of the less obvious ones apply.

The following effects on the petitioner are unlikely to qualify, unless they can be shown to be caused by the respondent's behaviour (though they might be sufficient if *injury to health* results and if the incidents relied on are carefully pleaded to link them to some identifiable fault on the respondent's part): emotional dissatisfaction (but is there *neglect, insensitivity* or *selfishness*?), sexual dissatisfaction (but is this neglect or caused by the *respondent's serious illness*?), desertion (but is it *neglect* or the respondent *not appreciating the commitment of marriage*?), and boredom or growing apart (but is it *insensitivity, inability to communicate* or *general neglect*?).

It is essential in these latter cases to be able to show that the respondent has breached some marital obligation, even if that is only the mutual enjoyment of each other's company socially, and the affection and moral support which one spouse is entitled to expect from the other.

8.5.4 Violence

Where there is actual physical violence it is obviously best if the petitioner has reported the matter to a doctor or the police. Not doing so will not necessarily lead to the conclusion that such violence has been tolerated, but evidential problems clearly might arise as in *Bergin v Bergin* [1983] 1 All ER 905. Although the petitioner can always give such evidence without corroboration, and may be believed if the suit is not defended, some independent evidence is obviously helpful. Lack of this might lead to a hearing, whereas with a doctor's letter the matter would have gone through on the papers in the usual way. Any psychological violence, such as what used to be referred to as mental cruelty, should also, if possible, be substantiated by medical or psychiatric evidence for the same reason.

8.5.5 Insensitivity, lack of communication, excessive unsociability or general neglect

If any one of these is alleged, it is essential that some conduct can be imported to the respondent and tied to incidents which can be given as examples. In *Buffery* (see 8.2, above), this did not succeed as the parties had really each gone their own ways and neither was more to blame than the other. However, in *Bannister* (see 8.5.1, above), the petition was successful because it could be said that the husband never took the wife out and never told her where he was when he went out himself, sometimes at night, and indeed never spoke to her if he could avoid it! A practitioner would tackle this problem by obtaining some detail when interviewing the client and relying on careful drafting to present a picture of unacceptable behaviour. The academic student will need to develop similar imagination in order to identify circumstances in which what may appear a thin case could succeed in practice.

8.5.6 Bullying or constant criticism

Bullying or constant criticism which fall short of violence, or strong verbal abuse which might otherwise appear to be trivial, will also need to be carefully particularised to show an overall picture which is unacceptable. In *Livingstone-Stallard*, for example (see 8.5.1, above), the incidents individually were insufficient, but together presented such a horrible picture of life in the Livingstone-Stallard household that the court had no difficulty in drawing the necessary conclusion.

8.5.7 Financial irresponsibility or excessive financial restriction

This is established Fact B behaviour, especially where it adversely affects the family and causes stress as in *Carter-Fea v Carter-Fea* [1987] Fam Law 131, and this may also be 'conduct' within the meaning of s 25(2)(g) which would reduce the respondent's entitlement in subsequent ancillary relief proceedings (see Chapter 12), especially if it has had the effect of dissipating the family assets.

Similarly, excessive financial restriction will usually be behaviour but will need to be carefully pleaded with some concrete examples, since a wife's cry of 'not enough money' is often seen as a classic 'sitcom' joke. If a wife has managed to live frugally despite the husband's parsimony, this may have repercussions in establishing what she needs for the purposes of ancillary relief.

8.5.8 Obsessive DIY

The classic case on obsessive DIY is *O'Neill v O'Neill*, mentioned at 8.5.1, above, where the court at first hesitated to decide that two years of 'home improvement' was not something that the wife and daughter should have been called upon to endure – although this was a particularly bad instance of living in discomfort for the sake of financial gain, since it included mixing cement on the living room floor and leaving the lavatory door off for eight months (which particularly embarrassed the teenage daughter). At first instance, the petition was unsuccessful as the incidents complained of were said to be no more than the ordinary wear and tear of married life undertaken for the benefit of the family as a whole, but the Court of Appeal eventually accepted that the situation went beyond such a mundane description and that marriage ought not require such stoic endurance! However, it may be that what really tipped the balance was that, in addition to making life so physically uncomfortable, the husband also cast doubt on the paternity of the children of the family. (In the absence of some evidence this is never regarded as good matrimonial conduct and would also qualify as bullying or verbal abuse.)

8.5.9 Emotional dissatisfaction

This has not been conspicuously successful in Fact B case law to date, the leading case being *Pheasant v Pheasant* [1972] 2 WLR 353; [1972] 1 All ER 587, but this was probably because the wife in that case had done absolutely nothing wrong in matrimonial terms, and the husband was to say the least a little strange, as he claimed that he needed an excessive amount of demonstrative affection due to his particular nature and personality, and that his wife had failed to provide it.

It can probably be safely said that in the ordinary case, if a petitioner were able to show emotional dissatisfaction linked to some aspect of the respondent's conduct which could be said to breach a matrimonial obligation, while the petitioner remained a committed, if perhaps less than sparkling, spouse, then there is no reason why emotional dissatisfaction (which is, after all, the usual reason for marriages breaking up) should not be a basis for a successful petition. However, such emotional dissatisfaction should be *evidenced* by the normal 'distress' which every well drafted behaviour petition alleges the petitioner suffers as a result of the respondent's unacceptable behaviour. In cases of emotional dissatisfaction, it is essential to look for instances of insensitivity, selfishness, and general lack of the mutual consideration which in any civilised relationship one spouse is entitled to expect from the other.

8.5.10 Sexual dissatisfaction

Although not found sufficient in *Dowden v Dowden* [1977] 8 Fam Law 106, sexual dissatisfaction is probably in a similar category to emotional dissatisfaction. In *Dowden*, the wife's petition was unsuccessful, despite her claims of frustration and tension as a result of the husband's lack of interest in sex. However, in view of the decisions in *Katz* and *Thurlow* (see 8.5.2, above), had the petition alleged some disorder on the part of the husband which had caused the conduct complained of, as well as emphasising the effect on the petitioner, it is difficult to see how, in the light of the now established proper test for Fact B behaviour, the petition could have failed. The same might be said of *Mason v Mason* [1980] 11 Fam Law 144, where the Court of Appeal in effect held that sexual incompatibility leading to a wife's refusal of intercourse more often than once a week was incapable of being a basis for a behaviour decree. In *Sheldon v Sheldon* [1966] 2 All ER 257, the wife's petition for lack of sexual intercourse on the basis of the then ground of cruelty was unsuccessful at first instance but allowed by the Court of Appeal.

8.5.11 Desertion

It goes without saying that ordinary cases of desertion are not behaviour and should therefore be categorised as Fact C and not Fact B (see *Stringfellow v Stringfellow* [1976] 1 WLR 645; [1976] 2 All ER 539, where the parties' falling out and going their separate ways were said to be only the steps preparatory to separation and not what is normally understood by the word 'behaviour', which suggests some actual positive conduct). Again this might be a little harsh in the light of the modern test for behaviour, since if the parties grow apart from each other, go their separate ways and in the process one is *inconsiderate, insensitive, neglectful* and *boorish* there is logically no distinction between that happening immediately prior to separation and it happening years before. Parties in this situation want a divorce, and provided the petition is properly pleaded and not defended it should succeed. This is a classic example of circumstances in which good drafting practice will salvage what might otherwise be interpreted as insufficient in law to found a decree of desertion (by not having lasted the requisite time). What is essential is to *avoid pleading* the actual finite incident of desertion (where the respondent leaves and does not return to the matrimonial home) as an instance of behaviour. If previous instances are pleaded as 'being constantly away from home' (eg, 'staying out late', 'not telling the petitioner of the respondent's whereabouts', 'apparent lack of appreciation of the nature of marriage and commitment to it', etc), there should be no problem in obtaining a decree, since the district judge who considers the papers has every right to grant one on the basis of such allegations. This is also a classic case of a situation in which appreciation by the student of divorce procedure, as well as of the black letter law on which divorces are granted, is essential in order to make a correct assessment of whether a particular petitioner may be entitled to a decree. See Chapter 11 for these insights.

8.5.12 Boredom and growing apart

Where these are relied upon, meticulous care will again be needed to avoid confusion with simple desertion. The practitioner will need to detail enough incidents prior to the actual departure to make it clear that the petitioner has some actual behaviour to object to (irrespective of desertion, which will usually not yet have qualified for Fact C by not having lasted for two years (see Chapter 9)). Such a case where the drafting was probably to blame was *Morgan v Morgan* (1973) 117 SJ 223. Here the marriage simply 'petered out' when the parties were in their 60s. This was at a time when they sold their matrimonial home and began to live separately, which allowed their case to be dismissed as one of simple desertion, whereas had the reasons for their separating been examined, there might well have been enough 'behaviour' that properly pleaded would have justified a Fact B decree.

8.5.13 Potential bars to a decree

It should be noted that the same reconciliation provisions apply to adultery and behaviour, save that by s 2(3) if the parties live together for more than six months after the last incident of behaviour relied upon it will not *automatically* constitute a bar to obtaining a decree based on that behaviour, but the period of cohabitation will be *taken into account* by the court in deciding whether or not it is reasonable for the petitioner to be obliged to live with the respondent, given that the behaviour in question will have been tolerated for at least the last six months. In any case, *any* cohabitation will be disregarded if the petitioner has nowhere else to go, as in *Bradley v Bradley* [1973] 1 WLR 1291; [1973] 3 All ER 750, where the wife could not get rehoused until after decree.

The cohabitation bar applies even after decree *nisi* and the decree will not usually be made absolute if the parties are still living together when it is applied for. If the parties have cohabited briefly and then separated again between the two decrees, this will not usually affect decree absolute. Very often, the cohabitation is irrelevant anyway, since much 'behaviour', such as selfishness, insensitivity, verbal abuse, financial irresponsibility, etc, is of a continuing nature (so that there is no last incident of behaviour). However, care should be taken because in *Savage v Savage* [1982] 3 WLR 418; [1982] 3 All ER 49 the court refused to make the decree absolute because the parties resumed cohabitation three months after decree *nisi* and were still living together three and a half years later.

In *Court v Court* [1982] 3 WLR 199; [1982] 2 All ER 531, however, the court took the view that it had already been held at decree *nisi* stage that it was unreasonable for the petitioner to have to live with the respondent, so the fact that the parties had resumed cohabitation and then separated again if anything underlined this finding; thus, the subsequent delay and cohabitation did not change the situation.

8.6 THE IMPORTANCE OF DRAFTING AN EFFECTIVE PETITION

It is obvious from the above account that skilled drafting is essential for the success of a behaviour petition under the contemporary law. This is the more so because of the nature of the 'Special Procedure' (see 11.6, below) by which, contrary to the suggestion in the name, most divorces are now processed (that is to say now entirely on paper without an oral hearing of any kind). Thus, if the particulars of behaviour pleaded in the petition give the court any cause for wondering whether the ground and the Fact have been made out, queries will arise and delay will be inevitable. If this does happen, it is nearly always possible to get the suit back on track, either by amending or by supplying further evidence, but this will mean that additional costs are inevitably incurred. Conversely, if the petition is well drafted (ie, explicitly to reflect the literal as well as the spirit of the meaning of s 1(2)(b) of MCA 1973), what may appear to be unpromising facts to start with may well result in a decree being granted. Obviously, there will also be a difference between those cases where the suit is undefended (so only the minimum standard of behaviour to satisfy s 1(2)(b) must be clear on the face of the documentation before the court) and those which are defended (so that the case will be thoroughly tested by an oral hearing with the usual cross-examination of witnesses) and in the latter case a borderline situation might result in a decree not being granted. Nevertheless, much may still be achieved by positive drafting of the particulars of behaviour relied on.

The trick in establishing 'behaviour' for this purpose is to remember that the key word is 'behaved': this is on the face of it an active word, not a passive one. What needs to be shown is that the respondent has *done* something to which the petitioner may take exception and done it to the extent that the petitioner cannot be expected to live with the respondent. While this 'doing' element can be achieved by 'being' (as the cases of *Katz* and *Thurlow* have demonstrated), and without the necessity to show intention on the part of the respondent, it is nevertheless still essential to show, as a minimum, a state of affairs that can realistically amount to 'behaviour' such that the respondent cannot be expected to tolerate it in a normal matrimonial relationship. Thus, if illness or a passive physical condition is relied upon, and that results in involuntary behaviour, the resulting state of affairs must amount to something that the petitioner could not realistically be called upon to endure. For a situation that potentially falls into this problematic category, careful drafting can still make the difference between failure and success.

Post-1969, it is no longer the case that the petition should set out to disclose conduct which is outrageous in quality or quantity. Showing that the petitioner is entitled to a decree is a factual exercise, not a moral one, and a succinct, unemotional, impersonal, precise statement of the facts relied upon to bring the petitioner within s 1(2)(b) is what is required. This is not Booker Prize literature, still less is it the purple prose of the indignant old fashioned advocate. Instead, the petition should be factual, *unemotional* and, as far as possible, *precise*.

This is, in fact, the spirit of the SFLA approach adopted by the best contemporary practitioners, but the style and format of such drafting in behaviour petitions has an earlier origin. In the opinion of the late and distinguished family judge Sir Roger Ormrod, if neither party had committed adultery (the easiest Fact to use for an immediate divorce desired by both parties), what he called 'the mild behaviour petition' was the next best choice. What he meant by this was that the petition should both show the *minimum safe level for the grant of a decree under Fact B* (in other words it had to meet what is now the *Buffery* test) and at the same time not be *unnecessarily offensive* to the respondent. In making this suggestion, Ormrod, who was an early champion of civilised divorce suits, thought first of the desirability of not making it impossible for the parties ever to speak to each other again (as was often the case under the pre-1969 law and an obvious consideration where the presence of children meant there must be ongoing parenting), and only second of the benefit to divorce procedure if behaviour particulars are kept within a sensible framework.

The original Ormrod suggestion was that behaviour particulars should ideally be limited to about three incidents. These he categorised as 'the first, the worst and the last'. The phrase has subsequently often been expanded by practitioners to the 'first, worst, last and witnessed' and it is generally accepted that the most extensive particulars should not detail more than about six incidents; more and the court may think that the petitioner's case must be somewhat weak if so many incidents have to be relied on. In any event, dates, times, places and any other details should in theory be as specific as possible although the lack of defence in most cases means more generalisation is in practice acceptable. Thus, a good précis may be necessary in some cases, particularly where the marriage has been long and the parties have apparently soldiered on against the odds for some time.

While the academic student is unlikely to be tested in drafting, a working knowledge of the above best practice is essential in understanding what conduct is, or is not, likely to result in a decree of divorce being obtainable.

THE GROUND FOR DIVORCE, ADULTERY AND BEHAVIOUR

THE GROUND FOR DIVORCE AND THE FIVE FACTS

There is a distinction between the sole ground for divorce (irretrievable breakdown of marriage) and the five Facts (adultery, behaviour, desertion, separation for two years with consent of the respondent or separation for five years), one of which must be shown in order to prove the sole ground.

PROOF OF THE GROUND

Both the ground and one of the five Facts must be proved separately; one without the other is insufficient. But proof of a Fact raises a presumption of proof of the ground unless the court has reason to believe otherwise.

ADULTERY

Adultery is defined in s 1(2)(a) of the MCA 1973 as follows: 'That the respondent has committed adultery and the petitioner finds it intolerable to live with the respondent.' There need be no connection between the two limbs of the sub-section. Adultery must be voluntary, between persons of the opposite sex, one of whom is married (but not to the other!) and must involve an ordinary act of heterosexual intercourse; indecent familiarities are not enough. Adultery if not admitted must be proved (eg, by blood tests, confession, birth of a child of whom the petitioner is not the father (though there is a strong presumption of legitimacy), circumstantial evidence or findings in other proceedings). Proof of the intolerability element is subjective. A petition must be brought within six months of discovering an act of adultery to be relied on.

BEHAVIOUR

The requirements of the 'behaviour' Fact are defined by s 1(2)(b) of the MCA 1973 as follows: 'That the respondent has behaved in such a way that the petitioner cannot reasonably be expected to live with the respondent.' The test of behaviour within this sub-section is a hybrid one, part objective and part subjective. Behaviour can be involuntary: the role of intention is a minor one and intention can be completely absent in an appropriate case, such as where the respondent is ill.

There is no finite list of qualifying behaviour; any gratuitously anti-social conduct is likely to be sufficient if it derogates from matrimonial obligations. Behaviour must be distinguished from desertion. Careful drafting of the particulars of behaviour in the petition to bring them squarely within the meaning of s 1(2)(b) may make the difference between success and failure to obtain a decree. The distinguished family judge, the late Sir Roger Ormrod, considered the 'mild behaviour petition' (alleging the minimum safe level of behaviour to secure the grant of a decree) the most civilised method of obtaining a divorce if neither party had committed adultery.

CHAPTER 9

DESERTION AND CONSTRUCTIVE DESERTION

9.1 DESERTION: FACT C

To establish this Fact the respondent must have deserted the petitioner for a continuous period of at least two years immediately preceding the presentation of the petition (Matrimonial Causes Act (MCA) 1973, s 1(2)(c)).

Academic courses still study this Fact along with the others in s 1(2), and it remains available as the basis for proving that a marriage has irretrievably broken down despite a drop in use in recent years evidenced by the lack of up to date case law in this sub-paragraph. However, unless the case is extremely clear-cut and definitely will not be defended, it is rarely used in practice because of its technical requirements. Moreover, a respondent who has deserted a petitioner for two years as required for Fact C is unlikely to resist a request to consent to a divorce on the basis of Fact D (ie, the same two years' separation plus the respondent's consent to the decree: see Chapter 10).

In theory, 'desertion' under Fact C can take two forms: either simple desertion, where the petitioner is left by the respondent without just cause and without the petitioner's consent, or 'constructive desertion', where it is actually the petitioner who leaves the respondent, but there is just cause for his or her departure. However, 'constructive desertion' is even more rarely used in practice as a basis for divorce than actual desertion itself, which is why there have been very few reported cases since the early 1970s. This is because any petitioner who can show constructive desertion can also show behaviour under Fact B more easily. Thus, apart from being able to present such a petition immediately without waiting for two years to accrue, the test for behaviour (see Chapter 8) is actually much easier to satisfy than that for constructive desertion. This is because for constructive desertion the standard of conduct must be 'grave and weighty' which, as was expressly stated in *O'Neill v O'Neill* (see 8.5.1, above), is not necessary for a successful behaviour petition. The reason for this is precisely because desertion increasingly fell out of use following the introduction of Facts B and D in the Divorce Reform Act 1969 and thus, unlike behaviour which also used to be interpreted as needing to be 'grave and weighty', desertion has missed being modernised by developing case law.

9.2 THE FOUR ELEMENTS OF DESERTION

The following must be separately established:

- actual separation;
- intention to desert by the respondent;
- lack of consent to the separation by the petitioner; and
- that the separation is without just cause.

9.2.1 Actual separation

This is often clear because one party has left the other and gone to live elsewhere. Sometimes, however, it is less clear because there is coming and going, or the parties consider they are separated but live at the same address.

Establishing that actual separation has occurred is important not only for desertion but also for Facts D and E (see Chapter 10), especially where the parties are still living in the same house. The principles are the same for Facts C, D and E, namely that it is essential that the parties, even if living at the same address, are in truth living in separate 'households' (more in the style of flatsharers living independent lives rather than in a cohabitational sense as husband and wife). A distinction is drawn between one 'unhappy' household, where there may be little contact, and two separate households where the parties usually only still occupy the same premises because there is no alternative. Thus, desertion may be available in situations where at first sight it appears unlikely. An example of this may be seen in *Naylor v Naylor* [1961] 2 WLR 751; [1961] 2 All ER 129. The wife removed her wedding ring and decided never to perform any domestic services for the husband again, while he in turn gave her no housekeeping money. They shared no family or communal life and the wife was held to be in desertion.

Naylor is the basic situation which will suffice for separation to be established where the parties are still living under one roof. Other cases fall one side or the other of the shared life marker and accordingly either amount to sufficient or insufficient separation.

Basically, the fatal flaws to check for in an alleged separation under the same roof are:

(1) Mending, washing or cooking done by the wife specifically for the husband. In *Le Brocq v Le Brocq* [1964] 2 All ER 464, the parties had separate bedrooms, sexual intercourse had ceased as the wife bolted the husband out of her bedroom, they did not even speak to each other and they communicated by note only when essential. However, the wife *did* carry on cooking her husband's meals – which proved fatal to her claim of having separated from him. It should be noted that a wife who returns to domestic tasks which she has abandoned will bring her separation to an end even if she refuses to resume sexual intercourse (*Bull v Bull* [1953] 2 All ER 601).

(2) Shared cleaning, as in *Mouncer v Mouncer* [1972] 1 All ER 289, where the parties were held not to be separated because they shared the general housework despite the fact that the wife did no laundry for the husband, the parties were on bad terms and they had separate bedrooms.

(3) Communal life, especially eating meals with the family. In *Hopes v Hopes* [1948] 2 All ER 920, no domestic services (as in *Le Brocq*) complicated the issue, and there was no shared bedroom or sexual intercourse, but there was a certain amount of communal life, including eating meals with the family in the dining room and sharing the remainder of the house. The separation was held to be insufficient, as Lord Denning said, because there were not two separate households but one unhappy one in which there was chronic discord and gross neglect.

One aspect of the shared (albeit inharmonious) life which convinced the court that the parties were not separated in *Mouncer v Mouncer* was that, while the husband had no desire to remain in the house, he in fact did so in order to help look after the children. This case was, of course, decided long before the Children Act 1989 put into statutory form an expectation that parents would remain good parents in the interests of the children. As there clearly was only one unhappy household and not two separate ones, it is unlikely that the same facts would be decided any differently merely because of the more recent concept of parental responsibility. However, it may be that if the parents are otherwise living discernably separate lives under the same roof, helping to look after the children would not be fatal to establishing separation, especially if the parties have nowhere else for the children to spend time with the parent in respect of whom a separate life is claimed.

This must be especially so in view of the fact that in some cases separation has been recognised where the petitioner had nowhere else to go, as in *Bartram v Bartram* [1949] 2 All ER 270. Here, the parties had separated, but were forced to resume living under the same roof, even sleeping in the same bed and eating at the same table, without sharing any common household tasks (although it is fair to say that Mrs Bartram made her feelings clear by treating her husband like a lodger whom she cordially disliked). Obviously, petitioners in these circumstances must be advised that great care is needed in showing separation under the same roof save for occasions for the specific benefit of contact of the other parent with the children.

Bona fide residence in the home as a lodger will always qualify as separation. An example of this is *Fuller v Fuller* [1973] 2 All ER 650, where the parties separated in the normal way, the wife leaving the husband for another man and taking the children with her. When subsequently the husband went to live with them as a lodger (he had been told that he had a terminal illness and only a year to live during which he should not be alone), the separation was held to have continued, even though he shared the entire life of the household, having all his meals with them and his laundry done by the wife, as this was in his capacity as a lodger. (In the event, he turned out not to be terminally ill after all – which was presumably why the decree was ultimately necessary.)

9.2.2 Intention to desert by the respondent

The intention to desert permanently is called the *animus deserendi*. It can be formed when the parties are already apart without having originally parted with the requisite intention, and can continue even if the respondent gets into a situation where the intention could not be demonstrably revoked (eg, where the respondent is sent to prison).

An example of the first point was demonstrated in *Beeken v Beeken* [1948] P 302, where the parties were prisoners of war. The wife started an affair with another man and ceased sexual intercourse with the husband, who knew of the association. When she was moved to another camp and told the husband she had decided never to return to him she was held to be in desertion.

The latter point was demonstrated in *Drew v Drew* (1838) 13 PD 97, where the husband had deserted his wife and was then arrested and sent to prison, and where it was held that he would not have returned to her even if he had been free to do so.

Clearly, a person who is insane cannot be in desertion as the *animus deserendi* cannot be formed (*Crowther v Crowther* [1951] 1 All ER 1131). Whether an insane person who formed the intention before becoming insane will remain in desertion depends on what evidence there is that the intention would have been sustained if insanity had not supervened.

It should be noted that the cases on intention afford just one example of the technicalities of desertion which encourage practitioners to keep away from Fact D unless there is no alternative.

9.2.3 Lack of consent to the separation by the petitioner

There are two elements of this lack of consent:

* no agreement to the respondent's leaving; and
* no refusal of a reasonable offer to return.

9.2.3.1 No agreement to the respondent's leaving

This first element is not as straightforward as it looks at first sight. Clearly there must be no express agreement, but there must also be no indirect agreement. This therefore precludes:

(1) A decree of judicial separation, because this will end the duty to cohabit and desertion will therefore be impossible.

(2) A deed of separation for the same reason as in (1) above – but not a maintenance agreement which does not contain a clause that the parties expressly agree to live apart (*Crabtree v Crabtree* [1953] 1 WLR 708; [1953] 2 All ER 56). However, where there is a deed of separation precluding or ending desertion, this can be cured by repudiating the agreement, which can have unintended results. This is seen in *Pardy v Pardy* [1939] 3 All ER 779, where the parties had separated by agreement due to the husband's drinking. When the husband stopped paying maintenance under the clause requiring him to do so, the wife tried to effect a reconciliation, but the husband refused. This had the effect of his repudiating the agreement, so *he* was then, quite unintentionally, in desertion.

(3) Any conduct implying consent to separation, for example, changing the locks on the matrimonial home, as this would stop the respondent returning, or obtaining a Jewish religious divorce which, although not valid to dissolve the English civil marriage, indicates that the party obtaining it does not want the other spouse back (*Joseph v Joseph* [1953] 2 All ER 710). An exclusion order obtained against a violent spouse does not, however, terminate desertion (s 4(4)).

It should be noted that it does not matter that the petitioner is relieved at the respondent's departure, or even helps with the packing, provided desertion is not actually encouraged in any way (*Pizey v Pizey* [1961] 2 All ER 658). However, the petitioner must not do anything which suggests he or she regards the marriage as over until the two years are up: thus, for example, there must be no celebration of the respondent's departure by starting up an adulterous relationship with a third party, as the essence of desertion is that the petitioner is complaining of breach of a matrimonial obligation to cohabit, and so must in theory expect the respondent back any time during the ensuing two years. Entering into a new relationship (unless it were not adulterous) would end the respondent's desertion by providing just cause for staying away.

Agreement to the respondent's leaving, initially given for good reason, may be revoked if that good reason no longer applies. The absent party will then be in desertion. An example of this situation is *Nutley v Nutley* [1970] 1 WLR 217; [1970] 1 All ER 410, where the husband consented to his wife living with her parents so she could look after them, but when she refused to return on their death she was in desertion. She was only in desertion when she told him she was not returning as, although she had formed the intention earlier, she had not communicated it, so he had had no chance to revoke his consent.

Desertion can also be ended by implied consent to separation deduced from conduct. An example of this situation is *France v France* [1969] 2 All ER 870, where the parties separated, the wife having constructively deserted the husband by falling in love with another man and asking the husband to leave the home. Later, the husband fell into the habit of visiting her and having sexual intercourse with her, although they did not resume cohabitation. This was held to end any desertion since the separation had thereby become subject to their agreement that the husband could come and go as he pleased.

Such sexual intercourse will not always end desertion if, as in the case of *Mummery v Mummery* [1942] 1 All ER 533, it does not establish a regular course of conduct.

9.2.3.2 No refusal of a reasonable offer to return

This second element is quite straightforward. Basically, there must be a *bona fide* offer of reconciliation on a proper cohabitational basis with no unreasonable conditions attached. It will not do, for example, that the offer is subject to the condition that the wife should merely return in the capacity of a housekeeper (as in *Slawson v Slawson* [1942] 2 All ER 527), or that the wife should agree to join a commune run by the Tramp Preachers Movement (as in *Fletcher v Fletcher* [1945] 1 All ER 382).

The offer must also be sincere (see *Everitt v Everitt* [1949] 1 All ER 903, where the wife did not believe in the husband's offer as she believed he was still committing adultery with the women for whom he had left her). However, if it is apparently a sincere offer, and it is turned down for the petitioner's own reasons, the petitioner can then be in desertion even if it turns out that the offer might in fact have been insincere (see *Day v Day* [1957] 1 All ER 848, where the husband had been committing adultery but the wife did not give this as her reason for rejecting his offer to return, and was held then to be in desertion herself).

9.2.4 That the separation is without cause

As already explained in relation to the alternative of constructive desertion, to establish a case of desertion under Fact C the separation must be without just cause on the part of the respondent. This means that while constructive desertion may not now actually be pleaded by the party who left (since if a divorce is desired, Fact B would be more appropriate) where the conduct of a petitioner has not been beyond reproach, the respondent will have a defence and desertion will not therefore be made out. However, a respondent may not actually make use of such a defence because, in practice, divorces are not normally now defended by parties who wish to obtain a decree, since there is realistically no longer any stigma to being divorced on whatever basis. Furthermore, the decree will usually have no effect whatever on the outcome of future proceedings for ancillary relief (see Chapters 12 *et seq*) or in proceedings under the Children Act 1989 in respect of child matters (see Chapters 24–26).

Naturally, a separation that starts out as being without just cause when the potential respondent leaves may become one for which there is just cause if the potential petitioner does something to give the respondent a good excuse to stay away (eg, commits adultery). This is fatal as it brings the desertion to an end.

There is a good deal of case law on what is and what is not just cause for leaving (another good reason for practitioners usually avoiding Fact C). All the usual reasons which would suffice for Fact B will probably be just cause for leaving and therefore both constitute a defence to a desertion petition and also, if serious enough, enable a petitioner who has left to establish a case of constructive desertion, plus in the alternative providing an opportunity to cross-petition for behaviour. Examples of this type of case include:

(a) keeping 30 dirty cats so that the house is uninhabitable (*Winans v Winans* [1948] 2 All ER 862);

(b) being overbearing, dictatorial and violent (*Timmins v Timmins* [1953] 2 All ER 187);

(c) being lazy and slovenly to the extent of driving out a moderately civilised spouse (*Gollins v Gollins* [1963] 2 All ER 966); and

(d) contracting a second polygamous marriage even where the first wife was also a Moslem – here the decision was also logical because the parties were Westernised and the first wife had expressly requested that the husband should not take a second wife (*Quoreshi v Quoreshi* [1985] FLR 760, one of the very few modern cases of constructive desertion).

In the light of the contemporary ease of obtaining a decree on the basis of behaviour or adultery, it seems strange that such petitions should have been brought in the past on the much more roundabout basis of constructive desertion. All the above cases were fought hard at the time they were decided, as it was by no means a foregone conclusion that the circumstances would be sufficiently 'grave and weighty' to justify the wife in leaving. Indeed, in defending, Mr Gollins, and probably Mr Timmins too, must clearly have taken the view that there was nothing at all 'grave and weighty' about staying in bed, not washing, telling the wife off and knocking her about a bit.

Problem areas still remain, which make using desertion and constructive desertion inadvisable and, with Fact B available for less serious behaviour, unnecessary. It was held in *Bulcher v Bulcher* [1947] 1 All ER 319, for example, that a wife who left her husband, who had formed a strange relationship with one of his farm hands which fell short of homosexuality, did not have just cause for leaving (and therefore was in desertion), although she was upset by it, embarrassed by local gossip and felt 'left out' and starved of affection. This is an old case which might have been decided differently today, but in any event she could now have easily obtained a Fact B decree on the basis of such allegations, *Wachtel* having now established that non-adulterous relationships can be more hurtful than adultery itself.

Similarly, there is still some intellectual dispute over whether on the old authorities refusal of sexual intercourse is just cause for leaving, although in the light of contemporary expectations this could probably be addressed, as other grey areas are, with careful drafting. In *Weatherly v Weatherly* [1947] 1 All ER 563, the wife was held not to be in desertion for such refusal, but in *Hutchinson v Hutchinson* [1963] 1 All ER 1 it was held that a wife could actually leave a husband who refused to have sexual intercourse. Despite the decision in the behaviour case of *Dowden* (see 8.5.10, above) it is probably correct to say that refusal of sexual intercourse, if coupled with other insensitive and non-communicative behaviour, must now be sufficient for Fact B (a further reason, if refusal of sexual intercourse must be relied upon, for avoiding desertion and choosing behaviour).

Insane delusions will not always be just cause for leaving, as in *Kacmarcz v Kacmarcz* [1967] 1 WLR 317; [1967] 1 All ER 416, where the wife believed her husband was committing a grave sin by having sexual intercourse with her. However, in *Perry v Perry* [1963] 3 All ER 766, the wife's delusion that the husband was trying to murder her enabled the court to decide that she was not in desertion herself since she should be judged as if her delusion were true. If delusions are not insane, but based on flimsy and unreasonable grounds, then usually there will not be just cause for leaving and such petitioners will be in desertion themselves. For example, in *Marsden v Marsden* [1967] 1 All ER 967, the husband deluded himself into believing, on no serious basis, that the wife was committing adultery, so he was not only unable to petition successfully, but also put himself into desertion.

It should be noted that although a spouse must not normally lock out a deserting spouse, or desertion will be brought to an end (and moreover the spouse who excludes the other will be in desertion instead of the other), it *is* permissible to exclude a spouse whose conduct is frightening to the other party and/or children of the family without that spouse being in desertion. Such behaviour will constitute just cause for leaving (and therefore for the locking out) (see *G v G* [1964] 1 All ER 129, where the husband was mentally ill and the wife waited for him to go away on a journey before taking her opportunity to change the locks).

It goes without saying that any conduct which is said to be just cause for leaving must actually have acted upon the mind of the spouse when deciding to leave. See *Herod v Herod* [1938] 3 All ER 722, where the husband had actually committed adultery, but the wife did not know and so was uninfluenced by it, thus herself being in desertion when she decided to leave.

9.3 TIMING

The two year period relied on for Fact C must immediately precede the presentation of the petition (or cross-petition if desertion is alleged in the answer). However, if a decree of judicial separation has already been obtained on the basis of an existing period of two years and the parties have not resumed cohabitation, that period can be relied on as if it had immediately preceded the presentation of the petition (s 4(1)).

There are similar reconciliation provisions to those in connection with Fact A, in that the parties may live together for a period or periods totalling less than six months and no account will be taken of any periods of cohabitation in calculating the necessary two year period to found desertion under this Fact. However, desertion must in total last two years immediately preceding the presentation of the petition, so if periods of cohabitation less than six months in total are to be disregarded, clearly the original desertion will have taken place up to two and a half years prior to the presentation of the petition.

9.4 PROBLEMS IN RELATION TO THE LOCATION OF THE MATRIMONIAL HOME

There are sometimes problems in relation to where the matrimonial home should officially be located and, further, as to who has the right to decide that point. Basically this is usually a point for behaviour under Fact B rather than a desertion matter and should probably be dealt with as an instance of lack of commitment to the marriage, both for simplicity and for all the reasons previously noted as to why Fact B is preferable to rely on than Fact C.

First, desertion is withdrawal from a state of affairs and not from a place. Thus, there may be desertion even though there is currently no matrimonial home and even where there has never been a matrimonial home, as in the case of members of the armed forces. In *Milligan v Milligan* [1941] 2 All ER 62, for example, the husband, who had lived with his wife in a series of hotels and in rented accommodation, was held to be in desertion as soon as he left her to live alone in the officers' mess and refused to return to her. This situation can also apply to domestic servants who live in their employers' homes, as in *Bradshaw v Bradshaw* [1897] P 24, where the parties visited each other at the husband's employer's home. They even had children together; however, the husband was in desertion as soon as he refused any longer to have her to visit or to maintain the children.

Alternatively, where there is supposed to be a matrimonial home, problems sometimes arise because the parties cannot agree where that should be, so if the impasse persists it is difficult to decide who has deserted whom. Even prior to the modern practice of presuming equality between the sexes and of regarding marriage as a partnership of equals, it was not necessarily the husband who had the right to dictate the location of the matrimonial home, even if he was the breadwinner. There may be other reasons why the choice of residence may realistically only be the wife's. An example of this situation is afforded by *Dunn v Dunn* [1918] 2 All ER 822. The wife was acutely deaf and very shy and did not want to move from the place where the parties had first set up home when the husband's posting in the Navy required him to live elsewhere. Due to her reasonable cause for refusing to move, the wife was held not to be in desertion, whereas the husband was as he had unreasonably refused to agree to the location of the matrimonial home. This is clearly the sort of situation which, while technically possibly desertion, is more amenable to Fact B than Fact C and should be treated accordingly.

DESERTION AND CONSTRUCTIVE DESERTION

THE FOUR ELEMENTS OF DESERTION

Desertion is a highly technical subject and is defined in s 1(2)(c) of the MCA 1973 as follows: 'That the respondent has deserted the petitioner for a continuous period of at least two years immediately preceding the presentation of the petition.' This requires the four separate elements of actual separation, intention to desert by the respondent, lack of consent to the separation by the petitioner and absence of just cause for the respondent's leaving.

Actual separation means that the parties must be living apart or, if still under the same roof, in separate households, rather than in one unhappy household. Lack of the petitioner's consent means that there must be no agreement to the respondent's leaving, nor refusal of a reasonable offer to return, but this does not preclude the petitioner's being glad to see the respondent go, or giving practical help, such as with packing. Any offer to return must not be subject to unreasonable requirements or conditions.

TIMING

The parties must not be living together at the time of the presentation of the petition and the two years are not fatally interrupted by periods of cohabitation, so long as these do not exceed six months in all.

PROBLEMS IN RELATION TO THE LOCATION OF THE MATRIMONIAL HOME

There are sometimes problems in deciding who is in desertion as neither party generally has the right to dictate where the matrimonial home should be, nor is there a need in fact for such a home, as desertion is from a state of affairs rather than from a place.

CHAPTER 10

THE SEPARATION DECREES

10.1 FACTS D AND E

These decrees were introduced in 1969, initially to an ambivalent reception from lawyer and layperson alike, not unlike that which greeted the introduction of the Bill which became the Family Law Act (FLA) 1996. The reasoning behind this initial opposition to the introduction of the two separation decrees was simple: Fact D brought divorce by consent into English law for the first time, and this was seen as a mixed blessing, while Fact E enabled an 'innocent' respondent to be divorced against his or, more usually, her will. Public opinion did secure protection for 'innocent' respondents on the basis that, as they did not themselves seek divorce, and indeed generally opposed it, it was right that adequate financial protection should be provided. This was thought to balance the mutually exclusive aims of recognising the sanctity of marriage, and giving due weight to one of the key principles of the divorce reform movement (that those marriages identified as dead should be given decent, timely and dignified burials).

10.2 TWO YEARS' SEPARATION WITH THE RESPONDENT'S CONSENT: FACT D

The requirement to establish Fact D is that the parties have lived apart for a continuous period of at least two years immediately preceding the presentation of the petition and the respondent consents to a decree being granted (s 1(2)(d)).

10.2.1 Living apart

The principles used to decide in desertion cases whether the parties when living at one address are living in one household or two (see Chapter 9) also apply to cases under Fact D, save that the FLA 1996 provides that the parties are to be treated as living apart unless they are living with each other in the same household (s 2(6)).

In addition to actual separation, a successful petition under Fact D requires recognition that the marriage is at an end, and when the parties are already living apart at the time that that decision is taken, some evidence of the changed status of the marriage will also be required. An example of this may be seen in *Santos v Santos* [1972] 2 All ER 246, where the husband lived in Spain and the wife in England, although they visited each other. For their divorce to be granted, it was held that a mental element was required to indicate the changed circumstances of the separation, and that the two years could only start when one party recognised that the marriage was over, but that once that had been done there was no need actually to communicate the decision.

However, it will be necessary, where the decision is unilateral, for the petitioner to pinpoint the moment when he or she decided the marriage was over and for there to be some evidence of that. In practice, this means no more than that the petitioner is able to say in the affidavit in support of the petition both when the decision was made and when the separation began if, as is usually the case, that was at a different time.

Sometimes there is actual evidence of a positive step (eg, one party writing a letter) or at least a change in the pattern of behaviour (eg, discontinuing visiting a spouse who is in prison or in hospital or elsewhere away from home, a cessation of communication with a spouse working overseas, or setting up home with a third party).

10.2.2 Consent of the respondent to the decree

Positive consent is required and not mere failure to object.

An example of this requirement may be seen in *McGill v Robson* [1972] 1 All ER 362 where the husband was living in South Africa and the wife's solicitors, in serving the papers, somehow managed not to send him a form of acknowledgment of service (upon which a willing respondent normally consents to the decree). He nevertheless acknowledged service and wrote saying that he wanted the proceedings completed as soon as possible – but in the absence of a specific written consent no decree could be granted.

One drawback of using Fact D instead of risking the complications of Fact C is that as consent must be positive – and the suit simply cannot proceed under Fact D without it – the respondent can exact conditions in return for the essential consent. The common condition is that the respondent will pay no costs, as in *Beales v Beales* [1972] 2 WLR 972; [1972] 2 All ER 667, but as it is now usual in Fact D cases for each party to pay their own costs this is not of far-reaching importance.

A more tedious condition can be that the respondent wants to exact a sharp deal on ancillary relief but, in general, if both parties want a divorce and the respondent sees that one will not be obtainable without some sort of suitable ancillary relief package, consent will usually be forthcoming. If the marriage has broken up anyway, the alternative might be to risk a petition being served on a fault based Fact, such as behaviour. As allegations need not be profoundly shocking for such a petition, it would usually not be possible or desirable to defend such a petition successfully, so this is sometimes the remedy where an expected consent turns out to be lacking. Moreover, costs, unlike in Fact D cases, might legitimately be asked for in such a case, especially if the respondent has refused to consent to a Fact D decree. In these circumstances, the best practical course is to suggest that all outstanding matters are agreed before a Fact D petition is filed and then the agreed ancillary relief package can go ahead by consent.

It should be noted that a respondent must have capacity to consent to a Fact D decree: see *Mason v Mason* [1972] 3 All ER 315, where it was established that the test for capacity is usually the same as for contracting marriage. This test, laid down in *In re the Estate of Park* [1953] 2 All ER 1411, is basically: 'Is the respondent capable of understanding the nature of the contract in to which he is entering?' In case of any doubt it will be up to the petitioner to establish that the respondent had capacity.

A further hazard of Fact D is that there is power to withdraw consent at any time before decree *nisi* and also power to apply for rescission of the decree *nisi* where the respondent has been misled in relation to any matter taken into account in deciding whether to give consent (s 10(1)).

10.2.3 Timing

Fact D requires a period of separation of at least two years prior to the presentation of the petition. *Warr v Warr* [1975] 1 All ER 85 shows that this period is crucial – the day of separation was included in the calculation of the two years in that case and a new petition had to be served. Thus it is good practice not to file the petition until two years and one day from the separation.

The usual reconciliation provisions apply to Fact D and the parties must not cohabit for more than six months so as not to break the period of separation. No account will be taken in calculating the two years of any periods which do not qualify because the parties were cohabiting (s 2(5)).

10.3 FIVE YEARS' SEPARATION: FACT E

The requirement to establish Fact E is that the parties have lived apart for a continuous period of at least five years immediately preceding the presentation of the petition (s 1(2)(e)).

This Fact is substantially the same as Fact D save that the period of separation must be five years and no consent is required from the respondent. The respondent may be divorced unless able to use the defence of 'grave financial or other hardship' provided by s 5(1) to preclude the grant of a decree in certain cases (see below).

10.3.1 Grave financial or other hardship: the s 5 defence to Fact E petitions

This special defence applies only to Fact E cases (and not to those brought under Fact D) and only where no other Fact is alleged in the petition. It is of limited application because the number of cases where grave financial or other hardship can successfully be shown is very limited.

It should be noted that 'grave financial hardship' within the meaning of s 5 is now virtually entirely limited to loss of pension rights cases, and only where the petitioner cannot make alternative provision to compensate for pension rights which will terminate for the defending spouse with the status of marriage. The importance of this defence has recently been further reduced since pursuant to the Welfare Reform and Pensions Act 1999 from 1 December 2000 it became possible to share a pension by asking in the prayer of the petition for a pension order (see Chapters 11–13).

The defence is also limited because where such marriages have broken down more than five years previously and the respondent has been obstructive in refusing consent to a Fact D decree, the petitioner often ultimately feels inclined, even if this was ruled out before, to petition on the basis of a fault based Fact which the respondent will at least be put to some trouble to defend. Moreover, the respondent will then be precluded both from defending the petition on the fault based Fact and from cross-petitioning, as once the five year separation period is admitted there is no room for the respondent to obtain a decree because the petitioner is already entitled to one (*Parsons v Parsons* [1975] 1 WLR 1272; [1975] 3 All ER 344).

In order to invoke the defence, the respondent must file an answer, thus making the suit defended and, unlike most divorce suits, eligible for public funding (see Chapter 11).

It must be shown that it would be wrong in all the circumstances to dissolve the marriage, which, of course, will not be possible if the petitioner can also rely on Fact A, B or C, and which is why the defence is exclusively reserved for petitions brought under Fact E alone. The rationale for this is that when the law was fundamentally changed in 1969 to introduce Fact E, it was realised that special arrangements would have to be made to avoid injustice either to petitioner or respondent. Fact E and s 5 were therefore combined to achieve two independent but linked results:

(a) to enable spouses who were previously unable to obtain decrees to petition. Previously, such spouses were technically the 'guilty' party (usually having left to form other relationships but not having divorced their spouses) and had no possibility of petitioning under the law which provided no separation decrees; and

(b) to protect the elderly, and especially financially dependent, spouses (usually wives), who could now be divorced against their will, from being cast off without at least proper financial provision being made for them.

The reason for combining the new Fact E with the s 5 defence was because Fact E was at the time regarded as something of a 'Casanovas' charter', enabling as it did those husbands who had traded in faithful, if now boring, middle-aged wives for a newer model to obtain divorces against their wives' will. Husbands who availed themselves of Fact E in order to bestow a marriage certificate (and the future status of widow entitled to their pensions) on the 'bimbo' whose existence their wives had always refused to recognise (by declining to take the divorce proceedings only they, the deserted wives, had grounds for) therefore benefited from the new law in being able at last to make an honest woman of a sometimes long time cohabitant and found there was a penalty to pay. However, they were also obliged to make effective financial provision for the discarded wife in order to obtain the decree.

A further class of spouses whom s 5(1) was intended to protect were those for whom religious objections to decrees were a serious consideration, especially in relation to foreign ethnic communities where divorce was said to be a social disgrace. These cases have, however, never really had much success, and have only infrequently been brought since the 1970s.

Furthermore, Fact E is now largely irrelevant as the stockpile of old cases where it benefited the errant husbands and the second families they had set up were all worked through in the 1970s. Section 5(1) defences are, therefore, usually now only employed as a bargaining tactic where divorce is likely to be inevitable and the only question is whether better financial terms can be exacted in return for truncating the delay and expense which a s 5(1) defence will cause. Generally, as good if not better terms can be secured at the earlier stage of consenting to a Fact D decree (see below).

The eventual replacement for the FLA 1996 – if a drastically recast statute is ever introduced – may considerably strengthen the position of a respondent claiming hardship, including on religious grounds, as this seemed to be one of the few components of the 1996 Act which found favour with a section of the public.

10.4 CHOOSING THE STRONGEST FACT ON WHICH TO PROCEED

As most divorces are undefended, it is best, if everything can be agreed, to proceed either on Fact D – provided there has been sufficient separation – or on a Fact which is the most easily and inexpensively proved, and to remember that most Facts can be proved without difficulty as long as the suit remains *undefended*. Esoteric points of law are usually only going to arise if the respondent disagrees so violently with the Fact on which the decree is sought that an irresistible desire to *defend* arises which cannot be headed off either by the respondent's own good sense or second thoughts or the combined advice of lawyers and friends. These cases therefore come to court for a contested oral hearing.

10.4.1 Multiple Facts

If there are multiple Facts on which a petition could proceed, it is not usually a good idea to proceed on the basis of more than one Fact even if the situation qualifies, as this merely makes the petitioner's case look weak. If the case is weak, using more than one Fact will usually make it look weaker, except in the case of combining a fault based Fact with Fact D in the hope that the respondent will consent to the Fact D decree and the other Fact need not be proceeded with. Thus, capable practitioners usually select the strongest Fact and only fall back on the suggested alternative in rare cases, since if there is a fault based Fact available, a draft petition shown to the respondent or respondent's solicitors before it is served may result in an agreement that consent will be forthcoming to a Fact D decree. If, on the other hand, the respondent is actually felt to be untrustworthy, then it may be better to plead the two Facts in the alternative, and if the desired consent is then given, the petition can be amended to delete the other Fact and particulars of it. This is preferable to having to change Facts after filing, as that always looks rather foolish. Amending the petition to delete one Fact may be done without the leave of the court unless an answer has been filed in the suit.

10.4.2 Choosing Fact D

If the parties are on good terms and it appears that everything will be agreed, Fact D is the most civilised procedure, although it does have drawbacks if the respondent is likely to drive a hard bargain in return for the necessary consent. The practitioner's answer to this problem has already been mentioned above.

If Fact D is not available, or is thought to be problematic, and there is more than one Fact available, then a choice will have to be made.

10.4.3 The alternatives to Fact D

Although Fact D is supposed to be the 'divorce by consent' Fact, in practice, because of the hazards of a respondent imposing conditions, behaviour and adultery tend to be the 'consent' Facts. However, strictly there is no such thing known to English law as a divorce by consent on the basis of either adultery or behaviour. This does not stop laypersons stating that they have obtained a 'divorce by consent on the grounds of adultery or unreasonable behaviour', a statement which contains more inaccuracies than that no respondent can 'consent' as such to a divorce on either ground. If it is *agreed* that there shall be a divorce and the basis selected is either adultery or behaviour, the divorce decree is achieved not by either party's *consenting* to the divorce but by the respondent *not defending* a petition brought by the petitioner – a significant difference. Nevertheless, whether or not the parties have agreed that there shall be a divorce, it will still be necessary for the petition and supporting documents to show a sufficient case of adultery or behaviour to enable the court to pronounce that the petitioner is entitled to the decree. This is so because, in view of the paper based nature of the routine divorce process, there will be no other evidence on which the district judge deciding the case can rely to form the view that a decree is justified.

10.4.3.1 Adultery

Adultery, if available, should always be the first choice of alternatives, since it is the most straightforward Fact:

- provided there is proof even when it is anticipated that there will be no unexpected defence; or

- where an admission is likely.

And of course provided the suit is genuinely unlikely to be defended in such circumstances.

Defended adultery is not to be recommended. The chances of a defended adultery suit must be at an all time low since it is not now necessary to name a co-respondent. Thus, the names of any new partners can be kept out of the suit. This may be desirable if there are children and the new relationship is to be permanent.

Officially, no stigma is now attached to being divorced for adultery, even where a co-respondent is named, because adultery is best considered as a symptom rather than a cause of marriage breakdown. However, practitioners consider that they should always check the position with their clients in case any client holds different views and in case there might be any unforeseen complication which the client has neglected to mention (eg, the respondent or co-respondent is a clergyman or holds an ecclesiastical post of some kind when a decree of divorce on the basis of adultery might amount to a professional slur hindering career advancement). If in doubt, the Solicitors Family Law Association Code gives clear guidance that practitioners should discourage the naming of a co-respondent without good reason.

While there is no defence to a petition if there is proof of the adultery in question, divorcing a respondent for adultery who might strongly object to that may make agreeing ancillary relief and/or child matters more difficult and costly in both emotional and financial terms.

10.4.3.2 Behaviour

Behaviour is likely to be the next alternative choice, preferably the 'mild behaviour petition' as envisaged by Ormrod, restricted to no more than three to six carefully drafted paragraphs. Most respondents do not mind this, especially if the allegations are not too exaggerated, since it seems to be accepted (particularly for some reason by men, which is as well as statistics show that most petitions are filed by women!) that spouses who want to complain about their marriages and to obtain a decree will be able to do so under the existing law, and that there is little point in resisting the determined petitioner. In particular, it seems to be accepted that women habitually complain about and divorce their husbands for relatively trivial reasons and most men are therefore unlikely to defend a behaviour petition which restricts itself to moderate language and what men regard as run of the mill 'women's complaints'.

This is, therefore, a good choice of Fact if a potential petitioner's statement shows reasonable material on which a good piece of drafting can be executed so as to establish the minimum safe level for a behaviour decree. It will obtain the decree quickly and easily without fuss and should not prejudice the ancillary relief and/or child matters.

10.4.3.3 Other Facts

Once the above Facts are exhausted, the practitioner enters the danger zone. For all the reasons explained in Chapter 9, Fact C should be vehemently avoided unless the case is absolutely straightforward and the respondent will not defend. While Fact D can be dangerous if the respondent is grasping, Fact E should only be used if there is no better and earlier alternative, or the respondent is very sweet-natured. Fact E is problematic because a potential respondent will usually have failed to agree to a Fact D petition long before the two years' separation necessary is established because the respondent anticipates being able to cause a lot of trouble to the petitioner when a Fact E petition is finally brought after five years. Usually, such a respondent can extort a high price for Fact D consent (as otherwise the petitioner will have to wait three more years and still face a costly ancillary relief package to secure a decree). The inescapable moral (for petitioner and respondent alike) is to use Fact D if at all possible. It is rare that any respondent gets a better deal after having kept the petitioner waiting five years: it is better for any respondent to threaten the three year delay and stand out for a good financial package in return for consent at Fact D stage, than to be on the defensive after five years (when the respondent has nothing left to bargain with).

10.5 PRACTICAL CONSIDERATIONS

Divorce is not a field of law which can usefully be studied academically in isolation from practice since, while the Matrimonial Causes Act (MCA) 1973 provides a legal framework for the grant of decrees, other provisions of the Act, and also divorce practice and procedure, significantly limit the impact of the purely substantive law in the MCA 1973, ss 1 and 2. It is therefore essential to understand the way in which the law works in practice or the conclusions drawn on the effect of the law, although technically correct on a reading of ss 1 and 2, will in fact be significantly different from how the law works in practice. Knowledge of what actually happens when a petition is presented and then goes through the various stages of divorce procedure as regulated by the Family Proceedings Rules (FPR) 1991 must be taken into account. In practice, the interaction of the ground for divorce with other sections of the MCA 1973, as amended, will often have a profound influence on the conduct of the divorce suit and ancillary relief or other related proceedings.

For example, a weak petition on the basis of behaviour under s 1(2)(b) will appear in the academic view, and in the absence of experience of practice, to lack sufficient behaviour to establish Fact B, since in such a case there always is room for intellectual argument as to whether the test in *Buffery* (see Chapter 7) is met. The student who looks through the eyes of the practitioner, however, knows that the petition will almost certainly succeed, provided the particulars of behaviour are carefully drafted so that it appears on the face of the petition that the petitioner could be entitled to a decree, and provided the respondent also wants a divorce and does not mind being divorced on the basis of that particular Fact, so that the petition remains undefended. Moreover, it is entirely proper, despite the weakness of the allegations, for the practitioner to present such a petition since the law permits a decree to be granted provided a minimum level case is made out which complies with the wording of the statute. There are also good reasons for choosing Fact B even when the qualifying facts are weak, despite the possibility that the respondent might have been coaxed into consenting to a decree under Fact D. If Fact D had been chosen instead, the respondent could have attached unwelcome conditions – which cannot be used in a Fact B suit – so that the necessary consent for a Fact D decree might have become unduly expensive.

It should be clear, therefore, that a number of practical considerations are relevant to the successful attainment of the decree of divorce (which will enable the parties to remarry), and that it is essential to understand how this goal fits together with other matters with which the petitioner may be concerned on the way to the successful conclusion of the case. Of these, the financial protection available to respondents to Fact D and E petitions is one of the most important issues.

10.6 FINANCIAL PROTECTION FOR RELUCTANT RESPONDENTS TO FACT D AND E PETITIONS

Every divorce will usually provide some fair financial provision for both parties on decree of divorce. This is built in under the ordinary law of ancillary relief, where the court (which is usually not in any way influenced by the Fact on which the decree was obtained) will seek to divide the assets as cleanly and fairly as possible, irrespective of which party technically 'owned' them while the parties were married. However, the two 'separation' Facts – Facts D and E – have their own protection: this is expressly because prior to their inclusion in the present divorce law, decrees were possible only on proof of fault. It was thought, therefore, that such a radical change as a separation decree – either on the sole basis of a short separation and consent, or a lengthy separation and against the respondent's will – should only be granted if the respondent could be sure that the post-decree financial position was definitely going to be satisfactory. This is achieved in different ways for Facts D and E.

10.6.1 Matrimonial Causes Act 1973, s 10

The first important provision of s 10 may or may not have any connection with financial protection, but is an extremely powerful bargaining chip where the petitioner wants a divorce badly and has no other Fact to rely on. Therefore, it may well be used in a financial context.

Since consent to a Fact D decree must be positive and not merely amount to the respondent not objecting, the respondent will have had to signify consent on the Acknowledgment of Service form. Furthermore, the consent can be withdrawn, for any reason, at any time up to pronouncement of the decree *nisi* which conditionally dissolves the marriage (see Chapter 11).

It should be noted that decree *nisi* is the first of *two decrees* required to fully dissolve a marriage, and must be distinguished from the second (decree absolute) after the issue of which the parties are both free to remarry (they are not, in any jurisdiction in the world, allowed to remarry between decree *nisi* and decree absolute, although this has sometimes not stopped people claiming they believed themselves to be free to marry again at this stage and doing so bigamously). There is normally a *minimum* period of six weeks between the two decrees, largely for the court's administrative purposes, although it can in practice be much longer at the will of the parties if there are good reasons (eg, hard bargaining in the ancillary relief context, especially where there is no satisfactory compensation for pension rights which depend on the continued status of marriage). In financial terms, this limbo period can be used to good tactical effect both by petitioners and respondents.

First, if it transpires in a Fact D divorce that the respondent has actually been *misled* in any way, in relation to any matter which was taken into account when consent was given, s 10(1) permits the consent to be withdrawn after pronouncement of decree *nisi,* provided action is taken before the decree becomes final at the decree absolute stage (see Chapter 11). The section permits such a respondent to even apply to have the decree *nisi* rescinded (so that if the petitioner still wants a decree another Fact will have to be used, or a new deal negotiated with the respondent). This is obviously a powerful weapon in the hands of the respondent and in theory can apply to any condition which might be expected, no matter how ridiculous, although there are no reported cases on the degree of absurdity to which this might be taken.

Secondly, by s 10(2), Fact D respondents who cannot claim to have been misled in any way, and also Fact E respondents unable to defend the Fact E petition (see below), can still hold up the final decree dissolving the marriage by applying to have their financial position specially considered by the court, and this too can be a powerful weapon if the petitioner is in a hurry to remarry. Indeed the petitioner in a hurry to remarry who has to rely on Fact D is giving hostages to fortune all along the way, and obviously only uses Fact D if there is no fault based Fact available.

Thirdly, by s 10(3), the court will consider the s 10(2) application and will not allow the decree *nisi* granted on the basis of the respondent's consent to be made absolute until they are satisfied that either:

(a) the petitioner does not need to make any such financial provision for the respondent; or

(b) the financial provision made for the respondent is reasonable or fair or the best that can be made in the circumstances.

Finally, by s 10(4) the petitioner can rescue the position – which may be desperate if, for example, he has promised early marriage to a pregnant new partner who insists on being married at the birth, or where the respondent or the new partner has a terminal illness – by applying to the court to relax the provisions of s 10(3), in that:

(a) there are circumstances which make it desirable to make the decree absolute without delay; and

(b) he will make such financial provision for the respondent as the court may approve, *and give an undertaking to the court to that effect.*

Grigson v Grigson [1974] 1 All ER 478 establishes that any undertaking must be sufficiently precise to be useful (in that case the general formula 'such provision as the court may approve' was rejected and precise proposals required); and *Parkes v Parkes* [1971] 3 All ER 670 shows how important it is that the s 10(3) power exists, as the agreed provision in that case was not sufficiently clearly defined to prevent the petitioner from exploiting ambiguities and in effect depriving the respondent of the fruits of the agreement. Had there been no s 10(3) power enabling the respondent to insist on the petitioner keeping the spirit as well as the letter of the agreement, the respondent would have lost out significantly.

On the other hand, *Lombardi v Lombardi* [1973] 3 All ER 625 demonstrates that some applications are entirely unnecessary (in that case no more was awarded than the approximate offer under the one third rule already made by the husband), and *Krystman v Krystman* [1972] 3 All ER 247 was even more absurd (where the Fact E wife respondent was better off than the husband and the parties had cohabited for only two weeks out of a 26 year marriage; not surprisingly, the court decided that this hasty and long abandoned wartime marriage should be dissolved without further provision). However, in *Garcia v Garcia* [1992] 2 WLR 347, the petitioner was able to delay the decree because her Spanish husband owed her £4,000 in unpaid maintenance for their child.

By s 10(3), this consideration of the respondent's financial position is a thorough stocktaking of that position as it will be after decree absolute and if the petitioner should die first, taking into account such matters as the age, state of health, conduct, earning capacity, financial resources and financial obligations, exactly as under s 25 of the MCA 1973 in relation to ancillary relief (Chapter 12). Indeed, a s 10(2) application and the usual comprehensive claim for ancillary relief are usually heard together, supported for convenience by one affidavit, although the FPR 1991 require a separate s 10(2) application to be lodged alongside the application to activate the routine ancillary relief stage of the divorce.

It is thus hard to see the need for the technically separate procedure, as all the separate form does is to alert the court hearing the ancillary relief application to the fact that the case is a s 10(2) situation, and that as the ancillary relief package is not satisfactory to the respondent, the decree finally dissolving the marriage will have to be held up unless the court relents pursuant to s 10(4).

A s 10(2) application is therefore a useful delaying tactic which tends to secure better financial terms in many cases. Even where it may not actually work at the substantive hearing, it will still have a nuisance value in that the final decree will be held up at least until that hearing, whereas otherwise the marriage might have been dissolved on the petitioner's application for the final decree earlier than the financial hearing could be arranged. This is because a court date for such a hearing will not be fixed until the parties' advisers have worked through all the stages of the new ancillary relief procedure and it is clear how much court time will be required for the hearing. From this point the state of court lists generally means the wait for a hearing could still be some months.

However, s 10(2) can *only* be used where Fact D or E is the *sole* basis of the petition, so in practice it is not available where a fault based Fact can be used, and a petitioner who fears a s 10(2) application from the respondent therefore usually petitions on a fault based Fact if at all possible.

10.6.2 Matrimonial Causes Act 1973, s 5

Instead of being merely a useful delaying tactic, s 5 provides an actual *defence* which if successful will stop a decree being granted at all. This section applies in Fact E cases only – it is *not* available to Fact D respondents. Fact E respondents who cannot use s 5 can still obtain some tactical advantage by using s 10 above to *delay* a final decree which they know they cannot ultimately *prevent* in due course.

The section provides that the respondent may oppose the grant of a decree under s 1(2)(e), despite proof of five years' separation, if it can be shown that the dissolution of the marriage will result in *grave financial or other hardship* to the respondent *and* that it would be *wrong in all the circumstances* to dissolve the marriage (MCA 1973, s 5(1)). If the respondent is successful the court will have to dismiss the Fact E petition.

Obviously it is only worth using the defence if the petitioner cannot rely on any other Fact, as if the Fact E petition is dismissed the petitioner is only likely to present another one, this time on Facts A, B or C.

In order to use s 5, the respondent must file a formal defence to the petition, called an 'answer' (see Chapter 11). For technical reasons it is never possible to cross-petition on a s 5 defence, so unlike in cases under s 1(2)(a)–(d) the defence will be a simple answer not incorporating a cross-petition based on any other Fact, even if one exists. This is because, as shown by *Parsons v Parsons* [1975] 1 WLR 1272; [1975] 3 All ER 344, once the five year separation period is *admitted*, which is essential in order to invoke the s 5 defence at all, there is no opportunity for the respondent to petition since the petitioner is already *entitled* to a decree. The whole purpose of s 5 is to ask the court to formally not grant the decree to which the petitioner has shown entitlement (by proving the five years' separation – the period of separation being the sole requirement of s 1(2)(e)) because of the special circumstances afforded by s 5 (ie, if the respondent can prove that those special circumstances apply in the particular case).

It should be noted that where a five year separation already exists and one party petitions not on Fact E but on a fault based Fact (eg, Fact B), the respondent can defend the Fact B petition and cross-petition on Fact E, but in that situation, as is shown by *Grenfell v Grenfell* [1977] 3 WLR 738; [1978] 1 All ER 561, the original petitioner will not be able to use the s 5 defence against the Fact E cross-petition. This is because the petitioner cannot then say that s/he does not want a divorce nor that it would be wrong in all the circumstances to dissolve the marriage when, as in the case of Mrs Grenfell, a petitioner has him or herself already petitioned for divorce! Mrs Grenfell's s 5 defence was struck out as an abuse of the spirit of the defence.

Section 5 defences rarely succeed, except in cases where the respondent can show that the dissolution of the marriage will have adverse financial effects which cannot be compensated for (eg, in the past where lucrative pension rights would have been lost). The scope of this defence is now severely limited because of the court's new power to share pensions in the case of all petitions presented after 1 December 2000 pursuant to the Welfare Reform and Pension Act 1999. It is usually impossible to show 'other hardship' in the sense of some social disadvantage, even in the lives of ethnic minorities where divorce is a disgrace which impacts on children's marriage prospects. Such cultural stigma does not usually apply in a Westernised context and in most overseas communities divorce is either now tolerated or separation, and not the actual dissolution of the marriage, has already done the damage complained of. The court usually looks to terminating such empty marriage ties, as in *Talbot v Talbot* (1971) 115 SJ 870, where a Catholic husband wanted to marry his mistress, with whom he lived in Italy, by converting his decree of judicial separation into one of divorce. The wife was young, employable and not losing any pension rights. The court could not see any argument for not ending the marriage.

Wives' pension cases might still succeed in some cases, since the complex rules of pension schemes may still preclude the wife genuinely sharing in the husband's pension rights where they cannot conveniently be shared and the scheme for some reason does not agree to pay his benefits to her. In these circumstances a decree of divorce may be undesirable because it ends the status of marriage (and therefore her pension entitlement). However, if there is nothing in the pension scheme to preclude the wife receiving the widow's pension on the husband's death regardless of whether they live together, judicial separation will mean that the wife will still be provided for if the marriage is not actually dissolved. For post-December 2000 petitions, this is likely to be a remote possibility (eg, where there is a non-UK based pension scheme).

However, usually the husband is able to provide for the wife in another way so as to compensate for the lost pension rights and in this case the s 5 defence will fail, as in *Dorrell v Dorrell* [1972] 1 WLR 1087; [1972] 3 All ER 343. Here the parties were both over 60 and the wife was living on welfare benefits. Although the husband claimed she could quite well manage on this without the widow's rights from his small local government pension, the defence was upheld as the court said that the amount – tiny as it was – was a significant part of her small income and, as there was apparently no way of compensating her, the marriage should not be ended. The same happened in *Julian v Julian* (1972) 116 SJ 763, a case of a police pension where the husband could not close the gap between what was lost and what was required to compensate, and nearly happened in *Le Marchant v Le Marchant* [1977] 1 WLR 559; [1977] 3 All ER 610, where there was a Post Office pension and only at the last minute was the husband able to take out an insurance policy to compensate the wife, though the court would not make the decree absolute until he had actually done it. Nevertheless, the court can only act within its powers as set out in ss 22–24 of the MCA 1973. It can hold up a decree absolute while the husband 'volunteers' a solution to enable a decree to be made absolute, but it has no power actually to order the husband to take out an insurance policy or to compensate the wife in other ways, except within its ordinary powers to order lump sum payments or property transfer from one spouse to another under s 22 or 23 (see *K v K (Financial Relief: Widow's Pension)* [1997] 1 FLR 610 and Chapter 12).

Sometimes welfare benefits can be sufficient, as in *Reiterbund v Reiterbund* [1975] 2 WLR 375; [1975] 1 All ER 280, which was complicated by the fact that the parties were in their 50s and the wife could not show that she was likely to suffer hardship by the husband dying before her and also before she became entitled to her own pension at age 60. The court thought this remote possibility could be covered temporarily by welfare benefits if it arose.

The s 5 defence will not work where the wife is young and/or the marriage has been short as in *Mathias v Mathias* [1972] 3 WLR 201; [1972] 3 All ER 1. In this case, the parties were in their 30s and the marriage had lasted only three years. There was a discretionary Army pension at stake as well as the State pension, but the court said the wife was young and employable and retirement was too far into the future for the pension to be a significant consideration.

Nor will the defence succeed where the respondent cannot establish that it would be wrong in all the circumstances to dissolve the marriage (ie, where the respondent has to shoulder some blame for the breakdown of the marriage, although the decree is sought under Fact E). This was the situation in *Brickell v Brickell* [1973] 3 All ER 508, where the wife had no difficulty establishing financial hardship on the loss of a Ministry of Defence pension, but her behaviour during the marriage was fatal, since she had had an obsessive belief that the husband had committed adultery with someone who worked in their business which had so adversely affected the business that it had had to be closed down.

It should be noted that despite initiatives to achieve a fair division of the husband's pension rights on divorce, this problem of compensating the divorced wife for lost pension rights still subsists, despite the fact that sharing will now be possible, because in practice the cash equivalent transfer value of the lost rights is not fully compensating since it ignores the future payments that would have been made up to retirement age. Some pensions can still be shared more effectively in other ways outside the statutory scheme, as in *Brooks v Brooks* [1996] AC 375, where Lord Nicholls of Birkenhead accepted that some such pensions (set up by the spouses themselves as part of a private company scheme) could be varied under s 24(1)(c) of the MCA 1973 as a post-nuptial settlement.

The wife's solicitors have a duty to obtain an actuarial valuation of the pension rights and to seek a substantial sum in compensation, or run the risk of a suit for negligence. Above all, whether or not s 5 is invoked, they should never seek a final decree dissolving the marriage except on express instructions of the client where pension rights may be lost as a result, since while application may be made for all available forms of ancillary relief at a subsequent ancillary relief hearing, leverage will have been lost if the marriage is already dissolved and the pension rights have actually gone.

Cases of financial hardship other than on the basis of pensions are not common, but in *Lee v Lee* (1973) 117 SJ 616 a divorce was refused due to inability to provide a satisfactory ancillary relief package outside a pension context. In that case the problem was the financial and other demands made on the wife by a seriously ill son and, since the husband could not give the wife enough money for her to cope with this situation, the court declined to dissolve the marriage.

It should be noted that such successful defences could undoubtedly increase if and when there is a replacement for Pt II of the FLA 1996 as the new divorce and procedural provisions in that Act would have multiplied the opportunities for objecting to a decree on the basis of hardship other than for financial reasons, and it may be that these provisions which were not at the heart of the objections to the 1996 Act might be replicated. On the other hand, the opportunity to object to divorce under that Act or under the MCA 1973 on the basis of loss of pension rights is likely to be reduced now legislation is in force to enable all pension rights to be shared, that is unless the pension arrangements can still be shown to be unsatisfactory in the particular case.

10.7 THE EFFECTS OF COHABITATION FOLLOWING MARRIAGE BREAKDOWN

It is essential to be aware of the operation of the reconciliation provisions in s 2 of the MCA 1973 on the different Facts when choosing which Fact to petition on. The adultery and behaviour position is very straightforward but cohabitation in separation suits needs careful consideration.

10.7.1 Adultery and behaviour

Cohabitation of six months or more after discovery by the petitioner of the last act of adultery will be fatal to the success of the petition. It should be noted that it is after the petitioner *finds out* about the adultery, not six months after the *last act* of adultery has actually been committed, so as long as the petitioner leaves immediately after finding out about it, very old adultery may indeed suffice for a decree. Once six months' cohabitation is completed, however, another act of adultery is required (MCA 1973, s 2(1)) and, where cohabitation was for less than six months, this must be mentioned in the petition (s 2(2)). Similarly, cohabitation of six months or more after the last act of behaviour is *not* necessarily fatal to the success of the petition, for two reasons:

(1) The behaviour may be of a continuing nature, so that there may still be a sufficient case without relying on the older incidents.

(2) In any case, cohabitation is not an absolute bar to the use of incidents prior to renewed cohabitation in the petition, since cohabitation is only relevant to consideration of whether the petitioner may be 'reasonably expected' to live with the respondent. Moreover, as in *Bradley v Bradley* [1973] 1 WLR 1291; [1973] 3 All ER 750, especially if the petitioner is a woman without independent resources, she may only still be technically cohabiting because she genuinely has nowhere else to go (MCA 1973, s 2(3)).

10.7.2 Desertion and separation suits

The position in the case of these suits is quite different, since cohabitation in the technical sense strikes at the very heart of the Facts in question. Cohabitation of six months or more since the start of the two year desertion or separation periods will break the continuity of the period and the two years must be started again. However, less than six months (whether the cohabitation was in one or more periods) will not break the accrual of the total two year period required to petition, although any months cohabiting will not count towards the total of two years' desertion or separation required (MCA 1973, s 2(5)).

Where there is cohabitation, for the purposes of these Facts the circumstances of the cohabitation should be examined carefully in accordance with the principles in *Mouncer v Mouncer* and *Hopes v Hopes* (see Chapter 9), since it may be that the parties can be said not to be cohabiting at all. Obviously, the court must not be deliberately misled or deceived (which the Codes of Conduct of both the Bar and the solicitors' profession prohibit), since this would be a matter of professional misconduct, but the Act does address the point by providing that the parties are treated as living apart unless *living together in the same household* (s 2(6)).

It should be noted that there will be an opportunity for the petitioner to establish that the parties have been living apart under the same roof in that the printed form of affidavit in support of the petition asks for details of living arrangements to be specified in such circumstances, including details of whether the parties have shared a bedroom, whether they have taken their meals together, what arrangements have been made for cleaning the accommodation and what arrangements have been made for paying the household bills (see Chapter 11). There may be a perfectly *bona fide* case to be made out for their living apart at the same address.

THE SEPARATION DECREES

THE SEPARATION DECREES: FACTS D AND E

These decrees were introduced in 1969 to provide divorces after periods of separation respectively of two and five years, without any matrimonial fault having to be shown. A Fact D decree requires the positive consent of the respondent who may exact conditions for that consent. A Fact E decree is available without the consent of the respondent, but there is a special defence under s 5 of the MCA 1973. This is provided to Fact E respondents only, and solely where they can show grave financial or other hardship if a decree were granted, and where no other Fact besides Fact E is relied upon by the petitioner. The s 5 defence requires an answer to be filed to the petition, and if it is successful the petition will be dismissed and no decree will be granted at all.

CHOOSING THE STRONGEST FACT TO RELY ON

Whether one of the separation decrees or one of those relying on a matrimonial fault is best chosen depends on all the circumstances of the case, and will be a tactical decision depending on whether the respondent wants a divorce, or is opposed to it or indifferent, whether it is likely to be defended (which is nowadays very uncommon) and on whether ancillary matters, such as a financial settlement and a shared approach to child matters, can be agreed. The basis of the divorce is usually entirely irrelevant to these separate matters so the choice of Fact will usually be dictated by separate considerations, most often in relation to the financial settlement to be expected.

PROTECTION FOR RELUCTANT RESPONDENTS

The Act provides mechanisms for respondents to both Fact D and Fact E petitions to ask for special consideration of their financial positions following dissolution of the marriage. These are contained in s 10 and include both delay of the final decree (decree absolute), where arrangements are not yet satisfactory, and rescission of the first decree (decree *nisi*), where the respondent has been misled.

The s 5 defence is most successful where a respondent can show that there will be severe financial hardship in relation to loss of pension rights which the petitioner cannot compensate in some other way. Claims of hardship on religious or social grounds have never been successful, since such hardship or disadvantage has usually already arisen following the separation, and is not generally made any worse by the grant of a decree formally ending the status of marriage.

THE EFFECT OF COHABITATION ON SEPARATION SUITS

It is necessary to beware of adversely affecting the qualifying period for either of the separation decrees through cohabitation, because separation is the essence of both Facts D and E, and also essential to Fact C. Periods spent by the parties together during the qualifying years prior to the presentation of the petition must be mentioned in both the petition itself and the affidavit in support (see Chapter 11), but with care such periods may not in fact amount to 'cohabitation' in the technical sense so long as the parties, though under one roof, can show they have maintained separate households.

DIVORCE PROCEDURE

11.1 THE RELEVANCE OF PROCEDURE TO THE SUBSTANTIVE LAW

Procedure is a subject seldom taught expressly on undergraduate courses, even those called 'Family Law and Practice', or even 'Family Law and Procedure'. It is nevertheless vital to an understanding of the heavily discretionary nature of family law. The following account is intended to enlighten the student as to how the law works in practice, which often has a profound effect on the statutory content, since there is little reliance on precedent due to the existence and application of the discretions, and the practice which has grown up around the black letter law.

11.2 FINANCING THE DIVORCE SUIT, ANCILLARY RELIEF PROCEEDINGS AND CHILD DISPUTES

A fundamental problem in making divorce accessible to women on the same terms as men was always that of how a divorce suit was to be financed. It was not until after the Second World War, when legal aid became widely available, that most women were able to consider petitioning. While women's growing independence due to their wartime experiences undoubtedly had some effect on the increase in divorce rates between the late 1940s and the 1969 Divorce Reform Act, it was also the availability of legal aid which swelled the statistics. The 1969 Act (at a time when legal aid was still plentiful) opened the floodgates and led to restrictions on public funding and, from 1976, to the simplification of divorce procedure so that costs could wherever possible be cut down, at least at the stage of obtaining the decree. After 1973 obtaining the decree was more a process to be gone through in order to access the more hotly contested ancillary relief stage than a case in which there was much doubt of the outcome.

Since 1977, no legal aid has been available for obtaining straightforward undefended divorce decrees: the contemporary position is that such assistance is only available for the *divorce suit* to obtain the initial decree where a divorce is defended (as opposed to resolving the *ancillary relief* and *child* matters, or for protection from domestic violence for which legal aid, now called 'public funding', is still available). Since April 2000, all legal aid (ie, public funding) which is still available, following the changes made by the Access to Justice Act 1999, is under the control of the Legal Services Commission (LSC) and its satellite body the Community Legal Service. The reformed system divides funding into various categories: 'legal help' (which replaces the old Green Form Scheme) and 'public funding' for more extensive advice, mediation and representation (which together replace the old legal aid for representation in litigation).

Provision of general information about the law, legal system and availability of legal services is free, as is initial legal advice consisting of whatever legal help is authorised to be provided under the individual supplier's contract without reference to the client's financial resources: only 'not for profit' sector contracts have such authority. Legal representation is also available for applications under the Child Abduction and Custody Act 1985 (see Chapter 28) and in connection with registration of foreign maintenance orders.

In every other situation, eligibility remains as it was under the former Green Form Scheme, where the only automatic qualification was for those on income support, income based jobseeker's allowance, Working Families' Tax Credit and Disabled Person's Tax Credit, although these applicants could still be disqualified on capital grounds, as disposable capital is assessed in all applications. Basically an applicant having a weekly disposable income over £84 is disqualified, and is ineligible if disposable capital is above £1,000 (rising to £1,335 with one dependant and £1,535 with two or more). As can be seen in Chapters 12–14, the aim of contemporary divorce funding is to encourage the key divorce issues, ie, financial matters, to be resolved in mediation rather than in court and, where the dispute does go to court, to hasten its settlement. It has already been held in the High Court of Justiciary in Scotland, sitting as the Court of Criminal Appeal, that restriction of legal aid is not a human rights abuse, so presumably such restrictions in relation to divorce and its ancillaries are not a breach of Art 6 either, since public funding is retained for other family law cases (see *Procurator Fiscal, Fort William v McLean and Another* (2000) *The Times*, 11 August).

11.2.1 The divorce suit

The divorce suit itself will therefore usually have to be conducted by the petitioner as a litigant in person, with such advice as is available if qualifying for non-contributory legal help, or else by a solicitor whom the petitioner pays privately, since there is no public funding of any kind for *divorce suits* as such (ie, for the relatively straightforward process leading to the grant of a decree), save in exceptional circumstances where:

- the suit is defended;
- there is to be a hearing in open court; or
- the petitioner is physically or mentally handicapped (which could include being unable to speak adequate English).

Once the initial proceedings up to decree *nisi* are over, public funding may then be available, subject to the applicant's means, for the financial settlement stage, which is technically called 'ancillary relief' despite the fact that under the modern law of divorce this, and not the divorce suit as such, is in practical terms the main stage of the proceedings. Nevertheless the 'ancillary' label persists as, in theory, such proceedings are only 'ancillary' to the divorce, and fall into the category of 'other proceedings' outside the divorce suit as such (and for which public funding for representation may be provided if appropriate).

11.2.2 Other proceedings

Apart from ancillary relief, other proceedings not necessarily connected with the divorce, but in practice often arising at the same time, may be conducted under the new scheme of 'public funding', which replaces all the former varieties of legal aid and comprises a portfolio of finance called 'licensed work', all subject to the 'sufficient benefit' test. There is 'general family help' for preparing a case (with a spending limit of £1,500), 'legal representation' and 'support funding'. The most common proceedings thus covered are those for ancillary relief. There are, however, two other types of proceedings which may also qualify as 'licensed work': contested Children Act (CA) 1989 applications (see Chapters 24–26) and domestic violence injunctions (see Chapter 23). Both of these may be started and pursued without divorce proceedings necessarily being on foot, though in the latter case, if a divorce suit is already in process, the application should, for technical reasons, normally be made latched on to the divorce suit. It should be noted that this does not mean that the divorce suit itself suddenly becomes eligible for public funding. The suit itself will continue to be financed by whatever means was originally decided, unless there is a change of circumstances affecting that decision, while the ancillary relief, CA 1989 or domestic violence proceedings are separately paid for by the LSC.

However, there are also arrangements for the funding of *mediation*, for which qualification is much the same as for legal help, as an alternative to going to court to resolve any of these matters. This has a spend limit of £350. In April 1999, when s 29 of the Family Law Act (FLA) 1996 was brought into force, a pilot scheme was developed for mediation referrals and has now been implemented fully across England and Wales. The Legal Services Commission contracts to provide family mediation services in the same way as other types of public funding are provided for those who qualify for them. Those seeking public funding for family proceedings are required to attend a meeting with a mediator in order to assess the suitability of family mediation before public funding for representation is granted for proceedings. There are certain exceptions to this rule. Franchised solicitors can apply for a contract to allow them to provide this advice and assistance to those who are eligible during and after funded family mediation.

The reason for this formal introduction is set out in s 1 of the FLA 1996, which *inter alia* addresses the cost of proceedings and seeks to keep them proportionate to what is in dispute and as low as possible. This was taken forward by s 29 of the FLA 1996, which restricted the availability of civil legal aid certificates in family matters where mediation was suitable. These provisions remain in force, despite the withdrawal of the new divorce system contained in Pt II of the FLA 1996. The current rules relating to family mediation are found in the Funding Code, established under the Access to Justice Act 1999 which adopted the provisions of s 29 of the FLA 1996 and which is now the overall source of public funding rules and regulations.

Subject to important exceptions, public funding for family matters is therefore now to be refused unless an applicant has first attended a meeting with a mediator to assess whether mediation is suitable to the dispute, the parties and all the circumstances, and in particular whether mediation could take place without either party being influenced by fear of violence or other harm, a key principle which relates back to the philosophy behind parts of the Family Law Act 1996. Public funding may also be refused having regard to the reasonableness test, which considers the outcome of the meeting with the mediator and the assessment of suitability of mediation as an alternative to litigation in the particular case. The object is not to force applicants to go to mediation against their will – forced mediation being a contradiction in terms – but to see whether the much less costly alternative of mediation, duly supported by legal advice and assistance, could save the costs and other perils of litigation.

The family matters affected are defined in the Funding Code, and are matters governed by English law in relation to which any question has arisen or may arise under the provisions of the Matrimonial Causes Act (MCA) 1973, the Domestic Proceedings and Magistrates' Courts Act (DPMCA) 1978 (see Chapter 19), Pts I to V of the CA 1989, Pt IV of the FLA 1996, and under any other enactment prescribed, under any prescribed jurisdiction of a court or tribunal or under any prescribed rule of law. (Currently no jurisdictions or rules have been prescribed under the last two heads.) Subject to the exceptions, the Funding Code applies to all new applications for public funding in family matters as defined above, which are received after 26 April 1999.

The exceptions to the Funding Code procedure affecting classes of business to which it applies include cases where there is an urgent need for emergency representation, where there is no suitable mediator, where one party is unwilling or where there is a reasonable fear of domestic abuse.

Mediation assessment meetings may take place either individually or jointly with both partners.

The governing regulations are the Legal Aid (Mediation in Family Matters) Regulations 1997.

11.3 THE DRAWBACK OF PUBLIC FUNDING

The problem with using any form of public funding in matrimonial cases is that, although the grant of public funding results in the fund assuming responsibility for paying all the legal costs of the assisted person while the case is going on, there is a duty to seek reimbursement of the money laid out in financing the case. Moreover, where, as in most divorces, money or property is recovered or preserved in ancillary relief proceedings, the Legal Services Commission will have first call on both money and property to pay the cost, *not only* of the ancillary relief proceedings, but also of any *other* costs incurred, such as of CA 1989 proceedings or proceedings for domestic violence protection. 'Money' in this context does not include periodical payments, but it does include lump sums unless they represent capitalised maintenance. 'Property' includes the former matrimonial home or any share of it. Just as under the Legal Aid Act 1988 and previous Acts, s 10(7) of the Access to Justice Act (AJA) 1999 provides that people pay towards the cost of their cases as far as they are able; this is supposed to encourage them to act reasonably and to put those who are publicly funded in the same position as a privately paying client.

This means that as before public funding is certainly not a *gift* and is usually not even a very generous *loan*. This is because although there is power to postpone the payment of the bill where the property in question is to provide a home for the assisted person and dependants (by deferring it against the security of the statutory charge), there is *no* power to *forego* collection of the money owed save in relation to legal help or help at court (the equivalent of the old Green Form Scheme) in cases of grave hardship or distress, or where it would be unreasonably difficult to enforce the charge against the property because of its nature. There is a similar power to waive the charge in relation to 'representation' (ie, old legal aid) in test cases or where the Legal Services Commission considers it cost effective on grounds of public interest. In this latter case, which is a very limited exception, the Legal Services Commission can only waive the charge if the case started out on this very specialised basis. The result is that generally the 'statutory charge' – like a second mortgage – is placed on the assisted person's home where that has been 'recovered or preserved' in the course of proceedings financed by the Legal Services Commission.

This is the reason for harsh words sometimes said in reported cases by judges about the foolishness of parties 'litigating on legal aid' and 'running up a bill out of all proportion to the costs incurred', instead of settling in a sensible and cost effective manner before the costs run out of control.

11.3.1 The statutory charge under the Access to Justice Act 1999

The rules remain much the same as under the previous legislation in the LAA 1988. Pursuant to s 8 of the AJA 1999, there is now a Funding Code and a Legal Services Commission Manual, and new Community Legal Service (Financial) Regulations 2000 (the 2000 Regulations). Where it applies, apart from use of the exemptions under reg 44 (largely the same as those formerly in the Civil Legal Aid (General) Regulations 1989 (the 1989 Regulations)), there is still no way of escaping the application of the statutory charge – on which simple interest will have to be paid at the current rate of money in court – except possibly by advising the assisted person who has the credit status to do so to refinance the debt elsewhere at a better rate of interest than will be charged by the Legal Services Commission. When the mortgage rate is low, as at the time of writing, this may be a realistic option for some, though not for those who have a cash flow problem, since one of the few advantages of the statutory charge is that, once the charge takes effect, interest on the amount outstanding is not paid monthly, as a mortgage would be, but only in the future when the home is finally sold and the public funding bill defrayed.

As before, the solicitor acting under the public funding certificate that generated the bill for proceedings is under a duty to inform the regional manager of any property recovered or preserved in those proceedings, so there is no concealing it, and it has been repeatedly held that the court should not even tailor its order to evade the statutory charge artificially by, for example, making orders in favour of children who are not the 'assisted person' within the meaning of the regulations. This was unsuccessfully tried in *Drascovic v Drascovic* [1981] 11 Fam Law 87. In fact, following the changes made in the AJA 1999, this authority is no longer needed to prevent such abuse, since the wording of the new Act catches property recovered or preserved whether for the assisted person 'or any other person'.

It should, however, be noted that district judges in ancillary relief proceedings have often in the past indirectly taken the statutory charge into account, since they usually required an up to date statement of the costs position of each party before making orders. In such cases, they took them into account so as not to make a futile order from which the applicant would receive no real benefit. This process has been formalised under the new Ancillary Relief Scheme, now in force nationally since June 2000 (see Chapter 14).

Nevertheless, there remain the traditional steps which can be taken to mitigate the effect of the charge:

(1) Restricting the property which is technically 'recovered or preserved' in the action by ensuring that it is not 'in issue' in the proceedings (*Hanlon v The Law Society* [1981] AC 124).

(2) Using the available exemptions within the meaning of reg 44 of the 2000 Regulations, which are similar to reg 94 of the preceding 1989 Regulations, save for the following:

(a) interim payments are no longer exempt (though the regional office can allow a solicitor to pay the applicant such a sum, rather than require it to be paid to the regional office) if necessary to protect the applicant's interests or welfare;

(b) the exemption for personal possessions is wider, though it can be disapplied in appropriate circumstances, for example, if the possessions are exceptional in quantity or value (eg, works of art); and

(c) lump sums capitalising spousal maintenance pursuant to s 31(7A) or (7B) of the MCA 1973 are exempt.

The Legal Services Commission's charge consists of the amount the Commission has spent on funding services at all levels, less any costs recovered by the applicant in the proceedings, and less any payment made by the applicant by way of contribution. The charge includes interest (s 10(4)(b) and (7)(b)). Regulations 40(2) and (3) and 43(2) make detailed provision for the calculation of the charge. The cost of assessing the supplier's bill is not part of the charge, but the cost of drawing up the supplier's bill is (see the 2000 Regulations, reg 40(4)). There are new provisions for taking a charge over a property with low or negative equity, so that when the property recovers in value, the Commission will be able to recover the value of the charge (ie, to the value of the bill for the assisted person's costs) rather than the value of the property at any previous point in time. In these circumstances, the assisted person is charged interest on the full value of the charge but on 'such lower sum as the Commission considers equitable in the circumstances' (reg 53(3)(c)(ii)).

11.3.2 Property which is 'in issue'

It was held in *Hanlon* (see 11.3.1) that where there is a dispute over *title* to a property which is jointly owned beneficially but not legally, and neither side agrees that the other owns at least a half share, the value of the *entire* property is in 'issue'. This is so because the successful party who achieves a transfer of the property from the legal owner has:

(a) recovered that party's share; and

(b) preserved their own.

Thus, the *whole* value of the property is available to secure the debt of the successful party's costs in favour of the Commission (otherwise they might have suffered a deficit in the settlement of their total bill if only *half* the house value had been available for their legal charge to attach to).

Curling v The Law Society [1985] 1 All ER 705 confirmed that even if there is no dispute as to *title* to the property (in this case the parties agreed they owned the home half each), the property will *still* be 'in issue' if there is a dispute as to when one party may realise their half share (in this case the husband sought a property adjustment order as he wanted to remain in the house, but the wife wanted an order for sale, and the compromise that the husband would buy out her share without a sale on the open market was held to be a sufficient dispute to put the property 'in issue' for legal aid purposes). This principle has been further confirmed in *Parkes v Legal Aid Board* [1994] 2 FLR 850, where in a case of two unmarried parents compromising an action so that the woman and child of the relationship should remain in the house where the man sought a sale order, the right to remain in a house with exclusive possession over a long period of years was said to be a 'property right' within the meaning of s 16(6) of the LAA 1988 (the predecessor of the new regime under the AJA 1999).

Thus, whether a property has been 'in issue' must be determined from an examination of the pleadings, evidence and judgment (merely including a complete prayer for all forms of available ancillary relief in the petition is insufficient to bring all the parties' property into issue). Where there has been *any* argument over property, this usually means that the property has been in issue, and the only remaining point to settle will be whether the *whole* property has been in issue or only part (eg, if one party has at least agreed that as a minimum the other owns a half or other proportional share). By s 16(7) of the LAA 1988, property recovered or preserved as a result of a compromise was still subject to s 16(6) and the same applies under the new regime.

It should be noted that money or property may be recovered or preserved in proceedings other than ancillary relief after divorce (eg, those brought under s 17 of the Married Women's Property Act 1882, s 27 of the MCA 1973, ss 2 and 6 of the DPMCA 1978 (see Chapters 18–20), or the CA 1989 (see Chapters 21–22)). Thus, where a client is on public funding applying for financial or property orders, the same considerations apply to trying to get the order made in a form which will make best use of the exemptions regardless of which proceedings are being taken. Moreover, where there are different sets of proceedings, practitioners recognise that it is a good idea if at all possible to obtain separate public funding certificates for *each separate matter*, and then to get them discharged separately, since then costs from one action (which may or may not have been successful) will not impact on another where significant property may have been recovered or preserved, as the costs of one public funding certificate will not be carried over into a subsequent one (*Watkinson v Legal Aid Board* [1991] 2 All ER 953, CA).

Where the statutory charge does apply, it is still important (as under the previous legislation) to check, when the order of the court is drafted, that it contains the appropriate recital to ensure that postponement of the payment of the Legal Services Commission bill for costs is achieved. This is done by inserting a formal certificate on the face of the order, detailing that the money or property has been recovered or preserved for the purpose of providing the assisted person with a home in accordance with *Practice Direction* [1991] 2 FLR 384.

If the assisted person wants to move from the home which is the subject of the statutory charge without repaying the LSC, this can be achieved by transfer of the charge to the new property to be acquired, providing there is sufficient equity in that new home.

11.4 THE DIVORCE PROCESS

It is highly desirable for academic as well as vocational students to acquire a sound grasp of the divorce process, without which they will never fully understand the working of ss 1 and 2 of the MCA 1973, and in particular the contemporary trend not to defend petitions as well as the reasoning behind the minor role now played in the divorce suit by post-divorce arrangements for children of the family (for which see 11.7, below).

A suit for divorce is commenced by issue of a petition. This may either be done through a solicitor, if the petitioner pays privately for this work, or (given the lack of public funding for the average divorce) by the petitioner personally. If a solicitor is used, the Solicitors Family Law Association (SFLA) Code of Practice recommends writing to the other spouse before issuing any proceedings, and if the solicitor belongs to the SFLA or observes the Code without actually being a member, this will be explained to the client. At the same time there is likely to be some discussion of the most convenient Fact on which to rely, bearing in mind the considerations discussed in Chapter 10. If a solicitor is consulted, it is explicit in the Law Society's Code of Conduct that both the ultimate cost and structure of the solicitor's fees must be explained to the petitioner at the same time, as well as the impact of the statutory charge should public funding be required to meet the cost of ancillary relief. Solicitors are also expected by their professional conduct code:

- to explain to the petitioner at this stage the impact of the change of status effected by a divorce decree (eg, in relation to entitlement under a spouse's pension); and

- to draw the petitioner's attention to consequential matters such as the laws of intestacy and inheritance as they affect divorced people; and

- to draw attention to the protection which is provided for spouses who do not own the matrimonial home (see Chapter 20).

The reason for this is that if, for example, there is any problem in realising a fair share of a pension, for which the continued status of marriage may be vital, it may not be appropriate for a divorce to be sought at all, but rather a judicial separation, or even a separation by agreement. Some potential petitioners do not even eventually issue proceedings at all, but decide on an attempted reconciliation and to go for marriage counselling, a situation which both the MCA 1973 and the FLA 1996, and the underlying research of both, have always contemplated.

11.4.1 Preparing the petition

If a petition is to be issued, this may be drafted either by the solicitor or, if there is no funding available (either public or private), by the petitioner. If there is a solicitor involved, the profession considers that, particularly where the petition is based on behaviour, it is good practice to let the other spouse know that a petition is to be presented and to supply a copy of the draft to them personally or to his or her solicitors where they have been instructed. The SFLA Code in any event recommends telling the other spouse before proceedings are commenced. Where the petitioner is acting personally, this is unlikely to happen but may still be good practice if there is to be no misunderstanding about the essentially co-operative nature of modern divorce (as set out in Chapters 7–10). There is no set format for a petition, although the Family Proceedings Rules (FPR) 1991 set out what must be included. These details comprise:

- the names of the parties;
- the date and place of the marriage;

- the full names (including surnames) and dates of birth of any children;
- details of any previous proceedings and assessments by the Child Support Agency;
- a statement that the marriage has irretrievably broken down;
- the Fact relied upon for the decree;
- particulars (but not evidence) of the matters relied upon to prove that Fact,

plus the prayer to the court, including:

- that the marriage be dissolved;
- any costs order sought; and
- the financial relief required for the petitioner and/or the children.

Since 'Brussels II', the precise basis of the court's jurisdiction must also be stated (see Chapter 7).

11.4.2 Supporting documents

Apart from the petition itself, either three or four documents, as appropriate, will also be required:

- the marriage certificate;
- the Statement of Arrangements for the children;
- the reconciliation certificate, if appropriate;
- the court fee, or a certificate of exemption.

Some points must be made about each of these, as the documentary approach occasioned by contemporary divorce procedure means that there will be no oral hearing. Everything needed by the court to decide if a decree should be granted must therefore appear on the face of the documents.

11.4.2.1 The marriage certificate

This means the original marriage certificate or a certified copy (FPR 1991, r 2.6(2)). Only one copy is required, since the certificate forms part of the court file and is not served with the other papers on either the respondent or any co-respondent. For a foreign marriage, the original or a certified copy will be required as usual plus a translation if the language in which it is recorded is not English, together with an affidavit from the translator verifying the translation. These documents usually cause no problems.

11.4.2.2 The Statement of Arrangements for the children

This form is required to enable the court to discharge its duty under s 41 of the MCA 1973, which requires a certificate that post-divorce arrangements for the children are satisfactory. It is submitted in Form M4 (FPR 1991, r 2.2), which provides that 'if practicable' the form should be agreed and both parents should sign it to indicate agreement to the arrangements detailed, and most parents do both sign, but if the respondent refuses to do so, the form may still be filed signed by the petitioner alone, with a covering letter explaining the circumstances.

Form M4 must be signed personally by the petitioner and the respondent. A solicitor, even if conducting the divorce, cannot sign for either of them. It is the petitioner who has the duty of filing the form, but where the children are *not* living with the petitioner it may not be possible for all the information required to be supplied on the form unless the respondent co-operates.

Where a Form M4 appears to be deficient in such information it is considered good practice for the respondent to file a separate Form M4 when returning the Acknowledgment of Service (see below). If this is not done, the court may ask the respondent to supply any further information in the form of a letter (FPR 1991, r 2.38).

However, it appears that the rules are deficient because it is not possible to require the respondent to do this if it is not done voluntarily. Nevertheless, the court is by no means left powerless in this situation since the ultimate solution is to direct that the court welfare office should prepare a welfare report giving details of the respondent's arrangements for the children, in the same way as might be done where the court is dissatisfied with the arrangements disclosed in a fully completed Form M4 and therefore unwilling to issue a s 41 certificate in a doubtful case (see below).

The form covers the following:

- accommodation;
- education;
- child care arrangements (particularly where the parent with whom the children reside is employed);
- financial matters, including maintenance orders and the Child Support Agency assessments;
- contact for the non-residential parent; and
- health (where a doctor's letter or a full medical report will be necessary if there is anything unusual to include, unless the health problem has been present from birth and there is nothing new to add).

Only one form is required regardless of the number of children in the family.

The form, which is daunting to laypeople, despite having been redesigned in recent years with heavy use of the 'multiple choice' style requiring the answers 'yes', 'no' or a tick in a box, is relatively straightforward for a solicitor unless there is a serious problem with the family which needs careful presentation. Where this is the case, as much useful information as possible should be included since, unless the district judge finds the form provides a wholly inadequate account of essential matters and asks for further information – which will in any case delay the s 41 certificate (see below) – this is the court's *only* means of acquiring a picture of the post-divorce lifestyle of the children. However, practitioners tend to consider that care should be taken not to cram the form full of *more* information than is actually necessary. A fairly laconic style is generally favoured, except where there is unusual information to be imparted in answer to any questions, such as in relation to the children's health. Failure to file a medical report in a case which obviously needs one is a common reason for the court asking for further information before issuing the s 41 certificate. A similar situation might arise where there have been proceedings in relation to one or more of the children and the copy order is not filed with the Form M4. If the court does take exception to any such omission, they will say precisely why and what is missing and at the same time ask the petitioner to renew the request for directions for trial (see below).

If there is to be an application for a formal order under s 8 of the CA 1989 for residence or contact, this should be stated on the form. The court will then not consider the children's arrangements at this stage.

11.4.2.3 Reconciliation certificate: Form M3 (FPR 1991, r 2.6(3))

This only applies where the solicitor is acting (ie, for a private client), and only requires the solicitor to indicate whether reconciliation has been discussed with the client and not whether it has been attempted or how or what the result was. (The solicitor is not 'acting' where the petitioner is being advised under the new legal help regime (the Legal Services Commission's replacement for the old Green Form Scheme), because such a person has the status of a litigant in person.) It is generally thought that the reconciliation certificate provision was intended in the early stages of the 1970s divorce reform to be developed so as to be an effective encouragement to reconciliation, but somehow it fell by the wayside and now exists only in the curious formality of the solicitor's obligation to file the form when technically acting for a client in the divorce proceedings.

11.4.2.4 Certificate of exemption

If applicable, a certificate of exemption from paying the filing fee will be required (alternatively a fee of £150). A petitioner receiving legal help through being on income support can claim such a certificate.

11.4.3 Filing

Filing is achieved by taking or sending all the above and the petition, with copies of the petition and Statement of Arrangements for service on the respondent, plus a further copy of the petition for service on any co-respondent, to the chosen court. This may be done at any 'divorce county court' which means any county court designated for the conduct of divorces. However, if there are children in the case it is advisable to file the petition at a divorce county court which is also a designated care centre, as any proceedings under the CA 1989 (eg, in relation to where the children should live, or their education or religion) would otherwise have to be transferred to such a court (because although in practice CA proceedings probably arise out of the divorce, they are technically considered separate (see 11.2, above)).

The court will then enter the case in the court books and assign it a number (which is its identity tag for the remainder of the suit and must be quoted on all contact with the court) and the petitioner, or the petitioner's solicitor where appropriate, is notified. At this stage, in the unattractive language of the press, the petitioner 'has filed for divorce' but the proceedings are not yet properly on foot before service is achieved.

11.4.4 Service (FPR 1991, rr 2.9(1) and 2.24)

The documents to be served are:

- the petition;
- Form M4 (plus a copy of any medical report);
- the notice of proceedings (Form M5, ie, notice to the respondent); and
- the Acknowledgment of Service (Form M6).

Service is normally effected by the court, generally by second class post, but since this obviously displays a touching faith in both the reliability of the postal system and the rectitude of the respondent (who could quite well put the papers in the dustbin and pretend they had never arrived), there are preferable methods:

- bailiff service (also called 'personal service by the bailiff');
- personal service (ie, other than by the bailiff); or
- substituted service.

Alternatively service may be *deemed* or *dispensed with* (FPR 1991, r 2.9(11)).

Both substituted service and dispensing with service are for exceptional circumstances only (ie, where some method is required for putting the proceedings into active mode regardless of the respondent's non co-operation). However, as either of these may have to be used if the Acknowledgment of Service does not come back duly completed, either by the respondent or a solicitor acting for the respondent, one of the first two methods might better be selected from the start: without some method of surmounting the service hurdle, the petition cannot be taken to be duly served pursuant to r 2.9(5) of the FPR 1991 and the suit cannot proceed. It will be convenient to look at the various methods in turn.

11.4.4.1 Bailiff service

This is also called 'personal service through the bailiff' to distinguish it from 'personal service through, but not by, the petitioner', for which see below.

The court will direct bailiff service if the petitioner applies on the appropriate form. Bailiff service is suitable where the petitioner can supply an address where the bailiff may find the respondent and a photograph for identification. There is a fee unless the petitioner has already filed a certificate of exemption from fees, and this is the cheapest way of effective service and therefore suitable for clients receiving any form of public funded legal help. The bailiff attempts to obtain a signature from the respondent, files a certificate stating how the respondent was identified, and if the respondent then does not return the Acknowledgment of Service, due service can be proved by the petitioner identifying either the respondent's signature or the photograph used by the bailiff to identify the respondent on whom the papers were served. The petitioner may do this in the affidavit in support of the petition.

This method can be used by private clients as well as public funded clients, but in that case the requirements of *Practice Direction (7 March 1977)* [1977] 1 All ER 845 will have to be complied with to show why bailiff service is chosen instead of the more usual (more expensive) alternative for private clients of personal service.

11.4.4.2 Personal service

The rules allow the petitioner to request personal service through, but never by, the petitioner (FPR 1991, r 2.9(2)(b)). This is suitable where postal service might not be satisfactory for the reasons explained at 11.4.4, above, and bailiff service is inappropriate because the petitioner cannot say where the respondent might be found – the bailiff cannot go searching for a respondent in a variety of places. While the *petitioner* cannot ever serve the documents personally (FPR 1991, r 2.9(3)), the petitioner's *solicitor* can do so, or alternatively an inquiry agent or professional process server can perform the task. This method can be used by persons in receipt of legal help where bailiff service is unsuitable because of the respondent's elusiveness.

Again the person serving the papers will attempt to obtain a signature, and if no Acknowledgment of Service is returned, due service can still be proved by the petitioner's identifying either a signature or a photograph of the respondent as in the case of bailiff service. However, the server does not file a certificate like the bailiff, but must swear and file an affidavit stating how the respondent was identified (FPR 1991, r 2.9(7)).

Personal service by an inquiry agent may have to be used because the inquiry agent must first actually locate the respondent. If this is necessary (eg, as a prelude to asking the court for substituted service or to dispense with service altogether), *Practice Direction (13 February 1989)* [1989] 1 All ER 765 should be followed. Basically, where the petition includes a claim for maintenance or there is an existing maintenance order, this enables the court to request a search of the Benefits Agency and Passport Office records, or where the respondent is in the Armed Forces the petitioner's solicitor may request an address from their records.

Obviously, any solicitor instructed by the petitioner would pursue all possible leads (eg, employers, clubs, trade union, friends, relatives, etc) before resorting to these more formal methods. If the petitioner had indicated at the first interview that there might be a problem with locating the respondent, the solicitor would usually arrange tracing before filing the petition and also think of how best to effect service before ordinary postal service had proved ineffective.

11.4.4.3 Substituted service

Where all efforts to trace the respondent's actual address fail, an order may be sought from the court for substituted service. There are various ways in which this might be effected, which basically fall into two categories:

(a) where the respondent is known to be around somewhere but always manages to elude personal service, even at an address or addresses which are not the respondent's own but which the respondent is known to visit; or

(b) where the respondent has effectively disappeared but has been seen in a certain area and is thought still to be there.

In the first case, instead of persisting in personal visits at great expense, the papers might be posted by way of substituted service authorised by the court to one of the addresses which the respondent is known to visit. In the second, service by advertisement might be authorised.

It is essential in both cases that the court is convinced that the petitioner has made all reasonable efforts to effect service. If there is to be an advertisement, the court will need to be convinced that the advertisement has a reasonable chance of coming to the respondent's notice and the court will settle the advertisement and decide where it shall be placed (FPR 1991, r 2.9(9)). Application is made *ex parte* on affidavit. Exceptionally, the court might authorise an advertisement to be placed other than by itself, in which case the publications concerned containing the advertisement must be filed at court (FPR 1991, r 10.5(3)). This might be done in the case of advertisement in a foreign newspaper (eg, where the respondent was last seen in Brazil and is thought to still be there, but despite his sometimes being briefly seen in public places no one has any idea where he lives between the sightings).

11.4.4.4 Deemed service

Deemed service is for the type of respondent who puts the papers in the dustbin. If the petitioner knows and can show that the petition and supporting documents have come to the attention of the respondent, even if they cannot be shown actually to have been destroyed or discarded, deemed service should be available. By r 2.9(6) of the FPR 1991, the court must be *satisfied* that the papers have come to the respondent's notice, and this may be proved in any way in which that can be shown, but the court no longer usually grants deemed service on the unsupported evidence (even sworn on affidavit) of the petitioner alone. They have had too many irate respondents appear out of the woodwork asking for the deemed service to be set aside on the basis that the petitioner knew perfectly well where the respondent was and merely pretended not to do so. Accordingly, an affidavit from another relative or friend will be required, for example, to the effect that the respondent was seen with the papers whether or not they were then thrown away in that person's presence. Alternatively, such an affidavit could be based on the respondent's statement to the person making the affidavit that the papers had been received but that nothing was going to make the respondent co-operate.

11.4.4.5 Dispensing with service

This is governed by r 2.9(11) of the FPR 1991 and requires the district judge to make an order dispensing with service in cases where, in his or her opinion, service is for some reason impracticable, or that it is necessary or expedient for other reasons to dispense with service. Application is again *ex parte* (ie, without notice to the other side) on affidavit and the affidavit should set out in full all the attempts to serve the petition. Obviously, the quality of the affidavit will be vital here since if the order is granted the respondent may be divorced without knowing anything about it. Thus, the petitioner will need to satisfy the district judge that even substituted service is not appropriate. Nevertheless, where the respondent has gone off and the petitioner cannot find him despite exhaustive efforts, the order may well be made.

11.4.5 Amendments

Once any service problems are dealt with, the next stage will normally be to request 'directions for trial', although in fact there will be no trial as such because the case will be dealt with under the 'Special Procedure' (now a misnomer, since although it was a special fast track paper-based route in the late 1970s (previously all cases had a hearing however short), since 1976 the 'special' procedure has been the normal (entirely paper-based) procedure). Before proceeding further along this route, it may be advisable for the petitioner to consider whether any amendments are required to the petition, and if so how to effect them.

Amendments to petitions often appear to the inexperienced to be difficult, but in practice they are not. There are various sorts:

(1) Simple amendments (basically, red ink on the existing text as in civil litigation generally), for example, deleting allegations or adding a new s 1(2) (of the MCA 1973) Fact arising before the date of the petition which you wish to amend.

(2) Supplemental petitions (a new document, read into the existing petition, rather like the looseleaf supplements supplied to practitioners' textbooks), for example, adding further allegations to particulars of a Fact already pleaded which have arisen *after* the date of the petition you wish to amend.

(3) Fresh petitions (in effect these start again, usually following *discontinuance or dismissal* of the existing petition, usually because the petitioner wants to change Facts and rely on a new one not included in the original petition).

By r 2.8 of the FPR 1991, there is no need for leave to file another petition if the first is already dismissed or discontinued. By r 2.6(4), leave *is* needed if the existing petition is still in existence through not having been finally disposed of in one way or another. There are sometimes technical reasons for keeping the existing petition alive until the new one is on foot.

The *date* of the existing petition will therefore be important if an amendment needs to be made: the *nature of the amendment* to be made will also have some relevance to the decision as to how to effect this. It is a question of what is already in existence in relation to the date of the petition to be amended. Clearly it is impossible logically to allege at the later stage of amendment a basis of divorce which must be inserted into a document with an earlier date! (Although the court can be brought up to date with current detailed developments.)

If it is desired to allege a *completely new Fact*, and if it arose *before* the date of the petition, this can be done by simple amendment (ie, on the text of the petition, in red ink). If it arose *after* the date of the petition, then a *fresh petition* will be required, as it will not be possible to amend the existing one in any way, not even by supplemental petition, to allege a Fact which did not exist at the date of the existing petition. For example, if the petitioner wants to allege a separation Fact where the relevant period had not been completed at the date of the earlier petition, a *fresh petition* will be required. If, however, all that is wanted is to add *fresh allegations* to the *particulars* of the existing petition, that can be done by building on to that existing petition either with a *simple amendment* (if the new information dates from *prior* to the petition) or with a *supplemental petition*, which is technically part of the existing petition although it is contained in a separate document (if the new information arose *after* the date of the petition). Here what the petitioner is doing is to add on further up to date particulars of a Fact which has already been alleged, and is not asking the court to indulge in time travel.

The standard red ink procedure is set out in r 2.11 of the FPR 1991. No leave is needed until the suit has reached the stage at which an answer is filed, and since few answers are filed, this occasion of leave is rare (r 2.11(1)(b)). However, leave will always be required once directions have been given (see below), so amendments at a later stage will always require leave (r 2.14). In theory, amendments may be made up to decree absolute but are unusual after decree *nisi*. Application is made for leave *ex parte* if the respondent consents in writing to the amendment, otherwise an application will need to be made on notice. For *very minor amendments* at the directions stage (see below), this can be done (eg, to correct a child's birth date, or add a missing middle name, correct a spelling, etc) in the petitioner's affidavit in support of the petition.

The amended petition is filed at court and re-served in the normal way.

11.5 THE 'DIRECTIONS' STAGE AND THE ROLE OF THE ACKNOWLEDGMENT OF SERVICE

'Directions' may be requested as soon as due service can be proved. This is normally achieved by proof of service in one of the ways mentioned at 11.4.4, above, or by return by the docile respondent of the completed Acknowledgment of Service (Form M6) sent out with the petition and accompanying documents. If none of these apply, an interlocutory application will have to be made for substituted or deemed service, or for service to be dispensed with before the suit can proceed further. In the vast majority of cases the Acknowledgment of Service is returned and it is this standard procedure with which the academic student will need to be primarily familiar.

The ordinary co-operative respondent should have no difficulty with return of the Acknowledgment of Service, which should be received back by the court within eight days of the receipt of the petition and accompanying documents by the respondent (r 10.8(2)(a)). Like the other standard forms designed for 'mail order' divorce, it is in question and answer format, and it is fully explained in the accompanying Notice of Proceedings (Form M5) which always goes out with it (see 11.4.4, above). While sometimes respondents do not get it back on time, in which case the court will usually send a reminder – and another copy of Form M6 in case the original is now at the bottom of the respondent's 'letters to answer' pile – late return is more likely to be due to forgetfulness or disorganisation rather than difficulty in answering the questions.

There are three points of particular importance to note about this form:

(1) The respondent's solicitor, if any, can sign the form for the respondent unless the divorce is on the basis of either Fact A or Fact D and the respondent is either admitting Fact A adultery or giving Fact D consent (r 2.10(1)).

(2) Although the form asks if the divorce will be defended, the respondent is not actually bound by the answer given in reply and can ultimately not defend after all if wiser counsel subsequently prevails. The result of stating that the divorce *will* be defended is merely that the proceedings will be held up after receipt by the court of the Acknowledgment of Service. This is to allow time for an answer to be filed, but it in no way forces the respondent to file an answer, so that if no answer is filed within the time allowed the divorce will eventually proceed as undefended (see below).

(3) Similarly, there is no obligation to follow through any other intention expressed on the form, such as in relation to the children, so that expressing no intention of asking

for an order in respect of the children does not mean that a CA 1989 order cannot afterwards be applied for after all.

When the court receives Form M6 it sends a photocopy to the respondent or the respondent's solicitor if appropriate (r 2.9(8)). If the form has indicated an intention to defend, the court will wait at least 28 days before the case will proceed further, so as to give an adequate opportunity for an answer to be filed (r 2.12(1)). If no answer is filed, the case proceeds as if undefended all along, unless of course a respondent subsequently obtains leave to file an answer out of time, which is not unheard of (see, eg, 11.6.1, below). However, in the vast majority of cases the suit is clearly undefended from the start and receipt of the Form M6 means that the case can proceed immediately to directions.

It is only in the minority of cases that no Form M6 is received and steps will then have to be taken to deal with this in accordance with the resolution of service problems (see 11.4.4, above).

11.5.1 Directions

The directions stage does not start automatically, as 'directions' must be requested. Moreover, 'giving directions' in the routine divorce amounts to no more than a junior judge of the court (called 'the district judge') acting on the petitioner's written request for directions, entering the case in the 'Special Procedure list' and ultimately considering the papers in an administrative manner, not in open court but in private, and without any hearing or participation by either party. Thereafter it is one of the district judges of the court who will handle the file, still in private and without a hearing, until it reaches the stage of pronouncement of decree *nisi:* this final stage must be done in open court, but this too may be undertaken by a district judge rather than a judge from the circuit bench by which the county courts are staffed at open court level.

The directions stage may be entered by requesting directions once due service can be proved (r 2.24(1)(a)) and it is certain that the case is undefended (ie, the Form M6 says so or if notice to defend has been given and the time for filing an answer has expired (rr 2.12(1) and 2.24(1))). There is a standard form on which directions are applied for by the petitioner's solicitor, or by the petitioner personally where a litigant in person, whether entirely unrepresented or merely on legal help (r 2.24(1)). It will be necessary for the district judge to be satisfied that all time limits have been complied with, so the first possible time for requesting directions will be eight days after service.

Although seeking directions might seem a simple and routine matter, if the divorce is to proceed smoothly, the directions stage is the next most vital stage after the skillful drafting of the petition. A crucial document if well drafted will ensure success. In this case the crucial document is the affidavit in support of the petition which must accompany the request for directions. In the absence of an oral hearing, the affidavit is the only evidence on which the court can base a decree, although there may sometimes be exhibits to that affidavit by way of corroboration (eg, medical reports in a violent behaviour case or witness statements in an adultery case). It follows that if the affidavit is not done well, problems may arise. It will therefore be convenient to examine the contents and purpose of the affidavit in detail.

11.5.1.1 The petitioner's affidavit

A pre-printed form is normally used, although this is not obligatory. If the affidavit is drafted from scratch it should follow the layout of the printed form so that matters are dealt with in the same order and providing the same information (r 2.24(3)). A practitioner might avoid the printed form and draft from scratch if the case is exceptional (eg, if the petitioner is alleging Facts in the alternative, ie, a fault based Fact plus Fact D). A petitioner acting in person will usually use the printed form and follow the notes which usually come with commercially produced high street packs for the public to handle their own divorces. The pre-printed forms are Forms M7(a)–(e), each respectively tailored to Facts A–E.

Besides comprising the evidence of the Fact relied on, the affidavit also serves the purpose of providing formal confirmation of various matters:

(1) Since the petitioner is required to swear that everything in the petition is true, the affidavit conveniently provides an opportunity to correct minor errors not worth the more formal amendment described at 11.4 (eg, correction of birth dates or names) without requiring the petition to be reserved, since the district judge will usually treat it as standing subject to the corrections.

(2) Since the respondent's signature will have to be identified on the Acknowledgment of Service for that document to be acceptable as evidence that the petition and accompanying documents were duly served, and of any Fact where the respondent's signature is necessary (ie, Fact A, admission of adultery, and Fact D, consent to the decree), the affidavit provides an opportunity for the petitioner to identify the respondent's signature.

(3) Since the Statement of Arrangements is vital to the Special Procedure, the affidavit provides an opportunity to confirm the accuracy of the Statement of Arrangements and to correct any inaccuracies or add any further information, and also for the petitioner to identify the respondent's signature on that document.

(4) Since a claim for costs may have been made in the petition by the petitioner (and resisted by the respondent, sometimes giving reasons, in the Acknowledgment of Service), the affidavit provides an opportunity for the petitioner to state whether it is really intended to pursue this claim.

However, the most important function of the affidavit is to persuade the district judge that it is just to grant the decree sought, and in this respect the solicitor's skill in drafting the relevant sections of the affidavit will be paramount. (Note though that with the aid of the commercially produced products mentioned above, members of the public are becoming ever more adept at this without the intervention of solicitors.) There are two distinct points here:

- how best to present the petitioner's evidence, given that there is no hearing;
- is any corroboration required?

11.5.1.2 The petitioner's evidence

It is essential that the solicitor (or other person) drafting the petitioner's answers to the relevant questions in the affidavit for each Fact should bear in mind the substantive law in each case (ie, the requirements of the MCA 1973, ss 1(2)(a)–(e)), and in particular the case law so that the petitioner's case is shown to fall squarely within what is established as sufficient for each Fact (see Chapters 8–10 above).

A particular danger area will be where the Fact relied on requires the parties to have been living apart, or where periods living together might amount to cohabitation exceeding that permitted by the MCA 1973. In such cases, great care should be taken to show that the parties were living apart in the *same home*, but not the same household, if circumstances required them to live under the same roof. This is particularly so where the parties are still living under the same roof when the affidavit is filed.

The aim should be to show unequivocally that the parties have used separate rooms (if possible not simply separate bedrooms) or have used the same rooms at separate times, that meals have not (or have rarely) been shared, and that no household services were performed by one for the other. A practitioner will look carefully at the evidence in comparison with the case law on this subject when dealing with this part of the petitioner's evidence, and will in particular consider *Mouncer v Mouncer* and *Bartram v Bartram* (see 9.2.1, above) which point to the distinction between one and two households, showing what may be done where the petitioner is obliged unwillingly to live in the same household as the respondent. If there has been apparent cohabitation because the parties have had to remain under one roof, it will usually be possible to deal with this satisfactorily in the affidavit by showing that there have been two separate households.

11.5.1.3 Where corroboration might be required

The district judge needs to apply a two part test before granting a certificate of entitlement to a decree *nisi* pursuant to r 2.36(1)(a):

(1) Would the particulars in the petition, if true, entitle the petitioner to a decree? This is a matter of law and if decided in the affirmative will entitle the petition to be in the Special Procedure list, on which point the district judge's decision is final (*R v Nottingham County Court ex p Byers* [1985] 1 All ER 735).

(2) Are the details in the petition in fact true? This is a matter of fact and evidence, which is where corroboration may be helpful.

Normally in an undefended divorce the petitioner's statements will be sufficient. After all, the affidavit is on oath. There are three danger areas where corroboration would obviously be helpful:

(a) adultery cases where the respondent admits the adultery but the co-respondent does not (rare now, since co-respondents are seldom used now they no longer need to be named and joined as parties in the suit);

(b) behaviour cases where the allegations are weak and insubstantial; and

(c) separation cases where the parties have remained under one roof and are alleging two households.

It should be noted that standards and practices are different from county court to county court, and some district judges are notoriously strict while others are not unduly demanding about corroboration. Practitioners therefore tend to follow the local practice as a yardstick of what is likely to be required. Students should therefore bear this in mind as another example of practice impacting on the substantive law.

Provided a suitable affidavit is supplied with the request for directions, the Special Procedure should follow automatically without hitches. It follows that great care needs to be taken in preparation of the affidavit as an ounce of prevention here may be worth a ton of cure once the district judge is alerted to any query over whether the divorce ought be granted at all. This is realistically the only part of the divorce process which is difficult for the layperson if legal help is not available, unless the living arrangements have been very straightforward, but the withdrawal of public funding is probably justified in that if a petitioner in person has a real problem, there are law centres and Citizens Advice Bureaux, and also various *pro bono* schemes which may be able to help.

11.6 THE SPECIAL PROCEDURE

As most divorces are now obtained via the Special Procedure, the only sworn evidence given by the petitioner will not be in the witness box but in the affidavit described above. Once all the papers are in the possession of the court, the next step is for the district judge to consider the file, on a private administrative rather than *ex parte* basis, usually taking a number of files to deal with each morning before beginning the day's list. Unless the papers suggest some problem when first perused (which will result in the case being withdrawn from the Special Procedure), the district judge's consideration of the petition and the supporting documentary evidence now comprise the petitioner's entire case and it will be obvious from the preceding sections that the petition and the affidavit in support must now always be prepared bearing this in mind – because the papers will be all the court (ie, the district judge alone in his private room) will have to go on in deciding whether the petitioner is entitled to a decree. It is therefore essential that each of these documents deals properly with the petitioner's case.

11.6.1 Consideration by the district judge of the evidence (FPR 1991, r 2.36)

If the district judge is satisfied with the evidence, a certificate will be completed to that effect, a day will be fixed for pronouncement of the decree in open court and a copy of the certificate will be sent to each party to notify them, although neither need attend and normally they will not do so.

It should be noted that although decree *nisi*, the first decree on the route to ending the marriage, is the effective moment at which the marriage is conditionally dissolved *unless cause to the contrary is later shown*, the district judge's certificate is virtually as important. Indeed, it has been described as tantamount to the decree *nisi* itself, lacking only the public element of pronouncement in open court, which is undertaken either by the judge or by the district judge (possibly the same district judge as issued the certificate, though not necessarily so, depending on how the work is allocated at the particular court).

In theory, decree *nisi* can be stopped before it is pronounced (eg, because the respondent wishes after all to defend), but it will first be necessary for the district judge's certificate to be set aside and this is no easy matter. This is demonstrated in *Day v Day* [1979] 2 All ER 187, where the husband kept changing his mind over whether or not to defend, and finally turned up on the day designated for pronouncement of the decree *nisi* to ask to file an answer out of time. The judge acceded to his request, at the same time removing the case from the Special Procedure list. On appeal this was held to be wrong, since once the wife had proved her case, the court was bound to pronounce the decree unless the respondent could show that there were substantial grounds to indicate that the decree had been granted contrary to the justice of the case. In the particular instance this did not apply since the husband had had ample time to defend if he had seriously wanted to and there was no injustice.

The decree *nisi* is thus virtually a certainty at this stage, *before* the district judge has even looked at the Statement of Arrangements. Hence the impact on the suit of the children in any case is now limited, if relevant at all, to delaying the decree absolute and not in any way to obtaining the decree *nisi* (see below).

Before dealing at all with the children, however, the district judge must decide any question arising in connection with the costs. The respondent and co-respondent are entitled to make representations about costs which are governed by r 2.37.

Normally costs will only be asked for in fault based cases, and sometimes not even then unless the suit becomes defended. If costs are asked for, the district judge will consider the claim and include an order for costs in the certificate: a legal help petitioner can obtain costs even if a litigant in person, though obviously only those small costs appropriate to such a case (Litigants in Person (Costs and Expenses) Act 1975).

If the petitioner has asked for costs, it is essential that the respondent contests them on the Acknowledgment of Service form, giving good reasons, or the district judge will usually grant the petitioner's claim. If the respondent's reasons are insufficiently full for the district judge to decide on the claim for costs, a further written statement can be required setting out more fully the reasons for the respondent's objections to paying the costs (r 2.37(1)), and the petitioner will receive a copy of this.

The petitioner can withdraw the claim for costs at any time, and may well do so between the petition and the directions stage, because, for example, the parties have reached an agreement that the respondent will consent to a Fact D decree if costs are not claimed, and in this case it would be in time for the petitioner to indicate change of mind in the affidavit in support of the petition. If this opportunity is missed, a letter can be sent to the district judge withdrawing the claim for costs at a later stage. If this is not done, and the district judge cannot decide the question of costs on the spot at the same time as considering the case for decree, costs will be referred to the judge and dealt with at the time that decree *nisi* is pronounced. This means that on *that* occasion when decree *nisi* is pronounced it *will* be necessary for one of the parties at least to turn up, namely the respondent to argue the question of costs. The petitioner may also wish to do so to defend the decision to claim costs, but need not. This is because if the respondent does not attend, the question of costs will at that stage be decided in favour of the petitioner.

It is also possible that the district judge will incorporate a financial agreement into a court order at this stage if the parties have reached agreement on financial matters, either permanently or temporarily.

If it is desired to do this (perhaps because the parties want an interim order anyway pending resolution of all outstanding matters at the usual ancillary relief stage), application should be made before the district judge gives directions. This procedure is governed by r 2.61 and, like other ancillary relief orders, the order will technically be made only after pronouncement of the decree *nisi* and will become effective (unless superseded) upon decree absolute (see Chapters 12–14 for the ancillary relief stage).

Finally, pursuant to r 2.39, the district judge considers the Statement of Arrangements for the children, and if *satisfied* will issue a certificate to that effect, but if *not satisfied* can do no more at this stage to protect the children than to hold up decree absolute where the cumulative test in s 41 of the MCA 1973 is applicable (see 11.7.1, below, for how this works). Normally, an agreed approach by the parents and a properly completed Statement of Arrangements signed by both will automatically produce a satisfied certificate. Where an application is already on foot for an order under the CA 1989, the district judge is excused from considering the Statement of Arrangements at all, since the children's future will be considered by another court (see 11.7.1, below, and Chapters 24 and 25).

The above is the normal procedure for undefended divorce decrees and applies in the vast majority of cases. However, some do not go smoothly.

If the district judge is *not satisfied,* the petitioner can be asked to file further evidence or alternatively (and if the further evidence is not filed or is still insubstantial) the district judge can remove the case from the Special Procedure list and list it for hearing before a judge in open court. The district judge has, however, no power to *dismiss* the petition – only the judge can do that if ultimately it becomes necessary. If the case is listed for hearing in open court, legal aid will be available.

11.6.2 Decree *nisi*

When decree *nisi* is pronounced in open court by the judge or district judge on the day appointed, a copy will be sent, by post by the court, to both parties. This does not finally dissolve the marriage, which is still a marriage until decree absolute.

11.6.3 Decree absolute

This is the final decree which permits the parties to remarry. By s 1(5) of the MCA 1973, this may not usually be granted until six weeks after decree *nisi*, although there is a rarely used power to expedite decree absolute in urgent cases (eg, terminal illness) so that one of the parties can remarry quickly. Such urgent applications are the subject of *Practice Direction* [1977] 2 All ER 714.

However, expediting decree absolute is not regarded as good practice, since six weeks is short enough in most cases, and is intended for the purpose of establishing that everything is in order to terminate the status of marriage – a step which may have far reaching consequences. Thus the better practice is for the solicitor to expedite the decree *nisi* by proceeding expeditiously at that stage instead and, having expedited the preparation of the petition and accompanying documents, writing to the court to press the urgency of the case, which will usually enable the court to save most or all of the six weeks between the two decrees at this earlier stage by expediting both the giving of directions and the pronouncement of the decree *nisi*.

Otherwise, in the ordinary course of events, the *petitioner* may apply for decree absolute six weeks after the grant of decree *nisi*, whereas pursuant to s 9(2) of the MCA

1973 the respondent must wait a further *three months after that* – a total of *four and a half months* after decree *nisi* – before applying if the petitioner has not done so. The petitioner's application is made on Form M8 pursuant to r 2.49(1) and Appendix 1 to the FPR 1991. No notice need be given to the respondent but another fee is due, unless the petitioner is fees exempt.

The work to be done by the district judge on receiving the application gives some indication of why the six weeks between the two decrees is required at all. Pursuant to r 2.49(2), the district judge must search the court records to check that:

(a) the court has complied with its duty under s 41 of the MCA 1973 in relation to the post-divorce future of the children and that there is no direction under s 41(2) delaying the decree absolute;

(b) no one is trying to upset the decree *nisi* already granted and that no appeal or rehearing is pending; and

(c) no one is intervening pursuant to ss 8 or 9 of the MCA 1973 to show cause preventing the decree being made absolute. By s 8 the Queen's Proctor (an official much more prominent in former times before Fact D and the agreed approach to divorce generally became the norm) may intervene to show such cause if there is any irregularity (eg, a collusive divorce based on fabricated evidence), and by s 9 any third party may also intervene if there are material facts not brought to the attention of the court.

If the results of these inquiries are satisfactory, the district judge will make the decree absolute and will issue a certificate to that effect, copies of which will be sent to both parties. If the district judge does not search the court records and grants the decree absolute regardless, it will be a nullity (*Dackham v Dackham* [1987] 17 Fam Law 345). The certificate is in Form 9 in Appendix 1 to the FPR 1991, indicating the date on which the marriage officially ended.

If the respondent has to apply for the decree absolute, this will be on four days' notice to the petitioner, by application to a judge or district judge (r 2.50(2)). There will be a short hearing, where the reasons for the petitioner's not having applied will be considered and, if found reasonable (eg, that ancillary relief orders are not in place and such security is required, perhaps because of the necessity to compensate the petitioner for benefits to be lost with the status of marriage), the decree absolute will not be granted, unless some way is found of satisfying the petitioner's objections. It should be noted that if decree absolute is not applied for after 12 months from decree *nisi*, an affidavit will have to be filed with Form 8 to explain the delay and in particular to deal with whether:

• the parties have resumed cohabitation since decree *nisi* and if so between what dates; and

• any child has been born to the wife in the interim, and if so stating the relevant facts, in particular as to whether the child might be a child of the family.

The reasons for this are obvious and the district judge can require any relevant facts to be verified on affidavit by the applicant. By r 2.49(2), the district judge must pay particular attention to whether s 41 of the MCA 1973 has been complied with in respect of any child born since decree *nisi*.

11.6.4 Defended divorce

Defended divorce is most uncommon but occasionally there are cases which ought properly to be defended. This takes them out of the Special Procedure. Only a tiny proportion of cases even start as defended and it is so uncommon that this area of the law and procedure is seldom taught even to vocational students.

11.6.4.1 The cost of defended divorce

The first most important point in relation to defended cases is whether the respondent can *afford* to defend. Although public funding is available in defended cases, the respondent must still satisfy the Legal Services Commission that there is a case worth defending. In other words, he or she must show reasonable grounds for defending at all and also that it is not unreasonable for public funding to be granted (ie, because there is a chance of winning).

Even if there is a chance of winning, it must also be shown that it is reasonable to fight it out at public expense, and that it is not reasonable that a divorce is obtained some other way (eg, under Fact D). If these points are not established in the respondent's favour, public funding will not be granted. The respondent must also be within the financial limits, so the first point is basically entirely a financial exercise. Of course, it may be that the respondent wants to pay privately, in which case the solicitor can do nothing but advise against a fruitless or futile defence.

11.6.4.2 Notice of intention to defend

If the respondent is really serious about this ill advised course, such notice should be given on the Acknowledgment of Service (see 11.5, above), but leave to file an answer can be given later, and can even be applied for well out of time provided that it is done before decree *nisi*. However, as in *Day v Day* [1979] 2 All ER 187, such leave can be difficult to obtain, because this would involve setting aside the district judge's certificate (not something district judges like to be done or judges to do, and technically not possible in ordinary circumstances as held in *Day*). The only situation where this really might be worth doing is if the respondent has for some reason received no direct notice of the date of pronouncement of the decree *nisi*, and if a decree *nisi* is pronounced without that notice being received the decree *nisi* itself would be set aside as it would be a nullity (*Walker v Walker* [1987] 1 FLR 31, CA).

Most respondents are best dissuaded if at all possible from defending and this should be done as early as possible in the suit. It is not necessary to defend to contest child matters or ancillary relief and the only case in which it might be worth defending is if the respondent expects an application for a domestic violence injunction and the petition already alleges serious violence. There is also some slight risk that such violence might be prejudicial in later child proceedings if not contested in the petition, but this is less so unless an interim order under the CA 1989 is anticipated, since there is usually plenty of time to deal with exaggerated petitions in later child proceedings without having had to defend them earlier.

A respondent who is dissuaded from defending is usually taking good advice, since defending normally achieves no purpose and is expensive in terms of legal costs, painful emotion and inordinate delay in disposing of the matter. Sometimes, respondents think they should defend 'so the truth is known' perhaps by the children, the public or third parties. As the press are not often interested in divorces any more unless the parties are famous or the suit extraordinarily colourful, this is pointless, as even the judge who hears the contested case is not interested in why the parties' marriage broke down, the children are unlikely to read newspapers which report such things, and if the suit is undefended only the district judge (and again not the children or third parties) will read the petition containing the petitioner's allegedly specious allegations.

Many respondents do not realise this until it is painstakingly explained to them, and if the children are the real concern the advice a practitioner will usually give such a respondent is to talk to the children personally in suitable terms at the next opportunity for contact. Ideally parents should not have to do this sort of thing individually because recent research indicates that children appreciate being kept informed of any fundamental step affecting them, such as the divorce of their parents, but that they prefer not to be involved in their parents' adversarial activities after proceedings are begun. Practitioners (particularly SFLA solicitors) will therefore usually strongly advise a client to tell the children what is happening, and how new arrangements will affect them, and that if possible this should be done *jointly* by both parents.

Talked to sensibly on these lines, there is anecdotal evidence that most respondents will agree that defending is pointless. Some men can often be persuaded that it is practically routine to be divorced by their wives for conduct which they see as more macho than socially unacceptable, and most do not mind being divorced for adultery as they often think that that reflects well on them, too! Women are reported by practitioners to be more difficult, but since most petitions are brought by women this is less of a problem.

Truly valid reasons for defending, where the determined client should not be dissuaded, include:

(a) wishing to dispute the grant of a decree at all, possibly if there is a s 5 defence, or for religious reasons;

(b) wishing to cross-petition (ie, to seek a divorce on an alternative basis) where the respondent really *cannot* accept the basis on which the divorce is sought by the petitioner; and

(c) sound reasons for disputing the basis on which the divorce is sought (eg, a clergyman might object to being divorced for adultery since he would almost certainly lose his living and not be able to obtain any other clerical post).

11.6.4.3 The answer

If notwithstanding good advice the respondent is determined, an answer should be filed within 21 days of the date of giving notice of intention to defend (r 2.12). A co-respondent can file an answer as well as a respondent.

Drafting an answer (and cross-petition if there is one) is similar to drafting a defence and counterclaim and legal help is really needed for this, which is presumably why public funding remains for this stage where there is good reason to defend. Normally, solicitors will send this out to counsel, and will also normally involve counsel immediately where public funding is needed, since the public funding certificate will almost certainly be limited to counsel's opinion to start with too.

A reply is possible from the petitioner (r 2.13), but this is even more unusual than an answer and cross-petition.

A more sensible respondent can still withdraw at this stage and let the suit go undefended. In such a case, it will revert to the normal course of the Special Procedure: many initially defended divorces do.

11.7 THE ROLE OF CHILDREN IN DIVORCE

It will be apparent from the above account that, despite the lip service paid to their welfare by the s 41 certificate procedure for which the Statement of Arrangements is provided, the role of children in divorce is now minimal. Although people seeking a divorce will often have problems (and arguments with their spouses) concerning their children, the resolution of these now has very little impact on the actual *divorce* process, although, as in any adversarial case, giving petitioners' spouses what they want may make agreement in other areas, such as over money, rather easier. For example, if the mother wants a good ancillary relief package from the father, for herself and the children, human nature being what it is he is likely to be more co-operative if matters are agreed about contact with the children (and may want more, less or none depending on the approach to parenting of the particular father). Equally he is more likely to co-operate if matters are discussed and it is agreed where they should live or go to school, than if the mother insists on taking him to court under the CA 1989 for a formal order with which he does not agree.

Although there is a minimal formal requirement for approving *agreed* ongoing arrangements for children whose parents are divorcing (see 11.6.1, above), where – at the stage the petition is filed – the parties are in fact already locked in combat over the children, the conduct and outcome of such battles is specifically excluded from the divorce suit and decided in CA 1989 proceedings completely outside the divorce process. Thus, the only matter with which the court granting the *divorce* will concern itself is that of what is to be done where supposedly *agreed* ongoing arrangements for the post-divorce lives of the children (or at least arrangements which are not formally being litigated) are *not* such as a conscientious, non-interventionist judge, applying the non-interventionist philosophy which is dictated to divorce judges by the CA 1989, can reconcile with common sense.

This is a big change in the pre-1991 position which both the parties to a divorce and the ordinary member of the public with a normal regard for the welfare of children may at first have some difficulty in taking on board.

Before 1991, when the CA 1989 came into force, it was impossible to obtain even a decree *nisi* of divorce unless the court was satisfied with the arrangements for the children of the family and pursuant to s 41 of the MCA 1973 *issued a certificate*, which was by no means rubber stamped, to that effect. This was called the 's 41 certificate' and also had to *specify* who had 'custody' of the child (ie, the power to decide everything of importance in the child's life), who had 'care and control' (ie, the management of the child's day to day life), and who had 'access' and sometimes even when (and whether this was to be arranged on a 'reasonable' basis or was 'defined' by the court, eg, 'every other Sunday between 10 am and 4 pm with four weeks staying access per year during the usual school holidays').

This approval of child arrangements does still survive in an emasculated form in the amended s 41, a new version of which came into force in 1991 to reflect the non-interventionist policy of the CA 1989. However, whereas the previous paternalistic approach of the court often kept the parties up to scratch by close enquiry and intervention in their arrangements (ie, by *automatically* making formal orders for custody, etc and *refusing* even decree *nisi* unless *satisfied* about the children), the *right* to a decree *nisi* is now always certified (if the petitioner is entitled to one) *before* the position of the children is considered at all.

Nowadays, again pursuant to the ethos of the CA 1989, there are no formal orders unless they simply cannot be avoided, and it is now rare for the court to refuse even a decree absolute on the basis of concern about the children, although in an appropriate case the final decree actually dissolving the marriage and permitting remarriage *may* be held up because of the children if the court has sufficient grounds to do so.

Thus, whatever the position in respect of the children, the decree *nisi* which ends the first stage of the divorce process is now completely independent of child matters. Although it is not actually pronounced in open court until after the s 41 certificate has been issued in one form or another, technically the decision has already been taken and recorded in the district judge's certificate that the petitioner is entitled to a decree *before* the position of the children is addressed and the s 41 certificate dealt with at all (see 11.6.1, above). Thus most divorces are already a *fait accompli* by the time the court even begins to consider the arrangements for the children and therefore there is generally no need to worry that the children may hinder the divorce suit as such.

This situation is supposed to be a positive development and was brought about due to the non-interventionist policy of the CA 1989, pursuant to s 1(5) of that Act, which enshrines the charming if sometimes naïve idea that parents are the people who will know what is best for their children and that they will be likely to observe the principle of parental responsibility created by the Act which requires them to continue in the role of parents despite the formal dissolution of their marriage partnership (see Chapter 24).

As a result, no routine formal orders are now made concerning either residence arrangements or contact with children following the divorce of their parents, which is the complete opposite of the earlier situation where someone had to have a formal order for what was then termed 'custody' and someone else usually had to have an order for care and control, without which the child was felt to be living in an undesirable vacuum.

The modern position is therefore that the court will wish to look at the Statement of Arrangements – jointly prepared by the parents in most cases – of the proposed living and educational arrangements for the children, and will then wish to certify that it does not need to exercise any of its powers under the CA 1989 (which do permit it to make formal orders for residence and contact in cases where the parents have not sorted the matter out themselves in the approved manner so as to obviate the need for a formal order). This is meant to place the responsibility on the parents, and enable the court to assume a role which is lightly supervisory but which does not cut across the non-interventionist policy of the CA 1989.

However, if this idealistic position is in fact *not* the situation in any particular case, the court may then reluctantly involve itself in a number of ways to regulate matters for children who fall within the court's s 41 jurisdiction, so as to bring the position disclosed in the Statement of Arrangements into line with what is felt to be reasonable.

11.7.1 Children to whom s 41 applies

The children with whom the court will concern itself are those termed 'children of the family'. This has a technical meaning, being defined in s 52 of the MCA 1973, as amended by the CA 1989, as:

- a child of both parties to the marriage, including a child of both born before their marriage; or
- any other child, not being a child who is placed with the parties to the marriage as foster parents by a local authority or voluntary organisation, who has been treated by both the parties as a child of the family.

A stepchild may thus *not* be a child of the family. Although in theory this is unlikely if the children in question have lived with the parties, sometimes a stepparent is able to establish a factual situation. Only children under age 16 are strictly the province of the court, or children under age 18 if they are still in full time education or training, though the court may decide if there are any other children in each case (eg, a disabled child not in full time education or training, over the age of 16, to whom s 41 should apply). It should be noted that even if there are no children of the family, the court must still issue the certificate which will simply certify that there are no children of the family to whom s 41 applies.

11.7.2 The satisfactory situation

Where both parents sign the form of Statement of Arrangements and the details provided in the form give the court no cause for concern, the court will automatically, without any further evidence, issue the s 41 certificate indicating that the court knows the identities of the children concerned and that it does not wish to intervene in the parents' arrangements. Prior to 1991 there was a formal oral hearing before the judge of the court (not the district judge, whose jurisdiction did not extend so far) which had to be attended by the parent with whom the children lived. Now neither has further involvement unless the Statement of Arrangements is plainly unsatisfactory.

11.7.3 The unsatisfactory situation

However, if the district judge, pursuant to r 2.39 of the FPR 1991, considers the Statement of Arrangements filed at court with the petition, and feels that there is a problem with, for example, the accommodation, education, health care, financial provision or some other similar matter, or that there are any other potential snags in future arrangements, he or she may be unwilling to issue the s 41 certificate. If this is the case, the court can invite the parties to file further evidence, order a welfare report or exceptionally call the parties before it in an effort to resolve the matter. If this still produces no satisfactory solution, then the certificate will take a particular form reserved for such cases. The district judge will apply the cumulative test in s 41(2), deciding such application because:

(a) the circumstances of the case require the court to consider the exercise of its powers under the CA 1989;

(b) the court cannot do so without further considering the case; and

(c) there are exceptional circumstances which make it desirable in the child's interests that the court should give a direction that the decree of divorce (ie, the final decree dissolving the marriage and permitting remarriage) should not be made absolute until the court directs otherwise.

It is clear from this cumulative test in s 41(2) that delay of the final decree is considered to be an exceptional step, and only the most proactive district judges tend to interfere. Most situations can be headed off by proper preparation of the Statement of Arrangements and filing with it any further documents which will deal with any potential area of difficulty (eg, where there is a child with a chronic illness, a medical report; where there is an accommodation problem, a letter from the local authority promising future accommodation as soon as possible, etc).

11.7.4 Where the matter is to go direct to a CA 1989 hearing for a formal order

Where the petition discloses that the parties are in any event seeking a formal order for residence or contact or in relation to another matter (called a 's 8 order') or where there is such an application already pending and the divorce suit is started, the district judge is excused from considering the arrangements for the children since they will be considered in the separate CA 1989 proceedings (see 11.7.1, above).

11.7.5 Grey areas

Where no *formal application* has been made for a s 8 order, but the district judge is not happy with the arrangements because, for example, there is a dispute about where a child shall live, some district judges will call the parties in to court to explain what orders might be applied for. A district judge will do this so that the matter might be formally resolved between the parties, and the court welfare service will often be involved if it is felt that they might help in resolving the parties' differences and putting them off the formal procedure under the CA 1989, pursuant to the non-interventionist policy of that Act. If an application is then made, the matter will pass (as described at 11.6.1, above) to the court hearing the s 8 application. However, if nothing is done, and if the district judge feels thoroughly unhappy about it, then a choice must be made between directing that the final decree be held up until the children's future is settled by the court making orders itself, and asking for further evidence which might enable the issue of a satisfactory s 41 certificate. For example, if doubtful accommodation is at the root of the problem, the district judge might ask the court welfare office to inspect it or for a letter from the local authority specifying when the party with care of the child will be adequately housed.

It will, however, be obvious from the above that the future of the children is very unlikely now to have any impact on a divorce suit, and therefore the children are unlikely to be a problem in relation to the *suit* itself, although there may well be hotly contested and emotionally charged child proceedings under the CA 1989 (see Chapters 24 and 25).

It should nevertheless also be noted that, where a solicitor is involved, the SFLA Code will always influence the conduct of divorce suits, either within the divorce suit itself or in separate proceedings under the CA 1989. In the absence of funding for divorces the contemporary trend for members of the public is to conduct their own proceedings and obtain a divorce first and argue about the children after; thus the court does not have much chance to protect children within these divorce suits. This has been repeatedly commented upon by academic writers, so far without significant impact, but tends to be justified by others due to the concept of parental responsibility introduced by the CA 1989, which is supposed to ensure continued joint parenting of children despite the dissolution of the marriage relationship. In many cases this has proved to be the triumph of hope over experience.

DIVORCE PROCEDURE

FINANCING DIVORCE AND OTHER FAMILY PROCEEDINGS

There is usually no public funding available for obtaining the divorce decree (neither legal help under the AJA 1999 nor civil legal representation), although public funding may be available to those qualified to receive it for the financial proceedings (ancillary relief) following the decree *nisi* and for child and domestic violence disputes. If public funding is obtained, the statutory charge taken over any property recovered or preserved means that the assisted person will pay interest on the value of the Legal Services Commission's bill for funding the proceedings, so that legal aid is a loan rather than a gift. The only ways of avoiding the statutory charge are to show that the property in question was not 'in issue', or to seek orders which do not recover 'property' (ie, periodical payments which are exempt even if capitalised). Pursuant to the Funding Code under the AJA 1999, those seeking public funding in areas where the Legal Services Commission contracted mediation services are available are generally obliged to be assessed for suitability for mediation, as an alternative to taking proceedings, before being allowed to apply for civil legal aid (public funding).

THE DIVORCE PROCESS

The divorce suit is commenced by petition filed in a divorce county court, and accompanied by the marriage certificate, and other documents including a Statement of Arrangements for the future post-decree welfare of any children of the family (which has a technical meaning pursuant to s 52 of the MCA 1973). It is the petitioner's obligation to file this statement, but if the respondent has the main care of the children this may be supplemented by a letter from the respondent. However, there is no duty on the respondent to provide such information. The petition may be drafted either by the petitioner personally or by a solicitor if the petitioner has funding, either public or private, for legal advice.

The court sends the petition and Statement of Arrangements to the respondent, together with a Notice of Proceedings and Acknowledgment of Service form. If the respondent duly completes this form, and does not indicate an intention to defend, the divorce will then be dealt with under the Special Procedure (which is in fact now the normal procedure). If the Acknowledgment of Service form is not returned, service must be satisfactorily effected, deemed or dispensed with before the divorce can proceed. The petitioner must then ask for directions and file an affidavit in support of the petition, which constitutes the petitioner's only evidence, although other documents (eg, a medical certificate) might be exhibited to it.

There is no oral hearing unless the divorce is either defended or there are some other complications. A minor judge of the divorce county court, the district judge, considers the file administratively and if satisfied by the documents makes a certificate indicating that the petitioner is entitled to a decree *nisi*, notifying the parties of a future date for pronouncement of the decree in open court. Neither party need attend unless there is a dispute about costs or some other unusual reason, such as a late desire to defend on grounds for which leave would need to be sought to do so out of time, and could properly be given (which is not often the case because the district judge's certificate is usually a final indication that the petitioner is entitled to the decree).

The district judge only then considers the arrangements for the children, and if satisfied issues the court's certificate of satisfaction pursuant to s 41 of the MCA 1973. Should the court not be satisfied, there is power under s 41 to delay the issue of the decree absolute until arrangements can be approved, but this is rarely used, and there is no possibility of refusing a decree *nisi*, in respect of which the district judge has already issued a certificate prior to consideration of the arrangements for the children.

The district judge has no power to dismiss a petition: only the judge can do that. Any cases where the district judge is not satisfied, even after asking for further evidence, will be dealt with at an oral hearing in open court.

DEFENDED DIVORCE

If a divorce is defended there will be a formal defence, called an 'answer'. In most cases the respondent could also cross-petition, and there will be an oral hearing in open court. This is rare, however, because of the cost and delay.

THE ROLE OF CHILDREN IN DIVORCE

Because of the sequence of the routine divorce process, the role of children in a divorce is now minimal, though pursuant to s 41 of the MCA 1973 the court can delay decree absolute in an appropriate case (but not decree *nisi* already granted prior to consideration of s 41). This is mainly due to the introduction of the concept of parental responsibility under the CA 1989.

PART III

FINANCIAL CONSEQUENCES OF FAMILY BREAKDOWN

CHAPTER 12

ANCILLARY RELIEF: THE BASIC LAW

12.1 ORDERS WHICH THE COURT MAY MAKE

Ancillary relief (ie, financial orders dealing with the spouses' money and property) is available following decrees of divorce, nullity, judicial separation and presumption of death and dissolution of the marriage. The range of the court's powers, contained in ss 23 and 24 of the Matrimonial Causes Act (MCA) 1973, arises in the case of orders for spouses 'on granting a decree', and is subject to the court's consideration of the matters contained in s 25 of the Act, which details the matters which the court must take into account when exercising its powers under ss 23 and 24.

Orders made in favour of spouses to take effect before decree absolute are called 'interim orders', but become 'final' on decree absolute. The various types of order are not mutually exclusive – a package of financial provisions may contain all the various orders or only those most appropriate to the case.

Orders for children are always called interim orders, because technically no order can ever be final in relation to a child whose maintenance may always come back before the court whenever appropriate. These orders can be made at any time if agreed between the spouses. Alternatively, if the children are 'children of the family' (see 11.7.1, above) who are *not* within the jurisdiction of the Child Support Agency (CSA) (which now deals with maintenance for all children whose biological absent parent the CSA can trace), an application can be made to the court by the parent with care even if the other spouse does not agree. If the child's parents save the CSA the task of assessment by agreeing maintenance for the child between themselves informally, the intervention of the CSA at that time can be avoided as the agreement may still be embodied in an order of the court which is made by consent. The CSA must, however, assess the child's maintenance and enforce payment against the absent parent if the child and/or the child's custodial parent are on welfare benefits or a court order is transferred to the Agency (see Chapter 15).

There is also in s 22 a power to order maintenance pending suit (MPS), prior to the ancillary relief stage and for the period between filing of the petition and decree absolute, although this is likely to be on a subsistence standard since its essence is that the court will not yet have all the information required to make a long term order. However, an MPS is wide enough to cater for an applicant's legal fees, this being part of the necessary subsistence. See *per* Holman J in *A v A (Maintenance Pending Suit: Provision for Legal Fees)* [2001] 1 FLR 377, Fam Div, where the wife, who was wholly dependent on her wealthy Muslim Arab husband, was without capital or income and already owed legal fees of £40,000, as her legal aid certificate had been withdrawn when an earlier MPS order had been made.

12.2 THE COURT'S DISCRETIONARY JURISDICTION

Subject to the constraints of ss 23–25 of the MCA 1973, the court has a complete discretion as to how its powers to make financial orders should be exercised (including whether they should be exercised at all), since there is no regime of matrimonial property under the law of England and Wales. This is criticised by some jurists overseas who are constrained by an inflexible code of automatic matrimonial joint ownership. They claim that the English law of ancillary relief is defective in that it is inappropriate to the modern concept of matrimony as a partnership, since it is 'a law of separation of assets'; and that it is illogical in a marriage partnership in which in theory there should be 'community of property' unless there are special reasons for contracting out of such a position. Prenuptial contracts make no difference to the discretionary nature of ancillary relief in English law, although they may be taken in account as part of all the circumstances of the case (see *per* Wall LJ in *N v N (Jurisdiction: Pre-Nuptial Agreement)* [1999] 2 FLR 745; and *F v F (Ancillary Relief: Substantial Assets)* [1995] 2 FLR 47, where Thorpe LJ took the view that such contracts have limited significance, although Cazalet J in *N v N (Foreign Divorce)* [1997] 1 FLR 900 considered that they may be relevant). Wilson J in *S v S (Staying Proceedings)* [1997] 2 FLR 669 considered that the day of such contracts would come, probably in serial monogamy cases where the enforceability of such a contract was crucial to a marriage taking place at all. The suggestion in the government's 1998 consultation paper, *Supporting Families* (Home Office, 1998), that prenuptial contracts should be made enforceable subject to specific conditions has not been implemented. The Family Division judges responded to the consultation paper in the March 1999 issue of the journal *Family Law* and distinguished them from the only similar pact now commonly taken into account by the court, namely the *Edgar v Edgar* ([1980] 1 WLR 1410) maintenance agreement. The Solicitors Family Law Association (SFLA), which publishes pre-marriage precedents, seems to be broadly in favour of introducing some sort of financial agreement on marriage.

The distinct approach of English law is often the reason for international multi-millionaire divorces being conducted in England rather than in the community property jurisdictions which exist in much of the rest of the world. The reason for the selection of an English forum for divorce in these cases is that these community property jurisdictions are unfriendly to the rich husband, since the law of those States usually considers that the spouses already actually or notionally own the matrimonial assets jointly whatever the spouses themselves desire or declare, whereas English law more usually proceeds on the basis of what provision is actually reasonably needed for the financially weaker spouse (who is generally the wife) rather than that the spouse should receive any particular proportion of the assets available for distribution.

This rejection of the purely 'arithmetical approach' was confirmed by the Court of Appeal in *Dart v Dart* [1996] 2 FLR 286, CA, where from assets of around £400m the wife received under £10m. The husband had carefully planned the family's 'habitual residence' in London so as to avoid the US jurisdiction of Michigan, although this approach has been criticised in cases such as *White v White* [2000] 2 FLR 981 and *L v L* [2002] EWCA Civ 1685.

The English scheme is thus one where the *actual ownership* in law of any asset which the court considers is available as a resource at its disposal is *irrelevant*, since by s 24, and subject only to s 25, the court has the power to rearrange ownership of the spouses' assets on divorce as they see fit.

Moreover, since the s 24 jurisdiction is a discretionary one, the court is not bound by precedent, a point stressed by the *Dart* decision, and not changed by the recent House of Lords decision of *White v White* [2000] 2 FLR 981. In *White*, Lord Nicholls of Birkenhead said that a judge should always check his award against the notional yardstick of equality, but a careful examination of his speech makes it clear that he thinks that closer adherence to the s 25 factors in the search for fairness between the parties is the route which English law should follow rather than attempting any specifically equal division, *inter alia*, because express equal division may not *be* fair, whether in average or big money cases such as *White*. This permits the distinctly English approach to the wife's reasonable needs to be interpreted in accordance with the particular circumstances, including age, length of marriage and former lifestyle of the parties, without any confusion over whether 'needs' is the same as 'reasonable requirements' where assets exceed the ordinary meaning of 'needs', even generously interpreted, and indeed in *L v L* (above) the Court of Appeal did comment that the award in the lower court did not take account of the wife's needs.

Conversely, as shown by Hale J (as she then was) in *B v B* (reported in the Court of Appeal *sub nom Burgess v Burgess* [1997] 1 FCR 89; [1996] Fam Law 465; [1996] 2 FLR 34), closely following the s 25 factors may *incidentally* produce a substantially equal division (about which Mr Burgess complained, on the basis that the judge must have misdirected herself in ignoring his allegedly superior needs as the result of her order was equality of division: however, Waite LJ found no fault with her meticulous application of the factors to produce what appeared to be a fair result).

12.3 APPLYING FOR ANCILLARY RELIEF

Pursuant to r 2.53(1) of the Family Proceedings Rules (FPR) 1991, all initial claims for any species of ancillary relief order must be made by a petitioner in the prayer of the petition, or by a respondent in the answer if the respondent files one (see Chapter 11). These claims should always be made at the outset of the suit (or if this has not been done, the petition amended – see Chapter 11). Alternatively, there is provision in the FPR 1991 for respondents to make such applications without filing an answer. The ancillary relief application is then activated and pursued within the relevant FPR 1991 constraints and this may be done at any time after decree *nisi* has been obtained, prior to which the ancillary relief aspects of the case cannot be progressed. This is because the power of the court to make orders for spouses arises 'on granting a decree ... or at any time thereafter'.

Thus all the long term orders in ss 23 and 24 are restricted to taking effect only upon decree absolute and the application for them made in the prayer of the petition may not be activated until decree *nisi* has been pronounced. Although the power of the court arises on making a decree of divorce, it is not unknown for applications to be made many years later for which leave would be required. This would only be granted if there is some reason for the delay and such delayed application would not cause injustice.

12.3.1 Income orders (MCA 1973, ss 22 and 23)

Basic maintenance in most cases – weekly, monthly or annually – will be provided by *periodical payments*, either for the spouse or the children or both – and will be awarded in the long term under the MCA 1973, s 23(1)(a) for spouses and s 23(1)(d) for children. The duration of such orders will depend on what the court orders as suitable for the particular case. For short term maintenance, MPS (under s 22) also provides periodical payments, but usually more at the rate of a subsistence allowance than to match the quantum of likely longer term orders, where more of the relevant facts are known about the payee's needs and the payer's ability to pay than at the initial stages of an ancillary relief application. Income orders or 'maintenance' are usually the core of an ancillary relief package unless there is to be a clean break with which they are incompatible. Sometimes it is found more convenient to apply to the Family Proceedings Court for temporary maintenance pending fuller consideration of the parties' financial positions after decree *nisi* (see Chapter 19).

12.3.1.1 Periodical payments

For a spouse, periodical payments (unless they are *secured*, as to which see below) usually last during joint lives of the payer and payee or until remarriage (MCA 1973, s 28), or for a limited period if intended to be part of a clean break arrangement (MCA 1973, s 25A, and see below). If no duration is specified at all, payments continue until further order of the court, which usually means until the payer or the payee applies to vary them under s 31 of the MCA 1973 (see Chapter 13).

Obviously a *payer* is likely to apply to vary the order *downwards* (because, for example, of job loss so that the payments are no longer affordable, or an increase in the payee's resources, so that they are no longer necessary) and a *payee* is likely to apply to vary the order *upwards* because, for example, the payments are no longer enough. This might be due to a combination of a rise in the cost of living generally and also an extension of the items of routine expenditure which the payee is called upon to fund. Variation commonly occurs where children grow up and become more expensive and their requirements for more space at home increases the regular outgoings, such as the ordinary utility bills (eg, when children are simply at home more, such as during the common occurrence of home study before A level or other public examinations). Any of these situations would produce a further order of the court whether that order reduced, increased or entirely discharged the original order.

12.3.1.2 Secured periodical payments

Where periodical payments are secured in favour of a spouse pursuant to s 23(1)(b), they can be made to last beyond the death of the payer. Secured periodical payments are not usual, since they require to be secured on assets, which are not generally available in most divorces in sufficient quantity to fund such security. Moreover, such an order would not be made without good reason, for example, that the payer had a bad payment track record, or might leave the country to work elsewhere, taking assets out of the jurisdiction at the same time. Secured periodical payments are therefore only likely to be applicable where the payer is particularly rich or particularly impecunious and it is necessary to protect the position of the payee by making a secured order. For example, in *Aggett v Aggett* [1962] 1 WLR 183; [1962] 1 All ER 190, the husband was so irresponsible that in case he left the jurisdiction (as anticipated) payments were secured on his house, and in *Parker v Parker* [1972] 2 WLR 21; [1972] 1 All ER 410, a second mortgage was taken out on the husband's house to secure an annuity.

Secured periodical payments for a child, which are possible pursuant to s 23(1)(e), are extremely uncommon, although there are sometimes good reasons, for example, to secure continued payment out of a payer's estate after his death without the necessity of taking further proceedings. For the court to make such an order a father would generally have to be a persistently unreliable payer: also, since the court only retains jurisdiction in cases where the CSA would assess contested orders, secured periodical payments for children will be restricted to consent orders where the payer agrees to the security or to cases where the payment is sought in contested proceedings for children of the family who are not within the CSA's remit (ie, stepchildren whose absent natural parent the CSA cannot trace, either because of the parent's death or disappearance or in some cases where the father of a stepchild is not actually known).

12.3.1.3 Children's periodical payments

The normal form of routine maintenance for a child who is within the court's jurisdiction will therefore be:

- unsecured periodical payments, and by the MCA 1973, s 29(2) these will last in the first instance until the child's 17th birthday; or

- by the MCA 1973, s 29(3) until the child finishes full time education or training.

The same section permits a child who is over 18 to continue to receive periodical payments if his or her welfare permits it (eg, if he or she is handicapped). All child orders terminate on the death of the payer in the same way as those for spouses, unless secured (s 29(4)). Prior to the grant of the decree *nisi* no order may be made under s 23 for a spouse (though this restriction obviously does not apply to periodical payments for children for whom an interim order may be made at any time) because the court's power to do so has not yet arisen, so if periodical payments are desired at this stage, it will be necessary to apply for MPS as soon as the petition is filed. These payments can be backdated to the date of the presentation of the petition and will automatically terminate at the end of the suit on grant of decree absolute. The amount of MPS will not be generous since it is regarded as a subsistence allowance and is granted *separately* from the main application for long term periodical payments, and at a more basic rate, precisely because it will not be possible until the ancillary relief proceedings are further advanced to determine what the terms and quantum of the final order should be.

12.3.2 Capital payment orders (MCA 1973, s 23)

Instead of or in addition to the basic maintenance of periodical payments, in some but not all cases a cash lump sum order may be made, either for a spouse or for a child or children, or all of them, and this also may be done under s 23(1)(c) for spouses and s 23(1)(f) for children.

The reasons for lump sums are many and various, although it was established as long ago as *Wachtel v Wachtel* [1973] 2 WLR 366; [1973] 1 All ER 829; [1973] Fam 72 (a case also famous for other reasons) that no particular purpose or justification is required before such an order may be made. A lump sum order may in fact be particularly appropriate in a variety of cases (eg, where the payee is likely to remarry, so that periodical payments would cease under s 28). An applicant may always prefer to seek a lump sum payment, since any lump sum will be outright, and will not therefore be affected by remarriage. However, in some cases, where the degree of bitterness has been such that periodical payments would be undesirable, a lump sum may also be a tactful way of ending the war between the spouses. The modern approach focuses on the needs of the parties (see *Dew v Dew* [1986] 2 FLR 341 where it was established that this approach was untrammelled, at least in the first instance, by ideas of proportionate division of assets, though the post-*White* concept of checking the order against a notional yardstick of equality may have some influence here in future).

However, in cases where remarriage is not ruled out, care would have to be taken that the lump sum order was not *specifically* made as a form of capitalised maintenance, as it could then be attacked and possibly set aside if there had been any deliberate misrepresentation over whether the payee was planning to remarry. This was the case in *Livesey v Jenkins* [1985] AC 424; [1985] 2 WLR 47; [1985] 1 All ER 105, where the wife omitted to mention that she was already engaged to be married shortly after the order was made.

Established cases particularly suitable for a lump sum include:

(a) where there is available capital of which the wife should have a share, as in *Trippas v Trippas* [1973] 2 WLR 585; [1973] 2 All ER 1, where the wife had been promised a share of the proceeds of the business because of her moral support in setting up and establishing it;

(b) setting up a business, as in *Nicholas v Nicholas* [1984] FLR 285 and *Gojkovic v Gojkovic* [1990] Fam Law 100, in which money was needed to set up respectively a guest house and a hotel where the payee spouse would thus be able to become self-supporting;

(c) reducing or replacing periodical payments, as in *Gojkovic* above, where the degree of bitterness and the capability of the payee spouse were both such that this was desirable, and in *Duxbury v Duxbury* [1987] FLR 7, CA, in which the now famous *Duxbury* calculation was first used to identify a sum which could be invested in a planned and cost effective manner so as to provide a particular applicant with lifelong maintenance by living at various times off both the income and the capital and at others a combination of the two;

(d) achieving a clean break as in *Duxbury*;

(e) compensating for loss of a matrimonial home, as in *P v P (Financial Provision: Lump Sum)* [1978] 1 WLR 483; [1978] 3 All ER 70;

(f) replacing maintenance where enforcement is likely to be difficult or as a punishment for concealing assets as in *Martin v Martin* [1976] 2 WLR 901; [1976] 3 All ER 625 and *Nicholas*, where the husbands were both potential bad payers and/or had tried to conceal their wealth, so that a clean break was clearly a better alternative to periodical payments.

Where a lump sum payment is made to a spouse, only one such lump sum may be ordered, though the lump sum may be *paid* in instalments and expressed in the order to be so payable (s 23(3)(c)) and such payment secured to the satisfaction of the court. It is a drawback of instalments that they may always be varied, or extinguished altogether, although Balcombe LJ has said that this power should be exercised with caution (see *Penrose v Penrose* [1994] 2 FLR 621).

Where a lump sum order is made in favour of a child, this restriction does not apply and therefore successive lump sum orders may be made.

In both cases, interest can be ordered if payment is deferred (s 23(6)), provided provision is made in the order. If this is so, then the interest will be payable from whatever date was specified in the order (see *per* Ewbank J in *L v L (Lump Sum: Interest)* [1994] 2 FLR 324). This is obviously a very useful provision to include when drafting an order in case of default.

It used to be thought that lump sums were only appropriate where the parties were wealthy and there was substantial capital, but it is now established that the exercise of this power is not restricted to such cases, provided the payer can reasonably raise the sum required (*Davis v Davis* [1967] 1 All ER 123; [1966] 3 WLR 1157). A more recent instance of this is to be found in *P v P* (above), which is clear authority for the proposition that no more than is really needed by the payee, and no more than can realistically be raised, will be ordered to be paid where it has to come from a business, or home and business, which is needed for the family to live on. In that case the wife owned the property, a farm on which she and the three children of the family lived and on which the parties had worked. It was accepted that the husband owned £8,000 of the stock and contents of the farm (the total value of which was £102,000) and he appealed against an order of only £15,000 payable in three instalments over a year, having asked for a lump sum and also a transfer of property order. It was held that the wife could not realistically pay more, since she would need the property to remain unencumbered by no more than the £15,000 that would suffice for an alternative home for the husband, in order to maintain herself and the children (having accepted only a nominal periodical payments order in favour of the children and nothing for herself).

12.3.2.1 Restriction on the grant of lump sums

The court will not cripple a spouse's earning power, nor a business off which the family has to live, nor put a home at risk, as was shown in *Martin v Martin* (see 12.3.2, above). In *Martin* where an order was reduced from £5,000 to £2,000 to avoid a husband's having to sell his hotel and thus lose his home as well as his business. Similarly, in *Smith v Smith* [1983] 4 FLR 154, the lump sum of £40,000 awarded was cancelled altogether because to raise it the husband would have had to sell shares in his company which was his only income-producing asset, and that would have benefited nobody. Again, in *Kiely v Kiely* [1988] 18 Fam Law 51; [1988] 1 FLR 248, the order was cancelled since to raise a £4,000 lump sum each for the children of the family would have meant selling the former matrimonial home, which was moreover not necessarily guaranteed to raise enough, but would nevertheless leave the husband in contempt of court through no fault of his own as well as unable to pay the order.

Otherwise if there are assets the court will not hesitate to make use of them for this purpose and does not much mind where the assets originated if they are required to do justice in the case and can reasonably be raised without violating the principles stated above.

It should, however, be noted that where a business is not to be sold, because the family lives off it, it is pointless to spend large sums of money on valuations. These are sometimes obsessively indulged in by spouses keen to get compensation for the value of an asset which cannot be sold but which they reckon they are entitled to a share of, and are determined that this shall be achieved by sale of some other asset.

A wife in these circumstances came in for some hard words from the court in *P v P* [1989] 2 FLR 248, where the argument was about the value of shares in a haulage company which on any view could not be sold. It was held that it was pointless to spend money on a precise valuation since the court only wanted a broad view of the value of matrimonial assets which were not being sold, and furthermore as there was another source of a lump sum for her – the proceeds of the matrimonial home, which was to be sold anyway – they could take the approximate value of the shares into account when making orders from those liquid funds. As a result, Mrs P received £240,000 out of the £260,000 sale proceeds of the matrimonial home and Mr P kept the shares, since it would have been reckless to put the business at risk by raising money from his fixed assets.

12.3.2.2 Adjournment until funds become available

Sometimes lump sum orders cannot be made because there are not, at the moment when the case is before the court, sufficient assets from which the court could order a lump sum, though it is anticipated that there will be in the foreseeable future. The solution here may be to adjourn the case, which may be done for up to a period of about five years (a period suggested in *Roberts v Roberts* [1986] 2 FLR 152) if this is the only means of achieving justice between the parties. In the same year, *Davies v Davies* [1986] 1 FLR 497 considered the general desirability of this type of adjournment and held that ideally the matter should be dealt with as soon as possible, but if there was a real possibility of capital becoming available in the foreseeable future, adjournment was permissible to achieve justice.

Adjournment, rather than making some sort of percentage order, is more appropriate where the future quantum of the anticipated asset is uncertain, such as the amount of a pension as in *Morris v Morris* [1977] 7 Fam Law 244, which concerned the likely amount of the husband's gratuity when he left the Army. He was a warrant officer and it was uncertain how much longer he would serve in the Army, which was directly relevant to the amount of the gratuity. The husband was ordered to notify the wife of the receipt of the money so that the application might be revived at that date. The principles applying to such adjournments were more recently reviewed in *MT v MT (Financial Provision: Lump Sum)* [1992] 1 FLR 362, a case dealing with the husband's prospects of inheriting from his 83 year old father on his anticipated death, which was said to be reasonably foreseeable. It was held that the court has a discretion to adjourn in any case where it would be suitable to do so because of the foreseeable prospect of capital becoming available.

12.3.3 Property transfer orders (MCA 1973, s 24(1)(a))

The court may transfer freeholds, leaseholds, protected and statutory tenancies within the meaning of the Rent Act 1977, secure tenancies within the meaning of the Housing Act 1985, and council houses and flats. The consent of the local authority is not required, but they have a right to be heard. The consent of a building society or bank may not be required, but they should be given a chance by the court to be heard (*Practice Direction* [1971] 1 All ER 896). This 'chance' may not make much difference, as is shown, for example, by *Lee v Lee* [1984] FLR 243, where the authority opposed the transfer because it disrupted its housing policy; the court did not consider that that merited the hardship that the wife would suffer and ordered the transfer. *Buckingham v Buckingham* (1979) 129 NLJ 52 was similarly rather hard on a private landlord when a transfer was ordered despite his objections, although a landlord's objection to a particular tenant is regarded as of significant importance in landlord and tenant law because of the close proprietorial relationship which they must have. *Tebbut v Haynes* [1981] 2 All ER 239 also indicates that the interests of third parties who live in the home (in this case the husband's mother and aunt) will be considered if the order will turn them out.

The most common use of the transfer of property power is to transfer the matrimonial home, especially if it is to effect a clean break (see 12.7, below, and Chapter 16). However, it may also be used to transfer ownership of chattels such as cars, furniture, works of art and indeed anything which needs to be transferred to achieve the necessary reorganisation of the parties' financial affairs.

12.3.4 Settlement of property (MCA 1973, s 24(1)(b))

This section enables the court to set up settlement orders in relation to the matrimonial home, such as the *Mesher, Martin, Harvey* and similar occupation orders which enable a spouse to remain in the home with the children until the latter are grown up, or even in some cases for longer (see Chapter 16). It can also be used to enable a spouse to establish a settlement of capital to provide for the other spouse and children, usually with reversion to the settling spouse or possibly ultimate remainder to the children.

12.3.5 Variation of settlements (MCA 1973, s 24(1)(c) and (d))

This is the power which allows variation of an ante- or post-nuptial settlement in favour of the parties or their children, including any settlement made by will or codicil. This provision, which permits the interest of a spouse to be reduced or extinguished, also sometimes permits variation of pension funds as in *Brooks v Brooks* [1995] 3 WLR 1292; [1995] 3 All ER 257, HL; [1995] 2 FLR 13, although there are very few cases where this possibility applies. In *Brooks* it was possible to vary the provisions applicable to the pension fund so as to give the wife an immediate annuity and a deferred index-linked pension payable from the date of the husband's death, going on to direct that these two pensions for the wife were to be provided in priority to the pension for the husband, so that if necessary he would take less. However, this could only be done as the pension scheme was the parties' own small company scheme whereas most pensions which would ideally be split on divorce were subject to the discretion of the trustees of the pension schemes in question, which were not subject to the orders of the court.

This problem has now been addressed by s 166 of the Pensions Act 1995, which inserted new ss 25B–25D into the MCA 1973 to provide 'earmarking' of pensions, now effected by an 'attachment' order and by the Welfare Reform and Pensions Act 1999, which inserted new ss 21A and 24B in the MCA 1973 to provide pension sharing in the case of all petitions filed after 1 December 2000. These provisions directly affect the resources to be taken into account by the court under s 25(2)(a) and enable the court to require pension fund trustees, whether of an occupational or personal pension scheme, to pay part of the pension or lump sum available to one spouse to the other according to the court's direction. However, it may still be more beneficial in some cases to obtain compensation by another route rather than actually to go through the process of valuing and dividing the share to be split off, which usually tends, due to the 'blunt instrument' method of valuation used, to result in the recipient in fact receiving a less valuable asset than the appropriate fraction would suggest.

12.3.6 Order for sale (MCA 1973, s 24A)

Whenever the court makes any of the above orders other than one which is simply for unsecured periodical payments, it may also order a sale of any property in which either of the parties has a legal beneficial interest. This power, not originally included in the MCA 1973, was introduced to provide the opportunity for the court not only to order a sale so as to facilitate payment of its orders – an obviously useful consequential benefit for the payee – but to make desirable facilitating arrangements, such as that the court's order be paid out of the proceeds of sale (s 24A(2)(a)), that the property be offered for sale to specified persons or classes of persons (s 24A(2)(b)) and to add any other condition of a practical nature that it thinks fit (eg, as to which party's solicitor should have the conduct of the sale). This can be very important since clearly the applicant's solicitors would ideally prefer to be in the driving seat in such a transaction, rather than having to keep contacting the respondents to try to push the matter along, whereas some respondents, especially the more pernickety, would (sometimes rightly) be anxious about not being in control of the disposal of major assets.

Like other orders, those under s 24A cannot take effect until decree absolute.

12.4 THE s 25 FACTORS, s 25A AND THE IDEAL
OF SPOUSAL SELF-SUFFICIENCY

A detailed consideration of s 25 is undertaken by the court in order to put together a suitable ancillary relief package in each individual case on which it is called upon to pronounce. A similar approach is taken by practitioners negotiating a package intended to be in the ballpark area of what the court would be likely to order after a contested hearing, with the intention of avoiding the costs and uncertainties of litigation.

The method is to look at the orders available under ss 23 and 24 (for which see 12.3, above), then to apply the s 25 considerations systematically to the facts and finally to propose the combination of orders which most suits the family's circumstances, and is fairest in relation to the relevant s 25 factors. Obviously any such scheme will give priority to the particular applicant's interests where possible, but will also take into account that what suits the family as a *whole* is also likely to be in that applicant's interests and will facilitate life after divorce, especially important where there are children and an ongoing relationship is likely to be essential. Practitioners therefore find that it is sometimes necessary to tell clients that what they think they want is not necessarily going to secure the best deal with the best chance of producing a happy solution for the client, whatever the client thinks, so that the black letter law may to some extent be adapted in practice by the circumstances. However, as always, the client instructs and the lawyer advises, but the lawyer must ultimately carry out the client's instructions. Good advice here as elsewhere may fall on deaf ears, in which case there is not much the solicitor can do but comply – or in an extreme case encourage the client to take the case elsewhere.

An inexperienced practitioner, or one whose regular work is outside family law, and most students, will need explicitly to work through the range of orders and the s 25 factors on the checklist principle, in order to build up a suitable package for any given set of facts. However, such a structured approach will not usually be necessary once some experience of the orders and factors is acquired, when it is usually possible to spot instantly the one or two points which will particularly favour the party to be advised and build the case around those. The academic student may find that to start with the structured approach is required, but in relying on this crutch should take comfort from the identical approach of Hale J (now Hale LJ but formerly Professor Brenda Hoggett, an academic of some distinction), which was upheld by the Court of Appeal in *Burgess v Burgess* [1996] 2 FLR 34, CA, mentioned at 12.2, above. Her consideration of the s 25 factors is pure textbook application. It is this closer relation to the provisions of s 25 which Lord Nicholls was advocating in the House of Lords' consideration of *White v White*, to which detailed further reference must inevitably be made in relation to the overall impact of the s 25 factors.

The considerations themselves are contained in the sub-paragraphs of s 25, which is conveniently broken into two sub-sections:

- s 25(1) sets out the court's 'general duty' in applying the whole of the section; and
- s 25(2) itself may rationally be broken into two sub-parts:
  - s 25(2)(a) deals with the resources out of which the court will make its orders; and
  - ss 25(2)(b)–(h) set out the checklist through which the court will work in deciding whether and to what extent it should make orders.

Additionally, s 25A has since 1984 given the court the power to *order* a 'clean break', if necessary, regardless of the parties' wishes, a power which in the absence of the *agreement* of the parties no court had prior to the 1984 amendment to the statute. The clean break is in accordance with the relatively new policy of spousal self-sufficiency by which, if a clean break is not possible immediately, the court at least likes to see even untrained wives working towards, if necessary taking part time work, acquiring a skill or, if older and out of the workplace for many years, perhaps retraining.

12.4.1 Welfare of children (MCA 1973, s 25(1): 'the general duty' of the court)

Section 25(1), while requiring the court to have regard to all the circumstances of the case, makes the welfare of the children the first consideration in every case where there are children of the family. It is important to understand the interaction of this principle with that of the clean break. The existence of children does not necessarily make a clean break impossible between their parents (though of course impossible between either of their parents and them), though it may make it inappropriate, or inappropriate for the time being. In *Suter v Suter and Jones* [1987] 2 FLR 232, the wife with young children received nominal periodical payments as the future was insufficiently clear to impose a clean break immediately, despite the fact that she was cohabiting with a lover who could make a substantial contribution to the household as long as he remained with her.

The children's welfare in the context of s 25(1) is usually interpreted as meaning that during their minority they must have a secure home and a sufficient income must be provided for them to live on. In *Harman v Glencross* [1986] 2 FLR 241, the occupation of the former matrimonial home had to be given to the wife, with whom the children lived, as otherwise they would have had no proper home.

This principle, articulated in *Harman*, but established much earlier, was the watershed from which sprang the now well established line of *Mesher* order variants, so called because their origin was in *Mesher v Mesher* [1980] 1 All ER 126 decided some five years earlier. Children in the context of s 25(1) means 'children of the family' within the meaning of s 52 (ie, a child of both parties, or a child of one who has been *treated* by the other as a child of the family). Stepparents can therefore successfully evade liability for their partner's children, but this would need to be done expressly as the court is slow to recognise any such situation. In *Day v Day* [1988] 1 FLR 278, the actual marriage lasted only six weeks, as Mr Day quickly decided that he preferred the bachelor life, although there had been lengthy premarital cohabitation. When he sought to avoid paying maintenance for the wife's two children, neither of whom apparently had a father available to maintain them, the court decided that he had fully understood his commitment and obligations towards the children for whom he had accepted responsibility and that he must therefore pay maintenance for them both despite the brevity of the actual marriage.

It should be noted that a secondary but also well established principle in connection with the court's general duty is the desire of judges to end financial dispute between the parties, a goal which will always remind the court of its duty to consider a clean break pursuant to s 25A in those cases where drawing such a line under the parties' disputes is possible (see, eg, *S v S* [1986] Fam 189, where £400,000 bought off annual periodical payments of £70,000 in an argument between a millionaire pop star and his wife).

12.4.2 Matrimonial Causes Act 1973, s 25(2)(a)–(h)

The first paragraph of the sub-section, s 25(2)(a), looks at the assets out of which provision may be made. The remaining paragraphs, s 25(2)(b)–(h), look at the considerations which must be weighed in dividing those assets.

12.4.2.1 Evidence of the parties' means (MCA 1973, s 25(2)(a))

This paragraph of the sub-section requires that all the parties' means must be taken into account so as to establish the nature and extent of the resources out of which the court will be able to make its orders. Clearly the size of the pie is the first relevant point before it can be divided, and the ingredients will be of the first importance in establishing both the precise make up of the dish and the size of the portions available.

The reality of the situation is that the court must consider more than the surface of the parties' respective financial positions. In order to do this, whether the case is to be contested or the subject of a negotiated settlement in the region of what the court might *order*, it is usual for both parties to make full disclosure.

If it is certain that the case will be contested, or at least that it must be started on that basis, then both parties formally and concurrently file a statement of means, now no longer in affidavits but in the much more precise and uniform 'Form E' devised for use with the Ancillary Relief Pilot Scheme (trialled in both the Principal Registry of the High Court (which acts as the divorce county court for central London) and in a number of designated divorce county courts around the country before in June 2000 being applied nationally).

Where a negotiated settlement is the aim from the start, it is common to make disclosure in some other convenient manner; for example, the parties may choose to exchange Form E informally in draft, or to provide each other with information by letter or in person at a meeting, supported by such bundles of documents as are necessary to verify the position. Where such negotiations are successful, the court may be invited to make an order by consent upon lodgement of a draft consent order, thus making a considerable saving in both time and costs (see Chapter 14 for the new ancillary relief procedure in full).

Section 25(2)(a) requires the court to take into account:

> ... the income, earning capacity, property and other financial resources which each of the parties to the marriage has or is likely to have in the foreseeable future, including in the case of earning capacity any increase in that capacity which it would in the opinion of the court be reasonable to expect a party to the marriage to take steps to acquire.

Looking below the surface, the court will therefore need to be alert not merely to what the parties have but to what they might have, such as:

(1) Both parties' *future* earning capacity as well as present earnings, including any *potential improvement* in earning capacity which might be acquired by retraining or other reorganisation of a party's lifestyle.

(2) Family money, such as from wealthy parents or a private company on which the family habitually draws, as in *Thomas v Thomas* [1995] 2 FLR 668, where a husband's appeal against some fairly onerous orders, including for school fees, was dismissed because the judge said the husband had no real complaint, provided his wealthy family came to his aid to pay some school fees as it had been understood would happen before the divorce. In the Court of Appeal, Waite LJ drew attention to the court's almost limitless powers in redistributing assets and to the necessity in modern times 'where the forms of wealth holding are diverse and often sophisticated, to penetrate outer forms and get to the heart of ownership'. This principal was returned to by the same court in the more recent *White v White* [1998] 2 FLR 310, CA, the now well known case of a husband and wife farming partnership where the wife objected to receiving only what the court took to be her reasonable needs when her partnership rights indicated that she was entitled to more. In fact, the husband did

finally receive slightly more of the family assets than the wife because his family had contributed more to start with (for *White* in the House of Lords, see [2000] 2 FLR 981).

(3) The principle of financial independence in so far as is consistent with the welfare of the children.

Besides family money, the variety of sources of means to be taken into account for this purpose will often include damages or compensation, anticipated interests under a will or settlement, the earnings of a new spouse or cohabitant, and property acquired since the separation and/or divorce, besides the spouse's *true* income or earning capacity where that is different from what is being claimed in disclosure. Welfare benefits are not a routine resource for ancillary relief purposes (see further 18.5, below).

12.4.2.2 Damages or compensation

The general rule is that damages for pain and suffering and loss of amenity are not taken into account. In *Jones v Jones* [1975] 2 WLR 606; [1975] 2 All ER 12, any alternative to the rule would have been particularly unsuitable, since the damages in question were an award of only £1,800 for injuries following a knife attack actually perpetrated on the wife by the husband, which had severed the tendons in her hands and made it impossible for her to continue to earn her own living as a nurse. However, general damages are normally regarded as a resource, as in *Daubney v Daubney* [1976] 2 WLR 959; [1976] 2 All ER 453, where the wife had used the general damages in question to buy a flat which necessarily counted as a resource of hers in the ancillary relief proceedings.

Nevertheless, where damages have been calculated to provide continuing care for a projected lifespan, these will not be counted (as, eg, in *Jones v Jones* [1983] 1 WLR 901; [1983] 2 All ER 1039, where the husband did not have to bring into account damages of £167,000 to provide care for the rest of his life after a motorcycle accident, and *C v C (Financial Provision)* [1995] 2 FLR 171, where the wife and child were on State benefits but a settlement was refused because all the damages were needed to provide for the husband's needs). This contrasts with a case where the sum actually received was in excess of that party's needs and some of that excess was needed to do justice between the parties by righting a disparity which would otherwise exist between their respective financial positions. In *Wagstaff v Wagstaff* [1992] 1 All ER 275; [1992] 1 FLR 333, the husband had received £418,000, also after a motorcycle accident, of which £32,000 was awarded to the wife, who had no particular need for the money except as an emergency fund, on the basis that she had contributed to a 12 year marriage, had a child to support, and the husband did not need all the money.

In *Wagstaff*, the court specifically took the opportunity to differentiate between smaller awards of damages specifically for pain and suffering (or any awards where the disabled spouse's needs used up all the money awarded) and those cases, like *Wagstaff*, where the amount of the damages, even if some of them were for pain and suffering, clearly indicated that they should be considered a resource.

12.4.2.3 Interests under a will or settlement

Here policy varies, and the proximity of the availability of the money, together with the likelihood of its actually being received in due course, will influence the decision as to whether the money will be considered a resource for the purposes of s 25(2)(a) (*Michael v Michael* [1986] 2 FLR 389).

The alternative, especially if justice cannot otherwise be done, is to adjourn a decision on the ancillary relief application until the money becomes available, which may be done for four or five years as in *Roberts v Roberts* [1986] 2 All ER 483; and *Hardy v Hardy* [1981] 11 Fam Law 153, or the court may make the order on the basis that the money will eventually come in, if that is fairly certain, but that payment pursuant to the order should not be made until the funds have actually been received, as in *Calder v Calder* [1975] 6 Fam Law 242.

However, the eventual availability of the assets must be reasonably certain: it is not possible to subpoena aged and ailing parents to state their testamentary intentions, as was discovered in *Morgan v Morgan* [1977] Fam 122. Cases do arise where, while it is by no means certain whether or when such an inheritance will be received, some account nevertheless has to be taken of the expectations and in this situation the wealth, degree of relationship, age and health of the testator or testatrix will all be relevant – how relevant will depend on the circumstances of the individual case (see *B v B (Real Property: Assessment of Interests)* [1988] 2 FLR 490, where there was a quantifiable interest under the will of a wealthy mother which the court could not ignore).

In a further case entitled *B v B* [1990] 1 FLR 20, advanced age enabled the court to take account of an expected inheritance without adjournment (the mother from whom one of the parties was to inherit was in that case aged 84 and the inheritance was held not to be too remote).

However, in *K v K* [1990] 2 FLR 225, the testatrix was only aged 79 and in good health and the court ignored the inheritance as a resource as being too remote. In the case of respondents with firm expectations in some foreign jurisdictions, the court is more likely to take those expectations into account, as in *MT v MT (Financial Provision: Lump Sum)* [1992] 1 FLR 362, where the wife's application was adjourned pending the death of her 83 year old German father-in-law, because under German law the husband would definitely inherit one eighth of the estate.

Where a spouse is a beneficiary under a settlement this can of course be varied pursuant to s 24(1)(c) or (d) if applicable but it is also common for the court to treat the spouse's beneficial interest as one of settled assets and to make an order on the basis that the paying spouse can borrow against his or her expectations (see *B v B* [1982] 12 Fam Law 92). Interests under offshore trusts are not safe from being counted as a s 25(2)(a) resource. In *Browne v Browne* [1989] 1 FLR 291, CA, the wife was eventually committed for contempt for not paying under an order which had been quantified on the basis that she had access at will to two offshore trusts where the trustees (who had previously handed over whatever money she had requested) refused to meet her request for funds for the purposes of the order.

While the court knows that no order is directly enforceable against offshore trusts outside the jurisdiction, judges do not hesitate to make orders taking into account offshore assets if they are satisfied that the money is normally at the disposal of the beneficiary.

Thus trustees cannot in fact help such a beneficiary by suddenly refusing to carry out requests to pay over money if they have been in the habit of doing so in the past (as is usually the case where offshore trusts are of the type designed to be of financial benefit both to the beneficiaries who obtain fiscal advantages by the money technically being owned by the trustees offshore and to the holding trust company which charges a large fee for the service).

12.4.2.4 Resources of a new spouse or cohabitant

This is always a problematic area. No order can be made which actually has to be paid out of the new spouse or cohabitant's pocket as such. In *B v B (Periodical Payments: Transitional Provisions)* [1995] 1 FLR 459, an order was held to be wrongly made against a father with a significant overdraft, which in effect meant that his partner had to pay the order, although it was right to take into account the fact that he was being supported by her having been out of work for two months. There are, however, two ways in which the new spouse or cohabitant can indirectly make money or assets available to the first family:

(a) by making over capital or property to the spouse as in *Ibbetson v Ibbetson* [1984] FLR 545, where the former wife's new cohabitant placed their new house into joint names, thus giving her a half share which had to be counted as an asset of hers in the ancillary relief settlement; or

(b) by paying some or all of the spouse's living expenses, thus releasing more of the spouse's income for the maintenance of the first family, as in *Macey v Macey* [1981] 11 Fam Law 248 and *Re L (Minors) (Financial Provision)* [1979] 1 FLR 39. Similarly, where the payee spouse had a new partner, his income was relevant (*Suter v Suter and Jones* [1987] 2 FLR 232).

On the other hand, if the former spouse simply gives up work and elects to be kept by the new spouse or cohabitant, no order will be able to be made at all against either the former spouse or the new partner. In *Wynne v Wynne* [1981] 1 WLR 69; [1980] 3 All ER 659, the former husband was supported in great style in a luxurious flat in Knightsbridge, but being a 'kept man' could pay no order himself, nor could the new partner be asked to pay that particular expense for him had an order been made against him despite her willingness to pay for anything else he might desire.

It is impossible to compel a new partner to make any disclosure, even to establish what the ex-spouse might reasonably have access to financially. The only way to obtain such detail is to compel the respondent to the ancillary relief application (ie, the ex-spouse personally) to give such detail as he or she knows of the new partner's means in the respondent's own disclosure (or in response to a questionnaire: these are still allowed under the new ancillary relief regime (see Chapter 14)). Even a production appointment under r 2.62(7) of the FPR 1991 will not help unless the information is forthcoming through the respondent since this only enables an order to be made to compel a person who could have been compelled to produce a document in the course of the proceedings to do so at an earlier stage than the actual hearing (*Frary v Frary* [1993] 2 FLR 696).

12.4.2.5 Assets acquired after separation or divorce

These are *not* excluded as a resource especially if needed to do justice between the parties (see *Schuller v Schuller* [1990] 2 FLR 193, where the wife inherited a valuable flat from a wealthy friend after the marriage had ended).

12.4.2.6 The spouse's true earning capacity

The court is not deceived by disclosure alleging a tiny income where the lifestyle does not match, as happened in *J v J* [1955] 3 WLR 72; [1955] P 215, where the husband was a property developer living far beyond his apparent means, but actually declared a tiny taxable income. The order was based on his lifestyle and not on his apparent income.

The court is even quicker to do this where they realise that they are being deliberately deceived, as in *Newton v Newton* [1990] 1 FLR 33, where they eventually decided that nothing the millionaire husband said could be relied on and based their order on his lifestyle: he had made his case worse by suggesting that his 53 year old agoraphobic wife should 'pull herself together and get a job'. Sometimes respondents positively insult the court's intelligence as in the well known case of *Wachtel v Wachtel* [1973] 2 WLR 366; [1973] 1 All ER 829, where the husband's income was supposed to be £4,000 pa, but he actually spent £5,000 and was in fact accumulating savings. He came from a wealthy family and the court took the obviously sensible step in the circumstances of treating his income as at least £6,000.

Where the respondent is from a wealthy family, it is not necessary for there to be actual deceit of this kind before the court will take the view that family money is likely to be available and that the respondent could reasonably expect to tap into those funds even to make a lump sum payment to his wife as happened in *O'Donnell v O'Donnell* [1975] 3 WLR 308; [1975] 2 All ER 993 and the 1995 case of *Thomas* (see 12.4.2.1, above) to pay school fees.

The court adopts the same sceptical approach when measuring actual earnings, even if the level of actual earnings is demonstrably true, but where the spouse in question could and should be earning more. It is no good such a spouse taking a low paid or *pro bono* job with a charity or working from choice for a friend at subsistence level if a more suitable level of earnings is genuinely realisable, as is shown by *Hardy v Hardy* (above) (where the husband went to work for his father, a wealthy racehorse trainer, on a stable hand's wage of £70 per week – the court had no hesitation in making an order of £50 in favour of his wife and children on the basis of what he could really earn) and *McEwan v McEwan* [1972] 1 WLR 1217; [1972] 2 All ER 708 (where the husband was actually already retired at the age of 59 on a police pension of £6 per week, but the court still made an order of that amount on the basis that he could still earn something as well).

This attitude is not confined to immediate decisions on current earnings. In *Mitchell v Mitchell* [1984] FLR 387, CA, the court also took the view that the mother of a 13 year old daughter could return to work and raise a small mortgage when the girl left school so as to give the husband a bigger share of the matrimonial home when the house was sold on completion of the daughter's education. However, where a spouse has genuine difficulty finding work and is obviously not simply workshy, an order will *not* be made on the basis of earning capacity. In *Williams v Williams* [1974] 3 WLR 379; [1974] 3 All ER 377, the husband was made redundant and while the judge at first instance took the view that he must be wilfully on welfare benefits and so made a maintenance order based on what he should have been earning, this was reversed on appeal when the court was satisfied of the true position. Equally, the chances of a middle aged woman's returning to the employment market after several years absence are recognised as problematic (*M v M (Financial Provision)* [1987] 2 FLR 1).

12.4.2.7 Pensions

The new s 25B inserted into the MCA 1973 by s 166 of the Pensions Act 1995 and the new ss 21A and 24B inserted by the Welfare Reform and Pensions Act 1999 require the court to examine the parties' pension position for the purposes of s 25(2). Resources now include both existing and likely future pension benefits, so as to enable the court to consider whether an order should be made pursuant to the amendments to the MCA 1973 to require payment of part of the pension to the applicant spouse, either by 'attachment' or sharing. The court takes into account all the possibilities, including attaching death benefits and nominations which could be deployed in favour of the applicant.

12.5 THE COURT'S CONSIDERATIONS IN EXERCISING ITS DISCRETION (MCA 1973, s 25(2)(B)–(H))

Once the s 25(2)(a) resources are identified, and the parties know on what figures their negotiations will be based, suitable orders will be worked out in accordance with the remaining s 25 considerations. This means looking at s 25(2)(b) as qualified by ss 25(2)(c)–(h).

12.5.1 The parties' needs, obligations and responsibilities (MCA 1973, s 25(2)(b))

Under this head, the court looks at the parties' needs and obligations – all the basic categories such as food, clothes, housing and expenses in connection with the upbringing of the children, whose welfare will be the first consideration. Obviously common sense is helpful here – some regard will have to be had to a suitable lifestyle for each of the parties, and some sort of budget in keeping with that, in order to assess what 'needs' actually means in each case. In deciding what the needs are, the court usually has two (sometimes inconsistent) aims in view, namely both to maintain a residence for the custodial spouse and children and to divide the family assets fairly (especially the matrimonial home, which is usually the largest asset).

The prime need will usually be for a home for each party, but while the court does operate on a rule of thumb of 'homes for both', because of the contact with the non-resident parent that s 25(1) will require, the roof will obviously be especially important for the party who has care of the children. *Mesher v Mesher* [1980] 1 All ER 126, decided in 1975 (although not reported until 1980), was the first case in which the need of the wife and children to be housed, which precluded the sale which might otherwise have been ordered, led to a settlement of the matrimonial home to enable them to occupy it for as long as necessary and then for the proceeds to be divided later on the deferred sale.

This case, the origin of the term 'Mesher order' as a generic description for occupational settlement orders in relation to the matrimonial home, has led to many variations on the theme, such as the Harvey order (where instead of leaving at the end of the occupation period, the spouse in occupation pays to the other an occupational rent assessed at a fair market rate), and the Martin order (where the spouse in occupation, usually the wife, controls the date at which the home is ultimately sold since the trigger event is that of her remarriage, cohabitation, voluntary removal or even death).

Husbands can benefit from the court's policy of requiring that each party should, if possible, have a home, as in Calderbank v Calderbank [1975] 3 WLR 586; [1975] 3 All ER 721, where the husband was held to need a house in keeping with the lifestyle he had enjoyed during the marriage to a wealthy woman, in which to receive access visits by the children, and Browne v Pritchard [1975] 1 WLR 1366; [1975] 3 All ER 721, where the husband and children remained in the matrimonial home since the wife had a council house and the unemployed husband could not afford to buy out her share of the former home. These occupational orders have therefore established a principle that ownership of the matrimonial home is relatively unimportant: what matters is where everyone is going to live. Obligations to a second family must be fully taken into account, though extravagant expenditure when resources are limited will be ignored (Slater v Slater [1982] 3 FLR 364).

The reasonable needs of affluent parties may include a luxurious standard of living. In R v R (Financial Provision: Reasonable Needs) [1994] 2 FLR 1044, it was reasonable for a wife to remain in a 'superb Queen Anne style house' worth £1.3m, especially as the husband had moved with his mistress to one costing £2.7m. This is not a new principle, having already been identified in the older case of Leadbeater v Leadbeater [1985] FLR 789 where the wife of a wealthy man was adjudged able to return to some sort of work to contribute towards the lifestyle she wished to maintain.

12.5.1.1 Special situations

The court will also have to take into account any factors which increase needs or reduce ability to pay because of other obligations: the two most obvious and frequently occurring of these are special needs and second families. The reasonable needs of affluent parties may cover a luxurious standard of living (eg, Mrs Dart in Dart v Dart [1996] 2 FLR 286, CA, who was nevertheless discontented to receive only £10m as she had wanted at least $200m; Mrs Gojkovic in Gojkovic v Gojkovic [1990] Fam Law 100, who needed £1m to set up her own business; Mrs R in R v R (Financial Provision: Reasonable Needs) [1994] 2 FLR 1094, whose award of £1.9m was for a short time the largest reported award (though it was said that there were many higher unreported), although this was soon overtaken by Mrs F in F v F (Ancillary Relief: Substantial Assets) [1995] 2 FLR 45, whose needs were £9m pounds' worth comprising a house in London, a mansion in the country, a villa in Switzerland and £5m in cash). The Duxbury calculation, devised in Duxbury v Duxbury [1987] FLR 7, CA, can detail the precise sum required to produce any desired level of annual income for this type of applicant.

12.5.1.2 Special needs

Needs will obviously take account of special needs in a health or education sense, especially where this affects the children, as in Smith v Smith [1975] 2 All ER 19, where the wife had to do part time work as she looked after a daughter with a kidney complaint. As a result she had no job security and clearly would not be able to rehouse herself if the matrimonial home were sold and the proceeds divided, even if the daughter were to leave home. In the circumstances, the court transferred the home to her absolutely.

12.5.1.3 Second families

However, it is now established that the needs of second families are just as valid as those of the first family – there is no 'pecking order' as such (*Barnes v Barnes* [1972] 1 WLR 1381; [1972] 3 All ER 872). *Barnes* established that no one is entitled to throw the burden of maintaining a spouse and family onto the State; they are expected to work to support them if at all possible. This is sometimes called 'the rule in *Barnes v Barnes*'; the case also settled the principle that the obligation to a second wife and family does not rank second after that to a first wife and family, so that the subsequent obligations must be given the same weight as any other responsibilities. *Stockford v Stockford* [1982] 3 FLR 52 and *Furniss v Furniss* [1982] 3 FLR 46 were both decided on the basis of this principle and resulted in the first wife coming off worse in her claim for what money there was since she, being alone and without a waged partner, could rely on welfare benefits if unable to work, while the new wife, having both a partner in work and younger children, was unable either to fall back on social security or to work herself.

These decisions have been followed more recently in *Delaney v Delaney* [1990] 2 FLR 457, where the judge, in justifying a similar decision, expressly invoked the principle that it is now recognised that 'there is life after divorce', although extravagant expenditure may be ignored (see *Slater v Slater* [1982] 3 FLR 364, where the court disapproved of a husband who had chosen to live in a country house with consequently high maintenance and transport costs).

12.5.2 The standard of living prior to the marriage breakdown (MCA 1973, s 25(2)(c))

This requires the court to consider how the parties lived during the marriage and is responsible for some of the apparently very generous orders in recent high value divorces.

Obviously, wealthier families may suffer no drop as in *Calderbank v Calderbank* (above), where the husband was able to maintain his previous lifestyle on the basis that the children would expect it when they visited him, and *Foley v Foley* [1981] 3 WLR 284; [1981] 2 All ER 857, where the wife had to be financed to maintain her lifestyle on a par with that to which she had become accustomed, including buying a house with a bit of land so as not to lower her usual standard of living.

The very wealthy husband usually benefits from this principle by invoking it in the form usually known as the 'millionaire's defence', in which it is claimed that a detailed account of such a husband's assets is not required to be sworn in an affidavit of means because the husband in question is so wealthy that he can easily meet any order the court might reasonably make based on the parties' marital lifestyle. This happened in *Thyssen-Bornemisza v Thyssen-Bornemisza (No 2)* [1985] FLR 1069, where the wife's request for full details of her husband's assets (so she could be sure she was getting a large enough settlement) was refused by the court since the standard of living criteria in s 25(2)(c) meant that they only had to provide for her needs in preserving her usual lifestyle, for which it was not necessary to put the husband to more expense in preparing financial detail than was actually required to satisfy the court that he had the means to pay the order made. It is questionable whether post-*White* the millionaire's defence is still available as the court must now check their s 25 based award against 'the yardstick of equality'. It would appear that a greater forensic search in relation to wealth and contribution is occurring. While the new Civil Procedure Rules which govern the remainder of civil litigation in the post-Woolf reforms era do not apply to family law, their philosophy of 'the overriding objective' (of dealing with cases swiftly and avoiding disproportionate expense and delay) is specifically reflected in the new Ancillary Relief Procedure (see Chapter 14).

Section 25(2)(c) will *not* be relevant where the marriage has been short and childless. In *Attar v Attar (No 2)* [1985] FLR 653, an air hostess who had been married to a wealthy Saudi Arabian with disclosed assets of £2m received only a lump sum equivalent to two years' pay at the rate of her former salary to enable her to readjust to the end of her marriage and dependence on the husband.

Low and middle income families tend, however, to have difficulty in sustaining the former lifestyle, although the court tries to leave the parties on similar standards of living so the drop is shared equally as in *Scott v Scott* [1982] 1 WLR 723; [1978] 3 All ER 65.

Where there is a dispute as to the appropriate standard of living (as in *Preston v Preston* [1981] 3 WLR 619; [1982] 1 All ER 41, where the wife had managed on a very small amount of money while the husband was building up the business on which they lived), the payee spouse is not expected to settle for the minimum level but can insist on a less frugal amount reflecting how the parties lived once their life had become more prosperous.

Nevertheless, sight should not be lost of the post-1984 goal of making the parties self-sufficient where that is possible (see *per* Ward J in *B v B* [1990] 1 FLR 20, p 26).

12.5.3 Age of the parties and duration of the marriage (MCA 1973, s 25(2)(d))

There is a clear recognition of the relevance of a spouse's non-financial contributions as well as of the realities of life. For example, a wife's age will clearly be relevant to her earning capacity (and therefore also to the clean break potential) and a husband's will be relevant to his retirement and ability to pay an order, whereas the duration of the marriage (which normally excludes any period of prior cohabitation) will be some guide to the contribution which the parties have both made to the relationship and which should be recognised in distributing the assets. It will thus be seen that the ages of the parties and the duration of the marriage in putting together a suitable ancillary relief package has nothing to do with the *merits* of the case and everything to do with the capability of the financially weaker spouse (usually the wife) to work and be self-sufficient following the divorce.

A v A (Elderly Applicant: Lump Sum) [1999] 2 FLR 969 shows how important the court's discretion is in cases of long marriage and older parties. Here, there was a 79 year old husband and a 76 year old wife, and a marriage of 43 years, with two adult children. Both parties had worked during the marriage; the wife had £1.034m including £750,000 in the bank, and the husband £61,000. A *Duxbury* calculation to produce an adequate income for his life expectancy would have given him a lesser lump sum than the length of the marriage and his contributions over the years appeared to warrant, and Singer J both rejected the wife's claim that a *Duxbury* fund of £87,000 would be sufficient and reduced the award at first instance of £389,000 to £350,000 to provide for his reasonable needs while reflecting the husband's contribution over 43 years.

An older wife who married in the tradition of non-working wives and mothers is less likely to be expected to work (and retrain if her skills are outdated or she has never had commercial skills or an employment history) than a younger one who has grown up used to the culture of working wives and mothers. Moreover, a younger wife who can work can raise a mortgage, whereas an older one with less earning capacity may not be able to.

Cohabitation before marriage is not normally relevant in calculating the length of a marriage, although in an exceptional case it may be, because of the difference recognised between formal commitment to marriage and the more flexible state of cohabitation, a difference emphasised in *Campbell v Campbell* [1976] 3 WLR 572; [1977] 1 All ER 1, where it was expressly noted that the obligations of marriage begin only after the ceremony, despite the fact that the marriage in that case was of only two years' duration, while it followed cohabitation of three and a half years. Cohabitation after marriage breakdown may or may not be a similar situation: see the overseas case of *Hewitson v Hewitson* [1995] 1 FLR 241, CA. Here, there had been a divorce and clean break financial settlement in California, after which the parties had resumed cohabitation and then separated again. The wife then sought an order in England based on the renewed cohabitation, but the court would not allow her 'two bites of the one cherry' as this meant acting as a court of appeal from the foreign jurisdiction. On the other hand, in *S v S (Financial Provision) (Post-Divorce Cohabitation)* [1994] 2 FLR 228, the 1977 consent order on the parties' divorce was set aside when they separated again in 1993 on the basis that the resumption of cohabitation had destroyed the fundamental assumptions on which it had been made.

This case has, with one notable exception, set the tone for subsequent decisions such as *H v H* [1981] 2 FLR 392, where the same approach was taken in respect of a marriage of seven weeks following on and off cohabitation of six years and the wife received only a small lump sum to enable her to adjust to the change in her circumstances. Similar principles were applied in *Foley v Foley* [1981] 3 WLR 284; [1981] 2 All ER 857, where the marriage was five years and the cohabitation seven – although as there were three children some small weight was given to the cohabitation by considering this to be part of 'all the circumstances of the case' under the general duty pursuant to s 25(1). In *Day v Day* [1988] 1 FLR 278, already considered in other contexts, the marriage was six weeks and the cohabitation four years. Moreover, in *Leadbeater v Leadbeater* [1985] FLR 789, Balcombe LJ, in restating the principle, defined a short marriage as anything less than about four and a half to five years.

The notable exception was *Kokosinski v Kokosinski* [1980] 3 WLR 55; [1980] 1 All ER 1106, where the marriage was extremely short but the period of cohabitation 22 years, and the wife, unable to marry the husband throughout almost the entire 22 year period because he was not free to do so, changed her name by deed poll, helped the husband in his business, bore him a son and, as the court specifically noted, gave him the best years of her life. Exceptionally, she received a large lump sum to enable her to buy a flat near her work.

However, more recently there has been a detectable tendency at least to look carefully at any period of cohabitation before deciding not to take it into account, and in *B v B* [1995] 1 FLR 9 Thorpe J specifically recognised the reality of the increase in pre-marriage cohabitation as a relevant factor. Were this approach to be adopted more generally it might effect a significant change in the law on this point.

Care should obviously be taken to obtain compensation, whatever the length of the marriage, where a spouse has given up a lot to marry in the first place and has lost out as a result (eg, a good job, a business opportunity or a residential tenancy as in *L v L* (above)). In the case of a short marriage this might not be a large sum in relation to the payer's assets, as in *Attar v Attar (No 2)* [1985] FLR 653. This *pro rata* approach is likely to be wrong, however, if there is a child, as the burden of the child's dependence is likely to cancel out the shortness of the marriage, and once more require an assessment of needs (see *C v C (Financial Relief: Short Marriage)* [1997] 2 FLR 26, CA).

12.5.4 Physical or mental disability of either party (MCA 1973, s 25(2)(e))

This is clearly relevant to earning capacity and capabilities generally. Such considerations will usually immediately identify themselves as in *Jones v Jones* [1975] 2 WLR 606; [1975] 2 All ER 12, the case already considered in another context of the wife injured by the husband's knife attack who could not continue to work as a nurse; *B v B* [1982] 12 Fam Law 92, where the wife needed extra money for her expenses since she had multiple sclerosis; and *Newton v Newton* [1990] 1 FLR 33, where the wife had serious physical and psychological difficulties which required a regular companion and help with transport.

Sakkass v Sakkass [1987] 2 FLR 398 was a similar case where the husband had multiple sclerosis, and the court felt that there had to be a *Mesher* order to enable the wife and children to remain in the home. In this case, however, the court could not decide on the eventual shares of the proceeds on sale until there was up to date information on the husband's condition because his future needs could not be properly determined at the time the house fell to be sold. This type of case may require an adjournment while the true position is ascertained.

12.5.5 The past, present and future contributions (financial and other) made or to be made to the welfare of the family by each of the parties (MCA 1973, s 25(2)(f))

Contribution to be considered here may be either positive or negative, and this paragraph has been the most significant of any provision in securing adequate recognition of the contribution of unwaged spouses who remain at home to care for the home and family. This contribution has been immortalised in such cases as *Vicary v Vicary* [1992] Fam Law 429 in judicial comments such as 'the wife had supplied the infrastructure and support in the context of which the husband was able to prosper and accumulate wealth'.

Wachtel v Wachtel [1973] 2 WLR 366; [1973] 1 All ER 829 is still good law on the value of the wife's unpaid work in homemaking and childcare as being every bit as deserving of recognition in money terms as the husband's in going out to work to earn a living for the family as a whole.

As Lord Denning said in that case, the wife contributes in kind to enable the husband to acquire assets for both parties, and the value of the wife's work in this area is clearly demonstrated merely by costing the price of hiring help to do the domestic work which she undertakes for the benefit of both spouses and the children.

The value of this contribution as an item in itself which earns the right to compensation is similar to a golden handshake on termination of employment after a lengthy period of service, and is quite independent of the need to maintain the spouse who has made that contribution. This is demonstrated by cases like *Smith v Smith (Smith Intervening)* [1991] 2 All ER 306; [1991] 2 FLR 432, where the wife committed suicide six months after an order was made giving her a substantial capital sum, and although the court rescinded the part of the order which represented capitalised maintenance payments, for which being dead she no longer had either a need or a right, it did not disturb that part of the order which represented recognition of her contribution over a 30 year marriage, and that sum survived for her estate.

A husband is equal before the court in this respect. In *B v B* [1982] 12 Fam Law 92, already considered above, the wife came from a wealthy family but the husband had worked hard to achieve success independently, had kept the family together despite the demands of his work, and on divorce obtained custody of one of the children. It was held that he was in the same position as a wife in similar circumstances who did not legally own the bulk of the family assets.

Contributions to the success of a business also count under this head, such as in *O'Donnell v O'Donnell* and *Gojkovic v Gojkovic*, already discussed above in other contexts, and this is especially so where a business in which the wife's hard work and willingness to turn her hands to everything has paid off so as to make the business profitable just at the time that the divorce occurred. Both the above cases involved hotels where initially the wives had given unfailing support, undertaking long hours of menial work to get the business off to a good start. There will usually be a similar approach where the spouses have endured some financial hardship in order to help initially struggling businesses, as in *Kokosinski* and *Preston*. Moreover, *Trippas v Trippas* [1973] 2 WLR 585; [1973] 2 All ER 1 shows that in appropriate circumstances mere moral support without actual work will be enough to establish a spouse's right to a share in the proceeds if there has been a promise to that effect that the court can oblige the other spouse to honour. In *Conran v Conran* [1997] 2 FLR 615, the high profile journalist wife's reasonable needs were supplemented by an extra award for her outstanding contributions over 30 years to the development of the Conran furniture and restaurant businesses.

Negative contribution under this head can be a way of recording due debit for less than supportive behaviour which does not amount to conduct under s 25(2)(g), as in *West v West* [1977] 2 WLR 933; [1977] 2 All ER 705, where the wife would not even set up house with the husband, but insisted on remaining with her parents, where she stayed with the children, for which lack of ordinary marital commitment she not surprisingly received a reduced maintenance order.

However, as always, the spouse who can show that any such reduction will not be in the interests of the children, whose welfare is required by s 25(1) to be given first consideration, can probably wriggle out of any adverse result that might otherwise be meted out under this section, as in the case of the appalling wife in *E v E* [1990] 2 FLR 233. Her extravagance and adultery, neglect of the children and walking out on the husband not only amazingly did not amount to conduct within the meaning of s 25(2)(g) but also failed to attract any reduction in maintenance despite the negative contribution this portfolio of shortcomings undoubtedly constituted. The court, while entirely agreeing about the negative aspect of such a contribution to the misfortunes of the family, had to conclude that leaving her in financial difficulties or even in severely reduced circumstances would not be in the children's interests, so she ended up with a large lump sum on a clean break. (Neither life nor the law of divorce purports always to be *fair*.)

Contribution and conduct appear to be on the opposite sides of the same coin, as has appeared in the more recent case of *Piglowska v Piglowski* [1999] 1 WLR 1360; [1999] 2 FLR 763. The parties actually spent their entire assets of £128,000 on the ancillary relief litigation, only to have the House of Lords uphold the assessment of the district judge at first instance who had concluded that the wife's contribution was such that she should have the lion's share of the limited assets, especially as the husband had left her to live in Poland with another woman before returning to claim a share of their matrimonial assets in order to buy a house in England.

However, the House of Lords did not take the opportunity of the recent appeal to examine the relationship between contribution and conduct which is clearly relevant, while the impact of s 25(2)(g) (below) is that conduct as such is not relevant except in very exceptional circumstances. Lord Hoffmann merely referred to 'value judgments' that had to be made in such cases 'on which reasonable people might differ', but like Lord Nicholls in *White* appeared to be sticking firmly to the remainder of s 25 without offering any illuminating guidance to the profession. The subsequent cases of *Cowan v Cowan* [2001] 2 FLR 192, and *L v L* [2002] EWCA Civ 1685 have, however, refined and debated the issue of contributions.

Contributions should usually be made over at least an average length marriage, in other words one that has lasted at least the four and a half to five years envisaged by Balcombe LJ in *Leadbeater* (see 12.5.1, above), but *Cumbers v Cumbers* [1975] 1 All ER 1; [1974] 1 WLR 1331 makes clear that such contributions if sufficiently significant will still be counted even in a short marriage, as it is the quality of the contribution *per se* which is relevant. Nevertheless, *Kokosinski* type cases apart, contributions usually need to be made during marriage and not during periods of cohabitation.

12.5.6 Conduct (MCA 1973, s 25(2)(g))

The wording of paragraph (g) requires the court to take into account any conduct of either of the parties which in their opinion it would be 'inequitable to disregard'. This means exactly what it says and no other extraneous descriptions or terminology need to be imported into the definition. Moreover, the trend in modern divorce law is to *disregard* conduct *unless* it is shown that it is or may be inequitable (unfair overall) not to take it into account because, as was stated in *Duxbury v Duxbury* (already mentioned above in another context), the application of s 25 is a financial and not a moral exercise (see also *Wachtel v Wachtel* [1973] Fam 72, CA). Consideration of 'conduct' is another opportunity to look at the extraordinary case of *Leadbeater v Leadbeater* [1985] FLR 789, where there was the most spectacular bad conduct on both sides, so much so that the unfortunate judge,

Balcombe J, could not avoid concluding that they were as bad as each other, so that he might as well disregard conduct altogether.

In any case, as was expressly recognised in *Vasey v Vasey* [1985] FLR 596, it is very difficult to discern what goes on in other people's marriages, an approach which has led to the essentially non-judgmental approach that is now felt appropriate, a distinct shift in both the general emphasis and the burden of proof in the matter which should be noted. This can initially be traced back to the decision in *Wachtel*, where the general non-relevance of conduct was first established, further to be refined in subsequent cases.

The overall result is that if conduct is going to be relevant at all it will have no relation to any ordinary considerations of morality, so one should abandon all 'normal' preconceptions in this regard, since in practice the conduct in question will need to be so appalling that it simply cannot be ignored. The following are (non-exhaustive) examples:

(1) *Murder and conspiracy to murder* will always qualify, as in *Evans v Evans* [1989] 1 FLR 351 (where the husband having regularly paid maintenance for 32 years was the victim of a plot by his wife and another to kill him – her maintenance order was discharged). Encouragement of suicide is in the same category as was held in *Kyte v Kyte* [1987] 3 All ER 1041, where the wife deceitfully set about ridding herself of the husband in order to set up house with another man, divorcing him for his behaviour as an unpredictable suicidal manic depressive, and obtaining an injunction to get him out of the house, and in the process lied to the court about her relationship with the other man. She had done everything she could to facilitate his demise in order to benefit from his estate: not even by taking his own conduct into account could the court possibly consider hers anything but inequitable to disregard.

(2) *Some violence* will be sufficient, depending on the frequency, nature and/or degree, especially if a weapon is used – such as in *Armstrong v Armstrong* (1974) 118 SJ 579, where the wife fired a gun at the husband; and *Bateman v Bateman* [1979] 2 WLR 377, where the wife stabbed the husband twice – and also especially if such conduct has financial consequences, as in the knife injuries to the wife which put an end to her nursing career and got the husband three years' imprisonment in *Jones v Jones* [1975] 2 WLR 606.

(3) *Financial irresponsibility* will generally be sufficient because it is directly relevant to financial orders (*Black v Black* [1995] 2 FLR 160). This is especially so where assets have been dissipated, as in *Martin v Martin* [1976] 2 WLR 901; [1976] 3 All ER 625, where the entire £33,000 lost by the husband in a string of unsuccessful business ventures set up with his mistress was counted as his share of the assets that he had already had, leaving the rest for his wife subject only to paying off his mortgage and giving him a small lump sum. Similarly, in the 1988 case of *Day v Day*, where the husband encouraged the wife to build up rent arrears so that money could be spent on other things, this qualified as conduct: even less serious financial irresponsibility as in *Suter v Suter and Jones* (another case already mentioned earlier, where the court looked askance on the young wife inviting her lover to live in her home without asking him to contribute to the household budget) was capable of amounting to conduct within the meaning of the section.

(4) *Misleading the court in financial matters*, especially deliberately, as in *Kyte* (above) and *B v B (Real Property: Assessment of Interests)* [1988] 2 FLR 490, is always sufficient conduct, as well as separately qualifying as contempt of court.

(5) *Alcoholism and laziness* if severe will in theory be relevant, again because of the direct effect on financial matters, but as in *Martin*, see above, tend not to deprive the culprit entirely of financial relief for the simple reason that a home will still have to be provided. This happened in *K v K* [1990] Fam Law 19; [1990] 2 FLR 225 where despite the husband's behaviour after being made redundant, as a result of which the matrimonial home had had to be sold, and which contrasted sharply with the wife's energy and industry which had resulted in a well paid job and a flat of her own, the court had to award him 60% of the proceeds of the home as this was the minimum he needed to rehouse himself. The court did, however, turn down his cheeky claim for maintenance from the wife.

(6) *Leaving the blameless spouse/being the sole cause of the breakdown* may carry some weight, but this will still tend to be reflected in the court's making an order at the lower end of a scale rather than in distinctly down-rating the award, and/or in the court's taking some care to try to see that the blameless spouse whose life has been disrupted is left as comfortable as possible. Nevertheless, in the relatively recent cases of *Robinson v Robinson* [1983] 2 WLR 146; [1983] 1 All ER 391; and *Ibbetson v Ibbetson* [1984] FLR 545 where the respondent wives could give no explanation for their actions their orders were reduced.

It should be noted that deliberately committing bigamy is conduct, and will preclude ancillary relief because the marriage could not possibly have been thought to be valid (*Whiston v Whiston* [1995] 3 WLR 405; [1995] 2 FLR 268, CA). Knowingly contracting an invalid marriage as a transsexual is obviously in the same category (*J v S-T (Formerly J)* (1996) *The Times*, 25 November, CA). Also, blatant marital, financial and litigation misconduct will be reflected in quantum, as, for example, in *Clarke v Clarke* [1999] 2 FLR 498, a notorious case in which the wife, in her 40s and in debt, ill treated her 80 year old husband over a marriage of six years, but never consummated the marriage during which she lived with her lover in the matrimonial home while making her husband live in a caravan in the garden. The wife nevertheless extracted large sums from the husband, who had assets in excess of £3m, lost money in speculative ventures after he paid off her debts, transferred his share portfolio to her and bought her several properties. On appeal, her first instance award of £552,500 was reduced to £125,000 and she was allowed to keep assets of £50,000.

Adultery alone is *never* sufficient, although really repugnant sexual behaviour will be (as in *Bailey v Tolliday* [1983] 4 FLR 542, where the wife had an affair with her father in law, and *Dixon v Dixon* [1974] 6 Fam Law 58, where the husband committed adultery with his daughter in law in the matrimonial home).

Moreover, if the adultery is coupled with some other generally gratuitous and anti-social behaviour it will count as conduct, as happened in *Cuzner v Underdown* [1974] 1 WLR 641; [1974] 2 All ER 357. The wife conducted an adulterous affair during the marriage, said nothing about it when the husband generously transferred their home (to which she had contributed nothing) into joint names and then applied for an order for sale so as to raise money to set up house with her lover, of which the court took a poor view.

Furthermore, what used to be called 'living in sin' – cohabitation with a new partner after separation from the spouse – is certainly not conduct within the meaning of s 25(2)(g) even if as in the *Duxbury* case both parties had had affairs during the marriage as well, and even though in *Atkinson v Atkinson* [1987] 3 All ER 849, such cohabitation following a decree absolute, but without remarriage, was found to be financially motivated. The most effect which such cohabitation will therefore have in financial terms is that the live-in lover will be expected to contribute to the ex-spouse's budget *if s/he can afford to do so*, but in the case of Mrs Atkinson the court was not even able to make an order on the basis that some such contribution would be made, because Mrs Atkinson's new man was so financially ineffectual that according to the court she needed her continuing maintenance even more because she was cohabiting.

Good conduct is of course as relevant under s 25(2)(g) as bad conduct, as *Kokosinski* (see above at 12.5.3) shows.

Where there are allegations of conduct, transfer for hearing by a High Court judge may be ordered (*Practice Direction* [1992] 3 All ER 151).

12.5.7 The value of any benefit lost on the dissolution of the marriage (MCA 1973, s 25(2)(h))

This paragraph requires the court to consider the value of any such benefit lost – in the past this was usually, but not exclusively, pension rights – and to award compensation. If such compensation was impossible there might have been a successful s 5 defence (see Chapter 10), or the applicant (if a respondent to a Fact D petition) may have been able to use s 10 to hold up decree absolute until financial provision was satisfactory.

The wording of s 25(2)(h) can still cover any benefit which is lost on dissolution of the marriage, although pension rights, which can now also be dealt with pursuant to the specific amendments to s 25, have always been the most likely losses for consideration under this head. However, despite the 'earmarking' provisions of the Pensions Act 1995, still preserved after the Welfare Reform and Pensions Act 1999's sharing provisions as an attachment order, there may still be financial benefits lost if the husband retires early or dies, as in *Milne v Milne* [1981] 2 FLR 286, where the husband therefore had to pay the wife the anticipated sum involved immediately. Except in the few cases where pension rights can already be split, as in the case of company schemes (like that in *Brooks v Brooks*) which can be varied under s 24, it is still incumbent on any solicitor acting in ancillary relief to obtain an actuarial valuation of the pension and to seek a lump sum in compensation if attachment or splitting pursuant to the new provisions is not suitable, since in such a case it may still be possible to achieve some compensation under this section.

In any event the value of the pension rights must be considered and the best recompense obtained for their value as well as for any other loss quantifiable under s 25(2)(h), such as in *Trippas*, where the court compelled the husband to pay the wife the share of the profits of the business in which she had been supportive, simply because he had promised she would eventually receive such a share.

12.6 THE CLEAN BREAK (MCA 1973, s 25A)

Making use of the range of orders available under ss 23 and 24 of the MCA 1973 must always be subject to the provisions of s 25A, only formally inserted into the MCA 1973 by the Matrimonial and Family Proceedings Act 1984, but prior to that already common practice in putting together ancillary relief packages. The practical result is that the court must weigh up whether there should be no periodical payments in the financial package (ie, a clean break) or substantive or nominal periodical payments (ie, continuing spousal financial interdependence), or whether any periodical payments that they consider must be ordered should be for a limited term so as to provide a deferred clean break (eg, because a solely capital package is impossible for the time being). The only difference made by the Matrimonial and Family Proceedings Act 1984 was that prior to the insertion of s 25A the court could not actually *impose* a clean break unless the parties themselves were willing to have one: now, whenever the court is making s 23 or s 24 orders, it can and does, such power being given by s 25A(1), (2) and (3) in the following manner.

12.6.1 Matrimonial Causes Act 1973, s 25A(1)

By s 25A(1), when exercising its powers under ss 23 or 24:

> ... it shall be the duty of the court to consider whether it would be appropriate so to exercise those powers that the financial obligations of each party towards the other should be terminated as soon after the grant of the decree as the court considers just and reasonable.

This is the general duty of the court to consider a clean break in general terms in every case, but not to impose one regardless unless that is suitable.

The importance of this point was emphasised in *Clutton v Clutton* [1991] 1 All ER 340, CA, where a wife's clean break order was cancelled on appeal because it transferred the matrimonial home absolutely to her in return for cancelling her maintenance order, which the court thought unnecessary for the following reasons.

First, it unjustly deprived the husband of his share of the matrimonial home acquired by their joint efforts, and that was in itself not even necessary since all that was required was an occupation order for the wife and the one child remaining at home, until she either remarried, cohabited or died.

Secondly, the court went on to say that if it was desired to achieve a clean break that could still be done, and much more fairly, by a *Martin* order, which would enable the house to be sold and the proceeds divided in the proportion of one third to the husband and two thirds to the wife, with the sale postponed until one of the triggering events occurred. As Lloyd LJ said, this solution, providing in effect 'a charge which does not take effect until death or remarriage which could only be said to offend against the principle of the clean break in the most extended sense of the term', is often acceptable and practical where a clean break is possible. Following *White v White* [2000] 2 FLR 381, it may be that there will be a marked emphasis on this approach, and a rejection of clean breaks, in order to do justice between the parties in favour of the husband.

12.6.2 Matrimonial Causes Act 1973, s 25A(2)

By s 25A(2), when making any periodical payments orders under s 23:

> ... the court shall in particular consider whether it would be appropriate to require those payments to be made or secured only for such term as would in the opinion of the court be sufficient to enable the party in whose favour the order is made to adjust without undue hardship to the termination of his or her financial dependence on the other party.

This is the section which requires the court to consider *limited term periodical payments*, though again to impose them only if appropriate, as part of an ancillary relief package.

12.6.3 Matrimonial Causes Act 1973, s 25A(3)

By s 25A(3), again when hearing any application for a periodical payments order under s 23:

> ... if the court considers that no continuing obligation should be imposed on either party to make or secure periodical payments in favour of the other, the court may dismiss the application with a direction that the applicant shall not be entitled to make any further application in relation to that marriage for an order under s 23(1)(a) or (b), above.

This is the section which empowers the court not only either to dismiss an application for periodical payments outright instead of setting a limit on the period for which they should be paid under s 25A(2), but also to direct that no further application should be made, either at all or to extend a limited term imposed under s 25A(2), and also to exclude future applications under the Inheritance (Provision for Families and Dependants) Act 1975.

12.6.4 Orders that can be made under the Matrimonial Causes Act 1973, ss 23 and 25A

Thus the three sub-sections of s 25A give the court wide and flexible powers either to approve what the parties have agreed themselves or to impose suitable terms if the parties cannot agree. Circumstances will dictate whether s 25A will be applicable at all and if so which precise type of order it will be most suitable to make. Orders may be made in the following forms.

12.6.4.1 Open ended periodical payments order: s 23

This is the simplest order, under s 23, ie an order for the amount of maintenance assessed as required by the payee, payable by periodical payments where the payer must apply to decrease or terminate the payments, or they continue indefinitely at the rate originally ordered, unless or until the payee applies because of a change of circumstances to increase the amount originally ordered. This is sometimes called a 'substantive' order, as opposed to a 'nominal' order (as to which see below). There is obviously no application of s 25A here.

12.6.4.2 Nominal periodical payments order: s 23

This is an open ended order, similar to that under 12.6.4.1, above, but for a *nominal* amount of maintenance, usually 5p or £1 per annum, which is meant only to indicate the payee's *continuing right* to maintenance, providing a long stop in case of future need for a substantive order. An example would be to protect the children if their mother loses her job, rather than the maintenance actually being needed as financial support at the time the order is made. It will continue in the same way as an ordinary open ended order unless terminated by the court.

Nominal periodical payments must be distinguished from 'small' periodical payments, which used to have a technical meaning, being paid (when maintenance was not tax free in the hand of the recipient) gross and without deduction of tax. Nowadays if anyone mentions 'small' periodical payments (although they will manifestly be for a small amount, probably for the good reason that the payee is cash restricted for the time being, but it is thought right to collect some contribution on principle), such orders will be for something other than 'nominal' amounts (ie, perhaps £10 per week, but not 5p per annum). However 'small', these periodical payments are only a sub-species of open ended periodical payments if not specifically expressed in the accepted nominal format.

However, neither open ended nor nominal periodical payments are compatible with a clean break because they continue the dependent financial link between the parties.

12.6.4.3 Fixed term periodical payments with power to extend the fixed term: s 25A(1) and (2)

This is the order contemplated by the philosophy of spousal self-sufficiency introduced in 1984 and is the only type of periodical payments order which can co-exist with a clean break, because it only preserves the dependent financial links between the parties for a strictly limited period. This will remain the case even if that period is subsequently extended by the court, since if limited term periodical payments were thought suitable in the first place such extension will not be granted lightly. Where limited term periodical payments are used there will be what is called a 'deferred clean break'.

It will depend on all the circumstances of the case whether there should be open ended or nominal periodical payments (ie, no clean break) or a clean break (ie, no periodical payments at all for the weaker spouse, since periodical payments may still of course be paid to the *children* without affecting a clean break between the *parties*). However, the important point to appreciate is which orders are *compatible* with a clean break and which are not, and then to decide whether or not a clean break is even feasible, which in turn will depend on whether the spouse who is financially weaker is capable of an independent financial existence without receiving regular maintenance from the other. Such independence may be achieved in a variety of ways.

The payee must apply to the court for variation under s 31 to extend the period of payment *before* expiry, unless there has been a direction that this is not permitted, otherwise the payments end at the end of the fixed term originally ordered.

12.6.4.4 Outright dismissal: s 25A(3)

This is the 'sudden death' tool for ending all claims by one spouse against the other, in life and in death, and is only appropriate as a clean break.

12.6.4.5 Lump sum order: s 23

Under s 23, a lump sum order can be made freely whether or not there is to be a clean break, since this is a once and for all payment, the only restriction being that only *one* lump sum order can be made per spouse. Thus, if lump sums are required for various different purposes, they must all be totted up and one global figure inserted into the order (see 12.3.2, above).

12.7 CLEAN BREAK OPTIONS

As may be seen in *Suter v Suter and Jones* [1987] 2 All ER 336, the existence of children does not necessarily preclude a clean break between the spouses, though a nominal order may be more suitable, as in *Day v Day* (already mentioned in another context). Generally there will be no clean break where there are children and the wife is unable or otherwise ill equipped to work, unless there is capital which could provide an alternative method of effecting a clean break, as in cases such as *Duxbury* where a sufficient sum of capital can be invested to provide an annual income that would otherwise have to be provided by the periodical payments which would preclude the desired clean break. There may be the same problem with older couples, where the wife's health and job prospects may be uncertain, as in *Scallon v Scallon* [1990] 1 FLR 193.

The clean break is therefore likely to be more suitable for short, childless marriage cases or those where there is sufficient money to provide the wife with capital.

If, however, there is to be a clean break, what is the most suitable way of dealing with a spouse's periodical payments orders? The two possibilities are:

* limited term periodical payments; or
* outright dismissal.

12.7.1 Fixed term periodical payments

Periodical payments on a temporary basis, but for a fixed term rather than an indefinite period, will be suitable where a spouse has or will have a recognisable earning capacity, and although unable to realise it immediately (eg, because of domestic responsibilities) can reasonably certainly be expected to be able to do so within the foreseeable future.

The type of case where this might apply would include that of the wife in *Mitchell v Mitchell* (see above) (where the trained secretary could be expected to earn a good salary once her daughter, who was 13 at the time of the divorce, had left school), and also any wife able to go back to work as soon as she has found a job using existing and recently used training and/or experience, such as the air hostess in *Attar v Attar* (although in her particular case, as she had no children, she received her two years' maintenance all at once in the capitalised form of a lump sum, which will always be preferable to limited term maintenance if there are no children).

Fixed term periodical payments would also suit any wife who embarks on a retraining course, or could be re-employed if she did (as in the case of Mrs Leadbeater (above), who although 47 and out of touch with modern methods had been a secretary before the marriage), since in all such retraining cases there are reasonable prospects of obtaining a job without difficulty either at the end of the course or within a reasonable period afterwards.

Sometimes the court expects the limited term to end as soon as children are at boarding school, as in *Evans v Evans* [1990] 2 All ER 147, where the wife was already a trained secretary, and *CB v CB* [1988] Fam Law 471, where the wife had capital of her own but no income and the court awarded limited term periodical payments only until the youngest child was 18 while she sorted out some other source of income. In both cases the order was clearly influenced by the acrimony and bitterness with which the divorce had been conducted obviously thus making a clean break desirable as soon as possible. Sometimes the limited term will be staged as in *C v C* [1989] 1 FLR 11, where there was an order for £10,000 for two years, then £5,000 for two years, then ending with dismissal of the payee spouse's claim.

The key to the use of limited term periodical payments is therefore *reasonable certainty* about the payee's future plans and prospects of employment. Limited term periodical payments are thus not suitable for older wives who cannot be employed or re-employed and who cannot therefore be expected to adjust to the absence of maintenance even after a generous term to allow for gradual change. Examples of such cases are those of *Morris v Morris* [1985] FLR 1176, where the wife was already 56; and *M v M* [1987] 2 FLR 1, where the 47 year old wife had only worked part time during the marriage and having lost her husband's pension rights on divorce would have been too much at risk at the end of the limited term, while the husband remained secure on his pension; it was accepted therefore that no s 25A(2) order could be made.

Other cases where limited term maintenance under s 25A(2) will be no more suitable than an immediate clean break under s 25A(1) is where there are young children, as in *Suter v Suter and Jones*, or where there are children, an older wife *and* uncertainty about job prospects, which all came together in *Barrett v Barrett* [1988] 2 FLR 516. Here the wife was age 44, without work experience and therefore of course also without a pension, and there were three children, including one still at home, after a 20 year marriage. In such cases the right approach is that the husband should pay ordinary open ended periodical payments (and apply later to vary them if and when the wife gets work) or if she is willing to have a go at earning her own living that there should be a nominal order (which can then either be dismissed if she becomes independent or varied upwards to a substantive order if her attempts at financial independence fail).

The court is cautious about limiting the right to apply for an extension of a limited term maintenance order and do not like to do so if there is any chance that an extension will be needed, as is shown by *Waterman v Waterman* [1989] 1 FLR 380, where a wife with one young child appealed both against a five year limited term order following a short marriage of one year and against the restriction on applying to extend the five year term in appropriate circumstances. The appeal court did in fact confirm the five year limited term, but said there was no justification to exclude the wife's application to extend the limited term after the initial five years which she might need to do if circumstances changed. Thus it will only be in the clearest of cases that such a final cut off as excluding the right to apply to extend the limited term would be ordered, and if an application is made to extend before the end of the term the court can grant a further term, though they will take into account the reasons for the original order to limit the term (*Richardson v Richardson (No 2)* [1994] 2 FLR 1051).

12.7.2 Outright dismissal

This will only be suitable if the weaker spouse has a sufficient alternative source of income and does not need the transitional assistance of limited term maintenance. It will thus be suitable for wives who are going to remarry within a short period, wives who already earn a good income themselves, and wives who are to receive a capital settlement in lieu of any income orders, such as Mrs Duxbury, and will be especially suitable where there is plenty of capital such as in *Gojkovic*.

Alternatively, outright dismissal may be suitable where the parties are on welfare benefits and nothing is to be gained by trying to work out (and regularly vary) what sums should be paid by one to the other when neither could really afford any lifestyle outside social security, as in *Ashley v Blackman* [1988] 3 WLR 562 (also known as *A v B*). This was a courageous decision of Waite J who said that outright dismissal was the only solution:

> ... to prevent a couple of acutely limited means from remaining manacled together indefinitely by the necessity of returning to court at regular intervals to thresh out at public expense the precise figure one should pay to the other, not for the benefit of either, but solely for the benefit of the tax paying section of the community to which neither of them had sufficient means to belong.

The wife was mentally ill and living entirely off welfare benefits and the husband had remarried and had a wife and child to support, and he earned so little his income even fell below the lowest tax threshold. The only reason for the application was to see if the DSS could recover some of the money they paid to the wife when her maintenance order was unpaid; therefore, this decision can only be classed as a victory for common sense over bureaucracy.

Such orders will also be suitable in any case where the court is dividing the assets fully and finally on divorce and is at the same time minded to make an order under s 25A(3) also, as in cases such as *Seaton v Seaton* [1986] 2 FLR 398 already mentioned above in connection with s 25(2)(e). In *Seaton*, the quality of life of the severely disabled husband meant that there was no point in preserving his right to apply for maintenance from the wife because nothing she could pay him could improve it or improve on the existing financial security sufficient for his tiny needs, which were already provided for by his living with his parents on a disability pension.

For the sake of completeness, all possible applications for ancillary relief in all its forms should be made or be deemed to be made and be formally dismissed, including where appropriate an order made under s 25A(3) prohibiting a future application by either party against the estate of the other under the Inheritance (Provision for Family and Dependants) Act 1975.

12.7.3 When is a clean break likely?

Traditionally clean breaks are for short childless marriages and for older couples where the family has left home and there are sufficient resources to provide each party with a home and to divide everything else without leaving the wife on social security in retirement.

They are also big money cases such as *White* which are obvious candidates for a clean break. A clean break in that situation should usually be for a split of assets, based on 'fairness', and probably approaching equality, due to the House of Lords' *White* requirement of checking the judge's tentative award based on the s 25 factors against 'the yardstick of equality'. However, the post-*White* cases, such as *Cowan v Cowan* (2001) *The Times*, 17 May, CA, make it clear (as the Family Law Bar Association's Summer 2001 Newsletter wittily commented) that fairness, like beauty, is in the eye of the beholder: Mrs Cowan (like Mrs White) did not get 50%, and despite appealing her original 27% (£3.2m out of £11.5m) to the Court of Appeal, only obtained there 38% of the assets on the basis that it was Mr Cowan's 'Midas touch' which had accumulated the fortune in the first place. She should not get as much as he merely due to helping to set up the business and then keeping the home fires burning during a long marriage.

However, a clean break must now be *considered* on every divorce, although not necessarily *imposed* regardless if the circumstances are not suitable. Nevertheless, in every case the court likes to see the parties working towards a clean break even if that must be deferred. Wives of whatever social class, and of all ages except those nearing ordinary retirement age, are therefore expected in principle either to work or, if they come from a wealthy background where they have never been expected to work, that there will be a clean break provided by the available capital. The policy is now *spousal self-sufficiency* and *not* the 'meal ticket for life'.

12.7.4 Welfare hazards of the clean break

A word of warning should be said about clean breaks, following the little noticed amendment to the social security legislation by s 8 of the Social Security Act 1990, which amended the Social Security Act 1986 to make a spouse liable for the support of an ex-spouse even after decree absolute if the ex-spouse is in receipt of welfare benefits.

The effect of this is that if a clean break is achieved by an order for outright transfer of the matrimonial home to the wife in return for surrender of her right to periodical payments under whichever limb of s 25A, then there will be nothing to stop the Benefits Agency attempting to recover any benefits paid to the ex-spouse if that ex-spouse gets into financial difficulties and is obliged to claim them. This is a direct reversal of the previous position, where spouses could be advised to make such transfers as, if the other spouse got into financial difficulties without periodical payments, an application could always be made for social security payments. Now it will be unwise to achieve clean breaks by capital payment or property transfer unless the payee spouse is thought to be responsible and likely to be able to achieve financial independence without difficulties which might involve an application for welfare benefits. This is subject, of course, to the qualification that at no time will the Benefits Agency be able to recover any money from a spouse who has not got any. Thus, if such a husband were himself on benefits, or of very limited means, the Benefits Agency trying to recover money it has paid out will be out of luck.

The liability to pay maintenance to children under the Child Support Acts 1991 and 1995 must also be remembered, since whatever the parties agree between themselves, this ongoing liability will remain. Also, if a wife applies to the CSA the husband will have to pay again subject to small relief introduced for capital payments in 1995.

A clean break is possible *only* between spouses but *not* between parent and child, even if a lump sum is paid to the custodial parent on the understanding that that is in consideration of the payee parent assuming responsibility for maintenance of a child (*Crozier v Crozier* [1994] 1 FLR 126). While there are now rules which permit capital settlements to be taken into consideration by the CSA in computing the non-custodial parent's obligation to pay maintenance to a child, they are not particularly generous, and the only way of achieving the former situation where a custodial parent got the lion's share of the assets in return for assuming full responsibility for the children would be by means of an express trust. See further Chapter 15.

ANCILLARY RELIEF: THE BASIC LAW

ORDERS THE COURT CAN GRANT

The orders which the court can grant following a decree of divorce or judicial separation are contained in ss 22–24 of the MCA 1973, and comprise money orders (periodical payments, secured and unsecured, and lump sums) and property orders (transfer or settlement of property, variation of settlements and pension orders) in favour of both spouses and children of the family, in the latter case only for children whose maintenance is not assessed by the CSA. The court's jurisdiction is discretionary, and there is no regime of matrimonial property dividing property of the spouses on marriage breakdown either equally or in any other proportion. Prenuptial contracts are unenforceable in England and Wales, though they may be taken into account.

Final orders take effect on decree absolute, save in the case of children, whose orders always remain 'interim', since they can come back before the court at any time. For ancillary relief procedure, see Chapter 14.

APPLYING FOR ANCILLARY RELIEF

Application is made in the prayer of the petition and activated following the grant of decree *nisi*. Interim orders can be made for both spouses and children.

INCOME ORDERS

Income orders or 'maintenance' are usually the core of an ancillary relief package, unless there is to be a clean break with which they are incompatible. Their duration varies.

CAPITAL ORDERS

There is no special reason required for a lump sum order, although there are some specific situations for which lump sums are appropriate (eg, to start a business, compensate for loss of a share of the former matrimonial home, or to capitalise maintenance).

PROPERTY ORDERS

These generally concern the home but enable the court to transfer any property from one spouse to another, or to vary settlements, and also to order sale and make consequential orders in respect of the proceeds.

THE s 25 FACTORS AND THE COURT'S DISCRETION

The general duty of the court is to take into account all the circumstances of the case, giving first consideration to the welfare of the minor children of the family. In practical terms this means to see that they have a roof over their heads and adequate funds to live on. The court then works through the s 25 factors and applies them to the facts of the case.

THE ASSETS OVER WHICH THE COURT HAS JURISDICTION (MCA 1973, s 25(2)(A))

The court requires that full and frank disclosure is made of all assets of both parties and if necessary is at liberty to make use of any or all of them in redistributing ownership to arrive at a fair resolution of the couple's outstanding financial disputes on the dissolution of their marriage. Assets commonly include capital and income, earning capacity, damages, future inheritances, pensions and any other resource (actual or potential), including assets acquired after separation or divorce. If actual earnings declared are suspect, the court will assess resources based on lifestyle. The resources of a new spouse or cohabitant are taken into account if they release funds which, but for reliance on the new partner's assistance, would otherwise have had to be expended by a divorcing spouse in his or her own support. Earning capacity is regarded as important and any unrealised capacity in this respect is expected to be accessed, if necessary by retraining. This is because of the philosophy of spousal self-sufficiency, which has generated the concept of the clean break.

MATTERS THE COURT TAKES INTO ACCOUNT UNDER THE MATRIMONIAL CAUSES ACT 1973, s 25(2)(B)–(H)

These include the ages of the parties and length of marriage, all their contributions, financial and non-financial, to the marriage (including that of the housewife and mother who does not work outside the home and including future contributions such as by bringing up the children or maintaining the family), the parties' lifestyle during the marriage, the health of the parties including any disability, any other special factors, and any loss that has been or will be occasioned by the dissolution of the marriage (eg, loss of pension benefits). Conduct is not taken into account unless inequitable to disregard, although positive or negative contribution may affect the quantum of any award by placing it at the upper or lower end of a scale of generosity.

THE CLEAN BREAK

The court has no obligation to order a clean break, but only to consider one (*Clutton v Clutton* [1991] 1 All ER 340, CA).

Appropriate cases for clean breaks include young childless spouses, and older spouses whose children have grown up. A clean break is not incompatible with a young family but is less likely to be practical unless the carer is also able to work full time and/or there is sufficient capital.

Options for a clean break include limited term periodical payments, leading to a deferred clean break, or sufficient capital provision for an immediate one, so that periodical payments can be dismissed outright, or some combination of the two.

CHAPTER 13

QUANTUM, VARIATION AND APPEALS OUT OF TIME

13.1 QUANTUM – CALCULATING SPOUSE MAINTENANCE

Quantum is always the most difficult part of ancillary relief: the basic law is straightforward and logical enough, but assembling any ancillary relief package, whether in a capital or income context, challenges many an academic and vocational student alike. The underlying problem is lack of practical experience, very often both of money and how household budgets and financing a family work in practice, and also of how to fit together the various provisions of ss 22–31 of the Matrimonial Causes Act (MCA) 1973.

It is first important to grasp that maintenance for the spouse and maintenance for the children are two completely different and separate assessments and the calculations must be made independently of each other. However, they will naturally have a knock on effect on each other, except in cases where the parties' means are not limited. This is exactly the same whether the family whose package is to be put together exists in a seminar or in reality.

The pre-Child Support Agency (CSA) method used to be to work out maintenance for the spouse, including what might be called the 'roof element' of the general household expenses, and then to tack on something for each child according to their ages, finally making an order for £x per annum for the spouse (which would be the larger of the two figures) and £y (which would often be a miniature amount for food and clothes) for each of the children. The advent of the CSA has meant that this can no longer be done, as most children's maintenance is now assessed separately by the CSA (either in fact, or in a notional calculation carried out by the parties' legal advisers if they are intending to contract out of the CSA system, as can still be done, by agreeing maintenance between the parties – NB this can only be done if the carer parent is not claiming welfare benefits). Thus, now the child maintenance must be worked out first in order to see what is left for the spouse (if anything). It is no good using the old 'roof element plus' system as this is susceptible to breach by later application to the CSA, regardless of any agreement to the contrary.

Previous complaints about the CSA have not so far included inconvenience of the CSA system to law students, but it is certainly a fact that it is now more difficult to work out quantum, especially in the wake of *White v White* [2000] 2 FLR 981, HL and subsequent decisions attempting further refinement of that decision, as it is by no means certain to what extent the *White* principles apply to 'small money' cases. The approximate answer to that question appears to be that *White* does apply, but only in so far as it is convenient to the facts of the case and the application of the s 25 factors. See *per* Connell J in *B v B (Financial Provision and Conduct)* [2002] Fam Law 173, where the judge said that where there were findings of non-disclosure and removal of assets by the husband, and the district judge had ordered transfer of the sole asset (the proceeds of sale of a modest house) to be transferred to the wife to house herself and the child, the husband was not entitled to receive some of the equity on *White* fairness and equality principles, as there was only room for equality and the yardstick of equality test when the housing needs of the carer parent in small money cases had been addressed.

Nevertheless, the impact of *White* on ancillary relief cannot be underestimated because of the House of Lords' ongoing reference back to the s 25 factors, which appears to be a meal ticket for life for the Family Bar where husbands want to run the equality point. The Family Law Bar Association's annual Court Tables publication, *At a Glance 2001–02*, has even found an apt Biblical quotation for their Preface, mentioning the 'seismic changes' currently taking place in ancillary relief: 'Lift up your eyes and look at the fields: they are *White* with the promise of harvest already' (John 4:35).

There has already been a post-*B v B* case in which it was decided by Thorpe LJ that there is no need for a district judge to produce an equality of outcome unless there are good reasons for departure, again emphasising the s 25 factors and housing the carer parent in limited means cases (*Cordle v Cordle* [2002] 1 FLR 207). This seems to be following the trend of cases subsequent to *White*, where judges have been emphasising 'fairness', sticking to the security blanket of s 25, and a slightly different approach to a wife's contribution to the success of a business which no longer needs to be emphasised because different contributions to family life are now accepted as equally valuable (see *Dharamshi v Dharamshi* [2001] 1 FLR 736, CA, where it was made clear there was no presumption of the liquidation of a business to achieve equality if that 'brought down or crippled the whole family's financial edifice'). No doubt this will continue to develop. As Sachs LJ said in *Porter v Porter* [1969] 3 All ER 640 (apparently approved of by Lord Nicholls in *White*), 'The law is a living thing moving with the times and not a creature of dead or moribund thought'.

Whatever the impact of *White*, if the family is cash limited and either on benefits or likely to be so, and as the CSA's calculation allows for no discretion and will simply provide a computer generated figure as soon as the carer spouse applies for an assessment (out of which eventuality it is *not* possible to contract if benefits are involved), it is essential to know the amount which will have to be paid to the children, or any other calculations, even rough estimates, will be meaningless.

Specialist family solicitors and counsel now use tailor made software to produce these calculations swiftly and painlessly so as to discover this extremely relevant figure as soon as possible before trying to calculate fair spouse maintenance. In wealthy families, this exercise is often an incentive to a clean break where the spouse will not receive maintenance at all, the reason being that capital payments are completely outside the CSA system, and it is possible to make provision, in draft orders of the court, for clawing back capital if a CSA application is made contrary to agreement.

Spouses from families above the breadline will in any case have their maintenance based on *reasonable needs* if there is *not* a clean break obviating maintenance, so in practice a budget will need to be prepared for the spouse to ascertain what those are and the order tailored accordingly.

Spouses from middle and low income families will need to have their maintenance measured against the yardstick of one of the long accepted guidelines, namely:

- the net effect calculation; or
- the one third rule.

Any or all of these calculations may be affected by the 'fairness' decision in *White v White*, which did not expressly deal with whether there should be an attempt at equality in income terms as well as in division of capital assets.

13.1.1 The net effect calculation

Irrespective of which guideline is used, a net effect calculation is good practice to check the feasibility of the orders to be made and most district judges will want one so they can see how the proposed orders will work out for each party. Thus this is a clear example of the law working only in explicit conjunction with the practice and both academic and vocational students need to become accustomed to the same. Indeed, this will be essential to estimate quantum for the poor family where every penny counts, as for such a family the so called one third rule (which is only a starting point anyway (see 13.1.2, below)) will be hopelessly inappropriate.

The net effect calculation is achieved by taking either an existing order or a hypothetical offer by either party, establishing the *net effect* of the proposal by calculating the parties' *respective spendable incomes* net of:

- tax, national insurance, pension contributions and work expenses (ie, travel);
- reasonable mortgage rent and council tax; and
- proposed maintenance,

which will give the parties' net resources, and then calculating each party's actual needs, that is reasonable expenses for:

- food, clothing, etc; and
- gas, electricity, telephone, TV, etc.

This will show whether the proposed maintenance is the correct figure and if it fails to meet either of the party's actual needs then it must be adjusted accordingly until it produces a fair result.

These methods were pioneered as long ago as *Furniss v Furniss* [1982] 3 FLR 46; and *Stockford v Stockford* [1982] 3 FLR 52, which attacked the then favoured one third rule on the basis that the net effect calculation suited low income families better because it enabled the court to see precisely what each side would have to spend.

Despite the long established principle in *Barnes v Barnes* [1972] 1 WLR 1381 that those with means to pay must not throw their financial responsibilities onto the State, in genuinely low income cases welfare benefits may have to be a resource as in *Delaney v Delaney* [1990] 2 FLR 457, already mentioned in the context of resources for the purposes of s 25(2)(a) in Chapter 12, above, and it is in many low income cases that the CSA's prior claims may mean that the paying spouse cannot afford to pay any spouse maintenance at all and the clean break or nominal payments, whichever is appropriate to the particular case, will beckon as the only alternative.

The court has a *subsistence level approach* to orders in low income families. It will obviously not make an order which depresses the payer below subsistence level as this would be pointless (see *Allen v Allen* [1986] 2 FLR 265; and *Billington v Billington* [1974] Fam 24), although the relevant level, which may be that which the Benefits Agency permits before requiring a contribution from a liable relative, is in fact slightly more generous than actual subsistence since it preserves 15% of the liable relative's earnings above income support and allied benefit rates before contribution is required.

13.1.2 The one third rule

This 'rule' had its origins in the pre-1988 tax regime and the pre-CSA idea that one third was the right proportion of assets to give to the wife since the husband would usually also maintain the children separately, pay school fees where incurred and also build up a pension out of which the wife, in the days of the 'meal ticket for life' philosophy of ongoing maintenance, would continue to be maintained when he had retired.

In fact it is, especially nowadays, a so called rule which has always been regarded as a *guide* rather than a rule: this is because, having no law of matrimonial property as such, English law has always proceeded until *White* on the basis of the *wife's reasonable needs balanced against the husband's ability to pay* rather than on any proportional share of assets being awarded on divorce. Thus the 'rule' has now probably passed its heyday, increasingly so since the net effect calculation has proved in practice so much more useful for rich and poor alike. Nevertheless, the one third rule has been difficult to kill off, because in certain circumstances, where the payer is the sole breadwinner and there are children, it can be a useful reference point still.

Indeed, occasionally cases have continued to crop up, even over the last decade or so, in which a judge will say that for one reason or another it is still a useful starting point, particularly in middle income cases where it may be a fair guide as to what is right to order, pointing to cases such as *Slater v Slater* [1982] 3 FLR 58 and *Bullock v Bullock* [1986] 1 FLR 372, where one third of the husband's assets was ordered, and noting that although the 'rule' had not always recently been followed it had never actually been disapproved, so was still a useful starting point, even if quantum was subsequently adjusted for other matters which had to be taken into account.

The cases mentioned in connection with variation at 13.3, below, indicate how it does not suit the poor. The case of *Preston v Preston* [1981] 3 WLR 619; [1982] 1 All ER 41 shows how it may not suit a wealthy family either because of the principle of *needs* (especially post-*White*), or the impact of businesses as in *Dharamshi*, and in the contemporary context of horrific house prices for quite ordinary properties, quite apart from the impact of other s 25 factors. Mrs Preston wanted £770,000 out of her husband's net assets of £2.3m, which included the business built up while she economised, but only obtained £600,000, enough to buy a suitable house and to give her the right income to maintain herself in it.

B v B (Real Property: Assessment of Interests) [1988] 2 FLR 490, already mentioned in the context of failing to make adequate disclosure to the court, which tends to be regarded as obstructing a spouse in the pursuit of just remedies as well as contempt, also shows that a one third approach will not be regarded as appropriate where the marriage is short. This is almost certainly not disturbed by *White*.

Even if the rule still exists, as it may for income calculations, cases like *Preston* – which emphasised the principle of the wife's reasonable needs balanced against other considerations such as the business, and *Potter v Potter* [1982] 3 All ER 321; [1982] 4 FLR 331, where the husband had a small, one man photographic business worth only £60,000 and the wife's capital award was reduced on appeal from £23,000 to £10,000 – show that it is not appropriate for capital calculations, especially where any capital order must take into account the principle of not threatening the viability of a business on which the family depends for any payments at all to be made. This was underlined in *Dew v Dew* [1986] 2 FLR 341, where considerations of preserving the husband's business and focusing on the wife's reasonable needs resulted in an order of only £135,000 where the wife's notional entitlement if the one third rule was applied was £350,000.

To make a one third calculation, the court adds together the parties' joint incomes less the expenses of earning them, divides by three, subtracts the applicant's existing income from the one third figure arrived at, and the resultant figure is the amount which the spouse with the lesser income can claim from the better resourced spouse. Of course, if the potential applicant already has more than one third of the joint incomes, an application is ruled out unless it can be justified on the completely separate basis of reasonable needs balanced against the other spouse's ability to pay, taking into account the payer's other obligations and whether it is still 'fair' in the *White* sense.

13.2 CHILD MAINTENANCE

Maintenance for children has to some extent been taken out of the hands of the courts by the Child Support Act 1991 (CSA 1991), which set up the CSA, a new system designed progressively to take over the assessment and enforcement of child maintenance except in the few cases where the court still has jurisdiction. The CSA started work in 1993 immediately after the Act came into force (on 5 April of that year). Although it was intended that at first new cases only would be dealt with, but that ultimately the CSA would also deal with variations of existing orders, this has never happened, and the 1991–95 Acts which were refined by a steady stream of regulations are to be progressively replaced from 2002 by the implementation of new legislation in the Child Support, Pensions and Social Security Act 2000 (see Chapter 15). This process is not even initially expected to be completed for a couple of years, and is to be phased in gradually, following a delayed start, up to about 2009.

The court has therefore in most non-exceptional cases lost its jurisdiction to make orders for children in contested proceedings (CSA 1991, s 8(1) and (3)), though it retains a power to revoke a maintenance order (s 8(4)) and can vary a pre-1993 maintenance order under s 31 of the MCA 1973 or a pre-1993 maintenance agreement under s 35 of the MCA 1973. Children whose maintenance orders may still be assessed by the court are all children of the family, other than biological children subject to the CSA regime:

(1) up to the age of 16 (or 19 if remaining in full time non-advanced education after the school leaving age);

(2) whose custodial parent (called the 'carer' in CSA parlance) already receives the maximum amount assessable by the CSA but requires further periodical payments, sometimes called 'topping up' cases (CSA 1991, s 8(6)). This may be specifically for school fees (see s 8(7)) or where extra expenses are caused by a disability (s 8(8)).

Where the order sought is to be made against the carer (resident) parent and not the absent (non-resident) parent (s 8(10)), all children of the family means those:

(a) over the age of 19;

(b) for whom lump sum or property transfer or settlement orders are sought;

(c) one or both of whose parents is not habitually resident in the UK;

(d) where an application for their maintenance was pending before 5 April 1993; and

(e) whose absent natural parent cannot be assessed by the CSA to pay maintenance for whatever reasons (eg, that parent has died or disappeared), so that an application is necessary against a stepparent.

Such orders can either be made for children under ss 23 and 24 of the MCA 1973 (though transfer of property orders for children are rare) or under ss 2, 6 or 7 of the Domestic Proceedings and Magistrates' Courts Act 1978, although if the child orders are sought in ancillary relief proceedings MCA orders are most likely.

However, *agreed orders* can still be made and this can be done by the court in relation to *all* children of the family, even those in respect of whom an assessment could be made by the CSA, if the order is incorporated into a consent order and is pursuant to an agreement in writing made between the parents. *But* this will not preclude an application being made at any time to the CSA for a CSA assessment to be made as any such attempted restriction is void (CSA 1991, s 9(4)). In particular, if a party goes on to benefits, it will be mandatory for the CSA to make an assessment even if a there is a court order in force at the time. For this reason, when drafting consent orders it is usual to include a recital to the effect that if such an assessment is made, the amount payable under the consent order shall be reduced by the amount of the CSA assessment, so that the payer is not legally obliged to pay twice or to incur the expense of applying to the court to have the consent order varied.

The detailed operation of the CSA is beyond the scope of this book but, of the numerous statutory instruments making regulations under the Acts, the following are the most useful for the working knowledge required so as to understand the law of ancillary relief:

- Child Support Act 1991 (Commencement No 3 and Transitional Provisions) Order 1992 SI 1992/2644;

- Child Support Act (Commencement No 3 and Transitional Provisions) Amendment Order 1993 SI 1993/966; and

- Child Maintenance (Written Agreements) Order 1993 SI 1993/620.

Because of the way in which the calculations work, a CSA assessment is not usually as advantageous either to the payee or to the payer as an agreed order which is part of a package embodied in a consent order, and the negotiated package will probably also be more advantageous overall to the payee than relying on strict CSA rights in respect of the children. So the trend is for both parties still to attempt to negotiate the ancillary relief package as a whole and only to have recourse to the CSA where essential.

However, some carers have wanted to obtain a CSA assessment in lieu of existing orders, in which case it is necessary (unless the carer is on State benefits) to apply under s 8(4) of the CSA 1991 to revoke the order (because by s 8(5) and the transitional provisions the CSA cannot make an assessment if there is in force an existing order or maintenance agreement, either of which could be varied). Yet the court might not in fact agree to revoke such an order to facilitate a CSA assessment, because (since the CSA assessments are notoriously higher than the court's usual orders and are also completely non-discretionary and inflexible) the judge might feel that if the payer had to meet a CSA assessment it would make continued contact with the child less affordable (a consequence which has resulted in many such cases).

The court therefore weighs up all the relevant facts in the interests of the child, and may insist on varying the order itself rather than revoking it to facilitate a CSA application. In *B v M* [1994] 1 FLR 342, such a revocation order was made at first instance and overturned on appeal, because the judge said that the proper course was an application for an upward variation of the order and not a revocation to permit a CSA assessment to take place.

13.2.1 Calculating child maintenance

In any case where the court is to make a consent order based on the parents' agreement and excluding the CSA's involvement, the order is still likely to be for periodical payments in the ballpark area of what the CSA would have assessed, albeit that under the CSA formula (to be repealed in the near future when the new CSA regime is implemented) the amount would not include the carer's premium.

Where the court is to *assess the quantum* of the order (rather than merely to embody the parents' agreement into a consent order), which of course will only be in any case where they still have jurisdiction, they must look at s 25(3) of the MCA 1973 which requires those s 25 considerations which are relevant to children to be taken into account in exactly the same way as when working out financial provision for spouses. This means they must take into account, for example, a child's:

- earning capacity (eg, of child models, actors and film stars);
- property (including any income derived from it);
- needs; and
- physical or mental disability (if relevant).

By s 25(3)(d), the court must take into account how it was envisaged by the parents that the child was to be educated or trained, as in *O'Donnell v O'Donnell* [1975] 3 WLR 308; [1975] 2 All ER 993 (see 12.4.2.6, above), where the children already went to boarding school so the husband was ordered to continue to pay the fees, and *Sibley v Sibley* [1979] 10 Fam Law 49, where the parties had envisaged a fee paying school so the husband was also ordered to pay the fees because that was what the parties had planned.

By s 25(4), the court must consider whether, in the case of an application for a stepchild, the stepparent against whom the order is sought had assumed responsibility for the child's maintenance and if so to what extent and for how long, whether that stepparent did so knowing that the child was another person's and also the liability of any other person to maintain that child. The case of *Day v Day* [1988] 1 FLR 278 is a classic example of this situation as the court had no difficulty in deciding that the stepfather had clearly understood his commitment to the wife and her two children and, as their natural fathers made no contribution, on the breakdown of the marriage he was obliged to support them as well as the wife, even though the marriage had been short.

Financial provision orders under s 23 (though not transfer or settlement of property orders under s 24) can be made for children even though the petition itself is dismissed (s 23(2)).

13.3 VARIATION

Variation of ancillary relief orders is governed by s 31 of the MCA 1973 and the general principles will be found in this section. Not *all* orders can be varied, however, and it is important to understand precisely what can be done on an application for *variation* under s 31, and what requires some other approach. In some cases where *variation* as such is technically not possible because of the provisions of s 31, there may be another way of achieving what is wanted: this is clearly important to the assessment of ancillary relief on divorce, which must look ahead to all eventualities, including those normally expected such as the children growing up and/or the carer or non-resident parent remarrying.

13.3.1 Routine variation

This is likely to happen some years down the line from initial order, simply for expected and unexpected life changes. Similarly, it may be important to preclude variation, in order to achieve certainty, at the point of initial assessment of quantum and type of orders. Thus it is impossible to assess appropriate quantum without taking into account the potential for variation, or lack of it. Generally, only *continuing* money orders may be varied, in other words periodical payments (whether secured or unsecured) including maintenance pending suit and interim maintenance orders, and instalments of lump sums (s 31(2)). There is no power to vary:

(a) *fixed term periodical payments* where a prohibition on extension of the fixed term has been attached pursuant to s 28(1A) of the MCA 1973;

(b) the *amount* of a lump sum order (although if it is directed to be paid in instalments, the *instalments* may be varied) nor the time within which the lump sum is to be paid *unless* the order itself provides for that, by expressly giving 'liberty to apply for extension of the time for payment' in an appropriate case;

(c) a property adjustment order under s 24(1)(a); and

(d) a settlement of property order under s 24(1)(b) or a variation of settlement order under s 24(1)(c) or (d) unless the order was made after a decree of judicial separation.

Prohibitions (c) and (d) are often unexpectedly found very inconvenient, such as in *Carson v Carson* [1983] 1 WLR 285; [1983] 1 All ER 478, where the wife wanted her property adjustment order varied to give her the husband's share of the matrimonial home in return for her giving up her periodical payments, a reasonable enough exchange often incorporated into clean break orders following divorce. The object of her proposal was so that she had enough money to buy a new home on the sale at the end of the *Mesher* period to which her existing home was subject, but the court could not help her because of the prohibition on varying property adjustment orders. The moral is that it is essential to consider at the time the *original* order is made whether the wife might eventually want to make such a swap, because it can be done at that stage (such an arrangement commonly being called a '*Hanlon* order'), but *not* later on *variation*.

There is a strange exception to this non-variation of property orders rule: an order for sale under s 24A, which certainly does not logically fall into the category of continuing money orders, *may* be varied by changing the date of the sale (s 31(2)(f)). It may therefore rightly be asked why the date of sale in a *Mesher* or similar order cannot similarly be changed – but unless the order has been specially drawn to cover that eventuality, in fact it *cannot*. Nor can the words 'liberty to apply' (usually added to consent orders to facilitate enforcement of the order) be interpreted so liberally as to permit this – they apply only to *implementation* of the order, so as to clarify the terms and to facilitate payment under it without there being unnecessary enforcement problems: such words do not permit actual changes in the order which, once the order is made, is a variation and is governed by s 31.

Moreover, until the recent amendment of s 31(7) effected by the Family Law Act (FLA) 1996, when any of the continuing money orders *were* varied, this could originally only be done by increasing or decreasing the amounts to be paid under those orders, or discharging them completely. It was *not* possible to vary such orders by discharging them and substituting a different *type* of order: for example, a periodical payments order could not be varied by making a *lump sum* order on the variation application, even though the applicant had received no lump sum in the original order which the application sought to vary, and even though it would have been convenient to order a lump sum as capitalised maintenance and this *could* have been done when the order was originally made (s 31(5)). Now that the FLA 1996 has inserted new ss 7A and 7B into the MCA 1973, periodical payments orders may very sensibly be varied by capitalising the payments into a lump sum order.

Notwithstanding the old s 31(5), it has always been possible to vary a *child's* periodical payments by ordering a lump sum. This is because it was always recognised that it might be convenient to give a child a lump sum (eg, for an older child who needs the money for higher education), and the approach to child orders has always been somewhat more flexible (eg, there has never been any need to wait for decree *nisi* to make orders for children and unlike spouses they can also have more than one lump sum).

The most common occasions of variation applications are when there is a change of circumstances in the lives of either the payer or the payee. In the case of the *payer* it will usually be because he or she has:

• been promoted, dismissed or made redundant or has lost opportunities for overtime (and therefore can afford more or less than the original order), constituting a change in the s 25(2)(a) considerations; or

• remarried, started to cohabit or acquired a new family (and therefore has new obligations), constituting a change in the s 25(2)(b) considerations.

In the case of the payee it will usually be because of:

• inflation; or

• the children being older and more expensive

(in both of which cases an increase is likely to be sought by the payee), or because of:

- cohabitation or receipt of financial support from a third party, but where there is no remarriage; or
- children leaving home, thus increasing the payee's earning capacity

(in both of which cases a decrease is likely to be sought by the payer).

When the court does vary orders in any of these circumstances it may increase, reduce, discharge, suspend or revive such orders (s 31(1)). The court also has the power to remit arrears, completely or only in part (s 31(2A)).

13.3.2 What the court considers when deciding whether to vary an order

On variation, the court is still expressly locked in by s 31 to the same s 25 considerations which had to be checked off before making the decision when the *original* order was granted, but this time it will focus on any *change* in those matters, in accordance with s 25(1), *still* observing the general duty to consider all the circumstances of the case, but *first consideration* being given to the welfare while a minor of any child in accordance with s 31(7).

Sometimes, changes will be *non-monetary* such as in *Evans v Evans* [1989] 1 FLR 351, already mentioned in connection with conduct, where the husband had paid maintenance regularly and uncomplainingly for 32 years, for which he was rewarded by the wife entering into a conspiracy to murder him. The court took the view that this was a sufficient change of circumstances to justify discharging the order.

13.3.3 The impact of the s 25A clean break principle on variation

Even if there has been no clean break at the time of the original order, by s 31(7) any court dealing with an application for variation must consider whether the order should be varied so as to impose a fixed limited term for periodical payments, after which the payee should have been able to adjust without undue hardship to their terminating altogether. However, marked reluctance has been displayed to make use of this section, and a payer is often left indefinitely vulnerable to a nominal order as the payee's 'longstop'.

As in other instances, the working (or as it happens failure to utilise) of the clean break in this situation is best illustrated by consideration of some hard cases. The leading cases are actually all somewhat graphic in their facts and results.

13.3.3.1 Atkinson v Atkinson [1987] 3 All ER 849

The case of Mrs Atkinson and her laid back lover was one where one might have thought the court would take the s 31(7) duty somewhat seriously. Mrs Atkinson was cohabiting with a man who had no intention of marrying her as he did not want to support her. Her husband, however, did not want to go on supporting her either, despite his wealth which made this extremely easy for him to do, because he thought her boyfriend should do so. But instead of the reasonably expected abatement or extinguishment of her periodical payments order, this case produced the rather curious result that (while expressly finding that Mrs Atkinson's reason for cohabiting rather than remarrying was financially motivated) the court nevertheless would not end her maintenance order, because (as they commented) a wife who cohabits might need the money more than one who was not cohabiting: this was because cohabitation is a relationship which by definition is even less permanent and committed a relationship than marriage, and in particular had none of the financial obligations which attend the dissolution of a marriage by divorce. The case was also complicated by the fact that the cohabitant was not even in a position to contribute to Mrs Atkinson's support, let alone to assume responsibility for it instead of the husband, since he had carefully chosen a low paid part time job.

13.3.3.2 *Hepburn v Hepburn [1989] 3 All ER 786*

Was Mrs Atkinson's an exceptional case, then? It was not.

Much the same happened in the case of Mrs Hepburn, another cohabitation scenario where the wife went to live with another man, after dissolution of a 10 year marriage, and then entered into business ventures with him which the husband claimed were financially irresponsible. When he was age 45 and she 40, the husband succeeded in getting her order reduced to a nominal one, but not in getting it discharged altogether: the court again talked of the backstop safety factor, saying that cohabitation is not the same as marriage and that unlike cohabitants, husbands did have obligations and should discharge them. It probably did not help Mr Hepburn that, like Mr Atkinson, he was himself wealthy and could afford to do so.

13.3.3.3 *Whiting v Whiting [1988] 1 WLR 565; [1988] 2 FLR 189*

Sometimes, however, one does find a dissenting judgment in this type of case, such as that of Balcombe LJ in the case of Mrs Whiting, where only he seems to have grasped what the legislation meant to do. In that case, in his famously forthright and well judged way, the late Balcombe LJ is at last on record as saying that it was absurd to keep a nominal maintenance order alive for purely safety net purposes, as it was clearly contrary to the clean break legislation which had been passed for good reasons of policy and which should not therefore be flouted unnecessarily.

In the case of the Whitings it is hard to fault his view, and curious that this is such a relatively lone view. Mrs Whiting, who had admittedly had to give up work in the early part of a 14 year marriage when the children were young, was by the time they were older a full time teacher with a good salary, whereas the husband, who had remarried, had been made redundant and had been forced to take a new job at a much lower salary than previously. He spent all his income on his second family and had therefore (not illogically) applied to end his first wife's nominal maintenance order once she was established in full time employment. The court of first instance refused to do this since they took the view that he was the wife's only longstop against ill heath or redundancy and that she could not be assumed to be independent of him indefinitely since she had limited capital resources. However, if there is not to be a clean break on variation in this type of case, it is difficult to see when that *would* be right.

13.3.3.4 Fisher v Fisher [1989] 1 FLR 423

It is Mrs Fisher who perhaps 'takes the biscuit' and makes it clear that it is not just the relative impermanence of cohabitation and commitment of marriage that prevents the court from imposing a clean break on variation applications where they otherwise might reasonably do so. *Fisher* shows that even where the parties' children have grown up, and the wife (having been maintained while they were young) might reasonably be expected to go out to work, this may not be possible. This will mean the husband's obligations continue, through no fault of his own, even though he may have been awaiting the day he could gain a certain financial freedom on the termination of what may have been a long period of obligation to an ex-wife with care of children.

In *Fisher*, the wife had care of a child who was 15 and applied for an upward variation of periodical payments due to inflation, which inspired the husband to cross-apply for discharge of her order altogether – after all their child was 15 and she should at that stage have been able to go out to work. Not so: in the meantime she had had another *much younger* child by another man as the result of an affair, and claimed she could not work due to her obligations to this younger child. The court agreed with her, holding that she had a limited earning capacity, but that due to her obligations to the younger child she was necessarily prevented from becoming independent of the husband and that it made no difference that the younger child who was the cause of this limitation on her availability for work was not the husband's. They examined the meaning and purpose of ss 25A and 31(7) and restated the principle that while their combined effect was to discharge the so called 'meal ticket for life', this did not extend to bringing about a clean break regardless in appropriate cases. They had regard to the meaning of the words 'undue hardship' in both sections and reiterated their wide discretion to do what was appropriate. They considered that it was much too soon because of the existence of the younger child to think about a limited term order (all logical reasoning as far as it went, and in accordance with other principles of family law, but not surprisingly the press, as well as Mr Fisher, were incredulous).

13.3.3.5 Ashley v Blackman [1988] 2 FLR 278

To some extent this story of the curious interpretation of s 25A does have something of a happy ending, though another word might be 'compassionate' in relation to the only other well known clean break case under s 25A, *Ashley v Blackman* [1988] 2 FLR 278 (already mentioned at 12.7.2, above). It was, however, an exceptional case where the judge (this time Waite J, like Balcombe LJ another luminary of the Chancery Bar who served both the Family Division and the Court of Appeal well in the incisiveness of such decisions) did courageously terminate the order.

This decision came despite the so called principle in *Barnes v Barnes*, which apparently did not permit the husband to give up paying maintenance and throw his burden onto the State. In *Ashley v Blackman* fortunately the judge realised that it was absurd that anything the husband paid would be surpassed by her benefits. Nevertheless, the exceptional facts appear to have precluded wider use of this approach in subsequent cases (see above).

13.3.4 Variation after a clean break consent order (MCA 1973, ss 25A and 33A)

Potential for variation after a clean break will necessarily be limited, since the entire philosophy of the s 25A clean break is supposed to be in full and final settlement. However, that does not necessarily mean that a *consent order* is not variable: it is but the scope for variation is likely to be limited since clean breaks and consent orders are supposed to deal with the matter once and for all, which is the whole point of the clean break legislation.

Therefore, if a consent order is to be variable, that should be made clear when it is made, as otherwise the parties may be stuck with the terms of it without possibility of alteration as in *Dinch v Dinch* [1987] 1 All ER 818. In that case, where the Court of Appeal had thought it could vary a property adjustment order but the husband was able to have the purported variation set aside, Lord Oliver of Aylmerton, in declining to confirm the variation to help the wife in unforeseen difficulties under the original order, had some hard things to say about practitioners who do not check the terms of orders sufficiently, to the detriment in such a case of their clients when there are new circumstances and nothing can be done to the consent order scheme to meet them. There are a number of different principles here which need close examination. For the power to make consent orders under s 33A of the MCA 1973 and the care required in their negotiation and drafting in case of possible future variation, see further Chapter 14.

13.3.4.1 'Liberty to apply'

This term, traditionally included in consent orders, is often mistaken for a passport to instant variation, but nothing could be further from the truth. Returning to the court which made the order, under the 'liberty to apply' term, the court will only permit working out of the existing order, not variation as such.

13.3.4.2 Where the welfare of a child is at stake

If it can be shown that the existing order does not make proper provision for a child, which may include not providing properly for the custodial parent, the court may reopen a consent order (*N v N (Consent Order: Variation)* [1993] 2 FLR 868), although they decline to do so in most cases.

13.3.4.3 Making a late application for relief where claims have not actually been made or dismissed immediately after the decree

Where comprehensive claims have been made at the time of a divorce and those not effectively pursued as far as obtaining an order of a particular type have actually been *dismissed*, then clearly no further application will be possible (*De Lasala v De Lasala* [1980] AC 546). However, if there has not been actual *dismissal*, whether because there has never been actual application (eg, defective prayer in the petition of a petitioner or no old ancillary relief Form M11 or new Form A filed by a respondent) or perhaps because neither the parties, nor their advisers, nor the court addressed the matter, then in theory a late application could be made, since the power of the court to make orders arises on or after the grant of a decree.

Nevertheless, the court does not like this because it is felt that parties should be protected against unexpected and stale claims long after the decree. Thus what may be a technically permissible fresh financial application to get around s 31 may not be allowed, as was the case in *Pace v Doe* [1977] 1 All ER 176, where a wife whose second marriage had swiftly failed tried to apply for a further order against her first husband to help her out of her unexpected financial difficulties.

Yet in an appropriate case, leave for such an application might be granted, as in *Chatterjee v Chatterjee* [1976] Fam 199, where the post-divorce situation had not yet settled and the wife was allowed to make an application for a property adjustment order and for a lump sum order.

It is (not surprisingly) now usual to deal in advance with the possibility of late claims by including an actual *recital* in a consent order that the provision is made in 'full and final settlement', thus avoiding the tedious problem of whether a claim should be allowed.

13.5 APPEALS OUT OF TIME

The alternative may be to appeal out of time, for which leave will be given in limited circumstances, on the principles set out in *Barder v Barder* [1987] 2 WLR 1350, HL; [1987] 2 All ER 440. That case had bizarre and tragic facts involving the death of both the wife and the two children of the family for whom provision had been carefully made, when the wife killed both children and then herself committed suicide. Four conditions need to be satisfied. These are that:

(a) a new event or events have invalidated the basis of the order *and* that the appeal is likely to succeed (this includes fresh evidence which could not have been known at the time the order was made, but *not* any new or more correct interpretation of what was then known all along);

(b) the new event has occurred within a few months of the order;

(c) the application for leave is made reasonably promptly; and

(d) no prejudice will occur to third parties who have acted in good faith and for valuable consideration on the basis of the order.

Similarly, tragic situations arose in *Smith v Smith (Smith Intervening)* [1991] 2 FLR 432, CA; and *Barber v Barber* [1992] Fam Law 436. In the former an appeal out of time was granted, but in the latter where the wife died three months after the order, recognition was given to the contribution a wife makes to the marriage and the building up of assets by distinguishing between the part of a capital order made by way of 'golden handshake' at the end of a marriage, and the part made actually to provide for a wife and children after divorce (eg, by buying a home or providing a lump sum to do so). In the latter case the court felt that the wife's share of the home should pass to the children of the marriage when they were grown up and did not accede to the husband's request that the order be rescinded on the basis that its whole purpose was nullified.

The court will not vary orders where the alleged basis is not really new but relies on facts which could have been ascertained at the time the order was made, as in *Barber v Barber* [1980] Fam Law 125. In that case, the wife knew about the husband's pension rights at the time of the order. Thus it is no good saying that tax calculations have been erroneous and that overseas legal proceedings have turned out differently from what was expected (as in *Penrose v Penrose* [1994] 2 FLR 621), nor that the payer's wealth has dramatically increased because of land values depending on planning permission if that could have been foreseen (as in *Worlock v Worlock* [1994] 2 FLR 689).

The courts do not like granting such leave, although they have done so. For example, in *Hope-Smith v Hope-Smith* [1989] 2 FLR 56, the husband wilfully delayed three years before paying a lump sum order calculated on the basis of the value of the matrimonial home, which meantime soared to £200,000, requiring a consequent upward adjustment of the wife's lump sum or injustice would have been done. Equally, such leave has been refused where the value of the home has *fallen* (as in *B v B (Financial Provision: Leave to Appeal)* [1994] 1 FLR 219) and where shares have shot up in value (as in *Cornick v Cornick* [1994] 2 FLR 530).

In order to succeed in cases like the last two it will be necessary to show that there has been some undermining factor such as fraud, mistake or incomplete disclosure which destroys the whole basis of the order. This is particularly the case where the order is a consent order, as in *Munks v Munks* [1985] FLR 576, where an appeal was allowed only because there was a procedural irregularity as the order had in fact been granted before decree *nisi* which it should of course not have been, and *Redmond v Redmond* [1986] 2 FLR 173, where the husband had agreed not to apply for redundancy and had then done so.

Cases of subsequent remarriage or cohabitation within a short time of the order being granted are not usually sufficient to undermine the order, unless blatant, and did not have that effect in *Cook v Cook* [1988] 1 FLR 521; nor *Chaudhuri v Chaudhuri* [1992] Fam Law 385; [1992] 2 FLR 73, though such an order was overturned after early remarriage of the wife in *Wells v Wells* [1992] Fam Law 386; [1992] 2 FLR 66 (this case was in fact decided in 1980 despite not being reported until 12 years later). A wife's change of mind about sale of the home fall into the same 'foreseeable' category as in *Edmonds v Edmonds* [1990] 2 FLR 202, where the husband failed to get the order overturned despite a rise in the price of the home when it was sold.

There still seems to be some doubt over whether the technically correct procedure in seeking to appeal against a consent order is to appeal to *vary* it or to have it *set aside*. This might be more appropriate in a case where an order should not have been made by consent in the first place (see *B v B (Consent Order: Variation)* [1995] 1 FLR 9, where Thorpe LJ said the wife's clean break should never have been ordered by consent as she had no chance of becoming financially independent).

13.6 VARYING *MESHER* ORDERS

This is no longer a problem following the amending of s 31(7), which is just as well since, post-*White*, such orders have become popular again, as they permit the family to be housed pending the end of the children's dependency, but also preserve the possibility of being 'fair' to the husband. *Mesher* orders often were not so fair: the wife usually obtained more than half the proceeds of sale at the end of the trust.

13.7 CLAIMS IN NEGLIGENCE AGAINST THE APPLICANT'S SOLICITOR OR COUNSEL

If none of the above are applicable, the ultimate remedy will be to sue the solicitors responsible for their client's being restricted by an invariable or unappealable order for negligence, entitlement being to damages for what would have been received if the matter had been properly handled. In *Dickinson v Jones Alexander* [1990] Fam Law 137, the solicitors used a junior member of staff, who did not realise that the husband was a wealthy man, to run a case without adequate supervision: proper disclosure of the husband's means was not obtained. The wife received a tiny lump sum of £12,000 and a maintenance order for the children of under £2,500. Eventually the husband did not pay even this and the wife had to go on to welfare benefits. Ten years later she sued and obtained a total of £330,000. Not surprisingly the solicitors admitted liability immediately.

Similarly, in *Re Gorman* [1990] 2 FLR 284, the wife received no property adjustment order so when the husband went bankrupt the trustee in bankruptcy sought possession and there had to be a temporary suspension of the order while the wife sued her former solicitors for having let the situation develop by not dealing with the matter properly on divorce and protecting her position. In *Griffiths v Dawson* [1993] 2 FLR 315, there was a similar negligence action where a decree absolute was obtained without compensation first being sought for loss of pension benefits.

Since *Arthur JS Hall & Co v Simons and Others* [1999] 1 FLR 536, where the Court of Appeal considered four appeals in which it was alleged that cases were settled on bad advice, suing counsel is also possible, Lord Bingham having said 'It is elementary that in any contested application for ancillary relief it is necessary to have full and proper valuations and financial information'.

QUANTUM, VARIATION AND APPEALS OUT OF TIME

QUANTUM – CALCULATING SPOUSE MAINTENANCE

The net effect calculation is now most used, the one third rule (always more a guide than a rule) having fallen largely into disuse, and being mostly as inappropriate to the rich as to the poor. Some judges still find it useful in middle income cases, however. Nevertheless, this must be of questionable value following *White v White* [2000] 2 FLR 981.

The CSA calculation will usually need to be done first if the CSA is to be involved, in order to discover what is left for the spouse. Even if the overall package is to be agreed and the children's maintenance is to be incorporated into their parents' consent order and the CSA not directly involved, children's maintenance will need to be allowed for within the ballpark area of what the CSA would order.

CHILD MAINTENANCE

The CSA is responsible for assessing all child maintenance for children within its jurisdiction other than those whose parents have entered into written agreements taking their children's maintenance outside the regime. Children excluded include those overseas or one or both of whose parents live overseas, those over 19, those over 16 in non-advanced education, and those whose natural absent parent cannot be found and assessed by the CSA. The courts assess maintenance in these cases, and also for 'topping up' orders for school fees or for disabilities requiring extra payments.

The legislation is contained in the Child Support Acts 1991–95, and a number of supporting statutory instruments. There is a new regime to be phased in from 2002 pursuant to the Child Support, Pensions and Social Security Act 2000.

Where the court assesses maintenance, their discretion is exercised under s 25(3) of the MCA 1973 on much the same lines as for spousal provision under s 25(1) and (2).

VARIATION

Most orders can routinely be varied, including consent orders. Periodical payment orders can now be varied by making lump sum orders (see MCA 1973, ss 7A and 7B, inserted by the FLA 1996). Consent orders tend to be more difficult to vary, unless provision has been made for variation, because they are intended to be in full and final settlement.

Late application, variation on the basis of the welfare of the child, appeals out of time varying *Mesher* orders, solicitors' negligence claims

All these means can be used to attempt to vary orders which appear otherwise unvariable.

CHAPTER 14

ANCILLARY RELIEF PROCEDURE

14.1 INTRODUCTION

The discrete topic of ancillary relief has in recent times become, like the law of divorce itself, an area of law which is impossible to understand fully without substantial knowledge of procedure. Whereas in the past an award of ancillary relief was rather a 'hit and miss' affair – whether a settlement was negotiated or whether the matter was fought out to the bitter end at the hearing, and possibly ultimately on appeal. New arrangements replicating for ancillary relief the spirit and to some extent the letter of the Woolf reforms in civil justice mean that there is now a structure which most cases will have to respect. Thus, whereas in the past it was not uncommon for ancillary relief so much to lack focus and reasonable deployment of resources as to drag on long after the decree *nisi* and indeed often after decree absolute – sometimes surviving a party's subsequent marriage and the breakdown of *that* – ancillary relief is now:

(a) generally resolved within a reasonable time; and

(b) conducted in a more structured manner.

This saves overall both expense and the stress and strain of uncertainty and sometimes deadlock which in the past could only be broken by the further expense and delay of protracted court appearances and preparation for them.

The new system is therefore another example of a topic which it is essential for both the academic and the vocational student to understand in order to assess the merit of the existing highly discretionary law of ancillary relief and to consider the now urgent matter of reform, which post-*White* is virtually daily called for by the judiciary, academics and practising profession alike.

The recent changes in the conduct of ancillary relief were designed to improve the efficiency of ancillary relief procedure which had become both slow and expensive. Initially a pilot scheme was inaugurated in some, but not all, courts in October 1996, introducing fundamental changes on a trial basis and offering an opportunity to assess the potential and pitfalls in its adoption nationally (see the *Ancillary Relief Pilot Scheme* [1996] Fam Law 612). The Principal Registry of the Family Division of the High Court in London, together with a number of divorce county courts around the country, participated in the scheme, which was evaluated by KPMG against a number of control courts not using it, and as a result of the positive results (which showed an increase in the speed and rate of disposal with no greater expense) the scheme was introduced nationally from 2 June 2000.

The prime reason for the reform was financial, since contested ancillary relief proceedings are so expensive that to litigate merely reduces the value of the assets available to provide for the family, as seen in the recent *Piglowska* case [1999] 1 WLR 1360; [1999] 2 FLR 763. Thus, control of the proliferation of paper in excessive disclosure, a strict timetable and early identification of the issues, plus structured opportunities for court-based negotiation and settlement, were seen as likely to produce better results. However, as all litigation is wearing for the client and matrimonial litigation arguably the most wearing of all, a secondary aim of such changes was to save prolonging the inevitable stress and strain. Under the new scheme the court encourages in a new Pre-Action Protocol optimum use of the dual approach of either attempting to negotiate without using the court process at all or, if that is unlikely to succeed, entering the court controlled framework of the scheme as soon as possible after deciding that the non-court approach will not suit the case in question.

The new ancillary relief process is also designed to bring the overriding objective of the Woolf reforms and active case management (including alternative dispute resolution) formally into family proceedings, together with equality of arms and proportionality of costs to assets, often missing in the past.

It should be noted that sometimes an applicant will still press advisers for a quick solution, as used to happen under the pre-2000 ancillary relief regime, and this may be a legitimate concern which will influence the conduct of the case in one way or the other. However, unless there are very clear instructions (eg, that full disclosure of the other party's means is specifically *rejected* in favour of an early solution which produces some financial provision immediately – perhaps because the client has some distressing outside pressure such as terminal illness in the family), practitioners are aware that it is unwise to believe what clients say in this respect, since settling early, particularly on disadvantageous terms which amount to less than the court is likely to order after a contested hearing, is often likely to lead to a later negligence action. Past cases have shown even the large specialist law firms that clients have notoriously short memories and are inclined to take the early settlement money and *then* try to come back for more, like the wife in the notorious case of *Edgar v Edgar* [1980] 1 WLR 1410, where Mrs Edgar's solicitors *told* her not to enter into a disadvantageous separation agreement because it would prejudice any later application to the court, but she would not listen and was subsequently disadvantaged when they were proved to be right: the court would have ordered more but held her to her agreement.

Ancillary relief is not an area where there are many litigants in person since public funding is available, and unless there are no assets worth arguing about, applicants and respondents will usually tend to be represented in this financial stage, whether in negotiation or litigation.

14.1.1 Terminology

Irrespective of who were petitioner and respondent in the *divorce suit*, for ancillary relief purposes the parties are called the *applicant* and the *respondent* (ie, in the technically separate *application for ancillary relief*, ie, financial relief ancillary to the divorce suit).

14.1.2 Tactics

Since contested ancillary relief actions are expensive and wearing, the aim in most cases will still be not to litigate at all but to settle despite the introduction of the new scheme.

Such settlements will lead to a consent order made by the court under the abbreviated procedure for approving orders previously agreed by the parties. Thus not every ancillary relief application will follow the full procedure set out below, although every case will have common initial and final stages.

Sometimes, the full ancillary relief package will be agreed before the divorce petition is even filed (and every detail of that suit will also have been previously agreed). For example, if the divorce is based on Fact D, consent may not be forthcoming from the respondent until every financial detail is to that respondent's satisfaction.

Thus, planning the case for ancillary relief may in fact begin at the first interview with the client, yet nothing may be processed through the court until much later; alternatively, at the first interview the client's statement may indicate that there is going to be a stand up fight over ancillary relief. Obviously (for reasons of costs) it would be unwise even in such circumstances to embark on a contested action before at least an exploratory approach to the other side, but it *may* be necessary to go through the full procedure, blow by blow, using every tactical weapon provided by the Rules. Sometimes, there will be a hybrid approach, when ancillary relief matters start out on a co-operative basis, and it then turns out to be necessary to make use of the court's powers to compel disclosure or locate and freeze assets. The new Pre-Action Protocol shows awareness of this practicality by suggesting that that may be the moment to bring the case which initially started out independently within the framework of the court process.

14.1.3 Commencement of ancillary relief proceedings

Ancillary relief orders cannot be made before decree *nisi* and cannot take effect until decree absolute. Nevertheless, practitioners start thinking about ancillary relief matters as soon as instructions have been received from the client, and the Form A to commence ancillary relief proceedings can be filed at any time after issue of the petition.

Indeed, in every case, although detailed planning may be left until later, some *brief* attention must be given to ancillary relief at the first interview, for three reasons:

(1) to apply for public funding where that will be necessary, and warn the client about the impact of the statutory charge on the relief obtained. The applicant seeking public funding must first be assessed for suitability for resolution of the case by mediation, for which there is separate funding called help with mediation (see Chapter 11) following which if appropriate general help for preparation and legal representation for conduct of the hearing may be available;

(2) to claim appropriate relief in the petition (see Chapter 11); and

(3) to begin negotiations as soon as possible.

Public funded ancillary relief cannot realistically be conducted on legal help, the successor to the Green Form, so the applicant will be either a private client or on one of the other forms of new generation public funding mentioned above.

14.1.4 The prayer of the petition

The initial application for all forms of ancillary relief (except an order for sale under s 24A) must be made in the prayer of the petition, or in the prayer of any answer filed by the respondent to the divorce suit (Family Proceedings Rules (FPR) 1991, r 2.53(1)). If no answer is filed, a respondent (ie, to the divorce suit) claims ancillary relief by notice in Form A (FPR 1991, r 2.53(3)). This is the single new form for starting proceedings, regardless of whether the applicant is petitioner or respondent, and which takes the place of the old Forms M11 and M13. Once one of the parties has claimed ancillary relief there will then be an *applicant* for ancillary relief purposes and a corresponding *respondent*, although the *respondent* in the divorce suit may not also be the *respondent* in the ancillary relief proceedings.

As mentioned in Chapter 11, above, in preparing the petition, *all* forms of ancillary relief should be included in the prayer, and even if some are inappropriate at the time, *none* should be omitted. Thus if the petition has not been prepared by the practitioners who are to conduct the ancillary relief stage, a first task in any ancillary relief case will be to examine the petition to *check* that it makes a comprehensive claim. In many cases a check will prove fruitful even where the petition *has* been prepared by the same firm and it is essential to verify the completeness of the prayer as a mistake will matter, in that it will have to be corrected before ancillary relief can proceed.

Moreover, while the petitioner's claims to ancillary relief are routinely made in the prayer of the petition, if the *respondent to the divorce suit* wishes to make any, it will be necessary to file the new Form A to give notice of that if there is no answer. Thus it is essential to be alert to the necessity of filing a Form A, claiming the full range of ancillary relief, as *routine* at some stage during the course of the divorce suit (and certainly before decree absolute) if ancillary relief is likely to need to be claimed by a respondent, and to do this promptly if acting for such a respondent who has not filed an answer. This is because it is still possible under the Matrimonial Causes Act (MCA) 1973 inadvertently to obtain a decree absolute before ancillary relief has been considered, thus ending the status of marriage, and if the applicant has remarried even putting any financial provision on the inconveniently different footing of a claim outside the discretionary ambit of the MCA 1973 (s 28(3)).

Had Pt II of the FLA 1996 been implemented this danger would have ended, since that Act required resolution of all child and financial matters before grant of the single divorce order, but under the MCA 1973 litigants still run the risk of being left without a resolution of outstanding ancillary relief even where a former spouse has moved on, and perhaps not only remarried but reached the stage of the second divorce. Thus this is the first adverse criticism which may still be levelled at the existing system of ancillary relief, despite the reforms in procedure which have brought other benefits.

While in theory the court can make any order on or after granting any decree, and leave may be sought to claim ancillary relief at a later stage – perhaps a long time after the divorce provided the applicant has not remarried, since s 28(3) would then preclude such application – the court tends not to like to grant such leave which may result in a party being taken by surprise by a stale claim which had reasonably been thought unlikely ever to be made.

14.1.5 Where the petition (or answer) does not make a comprehensive claim for ancillary relief

To correct an omitted application in the petition, the other side must agree to the applicant's making a claim without leave by notice in Form A, and this will almost certainly be accepted if the parties have agreed a settlement (FPR 1991, r 2.53(2)).

If the other side will not agree, what must be done depends on whether a decree *nisi* has been pronounced:

(a) if a decree has not been pronounced, there is still time to amend the petition or answer, with leave of course, and there should be no difficulty in obtaining such leave (see Chapter 11);

(b) if a decree has been pronounced, then a Form A will have to be filed, again with leave (FPR 1991, r 2.53(2));

(c) if a decree absolute has been pronounced and the applicant has remarried (as is sometimes the case, and even sometimes done by applicants without mentioning it to their lawyers: see Chapter 21), the discretionary jurisdiction of the MCA 1973 will have been irrevocably lost, an illogicality which must found a further criticism of the existing system.

14.2 STARTING THE ANCILLARY RELIEF PROCESS

The actual process, once it has begun, is actually quite a clever concept. Once within the court system, the matter rolls inexorably on to a timetable, and (as under the new Civil Procedure Rules (CPR) governing mainstream civil justice) the parties cannot get off the treadmill without the court's consent, so there is no scope for the former evasionary tactics which were so costly in financial and other terms. The practising profession let out a collective shriek of horror when the timetable was first implemented, but they have now apparently become used to its pressures, generally with advantageous effect.

An ancillary relief action starts with filing of Form A. The court serves the respondent. Before starting the process the parties are expected to have observed the guidance in the Pre-Application Protocol annexed to *Practice Direction (Ancillary Relief: Procedure) (25 May 2000)* [2000] Fam Law 509, which suggests that proceedings should not be issued if the matter can be agreed.

14.2.1 Filing

The following must be filed if the process is to be started:

- Form A, plus copy for service;
- public funding documentation if appropriate, ie:
  - certificate of public funding;
  - copy notice of issue;
  - notice of acting if not already on the record (ie, where the client was formerly on legal help or is a new client);

- the fee, if payable (ie, if the client is not on public funding when no fee is payable).

If there is a solicitor on the other side, service will usually be on that solicitor.

Where there is an application for a property transfer order, the land must be identified in the Form A, stating whether it is registered or unregistered, identifying the Land Registry title number, and giving particulars of any mortgage or other third party interest (FPR 1991, r 2.59(2)). Where a pension order is sought, this must be stated in the Form A.

There will now be a hearing date fixed at this stage for the First Appointment. This will be between 12 and 16 weeks ahead, and this cannot be vacated or even altered without leave of the court. In this time, most of the preparation of the case will be completed (which practitioners complain now front loads costs, although given the opportunities within the new scheme for settling the case before the final hearing this front loading tends to be cost effective). The district judge has a power to make interim orders at this stage, though 14 days' notice of any such application must be given, and a draft order and short statement of means will be required if an application is made before service of the Form E (see 14.3, below). The respondent must then file a statement of means within seven days of such an interim hearing if the parties' Form Es have still not yet been filed (see r 2.69F). Costs of such hearings will usually be costs in the cause.

14.2.2 Service

The other party must be served within four days of issue (FPR 1991, r 2.61A(4)) with:

- copy Forms A and C;
- notice of issue of public funding; and
- copy notice of acting.

Form A must also be served on any lender or pension provider (FPR 1991, rr 2.59(4) and 2.70(6)). The applicant is required to confirm to the court prior to the First Appointment that Form A has been so served and if it has not the First Appointment may have to be adjourned with a consequent costs penalty.

14.3 FORM E

The spouses' statements of means are now made consistently in Form E, and are most important documents calling for the assembly of detailed information and some skill in drafting. Affidavits are abolished unless specially directed by the court, usually at a later stage if affidavit evidence is called for. Older judges do still tend to direct affidavits (as was the case following the similar introduction of forms and statements for use under the Children Act 1989: see Chapters 24–26) as they feel that these sometimes 'tell the story' better and flesh out the forms, but this may not be strictly necessary since there are several electronic versions of Form E in use which permit expansion of the boxes to include detail to 'flesh out' the case, without negating the entire object of Form E which was to stop parties introducing irrelevancies, thus raising costs and the temperature of proceedings, and to collate all the information required in a standard format.

Nevertheless, narrative affidavits can sometimes be helpful to provide a financial history, especially in big money cases. Wilson J has indicated in a recent case that in appropriate circumstances directions should be sought, when listing a case for final hearing, for the parties to file such affidavits to set out the broader historical presentation of the financial circumstances of each party at the time of the marriage and the developments during the marriage which will illuminate the s 25(2) factors (*W v W (Ancillary Relief: Practice)* [2000] Fam Law 473).

Both parties must file and simultaneously exchange affidavit Form Es to support the application (r 2.61B); the complexity and expense of the former affidavits was the foundation of what has come to be known as the 'millionaire's defence', where a rich respondent (such as Baron Thyssen-Bornemisza in the case of the same name) successfully asks the court not to insist on filing of a detailed affidavit on the basis that the extent of his wealth is such that he can easily pay any order which the court might reasonably make for the support of his former wife, and that the expense and delay occasioned by compiling a detailed affidavit is therefore not justified. In theory this should no longer be necessary since the format of Form E, and the list of documents required to accompany that form, is designed to give the court the restricted amount of information it requires, and no more. Moreover, post-*White*, it is not clear to what extent the millionaires' defence is still valid, in that if in a case with a surplus of assets over needs the judge is to consider all those assets and make an order which is 'fair' and is then checked against the 'yardstick of equality', in theory knowledge is required of all the respective assets which should be considered.

14.3.1 Completion of Form E

Just as the precise form of each of the spouse's affidavits depended on which spouse the draft was for, so parts of Form E require a different approach depending on the party for whom it is filed, since the applicant will be claiming relief and justifying the claims made, whereas the respondent will be resisting the claims and justifying that resistance.

The Form is quite long and details the parties, their children, means, capital and income needs, standard of living, contribution, any seriously relevant conduct and any other relevant circumstances suggested by the particular case. The following means will need to be covered and are usually compiled from the budgets and schedules prepared for the purpose of advising on ancillary relief and then double checked against the client's income tax returns:

(1) *Income:* from all sources (ie, employment, or self-employment, or more than one of each, even State benefits; investments, including bank, building society and other interest, dividends, etc and, if the spouse is self-employed, accounts for the past three (or possibly five) years will be required, alternatively income tax returns for the same period).

(2) *Benefits in kind*: such as company car, tied accommodation, low cost loans, discounts, etc.

(3) *Outgoings*: including national insurance contributions, expenses of travel to work, meals at work, union dues and professional subscriptions, mortgage/rent, council tax, water rates, house and contents insurance, gas, electricity, TV licence, car and

associated expenses, school fees and extras, recreation and clubs, loans and credit cards, legal fees or public funding contributions, etc.

(4) *Assets:* everything owned by the spouse alone or jointly with the spouse or any other person or persons, all real property, and bank and building society accounts should be included, plus shares, unit trusts, PEPs, ISAs, cars, boats, antiques, works of art, jewellery, silver, etc. The history of the acquisition of some assets may be relevant (where, eg, one spouse has been a major contributor to the acquisition of that asset).

(5) *Pension rights, insurance policies, and interests under settlements or trusts:* should not be forgotten, and *expectations under wills or intestacies* may also be relevant.

Certain other matters will have to be dealt with in most cases:

(a) *actual or intended remarriage or cohabitation:* this will obviously be relevant to provision; and

(b) *conduct:* the court is only interested in conduct which it is inequitable to disregard and all other conduct will be irrelevant to the ancillary relief decision (see MCA 1973, s 25(2)(g) in Chapter 12).

Allegations of conduct in this context may necessitate transfer of the case to the High Court due to its difficulty or the complexity or gravity of the issues (*Practice Direction* [1988] 2 All ER 103; [1988] 1 FLR 540). Only the most essential and material allegations of adultery tend therefore to be indulged in at this stage, unless the spouses have time to spend and money to burn.

Whoever is going to argue the case before the district judge if it is not settled normally drafts the Form E, which is seen as a form of advocacy necessitating that the advocate should have the final say over how the case is to be put.

Specialist software packages enable the Form E to be conveniently completed electronically either by expanding and contracting certain boxes or creating explanatory addenda as necessary.

The following must be filed with Form E and copies exchanged with the other party:

- the last three payslips and last P60;
- bank/building society statements for the last 12 months for all accounts;
- any property valuation obtained in the last six months;
- the most recent mortgage statements;
- the last two years' accounts for any business or partnership plus any relevant documentation;
- valuation of any pension; and
- surrender valuations for any life insurance policies.

Any necessary explanatory documentation must be annexed. If there is late disclosure for any reason, the earliest opportunity must be taken to exchange and the defaulting party must enclose an explanation (FPR 1991, r 2.61B).

14.3.2 Preparation for the First Appointment

The parties must prepare, file and exchange at least 14 days prior to the date fixed for the First Appointment:

(a) a concise statement of the issues;

(b) a chronology;

(c) any questionnaire requiring further information and documents requested from the other side. This must refer to the matters raised in Form E. If there are no matters outstanding, the parties file a statement to that effect; and

(d) Form G – a notice stating whether that party will be in a position to treat the First Appointment as the Financial Dispute Resolution (FDR) appointment which will otherwise follow in due course after the First Appointment has effectively rendered the case ready for negotiation.

Each party must immediately before the First Appointment also file a Form H, detailing the costs incurred to date. This has been one of the major deterrents to unstructured handling of ancillary relief claims. The parties simply *cannot* any longer with impunity indulge in fanciful claims just as their advisers *cannot* quietly run up large bills, as the parties as well as their advisers are expected to attend hearings where the district judge will be keeping track of costs and bringing them to the attention of all concerned.

14.3.3 Insufficient disclosure

Under the old ancillary relief regime, there were two categories of defective affidavits:

- those not filed at all; and
- those actually filed but which were inadequate.

In the former case, where no affidavit had been filed, the remedies employed usually secured filing, and this has been overtaken by the new regime which requires simultaneous exchange of Form E. The new scheme retains the potential for interim periodical payments orders, which is likely, as it did in the past, to encourage the desired full disclosure since any respondent will want to establish that he is overpaying if that be the case.

In the latter case, where the affidavit received was so coy that it was hardly better than none at all, the remedies were either:

(a) a *questionnaire*, administered either informally by letter or more formally in a similar format to the request for further and better particulars used in civil litigation generally; and/or

(b) an *application* to the district judge for directions.

Clearly this was a game that could go on for a long time, so that it was recognised to be better *not* to deliver questionnaires in instalments, both because it saved costs, time and temper and because it was much more effective to hit the other side with a comprehensive shopping list of requirements. Instead the advice was to go for one big sortie, preferably of intelligent questions based on a little careful sleuthing beforehand, asking the respondent for as much detail as possible and then threatening to use r 2.62(4) to obtain documents and/or personal attendance for cross-examination and r 2.62(7) for a production appointment, whereby any person could be compelled to attend to produce documents at an earlier stage provided those documents could have been compelled for the actual hearing (r 2.62(9)).

This approach has been adopted in the new ancillary relief scheme. Any questionnaire must now first be authorised by the district judge, hence the requirement to submit it prior to the First Appointment, and only one now tends to be allowed. Moreover, the individual questions in it have to be authorised as necessary or desirable by the district judge. This is an integral part of the court's contemporary control of the case, including of proportionate disclosure.

The theory is that the documents requested and obtained under such procedures should thus always be carefully targeted and then carefully examined. For example, credit card statements can be very productive, since they often inadvertently reveal undisclosed accounts and certainly often bear witness to some very expensive habits and extremely costly non-essential consumption in parties who are resisting comparatively small maintenance for their former nearest and dearest, or even worse for their children, who in a spouse's new lifestyle may often be seen to come long after expensive club subscriptions and large regular payments to exclusive stores. However, under the former regime far too much disclosure was usually routinely required, often without essentially significant results, thus wasting much time, and increasing both costs and the paper mountain.

Unless the case is so simple that the First Appointment is already to be treated as the FDR, and notice has been given in Form G to that effect, the district judge will then decide at the First Appointment precisely what further documentation, over and above Form E and its accompaniments, will be allowed at the FDR and final hearing, and orders accordingly.

14.3.4 Discovery and inspection

The basic system is no different from that now pertaining in ordinary civil litigation under the CPR. However, matrimonial cases are distinct in that again it will usually be necessary to adopt an intelligent approach to what is produced and to look for clues about what is not being provided. The new regime provides for this in the district judge's stocktaking at the First Appointment, to assess:

- what questionnaires need to be answered;
- what documents produced;
- what valuations or other expert evidence is needed;
- what other evidence is needed (eg, schedules of assets or narrative affidavits).

Obviously the parties will not wish to have a pitched battle over every gas bill, but an analytical approach to the documentation is likely to yield reward, resulting in application being made for what is missing. The obligation is still to provide full and frank disclosure to the court, which cannot make orders properly without it, and this is made clear in the Pre-Action Protocol: while this was always the practice, as was made clear in *Livesey v Jenkins* [1985] 2 WLR 47, it has now also been formally enshrined in *Practice Direction* [1995] Fam Law 156 and the court does not take kindly to being misled, so the parties are more than entitled to probe.

Normally the following will be needed:

(a) valuation of the home by a joint valuer, appointed by the court if the parties cannot agree on one;

(b) similar valuation of a family business; and

(c) any available evidence of a new partner's means (which may not be much, as the court cannot order evidence from the new partner unless that party could already be compelled to come to court with any documents (see *Frary v Frary* [1993] 2 FLR 696)).

Either party can always ask the district judge for specific discovery of any document which he or she suspects is needed and has not been produced. This can be very productive, since one document often leads to another, until it becomes absolutely clear why the one first asked for at the beginning was not produced.

The district judge will then fix the date for the FDR, unless the case is:

• so complex that a second directions appointment is needed;

• so simple that it can go direct to final hearing;

• suitable for adjournment for mediation or negotiation; or

• one requiring adjournment generally.

The district judge can also make interim orders or make an appointment to consider an interim order before whatever is to be the next stage. He or she can also make costs orders at this stage, and any party who has caused the opportunity to be lost to treat the First Appointment as the FDR might receive an adverse costs order here.

There will be no further disclosure allowed between First Appointment and FDR. Thus has the mountain of paper relentlessly generated under the old system (and encouraged by the wide availability of relatively inexpensive photocopying) been controlled, with identifiable time and cost benefits, as well as improved focus and better deployment of the court's resources.

14.3.5 Offers

At this stage, between First Appointment and FDR, if it has not been considered or made before, it may be advisable to make an offer of settlement or one may be expected from the other side. This may be an open offer or a *Calderbank* offer.

The latter is an offer, called after the case of the same name, reported at [1976] Fam 93, which is expressed to be 'without prejudice, but reserving the right to refer to the offer on the issue of costs'. Obviously such an offer is better in writing and is usually in a letter. It is the matrimonial equivalent of a payment into court and is subject to the same rule of not being referred to at the hearing. If the district judge awards no more than was offered, the offer may then be referred to and should protect the party on whose behalf it was sent at least from having to pay the other side's costs from the date it was made, and may indeed enable the offeror's own costs to be recovered also.

There is a special system for disclosure of such offers under the new ancillary relief scheme which requires the applicant to inform the court of all offers, including those made without prejudice, and their status 14 days before the FDR. The court expects such offers to be made and considered, along with any counter proposals (see *Practice Direction (Ancillary Relief Procedure)* [2000] Fam Law 509).

There must be another Form H detailing costs to date immediately prior to the FDR.

14.3.6 The Financial Dispute Resolution

This is the hearing which attempts to settle the case, and must be attended by both parties and all legal representatives. All discussions and documents used at this hearing are privileged and records will not be kept on the court file. The district judge attempts to facilitate the parties' discussions by exploring common ground in the manner of a mediator. If settlement is reached, a consent order can be made. If no agreement is reached the district judge will take no further part in the case, but will consider if any further directions are required for the full hearing and may order narrative affidavits at this stage (eg, to show a wife's complex contributions, the financial history or the standard of living of the parties: see *W v W (Ancillary Relief: Practice)* [2000] Fam Law 473).

14.3.7 The hearing

The hearing will usually be in chambers before the district judge and will be private, although there is power to refer the application to a judge of the court (FPR 1991, r 2.65). Such hearings are normally very informal though occasionally a particular judge will prefer more formality. The furniture is usually arranged in a T shape in front of the judge and the parties and their lawyers sit either side of a table along the leg of the T with the judge at the top addressing the court seated.

The case will normally be opened for the applicant, witnesses called and cross-examined, the same order followed for the respondent, and then the advocates for the respondent and the applicant respectively will address the court. However, some district judges are much more informal and will indicate from the start what they are considering by way of order and will adopt an inquisitorial approach based on their reading of the file, inviting comment on specific matters before deciding on an appropriate order, which may be delivered in the form of a short judgment or alternatively they may merely announce the decision. An interim order would be made if a final order is not possible (eg, the employment situation of one party is still sufficiently fluid for a final order to be unjust). A good note is usually taken by both sides of the whole proceedings or at least the judgment, in case there is to be an appeal.

The hearing is also a clear indication of the arrival in the Family Division of all the finer details of case management which were building up in other divisions long before the CPR, but which under the old system were conspicuous by their absence. The present President of the Family Division and her predecessor have been working towards similar efficiency for some years and the full implementation of the new ancillary relief scheme appears at last to have achieved a degree of case management which has driven forward the reforms in an effective manner.

The 1995 President's Direction on case management, delivered in the Practice Direction referred to above, which followed those handed down in the Queen's Bench and Chancery Divisions, limited the length of opening and closing speeches, both of which were thereafter required to be 'succinct', and also the time allowed for examination and cross-examination of witnesses and reading aloud from documents and authorities. This has now been added to by two others: the *Practice Direction (Family Proceedings: Court Bundles) (10 March 2000)* [2001] 1 FLR 536; and the further *President's Practice Direction (Ancillary Relief Procedure) (25 May 2000)* [2000] 1 FLR 997 specifically contemplating the implementation nationally of the ancillary pilot scheme in June 2000.

Between them, these Practice Directions set out the standards required in documentation and hearings in all family proceedings except in emergency, so as to streamline and control both oral hearings and the paper mountain before the court; unless otherwise ordered, witness statements and affidavits have for some time been treated as evidence in chief and have themselves always been supposed to be confined to what is reasonably essential. Moreover, there has been for a long time the requirement of a bundle to be agreed, and sufficient copies produced in A4 format, for the use of the court and parties, to be duly lodged with the court, properly paginated and indexed, two clear days before the hearing. (Such, obviously, had been the standard of previous preparation, that the 1995 Direction indicated that the President even found it necessary to require that such bundles be 'wholly legible' and 'arranged chronologically'.) A pre-trial review and skeleton argument was required in cases estimated to last five days or more. Following the 2000 Practice Directions, there is a format for the content of the bundle in all non-emergency cases which includes:

- a summary of the background to the hearing, if possible on one A4 page;
- a statement of the issues;
- a summary of the order or directions sought by each party;
- a chronology for a final hearing if the A4 summary is insufficient in this respect;
- skeleton arguments; and
- copies of all authorities relied on.

While in 1995 it seemed that the court retained such a realistic view of the general standard of preparation which was likely to be achieved notwithstanding these instructions (since provision was made in cases where there was 'no core bundle' for parties to furnish the court 'with a list of essential documents for a proper understanding of the case'), no such leeway is now contemplated, as was made clear by Wall LJ when, following patchy observance of the March 2000 Practice Direction, he issued a lengthy and irritated comment on what was expected in the May 2000 case of *Re CH (A Minor)* (2000) unreported.

It might have been supposed that any advocate with any experience at all would have swiftly seen how essential to the proper presentation of a case the requirements of the 1995 Practice Direction were and wondered why it was necessary to formalise those requirements in such a manner then, let alone to repeat them with further detail in 2000. Clearly such preparation makes all the difference between a case with which the advocate is familiar and which can be presented in a readily digestible manner likely to produce the desired order and one where the district judge is obliged to dig and delve to discover what it is all about, and as a result might well not be drawn to the inevitable conclusion that the order sought was the one that should be made. However, as a result of this negative experience, the 2000 Practice Directions appear to have served notice that court documentation is now expected to follow the President's requisitions.

14.4 THE ORDER

Drafting of an order is as important as the substantive content: the practical results of many cases have turned on the drafting employed:

(1) Periodical payments do not necessarily run from the date of the order but can be backdated to the date of the application (though the court might not want to make them if this produces large arrears which cannot conveniently be met).

(2) The order may be registered in the Family Proceedings Court (see Chapter 17).

(3) Costs should always either be ordered or allowed for in the order, as this is always a vexed question in ancillary relief where there may be no clear winner (see *Gojkovic v Gojkovic (No 2)* [1991] 2 FLR 233), and where one or both parties may be on public funding. Costs are required to be proportionate, and the new CPR costs rules apply to family cases, including summary assessment and penalisation of obstructive behaviour (CPR 1988, Pts 43, 44, 47 and 48; Family Proceedings (Miscellaneous Amendments) Rules 1999; *Practice Direction (Family Proceedings: Costs)* [1999] 1 FLR 1295).

(4) Public funding taxation is expressly ordered (and must therefore be expressly asked for) to enable costs to be recovered from the Legal Services Commission where appropriate.

Liberty to apply should be included to enable the parties to return to court if difficulties subsequently arise in the implementation of the order, though this means strictly for the purposes of *implementation*, not *variation* (see Chapter 13).

The order will be drawn up and available for the parties usually within a few days of being made. Unless there is an appeal, or enforcement problems, that is the end of the ancillary relief matter. It appears that certificates for counsel are no longer required where counsel are instructed.

14.5 APPEALS

Either party may appeal from the district judge to the judge within 14 days of the order (FPR 1991, r 8.1(4)), setting out the grounds of the appeal. The judge will exercise a complete discretion in hearing the appeal, but will give such weight as is thought fit to matters determined by the district judge – the judge decides to what extent such matters are to be reopened and has a complete discretion over what further evidence may be admitted (*Marsh v Marsh* [1993] 2 All ER 794).

Consent orders (see 14.6, below) can also be appealed, but it seems that the correct way to do this is to apply to set the order aside (FPR 1991, rr 1.3(1), 8.1 and 8.2; County

Court Rules (CCR) 1981, Ord 37, r 6). Pursuant to Ord 37, r 6, a rehearing will be ordered on application within 14 days, or later with leave to make the application out of time.

14.6 CONSENT ORDERS (MCA 1973, s 33A)

The full procedure described above is not necessary if the parties succeed in what is now often the original aim of agreeing a consent order from the start. In that case, s 33A of the MCA 1973 gives the court power to make a consent order, r 2.61 of the FPR 1991 will apply and the abbreviated procedure may be followed:

(1) If agreement is reached before Form A is filed, application is simply made by one party or the other on Form A as appropriate for an order in the agreed terms, lodging with the application two copies of a draft order, one of which must be endorsed with a statement signed by the respondent agreeing to the terms.

(2) If agreement is reached at any time *after* Form A is filed, and before the First Appointment, the same procedure may still be followed.

(3) In either case, pursuant to r 2.61 the full procedure need not be followed but the court will require a short statement of financial information on which it may base its order. There is a form, called a 'Rule 2.61 Form', for this purpose, although it is not strictly necessary to use it. It is usually convenient to use the form, but the information required *may* be given in another manner, if desired in more than one document, so that existing disclosure might satisfy the rule such as where Form Es have already been filed.

The purpose of this procedure is to avoid the court making a consent order on inadequate information regarding whether each of the parties intends to remarry or cohabit (clearly relevant to the provision in the order), where each party is to live and, briefly, what capital and income is at the disposal of the each of those parties. Without this the court is unable to have an opinion on whether the order is broadly fair, and might make an order such as in *Livesey v Jenkins* (see 14.3.4, above) where the wife who was receiving a generous order suitable to her not remarrying immediately neglected to mention that she was engaged to be married and proposed to do so with indecent haste.

Where agreement is reached only long after the proceedings have been established, and perhaps at the door of the court, the court does have the power to dispense with the strict requirements of r 2.61 and can both manage without the draft order and direct that the r 2.61 information be given in any form that is convenient, thus enabling an order to be made before the parties change their minds (r 2.61(3)).

Xydias v Xydias [1999] 1 FLR 683 shows that heads of agreement, or some clear record of what has been agreed, should be prepared and signed by the parties, so that there is no confusion over the status of the agreement, which will not be enforced by the court as a contract, though they may regard it as their prerogative to decide whether agreement has been reached and to decide to make an order in the terms of the agreement.

It is the *practitioner's* responsibility, and *not* the court's, to see that the order is carefully drafted so as to reflect accurately and comprehensively what the parties have agreed: see *per* Lord Oliver of Aylmerton in *Dinch v Dinch* [1987] 1 WLR 252 in Chapter 13 and

Sandford v Sandford [1986] 1 FLR 412, where it is made crystal clear that this is not the *court's* responsibility since the court, not being fully aware of what it is desired to achieve, is not there to pick up the parties' legal advisers' potential errors. It is for this reason that solicitors are advised that it is a good idea to take some time to settle the terms of the order, possibly to have them approved by counsel, and then to bring a properly agreed draft to the court. Otherwise, in the haste attending the order drawn up in the court corridor, far from protecting their clients from the results of the other side's aggressive negotiation, it may be their opponents who are enabled to get back on the drafting what they have lost on the negotiation, a well established practice in the supposedly co-operative atmosphere of 'doing the best for the family as a whole'.

There are many good sets of precedents (eg, those of the Solicitors Family Law Association) which can be reviewed in order to assess the best way of putting together a satisfactory settlement expressed in an effective draft order, and these are commended to academic students for a better understanding of the substantive law.

14.7 GOOD PRACTICE IN ANCILLARY RELIEF

It must be stressed that the entire philosophy of ancillary relief in English law is that the only good settlement is one which is made on the basis of full and frank disclosure, and the only good consent order is one which is fair in relation to all the matters that must be taken into account in arriving at a balanced result. Any consent order should therefore be for relief in the ballpark area of what the court would be likely to order after a contested hearing at which the parties had both been properly represented.

Practitioners therefore consider that it may be a good idea, in cases even where the full ancillary relief procedure is not to be followed, to ask for Form Es to be exchanged in draft, although disclosure may be made much more informally, either orally at meetings, supported by such documents and vouchers as are reasonably required to verify what is being said, or in correspondence. Acceptable documentary support would often be tax returns and such other more detailed documents as the other party's advisers might reasonably request. This achieves as full and frank disclosure as is really necessary and saves a lot of time and expense since the greatest part of a contested ancillary relief matter is not the hearing but the preparation.

The abbreviated procedure may then be used with some confidence to obtain the actual order once it is agreed. This approach usually does *tend* to produce the best result for the family as a whole, since the best use may be made of tax planning, and it may also generate a more co-operative attitude which may benefit everyone in other ways.

The only situation in which full and frank disclosure on the approved model might not be insisted upon is where the parties are obviously co-operating well, and nothing is to be gained by turning down or querying good offers which are being made. Nothing is to be gained by putting either or both of the parties' backs up and if there are still small areas of disagreement in such a case, either small concessions can be made (it is unusual for a party to have to make no concessions at all) or a persuasive solicitor can often put the final touches to an agreement which has already been substantially made by the parties by coaxing the last items of detail out of a party who has already showed more than willing. Similarly, it is necessary to be careful if there is any suggestion of revenue fraud, as recent cases have indicated that where such evidence comes to light in the course of ancillary relief the administration of justice will usually require the court to take appropriate action. In *A v A; B v B* [2000] 1 FLR 701, this point was considered, and the argument that the requirement for full and frank disclosure between the parties entitled the perpetrator of any such fraud to immunity was found to be flawed and unattractive.

If a halfway house is desired between an agreed order and a court hearing, there is available a service provided by the Family Law Bar Association Conciliation Board which provides an adjudicator from a panel of senior barristers to consider the papers and make a recommendation, which may or may not be binding on the parties as they wish themselves to provide before seeking the adjudicator's help. It is only available where both parties are represented by solicitors. It is not a free service, but can be useful in avoiding much more expensive proceedings. Some family law chambers at the Bar, and also many solicitors practising family law, offer mediation services which can be cost effective in comparison with litigation, yet offer a more independent quasi-judicial service than negotiation between the parties' solicitors.

ANCILLARY RELIEF PROCEDURE

NEW ANCILLARY RELIEF SCHEME

There has been a new ancillary relief scheme in use nationally since 2 June 2000. This was designed to address the problems of expense and delay in the former ancillary relief procedure. There is a new Pre-Action Protocol giving guidance for the pre-litigation stages of ancillary relief disputes. Ancillary relief may be obtained through negotiating a financial settlement privately through the parties' solicitors and obtaining a consent order from the court to formalise the settlement, or by means of the court's formal framework which controls timetable and documentation.

TERMINOLOGY

In ancillary relief the parties are the 'applicant' and the 'respondent'. The petitioner in the divorce suit may not necessarily be the applicant in ancillary relief.

APPLYING FOR ANCILLARY RELIEF

The first application is made in the prayer of the petition, and if the matter is not to be settled informally pursuant to the Pre-Application Protocol, which counsels against proceedings if settlement can be achieved, the claim in the petition will be followed by activation by Form A. If the applicant is the respondent, then application is made on Form A which is filed by the applicant with a copy for service. In either case this is served by the court on the other party, and a date given for the First Appointment 12–16 weeks ahead. Public funding is available for ancillary relief. Interim orders can be made at this stage, upon basic financial information. If no application was made by the petitioner in the prayer of the petition, the petition can be amended to include such a prayer, unless decree *nisi* has been granted. If the applicant has remarried without having made an application for ancillary relief, it is then too late to do so and the applicant will instead have to rely on other remedies outside the discretionary ambit of the MCA 1973.

DISCLOSURE

Full and frank disclosure is expected in Form E and accompanying documents, which must be filed and served on the other party 35 working days before the date of the First Appointment. After filing and serving Form E, the parties must still produce for the First Appointment a concise statement of issues, chronology, a draft of any questionnaire desired to be administered to the other party and a Form G notice as to whether that party is in a position to treat the First Appointment as the FDR appointment, and also in Form H an up to date statement of costs incurred so far.

FIRST APPOINTMENT

This is basically for directions (eg, ordering experts reports (generally one agreed by the parties or appointed by the court), settling any questionnaires, ordering extra evidence, etc). If it is treated as an FDR, the case may settle at this stage and a consent order, including an order for costs, may be made. If not, the case proceeds to FDR, possibly with further directions at that stage, unless a further directions appointment is needed, or an adjournment for mediation or other purposes. Interim orders can be made. No further disclosure is allowed without leave of the court.

FINANCIAL DISPUTE RESOLUTION

This is without prejudice and intended to settle the case if possible, through the facilitation of the district judge, who must receive notice of all offers made prior to the hearing, including any made without prejudice. Offers are expected to be made and considered at the hearing and settlement seriously explored. If it does not settle, that district judge will take no further part in the case, all documentation is privileged and does not remain on the court file, and the case proceeds to hearing. The district judge might order affidavits to be prepared if this would assist a complex case (eg, to understand a wife's contributions, or the financial history). An up to date costs statement will again be required.

THE HEARING

This follows the usual format of a hearing in private before the district judge, with the applicant presenting his or her case, including evidence from witnesses if applicable, followed by cross-examination of them. Then the respondent does the same and the district judge makes an order, either final or interim if a final order is not possible. Costs will be dealt with pursuant to the latest up to date costs statements required of the parties, and the order drawn up.

CONSENT ORDERS

Consent orders can be planned from the start or entered into at any time on the basis of the usual disclosure in r 2.61 of the FPR 1991 unless that format is dispensed with or substituted by order of the district judge. It is the responsibility of the parties, not the court, to have the order drafted to reflect their agreement.

CHAPTER 15

CHILD SUPPORT

15.1 INTRODUCTION

One of the definable aspects of parental responsibility (see Chapter 24) is the obligation to support a child financially. This has resulted over the last decade in the separation of child maintenance from assessment of support and financial provision for the spouse, whether on divorce or within marriage, and in the creation of a uniform regime for child support regardless of whether the child's parents are married or not – so that all children, marital and non-marital, are to be treated equally for this purpose. The magic vehicle was supposed to be the Child Support Agency (CSA), set up to implement the Child Support Acts.

In theory this was an excellent idea, as many individual such theories in family law have undoubtedly been. In practice it has proved to be more disaster than magic, and has offered one of the most obvious examples of the real necessity to treat family law holistically, rather than as the sum of its independent parts, in order to avoid unexpected knock on effects in other areas of the law.

The fault does not appear to have been in the concept of child support itself – although the substantive law and practical application as originally set up was certainly unnecessarily complicated, and suffered from an ongoing rash of unnecessarily complex (and sometimes even muddled) amendments – but in the administrative disaster of the CSA. The CSA immediately caught the attention of the popular press, who recorded with glee the ongoing story of the fatally flawed rigid calculations which produced astronomical sums said to be owing by quite ordinary people, and drove some children's non-resident parents to suicide in despair of ever stopping the manic machine which endlessly churned out these frightening demands.

Moreover, the CSA seemed always to pursue those who were actually already paying for their children (although according to the CSA's calculations they were not paying enough), but never seemed to catch those who were paying nothing, and through a series of embarrassing mistakes sometimes broke up marriages when in cases of mistaken identity they targeted the wrong person as allegedly the absent parent of a child. The unfortunate victim was sometimes completely unable to convince a wife, who took the assessment at face value, that he was not and could not be the father.

Additionally, there were cases of assessments so large that attentive fathers who had kept in touch with their children, and would have liked to remain so, were unable to afford the costs of continued contact as well as being stretched to pay the new assessment. In particular, capital given to their families at the time of divorce, including obligations under loans sometimes taken out by absent fathers on their families' behalf to provide both necessities and luxuries, were disregarded as the assessment regime made no allowance for them, and no allowance was originally made for obvious costs such as travel to work to earn the money out of which the assessment would have to be paid, nor for the expenses of a subsequent family to which the father had concurrent obligations. This was despite the recognition of the importance of such obligations in case law recognising relevant contemporary issues, such as *Delaney v Delaney* [1990] 2 FLR 457 in which a father's aspirations for a life after divorce had been expressly acknowledged by the court.

Of course, the previous situation was scandalous, in which many absent fathers got away with miniscule child maintenance payments (and then often had to be let off by the court when they built up arrears and could not pay them). Baroness Thatcher is credited, when first Prime Minister, with vowing to reverse this unsatisfactory state of affairs, and the implementation of the scheme in the hands of a government agency was in character with the philosophy of her term of office. However, while other agencies were more successful it seemed that the CSA was doomed from the start and a series of resignations identified it to those likely to be appointed to such agencies as a poison chalice particularly important to be avoided. Parents, too, flocked to avoid its intervention wherever they could, which the Child Support (Written Agreements) Order 1993 enabled them to do, as long as they were not on welfare benefits. Those unlucky enough not to be able to avail themselves of this escape route were therefore trapped within the apparently unstoppably catastrophic system. Moreover there were 'silly' cases, such as where a millionaire father could not be assessed for payments as he had no assessable income, which should not have been an insuperable problem when drafting the regulations in the first place since tariff income from capital has always had a place in the welfare benefits regime and surely could have been included in the CSA's system.

15.2 THE DUAL CSA-COURT APPLICATION SYSTEM

Application to the court for child maintenance to be included in consent orders under the Matrimonial Causes Act (MCA) 1973 has already been discussed in Chapter 12. This chapter therefore looks mainly at the statutory arrangements for child support under the Child Support Acts, and also under the Children Act (CA) 1989 (which provides much the same supplementary financial orders for children of unmarried parents as the MCA 1973 does for those of parents who have been married and are divorcing) and at the interface between the CSA and the court.

As explained in Chapter 12, unless it is agreed between the parents, most child maintenance is now obtained pursuant to assessments under the Child Support Acts 1991–95, as amended by the Child Support, Pensions and Social Security Act 2000 passed on 28 July 2000, and supposed to be progressively operational from 2002, which has not in fact occurred. There is expected to be a gradual phasing in of the new provisions, probably up to 2009. The 1991–95 system is therefore currently still in use and for a while there will be two systems, for which the current version of the leading practitioner software *Child's Pay* has carefully catered so that calculations can be made under both systems (see 15.3, below). As the entire framework of child support, both old and new, is quite complex, but nevertheless forms an integral part of many undergraduate syllabuses, it may be that the best way to grasp it for those undergraduates whose universities offer vocational law courses, and are therefore likely to have *Child's Pay* in their electronic resources, will be to go to the software to find out for themselves in making the calculations how the assessments work. They will thus be able to form a view at first hand of whether the current reforms are effective or not.

15.2.1 Child Support, Pensions and Social Security Act 2000

The 2000 reforms followed a Green Paper, *Children Come First* (Cmnd 3992, 1998), which has generated much academic and practitioner comment. See, for example, 'Third time lucky for child support?' by Professor Chris Barton in [1998] Fam Law 668; and 'The Green Paper and child support – children first: a new approach to child support' by Nicholas Mostyn in [1999] Fam Law 95. Professor Barton, who has a longstanding interest in child support, also writes regularly on the subject in *The Times* legal pages and Nicholas Mostyn QC, a leading member of the Family Law Bar Association, is a co-author of the *Child's Pay* software package (see above). Their commentary is therefore particularly valuable since they have devoted many years of commitment to analysing the subject with some intellectual rigour.

It should be noted that child support has during the decade since its introduction become so complex that there is a specialist series of reports (the Child Support Commissioners Reports) which record decisions both on substantive law and procedure. There is also now an Independent Case Examiner (ICE), who deals with complaints outside the appellate structure of the CSA, although alternative recourse may also be had to the Ombudsman who may entertain a case after the ICE, though not *vice versa*. In other words, child support has grown into a significant specialist area of family law.

15.2.2 The court's residual jurisdiction

As explained in Chapter 12, there remain alongside the CSA system the residual powers of the court to make orders outside the CSA framework, in other words, all lump sum and property adjustment orders (as the CSA deals only in periodical maintenance payments) and periodical maintenance orders for children who are:

(a) over age 19, or who are still under 19 but have finished their non-advanced education;

(b) 'non-qualifying children' within the meaning of the Child Support Acts, in that there is no natural 'absent parent' (under the new legislation called the 'non-resident' parent) who can be assessed, so that the CSA may make no assessment but the court may make an order against a stepparent if a child is a 'child of the family' pursuant to s 52 of the MCA 1973;

(c) overseas residents or one or both of whose parents are not resident in the jurisdiction, so that the CSA may make no assessment but the court, if it has jurisdiction in divorce, nullity or judicial separation, may make a court order for child maintenance;

(d) applicants for top up payments, for example, for disability, school fees or other educational expenses in addition to the computerised calculation of the maintenance requirement which does not include such expenses.

The other statutory sources of financial orders for children, apart from ancillary relief under the MCA 1973, which supplement the CSA either:

• instead of the CSA assessment in the relevant cases mentioned above; or

- to top up the CSA assessment when that has reached the limit of its remit,

are:

- the Domestic Proceedings and Magistrates' Courts Act (DPMCA) 1978 (see Chapter 19);
- s 27 of the MCA 1973 (see Chapter 19);
- s 15 of and Sched 1 to the CA 1989 (see below).

Generally the last named will be used by the unmarried, since married parents can secure the same or better provision under one of the other jurisdictions.

15.3 CHILD SUPPORT ACTS 1991–95 AS AMENDED

The language of the original statute is distinctive (although there are subtle changes in terminology in the 2000 reforms which have yet to be implemented). The original *dramatis personae* comprises:

(a) The *qualifying child* (the child who needs the maintenance) who is a child one or both of whose parents is in relation to him *absent* (now called the 'non-resident' parent) (s 3(1)).

An adopted child or a child born by artificial insemination by a donor is included as a qualifying child unless in the latter case the husband is proved not to have consented to the treatment (Human Fertilisation and Embryology Act 1990, s 28(2)). But a child who is or ever has been married is excluded from the operation of the CSA 1991 (s 55(2)).

(b) The *absent parent* (any parent who is not living with the child where the child has a home with someone else who has care of that child) for the pursuit of whom the CSA was created (now called the 'non-resident' parent) (s 3(2)).

(c) The *person with care* (the person with whom the child has a home who provides day to day care for that child, whether exclusively or in conjunction with any other person, sometimes also called the *carer parents*) (s 3(3)).

The local authority does not appear anywhere in this cast of actors as the CA 1989 provides alternative means of their recovering the cost of caring for children when appropriate.

The CSA operates on the basis of the statutory duty to maintain a qualifying child, which is set out in s 1(1) of the CSA 1991 and makes each parent equally responsible, but by s 1(3) it is the *absent* ('non-resident') parent who has the duty of making the payments under a CSA assessment. The CSA then uses a computer based formula to make assessments, as to the operation of which see below.

15.3.1 The Child Support Agency and benefit cases

Where a carer parent is in receipt of specified State benefits, it is a requirement that the Secretary of State be authorised to take action to recover the amount paid out to the child in maintenance from the absent parent (CSA 1991, s 6(1)) and by s 46 benefit may be reduced if co-operation is not forthcoming from the carer parent either in refusing authorisation or in refusing essential information (ie, the identity of the natural father to pursue). However, in an appropriate case the carer parent can decline to do this without losing benefit provided the child support officer accepts that if the carer parent were to co-operate there would be adverse consequences of some kind. This normally means showing a likelihood of violence to the carer or the child since the officer has a discretion but must have regard to 'the welfare of any child likely to be affected by his decision' (CSA 1991, s 2).

15.3.2 Review of assessments

There is provision for review of assessments every two years (CSA 1991, s 16 as amended). Either the absent ('non-resident') parent or carer can apply at any time for a review if there has been a change of circumstances (s 17).

Although there is no room for discretion in making assessments and if the figures fed in are right the result should also be correct, any assessment which is thought to be wrong should be appealed within 28 days. Further appeal is possible to the Child Support Appeal Tribunal, then to the Child Support Appeal Commissioner on point of law, and subsequently to the Court of Appeal and House of Lords in the normal way (Child Support Appeal Tribunals (Procedure) Regulations 1992 SI 1992/2641).

Collection and enforcement are also provided for by the Act. When the original Act was passed it was ultimately intended that the CSA would take over the assessment, enforcement and collection of all child maintenance, although this was progressively postponed as the CSA clearly found its existing workload onerous and complex. It remains to be seen what will happen under the 2000 reforms. Meanwhile the usual methods of enforcement can be used, but additionally the regime offers the administrative procedure of a deduction of earnings order for which no court order is needed and there are also liability orders obtainable from the magistrates. Interest is available on arrears in excess of 28 days old.

15.3.3 The effect of clean break settlements

Originally any capital given to the carer parent at the time of divorce had no effect on liability for a CSA assessment under the non-discretionary rules (causing much hardship), but the Child Support and Income Support (Amendment) Regulations 1995 SI 1995/1045 have since April 1995 enabled past capital settlements to be taken into account. However, although these provide some relief where before there was none, the effect is hardly dramatic. The maximum deduction is £60 per week if the value of the transfer made under the capital settlement exceeds £25,000, and if it was less than £5,000 it does not count at all. Up to £10,000, the absent parent gets £20 per week off maintenance and up to £25,000 it is £40 per week.

The capital settlement must have been made by court order or written agreement prior to 5 April 1993 (ie, when the Act came into force), and must otherwise have satisfied the normal conditions of a clean break capital settlement, in that while the parties were separated (though divorce is not necessary) an outright transfer of property or payment of capital must have been made by the absent parent to the carer in circumstances other than to buy out the carer parent's share of an asset.

While this may be some help for people caught up in the maelstrom behind earlier settlements before the CSA was even a twinkle in the government's eye, this is a further incentive to contemporary parties to clean break settlements to take warning and attempt to deal with matters in a manner which benefits the family overall by agreement while they still can.

15.3.4 The parties affected by the legislation

The Child Support Acts affect all absent natural parents of qualifying children, whether they were ever married to the carer parent of the child or not.

15.3.5 The assessment formula: how maintenance is assessed under the pre-2000 framework

Both parents complete detailed forms to give the Agency full information about their financial position. Maintenance is then assessed, not on the basis of any discretion, but by applying a rigid computer based formula which is aimed to achieve consistency in assessments and to provide a realistic sum which recognises the true costs of child caring and rearing. Unlike in the case of the old court assessed orders, which were usually tacked on to a substantive order for the custodial parent, this is supposed to provide a realistic amount towards the real costs of bringing up a child, and this is generally the case even where the custodial parent is no longer being maintained (eg, because of remarriage). Under the former system, in that sort of case the child would have been left with an uneconomic order, frequently too low actually to provide food and clothing let alone contribute to the cost of keeping a roof over his or her head. Thus, if the CSA assessments have done anything, they have helped remarried parents and stepparents, since the natural father will usually have to pay something closer to the true cost of bringing up the child, removing some financial strain from stepparents and also from stepparents' first families who often suffered under the former system.

The formula for calculating the child's maintenance is complicated, and is related to other social security benefits, mainly income support (for a general explanation of which, see Chapter 18). The formula has four parts.

15.3.5.1 The maintenance requirement

This is the income support level for the child *plus* an allowance for the carer minus child benefit (but not minus the extra lone parent benefit).

This is the element of CSA assessments which annoys some absent parents as they then indirectly have to maintain the child's carer, usually the mother, through the carer's personal allowance. It is annoying where the father does not want to maintain the mother anyway, because, for example, there is a clean break, but as it applies even where the parties were not married and there was never any obligation to maintain the mother as such, that category of absent father tends to be even more irritated at having to pay through the CSA. This is obviously a case where an agreed solution outside the CSA framework usually is demonstrably better.

15.3.5.2 The assessable income of each parent

This is the net income of each parent after deducting income tax, national insurance, travel expenses to work and half pension contributions, *minus* the parent's exempt income for basic living expenses at income support rates, though anyone on income support is treated as having no assessable income (CSA 1991, Sched 1).

The *actual* living expenses are irrelevant as those taken into account will be based on the income support formula. This is another item which irritates absent parents as even if they are, for example, buying a car or a TV on hire purchase for the ex-spouse and child, the regular payments do not count. If the mother and child *want* such a car or a TV, this will be another incentive to contract out of the CSA assessment.

15.3.5.3 The basic deduction rate

This means the two parents' total assessable income is divided by two and if the resulting figure is equal to or less than the maintenance requirement above, then each parent is liable to pay half their assessable income for the children.

Where the absent parent is on income support, he or she will still have to pay a minimum amount per week out of the income support received unless he or she is living with other children and already receiving family premium or comes into other specified exceptional categories. Thus, even absent parents on income support have to pay something nominal which perhaps generates some awareness of responsibility towards children.

15.3.5.4 The additional element

This is where the assessable income is more than the amount needed to satisfy the maintenance requirement above and enables those absent parents with more money to pay more maintenance, the maximum amount of which was halved in April 1995 due to complaints from absent parents that this took away further sums from their incomes which they could not spare. There is also a protected income level which is applied to prevent the absent parent from falling below subsistence level.

15.4 REFORM OF THE CSA REGIME

The result of the ongoing tinkering with the 1991–95 Acts has been a large number of gates to a 'departures' order where parents were obliged to be within the CSA system and yet had special circumstances which morally required consideration within the CSA assessment, and yet were initially excluded by the computerised framework. This in turn generated a wholesale exodus to agreed orders pursuant to s 8(5) because of the complex formulae adopted. Attempts to try to provide fair assessments within the rigid computer driven scheme, so that there were 'safety nets' for low earners, became too complicated, especially because of the concepts of syphoning off first a basic element of 50% of the payer's assessable income up to the threshold of £75–£110 per week, followed by a stepped 'additional element' depending on the number of children – 15% for one child, 20% for two, 25% for three or more up to a ceiling (calculated by another formula) of about £55 per child.

The CSA 2000 scheme will adopt a simpler approach. This will be based on:

- the children who are the subject of the assessment; and
- the circumstances of the payer (now to be called the 'non-resident parent' rather than the insulting 'absent parent').

15.4.1 A new six point framework

15.4.1.1 Circumstances of the 'resident parent' (formerly the parent with care (PWC))

The circumstances of the resident parent are to be completely ignored, as will the non-resident parent's housing costs, both allowed under the present scheme.

15.4.1.2 Reduced liability of the 'non-resident parent' (formerly the 'absent parent')

Children's overnight stays with their non-resident parent (NRP), as now, will bring down the NRP's liability (instead of the present reduction for more than 104 nights per annum, 52 nights will operate as a reduction by one seventh, moving up a scale of further reductions up to 175 nights which cuts the liability by 50%).

The NRP's circumstances will include his or her (but usually his) income, pension contributions (now 100% as against only 50% formerly allowed) and all the children in his household, including stepchildren, whether of a legal marriage or unmarried partnership (to qualify in this respect the NRP will have to show receipt of child benefit by himself or his partner). Professor Barton is concerned about this, as it is a clear invitation to the unmarried man to obtain potentially undeserved relief from obligations to women and children in a series of relationships.

15.4.1.3 New straight line formula for percentage assessment

There will be a straight line rather than a stepped formula from the start so that the NRP will simply hand over 15%, 20% or 25% of his entire assessable income, up to a ceiling of £2,000 per week, depending on the number of children to be supported. This means that the maximum assessment will be £15,600 for one child, £20,800 for two and £26,000 for three or more. Top ups are retained, so that it will still be possible to go to the court for more where appropriate, though there is to be a ceiling on these payments and they are only to operate when the CSA assessment ceiling is reached.

There is, however, a complex system for protection of parents at the lower end of the scale, which is intended to specify who pays what. Moreover, the CSA will be able to assess NRPs working overseas for UK and UK based companies or for government employees such as the armed services or diplomatic service.

15.4.1.4 Variations (formerly called 'departures')

Departures are retained but renamed 'variations' (conveniently the same term as for court order variations).

15.4.1.5 New operating procedures

Further changes make it easier for the CSA to operate. It will be a crime to give false information (s 13 of the 2000 Act). The CSA will find it easier to fix paternity, as if the father was married at some time between the conception and the birth a presumption of paternity arises, as is also inferred from registration of the birth showing the person's name as the father. This obviously links to the current Lord Chancellor's Department initiative to give parental responsibility to those unmarried fathers who live with the mothers of their children at the time of the birth and registration which should become law in the Adoption and Children Act 2002, despite having been lost in the failure of previous Bills.

15.4.1.6 Enforcement

Enforcement is also stepped up. Instead of getting a liability order from the magistrates and then going for distress, or any of the usual forms of civil enforcement, even committal if complex rules are followed, the CSA can now get the defaulter disqualified from driving for up to two years, and/or imprisoned much more easily. Equally, instead of the complex penalty and interest provisions under the earlier Acts, the CSA will have the power, like the Inland Revenue, of issuing penalties. Commentators think that the driving disqualification is a brainwave!

15.5 PROGNOSIS FOR THE FUTURE

The result is likely to be that the exodus to court will be stemmed, as a new provision enables either parent to go to the CSA on two months' notice even if there has been an agreed court order, once the court order has been in force for a year. This will, however, only apply to new orders obtained after 2002: earlier orders will remain with the courts for variation as previously, unless a parent goes onto benefits. This should provide extensive drafting potential for family lawyers who will struggle to keep their clients' child maintenance in the hands of the court. There may be regulations made under s 45 of the 1991 Act to deal with the potential for ongoing conflict between the court and CSA variation applications. This could be a key area in which the law is temporarily uncertain, especially if courts take a robust view of their ongoing jurisdiction as happened when the first Act was introduced in the early 1990s.

Mothers will still have to name the father of their children pursuant to s 6(2) of the original Act, unless on Working Families' Tax Credit, when they are exempt.

NRPs on welfare benefits still have to pay some Child Support – formerly £5.10 per week, and now a flat rate of £5 per week, avoided if the child has 52 nights of staying contact, and there will be a power to assign an NRP a notional income for assessment purposes.

15.6 FUTURE SETTLEMENT OF CHILD MAINTENANCE

All new applications from 2002 will be either via the CSA or to the court if the parties agree, but after one year of the order being in force either party can apply to the CSA on two months' notice when the court's power to vary will be lost forever.

Thus, those parents who want to fund a child by joint parenting agreements will have to rely on the skill of practitioners in drafting their agreements, which may or may not be able to protect them from the CSA's intervention (eg, by a consent order including a chargeback where the CSA is relied upon following an agreed financial settlement). The Family Law Bar Association has been piloting this since well before the 1991 regime was implemented, with mixed success, but in that case tended to be aided and abetted by robust judges who hung on to the court's power to vary even when the CSA was claiming that they had no jurisdiction to do so: at that time the CSA's teething troubles much assisted this outcome.

It remains to be seen whether the implementation of the new regime in new cases in the first pilot year (whenever it actually starts) is more successful and less controversial so that radical changes do not have to be made as happened on the last occasion. One idea currently being floated in the *Child's Pay Bulletin* is that an annual order, lasting for a minute less than a year, expiring on Christmas Day (so no one will be able to make an application to the CSA) and automatically reviving the next day, would mean that no order had ever lasted for the qualifying year.

By s 9(4) of the 1991 Act, any provision in an agreement not to apply to the CSA is void and this remains, and the existence of an agreement will not prevent access to the CSA (s 9(3)). However, there are often good reasons why there should not be an assessment, for example, if there is to be a nominal maintenance order for the child because provision is to be made out of capital (sometimes extremely effective for inheritance tax planning purposes because this will usually be exempt if pursuant to a court order either as a disposition for family maintenance or as not intended for gratuitous benefit: see Inheritance Tax Act 1984, ss 10 and 11). This enables the court subsequently to vary the nominal order and is the normal route for obtaining an increased level of provision for children from the court, as pointed out by Wilson J in the recent case of *V v V (Ancillary Relief: Power to Order Child Maintenance)* [2001] 2 FLR 657, in which he distinguished *Philips v Pearce* [1996] 2 FLR 230 which had been an attempt indirectly to challenge a nil CSA assessment of a millionaire father with no assessable income, an entirely different process from the parties both inviting the court to determine child provision, although the court had of course *still* been able to make capital orders in the latter case. The alternative is for the resident parent to apply to the CSA for an assessment and then to the court for a 'top up' order.

It has been suggested that the CSA regime may be contrary to the welfare of the child (see 1991 Act, s 2).

As before, there are strong pressures on both the NRP and the resident parent to evade the CSA system as any changes in child support impact on other ancillary relief orders (eg, pension sharing and clean breaks by *Duxbury* lump sum). Moreover, there will only be a 25% limit on the high earner NRP's liability if all the children are dealt with under the CSA scheme. It will make settlement of an ancillary relief package much more difficult until the impact of the CSA figures are known in a particular case, so that an umbrella figure including child maintenance may have to be agreed for spouse and children if a private settlement is negotiated. Indeed, it may mean that the law in this area is somewhat uncertain for a period.

Students should watch the academic journals, in particular *Family Law* and *Child and Family Law Quarterly*, for articles about the new regime as commentary on it develops.

15.7 CHILD MAINTENANCE AND PROVISION UNDER THE CHILDREN ACT 1989

The provisions in s 15 of and Sched 1 to the CA 1989 provide for the triple tier of family courts, including the Family Proceedings Court, to make orders against the child's parents which can still usefully supplement other jurisdictions, in particular in the case of lump sum and property transfer orders which are outside the remit of the CSA. The criteria are similar to those governing the DPMCA 1978 and the MCA 1973.

Any person may apply for such an order who has a residence order in respect of the child, for example, relatives of the child with whom the child prefers to live than with the parents, a common situation involving children who think this is a way of 'divorcing their parents' (legally impossible of course because of the enduring nature of parental responsibility, but it does allow such relatives who are willing for a residence order to be made in their favour to obtain support which they would not qualify to obtain from the CSA). Similarly, a guardian, or step or adoptive parent, will qualify under the Schedule, as will an adult child over age 18 in education, providing that the child's parents are not living together.

Most commonly this route is convenient to obtain a property transfer in favour of the parent of a child with whom the child is residing, and who was not married to the child's other parent and is therefore unable to use the MCA 1973 to secure a home for the child's minority. Such a transfer is usually expressed to be for the benefit of the child until independence, which is now recognised to be more likely to be age 21 than 18, due to the lack of public support for undergraduate degrees, an argument which originated with Hale LJ, formerly the Law Commissioner and distinguished family lawyer, Professor Brenda Hoggett. The property will usually then revert to the transferor (*T v S* [1994] 2 FLR 883).

This provision is able to address the otherwise possible gross disparity between the father's circumstances and those of the mother and the child by the advancement of capital for the mother and child's housing needs.

This problem was examined in detail by Hale J (as she then was) in *J v C* [1999] 1 FLR 152, when she concluded that the relevant criteria, although not expressly included in Sched 1, para 4 to the CA 1989, must include the child's welfare while a minor, part of which should include entitlement 'to be brought up in circumstances which bear some sort of relationship with the father's present standard of living'.

It seems the father does not, however, have a right to dictate where the property in question should be, or its type, and this would appear to be confirmed by Art 8 of the European Convention on Human Rights, unless the court's interference was for some reason legitimate, necessary and in proportion to the restriction proposed, since it was established, *per* Johnson J in *Philips v Pearce* (see 15.6, above), that it is not for the court to decide where the parties should live, although this may be a part of the factual decision making process in granting any CA order.

On the other hand, the father's financial investment can be properly protected by trust deed (see Robin Spon Smith on this topic at [1999] Fam Law 763).

The court can also make these s 15 and Sched 1 orders of its own motion when making, discharging or varying a residence order.

CHILD SUPPORT

PARENTAL RESPONSIBILITY AND CHILD SUPPORT

The background to the current regime of child support is in the concept of parental responsibility and the obligation to support a child which falls on all natural parents of that child, whether the parents are married or not. This is now formalised in a regime of statutory child support under the Child Support Acts, and is supplemented by provisions for child maintenance in the MCA 1973 and CA 1989. Under the MCA 1973, where parents are agreed on maintenance provisions, their arrangements can be included in the consent order formalising their own financial arrangements on divorce: otherwise contested cases must be assessed by the CSA under the Child Support Acts 1991–95, unless the arrangements are in respect of a child outside the CSA remit (ie, stepchildren whose natural parent cannot be found, children outside the age and other qualifying limits, and children requiring capital, property and/or top up orders). The CA 1989 provides for similar capital, etc orders to be made in the case of unmarried parents who are not therefore able to use the MCA 1973.

The earlier regime of child support is to be progressively reformed from 2002 pursuant to the Child Support, Pensions and Social Security Act 2000.

CHILD SUPPORT ACTS 1991–95

These Acts created a framework of 'qualifying child', 'carer parent' and 'absent ('non-resident') parent'. The CSA assesses the qualifying child's maintenance requirement on the basis of financial disclosure of both parents, and the child's needs which are linked to welfare benefit rates. Where the carer (now called 'resident parent') is on benefits, the Acts require that parent to authorise the Secretary of State to recover the moneys paid in benefits through the CSA system. A resident parent who does not assist in this respect is liable to lose benefits unless there is a good reason for not identifying the absent parent (now 'non-resident parent') such as that it would be likely to bring harm to the child or carer. Reforms in 1995 created 'departures' to recognise more fairly than before the payer's other obligations (eg, costs of contact and travel to work, and also capital paid over on divorce clean breaks), but this system became so complicated, without really delivering increased fairness, that departures have been completely reformed in the 2000 Act, and renamed 'variations', and the entire scheme has been simplified.

REFORM OF THE CSA REGIME

The 2000 Act creates a flat rate of child support depending on the number of children, so that 15%, 20% or 25% of the payer's assessable income will be paid depending on whether there are one, two or three or more children. There is an allowance for payers with 'stepchildren', whether those are children of a formal marriage or informal cohabitation. The CSA will in future be able to assess British parents resident overseas and enforceability is improved. There is also an increased likelihood of application to the CSA after an initially agreed court order, since as soon as such an order has been in force for one year either party may in future apply to the CSA, rather than the order remaining with the court for variation as now.

CHILDREN ACT 1989

The CA 1989 provides for capital and property orders to be made in favour of children who do not have access to such orders through their parents' divorce under the MCA 1973, and also for maintenance orders in favour of persons with residence orders (eg, relations other than the parents with whom the child prefers to live).

CHAPTER 16

THE MATRIMONIAL HOME

16.1 THE POLICY OF HOMES FOR ALL

The fate of the matrimonial home will usually be the linchpin of any ancillary relief package for the simple reason that every family needs somewhere to live: whether it is to be sold, transferred outright to one party or made the subject of a deferred settlement the fate of the home will have a profound effect on the remainder of the provision ordered. It is therefore usual in our contemporary homeowning times for the court to view the resolution of the various competing claims to what may loosely be termed the 'matrimonial assets' (although in English law there is technically no such thing) by making one order dealing with all aspects of the parties' ancillary relief applications, and unless there is (rarely) no former joint home involved, to build their order holistically around the disposal of the home. This highly discretionary duty of the court to make appropriate orders in relation to the home has developed naturally as a consequence of the post-war expansion in home ownership generally, and also from the development over the past 25 years of the trend towards regarding marriage as an equal partnership, the routine joint tenancy of the matrimonial home and of the normality of the wife's working in order to help fund the mortgage payments and the expenses of bringing up a family which appears no longer to be possible out of one salary.

Within the spirit of these social trends, and the letter of the Matrimonial Causes Act (MCA) 1973, the outcome of the dilemma surrounding the destination of the home may well be decided at the outset by the court's duty under s 25(1) to give first consideration to the welfare of the minor children of the family. Alternatively, there may be considerable choice as to the precise manner in which the parties' assets should be distributed, but whichever is the case it will usually be easier to put the overall package together if a practical decision is reached *first* about the home. This is especially so as, with the possible exception of the husband's pension rights which have only recently received anything like the same attention from either the law or the parties as the importance of the disposal of the home, the home will usually be the parties' most valuable asset.

The home is therefore almost always the most important ingredient of whatever financial mix is to be proposed, since it will usually be not only the most valuable asset but also potentially either a roof for one of the parties or the source of two new post-divorce homes. Only rarely is there so much money available that the destination of the home is completely irrelevant.

Quite apart from its duty to the children under s 25(1), the court operates (where resources permit) a policy of 'homes for all' (see *M v B (Ancillary Proceedings: Lump Sum)* [1998] 1 FLR 53, where this aim was articulated, although the principle is much older, expressly surfacing in *Calderbank v Calderbank* [1975] 3 WLR 586, one of the early post-1973 cases where a wealthy wife had to provide a home for the husband to receive access visits from their children in suitable surroundings: thus any order will be driven by the principle that each party must if possible have a home, so that an order that leaves one of the parties potentially homeless is, in the absence of special circumstances, unacceptable.

However, it should be noted that while the court frequently restates the principle of 'homes for all', which appears to be a laudable basic goal, it is sometimes inappropriate in the particular circumstances of a case. For example, in the recent case of *Piglowska v Piglowski* [1999] 2 FLR 763, the House of Lords stressed that, especially where resources are limited, there is no *right* for a party to receive a home – especially the freehold ownership of a home – as a part of the ancillary relief package. In that case the Court of Appeal does seem to have been unduly influenced by the husband's claim for a home in this country, although he appeared still to have one in Poland.

Nevertheless, the requirement of s 25(1) that, while giving first priority to the welfare of the children, the court must consider 'all the circumstances of the case' does often create a potentially insoluble problem for the court, in that it is usually trying to achieve at least three (often inconsistent and mutually exclusive) aims, namely to:

- maintain a residence for the minor children and the custodial parent;
- provide a home for each party; and
- divide the family assets fairly, especially the matrimonial home.

16.1.1 Potential solutions

Thus, in addition to looking for guidance in the detail of the various s 25 factors in order to obtain a general picture of each party's overall claims on what resources there are, recourse must also be had to the various well tried home disposal packages which have been put together in cases which have come before the court for consideration in the past.

These packages tend to go by the name of the case in which that particular method of dealing with the matter was first used, such as the well known *Mesher* and *Martin* orders. This sometimes confuses the inexperienced who are bewildered by the range of what appear to be mere drafting solutions, and unsure which precise variety to select – until they remember that these precedents are meant to be a useful tool and not a shackle: none of the orders necessarily has to be adopted in total and unchanged, since most cases which arise in practice are not precisely the same as that of the Mesher or Martin family.

It follows that whatever order is ultimately drafted for any case will only be *generically* a *Mesher* etc order, but will in fact be *individually drafted* for the case in question. Thus if the name of the family in the case is Smith, and some practitioner's ingenuity produces a useful variant of a *Mesher* order, that particular precedent may be filed away, at least in the firm's library, as a precedent for a *Smith* order (and if it is ingenious enough may also become more widely known in the profession under that tag).

Practitioners and judges are not therefore afraid to innovate where nothing suitable has yet been used for a particular situation, providing the components of the order proposed are not mutually exclusive (eg, no draft will be using any form of ongoing periodical payments for a spouse where a clean break is desired, since in that case limited term periodical payments will be required in order to sever the former financial interdependence as envisaged by s 25A of the MCA 1973). In working out the best destination for the former matrimonial home, it is safe to assume that good drafting will be likely to be able to effect any sensible package which negotiation and settlement is likely to propose.

The potential offered by the comprehensive ancillary relief order is a fascinating development, in the full tradition of the complex layers of legal and beneficial ownership created by trusts, and of the deployment of the ownership and occupation of land for the use and benefit of different members of the former single family unit. This enables the law of ancillary relief to adapt in a super flexible manner to the changing needs of the family members, even the challenge of the latest twist in trends, the post-*White* era.

16.1.2 Order of priorities and alternatives

Because of the welfare of the minor children which by s 25(1) must be given first consideration, the first priority, whether of practitioner or court, will be to:

(a) look to the *purpose* for which a home is required (ie, *residential occupation*); then

(b) see how the children and the parent with care of them can best be housed; then

(c) see how the other parent can be housed; and only then

(d) check on the fairest way to divide actual *ownership* of such assets as there are.

Thus, the first step will be to seek to arrange matters on an *occupational* basis, for the moment disregarding questions of *ownership*. The second will be to consider ownership and property rights quite separately.

By s 24, whatever changes of ownership need to be made can be effected by the court at will, so who owns the various assets (including the matrimonial home) is of less importance than what the court wants to do with that asset. Unlike in strict property law, the approach here is not 'whose is this?' but 'to whom should this be given?'.

Priorities are therefore likely to be approached in the same order as the court's competing aims, namely:

- Where are the children and the spouse with care of the children going to *live*?
- Where is the other spouse going to *live*?
- What is to be done about *ownership* of the home?

This leaves three possible alternative fates for the matrimonial home:

- immediate sale and division of the proceeds;
- outright transfer to one party; or
- a trust for sale.

Each needs to be looked at in more detail.

16.1.2.1 Immediate sale and division of net proceeds
(often, but not necessarily, in equal proportions) (MCA 1973, s 24A)

Obviously, the parties can always agree to sell the house, but sometimes the court will order sale even if the parties are not agreed. This is suitable for three situations, where there is:

- sufficient equity in the home;
- enough equity to make a sale worthwhile but one party already has alternative accommodation; or
- no significant equity in the home and neither party, nor even really both of them together, can afford the home at all.

Thus, the court may *order* a sale in three typical cases:

(1) Where there is sufficient equity in the home (with or without the aid of a mortgage) to buy two new homes, one for each party, including *suitable* accommodation for the parent who will have the children to house. However, as this does have a disruptive effect on the children and possibly on their schooling if a move of area and school is also involved (as it sometimes may have to be if downsizing is essential), the court might be dissuaded from ordering such a sale if the carer parent does not want it.

(2) Where there is enough equity to make a sale worthwhile but one party already has alternative accommodation (eg, where one spouse has already moved in with a new partner who has secure accommodation). Immediate sale can then raise some essential capital for both parties, which can be used by the spouse without accommodation to buy a new property and by the one who already has accommodation either to upgrade that accommodation, or for some completely unrelated purpose: eg, if a new family is to be started but this has not yet happened, the funds realised can be simply taken as that party's share of the assets and invested until they are required, the point being that that spouse will then have had some proper share of the housing capital. In these circumstances the court is likely to *order* sale, unless there are children to be housed, as in (1), above.

If in the end this share of the housing capital money is never needed for housing, there is nothing to stop that spouse from using it to go on a world cruise – the money is the spouse's share of the sale proceeds of the matrimonial home and no obligation to use it in any way, nor any form of trust express or implied, is to be imposed on the award.

(3) Where there is *no significant equity* in the home and neither party, nor even really both of them together, can afford the home at all. This is the type of marriage which breaks up over financial pressures and the best course will usually be to sell the home and divide the tiny proceeds, putting both parties into rented accommodation. Sometimes one or both parties can return to live with parents. This is even sometimes possible for the custodial parent where there is a child or children, if a contribution is made by that parent to the household expenses. In recessions where there is unemployment compounded by mortgage problems, this has often been the solution. In these circumstances the court is practically certain to order a sale.

16.1.2.2 Outright transfer to one party (MCA 1973, s 24)

This is suitable as part of a clean break or where one spouse must receive a transfer as the only means of security which the court can award, as in *Bryant v Bryant* [1976] 6 Fam Law 108; (1976) 120 SJ 165, where the husband was a walking disaster: he had paid neither maintenance nor the mortgage on time, had assaulted the wife and been found guilty of persistent cruelty, and had three times been to prison for contempt for disobeying court orders. The court said they could never see him supporting the wife and children and the only way to protect them was to give the wife his half share of the house.

An outright transfer can be effected in three ways:

(1) On immediate payment of a cash sum by the transferee to compensate the other spouse for losing their interest in the home, or in other words a 'buy out' as in *Wachtel*, the well known case already mentioned in other contexts (although the mania for dubbing the various orders with the names of the cases in which they were first noted has not for some reason extended to this being habitually known as a *Wachtel* order).

(2) In return for a charge over the home either for a fixed sum or for a percentage of the sale proceeds either at a fixed date or upon a certain event or when the transferee chooses to sell (and since in the latter case this choice may *never* be made it may mean that the charge is not enforceable until the transferee's death).

(3) With *no* cash payment and *no* charge, but in return for some other benefit which will accrue to the spouse losing their interest in the property, such as the transferee foregoing periodical payments (this is called a *Hanlon* order).

Any *Hanlon* order must be effected *at the time that the order is first made*, since property adjustment orders under s 24 *cannot be varied* later under s 31 (see Chapter 13). This caused a problem in *Carson v Carson* [1983] 1 WLR 285; [1983] 1 All ER 478, where the wife had a *Mesher* order incorporating periodical payments for herself. Later she ran into financial difficulties and wanted the order changed to an outright transfer of the husband's share of the home in return for surrender of her periodical payments. Of course the court could not accede to her request, although an ingenious way has since been found round the difficulty: following amendment of s 31 of the MCA 1973 by the Family Law Act 1996, the periodical payments order can now be varied by ordering a lump sum to be paid to capitalise them, and the wife can then use that money to compensate the husband (if he is willing, as he usually will be if he has to find the capital sum anyway) for his share of the home (see the string of cases *S v S* [1987] 1 FLR 71; *Boylan v Boylan* [1988] 1 FLR 282; and *Peacock v Peacock* [1991] 1 FLR 324, where in each case a way had to be found round the pre-1996 problem of being unable to vary a periodical payments order by making a lump sum order). However, the principle is equally applicable to property adjustment orders, which still cannot be varied, in that providing the parties arrange the matter themselves rather than the court illegally varying a property adjustment order, the *Mesher* order can be unlocked to their mutual satisfaction.

A *Mesher* order cannot even be changed into a *Martin* order as the wife tried to get the court to do in *Dinch v Dinch* [1987] 1 WLR 252; [1987] 1 All ER 818, where she applied to the court when the youngest child reached 17 because the husband had become voluntarily redundant and had stopped paying periodical payments for his share of the mortgage: as a result she was in financial difficulties. She wanted a postponement of the sale, a lump sum and a further transfer of property order. The Court of Appeal tried to help by changing the *Mesher* to a *Martin* order so she at least need not sell the house until she chose, but the husband appealed to the House of Lords who agreed with him that the Court of Appeal had no power to change the format of the order, although they realised that this left the wife in a very difficult position. In the earlier case of *Dunford v Dunford* [1980] 1 All ER 122, the court saw the problem coming and immediately changed the initial *Mesher* on appeal to an outright transfer.

It always used to be recommended that any deferred charge should be for a *proportion* of the sale proceeds, in order, when house prices rose dramatically from year to year, to protect the value of the share which the spouse out of occupation would ultimately receive, as in *Browne v Pritchard* [1975] 1 WLR 1366.

However, in a falling property market, where there is a possibility of reduced or negative equity, it may be better to arrange for a *fixed sum* to be paid (as in *Hector v Hector* [1973] 1 WLR 1122), rather than that a proportion of the proceeds should be payable, especially as for tax purposes this will count as a debt and not as a share of the sale proceeds on which capital gains tax might be levied if the sale takes place (as it usually will) outside the period during which an owner out of occupation must sell in order even to claim the main residence exemption even under Extra-Statutory Concession D6 (see Chapter 18).

When a deferred charge is the right solution, a *Browne v Pritchard* (proportionate proceeds) or *Hector v Hector* (fixed sum) order can conveniently also be combined with *limited term periodical payments* to produce a deferred clean break under s 25A(2) of the MCA 1973.

16.1.3 A trust of land (MCA 1973, s 24)

This is the method of effecting a *Mesher* order and also all the variants, including the *Martin* and *Harvey* orders. A *Harvey* order may sometimes also be referred to as a *Brown* order after *Brown v Brown* [1982] 3 FLR 161, in which a somewhat similar order was made.

Where any of these settlement orders are made, the order may also provide for the payment of the outgoings, whether of the mortgage only or also of others such as repairs, insurance, utilities, etc precisely as it seems fair to the parties and their advisers that these should be paid by one party or the other or both equally or unequally.

16.1.3.1 Mesher orders

The *Mesher* order is suitable where children and the custodial parent need to be housed until the children are independent: the order vests the matrimonial home in both spouses on trust for sale, giving a right of occupation to the custodial parent *either* until the children reach independence (which will in some cases be when the youngest child is 17 *or* where appropriate when the youngest finishes full time education or training), upon which event the house is to be sold and the proceeds divided in an appropriate ratio, such division of the proceeds being decided by the court at the time the order for settlement is made.

The parties may *already* be trustees of the matrimonial home, as joint tenants in law and in equity (since joint ownership of their home is now the norm rather than the exception in the case of most couples), so it will only be necessary for the order to vest the home in the parties as trustees if one was formerly the sole legal owner. However, even if the parties are already trustees, so the order will then direct that the home *remain vested* in the joint names of the parties, it will still be necessary to go on to declare new trusts (because the standard trusts under the former joint ownership would usually merely have been that the parties should hold the property on trust for themselves beneficially, which is obviously no longer appropriate once a *Mesher* order is to be imposed giving sole occupation to one spouse for a period, and then declaring the ultimate interests in the proceeds of sale).

However, the order is only suitable where the proceeds of sale will be sufficient to rehouse the occupying spouse on sale and the spouse out of occupation has somewhere else to live.

A *Mesher* order is final and cannot be varied (so as, eg, to postpone the date of sale). For this reason the circumstances always need to be thought through very carefully by the parties and their advisers. While the order was first greeted with great enthusiasm as a solution to the problem of otherwise having to sell the house and disrupt the children's lives, it was quickly realised that it only stored up trouble for the future in a number of cases. This was because in the late 1970s and early 1980s house prices were unstable and many victims of the *Mesher* order found that when they came to sell there was not enough money to rehouse the occupying spouse and yet the order could not be varied, so other methods had to be found to deal with the situation.

Further, following the introduction of s 25A in 1984, the then latest fashion was for the clean break, with which the *Mesher* order is incompatible. However, following the property market collapse at the end of the 1980s, *Mesher* orders came back into fashion more or less by default since houses which were not actually repossessed for negative equity were often actually *unsaleable* so that a *Mesher* order was the *only* solution. At the present time *Mesher* orders are favoured again because of the necessity, post-*White v White* [2000] 2 FLR 981, to consider the concept of fairness and the yardstick of equality – so that an outright transfer to the wife may not be appropriate – coupled with the need in families of limited means to house the family until the children are grown up. These practical considerations are of course at the very heart of a family lawyer's advice on property division following marriage breakdown as a result of which both practitioners and the court, and academic students therefore, need to be fully abreast of current economic affairs as they will affect the ordinary family. This may prove to be a new lease of life for *Mesher* orders in an increased trend towards orders supported by periodical payments so as to give a fairer division of capital assets to husbands and income to wives.

16.1.3.2 Martin orders

A *Martin* order differs from a *Mesher* in that while the settlement is the same, the period of occupation is *not* linked to the children in any way; indeed there may be a *Martin* order where there are no children, as in the original case, provided the only other essential requirement (that the other spouse has secure alternative accommodation) is met. In the original *Martin* case, Mr Martin had a council flat, and although the Martins had no children, Mrs Martin needed somewhere to live; there had been a 15 year marriage and the court was of the opinion that but for the divorce the house would not have been sold for another 20 years. Thus instead of the children reaching adulthood, the triggering event in a *Martin* order case will be either the occupying spouse's death, or earlier remarriage, sometimes cohabitation or becoming dependent on another partner, or voluntary removal.

Obviously this order is less attractive to the spouse out of occupation than a *Mesher* order, since the non-occupying spouse might never see the proceeds of sale which may ultimately only accrue to that spouse's estate many years later, but it does preserve the capital of the spouse out of occupation, rather than giving it up completely as would be the result if there were an outright transfer for no value. This was the entire rationale of *Clutton v Clutton* [1991] 1 All ER 340, CA, and since the sale is postponed for so long and is under the occupying spouse's control (and the order is therefore in effect virtually indistinguishable from an outright transfer with a deferred charge) it does not fall foul of the clean break rules as was confirmed in *Clutton*. Nevertheless an outright transfer with a deferred charge payable on any of the usual *Martin* triggering events will usually be preferred by the occupying spouse and really makes no significant difference to the spouse out of occupation.

16.1.3.3 *Harvey order*

This order, sometimes also called a *Brown* order, is a variant of the *Martin* order where the occupying spouse still has the right to remain indefinitely in the property but, upon the children becoming independent or the mortgage being paid off (usually whichever is the later), the occupying spouse is required to pay a market rent to the spouse out of occupation for that spouse's share of the property, so as to provide some return on the capital tied up in the house for that spouse. Such rent is usually to be determined by the district judge in accordance with market rates at the date at which the triggering event occurs.

Another feature of the *Harvey* order is that it may specify a greater share of the ultimate sale proceeds for the occupying spouse who is paying the mortgage and the outgoings in recognition of the fact that whoever is in occupation will probably end up paying more of the mortgage than the spouse who is out of occupation. However, this provision may always be written into any order drafted, since as explained at the outset it should always be remembered that the order being drafted is a *customised order* for *the case in hand* and all clauses of all these well known orders may be swapped about to produce something totally original, provided the resulting package does not put incompatible clauses together.

When deciding upon a suitable order, it should of course be remembered that there are hazards in any form of outright transfer, unless in 'buy out' form, in relation to potential future claims for welfare benefits by the transferee and also the very limited account taken of such capital transfers by the Child Support Agency (CSA) (see Chapters 15 and 18). Thus a *Hanlon* order would pose potential risks for the husband today unless the wife were thought to be a responsible sort of person who would use the opportunity of receiving the house outright to make secure overall provision for herself for the future by working hard to guarantee her income.

16.2 LEGAL SERVICES COMMISSION STATUTORY CHARGE (AJA 1999, s 10(7))

It will be recalled that new generation public funding pursuant to the Administration of Justice Act (AJA) 1999 has preserved the statutory charge imposed in s 16 of the Legal Aid Act 1988 (which is the section referred to in the case law on this subject). This requires the Legal Services Commission (LSC) if possible to recover its costs of the ancillary relief proceedings (and also of any other proceedings financed on behalf of the assisted person, such as for an order under the Children Act 1989). The impact of this is normally felt in relation to property recovered or preserved in the ancillary relief package obtained, in particular usually in the form of a statutory charge taken over the home to avoid the property having to be sold in order to finance the very proceedings in which it was recently awarded to the assisted person (see Chapter 11). It will therefore always be necessary to bear the statutory charge in mind if it applies when deciding on which particular ancillary relief package to go for, another clear example of the influence of procedural matters on the black letter law.

16.2.1 Drawbacks for the assisted person

As has already been explained (see Chapter 11), public funding is a loan, not a gift, and also a somewhat ungenerous loan in that the interest charged on the unpaid bill of costs, which has to become the subject of a statutory charge over the assisted person's property preserved in the ancillary relief proceedings, will not be cheap, since it is at the rate of money in court for the time being.

Thus the public funded applicant for ancillary relief not only has a charge over the home that has just been recovered but will also be paying a higher rate of interest for the privilege than could be obtained on the mortgage market. Sometimes it will be possible for the litigant to refinance this bill by taking a mortgage or second mortgage over the home and paying the LSC off as soon as possible, but this will only be feasible where that person's status permits such a loan to be raised – sometimes a litigant will have insufficient status to do this, which will leave the LSC's finance through the statutory charge as the only possibility.

It must therefore always be remembered that the costs will have a profound impact on the net effect of an order, whether made by consent or after a hearing, since there are more hidden costs to the statutory charge than meet the eye.

Litigants, their advisers and the court have to be sure to bear this drawback of the statutory charge in mind throughout the ancillary relief proceedings and particularly in relation to the settlement. It must be recorded on the face of the order that the home was recovered or preserved as a home for the assisted person (including the assisted person's dependants if applicable, but it is not essential that there should be dependent children) or it will not be possible to make use of the statutory charge at all. Furthermore, the rising bill for costs must be constantly drawn to the litigant's attention and every effort made at every stage both to keep costs down and to settle at the earliest possible moment for the least cost possible so as to avoid decimating the value of the applicant's victory (and provision for the applicant's future) by running up a disproportionate bill of costs.

In this connection, as mentioned in Chapter 13, the new ancillary relief scheme now in force nationally requires a regular up to date statement of costs to be provided by each party at each hearing, so that the parties as well as the district judge can clearly see the impact of the statutory charge on the case.

It should also be remembered that, pursuant to s 10(7) of the AJA 1999, compromises of all kinds are caught in cases which have been contested. Therefore, a balance must be struck between persevering in the hope of getting a better deal and persisting in a weak case in such a manner that good money is thrown after bad.

16.2.2 Mitigation of the statutory charge

Obviously use will be made of the most obvious mitigation already mentioned above in Chapter 11 – obtaining periodical payments for the spouse and/or the children wherever appropriate since these are exempt from the charge regardless of amount; the first £2,500 of any money or property recovered or preserved will be exempt from the charge anyway. The court will usually make a charge efficient order if it can (see, eg, *Mortimer v Mortimer-Griffin* [1986] 2 FLR 315). There are a number of other methods which need to be considered in the overall game plan.

16.2.2.1 Costs from the other party

The next step is usually to try to obtain costs from the other side since this will be the first source of recovery of the money they have spent for the LSC to tap.

In some cases this will be impossible (eg, where the other spouse is also on public funding), but in every case where costs *are* potentially recoverable this possibility can be rigorously pursued. Nevertheless, it sometimes has to be recognised that while they *may* ultimately concede money or the home, especially to a spouse who has to look after the children, some respondents have a congenital dislike of paying costs. In this case canny practitioners recognise that it may be better to try to obtain a slightly higher order the better to enable the assisted person to pay the costs or support the burden of the statutory charge over the home that has been recovered or preserved, than to attempt to extract costs from the other party.

16.2.2.2 Keeping costs down generally

The one thing that is certain is that if energetic steps are not taken at the outset and throughout the case to keep costs down, the court will not be sympathetic to parties who want to litigate at public expense and then expect the court to wave some kind of magic wand to manufacture added value out of the order made.

The court is not moved by pitiful tales, such as of Mrs Hanlon who won £10,000 from Mr Hanlon only to see it nearly all swallowed up in costs of £8,025.

The court also becomes very irritated by wastefulness in conducting the case, as in *Evans v Evans* [1990] 2 All ER 147, where the Court of Appeal said it simply despaired – the costs of both parties were £60,000 (£35,000 the husband's and £25,000 the legally aided wife's) and the total assets only £110,000, two mortgaged houses where the parties respectively lived, and a small company belonging to the husband, the wife having no independent means.

The court suggested the most obvious of economies would have been to use shared valuers or at worst agreeing valuations where such expense as had been incurred really could not be justified and would have such serious consequences for the parties.

This type of situation is now avoidable as pursuant to the new ancillary relief scheme the court will usually *order* shared valuers and the managerial approach of the district judge is likely to be able to prevent waste, and to sanction it in costs at the end if litigation behaviour has been unsatisfactory (see Chapter 14). The recent 'Micawber misery' type case of *Piglowska v Piglowski* (see 16.1, above) (assets £127,000, including a home worth £100,000, costs £128,000) is a good example of a case which *would certainly* have been cost effectively managed under the new ancillary relief scheme.

16.2.2.3 Appeals

Appeals are possible if the costs destroy the whole scheme of distributing the assets between the parties, as was established in *Simmons v Simmons* [1984] 1 FLR 226 and followed in *Anthony v Anthony* [1986] 2 FLR 353.

The latter was a particularly badly run case where both parties were legally aided and initially the husband obtained the home and the wife £9,000, nominal maintenance for herself and maintenance for the two children. However, she and the children were going to be homeless as her costs left her only with the initial £2,500 which is exempt from the charge. So, the court started again, remaking the order to use all the available exemptions by abandoning the lump sum, which was otherwise going to be swallowed up by the costs bill, giving her a *Mesher* order so she could stay in the home and the husband still got some capital out of it at a later date, and making a more generous periodical payments package, an altogether different result.

A similar case was that of *Stewart v The Law Society* [1987] 1 FLR 223, where the costs were £4,600 and someone had been sufficiently innumerate as to allow the court to make an order of £7,000 for capitalised maintenance, leaving the wife with very little of the money which had been meant to provide for her. This is precisely the sort of case in which to use the exemptions, and if necessary go for limited term periodical payments, which like all periodical payments will be exempt from the charge.

However, the court much prefers to make orders which give the parties the benefit of exemptions in the first place than to be asked to make some last minute alteration. Even if an appeal is entertained at all, it is unlikely to be heard without some extremely sharp things being said on the Bench about such a situation being allowed to develop in the first place.

Moreover, the court is much less likely to intervene on appeal now the principles of running ancillary relief cases on public funding without spending all the gains on costs are well established, particularly as if cash is awarded in the form of a lump sum, provided it is earmarked for the purchase of a house so that the statutory charge can be invoked, it will not be necessary to pay the costs bill immediately, as was previously the situation.

Also, now the statutory charge may operate against the new home once bought, which was the outcome in *Scallon v Scallon* [1990] 1 FLR 193, there is less need for the court to intervene. In that case the wife appealed against an order for sale of the matrimonial home of which she was to receive a proportion, relying on the decision in *Simmons*, because the effect of the legal aid bill meant she had too little money to buy a house with. The court refused to help her since the revised operation of the statutory charge meant she could postpone the bill by means of a charge on the new home, which they took the view the Legal Aid Board would be unlikely to refuse to entertain if it frustrated the court's order.

16.2.2.4 Avoiding child proceedings on public funding

The saddest cases are where the bulk of the bill has been substantially run up in child proceedings (in which no property is recovered and often little is achieved except the guarantee of constant future expense on the children concerned) and the costs of both child proceedings and the ancillary relief proceedings have to be set against the property recovered in the latter, as in *Mason v Mason* [1986] 2 FLR 212.

In that case the parties ran up a huge bill by energetic litigation against each other in an acrimonious case involving both adultery and behaviour, which ultimately had to be compromised so that there was a decree under Fact D, followed by a long drawn out custody suit which also ultimately had to be settled. The costs were £23,000 and the home was only worth £53,000 so that little was eventually left. This is the sort of case which should be an awful warning to parties on public funding and the court usually comments on this sort of situation when they realise that what has happened has been entirely due to the parties' recalcitrance. It is also of course a warning against interpreting the black letter law of ancillary relief in the vacuum created if costs and other procedural and practical matters are not also incorporated into a holistic assessment of potential entitlement and the likelihood of achieving it.

16.3 DRAFTING OF ORDERS

Whatever ancillary relief package is finally agreed on, it must be formally incorporated into an accurate and comprehensive draft order to be placed before the court, so that, subject to such amendments (usually of style rather than substance) as the district judge may wish to make, the court can actually make the order sought in that form. Some understanding of drafting skills and the content and shape of an order is helpful for an understanding of the subject matter of this chapter, and those earlier chapters dealing with ancillary relief, because of the importance of grasping the issues in relation to the matrimonial home which do not depend at all on strict property rights but upon a proper exercise of the court's discretionary jurisdiction.

16.3.1 Drafting the order

Knowing what to put into the order is obviously an essential prerequisite of actually drafting it, so that the practitioner will usually start by making a *list* of all the terms for incorporation into the order, and in practice this is as far as the average academic student will wish to go. However, this can also be useful in appreciating the shape of an ancillary relief settlement or award, which *is* often a package, the individual items of which would certainly not stand satisfactorily alone.

Any of the following may be included:

- periodical payments for the payee spouse (or dismissal of such claims);
- periodical payments for children, often both for general maintenance and for school fees;
- transfer, settlement or sale of the home;
- transfer of other items, whether of real or personal property or chattels;
- payment of a lump sum to a spouse;
- possibly payment of lump sums to children;
- restrictions on future application to the court, in life and on death of each of the parties;
- costs, including detailed assessment (formerly called 'taxation') where appropriate;
- certificate for the purposes of the statutory charge.

It is worth considering all these in practical relation to one another and with regard to the principles of the law contained in Chapter 12, since the highly discretionary nature of ancillary relief law is that *any or all* of the possible orders can be assembled in a tailor made solution to a particular family's needs. This has always been the entire justification for our jurisdiction's clinging on to a discretionary regime of ancillary relief because it is believed this in principle provides better for the individual case than any variant of community of property in marriage.

It should be noted that following *Xydias v Xydias* [1999] 1 FLR 683, when settling a case with the other side, it is now considered advisable (if not also usual) for practitioners to incorporate the agreement made into written Heads of Agreement so that both sides know what is supposed to be in the order, prior usually to one of them drafting it for submission to and agreement by the other, although sometimes both parties' lawyers will prepare the draft together.

This is particularly important if there is a dispute over whether there is an agreement at all, as in *Xydias*, where the husband wanted to reinstate a full hearing date, on the basis that the case was *not* settled, due to disagreement as to some detail, although in principle the parties were *ad idem* generally.

Following some reported cases in which sloppy drafting has had catastrophic consequences (see, eg, *per* Lord Oliver of Aylmerton in *Dinch v Dinch* [1987] 1 WLR 252; [1987] 1 All ER 817), practitioners have developed drafting into an art form, often 'getting back on the drafting what was lost on the negotiation', but Lord Oliver's warning remains highly relevant: in *Dinch* the (combined) awful drafting of several lawyers produced such a result that he felt obliged to criticise it at length, not least because it seems that the draughtsmen in question, having failed to give effect to what was apparently agreed about the disposal of the petitioner's claims for ancillary relief, then tried to blame the court for not picking up and correcting their mistakes! Lord Oliver commented as follows:

> I feel impelled once again to stress in the most emphatic terms that it is in all cases the imperative professional duty of those invested with the task of advising the parties to these unfortunate disputes to consider with due care the impact which any terms that they agree on behalf of clients have ... and to ensure that such appropriate provision is inserted in any consent order ... as will leave no room for any future doubt or misunderstanding or saddle the parties with the wasteful burden of wholly unnecessary costs. It is of course also the duty of any court called upon to make such a consent order to consider ... the jurisdiction it is being called upon to exercise ... I would however like to emphasise that the *primary* duty [author's emphasis] in this regard must lie upon those concerned with the negotiation and drafting of the terms of the order and that any failure to fulfil such duty ... cannot be excused simply by reference to some inadvertent lack of vigilance on the part of the court or its officers in passing the order in a form which the parties have approved.

Lord Oliver was referring to consent orders (and the power to make them) which, after they have been agreed between the parties, is by s 33A of the MCA 1973 expressly given to the court *without* conducting a full hearing as would happen where the orders were made after a contested application, but what he had to say in principle actually applies to all forms of order, which the parties' advisers, and not the court, have the obligation to check. This includes those orders drafted after a *decision of the court* following contested proceedings, where it is normally counsel or solicitors, and not the judge, who draft the order, a procedure adopted precisely so as to see that the order accords with what the parties think was asked for and that it contains what the judge actually ordered after the hearing. The impact of Lord Oliver's words is therefore directed to how the order will actually work out in practice, in effect requiring the parties' advisers to try to envisage any difficulties or ambiguities and cater for them. If the *judge* has made a mistake, most judges would rather hear that sooner, before the order has been drawn up let alone sealed, rather than later when making amendments under the slip rule or setting aside an order that has somehow become mangled at the drawing up stage, so that Lord Oliver's advice is severely practical.

Practitioners normally consult the usual volumes of precedents for the proper format for consent orders of the various types mentioned. However, there is a legitimate academic interest in the composition of orders. This is because of the distinction between what may be incorporated in the operative part of the order (usually called 'the body') and what other ingredients may be introduced by way of 'undertaking' (ie, because no statutory provision allows such items to be 'ordered' as such, but the respect due to the court enables judges to take and to incorporate into their orders such undertakings to do voluntarily as a condition of the order being made certain desirable additions, and to punish any later disregard of such undertakings as contempt of court). Thus may the court insist on a party honouring a promise which was an essential part of the deal struck between the parties and sanctioned by the court (eg, for a husband to take out an insurance policy to compensate a wife for lost pension rights, as in *Milne v Milne* [1981] 2 FLR 286, or a wife to keep the home the subject of a *Martin* order in good repair). The drafting of orders to reflect both the statutory provisions and the practice underpinning ancillary relief is another example of the importance for the academic student of understanding procedural aspects of the law in order to achieve adequate analysis of its effect.

16.3.2 The layout of the order

Every order has at least two parts and some have possibly three or four parts:

- the heading (essential);
- recitals and/or undertakings as explained above (but neither of these is essential);
- the body of the order (essential).

16.3.2.1 The heading

This is copied directly from that of the suit, showing the court, identifying number and parties.

16.3.2.2 Recitals and undertakings

Recitals and/or undertakings come next, before the body of the order, and are not essential. As explained above, they exist to record any term which it is desired to incorporate into the order, but which cannot be comprised in the body of it because that item does not fall within the scope of what the court can order under ss 23 and 24 of the MCA 1973.

Recitals which may be appropriate include those concerning contracting out of the CSA regime and the intention to create a clean break or the compulsory recital which must record the status of the home for the statutory charge.

In addition to the examples given above, *undertakings* may conveniently cover a promise to invest the ancillary relief funds in the purchase of a home for the payee and children, or for a wife whose earning capacity needs improving to undergo a training course.

These immediately follow the recitals, and have the same force as an order of the court, since the undertaking is given to the *court*, making breach contempt.

16.3.2.3 The body of the order

This contains the paragraphs which will effect the provisions which have been won from the other side and which the court has the power pursuant to statute to order, in the same way that the recitals and undertakings embody those provisions of the parties' agreement which the court cannot order. Such operative clauses will cover periodical payments, as well as the appropriate clause for disposal of the home, and if there is to be a clean break, dismissal of all future claims, and costs.

THE MATRIMONIAL HOME

HOMES FOR ALL

The court attempts to provide a home for both parties from the assets to be divided, although pursuant to s 25(1) their first priority will be the welfare of the children of the family, which means a secure roof over their heads and sufficient income to live on during their minority. Sometimes a home for the non-custodial spouse cannot be provided.

POSSIBLE DISPOSALS OF THE HOME

Sale and division of the proceeds is appropriate where there is sufficient equity for two homes, or where one spouse has other accommodation, or where there is insufficient equity and sale is the best option to provide some liquid capital for both, both parties then going into rented accommodation.

Outright transfer to one spouse is appropriate where one spouse can compensate the other, where one spouse will take a deferred charge, or where there is a trade off of the home for some other benefit given up (eg, where the wife takes the home and no periodical payments).

Trust of land is appropriate where there needs to be a home provided for the children and custodial spouse, resulting in a deferred sale at the triggering event (eg, when the children are grown up, or the wife remarries, cohabits or elects to move). There are many variants of this (eg, *Mesher, Martin, Harvey/Brown, Browne v Pritchard*, etc orders).

THE STATUTORY CHARGE

This enables the public funding bill to be deferred against a charge taken by the LSC on the matrimonial home 'recovered or preserved' in the proceedings. The drawback of the charge is that eventually it will have to be repaid. Therefore it is essential that it should be mitigated by keeping costs down, settling where possible and as soon as possible and obtaining orders which do not attract it (eg, periodical payments orders) where possible. The new ancillary relief pilot scheme assists in attaining this goal as the district judge will seek to manage the case cost effectively, with shared valuations, regular costs statements brought to the notice of both parties and cost sanctions for wasteful litigation practices.

DRAFTING

The drafting of an order is as important as the content, and Lord Oliver has criticised and rejected the assumption of some practitioners that the court is responsible for checking the effect of any order presented to it for approval.

CHAPTER 17

PREVENTING EVASION OF LIABILITY OR ENFORCEMENT OF ORDERS

17.1 PRESERVING THE ASSETS AGAINST WHICH ORDERS ARE MADE

Some respondents never intend that ancillary relief orders will be made against them or, even if they are, that such orders will never be successfully enforced. However, the powers of the court would be empty if respondents to financial applications could get away with such schemes. If a party entitled to ancillary relief suspects such a situation to exist or that it might arise, urgent steps can be taken to prevent assets being moved out of the jurisdiction (or in any way put beyond the applicant's reach, for example, by their being transferred into the names of third parties).

Especially in cases where there is an international element, this matter is routinely considered at the first opportunity, when it is usual in any event to establish at the outset of a divorce case whether any action needs to be taken to register a party's matrimonial home rights (ie, of occupation, regardless of ownership) under s 30 of the Family Law Act (FLA) 1996. If protection is also required for other assets not within the FLA 1996, there is special provision in s 37 of the Matrimonial Causes Act (MCA) 1973 which will usually meet the applicant's needs. However, in an appropriate case a freezing order (formerly called a *Mareva* injunction) or a search order (formerly an *Anton Pillar* order) is also of course available just as in other types of civil litigation, although due to the expense and strict requirements for such orders the use of s 37, which does not have such disadvantages, will generally be sufficient, unless the respondent is very rich and the assets very widely spread around the world. All or any of these remedies may be used individually or together.

In view of the ongoing harmonisation of European family law pursuant to the new EU divorce jurisdiction rules, this particular provision may increase the attraction of commencing divorces with an international flavour in England and Wales, since other European jurisdictions, which are generally quite behind England and Wales in practical procedural and evidential matters, do not have legislation as effective. In matrimonial property cases, this is probably because most European jurisdictions operate a system of community of property and compulsory testamentary obligations, so that there is less opportunity and therefore incentive to indulge in the concealment or dispersal tricks possible under the English system where there is no regime of matrimonial property as such, although in general terms litigation in Europe is much less advanced a science overall. Conversely, the past background of English matrimonial law in property – including the concept of the wife as the husband's chattel whose quality was damaged by the criminal conversation of adultery, and the single legal personality of husband and wife – possibly explains the strong restitutionary element in the contemporary law. It is after all incredibly still only just over 30 years since the abolition of the action for breach of promise of marriage! Thus, as Maitland remarked of the rigidity of the medieval writs which at the dawn of English law gave access to the court's remedies, do the shadows of past influences still impact upon the current system.

As with other procedural aspects, an understanding of prevention of evasion, and ultimate enforcement of orders available under the substantive law, is important for the academic student to analyse the effectiveness of the law.

17.2 MATRIMONIAL CAUSES ACT 1973, s 37

This section can achieve two distinct results:

- *preventing* a suspected disposal (s 37(2)(a));
- *setting aside* a disposal which has already taken place (s 37(2)(b) and (2)(c)).

By s 37(1)(b), a disposition made before the court has had time to make a financial order may be set aside, and by s 37(1)(c) a disposition made *after* the court's financial order, and with the intention of preventing enforcement, will be similarly caught.

In all cases the actual or intended disposition must be for the purposes of *defeating the applicant's claim*, that is to say:

(a) *preventing* financial relief being granted at all, either to the applicant or any child of the family; or

(b) *reducing the amount* which might be granted; or

(c) *frustrating or impeding enforcement* of an actual or anticipated order (s 37(1)).

Thus, if the respondent is wealthy and wishes to transfer property which is not in practice needed to meet any order that the court might make, the section cannot be used to prevent this, or commercial paralysis would follow.

17.2.1 Activating the protection of the Matrimonial Causes Act 1973, s 37

In order to use any of these provisions the applicant will need to have started proceedings against the respondent for financial relief. That means that:

- in divorce a petition must have been filed claiming ancillary relief in the usual way;
- if the applicant is not the petitioner a Form A must have been filed;
- in a variation case an application must have been made under s 31 (or s 35);
- in s 27 proceedings (see Chapter 19) an application must have been made for provision.

Once whichever of these steps is appropriate has been taken, an application can be made under s 37 immediately, sometimes with quite dramatic results, as in *Hamlin v Hamlin* [1985] 2 All ER 1037, where the husband was stopped from selling a house in Spain, which happened to be the only matrimonial asset.

There is a *presumption* that the disposition was in fact *designed to defeat the claim* if made within the past three years and if it would in fact defeat the claim if not set aside (s 37(5)). Such a disposal is called a 'reviewable disposition', and by s 37(4) includes *any disposition* made otherwise than for valuable consideration, other than marriage, to a person who at the time of the disposition acted in good faith and without notice of any intention on the part of the respondent to defeat the applicant's claim for ancillary relief.

By s 37(6) a 'disposition' includes a conveyance, assurance or gift of property of any description, by instrument or otherwise, except any provision contained in a will or codicil, for example, mortgaging a house, giving away assets or even dissipating money (although in the latter case some assistance might be required from the law of trusts under the doctrines of knowing receipt and dealing).

17.2.2 Effect of s 37 protection

In theory, s 37(4) and (6) leave very little room for the respondent to make off with assets, but since dispositions caught by s 37 are *voidable* and not void (a principle which has essential commercial importance), sometimes a technically *bona fide* transaction escapes, even though the respondent had every intention of defeating the section. This happened in *National Provincial Bank v Hastings Car Mart* [1964] Ch 665; [1964] 3 All ER 93, where the husband conveyed the matrimonial home to a company which he had formed for the purpose and then the company mortgaged it to the bank. The court held the conveyance to the company to be a sham and set it aside as it was clearly intended to defeat the wife's claim, but the mortgage to the bank was a *bona fide* commercial transaction and had to be upheld.

In particular, although transfers to a controlled company or a relative will be caught, dispositions for valuable consideration (other than marriage) cannot be set aside if a third party acted in good faith and without notice of any intention to defeat the spouse's claim. Therefore, the section may be insufficient protection without backing it up with registration of a spouse's claim as a pending land action, a situation which came to light in *Kemmis v Kemmis* [1988] 2 FLR 223. In that case, a bank was lending on mortgage to a husband. It was held that such a bank might have notice of the husband's intention if they knew of the wife's occupation of the home and that she might be making a financial application.

The difficulty in such a situation is that the bank might have no reason to know of the husband's personal circumstances, so there may be no constructive notice on their part: this problem is obviated by registering the pending land action and thus giving notice to any such third party who may need to have it.

Obviously if the mortgagee already has constructive notice such registration will not be necessary, as in *Perez-Adamson v Perez Rivas* [1987] 3 All ER 20, where the bank made a loan without bothering to search the register. However, the wife had duly registered her pending land action under the Land Charges Act 1972, so when the husband left the country with the money she took priority over the bank as mortgagee, although in fact it turned out that they had constructive notice of her occupation anyway. If there is any doubt about constructive notice, it is obviously better for an applicant to register and be safe rather than sorry.

In these complex circumstances, banks have become much more sophisticated in recent years and, pursuant to their own good practice which now includes a formal Code, have adopted routines designed to ascertain whether they are accepting from a husband a charge over a matrimonial home where the wife may have an interest, irrespective of whether there may be a divorce pending, and if so whether she understands the nature of any obligation entered into. In the alternative they may be at risk in a bankruptcy where the wife will obviously attempt to establish such an interest or to claim undue influence and to rank her claims before those of the bank (see Chapter 20).

In all cases evidence will be required, and fanciful imagining will not be sufficient, since the court must be satisfied that the respondent is about to deal with the property in question in the manner feared, or that such a disposition has been made. It can then make such order as it thinks fit to restrain such a disposition or to set it aside if it has already been made.

17.3 FREEZING AND SEARCH ORDERS AND THE WRIT *NE EXEAT REGNO*

A freezing order may be used to ring-fence assets pending resolution of the ancillary relief claim, or a search order to gather information from relevant documents, and finally the writ *ne exeat regno* to prevent the respondent personally leaving the country, but obviously these will be used sparingly in matrimonial proceedings because of their expense and complexity. Usually such extreme measures are reserved for cases where the respondent has a history of flouting orders, as in *Emanual v Emanual* [1982] 2 All ER 342, where the husband fell into this category, and *K v K* (1982) *The Times*, 25 October, where the husband had failed to make full disclosure and it was necessary to obtain details of his stock in trade.

17.4 ENFORCEMENT

Normally, payments under money orders will be left to the parties to make as they see fit, and this will usually be by direct payment by monthly cheque, or standing order, unless the order is payable through the Family Proceedings Court, where different arrangements may apply (see Chapter 19). Successful ancillary relief applicants are therefore in any event usually made aware of enforcement methods as soon as their orders are made so as not to delay in bringing to their lawyers' attention any problems that arise, which should preferably be straight away when they first occur, as, pursuant to s 32 of the MCA 1973, leave is required to enforce arrears more than 12 months old: indeed in the Family Proceedings Court arrears more than 12 months old will not be enforced at all (on the basis that if the applicant has managed that long without the money, it cannot be essentially required).

Similarly the payer is usually advised to keep records of payment, of both lump sums and periodical payments, such as by paying through a bank by cheque or standing order.

All the same methods of enforcement of orders as are routine in civil litigation are equally available to enforce matrimonial financial orders, in other words:

- warrant of execution;
- attachment of earnings order;
- charging order and order for sale; and
- garnishee order.

There are also some extra possibilities more particularly tailored to typical matrimonial orders:

- a judgment summons (FPR 1991, r 7.4);
- a s 24A (of the MCA 1973) sale order;
- enforcement of property adjustment orders (Supreme Court Act (SCA) 1981, s 39; County Courts Act (CCA) 1984, s 38; MCA 1973, s 30); and
- registration of periodical payments orders in the Family Proceedings Court.

Before any process is issued to enforce an order made in matrimonial proceedings, it will be necessary, pursuant to r 7.1(1) of the Family Proceedings Rules (FPR) 1991, as amended, to file a certificate specifying the amount due under the order (ie, the amount of arrears of periodical payments or the unpaid portion of a lump sum). It may also be advisable to make an application for an oral examination in order to ascertain the nature and extent of the defaulter's means and therefore the best way of proceeding to enforce the order. Application is to the district judge who can compel the production of any necessary documents.

17.4.1 Judgment summons (FPR 1991, r 7.4)

This requires the defaulting payer to attend before a judge to be examined as to his or her means, and the judge will then make such order as is thought fit in relation to the unpaid sums, whether they be arrears of periodical payments or an outstanding lump sum or both. The judge does have power to commit the defaulter to prison for non-payment, though this is unlikely actually to happen if the money is paid within a specified period as the more usual course is to suspend any committal order on condition that the payments are made.

17.4.2 Section 24A order for sale

This is a useful provision under the MCA 1973 since where it has not been thought necessary to use this section to include a specific order for sale in the original order made, it still permits the unpaid payee to seek an order for sale at a later date with a consequential direction that the proceeds of sale or part of them should be paid over to the payee in satisfaction of the existing unpaid order.

Vacant possession can be ordered to facilitate such a sale (FPR 1991, r 2.64).

17.4.3 Enforcing property adjustment orders

Lack of co-operation on the part of the respondent is by no means fatal here, since drafting of any necessary documents can be undertaken if necessary by one of the conveyancing counsel to the court who can settle the proper instrument for execution by all those who must be a party to them.

Execution can be effected by an order that, unless the defaulter does this within a specified time, the district judge shall execute the document (SCA 1981, s 39; CCA 1984, s 38).

Where the order has been made in divorce, nullity or judicial separation proceedings (ie, where there is a decree which can be withheld), pressure can be put on the defaulter by the court's providing that the decree shall be deferred until the instrument has been duly executed.

17.4.4 Registration of periodical payments orders in the Family Proceedings Court

This is by far the most effective way of getting a periodical payments order observed if there is likely to be any difficulty in enforcing it. It is not therefore unusual to obtain a certificate of public funding for ancillary relief proceedings which extends to registration of one substantive order in the Family Proceedings Court.

The magistrates have a long history of effective collection of maintenance payments. This is because their somewhat parochial methods have always enabled payment to be made *through* the court, thus putting the clerk on immediate notice when the money was not paid, and enabling swift enforcement to follow. However, the introduction of new powers under the Maintenance Enforcement Act (MEA) 1991 made them even more effective.

This Act came into force on 1 April 1992 and for the first time enabled the magistrates to specify how an order should be paid, whether by standing order or attachment of earnings or otherwise, and also to require the opening of a bank account to provide payment by standing order where that was appropriate (MEA 1991, s 2). The result has obviously been to provide an even more efficient system, making registration of other courts' orders even more worthwhile since the new methods in respect of their own order freed time to enforce those of other less effective courts also. Combined with the removal of much child support business to the Child Support Agency, the resulting streamlining of magistrates' courts systems makes it now more than worthwhile to register even overseas orders (in respect of which there are many longstanding and sometimes little known reciprocal enforcement provisions which may be found in *Rayden*).

While it has for many years been similarly possible to register Family Proceedings Courts orders (made under the Domestic Proceedings and Magistrates' Courts Act (DPMCA) 1978 (see Chapter 19)) in the High Court under the Maintenance Orders Act 1958, this is only worthwhile for a large amount of money (eg, accumulated arrears). The traffic is very much the other way around.

Pursuant to s 32(1) of the DPMCA 1978, all magistrates' courts orders can be enforced in the following ways:

- attachment of earnings (Attachment of Earnings Act 1971);
- committal to prison (Magistrates' Courts Act 1980, s 76);
- distress (Magistrates' Courts Act 1980, s 76).

There is also the diversion procedure, whereby the Benefits Agency will take over the order and enforce it, meanwhile paying the applicant social security benefits in lieu (see Chapters 18 and 19).

An additional advantage of registration of orders in the Family Proceedings Court is that that court can then vary as well as enforce them, which may sometimes be useful rather than the parties being obliged to return to the court granting the original order.

17.4.5 High Court and county court methods

If registration in the Family Proceedings Court is not, exceptionally, the complete solution in the particular case, it will be necessary to weigh up the alternative methods available in the High Court and county court and to pick the one most suitable to the circumstances of the defaulter. For example, the High Court affords the possibilities of the writs of *fi fa* and sequestration, though the latter is hugely expensive and a party would obviously beware of incurring costs which might not even meet the order defaulted on, and there is also the possibility of appointment of a receiver by way of equitable execution to compel sale pursuant to an order under ss 14 and 15 of the Trusts of Land and Appointment of Trustees Act 1996.

PREVENTING EVASION OF LIABILITY OR ENFORCEMENT OF ORDERS

PRESERVING THE ASSETS AGAINST WHICH ORDERS ARE MADE

There is specific statutory provision in s 37 of the MCA 1973 to enable assets required for the fair disposal of ancillary relief claims to be frozen pending resolution of claims. The section is equally effective either to prevent or to set aside dispositions caught by the legislation. To invoke the section, proceedings must have been commenced, in that in divorce a claim has been made in the petition or a Form A filed by a respondent, and in claims under s 27 or 31 of the MCA 1973 or under the DPMCA 1978, an application must actually have been filed.

Ordinary freezing or search orders may also be used as in any civil suit, but the customised s 37 has advantages in not requiring the same quality of undertakings as the other orders. Matrimonial home rights pursuant to s 31 of the FLA 1996 may also be registered, and all or any of these precautionary remedies may be used individually or in concert.

Not all assets may be frozen, however: those not required for satisfaction of the quantum of the ancillary relief claim or validly charged in priority may be beyond reach, for example, where a mortgage is given to a bank which a wife is unable to claim to set aside for undue influence.

ENFORCEMENT

All the usual civil methods of enforcement may be used, although there are some specific to the matrimonial jurisdiction (eg, an order for sale under s 24A of the MCA 1973), including consequential orders disposing of the proceeds of sale, a judgment summons, specific enforcement of property adjustment orders with the assistance of the conveyancing counsel to the court, and registration of orders in the Family Proceedings Court. The latter also permits the court to vary as well as enforce the order registered (including foreign orders where there is a reciprocal agreement to this effect), and also to use the diversion procedure where the applicant would otherwise be obliged to rely on benefits if the order were not paid regularly. Recourse is also possible to uniquely effective High Court and county court remedies, such as sequestration and Trusts of Land and Appointment of Trustees Act 1996 orders.

CHAPTER 18

WELFARE BENEFITS AND TAX
ON RELATIONSHIP BREAKDOWN

18.1 INTRODUCTION

The availability of welfare benefits in family support has a significant impact on financial provision which can be ordered for separated and/or divorced applicants to the court. Benefits may be needed either short term on marriage breakdown or permanently following divorce: in some cases, where the parties are of acutely limited means, welfare benefits will be needed in both situations. It is crucial to recognise the implications for welfare benefit entitlement of any ancillary relief orders obtained, and vice versa, since it is of course essential that if maintenance is to be received that disentitles the applicant to benefits, the order should deliver a significantly better financial result than if reliance is placed solely on welfare benefits. The court is aware that if this matter is not addressed the applicant risks falling into the 'poverty trap'.

Benefits are obtainable either from the Benefits Agency or in some cases from the local authority or through the Inland Revenue. It is for individual applicants, not their lawyers, to make the actual application. This must be done on the appropriate form, which will be completed at the local office of the Agency. This is usually followed by an interview for new claimants, following which those not required to be available for work will be given a book of orders to cash at a post office: if the claimant does have to be available for and actively seeking work, the benefit will be paid by fortnightly giro cheque which will include their unemployment benefit, now called 'jobseeker's allowance', if applicable.

However, a working knowledge of the system is still essential for the lawyer or appropriate advice cannot be given. In particular, a practitioner would not be able to prompt the client to apply where appropriate without an in-depth knowledge and this will certainly be a routine task for a high street general practice advising initially under the new generation Green Form, known as legal help (see Chapter 11). However, benefits have the same impact on the academic assessment of quantum in ancillary relief, without consideration of which any general assessment of entitlement to ancillary relief will be incomplete.

The main sources of the law are the Social Security Contributions and Benefits Act (SSCBA) 1992, as amended, and the various regulations governing each benefit (ie, for income support, the Income Support (General) Regulations 1987 SI 1987/1967; for Working Families' Tax Credit, the Family Credit (General) Regulations 1987 SI 1987/1973, as amended; for housing benefit, the Housing Benefit (General) Regulations 1987 SI 1987/1971; and for council tax, the Council Tax Benefit (General) Regulations 1992 SI 1992/1814). In social security law the Regulations are at least as important as the statute.

Any lawyer working in a practice where clients commonly use benefits would need to have regular access to a good up to date practitioner's book on the subject, such as the annual publication of the Child Poverty Action Group (CPAG), established some years ago as the 'benefits bible', although there are now a number of other authoritative works, since detailed changes in the way that benefits operate occur regularly. The CPAG guide is usually issued in paperback and regularly updated, since annual changes in the rates and sometimes applicability of the various benefits are generally announced each autumn for implementation at the start of the next tax year in the following April.

The Benefits Agency also publishes regularly updated leaflets and booklets describing the individual benefits, including a useful booklet entitled *Social Security Benefit Rates*, which explains and details the range and amounts available, and these may be obtained free from post offices and Benefits Agency offices. A practice dealing regularly with clients using benefits will usually have a stock of such material to hand out to clients, since this saves taking up precious legal help time in going over the detail, as where appropriate the client can be advised in outline, given the booklets and advised to go straight to the Benefits Agency office to claim.

18.2 TWO TYPES OF BENEFITS

Benefits are either:

- means tested (most benefits); or
- not means tested (the only one is now child benefit – often abbreviated to CB – including the lone parent supplement which used to be called 'one parent benefit').

18.3 NON-MEANS TESTED BENEFITS

The only remaining non-means tested benefit, child benefit, is also tax free, although it will count as income for the purposes of some other welfare benefits. The law is to be found in ss 141–47 of the SSCBA 1992.

At present, all potential applicants with children to care for are likely to be receiving child benefit, and some with protected rights may also have the lone parent supplement which provides an additional amount for the eldest child.

Child benefit, and where appropriate the lone parent supplement, is paid to every person, regardless of means, who is responsible for a child either up to the age of 16, or up to the age of 19 where a child is in full time, non-advanced education or training (ie, any course below university first degree level), but there is a current proposal to remove both for children aged 16–19 so as to provide further funds for youth training and similar schemes.

Every other benefit is now means tested. Like child support from the Child Support Agency (CSA), child benefit is only payable for children over the school leaving age (16) when they are in full time *non-advanced* education or training (ie, A levels or even a secretarial course qualify, a university degree does not in any circumstances). Where a child leaves school at 16 or later, or stops further non-advanced education under the age of 19, either or both of these benefits usually continue to be paid until the child obtains a full time job or goes into some form of training which does not qualify for the benefit, or ultimately when the child reaches 19, whatever that child is then doing.

18.3.1 Child benefit

Child benefit is claimed from the Benefits Agency for any child living with an applicant or to whose maintenance a potential applicant contributes at a rate not less than the weekly child benefit rate. This is a standard weekly amount, in 2002–03 £15.75 for the first child and £10.55 for each subsequent child. Those lone parents with protected rights still receive £17.55 for the eldest child. The benefit will usually be paid to a parent, but this is not necessarily always the case, if someone other than a child is living with or maintaining the child.

Sometimes when parents separate, there are arguments over which parent is entitled to the child benefit and one parent benefit which will then become available after 13 weeks' separation. While the parties are married and living together, child benefit is technically payable to either of the parents, and if it is paid by order book, both names will be on the cover of the book and either may draw the orders, but the mother usually has the prime claim to receive it. Historically, child benefit was introduced to provide mothers with the care of children with one reliable source of income to spend on the children. However, once the parties are separated either can qualify since in law a person is *responsible for a child* if:

- the child lives with that person; or
- that person contributes to the child's maintenance at a weekly rate not less than the rate of child benefit.

When the person receiving child benefit (usually the mother) separates from the other parent, she is obliged to inform the Child Benefit Centre of this change of circumstance, and thereafter child benefit will usually be paid to her if the child is living with her. If the other parent, usually the father, disputes this, there are rules which enable the dispute to be solved by the Benefits Agency. Once claimed, child benefit is paid four weekly, usually direct into the recipient's bank account.

Child benefit will continue to be paid where there is a claim to it regardless of whether the person responsible for the qualifying child or children is married, separated, divorced, remarried or living with a new partner, though this is not the case with the lone parent supplement.

18.4 MEANS TESTED BENEFITS

The means tested benefits are:

- income support/jobseeker's allowance (whether income or contribution based);
- Working Families' Tax Credit;
- housing benefit;
- council tax benefit;
- the Social Fund.

As there are a number of them the various benefits are often abbreviated to IS/JSA, WFTC, HB, CTB and SF, respectively.

These benefits form a framework, the main beam of which will be either IS/JSA or WFTC, as these benefits are mutually exclusive. Of the two it might be said that IS/JSA is the principle one, since that is the benefit for people with no income or negligible income (since, for example, there is a tiny earnings disregard which is increased, but not significantly, for single parents). Where an applicant cannot claim IS, because of earnings from working more than 16 hours a week, but is still low paid, in need, and having at least one child, WFTC will be available. In other words, while IS/JSA is the basic welfare benefit payment for the unwaged, WFTC is a benefit targeted at low paid families who *are* in work, and for whom not being able to obtain IS/JSA because they are working is a hardship. Applicants on public funding for family law actions will usually use WFTC if not IS/JSA, and whether they are also entitled to any of the portfolio of other benefits will depend on the detailed working of IS/JSA or WFTC respectively in relation to their particular circumstances.

18.4.1 Income support (SSCBA 1992, ss 124–27 as amended)

This has largely been replaced by jobseeker's allowance (see below). However, IS is still appropriate for lone parents with children to look after and who are therefore not available to seek work, and is paid to anyone whose income does not exceed the 'applicable amount' (see below) and who is:

- over 16 years of age;
- habitually resident in the UK;
- not in full time work (ie, not working more than 16 hours a week) and whose partner is not in full time work;
- available for full time work and actively seeking work or excused (eg, heavily pregnant women, the disabled, or a lone parent with a dependent child);
- not in 'relevant education' (full time non-advanced education) unless living away from home or responsible for a child.

A child up to the age of 19 who is receiving child benefit cannot claim IS. One claim is payable per household, and a household is either a married couple, cohabitants living together as man and wife or a lone parent with a child or children, and the income of the unit will be taken into account in calculating how much IS should be paid. The amount payable will vary with the needs and circumstances (eg, the numbers and ages of the dependent children).

Capital affects the claim. No claim is possible if the claimant has capital or savings over £8,000, and a reduced amount is paid if savings are between £3,000 and £8,000 (£1 is taken off for every £250 of capital). The capital value of the home is ignored.

18.4.1.1 Calculating income support

The means test works on the basis of how much a person needs to live on. This is called the 'applicable amount' and against it is set against the total of any income. The second figure is taken from the first and the balance paid in IS.

A person's applicable amount includes:

- a personal allowance for the claimant and any partner;
- a personal allowance for dependent children;
- a family premium (where there is at least one dependent child);
- a lone parent premium;
- various other premiums (eg, for the disabled or pensioners);
- mortgage interest where applicable.

Water rates, council tax and insurance are not included in the applicable amount.

A person's income includes:

- earnings of the claimant and any partner (net of tax and national insurance contributions and half any pension contributions);
- maintenance;
- child benefit and one parent benefit;
- 'tariff income', meaning the £1 per £250 or part thereof of capital over £3,000 mentioned above, since this is treated as producing income at that rate whether or not it in fact does so.

Maintenance is counted as income, whether paid voluntarily or under formal agreement or court order, *including* lump sums whether paid by instalments or not, as are statutory sick pay, maternity benefits *and* part time earnings over £5, though this disregard is raised to £15 for lone parents.

IS also entitles the successful claimant to a range of 'passport benefits':

- free school meals;
- free NHS prescriptions and dental treatment;
- free milk and vitamins for expectant and nursing mothers and pre-school children.

Loss of passport benefits is one way in which a claimant can fall into the 'poverty trap' by working and losing IS instead of remaining on benefit, and careful calculations should be done before deciding that it is worth the claimant giving up IS.

However, the greatest benefit of all is that mortgage interest (though not the repayment of the capital element of the monthly payments) can be included in the applicable amount, although there are now restrictions on the total amount of the mortgage on which interest can be paid, as well as a lengthy delay before the payments can commence. Claimants are expected to have mortgage protection insurance to cope with mortgage payments when they are out of work. This is a significant change in the former situation, where mortgages could always safely be taken over when the home was transferred outright to the occupational spouse on divorce (a situation which as may be gathered from study of older cases was routine in the 1980s), since if the client fell on hard times the State would pay until matters improved. Where mortgage interest is paid through IS, the interest will normally be sent direct to the lender.

Once mortgage interest relief is qualified for, loss of it is another way in which the claimant may fall into the 'poverty trap' by losing IS on going back to work.

18.4.1.2 Appeal and review

Review by the adjudicating officer is the first step in any appeal against a benefit decision with which the claimant is dissatisfied. Appeal can then be made to the Social Security Tribunal, which has a legal chairman and two lay members experienced in social security matters; then on point of law and with leave to the Social Security Commissioners, and finally with leave to the Court of Appeal.

Any lawyer working with clients using IS will need to become familiar with the Income Support (General) Regulations 1987 SI 1987/1967, which are usually amended annually, and with the latest benefit rates which are contained in the Social Security Benefits Up-Rating Order 1995 SI 1995/559.

18.4.1.3 The diversion procedure

Where payment of maintenance is erratic or insufficient to preclude IS, an applicant may be able to claim IS one week and not the next, which is irritating and time consuming to say the least. The solution may be found in the *diversion procedure*, which puts the claimant permanently on benefit but enables the maintenance order to be assigned to the Benefits Agency who can then pursue the maintenance payments. To use this procedure, the maintenance order must be registered in the Family Proceedings Court (ie, it must be one of their own or an order of another court, including a divorce county court (see Chapter 19)).

18.4.2 Jobseeker's allowance (Jobseekers Act 1995, s 1)

This is the 1996 replacement for unemployment benefit and therefore for many people IS. There are thus two types of JSA: income based (the old IS) and contribution based (the old unemployment benefit). The benefit is now therefore distinguished from IS as described at 18.4.1 above, as the name JSA suggests, where the claimant is not in employment, and having no dependent resident children should be seeking work. Eligibility is the same as for IS but the claimant must 'sign on' and actively seek work. Any capital of a partner will be added to the claimant's when assessing eligibility, save that the earnings disregard is £5 for a single person and £10 for a couple and the claimant's partner must not work for more than 24 hours a week.

18.4.3 Working Families' Tax Credit (SSCBA 1992, ss 128 and 129 as amended)

This tax credit, administered by the Inland Revenue, is designed to give help to low paid working families with children, and is paid to anyone with at least one dependent child who is:

- habitually resident in Great Britain;
- in full time work (or whose partner is in full time work, or if both partners are in full time work, ie, 16 or more hours per week).

The *family* can consist of a married or unmarried couple, but it seems that any other 'couple' or family grouping is excluded. From April 2003, WFTC will be split to provide two new credits (Child Tax Credit and Working Tax Credit) as part of the ongoing reform of taxation of the lower paid.

The capital limit is again £8,000, with a reduced amount payable if savings are over £3,000, so that as with IS a tariff income will be presumed of £1 per £250 of such capital or savings: the rules are the same as for JSA.

The amount of WFTC actually paid will depend on the claimant's circumstances, but if a claimant has less than a fixed sum coming in, called the threshold, currently £90 per week, the maximum appropriate WFTC will be payable. If it is over £90, then the WFTC paid will be reduced by 70p in the pound (not pound for pound as with IS). A claimant taking a job of over 30 hours a week obtains an extra premium of £11.05 per week. There is a further tax credit of 70% of child care costs up to £100 per week for one child and £150 for two.

Income for WFTC purposes includes earnings, all periodical payments either to the claimant or the child or children, however paid, over the first £15, most social security benefits and pensions, and any tariff income must also be added, but it excludes child benefit and HB, which are ignored for WFTC.

It should be noted that the £15 *maintenance disregard* is exclusive to WFTC, and does *not* apply to IS where there is a similar £15 *earnings disregard* for lone parents.

WFTC is claimed by post and once granted lasts for six months (26 weeks) regardless of all changes in the claimant's circumstances unless the claimant's job is lost, when it will be necessary to come off WFTC and go onto IS instead. WFTC does not carry the complete range of passport benefits applicable to IS, but it does now entitle the claimant to free NHS prescriptions, dental treatment and eye tests, and help with the cost of spectacles.

There is a 'fast service' for processing applications from newly employed and self-employed people. Payments are either made through the wage packet or direct to the claimant.

18.4.4 Housing benefit (SSCBA 1992, s 130 as amended)

This is a useful benefit which is:

* paid to anyone liable to pay rent for a home;
* whether or not the recipient is in receipt of IS or WFTC;
* who has capital not exceeding £16,000.

The payment will be made either to the person who is *liable* to pay the rent or to a person who is *obliged* to pay the rent in order to remain in the home because a third party has not paid it (eg, usually the partner of the person claiming).

It is claimed as a *rebate* on council rent or *direct to the claimant* to meet private sector rent payable to a landlord. Generally only one home is allowed.

It covers all eligible rent:

* 100% of rent where the claimant is on IS or with income not over the IS level;
* at a reduced level according to a formula for higher incomes.

However, the method of assessment was changed in 1996 and is now quite complex since it is linked to rent ceilings, average rents for the area and an appropriate size of accommodation for the claimant. 'Eligible rent' does not include water rate and sewage charges, nor some service charges. Moreover, eligible rent can be reduced by an 'appropriate amount' if the dwelling occupied is too large for the claimant or if the rent itself is unreasonably high for that accommodation. Rules about rent have recently been made more restrictive and HB at the full rate will no longer be paid where the rent in question is above the level for the area where the home is situated, or if the accommodation is shared with non-dependents not on benefits.

For the purposes of HB, 'income' is defined in the same way as for IS, and WFTC if claimed is *included* as income.

18.4.5 Council tax benefit (SSCBA 1992, ss 131–33 as amended)

This is a useful benefit usually automatically available to those on HB and IS/JSA. The maximum benefit is 100% rebate of the tax and it is available to those:

- on low incomes;
- with less than £16,000 capital;
- whether or not they are on IS, WFTC or HB.

The scheme is a national one, although it is administered by the local authorities collecting the tax, and the Department of Social Security makes the regulations which govern its operation. There is a reduced level for those on higher incomes. Income is defined in the same way as for IS, and there is a £15 *maintenance* disregard.

Married and unmarried couples are both responsible for each other's council tax while they are cohabiting.

18.4.6 The Social Fund (SSCBA 1992, ss 138–40)

The further source of benefit money was originally set up by s 32 of the Social Security Act 1986 to replace the former system of single payments for special needs, such as furniture, which could not be met out of the ordinary weekly benefit income. Whereas single payments were outright, those made under the SF are either grants or loans to those on low incomes for meeting exceptional expenses, and the new concept is that both loans and grants should be discretionary and cash limited.

There are two types of loans:

- budgeting loans; and
- crisis loans.

Both are interest free.

18.4.6.1 Budgeting loans

These are for persons on IS and are repayable, (out of the IS received), discretionary according to needs and limited to repayments affordable to the claimant. They are designed to spread the cost of larger items over a longer period, and besides furniture could include removal expenses.

18.4.6.2 Crisis loans

These are to meet immediate short-term expenses following disaster, or emergency where the health or safety of the family are at risk, discretionary according to needs and also limited to repayments affordable and in any case to £1,000. This type of loan can even cover living expenses for up to 14 days or travel costs.

Alternatively, there are community care grants, which are not loans and therefore not repayable, but their availability is both discretionary and cash limited. These are designed to help people lead independent lives in the community, such as when they leave residential institutional care, but may also be made to relieve exceptional pressures on families, and could include minor house repairs, travel or removal costs and furniture.

One or other of these payments may be available to deal with family crises such as smashed furniture or a fire following domestic violence, or travel or removal to be with a sick relative. Generosity depends on area and, although there is extensive and complex guidance for SF officers adjudicating on claims, inevitably some human element creeps in, besides which the cash limiting system will mean that some particularly deprived areas will exhaust their funds earlier than others.

There are also funeral grants, available to applicants making funeral arrangements who are on IS, WFTC, HB, CTB or the disability working allowance, and also maternity payments, designed to buy clothes and equipment for a new baby. The former are loans and are repayable out of the deceased's estate; the latter are not loans and are not repayable.

18.5 MARRIAGE BREAKDOWN AND WELFARE BENEFIT PLANNING

The basic principle is that welfare benefits are not a primary resource for s 25(2)(a) purposes, but that the facts of life are such that sometimes when there is not enough money to go round, particularly when a low paid man starts a new relationship or second family, somebody may have to go onto welfare benefits. This is most common where the man has left a first wife and children, caring for whom will prevent the first wife from working, and has set up house with a cohabitant or second wife, who is herself prevented from working by caring for a young child or children. As the second partner will have a partner who is working, welfare benefits will be unavailable to *her*, but the first wife who is now without a partner will *not* be debarred from benefit, since her problem will be that her husband has left her for the other woman. It will thus usually be the *first* wife or partner who will have to go on to welfare benefits, or when the children become older, will have to go out to work.

The Child Support Act 1991, which has been in force since 1993, is having some success in enforcing the support of children by their liable parents, so that wherever possible neither the State nor the stepparents are now paying for these children. Reforms to the child support regime from 2002 will give further recognition to the role played by stepparents in cases where they are in practice supporting their stepchildren (see Chapter 15). However, the problem is still not entirely eradicated, as some such children have no liable parents (if those parents are dead or have disappeared), in which case there are various principles which are applied in attempting to resolve the issue of who shall be supported by the State as fairly as possible.

18.5.1 The principle in *Barnes v Barnes*

The first principle is that a husband or father cannot throw the burden of maintaining his family onto the State, but equally that there is no sense in making orders that reduce him below subsistence level. This was initially established in *Barnes v Barnes* [1972] 1 WLR 1381; [1972] 3 All ER 872 and has been several times reiterated, including in *Ashley v Blackman* [1988] 2 FLR 278, where the judge courageously decided to terminate a wife's periodical payments on a variation application because the parties were both of such acutely limited means that the public money spent in their returning to court for such purposes at public expense (since both were on legal aid) was simply not justified when the mentally ill wife living off welfare benefits merely lost some of her benefits whenever the husband (who earned so little that he paid no tax) could afford to pay maintenance. In that case the judge, in expressly referring to the *Barnes* decision, said that it was a 'salutary principle, protecting public funds from feckless or devious husbands who seek to escape their proper responsibilities', but also recognised that sometimes it was simply not possible for a man to pay for two families out of one wage.

The Child Support Acts continue the recognition of the *Barnes* principle, but as tempered by the obvious sense of not exacting payments which reduce the payer below subsistence level, in requiring *all* liable parents, even those on IS, to contribute a nominal amount out of their benefit payments for the support of their children. Such parents have apparently most recently been paying £5.40 per week but under the new system this will be slightly reduced to a flat rate of £5.

Previously judges had for years been recognising the pointlessness of making orders which took the payer below subsistence level so that in turn he would have to claim benefits, and this became enshrined in *Stockford v Stockford* [1982] 3 FLR 52 and *Furniss v Furniss* [1982] 3 FLR 46, both already mentioned in earlier chapters, which are together credited with having produced the net effect calculation now widely used to assess the effect of potential orders in families of limited means, although there was an occasional backlash against the use of welfare benefits as in the notorious 1988 case of *Day v Day* [1988] 1 FLR 278. In that case, Mr Day's cheeky assertion that he should not have to pay maintenance for his wife and stepchildren because she would be in a better financial position on benefits did *not* find favour with the court.

As already mentioned in Chapter 10, the case of *Reiterbund v Reiterbund* [1975] 2 WLR 375; [1975] 1 All ER 280 carried the *Barnes* principle into pensions when it was decided that where there were limited resources the availability of State benefits was in the particular circumstances a viable alternative to the husband's pension, the right to which the wife would lose on decree absolute if he died before she was aged 60 and entitled to her own pension.

The more recent case of *Delaney v Delaney* [1990] 2 FLR 457 is a classic one of the first wife who had to be the one to go out to work or on to benefits because the husband could not afford to pay for both families even with his cohabitant's contributions, his second partner being unable to claim benefits due to living with him. In that case the judge, overturning an earlier order that the husband should pay substantial maintenance to the children of the first union, expressly said that the husband was entitled to balance his future aspirations for a new life against his earlier responsibilities, so that the proper course was to allow the wife, who was eligible for benefits, to claim them, thus preserving the husband's income, such as it was, for his second family.

The second principle is that if a husband is truly out of work and unable to find employment he cannot be assumed to have an unrealised earning capacity and ordered to pay maintenance on the basis that he should be working. The CSA requirement of a minimum contribution, lately the minimum sum of £5.40 per week, out of such a father's income support is the only exception to this rule. The CSA was in fact not the originator of this principle, which was first established in *Freeman v Swatridge* [1984] FLR 762, where the judge ordered an out of work father to pay 50p a week each to his two children, thus making it clear that being on welfare benefits did not automatically have to preclude the imposition of a maintenance order as a matter of principle. The CSA seems to have recognised this view, on the basis that if the court makes an order that is fair and reasonable – such as a total of £1 per week in this case – it does not necessarily follow that the husband will be taken below subsistence level, so there is no need for a *rule of law* that maintenance cannot be ordered against a husband on welfare benefits.

However, if the husband is out of work, a *nominal* order, which can later be increased when work is obtained, is the right one, as was made in *Berry v Berry* [1986] 3 WLR 257; [1986] 2 All ER 948.

18.5.2 The liable relative formula

There is a statutory duty on a man to maintain both his wife and (since relatively recent but little noticed amendments to the law) his ex-wife (Social Security Administration Act 1992, ss 106–08; Income Support (Liable Relatives) Regulations 1990 SI 1990/1777), and also his children, whether he is married or not, and similarly a woman is liable to maintain her husband and all her natural children.

Thus if a liable relative fails to fulfil this statutory obligation to maintain, and a dependant claims benefits, the Benefits Agency will want to be reimbursed. It is usual practice to attempt a voluntary agreement with the liable relative first but failing this the Agency will take proceedings if they think they can recover the money expended on benefits. Obviously, this has created hazards for those contemplating a clean break involving transfer of property or capital in lieu of periodical payments for a wife, as has been mentioned in Chapter 12, above, and to this is now added the right of the CSA to assess a non-resident parent for child support payments regardless of a carer parent's agreement not to ask for a child support assessment (which cannot in law oust the Act or CSA involvement).

The only complete defence against liable relative claims following a clean break is for the liable relative to be without the means to satisfy any judgment so that the Agency in question is forced to the conclusion that the liable relative is not worth their powder and shot! Otherwise some creative practitioners are apparently now abandoning clean breaks and returning to *Mesher* orders where the proceeds of sale that would otherwise be paid to the spouse who asks for CSA assessments are reduced by the amount of the assessment.

The liable relative formula is widely used by courts to assess what the subsistence level is for a potential payer before making orders that can on that basis be afforded.

18.6 STRUCTURING THE ANCILLARY RELIEF PACKAGE TO MAKE THE MOST OF BENEFITS

Where welfare benefits are widely relied on, it will obviously be necessary to pay close attention to whether it is worth applying for a maintenance order or not.

It will also be necessary to beware of the capital limits on the various benefits, and the tariff income deemed to come from capital above the lower limit, in deciding whether clients should or should not receive lump sum orders. In particular, capitalised maintenance in the form of a lump sum may be a problem, since the client will be expected to use this up over a period before being entitled to benefits. Even where a lump sum is in fact for another purpose, unless it is the potential applicant's share of a capital asset, and is earmarked for the purchase of a new home, it can be treated by the Benefits Agency as disguised maintenance. The proceeds of sale of a former matrimonial home will be disregarded if it is used to buy a new one within six months. On the other hand, the value of the home is ignored so it may be better to take a residential property which can be classed as a home in settlement rather than cash.

18.6.1 Relevance of the matrimonial home in welfare benefit planning

The value of the matrimonial home will be disregarded for welfare benefit entitlement, but there are other problems to watch out for.

18.6.1.1 The home and the Child Support Agency

Limited credit can now be given in CSA assessments for past capital settlements (see Chapter 15). However, this is not entirely satisfactory and prevention of the problems which have arisen in the past would now be better than relying on such imperfect cures.

Attention has already been drawn to the hazards of a clean break settlement where the transferee subsequently goes on to welfare benefits. This problem can also be particularly acute in relation to child support under the Child Support Acts 1991–95 where the former matrimonial home is transferred in return for the transferee agreeing to support the children, as in *Crozier v Crozier* [1994] 1 FLR 126. In that case, Booth J refused to reopen such a clean break settlement when the wife applied for a CSA assessment for the child, holding that there can never be a clean break between parent and child. If a spouse wants to make such a deal, transferring either property or cash with the intention that this would effect proper provision for a child's maintenance, a trust would have to be set up and this would only be suitable in an appropriate case where transfer of a share of the home and/or of capital could generate sufficient income to provide for the child's needs, which would restrict its application to a minority of cases.

18.6.1.2 Income support and mortgage interest on the home loan

While the Benefits Agency will pay some of the interest element if the payer is on IS, they will not pay all of it (see 18.4.1, above) nor any capital repayments. The best way round this problem has been found to negotiate with the building society or other lender to restructure the mortgage (eg, to suspend payments, to accept interest only, to extend the term and/or to capitalise arrears). The Benefits Agency does in fact have a discretion to ignore capital payments from the other party to the mortgage.

18.7 TAX CONSIDERATIONS

There is now little change in the tax position when a couple either *separates* or *divorces* because of:

(a) fundamental changes in the taxation of maintenance from 30 June 1988 whereby all orders made after this date are paid tax free into the hands of the recipient (Income and Corporation Taxes Act (ICTA) 1988, s 347A, as inserted by the Finance Act (FA) 1988, s 36); and

(b) the fundamental change to separate taxation of spouses which took effect in 1990.

Prior to 30 June 1988, extensive tax relief was widely available on divorce, and this made the payment of maintenance much more attractive to divorced people who could afford to pay generous orders off the top of their income by utilising the personal allowances of their divorced spouses *and also* of each child payee. Divorces for tax purposes were not unheard of, especially as orders could be made by the court in favour of children *which were technically orders against the payer*, thus providing tax relief to divorced people for expenses, ranging from ordinary food, clothing and household bills to school fees, which had to be paid out of taxed income by people who remained married.

Clearly, although it was originally thought to be right to help those who had suffered the misfortune of divorce in this way, the system was too good to last when numbers divorcing escalated and it was realised that such tax relief was not only unfair to those who managed to keep their marriages together, but was also morally indefensible, since it militated not only against marriage and intact families, but also against the concept of spousal self-sufficiency: this was because a wife who already received maintenance using all her personal allowances had no incentive to go out to work because if she did so she would begin to be taxed at a much higher rate than other people earning the same.

It is in this context that the general rule is that, pursuant to s 347A of the ICTA 1988 and s 36 of the FA 1988, maintenance is now tax free in the hands of the recipient, whether the payee is a spouse or former spouse or a child of the family, and this is the regime with which you should expect to be familiar during the training contract. However, some awareness of the previous system may be desirable in order to understand the fiscal concepts involved.

Happily, there have been no transitional arrangements in switching to separate taxation of spouses: *all spouses* will now be subject to separate taxation. Thus, a spouse who is separating and/or who wishes to obtain a divorce will only have to consider the few minor quirks of the system which have special application to married couples. This is relatively simple to master, even for non-specialists in revenue law, so it will usually no longer be necessary, except in the most complex and high value cases, for reference to be made to an accountant in planning ancillary relief.

The work lost to accountants when the fundamental change was made in 1988 has now, however, more than been replaced with forensic accounting work in many ancillary relief cases, especially those involving creative application of the assets to make best use of what there is to provide for the family as a whole. A *working knowledge* of tax is therefore essential for the family lawyer, so as to be able to:

- identify cases where an accountant will still be necessary; and
- understand what the accountant instructed is proposing,

but a *detailed knowledge* of revenue law is not.

Where tax considerations *are* relevant in divorce, it will depend on the individual tax in question whether it is *separation* or *divorce* which triggers a change. In the case of income tax (IT) and capital gains tax (CGT), any changes will take place at the end of the tax year in which the parties *separated*, but in the case of inheritance tax (IHT) the fundamental change will be when the decree absolute of divorce is obtained. In divorce, an awareness of the existence of value added tax (VAT) and national insurance contributions (NIC) will also be required, especially in relation to family businesses.

18.7.1 Cases involving a pre-1988 arrangement

Although the change to tax free maintenance took effect some 14 years ago, because the radical nature of the changes made in 1988 could not be accommodated in existing ancillary relief packages, some maintenance was until April 2000 still being paid subject to the old taxation rules, under arrangements which were referred to in the FA 1988 as 'existing obligations' which are defined by s 36(4) as:

(a) periodical payments orders made by the court before 15 March 1988;

(b) periodical payments orders made by the court before 30 June 1988 where application for the order was received on or before 15 March 1988;

(c) any maintenance agreement under a deed or set out in writing made before 15 March 1988 and sent to or received by an Inspector of Taxes on and before 30 June 1988;

(d) any oral maintenance agreement made before 15 March 1988 which is then confirmed in writing and those written particulars sent to and received by an Inspector of Taxes before 30 June 1988;

(e) any variation of any of these.

Tax relief still therefore benefited those paying under an 'existing obligation', and continued until April 2000 when such arrangements were varied. However, tax relief was pegged at the 1988–89 tax year level, though the parties could change to the contemporary system if they preferred. Since April 2000, however, all is now tax free in the hands of the recipient.

18.7.2 Contemporary spousal taxation

Each spouse is now taxed separately, whether during or after marriage, each setting off an annual personal allowance against IT, and the husband also receives a *married couple's allowance*, unless this is paid by choice to the wife or it is split between them (FA 1988, ss 32 and 35 and Sched 3). Capital taxation liability is also separate, although there are still some advantages in favour of inter-spousal dispositions.

18.7.3 Income tax

Where there is a child or children, a *single parent* left to manage alone, through death, divorce or the *wife's* total incapacity, could up until April 2000 have an allowance equivalent to the married couple's allowance, *on top of* the ordinary personal allowance to which there would be routine entitlement as a single person: where the married couple's allowance was available in this way it was then called 'single parent's allowance' (which is the term commonly used) or 'additional personal allowance', actually the correct title for the allowance in ss 259 and 260 of the ICTA 1988. Tax relief in respect of the married couple's allowance was pegged at progressively lower percentage rates until April 2000, when it was abolished and replaced with the new children's tax credit with effect from 5 April 2001.

Each spouse is now therefore taxed at that individual's appropriate rate (ie, the lower rate, basic rate or higher rate over the annually fixed thresholds). Spouses are individually responsible for making their own tax returns and paying their own tax on all income, a change which has reversed many years of wives' resentment of officially not existing separately from their husbands for tax purposes. This has also benefited the family law practitioner, since there will not now be much tax impact of the parties' separation and/or divorce. Changes will be restricted to any impact on the capital taxes and on the new children's tax credit, where if a child or children live with one parent part of the year and the other parent for the remainder the allowance will have to be split, since this allowance operates as one allowance per couple, whether married, cohabiting or divorced, and is restricted to the one allowance regardless of the number of children involved. The parties may agree how to split the allowance, in default of which the percentage apportioned to each will be determined according to the amount of time the child or children spend with each taxpayer.

18.7.4 Tax implications of separation and divorce in relation to capital taxes

Where the parties *separate*, the Inspector may not consider them to be separated for tax purposes immediately. By s 282 of the ICTA 1988, the separation is a fact for Inland Revenue purposes if they are separated in such circumstances that the separation is likely to prove permanent, but individual tax offices may operate different procedures and may consider a couple separated in other circumstances. As explained above, *separation* is relevant in IT and *divorce* has no independent IT implications. Thus it is no longer possible to make qualifying maintenance payments to a spouse or to a spouse for the benefit of the children pursuant to s 347A of the ICTA 1988, and there is no longer any mortgage interest relief at source (MIRAS) as the 'tax deductible' element of money paid in interest on mortgage loans. However, both separation and divorce will be relevant in the context of the capital taxes. While divorce is thus definitely not the fiscal bargain it used to be prior to 1988, or even prior to the phasing out of MIRAS (when divorcing spouses were at least then able to retrieve the two independent MIRAS allowances which had been reduced on their marriage to the single allowance permitted to married couples), there is still some room for ancillary relief tax planning in relation to the capital taxes.

18.7.5 Inheritance tax (Inheritance Tax Act 1984)

This is a tax which only impacts on spouses on *divorce*. During the marriage, no IHT is payable on transfers of value between the spouses (Inheritance Tax Act (IHTA) 1984, s 18), and this position will continue, regardless of separation, until decree absolute. Even then IHT is unlikely to affect any dispositions which, having been ordered by the court following decree *nisi*, will take effect in accordance with the normal ancillary relief rules only on decree absolute. The reason for this is that either s 10 or s 11 of the IHTA 1984 will probably cover the situation where IHT might otherwise have been payable because either it:

- does not confer gratuitous benefit (IHTA 1984, s 10); or
- is a disposition for family maintenance (IHTA 1984, s 11).

The rationale behind the first exception is that husband and wife are no longer 'connected persons' for the purposes of the IHT and CGT legislation after decree absolute (IHTA 1984, s 270; Taxation of Chargeable Gains Act (TCGA) 1992, s 286), and therefore transfers between them pursuant to an order of the court in ancillary relief proceedings will be transactions at arm's length and not intended to confer gratuitous benefit (IHTA 1984, s 10). For the avoidance of doubt, in 1975 the then Senior Registrar (now called the Senior District Judge) issued a statement on the point with the agreement of the Inland Revenue which is reported at (1975) 119 SJ 596.

The rationale behind the second exception is that a disposition is not a transfer of value if made by one spouse in favour of the other or of the children for their maintenance or for a child's education or training, and by s 11(6) a disposition in favour of a spouse 'on dissolution of marriage' or *varying* such a disposition is specifically expressed to be within s 11. It would therefore appear that, unless such a disposition were unduly delayed, no IHT is likely to be payable on divorce, though if it was in any particular case the parties may use their annual exemptions (currently £3,000 per annum in total under s 19 *plus* £250 per person in any number of small additional gifts under s 20; such gifts may include potentially exempt transfers under s 3A). No IHT will of course be payable if the disposition falls within the transferor's nil band, which is £250,000 for 2002–03.

While it is accepted that it is inadvisable to invite trouble from the Inland Revenue by abusing the rules, a practice has developed of recognising that the opportunity may be taken in the ancillary relief proceedings to have the court order any disposition which can reasonably qualify as maintenance. This will enable wealthier payers to pass property on to the next generation and at the same time to provide for the family with a saving in IHT.

This opportunity has increasingly featured in ancillary relief packages: normally the practitioner will in any case look behind the actual assets available (eg, trusts and trust property, and family companies) in order to ascertain their true nature and potential for providing for the family before making or agreeing to any proposals (see Chapter 12). However, when the parties are wealthy, and sometimes even when they are merely reasonably well off, the overall package can be designed to make the best use of the assets available in a tax efficient way which, because of the potential tax saving, costs the payer little (because of the tax saved) and yet brings disproportionate benefits to the payee. It has been noted that it is also surprising what some payers will do when the tax saving is explained, which they would not have considered at all in favour of a spouse whom they are shedding if they weren't able to find some virtue in relieving the Inland Revenue of some tax!

18.7.6 Capital gains tax (TCGA 1992)

This is a tax which impacts on spouses on *separation*, and can therefore be little more than a nuisance to divorcing spouses.

During the marriage, transfers between spouses which might otherwise give rise to a chargeable gain are treated as if neither a gain nor a loss accrues (s 58). This does not mean that the transferee will be able to dispose of it free of CGT, but that that transferee acquires the asset at the value at which the transferring spouse acquired it. This is a hangover from the days when the spouses were one person (and that one person was the husband) for tax purposes. Even while they are married, the spouses now have an annual CGT allowance each to set against gains, so there is no incentive to separate promptly for CGT as *separation* ends free inter-spouse transfers, although usually the Inland Revenue will regard the married rule as continuing, as they always did in the case of IT, until the end of the tax year in which the parties separated. There can therefore be CGT problems in relation to the division of their assets in ancillary relief proceedings:

(1) While there is no CGT on disposals of *cash*, so lump sum payments ordered under the TCGA 1992, s 23 will be exempt, there is no CGT relief on disposals of assets which have to be sold to enable the payer to pay the lump sum to the payee.

(2) Property transfer orders under the TCGA 1992, s 24 (and any similar arrangement made between the spouses *without* a formal s 24 order) may give rise to a disposal for CGT purposes unless the Inland Revenue can be convinced that the transferee already owned that asset (eg, a share in the home where legal ownership was in one spouse but both owned the property *beneficially*, ie, in equity).

For this reason, despite the court's powers under s 24 to rearrange family assets how they choose, subject only to s 25, it may still be necessary to know which spouse owned what according to the ordinary rules of property law (see Chapter 21).

Regardless of the annual exemption, certain assets transferred on divorce will be outside the CGT rules anyway, for example, cars and other household chattels, commonly transferred under s 24, and tangible moveable property which is a wasting asset (ie, with a predictable useful life of 50 years or less). The only potential problem in most cases is likely to be the home, and that will only be if, because it has not been occupied as such by one of the spouses for the whole period of ownership, it does not completely qualify for exemption from a charge to CGT as the principal private residence of both spouses (TCGA 1992, ss 222 and 223). Even here CGT can usually be got round by one means or another as the gain will be apportioned and only part, for the period(s) out of occupation, charged to CGT, but as the home is deemed to be the principal residence for the last 36 months of ownership there will have to be some delay in selling the property, or transferring the share belonging to the spouse out of occupation to the other spouse, or a *Mesher* type order, for a CGT problem to arise at all.

18.7.6.1 Avoiding or reducing capital gains tax on the matrimonial home

This will only be necessary if the home is sold or transferred more than three years after the transferor left.

The first line of defence is Extra-Statutory Concession (ESC) D6. This applies where the transferor spouse has moved out more than three years previously but has not elected any other property in lieu of it as the qualifying only or main residence for tax purposes. The spouse out of occupation is simply deemed to have remained in occupation right up to disposal and no CGT is payable. The divorce practitioner should point this out to the client, but in practice there is more to life than saving *all* possible taxes, an effort which may not be cost effective in other respects. A particularly irritating facet of CGT is that it is a costly tax which is levied on money which has probably already suffered IT, but there are various mitigations, not least of which is that the property market is sometimes so slow and inflation so stable at a low figure that the alternative worry in an eventual disposal of the home may be negative equity. After recent overheating in the property market, in which borrowing to buy property which many people could not really afford has reached record levels, capital losses may well now come with the market corrections already being seen.

Where ESC D6 does not apply, because the non-occupying spouse has a new principal residence, that spouse will therefore have to bite the bullet and take comfort from the following:

(1) Only the gain attributable to the period of ownership over the ESC D6 36 months while the spouse was out of occupation will be taxed, not the whole period of ownership.

(2) The gain can be index linked from March 1982 (although since November 1993 this cannot create a loss as it previously could – now it can only cancel or reduce a gain).

(3) The non-occupying spouse's annual exemption of £7,700 (2002–03) can be used.

(4) The gain may be held over under s 79 of the FA 1980 so that it is not payable immediately.

Certain orders create CGT settlements which bring special CGT rules into effect at the beginning and end of the settlement and while it is in force. All orders giving the wife a right to occupation for life, or until remarriage or voluntary removal, fall into this category (eg, the *Martin* order), and if a practitioner has to work on a case involving such an order it will be necessary to consult an up to date specialist practitioner's book on matrimonial finance and taxation for the taxation consequences of the order. However, a *Mesher* order is not in this category.

18.8 THE IMPORTANCE OF TAXATION IN ANCILLARY RELIEF

While tax considerations should not drive the ancillary relief package regardless of all other matters to be taken into account, the important point is to achieve a workable and acceptable overall package which suits the family as a whole, and this may involve consideration of the impact of the capital taxes, particularly sales which will attract CGT. In the circumstances, close attention must usually be paid to the family's requirements, and only *then* to consider the tax implications, to see if more value may be extracted than at first appeared (eg, in making use of the divorce to achieve some IHT planning), and also to see that the *net* effect when tax is taken into account is not radically different from what was envisaged when the package was proposed. While the family's future is usually more important than saving a little tax, it can be foolish to throw away any benefits that may be available by arranging matters in one way rather than another. For example, where a spouse is to retire from the husband's family company, tax advantage may be taken of giving her (and possibly the husband as well) a tax free 'golden handshake' which will provide both cash for her and a means for the husband to pay it.

It is also necessary for both practitioners and the court to be on the lookout for the *tax implications* of a spouse's personal circumstances when making or agreeing ancillary relief orders. For example, a wife who has been working in the husband's business during the marriage will need to establish whether she is a paid employee, a partner or working for nothing. If the latter, it will usually increase her share of any assets obtainable for her, although, following *White v White* [2000] 2 FLR 981, HL; [1998] 2 FLR 310, CA and the subsequent case of *Dharamshi v Dharamshi* [2001] 1 FLR 736, CA, that may no longer be necessary since all contributions to family life are now expressly taken into account when looking for 'fairness' in the ancillary relief package, and checking its validity against 'the yardstick of equality'.

It will next be relevant whether the business is run by the husband as a sole trader, or if it is a partnership or a limited company, and what its profits – or debts – are, and also whether the wife has paid IT and NIC. If the business is a partnership, is it registered for VAT and has this been paid? Has the wife outstanding tax liability in respect of this business, either *qua* partner or director, or personally, and in particular any liability for which the husband should be required to indemnify her? A family lawyer is not usually required to replicate the work of the accountant, but in general terms is expected to be able to hear alarm bells ringing and call the fire brigade where anything untoward appears to justify it.

Because of the net effect calculation (see Chapter 13), it will often be necessary to work out what is the net spendable income of each of the parties under the proposed order. This is not a complex calculation but a simple arithmetical task, and has always been much rewarded by the approval of district judges when it has been done, not only in a case where it was essentially necessary, but where it would be helpful to know the effect of the order, but the new ancillary relief procedure now really demands that the calculation should be prepared in advance without specifically having to be asked for.

WELFARE BENEFITS AND TAX
ON RELATIONSHIP BREAKDOWN

WELFARE BENEFITS

Welfare benefits are an important part of ancillary relief planning. There are means tested and non-means tested benefits available from the Benefits Agency, the local authority or the Inland Revenue as appropriate. The only non-means tested benefit is now child benefit. The means tested benefits are IS/JSA, WFTC, HB, CTB and access to grants and/or loans from the Social Fund. Anyone with qualifying children is entitled to child benefit, which has a lone parent premium incorporated where appropriate.

MEANS TESTED BENEFITS

JSA, either income based or contribution based, has replaced IS and unemployment benefit for most people. Sole parents with dependent children are not required to sign on for work to claim JSA and receive IS instead; working families receive WFTC if one or more dependent children live with a working family (which may be a single person or a couple) whose income is below the threshold despite being in work. IS and JSA have valuable passport benefits, including payment of mortgage interest, but WFTC does not, so the claimant for WFTC must assess whether it is worth working more than the hours permitted while still eligible to claim IS, for fear of falling into the 'poverty trap'. IS/JSA and WFTC are mutually exclusive benefits, depending on how many hours per week the claimant works, unless the claimant does not work at all, when IS/JSA will be appropriate. IS/JSA are calculated according to a formula based on the needs of the claimant, and claimant's partner and family, according to a framework of premiums to produce and 'applicable amount' in each case. There are certain income disregards, and capital limits requiring deductions to be made from the amount paid, culminating in no IS/income based JSA at all over a capital ceiling of £8,000, and tariff reductions between £3,000 and £8,000.

WFTC also enables tax credit help with child care to be claimed, is administered through the Inland Revenue, and paid either directly or through the pay packet.

HB pays rent for those qualifying, provided their accommodation is not too large for their needs, nor too expensive for the type and area. IT does not cover mortgage interest nor water rates. CTB pays for council tax for qualifying persons, including automatically those on IS or HB. The Social Fund provides budgeting and crisis loans and some grants (eg, maternity grants).

THE IMPACT OF WELFARE BENEFITS ON ANCILLARY RELIEF

The principle in *Barnes v Barnes* requires that applicants should not throw the burden of maintaining either themselves or their dependants on the State if they can afford to take this responsibility without such recourse. This is reinforced by the Child Support Acts 1991–95, which have had some success in securing support for children from absent parents. However, the facts of life are such that benefits sometimes have to form part of an ancillary relief package, and this may either be done by direct application for benefits, or sometimes by obtaining an order and then using the diversion procedure where maintenance orders registered in the Family Proceedings Court may be signed over to the Benefits Agency, which will then pay the applicant regularly and enforce the order against the defaulting payer. The Agency employs the liable relative formula to recover in these circumstances. The ancillary relief package is therefore generally structured to make best use of welfare benefits where necessary. However, there is limited opportunity for the CSA to take account of capital paid out on clean breaks.

TAXATION ON RELATIONSHIP BREAKDOWN

There is now little impact of taxation on relationship breakdown, whether the parties were married or not. This is because spouses are now independently assessed for tax, and MIRAS and the married allowance have been abolished. All maintenance is now tax free in the hands of the recipient. There is a new child tax credit available to replace the married allowance from 5 April 2002. Taxation impact is therefore restricted to the capital taxes. Chargeable capital gains may be incurred if assets have to be sold to provide money to fund a lump sum order on an ancillary relief application, and there might be a CGT liability on the sale of the former matrimonial home as CGT benefits for spouses are restricted to inter-spouse disposals and disposal of the former home while it is the parties' sole or main residence: liability for chargeable gains also arises on separation, not divorce. However, there is little chance of CGT arising on the disposition of the main home if the ESC D6 rules are followed. IHT seldom impacts, as although liability arises for inter-spouse disposals on decree absolute, when most ancillary relief orders take effect, these are seldom for gratuitous benefit and, if pursuant to the order of the court, will fall into that exception or the other which permits dispositions to be made for family maintenance. An order of the court may therefore present a welcome tax planning opportunity.

CHAPTER 19

FINANCIAL PROVISION WITHOUT A DECREE OF DIVORCE, NULLITY OR JUDICIAL SEPARATION

19.1 INTRODUCTION

Ancillary relief and/or welfare benefits are not the only source of financial provision on family breakdown. Ancillary relief will clearly only be available if there has been or is going to be within a short time a decree of some sort, but apart from going on to welfare benefits as a regular source of income, or possibly negotiating voluntary payments, the law provides the separated spouse who does not wish to petition for one of the principal decrees with three other possibilities for obtaining formal maintenance in such a situation:

(a) a maintenance order from the Family Proceedings Court under Pt I of the Domestic Proceedings and Magistrates' Courts Act (DPMCA) 1978 (ie, what used to be known as a 'matrimonial order');

(b) a maintenance order from the county court under s 27 of the Matrimonial Causes Act (MCA) 1973 (rather similar to the income element of ancillary relief, without the necessity to obtain a decree first); or

(c) a separation and maintenance agreement (a possibility frequently overlooked, although this does need to be handled with care with regard to the possible effect on later ancillary relief).

19.2 DOMESTIC PROCEEDINGS AND MAGISTRATES' COURTS ACT 1978 IN THE FAMILY PROCEEDINGS COURT

If welfare benefits are not appropriate (eg, in a *Barnes v Barnes* [1972] 1 WLR 1381; [1972] 3 All ER 872 situation: see Chapter 18) and there is no potential for negotiation of a temporary voluntary arrangement, so that an order of some sort does need to be sought, a maintenance order from the Family Proceedings Court is probably the quickest and easiest type to obtain. Moreover, such an order not only has no adverse impact on later ancillary relief, even if a later petition is contemplated: it can also be much more convenient than maintenance pending suit and it is not incompatible with petitioning for divorce. Unless the low £1,000 per applicant ceiling on lump sums does not provide for the expenses of the interim budget (such as where it is contemplated that there will be substantial legal fees to be met in processing the divorce or ancillary relief when it is now established that maintenance pending suit can cater for these in total) there is much to be said for using the DPMCA order as a temporary source of funds in the often financially awkward transitional period up to decree absolute.

While the magistrates have lost to the Child Support Agency (CSA) much of their former jurisdiction to make orders for children, they can still make orders for spouses and, at the same time and on the same application, include orders for children of the family not within the CSA jurisdiction. These orders include:

- orders for stepchildren;
- child orders outside the CSA's powers (ie, for lump sums as opposed to periodical payments);
- for 'topping up' of periodical payments above the CSA's ceiling (eg, for school or further or higher education fees); and
- orders for children over 19 who are then outside the CSA age limit.

The DPMCA 1978 is therefore a species of magistrates' court jurisdiction equivalent of the MCA 1973 for these purposes, for use when a decree is *not*, or not yet, being sought. Only a spouse can apply, but child orders can always be made at the same time provided, of course, the child in question qualifies in some way (DPMCA 1978, ss 1 and 6(1)).

The magistrates' court (which is called the 'Family Proceedings Court' when exercising its matrimonial and family jurisdiction, but is still only a distinct type of magistrates' court) is based on a commission area for which the magistrates are appointed. A particular Family Proceedings Court will therefore have jurisdiction to hear an application under Pt I of the DPMCA 1978 if either the applicant or the respondent ordinarily resides within the commission area in which the court is situated (DPMCA 1978, s 30). Domicile is irrelevant, unlike in divorce or one of the other principal decrees.

Three distinct orders are obtainable:

- under s 2, for which grounds set out in s 1 must be established;
- under s 6, which may be made purely on agreement of the parties;
- under s 7, where the parties have resided apart for at least three months and one has been making payments to the other for that party or for a child of the family.

As only spouses can apply under the Act, divorced (ie, former) spouses cannot use it, nor of course can cohabitants.

A 'child of the family' is defined in s 88 and is the same as that of a child of the family in s 52 of the MCA 1973 (see 11.7.1, above).

Children who are not children of the family cannot be included in any orders under the DPMCA 1978, but they may be able to claim maintenance under the Children Act 1989 (see Chapter 15).

19.2.1 The types of orders available

Both periodical payments and lump sums can be awarded but no property orders can be made under this jurisdiction (though they might be able to be made by the same court under the Children Act 1989, if appropriate).

Periodical payments can be made weekly or monthly, for whatever term the magistrates think fit, including for a limited period, as in the case of *Robinson v Robinson* [1983] 1 All ER 391; [1983] Fam 42, where the period was for five years. However, pursuant to s 4:

- no order can *begin* before the date of the application;
- all orders *end* on the *death* of either the payer or payee; and

- an order will end on the remarriage of the payee, although any accrued arrears will remain payable provided they are claimed within one year: as s 95 of the Magistrates' Courts Act 1980 as inserted by the Maintenance Enforcement Act 1991 gives the magistrates power to remit them in whole or part, they usually will remit all arrears over a year old and might do so faster in the case of remarriage. Therefore, application for enforcement in this case should be prompt.

Divorce has *no effect* on a Family Proceedings Court order. Cohabitation has very little effect. Both s 2 and s 6 orders can still be *made* if the parties are still living together, though s 7 orders cannot and a s 7 order will cease *immediately* if the parties resume cohabiting (s 25(3)). However, even s 2 and s 6 orders will be *discharged* if the parties cohabit for more than six months at any time (s 25(1)).

Orders for *children* are totally unaffected by their parents' cohabitation (s 25(2)).

Children's orders end at 17 (s 5(2)), unless s 5(3) applies which permits the court to make:

- an order for a child which will last beyond the child's 18th birthday;
- an order for a child already over 18.

In either case such an order can be made if:

- the child is in full time education or training (whether or not also in gainful employment); or
- there are special circumstances justifying the order.

Such periodical payments will always end on the death of the payer.

Lump sums are subject to a limit of £1,000 (s 2(3)), though where there are children more than £1,000 may be awarded by giving lump sums to each of them as well as £1,000 to the applicant spouse (*Burridge v Burridge* [1982] 3 All ER 80). Moreover, the £1,000 limit does not apply if the order is made by agreement under s 6.

Lump sums can be made payable by instalments or time can be given for payment (Magistrates' Courts Act 1980, s 75). There is no rule that lump sums cannot be ordered unless the payer has capital, since all that is necessary is that the payer should have capacity to pay, from income or otherwise (*Burridge v Burridge*, above).

Where a lump sum order is payable by instalments, these can subsequently be varied, on application to the court, either as to amounts or numbers of instalments or dates on which they are payable (DPMCA 1978, s 22).

Altogether this presents an extremely useful opportunity to obtain quick, easy and inexpensive provision, the only real drawback being the limit on lump sums (though the limit of £1,000 applies to each applicant, ie, spouse and any number of qualifying children) and the lack of a property order jurisdiction.

19.2.2 Orders under the Domestic Proceedings and Magistrates' Courts Act 1978, s 2

Periodical payments and lump sums can be ordered for a party to a marriage or to a child of the family if the other party to the marriage has:

- failed to provide reasonable maintenance for a spouse;
- failed to provide reasonable maintenance for any child of the family;
- behaved in such a way that the applicant cannot reasonably be expected to live with that other party;
- deserted the applicant.

The grounds can be relied on in the alternative. Brief details of any behaviour alleged must be given in the written application for a s 2 order, which must now be made on Form 1 specified under the current rules which are the Family Proceedings Courts (Matrimonial Proceedings, etc) Rules 1991 as amended.

19.2.2.1 How 'reasonable maintenance' is determined

There is no formula in the Act or elsewhere. The court simply:

- takes the figure which it would have ordered if making an order from scratch on the basis of the s 3 considerations set out below at 19.2.2.3;
- compares it with what is being paid; if it is significantly less, the respondent is not making reasonable provision.

There is no need to prove that the respondent's failure is morally reprehensible, indeed the respondent need not even know that maintenance is required, so the ground can even be proved by a wife in desertion, as in the case of *Robinson v Robinson* mentioned above, which would clearly be illogical if any moral element were required in the failure to pay.

The respondent is *probably* still *failing to provide reasonable maintenance* even if a suitable amount has been hurriedly paid between the application and the hearing. There is no specific decision on the point, although by analogy the case of *Irvin v Irvin* [1968] 1 WLR 464; [1968] 1 All ER 27 decided that in the case of *desertion* that must continue up to the date of the hearing, so the same approach would mean that if the track record of failure to maintain had not been sustained there would be no basis for the application. However, it is thought that it is equally logical that one or two payments cannot alter a well established pattern of *chronic* failure, since it would be ridiculous if a respondent could get out of paying regularly simply by making such trivial and token payments just before coming to court.

19.2.2.2 Establishing behaviour and desertion

These are the same as under the MCA 1973.

The test for *behaviour* is exactly the same (*Bergin v Bergin* [1983] 1 WLR 274; [1983] 1 All ER 905; [1983] 4 FLR 344). Cohabitation after the last incident of behaviour is irrelevant, although application must be made to the Family Proceedings Court within six months of the last incident relied on, unless it is a continuing form of behaviour which is alleged (Magistrates' Courts Act 1980, s 127).

The elements of desertion are also exactly the same as under the MCA 1973, save that it is not necessary for a period of two years to have passed since the desertion – simple desertion with no particular minimum period is all that is required.

19.2.2.3 Matters to which the court must have regard
when making s 2 orders (DPMCA 1978, s 3)

This is the magistrates' equivalent of s 25 of the MCA 1973.

By s 3(1), there is the same general duty as under s 25(2) of the MCA 1973, whereby the court must consider all the circumstances of the case, giving first consideration to the welfare while a minor of any child of the family who has not attained the age of 18.

The s 3 factors are virtually the same as those under s 25 of the MCA 1973 except for the following:

(1) Section 3(2)(c) directs the court to have regard to the standard of living enjoyed by the parties to the marriage before the *occurrence of the conduct alleged* (cf s 25, where the standard is that before the breakdown of the marriage).

(2) There is no s 3 equivalent of s 25(2)(h) whereby the court considers the value to each of the parties of any benefit that might be lost by the dissolution of the marriage (eg, a pension), as the magistrates do not dissolve marriages and thus do not trigger any such loss depending on status.

The clean break provisions do not apply in the Family Proceedings Court again since the magistrates do not dissolve marriages.

The one third rule does apply if it is appropriate to the case, but often it is not because of the relatively limited means of those who normally apply to the Family Proceedings Court. There is, however, no rule that only those of limited means may use the Family Proceedings Court, nor is not at all unknown for it to be used as an easier alternative to maintenance pending suit (see 12.3.1, above).

The magistrates now take the same approach to conduct as is the case under the MCA 1973 in the higher courts. For a time between 1973 and 1978, when the magistrates finally got their own new MCA 1973 equivalent Act in the DPMCA 1978, there was a difference, since the magistrates were then applying the law as it had universally been before the Divorce Reform Act 1969 changed the approach of the divorce courts, while the county court and High Court was already applying the new regime.

19.2.3 Agreed orders under the Domestic Proceedings and Magistrates' Courts Act 1978, s 6

This is the magistrates' version of a consent order. The only grounds are that the parties have agreed the order (s 6(1)). The type(s) of financial provision agreed, and the amount and the term of any periodical payments, must be specified in the written application, which must be made on Form 2 specified for the purpose. Either party, payer or payee, may apply for the order to be made. However, it is not a rubber stamping procedure since there is still a general duty for the court to be satisfied that the provision is broadly right.

By s 6(3), the court has the right to approve financial provision for a child and will not do so unless it considers that the order makes a proper contribution towards the child's financial needs. Otherwise, the court will normally make s 6 orders if:

• it is satisfied that the applicant or the respondent as the case may be has agreed to make the provision; and

• it has no reason to think that it would be contrary to the interests of justice to exercise its powers under s 6.

If it is *not* so satisfied, the court will refuse to make the order unless the parties agree to make any amendments which the court wishes to see made, including that *either* party makes any further provision that the court requires (s 6(5)).

The *advantages* of having a s 6 order are that:

(a) the parties are more likely to observe an order which they had a hand in putting together, rather than one that is imposed on them from above;

(b) the terms of the parties' agreement are embodied in the order just as on a consent order after divorce; and

(c) neither party can repudiate the order unilaterally.

On the other hand, once made, the order can only be varied by agreement of both parties on returning to court for a variation, which might put some parties off.

The court can treat a s 2 application as one for a s 6 order if the parties agree terms before the s 2 application is heard.

19.2.4 Orders under the Domestic Proceedings and Magistrates' Courts Act 1978, s 7 to continue voluntary payments made during separation

The advantage of this order is that it can be made where the parties are living apart but where they cannot:

• make out any one of the four grounds required for a s 2 order; or

• come to a sufficient agreement for a s 6 order.

The parties *must* have been living apart for a continuous period of three months, neither being in desertion since that would permit an order under s 2. One of the parties must have been paying maintenance for the benefit of the other or of a child of the family.

The payee party must specify in the application the aggregate amount of payments made by the other to that party and the children of the family in the three months (s 7(1)). The respondent cannot be ordered to pay more under the order than the rate of payment during the three months (s 7(3)(a)). The court must check that the order is in line with what they would have ordered under s 2 (s 7(3)(b) and (3)(c)), in other words:

• not too much; and

• not to a child of the family who is not the respondent's child unless they would have ordered this.

The court will not make an order under this section if it thinks that it would not provide reasonable maintenance for a child (s 7(4)) or for the applicant and would then treat a s 7 application as one for a s 2 order.

The s 3 considerations apply to s 7 orders, including the standard of living enjoyed by the parties, prior in this case to their separation, rather than prior to the conduct relied on in s 2 (s 3(2)(c)).

19.2.5 Procedure

The Green Form successor legal help (which is 'controlled work' under the new franchised block contract system of public funding) and public funding for representation are normally used in the Family Proceedings Court.

Proceedings are commenced by written application, governed by the FPC(MP)R 1991, as amended by the Family Proceedings Courts (Child Support Act 1991) Rules 1993 SI 1993/627. The forms now give details of any assessment carried out by the CSA. (Specimen forms may be seen in the Rules.)

There are different forms for applications under the different sections for the different purposes mentioned above. The forms contain a statement of means of the applicant, which must be completed when the application is prepared, a notice of hearing (or directions appointment) which the court completes, and a blank form for the respondent's answer and statement of means (which the respondent will complete in due course).

19.2.5.1 Application, directions (if any) and service

The application is lodged at the court with a copy for service on the respondent (FPC(MP)R 1991, r 3(1)(a)). The justices' clerk (now called the 'legal or judicial advisor') will fix the date, time and place for the hearing (or directions) and enter these details on to the copy for service (r 3(2)(a) and (b)). The copy is then returned to the applicant for service (r 3(2)(d)). The respondent must have 21 days' notice of the hearing or directions appointment (r 3(1)(b)).

The justices' clerk must consider if there should be a directions appointment (r 6(1)). Directions can assume some importance. The clerk may give, vary or revoke directions which will usually cover a timetable for the proceedings, service of documents and evidence generally, and may consider written or (with leave) oral representations (r 6(1) and (3)). However, if a request is made in writing without the consent of the other party to the proceedings, the clerk must fix a date for a hearing of the request on at least two days' notice to both parties (r 6(4) and (5)). Both parties will then have to attend the directions hearing (r 8(1)). If the respondent does not turn up, the directions hearing can nevertheless proceed without him or her, provided the court is satisfied that due notice was given (r 8(2)).

Service can be in any of the usual ways, including personal service (r 4). A statement of service must be filed specifying the method of service used before the appointment mentioned on the papers (r 4(4)).

The respondent has 14 days to file and serve an answer, including the statement of means, indicating whether he or she will defend (r 5).

19.2.5.2 Evidence

Written statements of evidence in the usual form must have been filed and served on each other by each party before the hearing takes place (r 9(1)). Moreover, a chronology should be supplied, together with copy documents which each party intends to rely on (eg, payslips, loan and hire purchase agreements, and details of each party's outgoings); these can be supplemented where necessary (r 9(2)).

As in other courts, a party failing to comply with this rule will not be allowed to adduce the evidence in question without leave of the court (r 9(3)).

In other words, the Family Proceedings Court has opted for full advance disclosure on the lines of superior courts, with a view to encouraging early settlement once the parties have each seen the strength of the opposition case, thereby saving court time. For further saving of court time, before the hearing the justices are required to read the papers which have been filed (r 12(1)).

The justices' clerk is still nevertheless required by the rules to keep a note of any oral evidence at the directions appointment (r 11).

19.2.5.3 The hearing

The hearing is then conducted in the usual manner.

Pursuant to s 65 of the Magistrates' Courts Act 1980 as amended, the hearings are domestic proceedings and are held in private with a restricted attendance, including only court officers, the parties, their legal representatives, witnesses and other persons directly concerned with the case, the press and, pursuant to s 69(2) of the 1980 Act, 'any other person whom the court may in its discretion permit'. By s 67(2), it must be before magistrates from the domestic panel and there should be a man and a woman among them (s 66). The respondent is supposed to attend and failing such attendance there is likely to be an adjournment, although the court can proceed in his or her absence. A respondent to a s 6 application can send a statement of means and need not attend.

The allegation is put to the respondent, but such is the habit of centuries and the parochial manner of proceeding in the magistrates' court that the evidence is still heard anyway – even if the respondent admits everything.

The applicant opens the case, witnesses are called and examined, cross-examined and re-examined, and then the respondent (or his or her advocate) addresses the court. If there is a question of law, the respondent's advocate (if any) will be given leave to address the court on that and then, if there is a further speech for the respondent, the applicant will have a second speech also.

If either party is not represented, the court is under a duty to help that party (Magistrates' Courts Act 1980, s 73); in this circumstance, the case may take a long time since such help must be meticulous.

19.2.5.4 The decision

The magistrates will then consider whether the case is proved and a decision will be given as soon as possible (FPC(MP)R 1991, r 12(4)). By r 12(6), reasons must be given, stating any findings of fact. Costs may be ordered, in whole or in part (r 13(1)).

The court has power to make interim orders (DPMCA 1978, s 19), although this has been reduced by the CSA jurisdiction. Such orders can be backdated (s 19(3)), but will expire when the case is finally determined, or after three months or some other date specified by the court. By s 19(7), only one interim order is supposed to be made, but that can be extended if time is running out, provided it does not last for longer than three months from the first extension, so that an interim order has a maximum life of six months (s 19(6)).

19.2.6 Variation

All orders are variable, revocable or can be suspended. The format is to consider the case *de novo*. Some sort of change of circumstances will be required and the court can give effect to any agreement between the parties so far as it seems just to do so (s 20(1)). On variation, the court will be able to specify the method of payment of the new order if it has not already done so in respect of the earlier one (Maintenance Enforcement Act (MEA) 1991, s 4, amending the Magistrates' Courts Act 1980, s 60). Suspended provisions of an order can be revived under s 20(6). Curiously, periodical payments orders under ss 2 and 6 can be varied by making lump sum orders, but this power does not apply to those orders made under s 7.

19.2.7 Enforcement

The magistrates have always been well known for enforcement, since even before the MEA 1991 the clerk provided an excellent service in receiving and paying out maintenance and enforcing any order which was not paid, and for this legal aid certificates often extended to registration of one substantive order obtained elsewhere in the magistrates' court. Besides this, the diversion procedure described in Chapter 13 has always been extremely useful to those applicants who would otherwise be on welfare benefits one week and chasing maintenance payments the next.

The MEA 1991 was originally an interim measure pending the implementation of the Child Support Act in April 1993, but it has nevertheless made some useful permanent contributions to enforcement of maintenance payments generally. Pursuant to s 2, an amendment to s 59 of the Magistrates' Courts Act 1980 enabled magistrates for the first time to specify how payments should be made, for example, by standing order or attachment of earnings, previously only possible if the debtor consented or was previously in default on payments, due to wilful refusal or culpable neglect. The court could even for the first time require that a bank account be opened to enable a standing order to be set up.

Now any DPMCA 1978 money orders may be enforced as a Family Proceedings Court maintenance order (DPMCA 1978, s 32(1)) by:

- attachment of earnings (Attachment of Earnings Act 1971);
- committal to prison (Magistrates' Court Act 1980, s 76);
- distress (also s 76); or
- registration in the High Court under the Maintenance Orders Act 1958 (not generally worth it except for high sums, eg, accumulated arrears, but it does permit access to High Court methods of enforcement which may frighten the payer, eg, sequestration which is notoriously expensive).

Foreign orders are sometimes registered in the Family Proceedings Court for the area where a respondent resides when the clerk will enforce them in the same way as an English order. There are reciprocal enforcement provisions in respect of a number of foreign jurisdictions, which the trainee may sometimes have to research to enforce English orders overseas and vice versa. See *Rayden* (Butterworths, 1997) for full particulars of participating jurisdictions.

19.2.7.1 Committal

There are stringent conditions before this method can be used:

(a) the court must be of the opinion that the debtor has not paid due to wilful refusal or culpable neglect;

(b) attachment of earnings or some other method if available must be used first unless the court is of the opinion that that is inappropriate; and

(c) the debtor must be present when imprisonment is imposed (Magistrates' Courts Act 1980, s 93(6)).

The maximum is only six weeks (s 93(7)). However, pursuant to s 76 and Sched 4, a lesser maximum may apply, and payment of the debt will prevent imprisonment, or secure release if it has already been imposed, with reduction in the time to serve pro rata for part payment (s 79), and arrears do not accrue, unless the court otherwise directs, while the debtor is in prison (s 94).

It is, however, fairly easy to avoid committal. Any debtor can apply for the order to be reviewed and the warrant of committal cancelled (Maintenance Orders Act 1958, s 18(4)), and although the debt is not cancelled by time served, it is not possible to be imprisoned more than once for the same debt (Magistrates' Courts Act 1980).

Most usually the court will suspend any committal order if the debtor pays the maintenance in future and also pays something off the arrears each week (Magistrates' Courts Act 1980, s 72(2)). The debtor will be warned if he stops paying before the warrant is issued so as to have a chance to show cause why the committal order should not take effect, and only if that opportunity is not successfully seized will committal occur (Maintenance Orders Act 1958, s 18). Sometimes the court will merely adjourn the hearing to see what the debtor does. If no attempts have been made to pay by the time the adjourned hearing resumes, then committal may well follow.

19.2.7.2 Enforcement procedure

The clerk normally automatically brings proceedings for enforcement if requested in writing to do so by the payee (Magistrates' Courts Act 1980, s 59). This was the beauty of the clerk's service in the days before the MEA 1991 or the CSA and, as the court kept the record of payment (or non-payment), proof of default was easy. The clerk now has a standing authority to take proceedings if payment is normally made through the court. The Magistrates' Courts Act 1980 was amended by the MEA 1991 to insert new ss 59A and 59B to facilitate this type of enforcement, and s 59B imposes financial sanctions if the debtor fails to make payments by the methods which can now be specified. By s 94A (inserted by the MEA 1991, s 8), interest can now be ordered on all or part of unpaid maintenance.

The debtor will normally receive a summons for proceedings, but if necessary a warrant of arrest will be issued (s 93(5)).

19.3 MATRIMONIAL CAUSES ACT 1973, s 27

This section allows a freestanding application to the county court for financial relief *without* petitioning for any of the principal decrees, though a s 27 order can also be made after a decree of judicial separation.

By s 27(1), either party may apply if the other spouse has failed to:

- provide reasonable maintenance for the applicant; or
- provide or make reasonable contribution towards reasonable maintenance for any child of the family.

An order is available upon proof of the fact; it is apparently no longer necessary that the respondent should actually know of the requirement for maintenance and of course, as in the case of the DPMCA 1978, it is not necessary for the failure to pay to be morally reprehensible.

The possible orders available under this section are those for:

- periodical payments;
- secured periodical payments; and
- unlimited lump sums including by instalments.

Lump sums orders can be made for any purpose, including to defray debts incurred in providing reasonable maintenance for the applicant and/or children prior to the application. No maintenance pending suit is possible since the application is the whole suit, unlike in the case of ancillary relief following a divorce suit.

Orders are available for both spouse and children irrespective of failure to maintain only one or the other of them.

The s 25 considerations must be taken into account as on ancillary relief, and the duration of orders is the same as after one of the principal decrees (MCA 1973, ss 28 and 29).

This section is very little used as it involves county court costs and funding as for ancillary relief on divorce with the sole small benefit over the DPMCA 1978 that lump sums ordered are subject to no limit.

19.4 SEPARATION AND MAINTENANCE AGREEMENTS

It is often forgotten that a separation or maintenance agreement is a seriously viable alternative to a formal order from whichever court, and that if it is carefully drafted such an agreement can also actually be superior to an order where no proceedings for a principal decree are for the time being contemplated. They do have certain advantages:

(1) Within reason an agreement can be designed to incorporate virtually whatever provisions the spouses desire to include, thus importing more flexibility than even the

most advantageous consent or agreed order, which can only include either clauses which the court is able to order under ss 23 and 24 of the MCA 1973 or undertakings which the court is willing to accept. These categories exclude all orders which only the appropriate court (and not that granting financial orders) can make under the Children Act 1989, whereas an agreement is able to incorporate arrangements for the care of the children.

(2) Agreements are cheaper and less trouble than obtaining an order from the court.

(3) Agreements provide evidence of the fact that the parties regarded the marriage as at an end, which is essential for proving separation when that is necessary in divorce and judicial separation, and of the *date* of such separation (*Santos v Santos* [1972] Fam 247).

(4) An agreement which is observed will rebut any claim on the basis of failure to maintain under either the MCA 1973 or DPMCA 1978.

(5) Any tax relief available for a court order is similarly available for an agreement.

(6) Human nature being what it is, the parties are more likely to observe an agreement they have forged themselves with the assistance of their lawyers and more likely to embark on such observance in a non-confrontational frame of mind conducive to a fresh start which will benefit themselves as well as the children, than if they have just been engaging in adversarial litigation, which often brings out the worst in the parties even if the case settles.

However, there are *disadvantages* in that such agreements can be:

(a) more difficult to enforce;

(b) not so final, as the court's ultimate ancillary relief jurisdiction cannot be ousted;

(c) not so easily varied unless the parties agree; and

(d) unless the agreement is within s 34 of the MCA 1973 (see 19.4.2, below), consent of both parties will be needed to effect any variation. Care also needs to be taken with drafting as there are a few points to watch.

An agreement for *immediate* separation is legal, as is a *resumption of cohabitation* agreement containing provisions for *possible* future separation if the reconciliation does not work out. *Wilson v Wilson* (1848) 1 HLC 538 established that an agreement for future separation *per se* is *invalid* as being contrary to public policy because it prejudices the status of marriage, but such an agreement is *valid* if the parties are *already separated* or on the point of it since it may regulate their life following the *fact* of separation. *Re Meyrick's Settlement* [1921] 1 Ch 311 is a warning that even such agreements for *resumption of cohabitation* should be carefully drafted so that the overall effect of the agreement is to *promote reconciliation*.

Separation and maintenance agreements can be oral or written but are usually *written*, for obvious reasons, and are usually by deed.

19.4.1 Usual clauses

19.4.1.1 To live separate and apart

This clause terminates both the duty to cohabit and therefore precludes desertion whether it has begun or might otherwise begin: if such a clause is not included, the agreement is only a *maintenance* agreement so that desertion can *still* start or continue.

19.4.1.2 Not to take matrimonial proceedings

This must be expressly included and will not be implied. It is not contrary to public policy as ousting the jurisdiction of the court, because the effect is to forgive past conduct (none of which can then be used in proceedings in the future) rather than to preclude filing a petition.

The clause is sometimes called a '*Rose v Rose* clause' after *Rose v Rose* (1883) 8 PD 98, which gave it its name.

19.4.1.3 Non-molestation clause

This is a clause which excludes any act that would annoy a reasonable spouse and excludes any act done *with the authority* of the spouse as well as personally by that spouse. It does *not* preclude starting divorce proceedings, as was established in *Fearon v Aylesford* (1884) 14 QBD 792.

19.4.1.4 A dum casta clause

This must also be *expressly* included. It is sometimes inserted for the protection of husbands whose liability to maintain a wife who is committing adultery can then be ended.

19.4.1.5 Maintenance for either party

This can take the form of periodical payments, secured or unsecured, or lump sums and should again ideally be limited by some phrase such as 'while the parties are married and living apart', which coupled with a *dum casta* clause prevents the husband from assuming an open ended obligation which might otherwise last not only beyond adultery or cohabitation with another man but possibly even after the death of the payer when it could still be enforced against his estate.

The impact of the CSA on such agreements should not be forgotten – if anyone in the family is on benefits, the CSA assessment will take priority over anything agreed under such a clause, and such a clause would also not prevent the carer parent from asking the CSA for an assessment which again would take priority over the agreement (CSA 1991, s 9(2) and (3)). It would, however, be possible to link any such assessment to a reduced share of the division of any family property (eg, at the triggering event of a *Mesher* type order, which can be included in the property clause of the agreement: see below).

Great care is required in drafting this clause – there should be no covenant not to claim maintenance from the court (as this is void since it tends to oust the jurisdiction of the court). If such a covenant is included, the remainder of the agreement is valid (MCA 1973, s 34(1)), including any other financial arrangements (s 34(1)(b)), but this will *not* be the case if the *whole purpose of the agreement* can be interpreted as to oust the jurisdiction of the court, in which case the entire agreement, and not *just the objectionable covenant*, will be *void* and *of no effect*.

19.4.1.6 An agreement relating to property

This could be, for example, a *Mesher* or similar type trust regulating the occupation of the matrimonial home during the children's minority and providing for eventual sale and division of the proceeds.

19.4.1.7 Care and maintenance of children

This type of clause is only enforceable if for the benefit of the child or children.

19.4.1.8 Two very important points

(1) Stipulations encouraging the end of marriage will always be void.

(2) Both parties should have *separate legal advice* so as to obviate any suggestion of *fraud, mistake* or *undue influence*.

19.4.2 Applying to the court to vary written financial arrangements (MCA 1973, s 34(2))

This *only* applies to certain *written* agreements, and *oral* agreements *cannot* be varied under s 34. The reason is that ss 35 and 36 of the MCA 1973 permit variation of written agreements which meet the definition in s 34(2) *by the court* if the parties cannot agree this themselves, so it is essential first to know to *which* agreements this applies, and secondly, what are the precise *terms* of the agreement which is to be varied, which is hardly compatible with the variation of oral agreements of which the record, if any, may be disputed.

The agreements which are within the section are:

(a) *any* agreements containing *financial arrangements* whether made during the continuance or after the dissolution or annulment of the marriage; and

(b) *separation* agreements which contain *no financial arrangements* in a case where *no other agreement between the same parties* contains such arrangements.

There is a wide interpretation of 'financial arrangements': the term includes periodical payments and any dispositions for both parties and *any* child, *not* necessarily a child of the family.

19.4.2.1 Potential snags

There are a few points which need to be observed.

Observing all the rules

Sutton v Sutton [1984] 2 WLR 146; [1984] 1 All ER 168 shows how vital it is to be careful in observing *all* the rules applying to separation and maintenance agreements if one wants to apply to the court either for variation or enforcement. In that case the wife entered into an oral agreement which was not formalised as a deed or even put into writing after the parties were divorced. The husband was supposed to transfer the home to the wife and she was supposed to pay the mortgage and not to apply for maintenance. He did not make the transfer. The wife could not apply to the court to *vary* the agreement as it was oral and thus outside s 34. She could not apply to *enforce* it either as it purported to oust the jurisdiction of the court under ss 23 and 24 and therefore rendered the whole agreement void. She therefore had to fall back on applying under s 24 in the normal way for a transfer of property order ancillary to divorce as the only means of getting financial arrangements moving again.

It will be necessary to show that because of a change in circumstances (including a foreseen change) since the arrangements in the agreement were made, there should be an alteration to make different arrangements or that the agreement does not contain proper arrangements for a child of the family.

The court's discretionary powers on variation

Variation by the court includes revocation or insertion of such arrangements as appear just, having regard to all the circumstances (s 35(2)). *Gorman v Gorman* [1964] 3 All ER 739 established that this will be considered from an objective point of view.

Sometimes, the court *will* decide to vary an agreement because of subsequent change of circumstances. Sometimes the circumstances are adjudged not to be sufficiently changed. In *D v D* (1974) 118 SJ 715, for example, the fact that the parties had taken legal advice when making the agreement made them decide against variation when the home, which the wife had agreed to transfer for only £1,500, suddenly shot up in value, part of their reasoning being that by the time of the application the husband had remarried and had spent a considerable sum on the house so it did not seem fair to change the agreement.

In *Simister v Simister (No 2)* [1987] 1 FLR 194, however, they did vary the agreement. The husband had agreed to pay one third of his salary to the wife, and when he received a very substantial increase he tried to argue that it was in excess of her needs – clearly a different situation, especially because of the importance of needs in deciding what a wife should receive in accordance with the established rules of quantum.

The court's powers are wider on variation under ss 34–36 than under s 31. For example, s 35 variation can include insertion of a lump sum order which the court could not do to vary a periodical payments order under s 31.

Agreements are variable after the *death of the payer* if:

- they *provide* for payment after death; or
- the deceased died *domiciled* in England and Wales (MCA 1973, s 36).

An alternative is always available in this case, namely to apply under the Inheritance (Provision for Family and Dependants) Act 1975.

19.4.2.2 Procedure for application to the court for variation

Application may be made either to the county court or the Family Proceedings Court. The county court powers are wider and include inserting:

- unlimited lump sums;
- secured and unsecured periodical payments;
- property adjustment orders; and
- variation of periodical payment orders.

The Family Proceedings Court can only:

- vary or terminate periodical payments orders;
- insert unsecured periodical payments (MCA 1973, s 35(3)).

Transfer to the High Court is possible (Matrimonial and Family Proceedings Act 1984, s 37; *Practice Direction* [1987] 1 All ER 1087).

19.5 THE EFFECT ON FUTURE FINANCIAL APPLICATIONS OF ENTERING INTO AN AGREEMENT

The *existence* of such agreements will always be *considered* as part of all the circumstances of the case under s 25 of the MCA 1973 in subsequent ancillary relief proceedings because the jurisdiction of the court can never be ousted. Whether the substance of the agreement will influence the court is another matter and depends on the individual circumstances. Some principles emerge from the case law on the subject.

The basic principle is that *no* agreement will ever have the effect of preventing the court from exercising all its usual powers under ss 23 and 24 of the MCA 1973 because it is simply not possible to oust the jurisdiction of the court. However, the *fact* that it was entered into, whether that was done freely, whether advice was taken, and the extent to which it has been carried out by both parties, will all be relevant to the general duty under s 25 (*Dean v Dean* [1978] 3 WLR 288; [1978] 3 All ER 758).

Edgar v Edgar [1980] 1 WLR 1410 is an awful warning of what happens when advice *is* obtained and then *ignored*. Mrs Edgar entered into a maintenance agreement with her husband including a term that she would not later apply to the court for maintenance, although her solicitors told her that if she applied to the court she would get better terms. When divorce proceedings were started, she did apply to the court, thus breaking the agreement. However, the court decided in its discretion that it would not go behind the agreement since they took that she was bound, especially as she had had legal advice. The moral of this case would appear to be that if a client wants to do this sort of thing, it is better done behind the solicitor's back, since taking advice and ignoring it is fatal.

Nevertheless, sometimes the court does intervene even in situations like this, as in *Jessel v Jessel* [1979] 1 WLR 1148; [1979] 3 All ER 645, where they decided not to hold the wife to her agreement not to apply under s 31 of the MCA 1973 to increase an existing order.

Trends in the consideration of prenuptial agreements indicate that the weight to be given to the terms of any separation or maintenance agreement on subsequent divorce and application for ancillary relief is still uncertain unless there is a clear *Edgar* type situation. There have been initiatives (such as the proposal in *Supporting Families* (Home Office, 1998): see 5.9, above) which favour the introduction of binding prenuptial agreements in English law, none of which have so far come to fruition. The courts' approach to prenuptial agreements, fortified by all the case law to date, remains that such agreements are relevant as one of the s 25 considerations, and that the weight will depend on all the circumstances of the case, including the legal system under which the agreement was signed. The response to the *Supporting Families* proposals that 'pre-nups' should be binding met with a mixed response. An examination of the entire area of agreements outside court is overdue, but this is unlikely to happen until some steps are taken to reform the existing law of ancillary relief, on consideration of which the Lord Chancellor's Ancillary Relief Advisory Group has been engaged for years without result, since the relevance of agreements must be an essential part of the entire philosophy of division of assets on relationship breakdown, which at present remains heavily discretionary for married people and dependent on the ordinary law of property for the unmarried.

19.6 WHICH REMEDY?

The choice of remedy will obviously depend on the circumstances of the individual spouse, who should weigh up the pros and cons of each possibility and make a decision based on convenience to the case. However, if the rules are *observed* to avoid the hazards which can arise, and the agreement is carefully drafted, there is much to be said for an agreement which can be varied under ss 34–36, since on balance that combines the best of all the remedies.

FINANCIAL PROVISION WITHOUT A DECREE OF DIVORCE, NULLITY OR JUDICIAL SEPARATION

POTENTIAL SOURCES OF FINANCIAL PROVISION WITHOUT A DECREE

There are three possible such sources other than voluntary payments or welfare benefits: an order under the DPMCA 1978 from the Family Proceedings Court, an order under s 27 of the MCA 1973 or a separation/maintenance agreement.

DOMESTIC PROCEEDINGS AND MAGISTRATES' COURTS ACT 1978

The DPMCA 1978 provides the usual (normally contested) adversarial orders under s 2, agreed orders under s 6 or a formalising order (where there is a regular pattern of payments already established) under s 7. Orders under s 2 are made on the basis of failure to maintain either spouse or child, desertion (no particular period required) or behaviour, which has the same meaning as in the MCA 1973. The Family Proceedings Court makes orders in accordance with its own criteria under s 3 of the Act, which is similar to s 25 of the MCA 1973, save that the Family Proceedings Court will not dissolve the marriage so there is no room for an equivalent to s 25(2)(h).

Only periodical payments and lump sum orders may be made (no property adjustment orders) and lump sums are limited to £1,000 per person involved in the application (ie, each child may also receive £1,000). The CSA has removed the Family Proceedings Court's periodical payments jurisdiction over natural children whose absent parent can be assessed by the CSA.

Enforcement is particularly efficient in the Family Proceedings Court and orders obtained elsewhere, including overseas, may be registered there for enforcement. Such orders may be varied as well as enforced.

MATRIMONIAL CAUSES ACT 1973, s 27

Section 27 of the MCA 1973 provides a similar jurisdiction, without restriction on the amount of lump sums.

SEPARATION OR MAINTENANCE AGREEMENTS

While there are common standard clauses, separation or maintenance agreements may contain virtually any provisions the parties wish, provided that any child provisions are for the benefit of the child or children concerned, and the agreement is not void for seeking to oust the jurisdiction of the court or (if read as encouraging future separation) being contrary to pubic policy because such a provision undermines the status of marriage. Such provisions can either make the whole agreement void or, if severable, merely be disregarded. There are advantages of agreements as opposed to orders: for example, such agreements are flexible, cheaper and more likely to be observed if crafted by the parties, and disadvantages in that they are more difficult to enforce and vary unless the parties are in agreement. There is, however, statutory provision for the variation of written agreements (and separation and maintenance agreements are usually by deed).

Such agreements are always taken into account by the court on any future application to them for financial provision, but may or may not influence the subsequent decision. Usually if the parties have both had independent legal advice they will be held to their agreement, unless it is manifestly unfair, or disadvantageous to a child.

WHICH REMEDY?

The circumstances of the spouse (and if applicable children) requiring provision will dictate which is the most appropriate source of financial provision in their case.

CHAPTER 20

PROTECTING THE HOME AND CONTENTS
ON MARRIAGE BREAKDOWN

20.1 INTRODUCTION

Much influence on family law has been generated by the growth of home ownership and the central role occupied by the home in the theory of the division of assets on relationship breakdown. While the fate of cohabitants' homes still languishes under the provisions of the ordinary law of property, some recognition exists in the law for the key importance to the couple and the family of the matrimonial home.

Both during the marriage and on marriage breakdown, the home serves two linked but distinct functions:

(a) it is a roof for the couple or family, and may remain so for one of the spouses and any family after separation and divorce; and

(b) it is usually the couple's most valuable capital asset (although the value of pension rights may well come a close second to that and has been the subject of most recent development of the law on marriage breakdown).

It is therefore vital on separation that certain practical matters are addressed, possibly urgently, as first of all it will usually be necessary to establish the precise ownership of the matrimonial home with a view to registering matrimonial home rights under the Family Law Act (FLA) 1996 if that should prove to be necessary (ie, if the property is not jointly owned by the spouses). Matrimonial home rights protection applies to both *owned* and *rented* homes, so it cannot be assumed that a spouse's position in relation to the home is entirely safe simply because there is a only a tenancy.

In an appropriate case (ie, where the home is owned rather than rented but the other spouse normally pays the mortgage and it is not certain following a separation whether it is still being paid or not), it might also be necessary to give urgent further consideration to how the mortgage will continue to be paid and, if matters have already got out of hand, to whether it is going to be necessary to resist possession proceedings. If the answer to that is in the negative, it will still be necessary to consider what is going to happen to the spouse who will not remain in the home after separation, especially if there are children, since pursuant to the obligations imposed on the court by s 25(1) of the Matrimonial Causes Act (MCA) 1973 they will obviously need to be properly rehoused in some way.

The contents of the home will probably not be as urgent a matter at this stage, and (subject to, eg, distress on chattels which are the sole property of the other spouse) any problems in relation to contents can usually wait for solution at leisure under the Married Women's Property Act 1882 (see Chapter 21).

20.2 PREVENTING A SALE OR MORTGAGE OF OWNED HOMES

Especially if there is not much equity in the home, the spouse out of occupation is all too likely to default on the mortgage, whereas if there is significant equity there will be a temptation to raise money, or further money, by mortgaging the home or taking out a second mortgage or loan for which the equity in the home is again given as security. Case law has shown that legal advisers need to be on the watch for both of these situations.

20.2.1 Home in joint names

This is a relatively safe situation since, if the spouses are joint tenants, in theory the property cannot be conveyed, transferred, mortgaged or charged as security for a loan *without* the other spouse's signature – unless, of course, that is forged, which is not, unfortunately, unknown. Although banks and finance houses who are invited by one spouse, posing as single or separated, to lend on the security of a home have now become somewhat more alert about inspecting properties for signs of spousal occupation, and usually now require charges to be signed by both spouses in the presence of the spouses' own solicitor, nevertheless occasional cases continue to occur where one spouse, usually the husband, fraudulently disposes of the home, if necessary hiring a third party to pose as the wife for the purpose of executing the charge. Obviously there is nothing that can be done to protect a spouse against the occurrence of such determined dishonesty, although such a transaction might in due course be set aside, and it will usually be sufficient to obey the rules in those cases where swift pre-emptive action can preserve the priority of a deceived spouse's interests. This type of situation is perhaps now more likely to be obviated since the mechanics of such transactions have recently been considered in detail by the House of Lords in the conjoined *Etridge* appeals (*Royal Bank of Scotland v Etridge and Others* [2001] 3 All ER 449; [2001] UKHL 44, as to which see 20.2.2, below).

20.2.2 One spouse already a party to a prejudicial transaction

More problematic is the situation where it turns out that a spouse, usually the wife, is a genuine party to a transaction, such as a mortgage or sale, which has already taken place and which clearly prejudices that spouse's interests. Generally, where the client has apparently willingly and knowingly co-operated in the transaction, often a mortgage to secure the other spouse's business debts, or sometimes a mortgage for their mutual benefit, it will be too late to do anything to redeem the situation. However, if it can be said that there has been *undue influence* or *fraud* on the part of either the other spouse or of the third party, the mortgage or sale may not be binding on the client. See *Barclays Bank plc v O'Brien* [1994] 1 FLR 1, HL; and *CIBC Mortgages plc v Pitt* [1993] 4 All ER 433, HL, the leading cases on this point, which establish that:

(a) where a spouse (usually the wife) *relied on the other spouse* by placing trust and confidence in that spouse to manage their joint financial affairs, *undue influence will be presumed*, although the deluded spouse will in that case also have to show that the transaction was *disadvantageous* to her; *but*

(b) where the deluded spouse is not relying on such a *presumption*, but can *prove* that the other spouse did *exert undue influence*, then it will not also be necessary to show that the transaction was disadvantageous to the spouse who was influenced.

If a spouse is in one of these situations it may therefore be possible to have the transaction, usually a mortgage to a bank, set aside, where:

- the other spouse was technically acting in procuring the influenced spouse's agreement to the transaction as *agent for the mortgagee;* or
- the mortgagee had *actual* or *constructive notice* of the facts.

In the latter situation, the mortgagee will have to show that the spouse claiming to have the transaction set aside *entered freely into the obligation with knowledge of the relevant facts.* This will be quite hard for the mortgagee to show unless there has been a meeting with the spouse now claiming to have been prejudiced, where the other spouse was not present to exert influence, undue or otherwise, when the legal liability being taken on was explained, together with all the risks involved, and he or she was expressly advised to take independent legal advice, or such other reasonable steps were taken to apprise the deluded spouse of the risks. See *Barclays Bank v O'Brien* [1994] 1 FLR 1; and also *Banco Exterior International v Mann* [1995] 1 FLR 602, CA; *Dunbar Bank plc v Nadeem and Another* [1997] 1 FLR 318; and *Royal Bank of Scotland v Etridge* [1997] 3 All ER 628, CA, which have now been further refined by the House of Lords in *Royal Bank of Scotland v Etridge and Others* [2001] 4 All ER 449; [2001] UKHL 44, which laid down some precise guidelines as to how any transaction involving a wife offering security for her husband's debts should be handled. Lord Nicholls said in this case that as soon as the wife offers such security the bank is 'put on inquiry', and set out a framework of tasks for (i) the bank and (ii) the solicitor who is allegedly giving independent advice to the wife.

The bank's obligation is therefore now to see that the spouse who is to give security (usually the wife) gets independent advice, not to proceed until he or she has done so, and to make clear to him or her that once he or she is independently advised he or she will no longer be able to challenge the transaction if he or she proceeds with it.

The solicitor's obligation is not only to explain the documents to the spouse who is to be bound, who is often a wife who has left financial business decisions to the husband, but also to explain the seriousness of the transaction, including the potential for extending the initial loan facilities without further reference to her, to consider the couple's means in case of default, to state clearly that the decision whether to proceed is the wife's and hers alone, and expressly to ask her if she is content for the solicitor to write to the bank to say that she has had the documents and that their consequence had been explained to her.

The latter case, at the centre of a clutch of appeals heard by the House of Lords in the early summer of 2001, settled a number of detailed queries as to the precise duty of the lender, and the quality of the independent legal advice, but other queries remain. For example, what is the effect if the advice given is poor? Is the lender then deemed to be on the requisite notice, for example, where the legal adviser is also acting for the lender? This question recently arose in the case of a solicitor who was not merely an outside adviser, but also held an office with the lender, and therefore clearly had a conflict of interest. The question here, then, is still what are the precise circumstances in which deemed notice will be imputed to the lender? The cynic's answer to this appears to be that if anything goes wrong (ie, the security is unenforceable after all), the bank has in any case shifted the responsibility for the loss to the solicitor in negligence.

A question also arises as to the quality of the disadvantage which must accrue to the deluded spouse to make it voidable as between husband and wife, thereby giving rise to the very equity of which the lender is deemed to have constructive notice? This appears to be a question of fact, the duty on the spouse who is seeking the other spouse's agreement to be one of 'candour and fairness' and the disadvantage, while not necessarily large, must be so obviously disadvantageous that it must be presumed to have been brought about by undue influence. For example, clearly if the transaction bestows benefit on the wife, such as joint tenancy of a house which is bought with the money borrowed (as in *Dunbar Bank v Nadeem* [1998] 3 All ER 876), or if it supports an established family business rather than funds a speculative venture, this will probably require much less care on the husband's part to make clear the potential disadvantages.

However, *Etridge* has now confirmed that, depending on the facts of the case, advice given by a legal executive *is* generally sufficient to get round *O'Brien*, a question raised in the Court of Appeal in the other Barclays Bank case of *Coleman* [2001] 3 WLR 1021.

This whole area of law which has now been under review by the House of Lords, radically transforming the entire field, is both complex and of academic as well as practical interest, but a more detailed account is beyond the limited space available in a book primarily devoted to family law. The student is therefore recommended to read the report of the case which contains some very clear analyses by Lords Nicholls, Scott and Hobhouse.

20.2.3 Joint tenancies: to sever or not to sever?

The other matter to be considered where the home is in joint names is whether the joint tenancy should be severed so as to avoid the other spouse succeeding to it on the client's unexpected death before the divorce is finalised, since even filing a petition making a comprehensive claim for ancillary relief does not automatically sever any joint tenancy which exists (*Harris v Goddard* [1983] 1 WLR 1203). This is so despite the fact that issuing proceedings under the Married Women's Property Act 1882 does automatically operate to sever the joint tenancy. (However, if the client might succeed to the *other* spouse's half share (eg, if the other spouse is unwell and has a poor life expectancy), then this matter might be better left, as severance would of course preclude the client's gaining the other half of the home on that spouse's succession by survivorship.)

Any such notice is of course normally carefully drafted so as not to *admit* that there is a joint tenancy in *equity* under which the other spouse would be entitled to a half share, as this would prejudice future proceedings under the 1882 Act. The notice should sever any such joint tenancy if, which is not admitted, one exists.

It may of course be that there is an existing tenancy in common (so that there is no need to sever). A tenancy in common already exists if:

- the conveyance or transfer to the parties *expressly* states that they hold as tenants in common;
- there is a *separate* declaration of trusts to that effect;

- there is a *note or memorandum of severance endorsed or annexed* to the conveyance;
- there is a *restriction* to that effect on the Proprietorship Register.

However, as the building society usually has the deeds, in practice any solicitor advising may have to issue a notice pursuant to s 36(2) of the Law of Property Act (LPA) 1925 without knowing for certain what the position is!

20.2.4 Home in sole name of the other spouse

This situation can give rise to different problems. First, early registration of matrimonial home rights of occupation under the FLA 1996 would be prudent to avoid a sale of the property over the non-owning spouse's head. Secondly, if that is done too late to effect the usual protection, some thought might have to be given to non-matrimonial home rights which may protect the occupying spouse (ie, whether the client has an *overriding interest in registered land* or a *beneficial interest in unregistered land*), and whether in any event the client's ancillary relief claims should be registered as a *pending land action*, which may be done by lodging a caution in the Proprietorship Register, and any supporting action taken under s 37 of the MCA 1973 (see Chapter 17).

While the FLA 1996 registration will only apply to the home, a pending land action can be registered against *all* property (including, eg, a holiday home) and s 37 applies to *any* assets which may be needed to satisfy the client's claim for ancillary relief (see Chapter 17 for protection under s 37).

20.2.5 Non-matrimonial home rights interests which may protect the occupying spouse where the home is in the sole name of the other

These rights comprise the *overriding interest* and the *beneficial interest* in *unregistered land*.

For *an overriding interest* the claimant spouse must be in *actual occupation of registered land* (which means physically present, though not necessarily all the time) and must have a *beneficial interest* in the property as an equitable tenant in common by reason of contributing to the purchase price (Land Registration Act (LRA) 1925, s 70(1)(g)). This was established in *Williams & Glyn's Bank Ltd v Boland and Another; Williams & Glyn's Bank Ltd v Brown and Another* [1981] AC 487; [1980] 2 All ER 408, HL, a pair of cases heard together where the two wives were held to be entitled to resist the bank's application for possession as their husbands had mortgaged the homes without the wives' knowledge. As a result of these cases, however, banks now tend to ask everyone living in a home to sign a deed agreeing to postpone their interests to the bank's.

The same principles apply in the case of actual occupation of *unregistered land* in which the spouse has a beneficial interest, where knowledge of the spouse's occupation depends on the doctrine of notice, as was shown in *Kingsnorth Finance Ltd v Tizard* [1986] 1 WLR 783; [1986] 2 All ER 54. Unless the mortgagees actually enquire properly about the position they will have constructive notice of the occupation of such a spouse and their rights will be postponed to the occupying spouse's beneficial interest. Mr Tizard actually pulled a fast one on the bank in this case as he told them he was single and although the wife was at the house some of the time (she slept away but came daily to look after the children) he arranged for them to visit when she was absent. He then went off to the USA with the cash he had raised. The court held that the wife's occupation would have been discovered if the mortgagee had made proper enquiries and that her occupation was no less effective because she did not sleep there.

20.3 STATUTORY RIGHT OF OCCUPATION UNDER THE FAMILY LAW ACT 1996

Section 30 of the FLA 1996 gives a spouse who is not the owner of the matrimonial home a statutory right of occupation and gives the same right to a spouse who has an equitable interest. Where *both* spouses have ownership rights (eg, they are joint tenants), the Act gives them *both* the right to apply to the court to determine who shall occupy the home. The statutory right may therefore be enforced by either spouse regardless of in whose name the legal title is vested (ss 30(1) and (9) and 31(1)). Enforcement of these rights is pursuant to s 33. The right of occupation is an equitable charge binding on third parties as well as the owning spouse (s 34), and are registrable (s 31), in the same way as such rights under the preceding Matrimonial Homes Acts (MHA): the FLA 1996 repealed the last of these (the MHA 1983) in its entirety. (See FLA 1996, ss 30–32 and Sched 4.)

This statutory right of occupation applies only to homes which are, were intended to be or have been the matrimonial home (s 33(1)(b)) and do not apply, for example, to holiday homes, though if there is more than one home which might qualify as the matrimonial home the spouse seeking to register rights of occupation must choose which one to register against.

20.3.1 The rights conferred by the statute

What the precise rights are which may be enforced under the statute depends on whether the spouse applying is in occupation or not. The statutory right of occupation is defined in s 30(2) as:

(a) if *in* occupation, the right is not to be *evicted or excluded* from the home *or any part of it* by the other spouse *except with leave of the court* given by order under s 33;

(b) if *not* in occupation, the right is to *enter into and occupy* the home *with the leave of the court* (s 30(2)).

The court's power is wide and may exclude the owning spouse.

The court may regulate these rights in each case by:

(1) declaring, enforcing, restricting or terminating those rights;

(2) prohibiting, suspending or restricting the exercise by either spouse of the right to occupy the home or part of it (s 33(3)(b)); or

(3) requiring either spouse to permit the exercise by the other of the right (s 31(3)).

The court must regulate the rights of occupation in the light of the criteria in s 33(6) of the Act, namely in relation to:

(a) the parties' conduct in relation to each other and otherwise;

(b) the parties' housing needs and financial resources;

(c) the housing needs of any children; and

(d) any significant harm likely to be suffered by the parties or any relevant child on the basis of a new balance of harm test (s 33(6) and (7)), which in effect makes it mandatory for the court to make the order sought if the criteria for so doing are satisfied unless the respondent can show that the balance of harm test goes in his favour.

Each of these criteria is as important as any of the others.

For a discussion of how the criteria are applied in practice (usually, but not exclusively, in relation to domestic violence applications), see Chapter 23.

20.3.2 Termination of the statutory right

The statutory right is terminated by:

- the death of either spouse;
- the dissolution or annulment of the marriage (ie, on decree absolute); or
- order of the court under its wide power to regulate the occupation of the home during the subsistence of the marriage.

The court has power to direct that rights of occupation which would normally come to an end on decree absolute should *continue* beyond that event. In this case it is essential that application is made for such an order *before* the marriage has actually ended when the court may make use of s 33(5) to order otherwise (s 31(8)).

20.3.3 Registration of occupation rights

This is effected by registration at the appropriate registry of the spouse's right of occupation by means of:

(a) a Class F land charge in the case of *unregistered land,* which is effected against the *name* of the other spouse in the register of land charges (Land Charges Act 1972, s 2); or

(b) notice in the case of registered land, which is effected against the *land* in the charges register (LRA 1925 – see MHA 1983, s 2(8)(a)).

A spouse can register occupation rights while out of occupation, but in that case cannot enforce them without leave of the court (*Watts v Waller* [1972] 3 WLR 365; [1972] 3 All ER 257).

It is *essential* to register in the *correct form* at the correct place as otherwise the registration will be no use whatever, as happened in *Miles v Bull (No 2)* [1969] 2 FLR 389, where the wife lost her protection even though she was not the one to register at the wrong place.

20.3.3.1 How to find out if the land is registered or unregistered so as to register correctly

In order to discover whether the land is registered or unregistered, a search must be made on the Index Map at the district Land Registry, and if it is registered this will enable the title number to be obtained for identification.

Once registered, the spouse's rights will be protected against third parties because the registration is *actual notice* to the purchaser. However, the court can still determine the rights of occupation under s 33(3)(e) and can permit the other spouse to enter and occupy instead. In only one notorious reported case under the previous legislation does the spouse's priority seem not to have been secured by registration of the occupation rights, and that was because of the way in which the court applied s 1(3) of the MHA 1983 to give occupation to a third party against the wife, as to which the dissenting judgment of Sir Denys Buckley took the view that that decision was badly wrong. This was *Kashmir Kaur v Gill* [1988] 2 All ER 288; [1988] Fam 110, where the wife, who was out of occupation but had registered her rights thus binding her husband and a purchaser to whom he had sold the home, applied to enter and occupy. Unbelievably, the court refused her application, considering the interests of the purchaser, a blind man who particularly wanted the house, and deciding that he had a higher degree of socio-economic need than she did! The court said it would be different if the husband and the purchaser had colluded to exclude the wife and to nullify her registered right of occupation, but that this was not the case. Sir Denys Buckley, dissenting, obviously thought that this could hardly have been the result that was intended when the s 1(3) criteria were devised in a statute designed to regulate the rights of married people rather than to assist third parties. Such a decision would be highly unlikely under the new, much wider, criteria of s 33(6) of the FLA 1996.

20.3.4 Regulation of the right

This normally takes place on applications in connection with domestic violence in which case the court may make an *ouster* or *exclusion order* (see Chapter 23), although as has been seen above in *Kashmir Kaur v Gill* applications may be made for reasons unconnected with violence.

Regulation of the right of occupation can extend to excluding a spouse from a certain *part* only of the home, for example, a studio or separate office or study. It may also include requiring a spouse to pay for outgoings or repairs to the home (s 40(1)(a)), grant the use of furniture (s 40(1)(c)) and/or require a party to take care of such chattels (s 40(1)(d)).

20.4 RIGHTS TO PAY THE MORTGAGE AND IN POSSESSION PROCEEDINGS

A spouse entitled to occupy the matrimonial home may pay the mortgage and other outgoings and the money must be accepted (FLA 1996, s 30(3)).

A further advantage of registration is that a spouse with registered rights must be kept informed of mortgage enforcement proceedings and may be entitled to be made a party. The spouse wishing to exercise this right must apply to the court and will be entitled to be joined if the court:

- does not see any special reason against allowing joinder; and
- is satisfied that the spouse is likely to be able to contribute sufficiently towards the payments to affect the outcome of possession proceedings.

20.5 BANKRUPTCY

The statutory right of occupation may not provide protection in bankruptcy.

The court has a duty to balance the interests of the creditors, and the principle that a person should pay his debts, against the interests of the other spouse, usually in these cases the wife and family, as it tends to be the husband who goes bankrupt. In such a case, while the husband's property vests in his trustee in bankruptcy, the wife's right of occupation is *binding* on the trustee and creditors once it is registered, as is any right she may have to a legal or beneficial interest. However, her right of *occupation, even coupled with a beneficial interest*, may not be able to prevent an order for sale of the home being made to pay the husband's debts, since the trustee can apply for such an order under s 14 of the Trusts of Land and Appointment of Trustees Act (TOLATA) 1996 (formerly under s 30 of the LPA 1925, all references to which in texts which have not been since updated should now be construed as references to s 14 of the TOLATA 1996). The court will consider the criteria for a sale order contained in s 15(1) of the TOLATA 1996 and make whatever order is just and reasonable and s 336(4) of the Insolvency Act (IA) 1986, which is similar to the FLA 1996, s 33 criteria (without the balance of harm test), will have to be applied, taking into account (in addition to the interests of the creditors):

- the wife's conduct (if any) in contributing to the bankruptcy;
- the wife's or former wife's needs and resources;
- the needs of any children; and
- all the circumstances of the case,

other, that is, than the needs of the bankrupt husband (IA 1986, s 336(4)). After one year from the trustee in bankruptcy taking office, in the absence of any special considerations to be taken into account in that particular case, the court presumes that the creditors' interests outweigh all others (s 336(5)), but if in the meantime there has been a transfer to the wife in ancillary relief proceedings, even by consent order, this will be effective against the husband's trustee in bankruptcy as it vests the property in the wife (*Harper v O'Reilly* [1997] 2 FLR 816).

However, there are ways of dealing with this problem. Three separate situations need to be considered.

20.5.1 Where there is already a charging order over the home and the creditor seeks an order under of the Trusts of Land and Appointment of Trustees Act 1996, s 14

In this situation the creditor's claim is likely to prevail because the creditor's interest is one of the specific criteria under s 15(1)(d) which must be considered by the court, although a sale may be postponed to mitigate immediate hardship to the family (as in *Bank of Ireland Homes Mortgages v Bell* [2001] 2 FLR 809). Postponement tends not to be for long: for example, in *Re Turner* [1975] 1 All ER 5, the court balanced the interests of the creditors and the family and ordered the sale of the home within two months; this may be regarded as fairly average. In *Re Bailey* [1977] 2 All ER 26, the sale was ordered immediately – obviously tough on the family. In *Re Lowrie* [1981] 3 All ER 353, the sale was ordered in three months – a sufficient delay to provide some breathing space. However, in *Re Holliday* [1980] 3 All ER 385, the sale was postponed for five years until the youngest child was age 17. This is not at all the norm, especially in the light of more recent cases where the court appears to be getting tougher, initial longer periods being reduced drastically on appeal.

A prime example of this type of case is that of *Re Citro* [1990] 3 All ER 952; [1991] 1 FLR 71, where there were two brothers in business together, both married, both owning a half share in their homes and with young children who would not be age 16 for four or five years. Both had gone bankrupt and initially won a postponement of sale until the children were 16. On appeal this was cancelled and only short postponements substituted on the basis that the interests of the creditors were superior to those of the children whose parents would have to find alternative accommodation and schooling for them, though there was a dissenting judgment indicating that this might be wrong at a critical stage of their education. Basically, the message is that bankruptcy is now so commonplace that it will be unusual to find the lengthy periods of postponement that were achieved in the previous recession in the early 1980s.

The same year saw *Re Gorman* [1990] 2 FLR 284, where there was originally a two year postponement, ordered for the wife out of sympathy because before he had become bankrupt she had divorced the husband and claimed his half of the home, already owning her own half share; on appeal this was reduced to six months so that the husband's creditors were not prejudiced.

The moral must be to start the divorce proceedings and have the ancillary relief orders made before the husband goes bankrupt and, failing that, to look at the possibilities of the next situation.

20.5.2 Where the s 14 proceedings are transferred to the Family Division pursuant to the institution of divorce proceedings

This possibility is not a complete cure all as sometimes it will not be allowed. However, if it is, there is a much better chance of obtaining a more lengthy postponement of the sale, because the divorce court has greater flexibility in considering the needs of the wife and children, as was evident in *Austin-Fell v Austin-Fell* [1990] 2 All ER 455; [1989] 2 FLR 497. In that case the husband owed the bank £7,000 and they obtained a charging order over his half share of the home. On divorce the wife applied to set this aside and the registrar (now the district judge) found that unless he did this and gave her the whole house she would not have enough money left after settling the mortgage and the legal aid bill to rehouse herself, especially as the bankrupt husband was obviously not going to be able to pay any maintenance, so she would only just be able to keep the household going on her own earnings. The registrar therefore granted her application. On appeal the bank instead obtained a 10 year postponement of the sale to when the youngest child would be aged 18, on the basis that it was not fair not to enforce the charge just because the creditor was an affluent bank and that sometimes debtors' families would have to accept less security in life than might be desirable. Nevertheless, the 10 year postponement was a significant advance on the fate of the Citros in the same year.

However, in *First National Savings v Hegarty* [1985] FLR 80, transfer to the Family Division was refused even though the husband had forged the wife's signature in order to obtain the loan. The court gave the creditor a charging order and said that the wife's position should be considered if and when he applied to enforce it. Therefore it can be seen that application for transfer does not always work.

20.5.3 Where the debtor is bankrupt

As explained above there is little that can be done where the debtor is actually bankrupt as after one year s 336(5) will apply. Moreover, transactions designed to defeat the creditors will usually be set aside, as in *Lloyds Bank v Marcan* [1973] 1 WLR 1381; [1973] 3 All ER 754, where the husband leased his business to his wife, well knowing the bank wanted possession to sell it when he became bankrupt. The lease was set aside. On the other hand, *Re Densham* [1975] 1 WLR 1519; [1975] 3 All ER 725 was a case where the transfer to the wife of a one ninth share of the home survived the trustee in bankruptcy's application to set it aside, so she got her one ninth share of the sale proceeds.

Usually the trustee in bankruptcy will be able to set aside any transactions designed to prejudice the interests of creditors or to put assets beyond their reach (IA 1986, s 423). Transactions at an undervalue suffer the same fate within five years of the presentation of the bankruptcy petition (s 339). However, in the case of those more than two years before the bankruptcy it will be necessary to show that the debtor became insolvent as a result of the transaction, or that at that time the debtor could not pay debts as they became due (s 341).

In these circumstances the best hope for a spouse who is not a joint tenant of the home, and who fears that the other spouse may dispose of the property and make off out of the jurisdiction with the proceeds, would be to ask for a share of the money *in lieu of* registering the FLA matrimonial home rights of occupation. However, for the spouse who *is* a joint tenant, there seems to be no solution to offer but tea and sympathy and encouragement to do what can be done with whatever is the value of the spouse's share of the sale proceeds. Even energetic opposition to the trustee in bankruptcy's claim for an order for sale is likely, after the one year delay, to result in nothing but a large private or public funding bill, and the money could obviously be better spent.

Cohabitants, curiously, often have a better chance. While unlike spouses they have no *registrable occupation rights* as such, and no rights under the IA 1986, if they have a beneficial interest in the property they can oppose the trustee in bankruptcy's application under s 14 of the TOLATA 1996 and should be able to operate the year's delay in that the creditors' interests may not be presumed to outweigh all other considerations for that year at least if 'all the circumstances' in s 336(5) include the cohabitant's interests.

20.6 RIGHTS WHERE THE HOME IS RENTED

The same matrimonial home rights of occupation apply even if the home is rented.

The spouse's occupation will also be effective for security of tenure under the Rent Act 1977 and the Housing Acts 1985 and 1988.

By the FLA 1996, rent paid by the occupying spouse must also be accepted by the landlord, just as the mortgagee must accept mortgage payments.

20.7 ALTERNATIVES WHERE THE HOME CANNOT BE SAVED

Since those on income support/jobseeker's allowance are able to have mortgage interest paid for them, the first attempt to save the home for one spouse (and children) should be to negotiate with the mortgagee for *interest only* to be paid on the mortgage, on the basis that the Benefits Agency will pay the interest after the qualifying period appropriate to the date when the mortgage was taken out. The mortgagee may agree to this, especially if the reliance on welfare benefits is likely to be temporary and there is every likelihood that the spouse who has been paying the mortgage (or both the spouses) will soon be back in work. The arrears will have to be paid off, or sometimes the mortgage can be restructured so that the arrears can be added to the capital element of the mortgage and the mortgage term extended, thus also lowering the monthly payment. Often the mortgagee would rather do this than repossess the home, and in the current cut-throat competition for mortgagors' business, many of them keep departments for working out schemes to retain mortgages of people who would otherwise leave them for other lenders. If the situation is not too bad an attempt to save the existing home and mortgage should always be made first and is likely to succeed if there is substantial equity.

Failing this, the possibilities are basically (other than living with relatives, or friends) renting privately (housing benefit will be available: see Chapter 18) or trying the local authority. A council house or flat is unlikely to materialise immediately, however, and if the local authority is obliged to house the family it may be in bed and breakfast accommodation. Children can now in an emergency be voluntarily accommodated by the local authority pursuant to their duty, without any danger of a care order (Children Act 1989, s 20). This includes situations where parents are unable to look after them temporarily (see Chapter 26).

20.7.1 Local authority housing

Housing the homeless is now dealt with under the Housing Act 1996, which imposes a (now more limited) duty to house the homeless. This obligation is now also restricted by various concepts, and what follows is only a very rough thumbnail sketch of the position. Spouses who need advice on local authority housing require research of the up to date position beyond the scope of this book. A specialist vocabulary also needs to be learned in order to follow the new law, including the appropriate definitions of the words and phrases in common use in local authority housing law, such as 'homeless', 'intentionally homeless' and 'priority need'.

20.7.1.1 Homeless

Persons are homeless who have no accommodation for themselves or their family or who are 'threatened' with homelessness as they have accommodation and must leave within 28 days (eg, under a possession order from the court), or if those persons have accommodation and cannot use it because of violence or threats of violence from someone else living there.

20.7.1.2 Intentional homelessness

People are *intentionally homeless* if they would not be homeless but for deliberately or carelessly giving up accommodation. For this reason it is usually better to wait for a mortgagee to obtain a repossession order in respect of the home rather than to hand in the keys. Moreover, any accommodation which may be classed as available does not have to be within the jurisdiction, as it could be anywhere within the EU territory. However, a battered wife leaving home is specifically excluded from the category of intentionally homeless.

20.7.1.3 Priority need

Those with *priority need* include people with children, old age pensioners, handicapped persons, pregnant women, disaster victims (eg, homeless as a result of fire or flood) or other vulnerable people.

20.7.1.4 Local authority duties

Depending on the interrelation of these key concepts, the local authority *may* have a duty to house a person either temporarily or permanently, or possibly not at all. For example, a homeless person who establishes a priority need must be housed temporarily while it is established whether their homelessness is intentional and, even if the homelessness *was* intentional, if such temporary accommodation is needed to enable the applicant to find alternative housing. If it is decided that a person's homelessness is *not* intentional, the authority must provide more permanent housing, in the first instance for two years, which period may be extended if the priority need continues. If the homeless person has no priority need, the only duty on the authority is to advise and assist, although there is an overriding duty to assist applicants to obtain other non-local authority housing if available (Housing Act 1996, s 197). Where a person has become homeless intentionally, there is still a duty to provide temporary housing if that person has a priority need.

There are also new 'local connection' rules to prevent people 'trading up' to better areas, so that an authority descended upon by people from other authorities can insist on transferring responsibility for those people back to their originating authority. This is obviously important as a local authority tenancy is a secure tenancy under the Housing Act 1985. Local connection can be established by family or work links.

PROTECTING THE HOME AND CONTENTS ON MARRIAGE BREAKDOWN

PREVENTING A SALE OR MORTGAGE OF OWNED HOMES

Where the home is in joint names, in theory there should be no difficulty in preventing unilateral disposition by one spouse, since the signature of both will be required for any disposal. However, it is not unknown for a third party, at the instigation of one spouse, to impersonate a spouse whose participation is required, in which case it may be possible for the disposition to be set aside. However, sometimes a spouse will already have been involved in a prejudicial transaction. This area of law is already subject to certain principles pursuant to the decision in *Barclays Bank plc v O'Brien* [1994] 1 FLR 1, HL, which require the lender to show that a spouse who participated in such a transaction at the behest of the other spouse, in whom reliance and trust was placed in financial matters, fully understood the nature of the transaction and nevertheless entered into it willingly and knowingly. If the spouse was so reliant, and the transaction can be shown to be disadvantageous to that spouse, it can be set aside, but where undue influence or fraud can actually be proved then it will not be necessary to show that the transaction was actually disadvantageous to the spouse who was imposed upon. Usually the lender will need to show that effective independent legal advice was obtained by the deluded spouse if the transaction is to stand, but this whole area of law has recently been surveyed by the House of Lords in the early summer of 2001 and this has effected radical changes in the law since there is now a prescribed task list for both lender and legal adviser to the spouse offering security for the other spouse's debt.

JOINT TENANCIES

It may sometimes be beneficial to sever joint tenancies, depending on the particular circumstances, since joint tenants inherit outright from each other on the death of one of them. Joint tenancies must be distinguished from tenancies in common by the language of the conveyance, although this may be difficult for the legal adviser to ascertain in the absence of the deeds of a property which are usually with the mortgagee.

HOME IN THE SOLE NAME OF ONE SPOUSE

In this case it may be necessary or desirable to register matrimonial home rights pursuant to s 30 of the FLA 1996 to prevent any unilateral disposal of the main or only home. Other homes and assets in sole names can be protected by a pending land action or pursuant to s 37 of the MCA 1973. Alternatively, if such a registration is too late or inappropriate, there may be non-matrimonial home rights which may be claimed (ie, an *overriding or beneficial interest in land*, depending on whether the land is registered or unregistered, for both of which an equitable interest plus actual occupation is required).

STATUTORY RIGHT OF OCCUPATION UNDER THE FAMILY LAW ACT 1996

The MHA 1983 has been repealed but the protection replaced and extended pursuant to s 30 of the FLA 1996. This protection applies to all spouses, whether owners, non-owners or joint owners. These rights permit the court to determine, declare, enforce, restrict and terminate matrimonial home rights pursuant to wide powers, including excluding the owner spouse. The criteria which guides the court is to be found in s 33, which has much extended the previous criteria under the former legislation, including introducing a new balance of harm test which requires the court to grant an occupation order unless not to do so would inflict greater harm on the applicant than that occasioned to the respondent. The statutory rights normally terminate on death of the parties or dissolution of the marriage, but the court can direct that they should endure beyond decree absolute where appropriate. The court can also make consequential orders (eg, for payment of the property outgoings and use and care of furniture).

Matrimonial home rights need to be appropriately registered in the correct register for registered or unregistered land. Registration can be effected while a spouse is out of occupation, though that spouse must then seek leave of the court to enforce the rights.

BANKRUPTCY

The statutory right of occupation may be effective protection in bankruptcy, as the IA 1986 balances the interests of the creditors with those of the bankrupt's family. This normally means that sale can be held up for a year, but not usually longer, unless where there is a charging order in force the court can be persuaded to postpone the sale for compassionate reasons (eg, children at a crucial stage of education), or where the application under s 14 of the TOLATA 1996 is transferred to the Family Division and consolidated with ancillary relief in divorce proceedings. Where the debtor is actually bankrupt, there is usually nothing to be done to save the home from sale and appropriation of the proceeds, unless circumstances are such that the bankrupt's spouse, usually the wife, is able to sustain a claim against the trustee in bankruptcy (eg, by establishing an equitable interest which gives her a share of the sale proceeds, or obtaining a transfer in ancillary relief proceedings) which will vest the home in her as against the trustee in bankruptcy.

RIGHTS IN RENTED HOMES

The same matrimonial home rights apply in the case of rented homes. A spouse may pay rent on behalf of a spouse and it must be accepted, just as mortgage payments must be accepted by a mortgagee. A spouse may continue occupation for the other spouse for the purposes of security of tenure under the Rent Acts.

WHERE THE HOME CANNOT BE SAVED

Those on income support/jobseeker's allowance can obtain mortgage interest from the Benefits Agency, and mortgagees are usually interested in entering into compromises whereby the capital repayments are suspended and the debt is spread over a longer period, if the prospect is that the mortgagor will return to work and soon be able to resume full and reliable payment.

Failing this, recourse may have to be had to local authority housing pursuant to the Housing Act 1996. There are now statutory restrictions based on the concepts of priority need, and intentional and unintentional homelessness, and also local connection with the area of the authority to which application is made. Regardless of whether an applicant qualifies for local authority housing, which once obtained on a permanent basis is a secure tenure, the authority is obliged by the overriding duty pursuant to s 197 of the Act to assist homeless applicants to obtain other accommodation if such is available.

CHAPTER 21

OWNERSHIP OF THE HOME AND CONTENTS OUTSIDE DIVORCE PROCEEDINGS

21.1 INTRODUCTION

Normally precise ownership of property belonging to a married couple, whether that property is the home itself, chattels used in their home or other property in the nature of an investment, is of no particular interest in divorce, since pursuant to s 24 of the Matrimonial Causes Act (MCA) 1973 the court has a wide power to effect whatever adjustments it perceives to be necessary by making a property transfer order. However, there are occasions when proprietary rights are important, for example, because the parties are not *divorcing*, so that the s 24 jurisdiction is not being invoked. The jurisdiction will then be that of the Married Women's Property Act (MWPA) 1882 (s 17 as amended), which is confined to establishing *strict property rights*, allowing *no s 24 discretion*. Pursuant to the recent House of Lords decision in *White v White* [2000] 2 FLR 981, closer attention may also be paid to the ownership of assets even in divorce proceedings, when the s 24 discretion will naturally be used, because of their Lordships' concern that the judge's award should (a) proceed from 'fairness', and (b) be checked against the yardstick of equality. In *White*, the husband kept more of the assets which had been accumulated over a long marriage as his family had contributed more to start with and it was in fact Mrs White's insistence that regardless of the marriage relationship she was also commercially a partner in the parties' farming business that was at the root of the long litigation history. For further discussion of the impact of *White* on the law of ancillary relief, see Chapters 12 and 13.

21.2 APPLICANTS UNDER THE MARRIED WOMEN'S PROPERTY ACT 1882, s 17

The section *may* be used by the following:
- either party to a marriage *during* the marriage;
- either party to a marriage within three years after dissolution/annulment of the marriage (Matrimonial Proceedings and Property Act 1970); and
- engaged couples within three years of termination of engagement (Law Reform (Miscellaneous Provisions) Act 1970).

Cohabitants are not included unless they have been engaged. They will have to rely on the general jurisdiction of the court under the ordinary rules of property law for:
- an order declaring and enforcing a resulting or constructive trust;
- an order for sale under s 14 of the Trusts of Land and Appointment of Trustees Act (TOLATA) 1996 (see 21.2.1, below);
- an order for possession of real property; and
- injunctions and damages for wrongful interference with chattels.

Thus, s 17 is in practice used by:

(a) *existing spouses* in a non-divorce situation (eg, where for tax or bankruptcy purposes precise ownership of an asset must be established);

(b) *former* spouses who have remarried without remembering to apply under s 24 for a property adjustment order, or where one spouse has died and there is a title dispute; and

(c) *formerly* engaged couples (but not mere cohabitants) whose property rights have become intertwined in anticipation of a marriage which has not after all taken place.

21.2.1 Orders: declaration or order for sale

The section is very widely framed. It enables the court to:

(a) consider any question 'as to the title to or possession of property' and make a declaration of the parties' property rights; and

(b) make 'such order with respect to the property in dispute as it thinks fit' (eg, an order for sale).

This dual power to make both *declarations* and *consequential orders* provides very flexible remedies, and may be exercised over every type of property, both real and personal, and chattels.

Whether an order for sale *will* in fact be made will of course depend on the court's discretion. While land held jointly is always automatically subject to a trust of land so that application may be made under s 14 of the TOLATA 1996 for a sale (*Bull v Bull* [1955] 1 QB 234), whether a sale *will* in fact be ordered will depend on whether the underlying purpose of the trust of land (ie, the purpose for which the property was acquired, usually to provide a home for the parties and any children) is still subsisting (*Re Buchanan-Wollaston's Conveyance* [1939] Ch 738).

The new ss 12–15 of the TOLATA 1996 are not identical to the former s 30 of the Law of Property Act (LPA) 1925 so that pursuant to ss 12–15 both the intention of the settlor and/or the purpose of the trust can be considered in relation to the beneficiaries' wish to occupy the land. Thus most co-owning cohabitants should be able to apply for an occupation order under s 33 of the Family Law Act (FLA) 1996, as s 12 gives a general right to beneficiaries to occupy the land if that land is available for occupation.

In deciding whether the underlying reason for the trust still subsists, the court must apply the criteria in s 15(1), which basically look at the intention and purpose in setting up the trust, the interests of any creditors, or other circumstances and the interests of any children.

It is thus usually only necessary to look at the facts since cases tend to fall clearly into one category or the other: for example, in *Jones v Challenger* [1960] 1 WLR 1327; [1960] 1 All ER 785, where the husband was left alone in the matrimonial home, the underlying purpose had clearly come to an end. On the other hand, in *Bedson v Bedson* [1965] 3 All ER 307, the home in which the husband was again left alone was in fact a flat over a draper's shop where he conducted the business on which he depended for a living, and besides the fact that the wife had deserted him the property had been bought out of his life savings, so in that case the court did not order a sale. Nor did they do so in *Re Evers' Trust* [1980] 1 WLR 1327; [1980] 3 All ER 399, where the property was a cottage in joint names bought by a couple as a home for themselves and their various children. The woman paid more than the man and when they separated he wanted it sold. However, the property was still needed as a home and he had no need either of the money or of the accommodation as he was living with his mother.

The fact pattern of any case must therefore be examined to decide on the basis of common sense whether the underlying purpose does or does not subsist, and this will provide the correct signpost for further action.

However, in view of the wide application of the section, it is irrelevant if when the application is made the property has *already* been sold. Not only can a *declaration* still be made, although the court will not be able to reinforce it with an order for sale, by s 7 of the Matrimonial Causes (Property and Maintenance) Act 1958 *payment of the proceeds of sale* can be ordered, or a sale can still be ordered of *another* property which represents the proceeds of sale of the property already sold.

Despite *White*, which looks mainly at the basic discretionary divorce jurisdiction of s 25 of the MCA 1973, it is important to grasp the difference of approach under s 17 of the MWPA 1882 and s 24 of the MCA 1973. In s 17 proceedings, the court will ask 'Whose is this?'. In s 24 proceedings, the question will be 'To whom should this be given?' – even if first the court looks at the initial ownership so as to decide who brought the property into the pot to be distributed. Thus only legal and equitable principles of property law will be relevant under s 17, and the old cases which attempted to buttress the weaker financial position of the wife by giving credit towards a property interest for the wife's contribution (which is *relevant* under s 24, but *irrelevant* under s 17) are no longer followed.

Section 17 is therefore *purely procedural and declaratory*: in *Pettitt v Pettitt* [1970] AC 777; [1969] 2 WLR 966, the judgment refers to 'a purely procedural section', and in *Gissing v Gissing* [1971] AC 886; [1970] 3 WLR 255; [1970] 2 All ER 780, it was said that 'the ... principles are those of the English law of trusts'. More recently the law has been augmented by *Lloyds Bank v Rosset* [1990] 2 WLR 887; [1990] 1 All ER 111, which has reaffirmed strict property principles, in particular that where there is no express agreement only evidence of direct contributions to the purchase price will be sufficient to confer an interest. It is this decision which some commentators have stigmatised as setting back the position of women as property owners by 50 years, when earlier it appeared that a more liberal approach had developed.

However, it seems that the strict direct contributions rule is already being eroded, as in *Midland Bank plc v Cooke* [1995] 4 All ER 562; [1995] 2 FLR 915, CA, where it was held that, once the applicant had *established a beneficial interest*, the court was entitled to draw inferences as to the *proportions* in which the parties held the property, especially when as in that case there had been a long married relationship and it was not easy for the court to deduce what the strict beneficial interests actually were. Thus, if on the basis of the complete financial history of the matter, it could be concluded that the parties had in reality meant to share equally, they will not necessarily hold the property in shares directly proportional to their original contributions. The court will first look for evidence of agreement as to the proportions in which the property was apparently to be held, and if it discovers none, may then fall back on the maxim, 'equality is equity'. In the case of contemporary marriages, where the parties seldom preserve individual proprietary interests, but generally view the marriage as a partnership, this pragmatic approach probably no more than reflects the two positions, but cohabitants should not expect the court to treat them in the same way, as the married status was really the crucial element in the judge's decision in this case.

21.2.2 How to establish ownership for s 17

In the case of *land* the first thing to do will be to check the deeds, and then to take action under s 17 if appropriate. In the case of *personalty* there are certain rules which may assist (see below).

21.2.3 Checking the deeds

Any declaration of the legal or equitable title in the conveyance will be conclusive evidence of the shares unless:

(a) the conveyance can be set aside for fraud or mistake. In *Goodman v Gallant* [1986] 1 All ER 311, the wife had her former matrimonial home conveyed to herself and her new cohabitant as joint tenants, thus giving him the half share she had just obtained from her husband, since she already owned the other half share herself. However, when she and the cohabitant parted, she was not allowed to claim that she should have the whole house, since the *conveyance was conclusive* unless set aside or rectified. A similar situation arose in *Re Gorman* [1990] 2 FLR 284, where a transfer was to a married couple in equal shares, although the wife had contributed more of the money;

(b) s 37 of the Matrimonial Proceedings and Property Act 1970 (with regard to improvements to the property) operates to confer a share or bigger share; or

(c) there is a separate trust deed dealing with the beneficial interest.

Any of these exceptions will override the provisions of the conveyance.

Thus, the first task is to *inspect the deeds* and, if the spouse claiming an interest receives no support from the deeds, the next step will be to see if there is any chance of fraud or mistake. If the deeds are not specific, then a resulting or constructive trust may apply; failing this, proprietary estoppel or a contractual licence may help the spouse to establish the desired interest.

21.3 RESULTING OR CONSTRUCTIVE TRUSTS

The ordinary rules applicable to these forms of non-express trusts will therefore apply when a declaration is sought under this jurisdiction.

Any equitable interest must be *evidenced* in writing under s 53(1)(b) of the LPA 1925, and by s 53(1)(c) any *disposition* of such an interest must be *made in writing*. Since 1989 there is now a requirement that such an interest should also be created by contract in writing, containing all the terms expressly agreed, and signed by or on behalf of each party (Law of Property (Miscellaneous Provisions) Act (LP(MP)A) 1989, s 2). However, since spouses, cohabitants and other persons purchasing property together do not always regulate their affairs as they should, such a person seeking to establish an equitable interest may ask the court to declare a resulting, implied or constructive trust where necessary, since these three types of non-express trusts are specifically excepted from the strict rules of s 53 (LPA 1925, s 53(2); LP(MP)A 1989, s 2(5)).

21.3.1 Resulting trusts

Resulting trusts arise from the *action of the parties* plus *the court's giving effect to their presumed intentions*. This is the first type of trust to look for, since it will exist wherever there has been a *direct financial contribution by one party* (by paying all or part of the deposit/legal costs/mortgage instalments) and the *property is in the name of the other*.

To establish a resulting trust it is necessary to prove:

(a) a common intention between the parties that although one has the legal title the other has a beneficial interest; and

(b) that the owner of the beneficial interest has acted to his/her detriment based on the common intention.

The common intention usually gives rise to the inference that the beneficial interest is in proportion to the financial contributions, but *Midland Bank plc v Cooke* (see 21.2.1, above) may now affect this conclusion. *Re Rogers' Question* [1948] 1 All ER 328 is the simplest example of the operation of the doctrine. There the house was in the husband's name and he paid the £900 mortgage while the wife had contributed £100. She did not work or make any other contribution and it was held that the property belonged to the couple in the proportions one 10th to the wife and nine 10ths to the husband.

Subsequent case law has shown refinements of this doctrine: for example, where the wife has worked in a business from the profits of which the home is bought, she may be entitled to a bigger share than her original contribution on the basis that her work in the business, as well as running the home for both parties, has a money value too, as in *Meutzel v Meutzel* [1970] 1 WLR 188; [1970] 1 All ER 443 (the wife in this case obtained a one third share having contributed £650, while the husband paid the mortgage of £3,150). Where there is a *joint venture* the share may be a half as in *Falconer v Falconer* [1970] 3 All ER 449, where the parties bought a building plot, built a house together and the wife paid the housekeeping and the husband, the mortgage, and *Chapman v Chapman* [1969] 3 All ER 476, where the parties had each sunk all their resources into a similar project in a similar way and it was held that they must have acquired equal interests.

The recent case of *Midland Bank plc v Cooke* enabled Waite LJ to throw further light on this sometimes tricky task of quantifying a beneficial interest under a resulting trust. He said that when determining:

> ... (in the absence of express evidence of intention) what proportions the parties must be assumed to have intended for their beneficial ownership, the duty of the judge is to undertake a survey of the whole course of dealing between the parties relevant to the ownership and occupation of the property and their sharing of burdens and advantages. That scrutiny will not confine itself to the limited range of acts of direct contribution of the

sort that are needed to found a beneficial interest in the first place. It will take into consideration all conduct which throws light on the question what shares were intended. Only if that search proves inconclusive does the court fall back on the maxim 'equality is equity'.

This is a broader interpretation than that of *Lloyds Bank v Rosset* but not necessarily inconsistent with that case.

Even in these egalitarian days, it seems that it is still essential to watch out for the *presumption of advancement*, whereby payments made to or in the name of a wife by a husband (or a child by a parent) are found to be a gift to the wife or child whereas the reverse, where the transfer is *from* the wife or child, does not apply. Cases (such as *Pettitt*) which have considered this rule have doubted its continued existence in modern times, although in *Tinker v Tinker* [1970] 2 WLR 331; [1970] 1 All ER 540, where a husband conveyed a house into his wife's name to evade claims from creditors, it was held to belong to her absolutely.

There are very few modern cases on the point (probably because social change has meant that no one in practice regards it as a presumption any more), but *McGrath v Wallis* [1995] 2 FLR 114, CA has relatively recently enabled the point to be considered and to confirm how the presumption, if it still exists, may be rebutted by the facts. In that case a father and son bought a house, and 70% of the purchase price came from the sale of the father's previous house. The property was, however, conveyed into the son's sole name as the father was aged 63 and unemployed, and could not get a mortgage. The parties did have a declaration of trust prepared (indicating 80% of the interest in the property going to the father and 20% to the son), but it was never executed. When the father died intestate and his daughter claimed a share of the property, the son claimed it outright. The judge at first instance said the presumption had not been rebutted. On appeal, the Court of Appeal referred to *Pettitt*, commented that the presumption was a judicial instrument of last resort and that it could be rebutted by comparatively slender evidence and reversed the decision.

This decision should be useful in any situation where there clearly has been such a practical arrangement as was adopted in this case, and it will probably be rare that if the presumption can be said still to exist in any case it cannot be rebutted by a simple explanation of what happened in the particular circumstances.

21.3.2 Constructive trusts

Constructive trusts arise from the same *preconditions* as for the resulting trust:

- common intention; and
- acting to detriment.

However, unlike a resulting trust, constructive trusts arise by *operation of law* whereby a trust is implied because it would be *inequitable to allow the legal owner to claim the sole beneficial interest* rather than from the court giving effect to the presumed intention of the parties as in the case of resulting trusts.

A constructive trust usually arises where the financial contributions are *indirect* rather than *direct*, as they would be in the case of the resulting trust, so this type of trust should be looked for where direct contribution sufficient to establish a resulting trust is absent. The constructive trust is the usual way to establish an interest or an increased interest where the contributions are in *money's worth* rather than in actual cash, or are by way of *purchases* made with money which has not been spent on *direct contributions to the acquisition of the property*.

It is much more difficult to establish the necessary *common intention*, when this is in doubt, where contributions, whether in money or money's worth, are *indirect*, especially where the parties are not married.

However, where common intention is already established, and has been relied on by the non-owner to that person's detriment, such indirect contributions, whether in money or money's worth, will *not* be necessary and this principle is expressly not disturbed by *Lloyds Bank v Rosset*, above, *per* Lord Bridge.

The type of evidence showing common intention varies: the important thing is that it must show in one way or another that whether or not the parties were to share was *discussed at all*, and not necessarily the outcome of the discussion, since that may be deduced from the parties' subsequent actions. For example, in *Eves v Eves* [1975] 1 WLR 1338, [1975] 3 All ER 768, the fact that the man lied to the woman as to why her name was not on the title to the property (he said it was because she was under age 21) showed that the matter had been addressed, and in a similar case the lie was that it might prejudice the woman's forthcoming divorce proceedings. In *Re Densham* [1975] 1 WLR 1519; [1975] 3 All ER 725, where the wife's name was omitted from the conveyance, a letter instructing the solicitors showed that this was due to a misunderstanding, and in *Grant v Edwards* [1986] 3 WLR 114; [1986] 2 All ER 426; [1986] 1 FLR 87, the parties acting as though they were joint owners was enough to show the necessary common intention, in this case receiving a fire insurance payment into their joint account.

The only relevance of marriage in the operation of these principles of strict property law is that it helps to show common intention where that is in issue, since marriage is regarded as a partnership.

There are three methods of making *acceptable indirect contributions*:

(1) Payments enabling the other party to pay the mortgage. In *Fribrance v Fribrance* [1957] 1 All ER 357, the wife worked and paid the day to day expenses, and the husband saved all his earnings and paid the mortgage. Lord Denning commented that the ownership of family assets could not depend on such a chance division of tasks and resources. In *Hargreave v Newton* [1971] 1 WLR 1611; [1971] 3 All ER 866, it was expressly noted that in such a situation the husband could never have afforded to pay the mortgage if he had also had to meet the household bills.

The share will not necessarily be a *half* share in such circumstances, however, as it depends on what is fair in the circumstances. In *Hazell v Hazell* [1972] 1 WLR 301; [1972] 1 All ER 923, a wife got a one fifth share as while she worked like the former two wives, the husband in this case had had help from his parents in buying the house on mortgage, and the wife's contribution had been limited to the housekeeping and the children's clothes.

(2) Substantially improving the property. In *Cooke v Head* [1972] 1 WLR 518; [1972] 2 All ER 38, the man bought the plot, and arranged and paid the mortgage, and the woman

undertook a lot of rough work including demolition and cement mixing, and acquired a one third interest for the value of her labour. In *Eves v Eves*, the woman got a quarter share for similar labour. Section 37 of the Matrimonial Proceedings and Property Act 1970 gives a statutory right to a share for this type of work for *married parties only* – unmarried parties must continue to use the principle in *Cooke v Head*.

The contribution, in either money or money's worth, must be substantial, such as installing central heating or other major work, eg, a new kitchen or loft conversion (*Re Nicholson (Decd)* [1974] 1 WLR 476; [1974] 2 All ER 386), and not mere DIY as in *Pettitt* or housework as in *Button v Button* [1968] 1 WLR 457; [1968] 1 All ER 1064, nor buying furniture, since it must be an improvement to the actual property (*Gissing v Gissing* [1971] AC 886; [1970] 3 WLR 255; [1970] 2 All ER 780).

(3) Helping in the other party's business where there will be entitlement to a share of both the profits of the business and whatever is bought with them. In both *Re Cummins (Decd)* [1971] 3 WLR 580; [1971] 3 All ER 782; and *Nixon v Nixon* [1969] 1 WLR 1676; [1969] 3 All ER 1133, the wives got a half share, and in particular Mrs Nixon's unpaid work enabled the husband to buy the home.

The following are *not acceptable* as indirect contributions:

(a) Marriage as such, especially where the property was acquired prior to the parties' even meeting, though this would not matter for s 24 of the MCA 1973 (*Kowalczuk v Kowalczuk* [1973] 1 WLR 930; [1973] 2 All ER 1042).

(b) Money or money's worth where there is *no common intention*. In *Thomas v Fuller-Brown* [1988] 1 FLR 237, the man who went to live with a woman who owned a house was held to be a mere licensee doing the work on his own initiative when he obtained an improvement grant, spent the money on materials and fixed up her house, especially as when the relationship ended the woman then had to obtain an exclusion order to remove him from the property so she could return to live there.

(c) Insufficient contributions where there is also no common intention. *Allen v Allen* [1961] 3 All ER 385 showed that the mere fact that the wife works and contributes her earnings to the house does not raise a presumption of a beneficial interest unless there is agreement or common intention (though social change may make this harder and harder to sustain in the case of married couples because of the inference that such conduct must imply that there was a common intention). In *Burns v Burns* [1984] 2 WLR 582; [1984] 1 All ER 244, the parties were not actually married, which made establishing common intention virtually impossible, although the woman did as much as any fully committed wife but only bought furnishings rather than improving the actual property. The man gave evidence that the woman had never actually raised the matter of a share of the property in return for the earnings she had used in the household – indeed he had never thought of it, as he did not in fact need her contributions in order to service the mortgage, and even had the effrontery to add that if she had asked rather than assumed he would have put her name on the title!

Windeler v Whitehall [1990] 2 FLR 505 underlines the fact, established in the *Burns* case, where the relationship was 19 years and had produced two children, that where there is no common intention nor sufficient contribution, the length of the relationship is irrelevant, as that only counts under s 24 where the parties are divorcing, and are therefore married in the first place. 'Mrs' Windeler (again unmarried, like 'Mrs' Burns) had done ordinary housework, looked after the decorators and entertained for Mr Windeler, and in the absence of common intention this was not enough. In *Richards v Dove* [1974] 1 All ER 888, a loan of £150 and some trivial bills and no common intention were also not enough.

(d) No acting to detriment on the basis of common intention. In *Midland Bank plc v Dobson* [1986] 1 FLR 171, the wife could not show that she had used her earnings for household expenses other than for an utterly trivial amount, to which may be compared *Bernard v Josephs* [1982] 2 WLR 1052; [1982] 3 All ER 162; [1983] 4 FLR 178, where the unmarried couple contributed unequally to the deposit but pooled their earnings and worked together on the house, which led the court to decide that they owned the property in equal shares.

There is *no share nor increased share* available under strict property law from doing housework or looking after the family, as Mrs Burns (who was not a wife and had changed her name by deed poll) unhappily discovered, and this will *always* be the case whether the parties seeking to establish whether there is or is not a constructive trust are married or not, since credit for such domestic duties is only available under s 24 of the MCA 1973. Moreover, when establishing the precise *share* which a party should have, some regard will be paid to the proportions in which the parties contributed.

Help may be obtained in this respect from cases involving joint purchases by members of the family other than mere husband and wife transactions. Examples are *Sekhon v Alissa* [1989] 2 FLR 94; and *Passee v Passee* [1988] 1 FLR 263. *Sekhon v Alissa* was a complex mother and daughter purchase, in which the daughter variously tried to pass off the mother's contribution as a gift or loan, and the court identified the necessary common intention and worked out a fair division of the value of the property acquired. In *Passee*, the purchase was made by a man, contributed to by his aunt and her daughter, and then supported by renting part of the property to other relatives. Again the court unravelled the *types* of transaction, establishing which relatives were paying rent and which contributing to the acquisition of the property by making *direct capital contributions* (rejecting the man's claim that those were loans) and came up with a fair division of the equity interests.

It should, however, always be remembered that a loan can be sufficient to give a beneficial interest, if it is *interest free* and there are no repayments as in the case of the woman's loan in *Risch v McFee* [1991] 1 FLR 105, which eventually played a part in obtaining a beneficial interest for her.

21.4 ALTERNATIVES TO A CONSTRUCTIVE TRUST

If it is impossible to establish even a constructive trust, the next stage is to look for evidence of two alternative legal relationships, either of which may assist cohabitants and mistresses, as well as wives, to establish useful rights:

- a contractual licence; or
- proprietary estoppel.

21.4.1 Contractual licence

A contractual licence is a contract like any other and requires:

- a legally binding relationship; and
- consideration.

It will not usually confer property rights other than of occupation, but will enable a wife, cohabitant or mistress to stay when the owner demands that they leave a property. For example, in *Tanner v Tanner* [1975] 1 WLR 1346; [1975] 3 All ER 776, there was only ever a 'visiting relationship' and no cohabitation, but a property was acquired for the woman to live in, whereupon she gave up her own rent controlled flat. When the man asked her to leave the house subsequently acquired for her and their twins to live in, she was held to have a contractual licence entitling her to damages for breach, and she was allowed to remain in the home until the children had finished their education or other suitable change of circumstances. Similarly in *Hardwick v Johnson* [1978] 1 WLR 683; [1978] 2 All ER 935, a wife was entitled when the marriage broke up to stay in a home rented from the husband's mother (but on which they had not been paying rent as they were short of money) as there was a contractual licence.

However, if there has never been a legal relationship this will not work. In *Horrocks v Foray* [1976] 1 WLR 230; [1976] 1 All ER 737, there was a relationship of 17 years, including the birth of a child, but when the man was killed in a road accident, the wife successfully sought possession from the mistress as the court could find no consideration and identified the man's generous provision for the woman as going beyond any possible contract. Similarly in *Coombes v Smith* [1987] 1 FLR 352, the woman was unable to show any consideration as she had left her previous marriage because it was unhappy (not for the benefit of the man) and left her job because she was pregnant (albeit by the man) so when the relationship ended she had to leave the property he had provided.

Where there *is* a contractual licence, there is no need to establish *detriment* (though if this exists it may be the required consideration), since the point of a contractual licence is that once existing it *cannot be revoked*.

21.4.2 Proprietary estoppel

Proprietary estoppel is a very useful remedy, especially as its very nature is that it is *flexible*. To establish proprietory estoppel one party must act to his or her detriment in the belief, encouraged by the other party, that this will result in some right being given over a property belonging to that other party; this right sometimes affects only the promisor, but sometimes binds third parties as well. There is no need to establish common intention, but only that the claimant has been misled. It is similar to a constructive trust, but different in that if the conditions are satisfied:

(a) the legal owner will be *estopped* from relying on an owner's strict legal rights; and

(b) the remedy will be flexible, in that it will be appropriate to the type of right the person misled thought he or she was acquiring.

Thus, there will not always be a conveyance of the freehold – some lesser remedy, such as a life interest, may be more suitable.

The most recent case in which the doctrine was exhaustively re-examined was that of *Re Basham* [1986] 1 WLR 1498, where the variety of situations in which it could apply was reviewed and the flexibility of the remedy was confirmed. Leading cases include *Pascoe v Turner* [1979] 2 All ER 945, where a conveyance was ordered to a housekeeper who had developed a relationship with her employer, but had refused his proposal and they had not married. She had settled in a house which he had given her for her life, together with its contents. Understandably she did not want to leave when their relationship ended, as she had spent a substantial part of her life savings on improving it. He was not allowed to take the house back and the court said only a conveyance would protect her adequately.

However, in *Greaseley v Cooke* [1980] 1 WLR 1306; [1980] 3 All ER 710, mere occupation was all that was wanted by the maid who had been promised that in lieu of wages she could remain for life in her employers' home, and this she got, despite the fact that her occupation (living with the family) was not exclusive. Similarly, in *Maharaj v Chand* [1986] 3 All ER 107, where a man and a woman lived together and the man provided a house for her and her children which he assured her would be a permanent home, she was allowed to stay when their relationship broke up as she had given up her own flat in reliance on his promise, and also used her earnings for household expenses, and the children needed a home until they were grown up.

Sometimes, proprietary estoppel appears in family purchases of property across the generations and the fact that this will create rights can cause particular ill feeling where step relationships are concerned. Such was the case in *Jones v Jones* [1977] 2 All ER 232, where a man bought a house near his own for his son and invited his son to move there, which the son did, giving up his job and his own house to do so. He paid the rates and did work on the house but he never paid rent, and when the father died his widow, the son's stepmother, failed in her attempt to take the house back as the father had represented that the son should have it for life.

Coombes v Smith had no more success as a case of proprietary estoppel than as a constructive trust, because the man had made no *representations* nor *promised the woman she should stay*.

On the other hand, the promise that a woman may remain 'for life' sometimes has strange results, as in *Ungarian v Lesnoff* [1990] 2 FLR 299, where the woman was Polish and had given up her accommodation in Poland and come to England to live with a man whom she did not marry. When he bought a house in his name for her and her children to live in and she and her two sons did substantial work on it, with materials bought by him, he did not succeed in turning her out at the end of their relationship because of what he had said. She could not establish either an outright gift or a constructive trust, as a result of which the court said if she was to have a life interest it must be as a tenant for life under the Settled Land Act 1925, entitling her to a vesting deed and all the incidents of that status.

21.5 PERSONALTY

Disputes over property other than the home tend to fall into four categories:

- chattels generally;
- housekeeping allowances;
- joint bank accounts; or
- wedding presents.

21.5.1 Chattels

The general category of chattels may be anything from cars to kitchen tables, and encompasses the whole range of utilitarian items which a family needs to cope with life, but might equally include valuable works of art, family jewellery or other heirlooms, and all sorts of property the ownership and use of which is taken completely for granted until the parties split up, whether or not they are divorcing, and for the first time it is therefore necessary to decide where that item shall be kept and used.

Chattels generally, whether in the utilitarian or luxury or investment categories, can always be transferred by s 24 of the MCA 1973 in a divorce situation, if their ownership is certain and it is desired to change it. Where their ownership is *not certain* and the argument must be resolved (eg, because of bankruptcy, inheritance or one of the other reasons for which precise ownership may need to be known), s 17 of the MWPA 1882 is available for the purpose exactly as in the case of real property. If there is no other way of resolving the matter, the court can order a sale.

There are special rules in the case of engaged couples. Engagement rings are presumed to be an absolute gift (Law Reform (Miscellaneous Provisions) Act 1970), but engagement presents from *third parties* are presumed to be given conditionally on the marriage taking place. However, engagement presents *between the parties* may be *either* an absolute gift if not related to the actual or planned life together *or* conditional on the marriage taking place. It is irrelevant who terminates the engagement (s 3(1) of the 1970 Act).

21.5.2 Housekeeping

Section 1 of the Married Women's Property Act 1964 provides that such allowances made by the husband to the wife for the expenses of housekeeping etc belong to the parties equally, as does anything bought with them.

In *Tymosczuck v Tymosczuck* (1964) 108 SJ 656, it was considered that mortgage repayments were not within the Act, since an allowance to pay them was not for 'the expenses of the matrimonial home or similar purposes', but a later case queried, *obiter*, whether this was in fact a logical interpretation of the Act.

21.5.3 Joint bank accounts

Ownership of funds in joint bank accounts depends on the intentions of the parties. As in other cases where *intention* is relevant, social trends may influence what the parties' intentions are thought to be likely to be. Probably now that marriage is considered an equal partnership, such accounts are generally regarded by spouses as 'our money' whereas in the past the man tended to buy investments and set up savings accounts in his sole name in order to provide for the two spouses, just as until the early 1960s the matrimonial home tended to be in the name of the husband, regardless of whether the wife had contributed. It is difficult to say when this system, which had its roots in middle class life in leafy suburbs before the Second World War, came to an end and when it became more normal for married couples to own their home together, but the 1960s, which is usually blamed for everything controversial, was probably in this instance the watershed, the era when we allegedly 'never had it so good' and young married couples began to be able to amass money and property.

There are therefore not many cases which help in deciding the ownership of money in bank accounts, since many of them are opened for pure convenience so that one party may pay certain bills and there is no intention to make a gift of the money in the account to the spouse who writes the cheques on it. However, if all else fails in deciding the intentions of the payer and payee, and the account is in joint names, the spouses will own both the money in the account and anything bought out of it jointly on the basis that equality is equity, unless perhaps where the account is regarded as a joint purse any items *bought* with the funds in that account are of a personal nature (eg, the wife is not likely to want Saville Row suits made to measure for the husband and the husband will probably not want to lay claim to Janet Reger knickers, though he might want to bid for half a Villeroy and Boch dinner service), and similarly there are likely to be joint claims in the case of any purchase which was in the nature of an investment, such as an antique or *objet d'art* or a monetary investment such as shares in a privatised industry.

These principles have to be applied to the facts of actual cases when they arise. In *Jones v Maynard* [1951] 1 All ER 802, there was a joint account which was fed by the husband's earnings and various funds paid in by the wife. The husband paid in more than the wife. There was no evidence of their intentions but it did seem that they used it as a common savings account. The husband normally took out money and invested it, in his sole name, as did the wife in hers, but to a lesser extent. When they divorced it was held to be a joint account and the investments were joint investments, being an extension of the savings from which they were bought. On the other hand, in *Re Bishop (Decd)* [1965] 2 WLR 188; [1965] 1 All ER 249, the investments bought in this way with money from a joint account were each held to belong to the spouse who had bought them, on the basis that the withdrawals of cash had been made in each case with the *presumed authority of the other* and to spend as the parties chose. However, the remaining money in the account belonged to the wife on the basis that she was the surviving joint tenant and so took by survivorship as is normal in such cases.

The presumption of advancement, whereby husband to wife gifts are the wife's and wife to husband gifts are still the wife's (on the basis that he intends to benefit her but she does not intend to benefit him), probably has no place in modern life. It was considered in *Re Figgis (Decd)* [1968] 2 WLR 1173; [1968] 1 All ER 999, where a husband paid his salary into a joint account and the money was presumed to belong to the spouses equally. However, in *Heseltine v Heseltine* [1971] 1 WLR 342; [1971] 1 All ER 952, the account was held to be for convenience only where the 'gift' was from the wife to the husband, and both the money in the account and the assets bought with it were held to belong to the wife alone.

In contemporary contexts, it will therefore be necessary to look carefully at the circumstances of each case. *If* there is still any presumption of advancement, which works in the case of parent to child gifts as well as in the case of those in a husband to wife direction, this can relatively easily be rebutted by facts showing a credible explanation for the property being in the 'donee's' name, as in *McGrath v Wallis* [1995] 2 FLR 114, CA, where a property was shown to be in the son's name although the father put up much of the money because the father was in his 60s and unemployed and could not get a mortgage, whereas the son was a credible mortgagee. Social conditions have changed so much that whereas such an arrangement might once have been interpreted as conferring a gift, it is now a common situation that families buy property together and by no means the case that parents (or husbands) will necessarily be in a position to give their children (or wives) handouts, so that the facts will usually dictate some other transaction.

21.5.4 Wedding presents

Wedding presents are usually presumed to belong to the party whose relatives or friends gave them, *not* to *both* parties, although it can also depend on the intention of the donor, if that was specifically different.

The leading case is *Samson v Samson* [1960] 1 All ER 653, where it was established that wedding presents do not necessarily belong to both parties. However, in *Kilner v Kilner* [1939] 3 All ER 957, where the gift was £1,000 from the bride's father, it was held to belong to both parties, although that may have been inevitable since the cheque was paid into a joint account the funds in which the couple had doubtless decided to use for joint purposes.

21.6 MARRIED WOMEN'S PROPERTY ACT 1882, s 17 OR THE MATRIMONIAL CAUSES ACT 1973, s 24?

The MCA 1973 will *always* apply on divorce, since it is not possible to oust the jurisdiction of the court under s 24. The object of s 24 is to give the court a wide discretion in regulating and reorganising all financial and property arrangements between the parties and their children where necessary. Thus the court will resist any attempt to evade their powers in this respect, such as by attempting to use the MWPA 1882 or s 14 of the TOLATA 1996. In *Williams v Williams* [1976] 3 WLR 494; [1977] 1 All ER 28, an attempt to make an application in the Chancery Division under s 30 of the LPA 1925 when divorce proceedings were pending was transferred to the Family Division, since it was obviously within their remit.

While the court may look at who brought what into the marriage, and act on that information (as in *White* mentioned above), such ownership information is not usually of central importance in the divorce jurisdiction since where resources exceed needs dispersal of what may loosely be termed the 'matrimonial assets' depends on 'fairness' checked against the 'yardstick of equality' overall. Where resources do not exceed needs it will still, in the discretionary ancillary relief jurisdiction of English law, be impossible to preserve individual ownership of assets, since the court will then use whatever assets are necessary, regardless of which spouse owns them, to do practical justice. However, where possible they may decide that previous ownership or more substantial contribution to acquisition suggests a deferred settlement, such as a *Mesher* order, rather than as might previously have happened in an outright transfer, since this would do greater justice to the spouse out of occupation of the home, usually the husband, by preserving his share of the capital locked up in it for distribution when the children are grown up and/or the wife is able to be housed in another way. This may therefore spell the end of what Thorpe LJ has graphically described as not a 'clean break' *penalising* the husband, but a 'clean getaway' *benefiting* him, since he usually leaves the marriage and the matrimonial home with his earning capacity intact, even if he has had to part with some substantial capital. On the other hand, the wife who remains in the home with the millstone of the children is generally handicapped by caring for them, while the husband is usually able to start again, by saving a deposit and paying a mortgage from his salary to get quickly back on the property ladder, unencumbered with the time consuming responsibilities of children.

It should always be borne in mind that the approach of the two statutes could not be more different:

(1) The MWPA 1882 looks *back* to how property rights arose, while s 24 of the MCA 1973 looks *forward* to needs and resources.

(2) The MWPA 1882 is purely procedural and declaratory, while the MCA 1973 gives the court unfettered discretion within the s 25 considerations.

(3) The MWPA 1882 declares and gives effect to existing rights, while the MCA 1973 alters them.

(4) The MWPA 1882 considers conduct irrelevant, while the MCA 1973 considers conduct occasionally relevant.

(5) The MWPA 1882 considers children's interests generally irrelevant, while the MCA 1973 gives first consideration to children.

(6) The MWPA 1882 considers conjugal services irrelevant, while the MCA 1973 considers such contributions important.

OWNERSHIP OF THE HOME AND CONTENTS OUTSIDE DIVORCE PROCEEDINGS

RELEVANCE OF PRECISE PROPERTY RIGHTS

For divorce purposes, it is not normally necessary to know to whom a married couple's assets belong in law, since s 24 of the MCA 1973 operates on the basis of a broad discretion to rearrange property ownership as appears appropriate to the court so as to do justice in the case. Following *White v White* [2000] 2 FLR 981 in the House of Lords, tracing of ownership may be more relevant in future, as where there are assets surplus to needs judges are to check their awards against the yardstick of equality. Where ownership is relevant either because the parties are not divorcing or for other reasons, s 17 of the MWPA 1882 may be used to determine proprietary interests. This is a procedural section and does not alter such interests, but only provides a machinery to declare them.

APPLICANTS AND ORDERS

Existing and former spouses and formerly engaged couples can use s 17. Cohabitants cannot unless they have also been engaged to be married. Cohabitants must rely on the general jurisdiction of the court under the ordinary law of property to obtain relief (eg, an order for sale under s 14 of the TOLATA 1996, an order declaring and enforcing a trust, a possession order or an injunction). The jurisdiction is very wide and the court may consider and make a declaration on any question concerning property and make any consequential order it thinks fit (eg, an order for sale). Orders may also be made in respect of the proceeds if a property has been sold. Orders for sale usually depend on the purpose for the trust having come to an end, for example, a trust of land intended to house the spouses and their children where the marriage has come to an end and the children have grown up.

ESTABLISHING OWNERSHIP FOR s 17

This usually means checking the deeds, in which any express declaration will be final. For example, a gift of half a share in a house so that the parties hold as joint tenants will usually conclusively mean that unless there is fraud or other reason to set aside, such as mistake.

RESULTING AND CONSTRUCTIVE TRUSTS

If money has been paid and the property taken in the name of another, there will usually be a resulting trust, which arises from the court's giving effect to the presumed intention of the parties based on their actions. Common intention will need to be proved (ie, that though one paid the money it was intended that the property should be held the in the other's name), and that the payer has acted to detriment based on the common intention (ie, paid the money on the understanding in question). Resulting trusts therefore require direct contributions.

This may mean that in a marriage a wife will have a beneficial interest in either or both the home and/or business, and that where there is a joint venture the shares may be half and half. Sometimes, once a beneficial interest is established, a court will look at the whole financial history of a marriage or other relationship so as to deduce what the parties should be presumed to have intended, and if unable to deduce an answer with accuracy may rely on the maxim that 'equality is equity'.

It is still necessary to watch out for the presumption of advancement in gifts from husband to wife and parent to child, despite their likely contemporary obsolescence.

The alternative possibility is to establish a constructive trust, which arises from the same preconditions as a resulting trust but on the basis of the operation of law to the effect that it would be inequitable to allow the legal owner to claim the whole (sole) beneficial interest in the particular circumstances. 'Indirect' contributions are generally of money or money's worth but made for collateral purposes (as if direct a resulting trust could be claimed). It is more difficult to establish common intention for a constructive trust, therefore, especially if the parties are not married. Acceptable indirect contributions include payments enabling the other party to pay the mortgage, substantially improving the real property and/or helping in the other party's business. Insufficient indirect contributions include marriage as such, money or money's worth in the absence of common intention, insufficient contributions, or no acting to detriment.

ALTERNATIVES TO A CONSTRUCTIVE TRUST

Contractual licence (a legally binding relationship and consideration) or the flexible remedy of proprietary estoppel may establish some remedy if a constructive trust is not made out. Proprietary estoppel enables the remedy to be matched to what the applicant expected, and was not disabused of that expectation by the respondent.

PERSONALTY

Such disputes usually involve chattels, including wedding presents, housekeeping and/or joint bank accounts. Chattels may be the subject of a s 17 declaration as much as realty, or may be transferred under s 24 of the MCA 1973 in a divorce situation.

Housekeeping accounts are governed by s 1 of the MWPA 1964 and belong to both spouses (as do purchases made from those accounts) when the allowance is provided by the husband for the wife to defray household expenses, but do not cover mortgage repayments, though this is thought to be an illogical interpretation of the Act. The ownership of funds in joint bank accounts depends on the intentions of the parties.

Wedding presents belong to the spouse whose relations or friends gave them, unless a contrary intention appears (eg, by express gift to both).

PART IV

REFORM OF THE LAW OF DIVORCE, SEPARATION ON MARRIAGE BREAKDOWN AND ANCILLARY RELIEF

DOMESTIC PARTNERSHIP BREAKDOWN
IN THE 21ST CENTURY

22.1 INTRODUCTION

Reform of the law of divorce has been discussed almost since the Matrimonial Causes Act (MCA) 1973 consolidated the Divorce Reform Act 1969 and the Matrimonial Proceedings and Property Act 1970. That bout of reform, it was said, had been insufficient to achieve a civilised framework for divorce in a contemporary society where, in the opinion of both public and lawyers (ie, both academics and practitioners), there ought to be a non-contentious means of dissolving marriages without requiring the parties to make allegations against each other and without requiring the periods of separation in the MCA 1973 for either divorce by consent or on the basis that the parties had lived apart for so long that the marriage must be dead and should be recognised as such.

Over time this argument was widened to take in the philosophy that there should be support for the family and commitment to marriage as the central core of the fabric of society; and also on the basis of an objection to the large amounts of public money spent in fighting the financial relief and child matters linked to divorce under the MCA 1973 with the assistance of demand driven legal aid.

As a result, by the time the Law Commission produced its two carefully thought out papers (*Looking to the Future: Mediation and the Ground for Divorce*, Law Com 192, Cm 2424, 1990; and *Domestic Violence and Occupation of the Family Home*, Law Com 207, 1992) the focus was as much on how to cut down the appalling divorce figures (the worst in Europe) and save money on divorces overall, as on the allegedly core philosophies. At the time that he introduced the Family Homes and Domestic Violence Bill, annexed to Law Com 207, in 1995 and the Family Law Bill in 1996, Lord Mackay, the then Lord Chancellor, was already repeatedly warning that legal aid could not remain an open cheque and must become cash limited and that other ways must be found to effect divorces more cheaply.

Thus, the Family Law Act (FLA) 1996 was eventually passed, but not without extensive savaging in Parliament and an earlier expensive skirmish when the Domestic Violence Bill (like its predecessor, the Domestic Violence and Matrimonial Proceedings Act 1976, quickly abbreviated to the 'Domestic Violence Bill') had to be withdrawn and recast as Pt IV of the FLA 1996, due to a misconceived campaign by the *Daily Mail*. This was because journalists had misunderstood the import of the harmonisation of the law merely to protect both cohabitants and spouses from domestic violence, and thought it was a sinister campaign to abolish the distinction between married and unmarried relationships, to the detriment of property owners who allowed short term cohabitational relationships to develop, based in their homes which they then thought they might be at risk of losing permanently. The ensuing campaign both inside and outside Parliament inevitably forced clearer distinctions between married and unmarried parties, regardless of the length of the relationships and the varying levels of commitment that might exist between those parties, and has not helped the cause of rational thought about the principles underpinning genuine family relationships, regardless of whether those involved traditional marriage or not.

22.1.1 What the Family Law Act 1996 set out to do

The Act was intended not only to change the basis for divorce and legal separation and the procedure for obtaining them, but also to change the whole approach to divorce and marriage, to bring the law of divorce closer to the philosophy of the Children Act (CA) 1989 and only *incidentally* (it was said, though cynics never believed it) to change the procedure and to save the galloping costs of both private and public funding of proceedings.

This was to be achieved in four ways:

(a) by enacting s 1, which embodied the alleged philosophy of the MCA 1973, but which was never stated in that Act (ie, to support marriage in general);

(b) failing that, by achieving relatively painless divorce for adults and children;

(c) by supporting relationships in the divorced family; and

(d) by controlling both domestic violence and escalating costs.

Section 1 was quickly brought into force, as was Pt IV which consolidated and clarified the law on domestic violence, although the remainder of the Act was shelved pending pilot schemes to try out and establish what were believed to be the best methods of moving into the new process, which was obviously essential before the new divorce law could be implemented. It was at this stage that the project foundered as far as a new divorce law was concerned, and when the Lord Chancellor discovered that the pilot schemes had mostly been unsuccessful and not liked by the public he announced in 2000 that the Act would not be implemented in its present form and in January 2001 that the parts not so far implemented would be repealed.

So far there is no word as to any replacement, but as the law of ancillary relief clearly also needs reforming, following the seminal case of *White v White* [2000] 2 FLR 981, HL, it may be that there will now be a fairly prolonged wait before a new Bill is presented, especially in view of the simultaneous calls for reform of the law of cohabitation, which seems rather nearer at present.

22.1.2 Divorce and separation under the Family Law Act 1996

The FLA 1996 envisaged five stages:

(1) a compulsory information meeting for the spouse initiating the divorce;

(2) a statement of marital breakdown (issued by that spouse or both jointly);

(3) a period of reflection and consideration, normally nine months, but longer if there were children or complications;

(4) settlement of arrangements for the future for both children and financial matters; and only then

(5) a divorce or separation order – one order only, not a decree *nisi* and decree absolute as now under the MCA 1973, and neither issued until the child and financial matters had been settled.

Regardless of the actual basis of the grant of a divorce proposed by the Act, which clearly caused doctrinal problems for some people, the bare bones of this new procedure (especially without all the inessential 'fiddly bits' which eventually doomed the entire process) would have overall delivered a far better divorce system than the present one, where (unless there are dire concerns which hold up the final decree) the children's future may still be in the hands of another judge when the decree absolute is obtained, and as a result spouses may also already be leaving their next marriage before all financial matters are settled in respect of the previous one!

It was envisaged that the FLA 1996 divorce process should be worked through and completed within a period of five years, or the parties would have to start again, but that some people might take the full five years due to the built in provisions for attempting reconciliation. It was further envisaged that the information meetings would be more cheaply conducted than by petitioners' obtaining public funding or paying privately to hear about the divorce process from a solicitor, that the information would be more effectively and independently imparted by information officers rather than by solicitors who hoped to be instructed to conduct the divorce, and that this might therefore turn some people back before actually issuing proceedings, but that, if it did not, this might still be achieved in the period for reflection and consideration.

Extra safeguards were built into the process for children in that no order could be made until their future was settled. This was said to be superior to the existing s 41 of the MCA 1973 (which everyone knows is something of a farce in view of the non-interventionist policy of the CA 1989, because many parents pretend that all is agreed until after the divorce, and then arguments break out about child issues which often have to be referred to the court at that later stage).

The FLA 1996 was also to take into account children's wishes in the same way as they are considered under the CA 1989 (since they are not at present considered at all under the MCA 1973) and in appropriate cases there was to be a 'no divorce' order if a new hardship bar was established. Moreover, religious objections (never successful under s 5 of the MCA 1973) were to be seriously considered under the hardship provisions, together with objections to divorce connected with the children (eg, that they did not want it).

It was also envisaged that one statement of marital breakdown could be used either for separation or divorce and that the parties could decide later, not only if they wished to go ahead with proceedings, but also whether they wanted to divorce or to be legally separated.

It was further envisaged that most of the divorce would be handled only by mediators, at less cost than lawyers, but that public funding should still then be available for the parties to obtain legal advice from their lawyers, and that they should be funded if necessary to use lawyers to process the legal documentation required to finalise the process. This would include, if the divorce or its ancillaries were ultimately contested, that there should be funding for such representation. There was to be a duty on mediators to refer parties to lawyers for advice on the law, complementing the duty on lawyers to refer parties to mediation.

22.1.3 What actually happened

This entire scheme unfortunately foundered on the misconception that the public would like the information meetings and would share the dislike of successive Lord Chancellors for the inflated legal aid bills and the concept that these were all caused by useless 'fat cat' lawyers. The public did not react as anticipated. It appeared that family solicitors had been right when they had said at the outset that the information meetings told the public nothing that a good Solicitors Family Law Association solicitor had not already been telling new clients for years. The public indeed told the researchers deployed by Professor Janet Walker of the University of Newcastle that 39% would go immediately to their lawyers rather than mediators as in the new system they would want their advice more, not less, and only 7% said they would be willing to do what the Lord Chancellor wanted, which was to mediate on issues relating to the divorce. This fall at the first fence meant inevitably the end of the Act, as without the first stage the rest could not (apparently) follow as planned – although it is hard to see why some immediate amendments could not have been made to the MCA 1973 to reflect the positive (and largely applauded) aspects of the new FLA 1996 which postponed the final decree until after all child and financial matters were settled. The current s 41 procedure does not sit well with either Art 8 of the European Convention on Human Rights, or with Art 3 of the UN Convention on the Rights of the Child in protecting children's welfare.

Such improvements could quite simply have been achieved by amending s 41 of the MCA 1973 (to hold up the final decree until child matters were settled), an amendment to s 5 of the MCA 1973 (to permit religious objections to divorce to be taken seriously) and a simple amendment to s 9 of the MCA 1973 (to postpone the grant of the final decree until appropriate ancillary relief was in place).

Instead, the Lord Chancellor implemented s 29 of the Act with a pilot scheme initially in selected areas. This meant that any person wanting public funding for divorce or child matters in a pilot scheme area had first to be assessed for suitability for mediation, and only if mediation was not suitable for the dispute or the parties would public funding be available. Despite criticisms of public funding related mediation, the Access to Justice Act (AJA) 1999 has entrenched the process envisaged by s 29 of the FLA 1996, and unless an applicant's case is covered by an exemption in all cases where public funding is needed, assessment for mediation services is mandatory.

Other minor implementations of certain sections of the Act have tinkered with the process in relation to the existing divorce law, in particular in relation to ancillary relief, which it is perhaps more urgent to address than the basis on or procedure under which divorce decrees are obtained under the MCA 1973. For example, an amendment to s 31 of the MCA 1973 now permits periodical payments orders to be varied by capitalisation into a lump sum, a sensible initiative in pursuit of the clean break which really remains the ideal in as many divorces as possible if there is to be a truly contemporary divorce law to address the serial monogamy which now appears to be the norm. However, statistics present an alarming picture of increasing divorce and decreasing marriage which suggests that the current overwhelming trend is towards cohabitation which, with care, can now be practised in much the same way as marriage and divorce but with less upheaval in the wallet. It may therefore be more urgent to look at the dissolution of both married and unmarried relationships into some consistency of approach, rather than to concentrate only on the minority relationships of marriage. Part IV of the FLA 1996 offers a successful precedent for such an approach (see Chapter 23).

22.2 THE FUTURE

This is anybody's guess. Critics (eg, Professor Cretney) famously said that the parties would never spend the period for reflection in that process, as they would already have decided on divorce by the time it was reached. Other critics said the extended periods to consider reconciliation would be manipulated by those not wishing to be divorced to bring the parties to the end of the five years, so they were timed out, as in an electronic game. Many people said it was unfair for a person to be divorced on a statement of marital breakdown with no chance to defend or to know what was the alleged fault or shortcoming which had generated the action (most of the *Hansard* reports of the parliamentary debate on the passage of the Bill record these doubts from far and wide). *No one* actually predicted that the public would vote not to shoot all the lawyers.

However, with the development of mediation and alternative dispute resolution generally, it may be that a reappraisal is what is really wanted in contemporary divorce law, and better integration of skilled mediation and traditional lawyering might keep down the costs and still afford the parties proper legal advice at a crucial time in their lives. What might best happen is a comprehensive reappraisal of the existing law with a view to retaining some recognition of breach of marital obligations as a basis for divorce, since in modern times marriage remains a contract of partnership which should be dissolvable either at will or for breach, and the Law Society has appeared in favour of the development of marriage contracts. Further, the outcry at the proposal for no fault divorce was deafening and, as Ruth Deech has pointed out, in *Divorce Dissent*, her 1994 paper for the Centre for Policy Studies, many of those US States which decided to opt for divorce by consent 30 odd years ago are now seeking to backtrack. It may therefore be that a comprehensive reform of the entire area of divorce law, including the fairly urgent issue of ancillary relief after *White* and the succeeding line of cases culminating most recently in *Lambert v Lambert* (2002) unreported, 14 November, CA is now essential alongside the proposed reforms of the legal effects of cohabitation. On any view, time will need to be taken to assess the public vote of no confidence in the FLA 1996.

It is fair to say that despite the negative reaction to information meetings in the research conducted by Professor Walker, the research into the experience of and attitude to mediation (conducted by Professor Gwynn Davis of the Department of Law of the University of Bristol) was on the whole positive as regards the principle: what the public seemed mostly to doubt was whether it would work in their case (a sort of family law version of the NIMBY approach to town and country planning applications!). It may therefore be that as mediation becomes better known and accepted in commercial and community disputes, it will become more acceptable in the family law context. In general terms the UK is far behind North America and Australia in the use of mediation as an integral part of the litigation process. Professor Davis' final research report, *Monitoring Publicly Funded Mediation* (Legal Services Commission, 2000), is available on the internet and has received extensive comment in [2001] Fam Law at 110, 186, 265 and 378. A summary is annexed to the Fourth Annual Report of the Advisory Board on Family Law.

DOMESTIC PARTNERSHIP BREAKDOWN IN THE 21ST CENTURY

FAMILY LAW ACT 1996

This Act was not welcomed by the public or the legal profession despite apparently careful research by the Law Commission. It appeared to founder on the dislike of the initial information meeting and the involvement of mediation, though a pilot scheme under s 29, now fully implemented by the AJA 1999, whereby parties are now assessed for suitability for mediation before public funding is granted, appears so far to be of limited success.

The divorce over time and no fault statement of marital breakdown appear to be disliked by the public and profession alike. Some alternative mix would seem necessary, perhaps based on the concept that modern marriage is a partnership contract. The Law Society has been in favour of the development of marriage contracts and formalisation of the law of cohabitation, and the urgent requirement to reform ancillary relief law at present may offer an opportunity to recast the whole area of the contemporary law of relationship breakdown.

PART V

DOMESTIC VIOLENCE

CHAPTER 23

THE REFORMED LAW OF DOMESTIC VIOLENCE

23.1 INTRODUCTION

This entire area of family law is now governed by Pt IV of the Family Law Act (FLA) 1996, which was implemented in the autumn of 1997, and repealed the former domestic violence specific law in its entirety. Although injunctions under the inherent jurisdiction of the court ancillary to other proceedings remain a possibility, now that there is a codified framework specifically to address violence and harassment within the family, neither such an ancillary order nor any of the other new statutory provisions designed to prevent and restrain such anti-social activity generally will usually be appropriate in a family context when the FLA 1996 has specifically provided for the purpose.

It is therefore *not* necessary, even for the academic student, to learn the earlier law in any detail, but such a student *will* need to have an overview of the repealed legislation in order to understand the beneficial effect of the codification effected by the FLA 1996.

In order, however, to understand fully how the codified law of domestic violence works, and *why* it operates as it does, it is essential to appreciate how the former piecemeal legislation came about, and why it thus needed codification around settled principles distilled from the sociological and legal developments of a quarter of a century.

The origin of domestic violence protection centred around the concept of a right to peaceful occupation of the home, at a time when increasing numbers of women (married and unmarried) were becoming joint owners with their husbands or cohabitants, but there were still substantial numbers who were not property owners at all. This in turn was linked to the rising rate of divorce and marriage breakdown and the shifting balance between marriage and cohabitation (the former decreasing steadily in popularity and the latter rising, initially as a form of 'trial marriage' and then as an alternative relationship in its own right, although in those days it was still fashionable to prefer marriage as the higher norm). Initially domestic violence protection was rooted in the concept of protecting the wife, whether she was a house owner or not, from being driven out of the home (often with the children) by means of successive Matrimonial Homes Acts, giving rights of occupation which could be invoked to remove violent husbands or to exclude them and allow the wife back in. Later, personal protection was added, and later still this was all extended to cohabitants (at that time illiterately referred to as 'cohabitees', which is the term that will be noted in those old cases which still have relevance to the modern law).

In these circumstances, it was not surprising that the eventual mass of 'bolt on' provisions needed codifying, the language bringing into line with contemporary conditions, and the codified law providing with new procedural uniformity, in tune with the present day approach to marriage and cohabitation as the two viable and virtually equally acceptable alternatives for family life. One change that particularly needed making by the FLA 1996 was to incorporate the Matrimonial Homes legislation and the domestic violence legislation into a single unified code, and to create separate rights of occupation for cohabitants (linking those to their property rights where such existed so as to create an alternative which did *not* leave the cohabitant without a property claim completely homeless, since it was easily identified as wrong that a woman without a marriage certificate should be necessarily worse off when thrown out of her home than she who had the certificate).

It should also be noted at this stage that *only* the three domestic violence specific statutory jurisdictions (under the Matrimonial Homes Act (MHA) 1983, Domestic Violence and Matrimonial Proceedings Act 1976 and Domestic Proceedings and Magistrates' Courts Act (DPMCA) 1978) have been repealed and that there may be cases where the facts indicate that the inherent jurisdiction of the Supreme Court to issue injunctive orders under the Supreme Court Act (SCA) 1981 remains more appropriate even where the FLA 1996 could be used, so that that court may still attach any protective injunction (now called simply an 'order') to any substantive suit before the Supreme Court. Clearly this inherent jurisdiction, formerly arising under common law, has also been statutory since the SCA 1981, and the county court, itself only a creature of statute, has a similar jurisdiction, originally under the County Courts Act 1984, and now pursuant to s 3 of the Courts and Legal Services Act 1990, and both courts will always use these flexibly to provide the best remedy in the particular case. Such orders may be granted in support of any legal or equitable right, and although the FLA scheme will be likely to serve most needs there may well be cases which do not come squarely within the statutory framework where an order ancillary to other civil proceedings will be necessary or desirable.

There remains, therefore, a choice of jurisdiction: where appropriate the inherent jurisdiction under the SCA 1981 *may* be used to latch an application for an injunction order onto an existing suit, or one begun for the purpose of obtaining the order, but in general terms the FLA 1996 is so comprehensive, especially in view of the large number of associated persons now identified by s 62 of that Act, that it is unusual to need another jurisdiction for obtaining either of the two available orders. Those orders are:

(a) a non-molestation order (which prohibits either particular behaviour or molestation generally, against the applicant or a relevant child (s 42(1) and (6)); or

(b) an occupation order (with a variety of possible terms) declaring existing rights in the family home or regulating its occupation and as mentioned above this is for present or previously married or cohabiting applicants alike.

The Act increases the range of categories of persons who can apply for these remedies, which are based on the concept of persons who are 'associated' with one another through family or domestic connections or by being parties to the same family proceedings. This is a new concept which did not exist before the FLA 1996 and has been the means of creating a coherent framework of persons who can be protected by non-molestation orders.

Regardless of which court in the triple tier of family courts actually grants the orders, only the two orders mentioned are used. Each court has the full range of identical powers provided by Pt IV (with a minor difference in the case of the Family Proceedings Court, which cannot decide an issue of title to land where that is relevant – not, however, likely to be a routine issue in their jurisdiction). Thus it is no longer necessary to distinguish between the 'non-molestation' and 'personal protection' or 'ouster' and 'exclusion' orders, nor to decide upon which court to apply to on the basis of that court's powers. Therefore, all these different terms which will be encountered in the old reports of domestic violence cases, the broader principles of which may still be relevant to the present law, can be disregarded.

Non-molestation orders are available to the entire class of associated persons mentioned in ss 62 and 63 of the Act.

In summary, occupation orders are available to current and former spouses and current former cohabitants, whether or not they have pre-existing rights in the property, and to other associated persons who have such pre-existing property rights.

23.2 RIGHTS OF OCCUPATION OF A *MATRIMONIAL* HOME

Because of the statutory right of occupation of the matrimonial home, which since 1967 has been protected under successive Matrimonial Homes Acts and is now incorporated into ss 30 and 31 of the FLA 1996 and protected under ss 36–38, married rights of occupation need to be looked at *first* before the law of domestic violence can be understood, because it is onto this concept that occupation rights for cohabitants (who by definition do not have matrimonial home rights!) were grafted, to create something 'similar' but sufficiently 'not the same' as to be politically correct at a time (in 1996) when there was still an indignant groundswell of public opinion in favour of the claim for a superior status of marriage. A thorough working knowledge of this legislation is therefore required for a successful grasp of domestic violence orders for both married and unmarried parties, since the FLA regime is dependent on distinctions between applicants who either have some *interest in a property* or have *matrimonial home rights*, which amount to much the same thing, and those who have neither a property interest nor such rights. While the MHA 1983 has been repealed, it has been substantially re-enacted as well as extended by Pt IV of the FLA 1996. Also, while this Act renames the married right of occupation, now called 'matrimonial home rights', the protection available continues much as before. Cynics say that *only* a link to an interest in property (always sacred in English law!) could have placed a cohabitant in a similar category to a married person in this context.

23.2.1 Matrimonial home rights

Obviously matrimonial home rights apply *only to spouses* and not to cohabitants (the word which has now replaced 'cohabitees' in the legislation) and are basically no different from the former statutory right to occupy the matrimonial home irrespective of which of the spouses is the legal owner, whether the claimant has an equitable interest or whether the parties own it jointly (FLA 1996, ss 30(1) and (9) and 31(1)). These rights may be enforced under s 33 pursuant to the criteria in s 33(6).

Matrimonial home rights still do not apply to houses other than the matrimonial home (such as holiday homes, although they do now affect a property which was *intended* to be a matrimonial home under s 33(1)(b)), a distinction from the former law. Nevertheless, where there is more than one possible house which could qualify as a matrimonial home, an applicant may – and must for the purposes of the application – choose only one to be the subject of that application.

The court may *regulate* matrimonial home rights as before, as follows:

(a) by enforcing, restricting or terminating those rights;

(b) by taking certain *criteria* into account (s 33(6)):

- the conduct of the spouses in relation to each other and otherwise;
- their respective housing needs and the financial resources of the parties;
- the housing needs of any children;
- any significant harm likely to be suffered by the parties or any relevant child on the basis of a new balance of harm test (s 33(6) and (7)) which in effect makes it mandatory for the court to make the order sought if the criteria for doing so are satisfied unless the respondent can show that the balance of harm test should go in his favour.

This last criterion *is* a substantially different provision from anything to be found in earlier MHAs of 1967 or 1983.

The statutory rights of occupation are now defined in s 30(2):

(a) if in occupation, the rights entitle the applicant spouse not to be evicted or excluded from the dwelling house or any part thereof by the other spouse save with leave of the court given by an order under s 33;

(b) if not in occupation, the rights entitle the applicant spouse with the leave of the court to enter and occupy the dwelling house (s 30(2)).

The court's power is wide and as before allows excluding the owning spouse.

Matrimonial home rights are an equitable charge binding on the owning spouse and third parties (s 34) and are still registrable (s 31) in the manner set out in 20.3.3, above, registration of the spouse's rights being actual notice to the purchaser (Law of Property Act 1925, s 198(1)), but the court can still determine the spouse's rights of occupation (FLA 1996, s 33(3)(e)). However, earlier decisions such as that in *Kashmir Kaur v Gill* [1988] Fam Law 110; [1988] 2 All ER 288, which oddly took into account the interests of a blind purchaser of the home from the husband on the basis that he would be prejudiced by the wife's rights, might now be decided differently under the much wider criteria of s 33(6). At the time Sir Denys Buckley (dissenting) said that he thought the decision wrong and that Parliament could not have meant a third party to take precedence over the spouse whose interests the legislation was intended to protect.

23.2.2 Additional orders on regulation of matrimonial home rights

It should be stressed that matrimonial home rights *exist* whether or not any order regulating them is applied for and that an order *may* be made regulating those rights completely independently of domestic violence, although domestic violence is the common cause of such an application. The fact that the right of occupation is a registrable property right can impact on ancillary relief even if no domestic violence order is sought.

The legislation also provides for ancillary orders which may be made if an order is applied for. This results in the applicant obtaining sole occupation of a home for the duration of the injunction order.

The other spouse may still be required to pay for outgoings (ie, the mortgage, insurance, council tax and water rates) and/or repairs to the home (s 40(1)(a)). The court can also grant the use of furniture, etc (s 40(1)(c)). Alternatively, the spouse in occupation receiving such an order can require a party to take care of such chattels (s 40(1)(d)). However, problems have been identified in relation to the enforcement of ancillary orders to pay the mortgage (see *Nwogbe v Nwogbe* [2000] 2 FLR 744). Basically, the payer cannot, apparently, be committed for contempt for failure to pay the ancillary orders, and as this is the ultimate sanction for breach of the occupation and non-molestation orders, the breach of such an ancillary order may be successfully committed without fear of incarceration.

A spouse entitled to occupy the matrimonial home may also pay the rent or the mortgage direct to the mortgagee or landlord, and the money must be accepted, as under the earlier legislation (s 30(3)). Moreover, such a spouse must be notified of mortgage enforcement proceedings and may be entitled to be made a party (s 56).

Matrimonial home rights in favour of a spouse not otherwise entitled to an interest in the property last until divorce or the death of either spouse (s 31(9)), unless the court makes use of s 33(5) to order otherwise (s 31(8)). This should always be remembered when dealing with the home in the context of ancillary relief on divorce as this will be relevant in every case where a spouse is still occupying the home, whether or not there are domestic violence issues.

23.3 DOMESTIC VIOLENCE INJUNCTIONS

These are now comprehensively catered for by Pt IV of the FLA 1996, although (apart from the inherent jurisdiction mentioned at 23.1, above) there is also a collateral statutory jurisdiction under the Protection from Harassment Act 1997. This is basically for cases outside the Act, having been created primarily to deal with 'stalkers', and is not appropriate unless the FLA 1996 is inapplicable, eg, because the parties do not come within any of the s 62 categories of 'associated persons'. There are two types of orders, as mentioned at 23.1, above, the least serious of which is the non-molestation order, which is therefore also the easiest to obtain.

23.3.1 Non-molestation orders (FLA 1996, s 42)

Despite the creation of the new class of 'associated persons', non-molestation orders are also the least complicated of the new orders. The reason for extending protection against molestation and violence to the larger class of associated persons (rather than as formerly to spouses and cohabitants only) was the recognition by the Law Commission that harassment and violence can occur in many types of relationship. While there is specific statutory protection against such tortious behaviour in the Protection from Harassment Act 1997, which now deals with most non-residential boyfriend-girlfriend situations not covered by the FLA 1996, it was thought appropriate when reforming the general law of domestic violence to provide injunctive protection for the whole family rather than simply those in a married or unmarried heterosexual relationship. For example, elderly people may need to be protected from abuse by members of the family with whom they are living and many women may need protection from violence at the hands of their teenage or adult sons. Engaged and formerly engaged couples are also included in the broad spectrum of associated persons.

23.3.2 Associated persons (FLA 1996, s 62)

'Associated persons' are defined by s 62(3) and the applicant for a non-molestation order must show that he or she is associated with the respondent, in that:

(1) they are or have been married to each other;

(2) they are cohabitants or former cohabitants;

(3) they live or have lived in the same household, otherwise than merely by reason of one of them being the other's employee, tenant, lodger or boarder;

(4) they are relatives;

(5) they have agreed to marry each other (whether or not that agreement has been terminated);

(6) in relation to any child, they are both persons falling within s 62(4), which provides that a person falls within its scope if he or she:

   (a) is a parent of the child; or

   (b) has or has had parental responsibility for the child; or

(7) they are parties to the same family proceedings other than proceedings under Pt IV of the FLA 1996.

'Cohabitants' are defined by s 62(1) as a man and a woman who, although not married to each other, are living together as husband and wife. 'Former cohabitants' is to be read accordingly, but the term does not include cohabitants who have subsequently married each other.

This means they must be of opposite sexes and have lived together as husband and wife, thus *excluding* homosexual relationships under this head, although the *Mendoza* case (see 1.1, above) may mean this will change.

Persons who 'live or have lived in the same household other than by reason of one of them being the other's employee, etc' comprise a new class of potential applicants, and would include persons living together who are neither spouses nor cohabitants nor related in any other way, thus *including* homosexual partnerships in this category.

23.3.3 Other essential definitions

A 'relative' is defined by s 63(1) as the father, mother, stepfather, stepmother, son, daughter, stepson, stepdaughter, grandfather, grandmother, grandson or granddaughter of a person or of that person's spouse or former spouse or the brother, sister, uncle, aunt, niece or nephew (whether of the full blood or of the half blood or by affinity) of that person or of that person's spouse or former spouse, and *includes* (in relation to a person who is living or has lived with another person as husband or wife) all these relationships which would have existed if the cohabitants in question had been married to each other.

It should be noted that this definition means that cohabitants and former cohabitants are *deemed* to have the same family relationships as if they had actually been married.

'Persons who have agreed to marry each other' are not specifically defined in s 63, but s 44(1) provides that written evidence must be available of such an engagement unless there has either been a gift of an engagement ring or a ceremony witnessed by one or more persons present for that purpose. Applications by such people must be made within three years of termination of the engagement (s 42(4)).

'Parental responsibility' has the same meaning as in the Children Act (CA) 1989.

'Family proceedings' are defined by s 62(3) to include any High Court proceedings in relation to children under its inherent jurisdiction (eg, wardship) and any proceedings under the MCA 1973, the DPMCA 1978 and the CA 1989.

The term 'relevant child' is comprehensively defined and means any child who is living with or might reasonably be expected to live with either party to the proceedings, any child in relation to whom an order under the CA 1989 (or the Adoption Act 1976) is in question in the proceedings, and any other child whose interests the court considers relevant.

'Harm' in relation to the balance of harm test (including where harm is applicable in relation to the grant of *ex parte* non-molestation orders under s 45: see 23.3.7, below) is defined by s 63(1) to include (for adults) ill treatment or impairment of health or (for those under 18) to include also impairment of development.

23.3.4 Obtaining a non-molestation order

By s 42(2), the court may make a *non-molestation* order either on the application of any associated person who can show qualification as such, or of its own volition if it considers that such an order should be made for the benefit of any party or any relevant child. Applications may be made either in the course of other proceedings or on a freestanding basis.

A child under 16 may apply for an order with leave of the court (s 42(1)) and such leave may be granted where the court is satisfied that the child has sufficient understanding to make such an application (s 42(2)). A child may also be separately represented in existing non-molestation proceedings started by others (s 64). Provision is also made by the Act for third parties (eg, the police or other agencies) to take proceedings on behalf of an associated person who is reluctant to apply for a non-molestation order personally (s 60). Orders may also be obtained *against* 'children' under 18, although there remain problems of enforcement as such a defendant could not be committed to prison for breach.

For procedure, see 23.5, below.

23.3.5 Scope of molestation

The FLA 1996 does not define 'molestation', which the Law Commission considered was a sufficiently well known concept long recognised by the courts. It is wider than violence and will usually encompass any form of harassing or pestering. There is a core body of case law which makes clear precisely what may fall within the ambit of 'harassing or pestering'. The following cases impart the general idea.

In *Vaughan v Vaughan* [1973] 1 WLR 1159; [1973] 3 All ER 449, a husband was a 'perfect nuisance', always making unwelcome visits to his wife from whom he was separated.

In *Horner v Horner* [1982] 2 WLR 914; [1982] 2 All ER 495, a husband made offensive telephone calls to his wife from whom he was separated.

Wooton v Wooton [1984] FLR 871 was a case where the behaviour in question was the result of epileptic fits, which shows that the conduct complained of can be involuntary rather than deliberate. More recently, this approach has been confirmed where the behaviour in question was induced by drugs (see *G v G (Occupation Order: Conduct)* [2000] 2 FLR 36).

Johnson v Walton [1990] 1 FLR 350 was more esoteric than most; this was a case of unwelcome publicity where embarrassing revelations about one of the parties was disclosed to the newspapers together with photographs, which brought down a plague of journalists on the unfortunate victim.

However, *C v C (Non-Molestation Order: Jurisdiction)* (1997) *The Independent*, 27 November made it clear that there is no non-molestation order available for the protection of privacy as such, and the *ex parte* order granted in that case (where revelations of conduct during married life were published some time after the marriage had been dissolved) was discharged on the basis that a 'higher degree of harassment' was required to invoke the protection of the statute.

23.3.6 The court's discretion

In deciding whether to exercise its powers to grant a non-molestation order, the court must have regard to all the circumstances including the need to secure the *health, safety and well being* of the applicant and/or any relevant child or, where the court decides to make the order of its own volition, the health, safety or well being of the associated person who the court decides should have the benefit of such an order (s 42(5)).

By s 63, 'health' is defined as including physical or mental health and would therefore appear to give the court a very wide discretion.

23.3.7 *Ex parte* orders (FLA 1996, s 45)

Such applications are no longer governed by case law (as prior to the FLA 1996) but by statutory provision in s 45. The court may now make such orders whenever it is just and convenient to do so (s 45(1)) and must determine whether that is the case in accordance with the guidelines set out in s 45(2), in that it must take into account all the circumstances of the case including whether:

(a) there is any risk of significant harm to the applicant or a relevant child attributable to the conduct of the respondent if the order is not made immediately;

(b) it is likely that the applicant will be deterred or prevented from pursuing the application if an order is not made immediately; and

(c) there is reason to believe that the respondent is aware of the proceedings, but is deliberately evading service, provided it is shown that the applicant or a relevant child will be seriously prejudiced by the delay involved:

- where the court is a magistrates' court, in effecting service of proceedings; or
- in any other case, in effecting substituted service.

The court must afford the respondent an opportunity to make representations as soon as just and convenient at a full hearing (s 45(3)) and any time which elapses between the initial *ex parte* order and the final order will be included in computing the duration of the final order; thus the final order is deemed to have commenced at the time the *ex parte* order was granted. Non-molestation orders are normally made for a specified period unless there are exceptional or unusual circumstances (*M v W (Non-Molestation Order: Duration)* [2000] 1 FLR 107), but the Court of Appeal has ruled that they *can* be made for an indefinite period, thus overruling Cazalet J in the above case who was of the view that a definite period was essential (see *Re B-J (Power of Arrest)* [2000] 2 FLR 443).

23.3.8 Undertakings (FLA 1996, s 46)

The court may always accept an undertaking instead of making an order (s 46(1)) and this is as enforceable as an order of the court (s 46(2)), ie, by applying for a warrant of arrest (s 47(8)). This is likely to remain the common means of settling domestic violence cases, although previously accepting such an undertaking was based on practice and not on statute. However, it will not be possible to accept an undertaking in lieu of making an order where a power of arrest would otherwise be attached (s 46(2), and see 23.3.9, below).

23.3.9 Power of arrest (FLA 1996, s 47)

By s 47(1), the court has a mandatory duty to attach a power of arrest to its order unless it is satisfied that in all the circumstances of the case the applicant or any relevant child will be adequately protected without it. This duty arises whenever it appears to the court that the respondent has used or threatened violence against the applicant or a relevant child (s 47(2)).

This is a significant departure from the previous practice where attaching a power of arrest was discretionary and only used if absolutely necessary. The new system may be especially harsh as it may now apply whatever the standing of 'associated persons', so might involve a very distantly associated person indeed. By s 47(3), the power of arrest may be attached to an *ex parte* non-molestation order provided s 47(2) applies.

Where a power of arrest is attached, the police may arrest the respondent without warrant if they have reasonable grounds for suspicion that the order has been breached (s 47(6)). This affords the applicant significantly greater protection than if a warrant of arrest must be applied for before such action can be taken (normally now the procedure replacing the former application to commit the respondent for contempt). Although the Act is silent on this point, it is assumed that the power of arrest will be attached only to those parts of the order dealing with violence and not to those prohibiting harassment or pestering.

Another significant change made by the FLA 1996 is that where a power of arrest is not initially attached, later application may be made for this to be done (s 47(8)).

Where the respondent is arrested, he or she will be brought before the court and may be remanded (s 47(10)), including for medical reports (s 48(1)). Where a respondent is remanded in custody, the court has the same powers as the magistrates under ss 128 and 129 of the Magistrates' Courts Act 1980.

As this power is more sweeping than its predecessor under the old law, it is perhaps useful that, when registered at a police station, the power of arrest must be accompanied by a statement on one of the newly designed forms produced for Pt IV proceedings setting out how the order was served or notified to the respondent.

A power of arrest on an order granted at an *inter partes* hearing should normally last for the same length of time as the order (*M v W* at 23.3.7, above), but can be for a lesser period if this would give the court flexibility to protect the victim while not restricting human rights more than necessary.

There is a discretion as to which parts of an order the power of arrest should be attached to (*Hale v Tanner* [2000] 1 WLR 237).

23.4 OCCUPATION ORDERS

Occupation orders have always been more difficult to obtain because it has always been accepted that it is a draconian act to turn a person out of his or her home. It is therefore usual always to ask for a non-molestation order, and to add an application for an occupation order if that is felt to be justified. It is rare in a case of domestic violence not to secure the former (especially as no actual *violence* is required: see 23.3.5, above) but an occupation order always requires more effort since the application of ss 33–38 is meticulously detailed.

The concept of associated persons is also relevant to occupation orders. However, application for an occupation order is slightly more complicated than that for non-molestation orders. This is because relief must be sought under the section of the FLA 1996 which is appropriate to the applicant and that in turn depends both upon the matrimonial status of the parties and on whether or not they have any property right in relation to the home of which occupation is sought. An occupation order can only be made in respect of a property which is or was an actual or intended home and never in relation to investment property (see ss 33(1)(b), 35(1)(c), 36(1)(c), 37(1)(a) and 38(1)(a)).

There are three types of potential *applicants*:

- entitled persons;
- non-entitled persons; and
- persons with matrimonial home rights (who are very similar to entitled persons).

The last of the three are those who used to have 'rights of occupation' under the MHA 1967 or the MHA 1983, these rights now being called 'matrimonial home rights' under Pt IV of the FLA 1996 and protected by ss 30 and 31 (see 23.2.1, above). Any of the associated persons identified in ss 62 and 63 may be respondents to occupation order applications.

23.4.1 Entitled and non-entitled persons

Entitled persons and *persons with matrimonial home rights* apply under s 33, while *non-entitled persons* must apply under one of ss 35–38:

- A *former spouse* with no existing right to occupy applies under s 35.
- A *cohabitant* or *former cohabitant* with no existing right to occupy applies under s 36.
- Where neither spouse is entitled to occupy application is under s 37.
- Where neither *cohabitant* is entitled to occupy application is under s 38.

The distinction between the different sections is important, since the wording of the respective sections is not identical, so that different conditions must be satisfied in the various different situations.

It should be noted that an *entitled* person can apply for a s 33 order against the entire wide class of associated persons identified in ss 62 and 63. Further, although normally matrimonial home rights only endure until decree absolute, the court has power to order that they shall continue in favour of a former spouse beyond that decree (s 30(5)). Thus some divorced spouses may be able to apply under s 33. If there has been no such order, a former spouse will apply under s 35 or 37 (see 23.4.4 and 23.4.6, below).

23.4.2 The court's powers under the Family Law Act 1996, s 33

(Ie, where the applicant has an estate or interest in land or matrimonial home rights.)

The court's powers where the parties are entitled are set out in s 33(3) and include:

(a) enforcing, restricting or terminating matrimonial home rights;

(b) prohibiting, suspending or restricting the exercise by either spouse of those rights to occupy the home or part of it;

(c) requiring either spouse to permit the exercise by the other of occupation rights;

(d) declaring the applicant's rights;

(e) requiring the respondent to leave the home or part of it; and

(f) excluding the respondent from a defined area around the home.

The fact that these powers are similar to those giving rights of occupation of a home to *married* people is no accident, since this section caters for: (1) spouses who own; (2) owners, married or not; and (3) spouses who are not owners but who by virtue of marriage have matrimonial home rights, which is entirely consistent with the history of this remedy (see 23.1, above).

23.4.3 The court's discretion under the Family Law Act 1996, s 33

New criteria to guide the court are introduced by s 33(6) (see 23.2.1, above). These criteria are:

(a) the conduct of the spouses in relation to each other and otherwise;

(b) the respective housing needs of the parties and any children and their respective financial resources;

(c) the likely effect of any order/lack of order on the health, safety or well being of the parties and any relevant child; and

(d) all the circumstances of the case.

The court must also consider whether, if the order is not made, any significant harm will be suffered by the applicant or a relevant child attributable to the conduct of the respondent, and in this case they must make an order unless the *balance of harm* test introduced by s 33(7) is in favour of the respondent and not the applicant.

These criteria are much wider than those in s 1(3) of the MHA 1983 which they replace, as s 33(6) includes a new guideline which requires the court to consider the likely effect of any order or of any decision of the court not to exercise its powers on the health, safety and well being of the parties or of any relevant child. Moreover, by s 33(7), this is to be considered on a *balance of harm* test and if harm attributable to the conduct of the respondent would be likely to be suffered by the applicant or a relevant child if the order is not made, the court should normally make the order unless that would lead to greater significant harm to the respondent or a relevant child. Thus this provision imposes a *mandatory* duty on the court which did not exist before, the effect of which is that, if the relevant conditions are satisfied and the respondent cannot show that the order should not be made, the court *must* make it.

It should be noted that these new criteria replacing s 1(3) of the MHA 1983 are exclusive to s 33 and are *not* repeated in relation to the other sections dealing with different classes of applicant – a significant departure from the pre-FLA 1996 law which used to use the same test (ie, that of s 1(3) of the MHA 1983 regardless of which jurisdiction was used by the various different applicants who at that time had to choose between different pathways to an order). Each section which provides a remedy under ss 35–38 has its own criteria which are repeated in that section. Broadly, the Act gives greater protection to spouses than to cohabitants.

With the addition of the balance of harm test, the new criteria clearly have some significant new elements, and it is debatable how much of the old case law on the former may still be helpful. In particular, children's interests are not only relevant but it may be necessary to balance the competing needs of different children (see, eg, *B v B (Occupation Order)* [1999] 1 FLR 715, where the comparison of relative harms meant the violent spouse remained in the home because of the interests of the child whose needs required this).

Recent case law (which has been sparse) suggests that an occupation order is still a draconian one to make: some harm or seriously anticipated harm to the applicant has to be shown before an order will be made at all and the balance of harm test must come out in the applicant's favour. For example, in *Chalmers v Johns* [1999] 1 FLR 392, 'considerable harm' was said to be required, as the order was for extreme cases only; in *Banks v Banks* [1999] 1 FLR 726, an order against the physically and verbally abusive mentally ill wife would have caused greater harm to her than to her husband if not made; and in *Re Y (Children: Occupation Order)* [2000] 2 FLR 470, CA, the order was said not to be for the ordinary tensions of divorce. Where children are concerned, schooling will generally be a critical factor. Contemporary decisions are confirming the earlier case law (as long ago established in, eg, *Summers v Summers* [1986] 1 FLR 343) (*Re Y*, above).

Some general principles derived from the earlier law therefore remain useful.

23.4.3.1 The parties' conduct

Elsworth v Elsworth [1978] 9 Fam 21 established that there must be some 'conduct' complained of which is good reason for the spouse wanting the injunction to seek it: here the wife left and refused to return until the husband moved out, but there was no identifiable reason for her objection to doing so and she did not get her injunction.

Two cases indicate that the parties may be made to share the property if it is large enough to divide on a temporary basis at least. *Myers v Myers* [1971] 1 WLR 404; [1971] 1 All ER 762 established that if the house is large enough so that the parties might be kept apart (and if they are relatively sensible and civilised and there is no violence), an injunction will not be granted merely because the situation is unpleasant and tense. *Phillips v Phillips* [1973] 1 WLR 615; [1973] 2 All ER 423, on the other hand, made it clear that this will not be the case if the premises are very small: here there was a council flat and the divorce had already been obtained. The wife said she and the son would become psychiatric invalids if the situation continued and there was medical evidence to this effect. The injunction was therefore granted.

Walker v Walker [1978] 1 WLR 533; [1978] 3 All ER 141 was a similar case where a clinically depressive illness could be proved and the injunction was again granted.

Summers v Summers [1986] 1 FLR 343 established that an order *cannot* be granted where it is not strictly necessary, for example, simply to give the parties a break in the *hope* that this will help towards a reconciliation, since this would not qualify as *necessary*. In this case the judge gave a two month exclusion order, as the parties were quarrelling loudly and upsetting the children, both being equally to blame, and the husband had to go and sleep on his grandmother's sofa. On appeal this approach was held to be clearly wrong, since the order is draconian and not capable of being adapted as a solution for this sort of situation.

Kadeer v Kadeer [1987] CLY 1775 was a similar case where the judge thought that two months apart might settle the parties after the wife had an affair and was sleeping on the floor of the study to escape the husband's excessive sexual demands: again on appeal the order was set aside as being wrong where there was no necessity (eg, because of violence).

Scott v Scott [1992] 1 FLR 529 shows that violence is not in fact essential if the order can be categorised as necessary. Here the husband was excluded on the basis that, if there is a sufficiently serious situation, an exclusion order will be made regardless of the absence of violence, but the emphasis is on the seriousness of the circumstances: the divorce was in process and the future of the 15 year old daughter of the marriage was not yet settled as contested proceedings were pending. The court nevertheless made an order as the husband was continually pestering the wife about a reconciliation, since he did not accept that the marriage was over. However, she was not amenable to his suggestions, and although he was never violent he had already breached a non-molestation order on numerous occasions: clearly something had to be done, as the parties could not live in the same house, and his appeal against the order on the grounds that the reasons for it were insubstantial was rejected.

23.4.3.2 The parties' needs and resources

This is not always easy to assess. Again cases suggest the right approach.

Thurley v Smith [1985] Fam Law 31 established that the court will require detailed information as to how easy (or difficult) it is for either party to be rehoused by the local authority.

Lee v Lee [1984] FLR 243 shows that the wife may have the edge if she has the children as they will handicap her in finding alternative accommodation, but this does not always work in wives' favour.

Wiseman v Simpson [1988] 1 All ER 245 is the leading case on the draconian nature of the order. In that case there was no violence but merely an 'atmosphere', so no order was made: the position was that the young couple who were cohabiting had merely fallen out of love with each other and the existence of a baby who needed to be with the mother was not conclusive in obtaining sole occupation for her.

23.4.3.3 Children's needs

Children's needs can sometimes swing the balance, as some cases demonstrate.

Bassett v Bassett [1976] 1 All ER 513 was quite a strong case on the needs of the children. There a couple and their baby lived in a very small (two roomed) flat and the husband brought his teenage son to live there also. The wife said that the husband drank and was violent. She went to live with her parents (where they were very overcrowded) and applied for an ouster order which she obtained and which was upheld on appeal. Presumably this was because the husband and the teenage son could find alternative accommodation more easily than a woman with a baby, who tend not to be popular tenants with private landlords, thus leaving them reliant on the local authority and possibly with no alternative to bed and breakfast accommodation.

Samson v Samson [1982] 1 WLR 252; [1982] 1 All ER 178 was a case where the wife's allegations of conduct were insubstantial, although they did include over-criticism of her and a resultant undermining of her confidence. Surprisingly, however, the court nevertheless gave her an exclusion order as the children needed to be accommodated in the house, and the wife would not return with them unless the husband left because of her extreme aversion to him, due to the matters alleged in the petition. While the Court of Appeal said they could not look into the adequacy of allegations in divorce petitions to see whether she was justified in leaving, they made the order on the basis of the children's needs.

Myers v Myers (above) was a case of exclusion after only one incident of violence and much verbal abuse, where the order initially obtained was based on the needs of the children and was set aside on the twin bases: (i) that the wife was possibly being unreasonable; and (ii) a reappraisal of the children's needs.

Richards v Richards [1984] AC 206 was a case where an exclusion order was refused because the wife's allegations were trivial and 'rubbishy' and the interests of the children were not paramount.

Anderson v Anderson [1984] FLR 566 was a case where there was a two roomed flat from which the wife departed with the two year old son due to the husband's violence: she refused to return until the husband left, was expecting a second child and was staying in a hostel for battered wives. The husband, however, proposed sharing the flat, with one bedroom for her and the children and one for him, and sharing the kitchen, bathroom and living room. Not surprisingly, the court rejected his proposals and made the exclusion order in the interests of the children.

Lee v Lee (above) was a case where there was an unmarried couple with two children, a son and a daughter, who made allegations of indecency against the father. While her mother was in hospital the daughter had to live with her grandmother, an arrangement which she did not like. The court gave occupation of the jointly owned council flat to the woman because the man on his own did not require such extensive accommodation, and the wife and children clearly had a higher degree of need for it.

Children may swing the balance of harm test in cases where other things are equal (see, eg, *B v B* at 2.4.3, above).

23.4.3.4 All the circumstances

Such circumstances may be quite varied, as again the cases show.

Jones v Jones [1971] 2 All ER 737 establishes that this may cover situations as varied as the husband installing his mistress in the matrimonial home (where the court made an immediate ouster order) to trying to pre-empt the ultimate property settlement (which has usually not worked as the emphasis on domestic violence protection has always been 'first aid' pending such final decisions). *Hadden v Hadden* [1966] 3 All ER 412 was such a case where one spouse was trying to evict the other.

It should be noted that it seems that in accordance with previous practice the order should be made only for a determinate period (s 33(10)) or should be expressed to be until 'further order', although no time limit is actually specified in the FLA 1996. This contrasts with the earlier practice of only making such orders as a 'first aid' remedy for a limited period pending long term resolution of outstanding property or underlying problems.

23.4.4 Orders under the Family Law Act 1996, s 35

These orders, in favour of *former spouses* without an estate or interest against *entitled* respondents, protect the former spouses from eviction or exclusion from the home, and if necessary permit the former spouse to re-enter, also requiring the other spouse to allow this.

These terms will be *mandatory* if the court decides to make an order at all. Whether such an order is made is within the discretion of the court, since a *former* spouse who needs to use this section will have no matrimonial home rights, as if such existed application could have been made under s 33.

There are guidelines for the court in exercising its discretion contained in s 35(6) and these are similar to those under s 33, but the court must also have regard to the length of time since the parties' separation and/or since the marriage was dissolved or annulled, and also to the existence of any pending property proceedings (whether under the MCA 1973 or otherwise). Finally, the court must apply the balance of harm test, which again imposes a mandatory duty to make the order unless the respondent shows why it should not be made.

Orders under s 35 are not to last in the first instance for longer than six months, though renewals are permitted (s 35(9) and (10)).

23.4.5 Orders under the Family Law Act 1996, s 36

Orders in favour of *cohabitants* without an estate or interest or *former cohabitants* but where the *respondent* is *entitled* are made under s 36. Protection and guidance to the court are virtually the same as under s 35, save that in the case of cohabitants s 36(6)(e)–(h) requires the court to consider the nature of the parties' relationship, the length of time for which they have cohabited, whether there are any children for whom both parties have parental responsibility and the length of time since they have ceased to live together. The balance of harm test under s 36(8) is also weaker than in the case of ss 33 and 35 in that there is no obligation on the respondent in a s 36 case to show why the order should not be made. It is clear from this and from s 41 which requires the court to have regard to the fact that the parties have not given each other the commitment of marriage that Parliament intended to give the strongest protection to those who are or who have been married and thus to distinguish between married and cohabiting couples in favour of those who have assumed the commitment of marriage.

23.4.6 Orders under the Family Law Act 1996, s 37

Orders in favour of *former spouses* (but where, unlike those under s 35, the *respondent* is *not entitled*) are made under s 37. Protection given and guidance to the court are the same as under s 33(3), (6) and (7) (see above). Both parties must still be residing in the home for this section to be used and orders are limited to six months plus one possible extension of a further six months.

23.4.7 Orders under the Family Law Act 1996, s 38

Orders in favour of *former cohabitants* (again where, unlike those under s 36, the *respondent* is *not entitled*) are made under s 38, for which the requirements are identical to s 37 save that the parties have never been married, and there is similar protection to that of cohabitants under s 36. Again, the order is limited to six months plus one renewal for the same period.

23.4.8 Powers of arrest

These are attachable to occupation orders or to non-molestation orders (see 23.3.9, above) but are not attached to ancillary orders (see 23.2.2, above) if such are included.

23.5 PROCEDURE

The new procedure involves both new forms and amendments to the rules comprising three statutory instruments and the Family Proceedings (Allocation to Judiciary) Directions 1997.

23.5.1 Family Proceedings Rules 1991 amendments

Procedure for obtaining the new orders has also been streamlined. Applications are governed by the Family Proceedings (Amendment No 3) Rules 1996 SI 1996/1778, which insert new rules into the Family Proceedings Rules (FPR) 1991 to provide one common application form. This is Form FL401 which is to be used in all cases whether the application is freestanding or made in existing proceedings and whatever the Pt IV remedy sought. On the form, the applicant must show in what way there is association with the respondent within the meaning of the Act (ie, the parties are or were married/cohabitants/related, etc). The applicant files a signed and sworn statement in support.

23.5.2 *Ex parte* orders

If the application is made *ex parte*, the statement must explain why this is necessary, since the court has power to abridge the time for service, which is normally only two days, making at least informal notice (eg, a telephone call) possible in virtually all cases. *Ex parte* orders are therefore still only likely to be allowed in the most drastic circumstances. See *G v G* [1990] FLR 395, where the husband obtained an *ex parte* occupation order (previously known as an ouster order) against the wife together with a non-molestation order restraining her from assaulting him, which was set aside on the various grounds that:

- she was readily available for service;
- there was a conflict of evidence;
- there was no danger of serious irreparable harm; and
- the order had been granted for seven weeks, which was far too long, since an *ex parte* order should only be for a very short period pending a hearing on notice.

23.5.3 Service

Service is normally to be effected personally by or on behalf of the applicant, but an applicant acting in person may ask the court to effect service, and the court may also order substituted service. Where the application is for an occupation order, any landlord or mortgagee must be served with a copy of the form together with notification of the right of such a person to make representations.

23.5.4 The hearing

The hearing is in chambers unless the court directs. By the Family Law Act (Pt IV) Allocation of Proceedings Order 1997 SI 1997/1896, there is a completely free choice between the county court and the Family Proceedings Court, and applications started in the Family Proceedings Court may be transferred to the county court, either because of the desirability of consolidation with other proceedings or because there is a novel or complex point of law or a question of general public importance involved, or if the proceedings are exceptionally complex.

The court is under a duty to keep a record of proceedings.

23.5.5 The order

The order will be made on a blank form FL404, which also provides a menu of standard clauses for incorporation, so as to achieve an appropriate mix of provisions to meet the particular case, into the draft order which the court is invited to make. 'Cutting and pasting' from the standard clauses, the desired text is entered on the form by the applicant, usually also incorporating in either Notice A or Notice B mandatory or discretionary penal notice as appropriate. There are different forms to vary, extend or discharge orders.

23.5.6 Applications by children

A child may make an application, but only with leave of the court (s 43(1)) and only if the child has sufficient understanding to make the proposed application (s 43(2)), in which case by r 3.8(2) of the FPR 1991 such application is treated in the first instance as an application for leave to make the application. This is clearly a significant extension of the former powers to regulate the occupation of the family home.

23.5.7 Children Act 1989 exclusion orders

Part IV has amended the CA 1989 to give the court power to make an order excluding a suspected abuser from the home where the court is making an interim care order under s 31 of the CA 1989 or an emergency protection order under s 44. This procedure is governed by a new r 4.24A. This exclusion order can be made without notice to the suspected abuser. The order is then served by the applicant on the suspected abuser together with a separate statement of the evidence, informing that person of the right to apply to vary or discharge the order. There is obviously some concern as to the evidential implications of this change.

23.6 VARIATION

Applications to vary or discharge an order may be made by either party on form FL403, or if the court has made an order of its own motion such variation or discharge may similarly be initiated without application by either party (s 49).

23.7 COMMITTAL FOR CONTEMPT

Breach of any undertaking or disobedience to a domestic violence injunction order will invite committal for contempt, a rigid procedure which must be strictly followed, whether the order was made or undertaking given under the FLA 1996 or pursuant to the inherent jurisdiction of the court.

23.8 TRANSFER OF TENANCIES

Tenancies (either local authority or privately owned) can also be transferred under the Act, providing a longer term solution than a temporary occupation order, pursuant to s 53 of and Sched 7 to the FLA 1996. This would enable one married or cohabitant joint owner to obtain the tenancy to the exclusion of the other (see *Gay v Sheeran* [1999] 2 FLR 519). Criteria in Sched 7 include the suitability of the parties as tenants and the circumstances in which they obtained the tenancy. For discussions of these provisions, see Bridge, S, 'Transferring tenancies of the family home' [1998] Fam Law 26; and Woelke, A, 'Transfer of tenancies' [1999] Fam Law 72.

THE REFORMED LAW OF DOMESTIC VIOLENCE

FAMILY LAW ACT 1996

The Act has codified the law of domestic violence by consolidating the law to provide two forms of order – non-molestation and occupation orders – available uniformly in the triple tier of family courts. The orders work on the basis of a concept of 'associated persons', a wide class defined in the Act. The Act additionally provides occupation orders for married, formerly married, cohabiting and formerly cohabiting heterosexual couples, additionally based on a concept of 'entitlement': this concept regulates the specific criteria on which the court will base its decision, the most protective criteria being accorded to cases involving married couples and those who have an interest in the property concerned. Financial needs and resources, children's needs, the conduct of the parties and all the circumstances of the case figure in all cases, but the balance of harm test, stronger or weaker depending on the relationship – married or not, existing or former – is a crucial factor. Ancillary orders can also be made to finance the occupation, which will be of longer or shorter duration depending on which section of the Act the parties apply under.

NON-MOLESTATION ORDERS

Orders to restrain harassment or pestering as well as violence may be made under s 42 of the Act. Such orders may be made without notice where pursuant to s 45 the applicant has good reason not to give notice (eg, fear of the applicant until protected by the court's order, or inability to find and serve the applicant, or urgency), and may be made when it is 'just and convenient', but a hearing on notice should follow as soon as possible. A power of arrest should be attached unless the court is satisfied that that is not necessary. Undertakings may be accepted in lieu but not where a power of arrest is indicated. Committal may follow for breach of an order.

OCCUPATION ORDERS

Such orders may also be made *ex parte* but only for a short period until a hearing can be held on notice. Occupation orders are regarded as draconian and will only be made when really necessary to restrain some identifiable harm and only where the balance of harm test in the appropriate criteria for the section under which the applicant's standing requires the application to be made is in favour of the applicant.

Such orders may have ancillary clauses to finance the occupation through payment by the respondent of the home's outgoings.

A power of arrest may be attached to all but the ancillary order clauses. Committal may also follow for breach of an occupation order.

TRANSFER OF TENANCIES

Schedule 7 to the Act permits the longer term remedy of transfer of either a public or private sector tenancy to one of joint tenants.

PART VI

CHILDREN

CHAPTER 24

THE CHILDREN ACT 1989

24.1 INTRODUCTION

The Children Act (CA) 1989 made major changes in both the public and private law relating to children. Following the marginalisation of the divorce suit, which 50 years ago formed the bulk of 'family law', the law relating to children, together with ancillary relief after decree, now forms the major part of the specialist family lawyer's workload, and some specialise in child law alone. This significant workload is divided between private law (cases about the respective rights and duties of children and parents *inter se*) and public law (cases about the duties of the local authority in respect of children living in their area, and of the rights of children and parents in relation to the local authority). Thus, an academic student requires:

(a) a sound working knowledge of the private and public law aspects of the CA 1989;

(b) some outline knowledge of how the public law provisions impact on and interrelate with the private law;

(c) an ability to watch trends and appreciate the importance of the latest cases (because of the lack of application of the doctrine of precedent – so that decisions are only a guide to how a court might interpret the exercise of its duty within the statutory framework, particularly since child law can be a fast moving field); and

(d) an ability to research the law where necessary in order to decide whether there are human rights implications which impact upon the established principles of English law.

The first step is a good working knowledge of the law and practice, so as to identify the *questions* that need to be asked, even if the answers to the more specialised and complicated ones are not known, since this is an area where there has been much recourse to the European Convention on Human Rights: the role of human rights will doubtless continue to play a major role under the Human Rights Act 1998.

24.1.1 Background to the Act

The CA 1989 came fully into force on 14 October 1991, and was intended to provide a comprehensive code for child law, mostly regardless of whether a child's parents were married or not – hence the separation of child orders from the divorce, nullity and judicial separation decrees. An overview of how the radical new system now works may be helpful to students who otherwise might be confused by reading reports of old cases, which are often still a useful guideline to the likely interpretation of the contemporary statutory provisions, but of course contain the old terminology.

Part I of the Act confirmed the basic principle that the child's welfare is paramount in both public and private law. The former concept of parental *rights* and duties (which had its roots since time immemorial in both historical and religious contexts) was replaced with the more modern one of *parental responsibility*.

Part II completely restructured the private law of children. It abolished the outdated concepts (and unhelpfully emotive wording) of *custody, care and control* and *access*, and replaced them with a power for the court to make individual orders to regulate in a manner perceived as less emotive and more specifically practical the issues of a child's *residence* (ie, where and with whom the child should have a *home*) and *contact* (ie, when and how the child should keep in touch with the non-residential parent or other relatives). It then provided for special orders to be made with regard to any *specific issue* or *prohibited steps*, in respect of which the court was empowered to make individual one-off decisions *without* making any other changes in the child's arrangements.

The remainder of the Act is concerned with the public law relating to children (see Chapter 26). Parts III–V reorganised the general powers and duties of local authorities in relation to children, also reorganised the emergency protection of children and created a new *emergency protection order* and *child assessment order*, which both together and separately assist the local authority to carry out their duties in relation to the protection of children in their area.

24.1.2 The new philosophy of Pts I and II

The package of new private child law provided by the Act, and the fresh air it has blown into this area of the law, has in the past few years contrasted very favourably with the former position, where in order to make a simple point about a self-contained decision – such as where a child went to school, or what religion the child should practise – a parent had to embark on a full blown custody application: this was because under the old law the parent with custody had the right to make such major decisions and impose them on the child and the other parent, whose only recourse was to go back to the court to ask for custody to be changed so that that parent could take over major decisions in the child's upbringing.

The new orders are provided by s 8 of the CA 1989 and are thus usually referred to collectively as 's 8 orders'.

The new structure owes much to concepts derived from the wardship jurisdiction of the High Court (see Chapter 27), for which it was designed to be an easier and cheaper alternative.

Procedural support for the Act alongside that for other family law matters is to be found in the two new sets of rules brought out in 1991:

(1) For the High Court and county court, these are contained in the Family Proceedings Rules (FPR) 1991 SI 1991/1247 as amended.

(2) For the magistrates' court (renamed the Family Proceedings Court by the Act), these are contained in the Family Proceedings Courts (Children Act 1989) Rules 1991 SI 1991/1395.

The rules are in fact much the same save for obvious procedural differences applicable to the two distinct sets of courts.

The overall effect is designed to achieve a completely new approach to child disputes, in which the *rights* of the child and the *duties* of parents and the local authority are emphasised, together with the *non-interventionist* policy of the law and the court, and the principle that in child cases there should be *no delay* in the resolution of the problem which has invited the court's involvement.

The concept of a child having rights rather than duties, and that of the parent having duties instead of rights, was not new in 1989, but rather traces its history back to the 1959 United Nations Declaration and 1989 Convention on the Rights of the Child to which the UK is a signatory. Earlier signs of such an approach in English law may be seen in the report of the working party of the law reform society JUSTICE in the early 1970s, which caused a stir at the time of its publication, but nevertheless took rather a long time to work its way through in our participation in the International Year of the Child, the establishment of a Children's Legal Centre and the 1980s work of the Law Commission which led to statutory 'parental responsibility' in the CA 1989 (see 24.2, below).

However, even in the single decade since the implementation of the CA 1989, it is clear that the new approach is largely successful. While it may take more than an Act of Parliament to confer on some feckless, damaged or inadequate parents the parental responsibility envisaged by the Act, the system clearly encourages better relations between parents, since it is no longer necessary in divorce for either parent to insist on having custody or indeed any sort of order at all, which in bitterly contested cases often meant merely obtaining legal possession of the children at all costs, usually for all the wrong reasons, in order for parents to get their own way in a relatively self-contained area of the child's life.

Moreover, while joint residence orders are not encouraged, on the basis that a child should generally have one home and not two unless it is already an established fact that that child divides the week entirely amicably between the parents – for example, where there is a shift arrangement which is working well – the provision of the system of residence, contact and specific issue or prohibited steps orders means that the child can often share time more fairly between both parents, who may thus *both* continue to influence a child who is living with one parent and having generous contact with the other.

The court can then contain any subsidiary arguments by deciding on any specific (educational or other) issue, *without* a pitched battle necessarily having to break out. This obviates the previous need to disrupt every aspect of the child's lifestyle with a change of custody simply because one parent or the other had strong views on some point and wished to enforce them if possible.

For those parents who can agree everything without recourse to the court, actual *orders* may thus never be necessary at all, while for those for whom losing custody would have meant *losing face*, a generous *contact order*, plus the right to go for a *specific issue order* if necessary, may be entirely satisfactory. This often proves to be so, even where the other parent obtains a residence order which was not initially acceptable until the full potential of 'generous contact' has been appreciated by the parent who has lost the residence order application.

All these innovative concepts need to be examined in detail.

24.2 PARENTAL RESPONSIBILITY

Parental responsibility (PR) is 'all the rights, duties, powers, responsibilities and authority which by law a parent of a child has in relation to the child and his property' (CA 1989, s 3(1)). It is central to the concept that a person with PR may not *surrender or transfer* any part of that responsibility (s 2(9)). It may, however, be wholly or partly *delegated* (eg, to a child's school or to the local authority), or *qualified* or *curtailed* (eg, as between the parents of the child either informally or by order of the court, ie, by a s 8 order) and one parent can in routine matters act independently, but not, obviously, in relation to important, irreversible decisions (see CA 1989, s 2(7) and *Re J (Specific Issue Order: Circumcision)* [1999] 2 FLR 678, discussed further in Chapter 25).

When PR is delegated, the parents remain responsible for the omissions of the person with delegated PR.

PR is not simply a philosophical concept but actually requires the parent to assume various responsibilities towards the child. 'Parental responsibility' is not defined in the Act but its meaning may be abstracted from case law and statute. Bromley has summarised the duties as follows:

(1) To provide a home for and care for and control the child (or have contact with the child) including disciplining the him or her until he or she is 18, marries, enters the armed forces or is adopted, to which consent must be given or dispensed with. As far as control goes, *moderate and reasonable punishment* is allowed, but any excess is assault (*R v Smith* [1985] Crim LR 42). As all parents know, this duty tends to be reduced to giving advice as the child grows older and (hopefully) matures, as is shown by *Gillick v Wisbech Area Health Authority* [1985] 3 All ER 402, where a Catholic mother took exception to a government circular which would have had the effect of allowing the family GP to give contraception to her teenage daughters below the age of 16. The House of Lords, up to which Mrs Gillick fought the case, decided there was nothing wrong with this if the girl in question had sufficient understanding to consult the doctor for proper and necessary medical treatment without informing the mother. A child with this level of understanding is now called *Gillick competent*.

(2) To consent to the child's marriage.

(3) To consent to medical treatment, although over 16s consent themselves (Family Law Reform Act (FLRA) 1969, s 8(3)): under 16s consent if *Gillick* competent, but doctors can always give emergency treatment without parents' consent anyway.

(4) To maintain the child financially, which is enforced by various statutes including ss 23 and 24 of the Matrimonial Causes Act (MCA) 1973; Sched 1 to the CA 1989; the Domestic Proceedings and Magistrates' Court Act 1978; s 106 of the Social Security Act 1992; and s 1(1) of the Child Support Act 1991.

(5) To protect the child from physical and moral harm, and determine the child's religion. This means not doing anything to cause such harm to the child carelessly (which if it caused the death of the child would be manslaughter, which is a crime) nor deliberately as in cruelty to children (which is also an offence where a person over 16 having charge of a child assaults, neglects, ill treats or abandons a child or exposes him or her to harm so as to cause unnecessary suffering or injury within the meaning of s 1 of the Children and Young Persons Act 1933: see *R v Lowe* [1973] 1 All ER 805 (a

case of simple medical neglect where a father of low intelligence failed to appreciate that his nine week old baby was ill and failed to call a doctor, so the baby died of dehydration and malnutrition); and *R v Shepherd* [1981] AC 394; [1980] 3 All ER 899). As far as *moral* harm goes, the parent should be aware of the Sexual Offences Act 1956, ss 10 and 11 (incest), ss 14 and 15 (indecent assault) and ss 25, 26 and 28 (permitting the use of premises by young girls for intercourse or encouraging them in prostitution, etc).

(6) To ensure that the child receives education. This is enforceable under s 437 of the Education Act 1996 by a school attendance order or under s 443 for failing to comply with a school attendance order, or by using other sanctions such as the local authority threatening a care order if the child is suffering 'significant harm' within the meaning of s 31 of the CA 1989.

(7) To consent to or veto the issue of a passport, or to emigration.

(8) To represent the child in legal proceedings.

(9) To agree to the change of the child's surname.

(10) To bury or cremate a deceased child.

(11) To appoint a guardian for the child.

(Professor Bromley's original version of the list may still be found in the current 9th edition (1998) of *Bromley's Family Law*, now edited by Nigel Lowe and Gillian Douglas, at p 350.) Some have argued that these duties should be made more specific by an amendment of the Act.

The leading classic article on PR remains that of Nigel Lowe in 1997, 'The meaning and allocation of parental responsibility – a common lawyer's perspective' (1997) 11 International Journal of Law, Policy and the Family 192.

The CA 1989 permits the court to make a 'prohibited steps order' to stop a parent taking any undesirable step in carrying out PR in one of these ways (see Chapter 25), or where appropriate the High Court may also make a wardship order so as to take over from the child's parents the task of making decisions in these matters (see Chapter 27). The 1990s high profile case involving a 13 year old schoolgirl allowed by her parents to contract a marriage with a Turkish waiter is an example of just such an appropriate scenario for a wardship order, although wardship is rarely used now since the prohibited steps and specific issue orders were expressly created so as to obviate the need to resort to the expense of High Court wardship, and the s 8 orders are available in all courts which have jurisdiction under the CA 1989.

24.2.1 Persons with parental responsibility

Parents who were married at the time of the child's birth, or who have married since, and pursuant to s 1 of the Family Law Reform Act (FLRA) 1987 have by the marriage legitimated their child, will have *joint parental responsibility* (s 2(1) and (3)). Pursuant to ss 2 and 3 of the Legitimacy Act 1976, the child is treated as legitimate from the date of the marriage provided the father is domiciled in England and Wales: this will be so even if the father is living in a country where legitimation by subsequent marriage is not recognised, provided the child is in England and Wales.

Mothers, where the parents are not married, will have PR.

Fathers *not* married to the mother (often called 'unmarried fathers') do not automatically have PR. However, the unmarried father can obtain PR in one of five ways, by:

(a) making a PR agreement with the mother (s 4(1)(b)) in the prescribed form (which is regulated by the Parental Responsibility Agreement Regulations 1991 SI 1991/1478);

(b) applying to the court for a PR order (s 4(1)(a));

(c) applying to the court for a residence order, in which case if the residence order is granted the court will automatically also make a PR order under s 4(1)(a);

(d) being appointed the child's guardian by the court; or

(e) being appointed the child's guardian by the mother or by another guardian (s 5),

or, of course, by marrying the mother and thus legitimating the child under s 1 of the FLRA 1987, as mentioned above, since this will result in the marriage's technically dating back for legitimation purposes to the time of the child's birth, and giving the father PR in the process, provided the parents were legally able to marry at the time of the child's birth.

It is not uncommon for fathers to apply for PR and the court will consider whether it is in the child's best interests for the father to have it. Naturally it will be necessary for the father to satisfy the court that he is the father, and this will be on the ordinary civil standard, namely on a balance of probabilities. The court will take into account any evidence of commitment (*Re P (A Minor) (Parental Responsibility Order)* [1994] 1 FLR 578) and it is important for a father seeking an order to be able to show that commitment in some way or other.

Re H (Illegitimate Children: Father: Parental Rights) (No 2) [1991] 1 FLR 214, CA shows that in addition to commitment and the degree of such commitment, two further points need to be satisfactorily demonstrated in the father's favour, namely the degree of attachment between the father and the child and the reasons for his applying for the order, although the child's welfare will be paramount and Hedley J, writing in the journal *Family Law* in September 1994, made clear that the award of PR is not 'a prize for good behaviour'. He suggests that the application should be scrutinised for any indication of an improper or wrong reason for applying, and if this is absent the court should make the order unless there is something special in the case which means that the child's welfare requires that the order not be made. See, for example, *M v M (Parental Responsibility)* [1999] Fam Law 538, where the father was violent due to head injuries in a road accident and the order was refused, and *R v P* [1998] 2 FLR 855, where the very elderly father was suspected of being a paedophile and of potentially using PR to undermine the much younger mother's care of the child.

Neither lack of actual contact between the father and the child as in *Re H (A Minor) (Parental Responsibility)* [1993] 1 FLR 484, CA, nor friction between the parents as in *Re P (A Minor) (Parental Responsibility Order)* [1994] 1 FLR 578, is therefore in itself a reason for refusing a PR order if the three point test in *Re H* (1991) is satisfied.

Similarly, the fact that a father does not obtain a contact order for any reason (eg, because he is convicted of possessing obscene literature) does not preclude his having PR, which is about duties and responsibilities and does not entitle the father to interfere in the child's day to day life (*Re S (Parental Responsibility)* [1995] 2 FLR 648, CA). Sir Stephen

Brown P reiterated this important point in *Re D (A Minor)* (1995) unreported, 24 May, where the Family Proceedings Court had refused a PR order on the basis of parental hostility and lack of mutual respect, which were irrelevant to the *Re H* (1991) criteria.

PR can always be terminated if the father does anything which is obviously harmful to the child (eg, assaulting the child: *Re P (Terminating Parental Responsibility)* [1995] 1 FLR 1048). However, cases have occurred where the degree of commitment and attachment has been found insufficient and it has been held that it is for the father to *demonstrate* that there is a sufficient degree of both. In *Re J (Parental Responsibility)* [1999] 1 FLR 784, the father of a 12 year old had never lived with the child with whom he had enjoyed only annual contact, and PR was refused although the child's mother was in prison for drugs.

Commitment does *not* have to be linked to maintenance. In *Re H (Parental Responsibility Order: Maintenance)* [1996] 1 FLR 867, a father successfully appealed against a judge's adjournment for him to demonstrate commitment by paying maintenance. *Re G (A Minor) (Parental Responsibility Order)* [1994] 1 FLR 504, CA and *Re H* (1996) have confirmed that the usual PR criteria of commitment, attachment and reasons for application, as set out in the early cases, are not exhaustive but indicative, but *Re G* established that if they are present they do raise a *prima facie* right to PR. Nevertheless, many family lawyers fear that this is wrong, as PR includes a right and duty to support the child financially, and there should therefore be some link between PR orders (and indeed contact orders) and some financial commitment.

It should be noted that although these criteria apply to all PR *orders*, there are no suitability controls if the mother chooses to enter into a PR agreement with the father, even if the child is in care (see *per* Wilson J in *Re X (Parental Responsibility Agreement: Children in Care)* [2000] Fam Law 244). It should be noted that, while it has repeatedly been held by the European Court of Human Rights that difference in treatment between married and unmarried fathers in relation to PR does not *necessarily* infringe Art 8 of the European Convention, the Convention is now incorporated into the Human Rights Act 1998 and is being continually raised in English PR cases (see *B v K* [2000] 1 FLR 1, but see also proposals for reform at 24.2.2, below).

If either parent misuses PR, the other can always apply for a prohibited steps order to stop this (see Chapter 25), and s 2(8) in any case prevents a parent with PR from acting in any way incompatibly with another order (eg, a s 8 residence order).

Stepparents do not acquire PR on marriage to the child's biological parent, although a stepparent caring for a child and treating that child as a child of the family will create the usual obligations towards such a child of the family, such as in respect of ancillary relief claims (see Chapter 12), irrespective of whether the stepparent has PR (s 3(4)(a)). A stepparent without PR who has care of a child may do whatever is reasonable to safeguard or promote the child's welfare irrespective of having PR or not (s 3(5)), as may any person who has *de facto* care of a child.

Other persons (including stepparents) may acquire PR as follows:

(a) guardians, who are thus equated with natural parents (s 5(6));

(b) adopters, when the adoption order is made in their favour (since they are then parents, and the biological parents will at the same time lose their PR);

(c) local authorities acquiring a care order (s 33(3)), though the parents will also retain theirs; and

(d) any person acquiring a residence order, however only for the duration of the order (s 12(1) and (2)) which means that this type of PR will cease at 16 when the residence order does, unless the residence order is exceptionally extended beyond 16. This is the normal way of giving PR to stepparents, rather than by adoption. Stepparents remain the poor relations of the extended family, with no specific duties unless asked for periodical payments under the MCA 1973, and few rights.

24.2.2 Reform of the law of parental responsibility and unmarried fathers

The Lord Chancellor issued a consultation paper, *Paternity and Parental Responsibility: The Law on Parental Responsibility for Unmarried Fathers*, in March 1998 concerning a proposed reform to give PR to fathers signing the birth register with the mother of a child at the time of its birth, and although no immediate opportunities arose for the law to be changed, the government did announce that there would be legislation as soon as convenient. The Adoption and Children Bill 2001 failed to reach the statute book but the relevant provisions are included in the Adoption and Children Act 2002 (see further Chapter 29).

An article by Ashley, J, 'Parental responsibility – a new deal or a costly exercise?' [1999] Fam Law 175, commented on the Solicitors Family Law Association (SFLA) response to the paper, and Branchflower, G, in 'Parental responsibility and human rights' [1999] Fam Law 34, discusses Arts 8 and 14 of the European Convention on Human Rights in the context of family life without discrimination. In *Marckx v Belgium* (1979) 2 EHRR 330, the European Court of Human Rights held that the Art 8 right of respect for family life applied to illegitimate as well as legitimate relationships. However, in *McMichael v UK* (1995) 20 EHRR 205, the differing treatment in UK law was unsuccessfully challenged by a Scottish father who apparently failed to establish a breach of Art 8 because of the wide variety of relationships between natural fathers and their children, and the subsequent case of *R v UK* [2000] FLR 1 achieved the same result when the European Court said there were 'objective and reasonable justifications' for the different treatment of married and unmarried fathers in English law. Branchflower criticises this approach on the basis that there is a similarly wide variety of relationships between married fathers and their children, and because the decision conflicts with *Marckx*. See also Stephenson's 'Parental responsibility: is there anything more to say?' [1999] Fam Law 296.

24.2.3 The termination of parental responsibility

PR acquired by an order of the court or by agreement ends when the child is 18 as of course it would do automatically in the case of any child reaching majority. PR is thus somewhat like a smile – it can be given out generously to all and sundry without necessarily diminishing the original supply, since despite delegation and even increase in the numbers of persons who technically have it, PR can be *lost* only on *death* or *adoption* or specific removal for good cause by the court where a father did not have it at the child's birth. There is no way of removing PR from a parent who has always had PR, regardless of how such a parent behaves, although a care order will restrict such a parent's exercise of PR (see Chapter 26).

Where more than one person has PR, each has power to act alone (s 2(7)) unless some specific requirement necessitates the consent of more than one (eg, to adoption). But s 2(8) prevents any unilateral action incompatible with another order.

24.2.4 Children divorcing their parents

Due to the enduring concept of PR, such 'divorces' are only possible in the minds of the children concerned, even where a residence order is granted for the child to live with other relations or the families of friends. See, for example, *Re AD (A Minor)* [1993] 1 FCR 573, an early case in a long line of decisions by which the court began to be troubled in the early and mid-1990s where children were determined to move house if necessary against their parents' wishes.

Andrew Bainham looked at this phenomenon in his article 'See you in court, Mum: children as litigants' (1996) 6 JCL 127. The basic approach taken by the court in any such cases, where usually the persons with whom the child desires to live will have to seek leave to apply for a residence order under s 10 of the Act, is to look at the criteria in s 10(9), which include the nature of the proposed application, the applicant's connection with the child, any risk of harm or disruption to the child's life through the application and, where the child is in local authority accommodation, the authority's and the parents' wishes and plans for the child. Where the child is applying personally, by s 10(8) the court must be satisfied that the child has sufficient understanding to do so, but the s 10(9) criteria do not apply. This same s 10(8) criterion would apply to the decision of any solicitor willing to represent the child, who will need to be represented in such proceedings since a child cannot apply as a litigant in person.

The SFLA, in its Code and guidelines, gives guidance to solicitors representing children, and these and the court, in a number of now accumulated decisions, suggest that, while the views of competent children should be taken seriously, both the solicitor and the court should be slow to accept children in litigation. One reason for this is that there is every likelihood that children as parties, who are entitled to see all documents in the case, and are liable to be cross-examined, possibly by parents, will be exposed to adult themes which are not appropriate for them. Some children do establish that their wishes are so strong that they must put them forward themselves and not through the court welfare officer (see *Re C (Residence: Child's Application for Leave)* [1995] 1 FLR 927).

The welfare principle does not apply to applications for leave (or the child might be denied the right to raise the issue of the s 8 order sought at all), but there is a *Practice Direction (Family Proceedings Orders: Applications by Children)* [1993] 1 All ER 820 which requires all such applications to be made in the High Court.

24.3 THE NON-INTERVENTION AND NO DELAY PRINCIPLES (CA 1989, s 1(5) AND (2))

These two principles are deeply rooted respectively in the philosophy of and the historical background to the Act.

The *non-interventionist* principle is also sometimes referred to as 'the presumption of no order', and s 1(5) provides that:

> ... where a court is considering whether or not to make one or more orders under this Act with respect to a child, it shall not make the order or any of the orders unless it considers that doing so would be better for the child than making no order at all.

This is a principle generated by the belief that parents are (or should be) the right people to decide what is best for their children. There must therefore be positive benefits to be seen in an order. In *Re K (Supervision Order)* [1999] Fam Law 376, a case in which a care or supervision order was sought, and the former was made, Wall LJ said that the court should start with the less interventionist approach.

Technically, it is *not* now possible to make s 8 orders by consent (as the old custody, care and control and access orders sometimes were, especially in relation to joint custody where the parents were agreed that that was the best thing in their particular circumstances and the court approved). The way that the court gives effect to agreements ultimately made at the door of the court is to make no order, which would have been what had happened if the parents had been able to agree in the first place. This is because the court prefers the parties to observe the spirit of the Act in negotiating and observing a proper parenting relationship. Sometimes, however, the court will override the united wishes of the parents: in *Re C (A Child) (HIV Testing)* [2000] 2 WLR 270, the presumption that the best interests of the child coincided with the joint wishes of the parents was actually rebutted, where the local authority wanted to test the child for HIV and the parents opposed the test. In other words, the united wishes of the parents cannot override the child's welfare, which is paramount.

The court therefore only goes on to make an order in such circumstances (ie, after the parents have agreed to settle their differences) when for some reason everyone thinks a formal order would actually help, and though the court in such circumstances will put into the order whatever the parents have agreed, *technically* it is *not* a consent order as such but an order handed down by the court for the purpose of providing certainty. This may be splitting very fine hairs, but there is good reason for it in that any order is regarded as, if not precisely a failure on someone's part, at least *undesirable* if it can be *avoided*, and so strictly reserved for when it serves some *useful purpose*.

Sometimes orders are made, despite the no order principle, where it is necessary to give practical status (eg, a residence order in favour of a non-parent).

Mediation services are widely used to attempt to avoid having to make orders, and there is a procedure for a meeting before a district judge with a welfare officer present (*Practice Direction* [1992] 1 FLR 228). However, judges who make no order purely on the basis of s 1(5) are now definitely seen as wrong, since if there is a dispute requiring adjudication an order is clearly needed (*Re S (Contact: Grandparents)* [1996] 1 FLR 158).

The *no delay* principle is stated in s 1(2) and requires that 'in any proceedings in which any question with respect to the upbringing of the child arises' the court should have regard to 'the general principle that delay in determining the question is likely to prejudice the welfare of the child'.

This sub-section owes its existence to horror stories of the past, such as *J v C* [1969] 2 WLR 540; [1969] 1 All ER 788, where delay in deciding the future of a Spanish boy brought up by middle class foster parents in an English green belt area resulted in his being unable to return to the working class background of his natural parents in a poor urban quarter of Madrid, as it had taken nearly 10 years to reach a final hearing. As a result, s 11 requires that a timetable be drawn up to progress s 8 orders (and s 32 makes a similar provision in relation to care and supervision orders in the public law part of the Act). The court takes this seriously, expecting the timetable to be adhered to and sometimes, for example, proceeding in the absence of some reports if the consequent delay to wait for them outweighs the disadvantage of delay. This is currently posing a dilemma in many cases as in some areas there is at least a 15 week wait for a welfare report to be prepared by the Court Welfare Service.

24.4 THE WELFARE PRINCIPLE (CA 1989, s 1(1))

This section provides that whenever a court determines any question with respect to the:

- upbringing of a child; or
- administration of a child's property or the application of any income arising from it,

the welfare of the child shall be paramount. There is no conflict with s 25 of the MCA 1973 in the law of ancillary relief, which states:

> It shall be the duty of the court in deciding whether to exercise its powers under ss 23, 24 or 24A above and, if so, in what manner, to have regard to all the circumstances of the case, *first* consideration being given to the welfare while a minor of any child of the family who has not attained the age of eighteen ... [author's emphasis]

nor with the interests of children in the reformed law of domestic violence and occupation of the matrimonial home, now contained in Pt IV of the Family Law Act (FLA) 1996 (see Chapter 23).

It is established that 'paramount' in s 1(1) of the CA 1989 means 'the welfare of the child should come before any other consideration in deciding whether to make an order' (*Hansard*, vol 503, col 1167). However, there is no guidance where more than one child is involved and their interests conflict.

A 'child' is anyone under 18 (CA 1989, s 105), but no s 8 orders are made for children over age 16 unless the case is exceptional (s 9(7)). This is for the obvious reason that at this age, which is also the school leaving age, such a 'child' might not observe them and cannot be compelled to remain in a parent's house nor to see an absent parent against the child's will. For the same reason, public law orders (ie, for care or supervision) are not made for children over 17 (16 if the child is married).

'Welfare' means (or so it is thought, as the term is nowhere expressly defined) the body of issues relevant to a child's satisfactory upbringing, which now appear in the *statutory checklist* under s 1(3) of the Act (see Chapter 25). This statutory checklist of welfare points to be taken into account in reaching decisions has now assumed crucial importance in making all s 8 orders, and was specifically referred to in order indirectly to define welfare in a 1995 case in the Court of Appeal by a judge skilfully emerging from a horrendously complex appeal against the denial of contact for a mother against the wishes of her children (see *Re M (Contact: Welfare Test)* [1995] 1 FLR 274, CA).

24.5 CHILDREN'S RIGHTS

It is often said that the concept of PR and the philosophies entrenched in s 1 of the Act negate the growing importance of children's rights. The usual answer to this is that in England and Wales children are perceived as having a right to a childhood and therefore to a right *not* to have to concern themselves with those matters which are addressed by the concepts of PR, welfare, non-intervention and prompt disposal of issues concerning children. There are, however, one or two areas where the theory behind the jurisprudence that has been developing needs considering.

The concept of *children's rights* in English law most commonly arises in practice (in a reactive rather than proactive manner) in connection with a child's right to determine his or her own medical treatment, whether pursuant to s 8 of the FLRA 1969 (which gives to 16–17 year olds the right to consent to their own medical treatment) or to the *Gillick* competence of a child under 16. Specific issues also arise from time to time, such as that of corporal punishment, ended in State schools by the Education (No 2) Act 1986 and in children's homes by the CA 1989: some cases have been taken to the European Court of Human Rights on this point though with the exception of one, involving a caning by the child's stepfather, the punishment in question has mostly been found to be generally insufficiently severe to be so degrading as not to be in the child's best interests within the meaning of Art 3 of the Convention, which requires those interests to be the primary consideration.

However, the UN Convention on the Rights of the Child does not have the force of law in England and Wales, although some of its concepts are enshrined in the CA 1989. The operation of the Convention is therefore only monitored by the UK as signatories and by the UN which has set up its own Committee on the Rights of the Child to monitor abuses in countries where the Convention has been adopted. The various articles guarantee such basic rights as that to life (Art 6), freedom of expression (Art 13) and of association and peaceful assembly (Art 15), protection of privacy and family life (Art 16) and thought, conscience and religion (Art 14), contact with parents (Art 9), protection from drugs, exploitation and torture (Arts 33, 34 and 37), the right to education, rest and leisure (Arts 28 and 30), the right to an adequate standard of living, health and medical care and protection from work interfering with education or development (Arts 24, 27 and 33). There is also an obligation on the part of the State under Art 5 to respect the rights and duties of parents to guide the child appropriately to his or her developing capacities.

24.5.1 The theory of children's rights

As a result of the limited concept of children's rights generated by the protective provisions of the CA 1989, which is not overly reflective of the UN Convention, the jurisprudential theory of children's rights has not received much attention in English law. Eekelaar's 1986 identification of a triple concept of basic, developmental and autonomy rights was a timely commentary that influenced the development of children's right to express their wishes, now reflected in s 1(3)(a) of the CA 1989, and this has been taken up by other commentators, notably Andrew Bainham and Jane Fortin. Nevertheless, the law as such remains primarily protective towards childhood rather than positively empowering of children. The *Gillick* case drew attention to the fact that we had moved on from the absolute rights of the father in *Re Agar-Ellis* (1883) 24 Ch D 317, CA, through the recognition of the modern reality of diminishing parental influence in *Hewer v Bryant* [1970] 1 QB 357 to the contemporary position of giving effect to the appropriate decision making potential of the child who is approaching adulthood. Nevertheless, limitations remain which have led some commentators to the conclusion that any theory of even limited empowerment is entirely hypocritical because where the child's life is threatened the court will always overrule the decision of even a *Gillick* competent child, as may be seen in the medical treatment cases which come to the inherent jurisdiction of the High Court for decision.

24.5.2 Medical treatment

While the *Gillick* case confirmed the *Gillick* competent child's right to *consent* to treatment, the courts have steadfastly reiterated that such a child cannot claim, pursuant to s 8(3) of the FLRA 1969, to refuse life saving treatment.

This was originally established in two landmark cases: *Re R (A Minor) (Wardship: Medical Treatment)* [1991] 4 All ER 177; and *Re W (A Minor) (Consent to Medical Treatment)* [1993] 1 FLR 1. In the former, the court authorised the administration of anti-psychotic drugs to a 15 year old (Lord Donaldson using the analogy of a keyholder – the competent child or the parent – unlocking the door to treatment and the consent providing a flak jacket to protect the doctor from suit for assault), and in the latter held that while the view of the competent child in refusing treatment for anorexia nervosa was important, there came a life threatening stage where the court was not bound by it, not least because anorexia nervosa is known to destroy the ability to make an informed choice.

This issue of consent to medical treatment for children was discussed by Michael Nicholls of the Official Solicitor's Office in an article, 'Keyholders and flak jackets – consent to medical treatment for children' [1994] Fam Law 10, and has been the subject of further comment, following the later case of *Re L (Medical Treatment: Gillick Competency)* [1998] 2 FLR 810, concerning a 14 year old who had signed a 'no blood' card and was declared not *Gillick* competent.

This in turn generated an article by McCafferty in [1999] Fam Law 335 entitled 'Won't consent? Can't consent! Refusal of medical treatment', in which the author points out that there are no reported decisions in England and Wales in which the court has allowed a Jehovah's Witness child to refuse a blood transfusion, or to have parents do so on the child's behalf. McCafferty took the view that it was better to follow the reasoning in *Re E* [1993] 1 FLR 386, where Ward LJ had held that the boy in the case was not competent as he had not fully understood the horrendous way in which he would die if he did not have the transfusion rather than to compare the child L to a teenager with a mental health problem. This view was supported by Downie in the article 'Consent to medical treatment – whose view of welfare?' [1999] Fam Law 818, which notes that it is clear that any assessment of the child's competence is almost a pretence as the court will base its decision on its view of the child's welfare. Nevertheless, the court did order the detention of a teenager in *Re C (Interim Care Order: Residential Assessment)* [1997] AC 489; [1997] 1 FLR 1, in which the House of Lords held that s 38(6) and (7) should be construed purposively since the purpose of the sub-sections was to enable the court to obtain the information needed to make a final decision.

However, there may be some justification for the court's approach, and for the overall approach of English law, in *generally* protecting what they see as the rights of childhood to have someone else overrule a decision which may be unwise. In *Re M (Medical Treatment: Consent)* [1999] Fam Law 753, the court, based on their right to override a child's veto as identified in *Re W*, above, gave consent to a heart transplant for a 15 year old who had refused it, though her mother consented. The girl had refused as she had thought having someone else's heart would make her a different person, and as she had been unwilling to face a lifetime of anti-rejection drugs, but later told the media that she was glad that the court had intervened. Johnson J, who decided *Re M*, took the opportunity in that case to set out the balancing test that the court goes through when making a decision, referring back to *Re W* and identifying the basic principles as twofold:

(a) in a case likely to lead to death or permanent injury, the court does first try to see the situation from the minor's point of view; but then

(b) if necessary, the court must choose the course of action which promotes the child's best interests, even if that goes against the child's wishes.

There may of course be appropriate cases where the court might allow a child to die where it was appropriate to withdraw medical treatment, just as in the case of severely damaged babies who cannot take a decision one way or the other and would not be competent to do so even if undamaged. See, for example, *Re C (A Baby)* [1996] 2 FLR 43, where artificial ventilation of a warded brain damaged child who was blind, deaf and in distress was switched off by order of the court. However, these cases are unlikely to come before the court on the issue of a competent child's right to consent, since in the nature of the facts a child of whatever age in such circumstances is unlikely to be competent.

Medical treatment cases, due to their urgency and importance, are not usually decided under the provisions of the CA 1989 but under the court's inherent jurisdiction or in wardship (for which see Chapter 27).

24.6 THE CHILDREN'S GUARDIAN (FORMERLY GUARDIANS *AD LITEM*)

Either parent with PR may appoint a guardian for the child in the event of that parent's death; but if on that parent's death the other parent with PR is still alive, the appointment will not be effective, and the surviving parent will take sole charge of the child, unless the deceased parent had a residence order, in which case the guardian will *not* be displaced, and the surviving parent will have to apply to the court for the guardian's appointment to be revoked (CA 1989, s 5).

From such testamentary guardians must be distinguished the position of the 'children's guardian' (formerly called the 'guardian *ad litem*' and abbreviated GAL) who is a person appointed to protect the child's interests in any 'specified proceedings' (ie, of a public nature, eg, care, supervision, emergency protection orders: CA 1989, s 41). The obligations of the 'children's guardian' include appointing and instructing a solicitor to represent the child, unless the child is already of sufficient age and understanding to do this personally. The guardian, who will be appointed unless the court is satisfied that this is unnecessary, should also advise the court if any party should be joined to the proceedings, on the appropriate forum and timing for proceedings, as to whether the child is of sufficient age and understanding to be served documents or consent to or refuse medical or psychiatric examination, and wherever appropriate to act as a channel for indicating to the court the child's wishes. The guardian should attend all hearings, and advise the court on the options available and their suitability. Renaming of the GAL follows recent changes in terminology and reorganisation of children's services in family courts (see 24.7, below), but the new 'guardian' is essentially the same as the GALs who appear in past decided cases.

24.7 WELFARE REPORTS

Section 7(1) of the CA 1989 provides for the preparation of welfare reports wherever a court is considering any question with regard to a child under the Act, and these are usually prepared by the court welfare officer who may be a social worker or probation officer. These reports should deal with 'such matters relating to the welfare of the child as are required to be dealt with in the report', and where such a direction is given the report is expected to be thorough and comprehensive (see *Scott v Scott* [1986] 2 FLR 320, CA; and *Re P (Welfare Officer: Duty)* [1996] 2 FLR 5, where it was emphasised that first hand and comprehensive research was required). In *Re P*, the case was remitted to the Family Proceedings Court for reconsideration when the mother appealed on the ground of the manifest inadequacy of the report: the welfare officer had held one meeting only at her office with all parties present and did not assess the quality of the relationships of the parties and the children. For the importance of the welfare report as a channel between the child who is not of an age to communicate ascertainable wishes and feelings to the court personally pursuant to s 1(3)(a), see Chapter 25. A welfare report will usually be essential in contested s 8 order cases (*Re V (Residence: Review)* [1995] 2 FLR 1010), including those generated by the inability of the court to give a s 41 certificate in divorce (see Chapter 11) and in public law cases. The court welfare officers are now provided by a new family court service called CAFCASS (the Child and Family Court Advisory and Support Service) and are now called Child and Family Court Reporters. Nevertheless their services remain the same as the former generation of court welfare officers, which it appears they continue to be referred to as by the practising profession. See further 26.7.2, below.

THE CHILDREN ACT 1989

CHILDREN ACT 1989

This Act has radically changed both public and private child law. It has abolished the concepts of custody, care and control and access, and replaced them with those of residence and contact, specific issue and prohibited steps orders under s 8 of the Act, and a new concept of PR. There have also been changes in public law. This has created a new approach to child disputes.

PARENTAL RESPONSIBILITY

There is no definition of PR, but it encompasses all the traditional protection and support which a parent has historically given to the child. Some commentators have claimed these obligations should be made more explicit in the Act itself.

Parents who are married at the time of the child's birth have PR automatically. Otherwise the mother has it and the father can obtain it by agreement with the mother or by order of the court. Parental responsibility is normally given by the court to those fathers who can demonstrate the criteria settled in *Re H (Illegitimate Children: Father: Parental Rights) (No 2)* [1991] 1 FLR 214, CA, and many times reiterated in successive cases since. Parental responsibility only terminates on death or the child's majority and can never be lost unless acquired PR is removed by the court following proof of misconduct towards the child by an unmarried father. There is some human rights impact on the concept of PR, but it is not necessarily a breach of the European Convention on Human Rights to treat married and unmarried fathers differently. The concept of PR means that children cannot 'divorce' their parents.

THE PRINCIPLES AND PHILOSOPHY OF THE ACT

The non-interventionist and no delay principles in s 1(5) and (2) require that no order is made unless making an order would be better than not making one, and that any delay is presumed prejudicial to the child. Parents are therefore encouraged to agree matters in issue and withdraw their applications rather than that the court should make a consent order (a technical impossibility under the CA 1989 in fact) and a timetable is drawn up and adhered to for disposal of all cases.

The welfare principle in s 1(1) means that the child's welfare is paramount in all decisions concerning the child's future or the administration of the child's property. 'Welfare' is not defined in the Act but is ascertained through application of the criteria in a welfare checklist in s 1(3), use of which is mandatory in contested cases. A welfare report is also usually crucial in such cases, and although the court is not bound to follow the report's recommendations, they usually do.

CHILDREN'S RIGHTS

Children do not have formal rights in English law, despite the UK being a signatory to the UN Convention on the Rights of the Child. However, the concept of PR acknowledges that the child's relationship with parents and State is one in which the child has some rights and parents and the State have more duties and obligations than rights, especially in relation to *Gillick* competent children. Nevertheless, the court retains a right to intervene in the decisions of such children where in refusing medical treatment such decisions pose a threat to those children's lives. This is usually explained as challenging the child's competence as affected by the illness in question, but has been the subject of much adverse comment by academics who consider there is a presumption that any life threatening refusal of treatment will be overturned and that the court's examining of the child's competence is not genuine.

GUARDIANS AND CHILDREN'S GUARDIANS

Guardians appointed to act after the death of both parents with PR should be distinguished from the children's guardian *ad litem* (also called simply a 'guardian'), normally necessary to protect a child in litigation under specified sections of the Children Act 1989. The latter acts as a channel between court and child and ensures that the child has a solicitor to represent them in proceedings.

CHAPTER 25

THE CHILDREN ACT 1989: SECTION 8 ORDERS

25.1 THE PORTFOLIO OF ORDERS

There are four s 8 orders:

- residence order;
- contact order;
- prohibited steps order; and
- specific issue order.

It should be noted that, due to the non-interventionist principle in s 1(5) of the Children Act (CA) 1989, these orders cannot technically be made 'by consent' (see 24.3, above).

25.1.1 A residence order

Pursuant to the new ethos of parental responsibility generating ongoing practical parenting, this order merely settles where a child shall live and no more. Parents will still share parental responsibility even if one obtains a residence order, and even if a non-parent obtains a residence order (which will give that person parental responsibility also) the parents will still retain their own parental responsibility.

Although the court prefers children to have one settled home, there may be (in appropriate established circumstances or where such a routine is likely to work) an order in favour of more than one person. This is variously called a split or a joint residence order. The opposite terms ought to mean distinct orders, but seem to be different ways of expressing the same idea, namely that the child will have a settled home with each parent and since the parties are (obviously) not living together the order can detail the periods to be spent at each house. Cases where such orders have been made include *Re H (A Minor) (Shared Residence)* [1993] Fam 463; and *G v G (Joint Residence Order)* [1993] Fam Law 615.

Residence orders are often used to give some standing to stepparents. See, for example, *Re H* [1995] 2 FLR 883, where the order was in respect of a son and a stepson since the two boys saw themselves as both equally 'sons'.

25.1.2 A contact order

This requires the person with whom the child lives (who may or may not have a residence order) to allow the child to visit or stay with a named person (generally called 'staying contact') or for that person and the child to have contact with each other in some other manner. The extent of such contact may either be left unspecified or alternatively be more precisely stated as *reasonable contact*, or even *defined contact* if the parents cannot agree a programme and prefer the court to order it in detail for them.

This is a complete change from the former system of 'access', which could be only by physical presence. Now the court may order that letters and telephone calls may be exchanged between the child and the recipient of the order, or sometimes (eg, where the child is too young to write or telephone personally) to a limited extent between the latter and the parent with care, though they generally cannot order the parent with whom the child resides actually to perform more extensive tasks (eg, personally to take any positive action in writing progress reports to or communicating news to the other parent if children do not do so themselves (or cannot do so, eg, if they are too young to write or even to speak on the telephone)). This was attempted in *Re M (A Minor) (Contact: Conditions)* [1994] 1 FLR 272, and the court held the view that such an order could not be made although it was deemed that a custodial parent could be ordered to *keep the other parent informed* of the child's whereabouts, so that contact could actually take place.

However, *Re O (A Minor) (Contact)* [1995] 2 FLR 124, CA did approve a mother being asked to send photographs, medical reports and nursery school reports, inform the other parent of serious illness of the child and accept delivery of presents and cards for the child, which clearly only really involves the ordinary civilised behaviour which might be expected of a custodial parent towards the other with whom the child does not reside. Lord Bingham also used the opportunity to spell out to the resident parent the responsibilities to allow and promote contact with the other parent which some parents still ignore, and hinted that as contact with both parents was so important to the child any obstruction was at their peril since the court could take appropriate action.

Technically, any conditions which are acceptable so as to achieve indirect contact where direct contact is for some reason impossible may be attached pursuant to s 11(7), which permits conditions to be attached to all s 8 orders. This power must be read in the light of the new concept of promoting indirect contact as an alternative to actually seeing the child, but not carried to extremes which require so much of that parent that the concept of contact with the *child* is distorted into a back door requirement for contact with the carer *parent*, which was clearly not the intention of the statute.

Contact orders will usually always be granted in the case of biological parent-child relationships, even though there is no statutory presumption to that effect, on the basic principle that it is for the good of the child living with one parent to remain in contact with the other parent. In *Re W (A Minor) (Contact)* [1994] 2 FLR 441, CA, the Court of Appeal made an order for contact despite a mother's hostility to the applicant (as she had remarried and was teaching the child to regard her new husband as the natural father). They allowed an appeal against the judge below who had not made an order, *inter alia* because the mother had said she would disobey it if it were made, so that judge had understandably thought that to make an order in that climate would only destabilise the child and not be in any child's interests. However, the Court of Appeal said he had abdicated his responsibility.

This must therefore be taken to be the contemporary trend, and that in the absence of complications, such as violence or sufficiently implacable hostility of either the custodial parent or of the children themselves to raise a query as to whether contact is or is not for the child's welfare, there *is* a basic presumption of some sort of a right to contact. This *can* and *will*, however, be displaced by expressly showing (in the words of the text now adapted by the Court of Appeal in 'implacable hostility' cases and with reference to the statutory welfare checklist) that the:

... fundamental emotional need of every child to have an enduring relationship with both its parents' – as contemplated by s 1(3)(b) – is outweighed by the depth of harm which in the light, *inter alia* of the child's wishes and feelings – under s 1(3)(a) of the checklist – the child would be at risk of suffering – ie, within the meaning of s 1(3)(e) – by virtue of the contact order.

Contact is therefore likely to be refused if that is absolutely necessary and in the child's interests (*Re B (Minors: Access)* [1992] 1 FLR 140; *Re H (Minors: Access)* [1992] 1 FLR 148), especially if the child personally opposes it and is of an age when his or her ascertainable wishes and feelings, within the meaning of the statutory checklist, are taken into account (*Re F (Minors) (Denial of Contact)* [1993] 2 FLR 677). Even indirect contact could be refused if that was in the child's best interests, although reported examples of this are rare due to the normal assumption that it is highly desirable that, if there can be no direct contact, indirect contact should be established (see *Re C (Contact: No Order for Contact)* [2000] Fam Law 699).

Whether an order should be made is less obvious where the hurdle is the *resident carer parent's* implacable hostility to the contact for the child, making the child potentially at serious risk of emotional harm if contact is compelled because it will have such a bad effect on the objecting parent (see *Re D (A Minor) (Contact: Mother's Hostility)* [1993] 2 FLR 1; *Re F (Minors) (Contact: Mother's Anxiety)* [1993] 2 FLR 830; *Re J (A Minor) (Contact)* [1994] Fam Law 316).

As indicated in *Re O*, above, courts disapprove of parents being obstructive about contact and in the past have indicated that a parent's attitude to contact might influence them to make an order for residence in favour of the other parent. For example, in *D v M* [1982] 3 WLR 891; [1982] 3 All ER 897, the father was reluctant for the mother to have contact and as a result the court was reluctant to let him have a residence order for the children. *Re S* [1990] 2 FLR 166 was a similar case where the children (two boys) each lived with one parent, and the court said that if the mother did not allow the boy in her care to visit the father and the other child she might have to give up the boy unless she became less recalcitrant, as she was depriving the boys of *each other's* company as well as the father of the company of the boy in her care.

It has of course been stressed that changing residence might be an empty threat, since in theory the grant of a residence order must be in accordance with the s 1(3) criteria, reference to which is mandatory in contested cases. However, by s 1(3), the welfare of the child is paramount, thus attitude to contact is very important in a s 8 order application, because the court can always hang its decision on one or more of the s 1(3) pegs (eg, the child's emotional needs or the harm to the child if contact with one parent is lost or fundamentally reduced).

Recently the court has taken more decisive steps to give weight to the fears of children and carer parents where there has been such violence and traumatisation that contact is resisted, usually by the mother where it is the father who has been violent. This issue was initially raised by the Children Act Sub-Committee of the Lord Chancellor's Advisory Board on Family Law, whose report indicated that the earlier position, whereby the court's view that violence was not of itself a bar to contact had prevailed, might not always be a suitable stance. For example, in *Re M (Violent Parent)* [1999] Fam Law 380, Wall J suggested that instead of requiring mothers to arrange contact regardless, the violent father might have to show that he was fit to have contact before it would be ordered. In *Re K (Contact: Mother's Anxiety)* [1999] Fam Law 527, the court found that the mother's traumatisation by the father's behaviour was such that it would inevitably impact upon the child, causing emotional harm, if contact were insisted upon.

The Court of Appeal has since reviewed the matter in four conjoined cases (see *Re L (Contact: Domestic Violence)* [2000] 2 FLR 334, CA) and indicated that there is no presumption either way, but that a balancing exercise must be undertaken to determine what is best for the child's welfare by using the s 1(3) checklist in the usual way but looking particularly at the past and present contact of the parties, the effect on the child and the carer and the motivation of the non-resident parent.

Contact orders do *not* confer parental responsibility so, like a stepparent without parental responsibility, a person with a contact order and no parental responsibility can do anything which safeguards and promotes the child's welfare during the contact but should not exceed that duty by doing anything which would be appropriate in a person exercising parental responsibility. It should be remembered that, apart from the case of parents with automatic parental responsibility, the key to other relations and associates of the child having parental responsibility is not the relationship as such but whether that person has a residence order which does confer parental responsibility (see Chapter 24).

It should be noted that contact has been traditionally the right of the child and that the non-resident parent, having no 'right' to it, could not be compelled to exercise any right or duty to have contact with a child. However, after the Human Rights Act 1998 came into force European jurisprudence started to develop in relation to the non-resident parent's right to family life and therefore contact. Nevertheless the English court has adopted a robust view based on the assumption of a duty to balance competing human rights, which inevitably, has followed the child's welfare (see, eg, the child abduction case of *P v P* at 25.4.1, below).

25.1.3 A prohibited steps order

This order (often abbreviated to PSO) is one which can prohibit a parent from taking any step which could be taken in meeting that parent's parental responsibility towards the child. The order is not intended to prevent parents doing anything else which does not amount to a step in meeting their parental responsibility, as is shown by *Croydon Borough Council v A* (1992) 136 (LB) 69 (FS), where the local authority had removed children from their home under an emergency protection order and placed them with foster parents because the father had sexually abused one of them. When the authority applied to the magistrates for an interim care order, the court refused that order and instead for some reason made two PSOs, the first preventing the father from seeing the children and the second prohibiting him from having contact with the mother. On appeal the second order was overturned because it did not fall within the statutory definition of a parent taking a step in meeting his parental responsibility, and the authority got their interim care order.

Similarly, in *Re H (Prohibited Steps Order)* [1995] 1 FLR 638, a judge made a PSO to forbid contact between a mother's former cohabitant and her children who were living with her, and over whom the local authority had supervision orders because the children had been sexually abused by the former cohabitant. He also attached no contact conditions to the supervision orders. On appeal, the Court of Appeal held that the PSO was wrong because it contravened s 9(5)(a) of the CA 1989, which specifically forbids a court to make a PSO as a back door means of achieving a desired result which could, and properly should, be effected by a residence or contact order, and that although conditions could be attached to the authority's supervision order (such as for medical or psychiatric examination) a condition for no contact could not be so attached, although the supervisor has other means under Sched 3 to the CA 1989 of achieving the same result.

Common use of the PSO is to prevent the two important steps prohibited by s 13(1) of the Act (ie, change of a child's name or removal from the jurisdiction: see below).

25.1.4 A specific issue order

This order, as the name suggests, enables the court to give directions to decide a dispute as to any major decision to be taken in relation to a child's future (eg, a change of surname, school or religion, or whether a child should or should not have a particular medical treatment, such as a blood transfusion, where one or even both of the parents are against it for religious or other reasons, or sterilisation or abortion, eg, where the child is advised not to have children for some sufficient medical reason).

Sometimes several issues are combined resulting in a specific issue and a PSO on one and possibly no order, under the s 1(5) principle, on another, as in *Re J (Specific Issue Order: Circumcision)* [1999] 2 FLR 678. Here the court first refused the Muslim father's application for a specific issue order that his son be circumcised as the boy's non-Muslim mother had vetoed this (and the court said this was a powerful welfare consideration) and it was not suggested by the father that the boy should attend the mosque or receive religious instruction, and secondly made a PSO to stop the father from arranging the circumcision himself. In respect of the child's religion, they did not consider that an order should be made to require the child to be brought up by the mother in his father's religion, since the father had made no proposals for such religious observance, so that the boy's religious instruction should fall within his contact with his father.

The court can either take the decision itself, as in the above case, or direct that a particular person should take it, for example, where treatment is directed by a specified doctor as the doctor deems appropriate. Such orders may be sought by non-parents (eg, a local authority concerned for the child's welfare).

In general the court now tends to order modern diagnostic treatment against parents' wishes, on the basis that the child him or herself is entitled to the benefits of science unless there is genuine scope for debate (see *Re C* (1999) BMLR 283, which concerned an HIV test on a five month old child, which the parents had resisted).

The same restrictions apply to these orders as for PSOs.

25.1.5 Interim orders

All s 8 orders may be made as interim orders and s 11(3) and (7) permit conditions to be attached or to allow the court to delay implementation, restrict the effect of the order to a certain period or attach conditions.

Tactically, obtaining an interim order is usually in the applicant's interests, because of the status quo element in the statutory checklist (see below) and the additional value of an interim residence or contact order is that it may cement a relationship, thus strengthening other statutory checklist points in the applicant's favour (eg, the child's ascertainable wishes and feelings in favour of remaining with the applicant if temporary arrangements are working out well).

25.1.6 Enforcement of orders

Enforcement can be a problem in the case of both residence and contact orders. Both may be enforced by using s 34 of the Family Law Act (FLA) 1986, formerly used to enforce old style custody and access orders, but expressly referred to in Sched 13 to the CA 1989 for enforcement of residence and contact orders. Schedule 14 to the CA 1989 also affords another method whereby such an order may be enforced under s 63(3) of the Magistrates' Courts Act 1980 by serving a copy of the order and requiring production of the child.

However, while fathers are often committed for contempt for failing to observe orders, mothers often tend not to be (as then children might have to go into the care of the local authority if there is no one else available to look after them). Yet committal is not really suitable for either parent and is only used in the last resort (see *Re N (A Minor) (Access: Penal Notices)* [1992] 1 FLR 134). The remedy is really to re-educate the parents into observing the philosophy and spirit of the Act, such as in the current 'Making Contact Work' initiative, and to the use of a neutral point of exchange, such as relatives, friends or one of the charity contact centres so the parents do not have to meet. A directory of all such centres may be obtained from the network of Access and Child Contact Centres at Nottingham.

25.2 WHO MAY APPLY FOR s 8 ORDERS

Certain persons are entitled to apply as of right:

- any parent or guardian of the child (s 10(4));
- anyone who has a residence order in respect of the child (s 10(4));
- any person with an old style custody, care and control or access order, called an 'existing order' (Sched 14).

A father who is not married to the mother will usually be classed as a parent, and will not require leave, but only if he can show that he is the father. Alternatively he may have resided with the child for three years (see below) and thus not need leave for that reason.

The following are entitled to apply for residence and contact orders only:

(a) any party to a marriage (whether or not the marriage is still subsisting) in which the child was a child of the family as defined in s 105(1);

(b) any person with the consent of all those with residence orders (or 'existing orders') or parental responsibility in respect of the child;

(c) any person who has the consent of a local authority which has a care order; and

(d) any person with whom the child has resided for three years (not necessarily continuously, but beginning not more than five years before the application is made).

Rules of court may extend this list (s 10(7)).

Other persons can still apply but will need leave of the court (eg, grandparents or any other relatives with whom the child has not established a three year residence qualification). The test for success is whether there is a good arguable case (*Re M (Care: Contact: Grandmother's Application for Leave)* [1995] 2 FLR 86). Where there is a contest between parents and other relatives, weight is given to natural parenthood (*Re D (Care: Natural Parent Presumption)* [1999] 1 FLR 134; *Re D (Residence Order: Natural Parent)* [1999] Fam Law 755).

The child itself may apply if of sufficient understanding (s 10(8)), and a number of such applications by teenage and sub-teenage girls have succeeded; a solicitor may accept instructions from such a child and obtain legal aid in order to pursue his or her application. It is clear, since children picked up the idea of 'divorcing their parents', that this may be a practice growth area.

Acting for children has become a specialism in itself for some family lawyers and, owing to the potential complexities, all such s 8 applications must be heard in the Family Division of the High Court (see *Practice Direction* [1993] 1 All ER 820). There is a growing corpus of authority on this area of law and practice (see Family Proceedings Rules (FPR) 1991 SI 1991/1247, r 9.2A; *Re CT (A Minor) (Wardship: Representation)* [1993] 2 FLR 278; *Re C (Leave to Seek s 8 Orders)* [1994] 1 FLR 26; *Re SC (A Minor: Leave to Seek a Residence Order)* [1994] 1 FLR 96; *Re H (Residence Order: Child's Application for Leave)* [2000] 1 FLR 780 which indicate the caution involved, in view of the fact that such an application can have a detrimental effect on parent-child relations and the query as to whether the formality of an order is necessary or whether informal resolution is preferable). It is uncertain whether the Human Rights Act 1998 gives increased scope for leave for children to participate in court proceedings. Not surprisingly, in view of all these doubts, the Solicitors Family Law Association also issues its own *Guide to Good Practice for Solicitors Acting for Children*.

It is incidentally, of course, despite all media misconceptions, *impossible* for a child to divorce his or her parents, since parental responsibility is for life or at least until adulthood or adoption of the child, though the child may naturally obtain a residence order to go to *live* with other relatives, or with anyone suitable, and maintenance may be obtained from the natural parent(s) to enable this to happen (see Chapter 15). Since the mid-1990s, when a child succeeded in making her own application in her parents' s 8 proceedings (*Re C (Child's Application for Leave)* [1995] 1 FLR 927), such initiatives by children have been accepted as appropriate in certain cases, but are by no means common.

If leave *is* required the court will base its decision on the following:

(a) the nature of the proposed application for a s 8 order;

(b) the applicant's connection with the child;

(c) any risk there might be of the application disrupting the child's life so that he or she would be harmed by it; and

(d) if the child is being looked after by the local authority, the authority's plans for him or her and the wishes and feelings of his or her parents.

Applications are often made in the course of a divorce, but this is in no way necessary (see Chapter 11), since application may be made at any time on a completely freestanding basis and the same form is now used irrespective of whether there is a divorce in process.

The court will have jurisdiction if the child is either habitually resident in England and Wales or present and not habitually resident elsewhere on the date of application or hearing. Jurisdiction is excluded if there are matrimonial proceedings elsewhere in the UK unless the other court has waived its jurisdiction, or stayed proceedings so that the matter might be heard in England and Wales (Family Law Act (FLA) 1986, s 3), though if the court thinks that the matter would be better determined outside England and Wales (ie, in any other jurisdiction) it has the power to direct that no order be made (FLA 1986, s 2(4)).

25.3 THE ALTERNATIVE TO A s 8 ORDER: THE FAMILY ASSISTANCE ORDER (CA 1989, s 16)

This is a short term alternative to a s 8 order, though it may be used for many purposes, such as even when a s 8 order has already been made and the parents need extra support. The order was introduced by the CA 1989 and is specifically designed to help at times of matrimonial breakdown. Such an order is only made in the most exceptional circumstances, and merely enables a social worker to give general advice and assistance. Everyone involved except the child must consent to the order (s 16(3) and (7)).

So far, there has not been great use of the family assistance order, though it has come in useful where it was held that a s 11(7) condition of supervision of contact could not be attached to a contact order (see *Leeds County Council v C* [1993] 1 FLR 269, where Booth J used a family assistance order to achieve supervised contact).

25.4 CHANGE OF NAME OR REMOVAL FROM THE JURISDICTION (CA 1989, s 13(1) AND THE PROHIBITED STEPS ORDER)

The prohibition of these two acts by s 13(1) provides a common example of the use of the PSO to stop a parent misusing parental responsibility by taking a step with which objectively the other parent cannot necessarily be expected to agree, thus making unilateral action clearly inadvisable. Where a residence order is already in force (ie, where the parents have already had recourse to the court for one reason or another), the section prohibits:

- changing the child's surname; and
- taking a child out of the jurisdiction,

in either case without the written consent of every person with parental responsibility or the leave of the court. The reasons for this are obvious. (It should be noted that if there is *no* residence order in force, the correct procedure to stop the removal or change of name is to apply for a PSO under s 8.)

25.4.1 Removal from the jurisdiction

The person with the residence order may in fact take the child out of the UK for a holiday of up to one month *without leave*. If leave is required for longer it is likely to be given by the court if the other parent will not consent, provided the holiday is not obviously intended as a cover for permanent removal beyond the reach of the court's authority. Moreover, a parent who has totally unreasonably withheld consent might find that he or she has to pay the costs of a court application.

The way in which this restriction may be dealt with in practice is to have in place either a general direction attached to the residence order to enable removal of the child whenever convenient subject to a return to the jurisdiction whenever required, or a general undertaking may be given to the court by the parent wishing to remove the child (eg, a father living abroad whom the child will visit regularly).

Permanent removal is more difficult, as this might in practice cut off all contact for the other parent. However, the court is aware of the difficulties that may arise if the parent with the residence order is thwarted in an attempt to emigrate, with consequent unhappiness for the whole family, as is shown by the accumulated case law.

Historically, the court's generally cautious stance is shown by cases such as *Chamberlain v de la Mare* [1983] 4 FLR 434; and *Lonslow v Hennig* [1986] 2 FLR 378, which indicate that while if the move is in the child's interests and is well worked out the court may consent, but that precedent has no role in the decision as each case must be approached on its own facts and merits. More recent decisions have indicated the reconfirmation of the longstanding presumption set out in *Poel v Poel* [1970] 1 WLR 1469 in favour of requiring a well worked out plan for emigration by the carer parent, in which case there is likely to be consent to leave unless that would be plainly contrary to the child's welfare (*Re H (Application to Remove from the Jurisdiction)* [1998] 1 FLR 848).

Among a rash of recent cases, possibly generated by the Human Rights Act 1998, there was an unsuccessful challenge to this position by a father who opposed the return of a child and her mother to the mother's home jurisdiction of New Zealand on the basis that it breached his human right to family life pursuant to Art 8 of the European Convention on Human Rights, but the Court of Appeal confirmed that the paramountcy of the welfare of the child meant that adult rights in conflict must give way (*P v P* (2001) unreported, 9 March, CA). Other similar recent cases include *Re K* [1998] 2 FLR 1006; and *Re M* [1999] 2 FLR 334. Despite this, Kirkconel, in 'Removing children from the jurisdiction' [1999] Fam Law 333, has argued for carer parents seeking leave to remove to have to prove that their plans were not merely reasonable but positively for the benefit of the child, which would create a stiffer test than at present. This was the approach adopted by the court in *Re X and Y (Children)* [2001] Fam Law 344, where it was said the applicant must make out a case of positive improvement in welfare terms, although this does lay the court open to creating more potential abductions where the decision led to the disruption envisaged by Thorpe LJ and therefore hardly be likely to be for the benefit of the child in the long run, especially if the Court of Appeal decision (where the bench included Hale LJ) in *P v P* is right.

Certainly reasonable contact proposals could be required before leave was granted, as in *Re M* [1999] 2 FLR 334, but any more stringent requirements might exacerbate an already serious problem area, in which Thorpe LJ has already said that there is no reason to tinker with the established classic case law where a carer parent has a reasonable wish to emigrate but has also emphasised that there is no presumption in favour of the carer parent: the obvious knock on effect, if serious consideration is not given to the reasonable plans of the carer parent, may be to inflate the incidence of child abduction which in the context of growing cross-border mobility is already a serious problem. The practice has therefore tended towards safeguards such as mirror orders, notarised agreements and the like, since it is desirable to prevent competing litigation in two jurisdictions with different traditions (see *Re K (Removal from the Jurisdiction: Practice)* [1999] 2 FLR 1084).

Looking back at the older cases, the court sometimes did refuse leave if the future picture presented was unsatisfactory, but generally did not, as in *Re F* [1988] 2 FLR 116, if a parent was remarrying, if the new partner seemed to be 'good news' and if there was a happy relationship between the applicant parent and the child or children and other positive indications. The key to a successful application is clearly that the applicant parent should already have a residence order or a settled *status quo* whereby the children are and have been for some time living happily with that parent. Applications for leave to take the children out of the jurisdiction to emigrate are obviously not best placed where the relationship between the applicant parent and the children is already slender and the other parent conversely has established a satisfactory lifestyle for them, especially if that includes an existing or interim residence order (eg, in *P v P*, above, there was an extended family, including grandparents, in New Zealand). Moreover, it has been held in *Re A* [2000] 2 FLR 2000 that *Poel v Poel* was not in conflict with the Human Rights Act, as both mother and father had a right to a family life under Art 8.

Lengthy, more temporary, removal may be a problem, as is shown by *Re K (A Minor)* [1992] 2 FLR 98, where the court would not allow a mother to take the child to the USA for her postgraduate study because it would seriously disrupt contact with the father, which does show that each case will genuinely turn on its circumstances as is intended by the requirement to balance the child's interests in accordance with the statutory checklist.

25.4.2 Change of surname

Both formal change by deed poll or informal change (eg, by instructing a school that a child is to be known by a certain name) is equally forbidden by the section, and if the other parent will not consent application will again have to be made to the court.

The court tends to resist consenting, because of the importance of preserving the formal link with the absent father and of the importance of his name as part of the child's identity regardless of the mother's new associations. The children's own wishes count exceptionally little in this situation, and much less than they might in others *because* of the importance placed by the court in the continuing connection with the father, as is shown by cases such as *W v W* [1981] 1 All ER 100; [1981] Fam 14, where the family were all emigrating to Australia and the 12 and 13 year olds wanted to take their mother's new name, which was that of their new stepfather.

With the general tendency towards serial monogamy and cohabitation, embarrassment at having a different name (or even several in the reconstructed family) is now unlikely to be felt by the children, or at least believed by the court, so that the chances of the court's agreeing to a change appear slimmer than ever, and the older cases where they did agree (except perhaps because of a *fait accompli*) are now probably out of date and no longer even a guideline. In particular, as in *L v F* (1978) *The Times*, 1 August, where the father is a person of stature and able to make a positive contribution to the children's lives the court is unlikely to approve the loss of his name, especially as contemporary psychiatric evidence shows that children need to know and acknowledge their biological origins. Conversely, a parent's best chance of success might be if the father were notorious (as has been successful in one well known case in the USA).

This situation has persisted into the contemporary context where consideration and often rejection of the wishes of *Gillick* competent children have generated many pages of appellate judgments (see Chapter 24). Some recent cases have both re-emphasised the importance of the link with the father for the reasons stated above and also held to the principle that *changing* a surname by which a child is already known is a significant step which places a heavy burden on the party seeking to make the change to show that it is in the child's interests. See eg, *Re S (Change of Name) Cultural Factors* [2001] 2 FLR 1005. Indeed, the court now appears to be saying that if any change is to be made, even where the mother alone has parental responsibility because the parents have never been married, good practice indicates that this should be approved by the court. This is no doubt in accordance with the contemporary social context, where neither married nor unmarried relationships are supposed to impact upon child status, but it does in theory conflict with the continuing position of sole parental responsibility for the mother unless the unmarried father has obtained parental responsibility in one of the usual ways.

In *Re C (Minors)* (1997) *The Times*, 8 December, the children had taken the mother's maiden name as their parents had never been married, and when she subsequently married another man and their father, with whom they lived, obtained a residence order, the court held that their name should be changed to his since there was no useful purpose in retaining their mother's maiden name, which she herself no longer used. In *Dawson v Wearmouth* [1999] 1 FLR 1167, however, the House of Lords upheld the Court of Appeal in supporting the decision of the mother of an illegitimate child, who had registered the child's name at birth under her own surname, which was that of her former husband, and not of the actual father, and restated the principle that, pursuant to the paramountcy principle, clear circumstances were required to justify changing a child's surname.

Between the Court of Appeal and House of Lords' hearings of *Dawson v Wearmouth*, the Court of Appeal laid down some guidelines in *Re T (Change of Surname)* [1998] 2 FLR 620, which acknowledged the right of a father with a parental responsibility order, but no residence order, to object to change of a child's surname, and articulated the principle that names are important to the issue of welfare so that in any dispute either consent of the other parent or leave of the court is required, particularly where both parents have parental responsibility. It seems, therefore, that s 13 has in no way changed the common law position that neither parent of a legitimate child could change the child's surname without the agreement of the other, and that where the child is not legitimate (so that historically the mother was the only one with parental responsibility) it is now considered at the very least good practice to refer any dispute about name change to the court, despite the *obiter* remarks to the contrary in *Re PC (Change of Surname)* [1997] 2 FLR 730. Basically, the position clearly now is that the old system, whereby the mother of an illegitimate child was its only parent, is completely dead, because at any moment the unmarried father can apply for parental responsibility if he has not already got it and in the absence of negative contribution to the child's life is likely to be given at least the status of a father.

Pursuant to s 10(8), a child of sufficient understanding can alternatively make his or her own application to the court to seek or prevent a change of surname. In *Re S* [1999] 1 FLR 79, a 15 year old *Gillick* competent child won an appeal against refusal to allow her to change her name to that of her maternal family on the ground that the judge had failed to give sufficient weight to her wishes, feelings, needs and objectives, to the views of the guardian *ad litem* and to the real motives of her father in objecting. This may indicate a significant trend since in *Re B* [1996] 1 FLR 79, the court had said that s 1(3)(a) was not to be given as much weight in specific issue cases about change of name, no doubt due to the importance that has always been given to retaining some traditional links with the father which dropping his name – the situation in most change of name cases – would sever. However, it was acknowledged that there is in fact little the court can do if the child does not accept this principle, such as by asking friends to use the preferred name.

The most recent case on which there was a useful discussion of the dynamics of disputes about changing the child's first name is *Re H (Child's Name: First Name)* (2002) *The Times*, 7 February.

25.5 THE STATUTORY CHECKLIST (CA 1989, s 1(3))

The CA 1989 for the first time reduces to statutory form the various matters which courts have always taken into account when making orders in relation to children, although the case law from which the new checklist was derived may still afford guidelines as to how the court interprets that checklist. The court's primary duty is now simply to work through the checklist itself, which is *mandatory* when making, varying or discharging any s 8 order which is opposed. There is therefore nothing particularly new in the content of the checklist, but prior to the Act, the principles on which decisions were made were to be deduced only from case law if any applied, whereas now the matters in the list must be addressed in a structured manner.

The list does not express or imply any order of importance among the following:

(a) the ascertainable wishes and feelings of the child concerned;

(b) the child's physical, emotional and educational needs;

(c) the likely effect on the child of any change in his or her circumstances;

(d) the child's age, sex, background and any characteristics of his or hers which the court considers relevant;

(e) any harm which the child has suffered or is at risk of suffering;

(f) how capable each of the child's parents, and any other person in relation to whom the court considers the question to be relevant, is of meeting the child's needs; and

(g) the range of powers available to the court under the CA 1989 in the proceedings in question.

In the 10 years of its regular use, the checklist has seemed to be a useful innovation: since there is no precise definition of 'welfare' in the Act, it provides a formula whereby it may be decided *whether* a particular action is or is not for the child's welfare, which in practical terms is probably more useful than an express definition of the term (as thankfully identified by Wilson J in the context of the implacable hostility syndrome which has beset contact cases in recent years).

The old case law is thus still of guiding importance, although it has to be read in the light of modern conditions; for example, children of every class now in fact appear to mature earlier, beside which our contemporary attitudes to children are less paternalistic than before.

Thus children's views generally tend to be taken into consideration more than they used to be in the past where they were expected to be seen and not heard and above all to do what their parents told them. This greater amenability to the consideration of the child's point of view has manifested itself not only in a semi-formal channel in the first head of the checklist under s 1(3)(a), where their ascertainable wishes and feelings are to be considered, but also in the recognition in s 10(8) of the capability of children of sufficient age and understanding to make their own s 8 applications.

25.5.1 The ascertainable wishes and feelings of the child concerned in the light of his age and understanding (CA 1989, s 1(3)(a))

Obviously the *wishes* of a very young child will not be a serious consideration, especially if contrary to the child's long term interests, but the *feelings* of such a child, in the sense of profound attachment to the parent to whom he or she is used and with whom he or she feels loved, secure and comfortable, must always be relevant. Thus, in *Brixey v Lynas* [1996] 2 FLR 499, the House of Lords acknowledged that though there is no legal presumption that a young child should be with his or her mother, there was a 'widely held belief based on practical experience' that this is appropriate.

The child's prime communication channel in this respect is the *welfare officer*, since in a contested s 8 application a welfare report will have been ordered. The welfare officer will have seen the child alone as well as with the parent with whom he or she lives, and possibly with the other parent as well, so will be in a position both to ask expressly if a child of suitable age to say so has views, and to judge independently from the child's body language and demeanour, alone and in the company of one or other or both of the parents, whether one of them has coached the child in rehearsed responses.

Alternatively, or in addition, the judge (but not the magistrates if the case is in the Family Proceedings Court) may interview a child over the age of about seven, in order to find out at first hand about the child's views or feelings. Obviously, the older the child the more likely the judge is to want to know his or her view and then if appropriate to take expressed wishes into account.

There are some milestone cases which should be noted along the way to this result.

Gillick v West Norfolk and Wisbech Area Health Authority [1985] 3 All ER 402 established the right of the teenage girl approaching age 16 to obtain contraceptive advice from a doctor without her mother's knowledge or consent, while in *Hewer v Bryant* [1969] 3 WLR 425; [1969] 3 All ER 402, it was realised that the parental duty to care for and have control of the child will ultimately end in nothing more than a right to give advice as soon as the child matures.

Age is always important, and although there is some room for degrees of maturity to be considered, an older child will obviously have more influence on the court's decision than a younger one, as is illustrated by *Stewart v Stewart* [1973] 3 Fam Law 107, where a 15 year old girl wanted to live with her mother and the court took her wishes into account, considering that she was old enough to express a wish sensibly in her long term interest rather than making a decision for childish reasons. Conversely, *M v M* [1977] 7 Fam Law 17, where a six year old girl wanted to stay with her father and her wishes were treated with caution, and *B(M) v B(R)* [1981] 1 WLR 1182, where the girl was seven and a half and her wishes were similarly cautiously treated, show the likely position in the case of younger children.

Marsh v Marsh [1978] 8 Fam Law 103 is particularly interesting since that was a case of two girls who wanted to live with their mother and when they were eight and five years old the court took no account of their views: however, when they were 12 and nine years old, and the mother reapplied, the court did listen to them and although there was nothing wrong with their father's care agreed to a move. This seems to suggest that children aged from about 10 to 12 may be able to dictate their future.

M v M [1987] 1 WLR 404 shows that the court may even split children if their views differ widely on where they should live. In that case there was a girl of 12 and a boy of nine; the girl wanted to stay with her father and refused to return with her brother to their mother, and the court upheld her wish to remain with the father.

The child's own wishes are what matters. In *Re S (Infants)* [1967] 1 WLR 396; [1967] 1 All ER 202, a 13 year old boy who had been coached by one of the parents expressed his 'view', which was ignored because it was not genuinely his and was in any case contrary to his long term interests.

It is now regarded as the duty of the court to have regard to the wishes and views of older children, especially if they are sensible, mature and intelligent (see *Re P (A Minor) (Education: Child's Views)* [1992] 1 FLR 316; and *Re W (Minors) (Residence Order)* [1992] *The Times*, 3 March, CA, where it was held that it was correct to take account of the views of children aged 10 and 12).

25.5.2 The child's physical, emotional and educational needs (CA 1989, s 1(3)(b))

There are six sub-points to consider here:

- Do mothers obtain care of young children and/or girls?
- Do fathers obtain the care of older boys?
- Do living conditions count?
- Will the court separate siblings?
- Does education play a significant part?
- Will religious and/or cultural differences be a significant factor?

25.5.2.1 Do mothers obtain care of young children and/or girls?

It was once thought that this was a *presumption*, and in *Re W (A Minor) (Residence Order)* [1992] 2 FLR 332, CA the court held that there was a rebuttable presumption that a tiny baby should be in the care of its mother, but except in such an extreme case it is generally now regarded rather as a *practice*, for obvious reasons, although there is no general rule of any sort that mothers have children of any age or sex living with them (see *Re A (A Minor) (Custody)* [1991] 1 FLR 394; *Re S (A Minor) (Custody)* [1991] 2 FLR 388). However, especially now custody and residence are distinct concepts, obviously the good mother in the right circumstances will always have a better chance of obtaining a residence order for babies and young children (*Re W (A Minor)*, above).

Indeed, there is a long line of cases showing the court's apparent preference for the mother's care in such cases, for example, *Greer v Greer* [1974] 4 Fam Law 187, where two girls aged eight and five were returned to the mother after they had been separated from her for some time subsequent to her departure from the matrimonial home, and it was even said that she had never taken much interest in them while the marriage had subsisted, preferring her career to either home or children. However, after she left she had kept in touch with them and was later successful in her custody application. In *Ives v Ives* [1973] 3 Fam Law 16, there was a similar or perhaps even stronger situation in favour of the father, where he had looked after the two daughters for four years, and even the welfare officer was in favour of their remaining with him, but the court still returned them to the mother for the traditional reason. There was the same result in *Re W* [1983] 13 Fam Law 47; [1983] 4 FLR 492, where the father again lost to the mother a girl whom he had looked after for the whole of the first two years of her life. In *Allington v Allington* [1985] FLR 586, there were even doubts about the mother whose new relationship was unstable, but the daughter was still taken away from the father and sent to live with her. In *C v C* [1988] 2 FLR 291, the mother succeeded in taking a four year old boy away from the father.

However, such traditional results are not always a foregone conclusion, and if in a particular case it is felt that a father has the merits on his side it is clear that it is worth his pressing on in the hope of demonstrating to the court that he should retain a child with him whatever its age and sex, especially since what used to be thought the *presumption* of the mother's better right seems to have been dislodged and is more precisely regarded nowadays as no more than a *practice*.

In *B v B* [1985] Fam Law 29, just such a positive result was achieved on the particular facts even though the case did not look promising to start with in the light of the decisions mentioned above. The father was left with an 11 month old child whom he assiduously looked after for two years before the mother sought custody, by which time the child was strongly attached to him and it was felt that the change might harm her. This fact obviously had something to do with the decision (see the checklist status quo (s 1(3)(c)), 25.5.3.1, below), but what *really* tipped the balance it seems was that the father was unemployed and could stay with the child all day – although the court was very unhappy about a man being out of work on a long term basis and barely stopped short of saying that he really ought to get back into regular employment.

However, this was in 1985, since when the unemployment situation has meant that *many* men now cannot find work whereas women, particularly middle aged women, *can*, and the role of the house husband and male child carer at the PTA and Toddler Group has perforce had to be accepted. Thus, while clearly it is *desirable* that a man should be working and supporting his family rather than remaining at home unemployed caring for house and children, there is actually no reason in *law* why a man should not do so if he wishes and it suits the family situation. Moreover, many of the younger middle aged men who have been made redundant or forced into early retirement without being able to find new employment now work from home, as those mothers who wished to do so in order to care for their children personally have traditionally done.

Re H [1990] 1 FLR 51, CA shows that a mother who leaves her child for a prolonged period may definitely now be regarded as at risk of the status quo operating against her. In that case a boy came to England from India to reside with an aunt and uncle, who neglected to send home any news of him, as did the father, while the mother it seems did not get around to asking for any. By the time the mother arrived in England to divorce the father, the boy had settled with his relatives with whom he had thrived and the mother lost custody to them. It seems that, if mothers behave in this way, only some extraneous circumstance will now save them from losing the child, as in *Re W* [1990] Fam Law 261, where the mother was young (18) and the father (47) was not of an age to relate as well to the child.

25.5.2.2 Do fathers obtain the care of older boys?

This has never been a *presumption* in the way that mothers having girls and younger children was thought to be, and as a *practice* was never as strongly established. *W v W and C* [1968] 1 WLR 1310; [1968] 3 All ER 408; and *Re C, C v A* [1970] 1 WLR 288; [1970] 1 All ER 309 seem to show a principle that fathers should have older boys with them (ie, boys older than about eight years when upper and middle class English boys traditionally went away to preparatory school as boarders), but it is far more shadowy than the mother principle in respect of girls and younger children. Probably another factor as well will need to be introduced into the equation for this point to be conclusive in favour of the father. Moreover, contemporary trends should always be borne in mind and it should be remembered that there is currently a significant and continuing statistical drop in boarding school numbers which may partly be due to the cost, which can no longer be met by many families, but is also undoubtedly driven by the recent social trend of preferring to keep children, even male children, at home during their formative years so that they may be in touch with their families and not isolated in a single sex environment away from home.

25.5.2.3 Do living conditions count?

Obviously, good living conditions will be superior to bad ones, but there is no argument for materialism as such. All other things being *equal,* good accommodation will always have the edge as in *Re F* [1969] 3 WLR 162; [1969] 2 All ER 276, but *not* where this is not so, as in *D v M* [1982] 3 WLR 891; [1982] 3 All ER 897, where the father's relative affluence did not score in contrast to the mother's somewhat more basic but nevertheless adequate living conditions, on the basis that she was in fact the *best* person to bring up the particular child. Indeed, in *Stephenson v Stephenson* [1985] FLR 1140, where the court was anxious about other negative aspects of the mother's case, any disadvantage in less good *accommodation* was thought to be of relatively little importance, and this was also the view in *B v T* [1989] 2 FLR 31 (where a semi-detached house with a garden had to be compared with a tower block flat with a play area some distance away).

The standard of *day to day care* rather than the accommodation itself is likely to be more important to the court in forming a view about the best environment for the child. The court is not interested in acrimonious squabbles between the parents about minor matters, since incompatibility between the parents and their approaches to many things is likely to have been a factor in the relationship ending in the first place, but they will begin to take notice if one parent regularly allows the children to be dirty, ragged, ill mannered and undisciplined.

Obviously a parent who is undertaking the child's care personally will always have an edge over the parent who is not able to be at home full time, but if there has to be substitute care, the quality of that provision will obviously also be part of the overall environment provided by the one home as opposed to the other, and here the age of the child will be crucial: older children have their own pursuits and married parents may not see much of them, so this is where the divorced working parent need be no worse off. A common sense approach is what is required here.

Where residence is contested, and accommodation is positively and unarguably *sub-standard*, then the parent in question can usually only be advised to make strenuous and preferably successful efforts to change it since otherwise such a negative factor is bound to be a handicap in s 1(3) terms.

If a move is proposed (obviously involving a child in moving schools, making new friends, settling in a new area, etc), the parent who is in the awkward position of having to disclose these plans to the court (which is *not* the ideal of most advocates conducting s 8 applications) will need at least to have clear and demonstrably workable plans for the child's future. As a minimum, an attempt would have to be made to supply particulars of the sort of house that the parent could afford in the new area, particulars of schools and if possible some plans for continuity of care, preferably from a relative rather than from paid help, so that something will remain unchanged in the children's lives.

Similarly, if council accommodation were to be depended upon, a letter would need to be sought from the local authority specifying what accommodation would be available and when. The better advice must, however, be that an applicant should *not* go in for moves at this precise stage, but either to have done it already before an application is initiated, or else not to propose it until the s 8 order is safely made, as it will merely create handicaps in presenting the case.

From this it will be clear that the results of such applications are much dependent on the skill of the advocates presenting them, and the level of practical preparation that has been undertaken by the parties, since sadly the state of the law is such that, in a divorce situation, parents who are co-operating are able to obtain a decree on the basis of a perfunctory statement of arrangements (see Chapter 11) and postpone their child arguments until a later stage where further careful scheming may enable a cunning parent to manipulate the court's decision, without there remaining any sanction through delay in the grant of a decree.

25.5.2.4 Will the court separate siblings?

The court does not like to do this (*Re P (Custody of Children: Split Custody Order)* [1991] 1 FLR 337), for the obvious reason that a divorce is upsetting enough for children without disrupting their ties with siblings as well as with their parents as a married couple, but it is sometimes necessary for one reason or another.

There has been something of an argument as to whether if the children in a family are split between the parents, this can be compensated for by generous and frequent contact. At first the answer was thought to be in the affirmative (*Re P* [1967] 1 WLR 818; [1967] 2 All ER 229), where the problem was thought to be completely solved by the children meeting in the holidays, but in *C v C* [1988] 2 FLR 291, this idea was strenuously attacked on the basis that meeting frequently was not the same for the children as being brought up together, and the four year old son was sent to live with his mother along with the seven year old daughter as the court said the children would be a mutual support to each other. However, this result could be equally explained by the fact that the boy was only four, so it might not be a strong guideline after all.

Nevertheless, in *B v T* (see 25.5.2.3, above), while the tower block flat versus the semi-detached home with a garden did not prove decisive, the Court of Appeal could not apparently themselves solve the problem of whether or not to separate a boy of three years and a girl of 15 months where the magistrates had initially given both children to the father, whereas on appeal the High Court gave both to the mother: their usual keen analytical powers obviously temporarily defeated, they sent the case back to the magistrates with instructions that the whole matter was to be gone into in depth and that the bench should consider the only solution so far not tried of giving the parents one child each! The answer to this sort of situation must be that other factors in the checklist must be used to flesh out the picture so as to indicate the right solution.

25.5.2.5 Does education play a significant part?

Education is now unlikely to be as important as it once was, other than applying the status quo under s 1(3)(c) so as to keep a child at the same school if possible, especially if the current stage of education is a crucial one such as that during a GCSE or A level course or examination years.

Where educational preferences of the parents might play a part is in the classic situation where one of the parents considers academic achievement to be important and the other does not, as in *May v May* [1985] Fam Law 106, where the father was insistent on a good education, and the mother and her cohabitant were not concerned about such matters. The father got the children, though this will often be the result where the father is willing to pay school fees. If the parties cannot ultimately agree on education, however, and are otherwise not genuinely disputing where the child shall live, the solution is a specific issue order to decide where the child should go to school rather than a contested residence order application, because now that custody as such has been replaced by parental responsibility, and residence and contact orders, it is usually possible to contain the dispute within limited bounds by using the specific issue order machinery to look at the area of dispute in isolation from the broader basis of the child's upbringing in a home from which regular contact with the non-residential parent may be arranged.

25.5.2.6 Will religion and/or racial and cultural differences be a significant factor?

Any one of these factors can be of importance since despite the apparent decline of the Christian religion in the UK, feelings can still run high within the minority for whom religion still matters. In fact, in the non-Christian denominations religion is still very much a live issue, especially where culture and lifestyle are really part and parcel of the religion (eg, both Islamic and Jewish families will almost certainly feel this). Alternatively, religion may be a significant factor where the religion is regarded by some judges as supporting principles which are in conflict with key tenets of English law, such as in the case of Scientologists, the Exclusive Brethren, the Mormons, Jehovah's Witnesses and similar 'sects'.

Re L [1974] 1 All ER 913 focused on the psychological damage done to a child who is uprooted from a familiar culture and language with further consequential damage to his or her identity and education. Such problems were considered by the House of Lords in *J v C* [1969] 2 WLR 540; [1969] 2 All ER 788, where they concluded that the young Spanish boy who had spent 10 years in England with a middle class family, learning English and going to an English school with his English foster brothers and sisters, could not be returned to his desperately poor urban background where his working class natural parents would have no points of contact with him. However, the House could do one thing for the Spanish natural parents – his English Church of England foster parents were required to bring him up as a Catholic, and this is not an uncommon direction in cases where the child's religion differs from that of the carers (in *Re E* [1964] 1 WLR 51; [1963] 3 All ER 874, a Jewish couple had to undertake to bring a child up as a Catholic).

Negative influence of religion on decisions about where and with whom a child should live may be seen in some other cases (eg, *Re B and G* [1985] FLR 493, where the father and stepmother, who were Scientologists, lost them although they had had the children for five years). While it is true that such judgments show a judicial wariness about such sects, it appears that the real concern in allowing children to remain under the influence of sectarian carers is the dire influence on young people due to actual incidents which have shown how dangerous this can be: these have ranged from mere isolation from other people (which militates against any balance which might otherwise counteract a sect's extremism) to actual psychological damage and disturbance. The court is also anxious about young people losing their property through unwisely giving it away to the movement.

Absence of normal social contact is also a negative aspect of the Exclusive Brethren, whose beliefs expressly limit such contact, which is not thought to be good for children, as was shown in the decision in *Hewison v Hewison* [1977] 7 Fam Law 207, whereas the problem with Jehovah's Witnesses is that in addition to permitting house to house visiting (which is again thought to endanger children's social development) they also believe that some medical treatment is wrong, so a Jehovah's Witness with care of a child would not be able to consent to any life saving emergency procedure such as a blood transfusion. Where the negative social aspect can be dealt with by ensuring regular contact with the child's other parent who does not belong to the sect, it was always possible under the old orders for custody, care and control and access to get round the medical treatment embargo by giving custody to the father and care and control to the mother, so that the former could, if necessary, consent to any urgent treatment such as a blood transfusion or other surgical intervention as in *Jane v Jane* [1983] 13 Fam Law 209. The same result could now be achieved either by a split or shared residence order or generous contact for the non-residential parent, provided of course the parent who is not a Jehovah's Witness genuinely keeps in regular contact, is likely to be told of an emergency and is therefore able to intervene thus preserving the right of the residential parent to belong to such a sect if he or she wishes to do so.

25.5.3 The likely effect on the child of any change in his circumstances (CA 1989, s 1(3)(c))

There are two separate points here: the status quo, which it will clearly be desirable to maintain if at all possible, and whether there will be continuity of care which really concerns the child's quality of life, already considered under s 1(3)(b), above, and which after divorce is the most likely to suffer necessary logistical changes anyway. For example, the mother goes out to work even if that were not formerly the case and has to employ child care help, so that if the father, who will presumably continue to work in the occupation which he followed prior to the divorce, wants to make a bid for the children, he might at that point succeed if it is a straight contest between working mother and working father. However, he probably would not get the children if his arrangements involve a more complex chain of carers, however worthy, rather than the mother with some help. Obviously, in this situation, the mother who is at home and able to offer satisfactory full time care or who works only part time has the edge over the father and even a highly trained nanny. Each case has to be taken on its particular facts, as the cases show.

25.5.3.1 The status quo

The status quo as such has always been important as the tragic result of *J v C* showed, even though it was the very adherence to the status quo principle which had produced the unjust result due to the delay in proceeding with that case. This belatedly inspired the express statutory 'no delay' principle now in s 1(2) of the CA 1989. Where *existing* care is *satisfactory*, it is difficult to get the court to change arrangements because of some *potential* but *untried* alternative. The better remedy in this sort of case will be generous contact, not a residence order in favour of the parent seeking a change of basic living arrangements for the child, as is shown by *S(BD) v S(DJ)* [1977] 2 WLR 44; [1977] 1 All ER 656, where a father had remarried and wanted to obtain custody of two children, a boy aged eight and a girl aged six, but the court did not think it was a good idea to move them from the mother and into a strange home and a strange area.

D v M [1982] 3 WLR 891; [1982] 3 All ER 897, already considered under s 1(3)(b), above (where the father's relatively affluent living conditions did not triumph over the mother's more basic but adequate lifestyle) was a similar case, where the attempt was to move a one and a half year old illegitimate boy from the mother, with whom he had lived all his life, to the father's home, following the father's marriage as a result of which he felt he could offer the child a better life: the court felt it inadvisable to disturb the status quo, as was also the decision in *B v T* (the case of the tower block flat versus the suburban semi-detached house with a garden already considered at 25.5.2.3, above, which concerned a 15 month old girl who had lived all her life with her mother) and in *Re H*, the case of the Indian boy left for an extended period by his mother with an aunt and uncle in England (also considered at 25.5.2.1, above). In the latter case, the mother *did* obtain generous access.

The moral to be extracted from these cases is that, where a mother is going to leave children in the care of a father or even of other relatives, it is absolutely essential to keep in touch with the children or a status quo will develop which it will be hard to reverse.

However, where lines of communication have been established and kept open, it is possible to convince the court that what looks like a new status quo which has perforce developed for good reasons, and which should therefore in theory be valued as such, is really only a temporary arrangement from which such a mother may retrieve her children when she is able.

Nevertheless, the ongoing relationship is the key, and if the children have really lost touch with the mother this approach will not work, as was shown by *Stephenson v Stephenson* [1985] FLR 1140, CA, where the mother failed to obtain custody of the seven month old daughter she had left with the father and his cohabitant for two years, during which she had set up house with a new cohabitant herself and had seen the child only six times. In fact the only hurdle to her success was that she had had the misfortune (or ill judgment) to pick as her new cohabitant a violent man with a criminal record, and the court made no secret of the fact that it was hanging its decision on the alternative peg of the status quo due to its dislike of the home circumstances into which it was invited to send the child owing to the mother's association with such an unsuitable surrogate parent.

However, in *Re DW* [1984] 14 Fam Law 17; and *Allington v Allington* [1985] 15 Fam Law 157, keeping in touch with the children during absence did enable both mothers to retrieve the children from the fathers, in the first case when a 10 year old boy was moved from a stepmother's care after five years, and in the second where a girl was removed from her father despite some doubts about the mother's new relationship.

25.5.3.2 Continuity of care

The cases unfalteringly go in favour of the parent who can provide personal care, as in *Re K* [1988] 1 All ER 214, where the father was a clergyman who (due possibly more to a sense of outrage at his wife's adultery than a desire to have the children himself) had assembled a team of worthy people to take care of them while he worked: however, the court lost no time in deciding that a child would prefer its own mother who was available for full time care. Similarly, the full time mother succeeded in *D v M* and *S(BD) v S(DJ)* (already considered at 25.1.2 and 25.5.3.1, above) where in both cases she was unemployed and the father and his new wife were both working, and so offered a similar chain of helpers to the clergyman's, and indeed in the latter case the father's new wife would clearly have been overstretched in trying to take in extra children on top of what she already had to do.

Sometimes the help of relatives in the extended family rates highly in the equation (as in the case of the Indian boy who settled happily and thrived with his paternal aunt and uncle), but this will not usually work where the contest is a mother's full time care against a father's care helped even by his mother, who as the child's grandmother clearly has something to contribute to the general family picture which is usually for the child's actual benefit. Again the mother obtained care in competition with such an arrangement in *S v S* [1990] 2 FLR 341, where the father was a builder who worked very long hours, and although he had a willing and suitable mother, they could not compete with a mother offering full time care. Where the mother works, the balance of power is of course immediately evened up.

Sometimes the court will solve such a competition by giving care (ie, now a residence order) to the person offering continuity of care and generous contact to the other, as in *Riley v Riley* [1986] 2 FLR 429, where one parent was always on the move and the other led a settled life, the latter obviously being preferable to the court.

25.5.4 The child's age, sex, background and any characteristics of his which the court considers relevant (CA 1989, s 1(3)(d))

This is really an extension of earlier categories and the cases mentioned in relation to them give sufficient illustration of the problems which arise and the principles involved in resolving them. For example, traditionally, if parents are really going to quarrel about contact, Christmas is often the catalyst because of the religious and/or cultural importance of that time of year and the key role in family life that it is supposed to assume in childhood, and certainly applications to the court escalate at that time of year. Thus, here background and religion may occasionally be more important than usual and due to the prevalence of intercultural marriages and divorces, arrangements may have to be made, whatever the normal residence situation, for a Christian child to spend that period with the Christian relatives rather than with those from whom he has obtained the other half of his genetic and cultural heritage.

25.5.5 Any harm that the child has suffered or is at risk of suffering (CA 1989, s 1(3)(e))

This means harm in its widest sense (ie, psychological as well as physical harm). Basically, the court wants to keep the child from influences that a good parent would keep children from (ie, violence, overt sex, crime and drugs), and any parent with a cohabitant who might bring such influences into the child's life will be a handicap to the parent seeking the s 8 order, especially if it is a residence order, as has already been seen in *Stephenson v Stephenson* (see 25.5.2.3, above). *Scott v Scott* [1986] Fam Law 301 was a similar case where the new partner had a record of violence and indecency, which did not at all help the mother's case and in fact lost her the claim to custody she might otherwise have had.

Where a child is not able to see both parents, as where one parent opposes contact with the other, this may be considered to be harm (*Re S* [1990] 2 FLR 166, and see under s 1(3)(f), below).

25.5.6 How capable each of the child's parents, and any other person in relation to whom the court considers the question to be relevant, is of meeting the child's needs (CA 1989, s 1(3)(f))

There are four points to consider here: the parent's conduct, the parent's new partner, attitudes to contact of both the parents, and same sex relationships.

25.5.6.1 Parents' conduct

The court is not concerned with moral judgments, and while it may regret the apparent injustice of having to decide against 'good' parents, will always consider the interest of the child first and the parent *qua* parent rather than *qua* conduct (although where the parent's new partner is an inherent disaster, such as in the cases of the new relationships of Mrs Scott and Mrs Stephenson, above, these adverse factors inevitably enter the equation *despite* the parent's ill choice not precisely being 'conduct' within the meaning of the term).

Conversely, the 'good' parent who loses the children to a 'bad' spouse because of care arrangements being inferior to full time parenting does not do so *regardless* of his or her conduct as such, but because the *interests of the children demand good parenting*, irrespective of personal shortcomings in relation to the marriage. The Rev K already considered above had perseveringly attempted a reconciliation with the children's adulterous mother, who had left him, no doubt thought he had done his best to provide a Christian home for the children and had taken pains to provide what in other circumstances might have been totally adequate childcare, so it must have been particularly galling that Mrs K was nevertheless given the children. Mrs S in *S(BD) v S(DJ)* was also definitely not an unimpeachable parent, as she had had three affairs, and still got the children, but these results are inevitable if it is only the availability of full time parenting as against carers which is in issue.

Obviously a parent's health is relevant to ability to care for a child, but if physical health is poor this will not affect such ability provided there is both adequate domestic help and the parent will be present and not, for example, absent for prolonged periods in hospital. As far as *mental* health goes, this will be relevant only in so far as it may affect the child adversely. A little instability, especially if drug controlled, may not matter, whereas full blown schizophrenia obviously would. In either case, comprehensive medical reports would be advisable if a s 8 application is to be made or defended.

25.5.6.2 The parent's new partner

The *Scott* and *Stephenson* cases have already provided a sufficient illustration of this point (see 25.5.3 and 25.5.5, above).

25.5.6.3 Attitudes to contact

D v M (25.5.3.1 and 25.5.3.2, above) was further influenced by the father's attitude to contact, which he was reluctant to allow, and the court regarded this as a very serious matter and did not want to give him the child as a result. Similarly, in *Re S* [1990] 2 FLR 166, where lack of contact with one parent was considered to be potential *harm* within the meaning of s 1(3)(f), there were two boys where one went to live with each parent and the wife would not allow the husband any access to the one in her care. This deprived that child of the society of his brother as well as of contact with the father. The court felt that the wife might have to lose the boy she had living with her unless she proved less recalcitrant.

25.5.6.4 Same sex relationships

This is not a matter to which the court has become much accustomed despite the general change in attitudes of the public. Recent cases on the subject still seem to suggest that the court does not want to allow a child to live in a same sex household if that can possibly be avoided. This is because of problems as the child grows up, at school and with friends etc. Where it is the *only* alternative, this leaves the court in some difficulty. It seems that where it can the court will hang the decision to remove the child on some other peg as in *Re C* [1991] Fam Law 175, where the wife's lesbian cohabitant had a criminal record, but in at least one case a child has been allowed to live in a lesbian household due to the role the father would play in the child's upbringing: in *B v B (Minors) (Custody, Care and Control)* [1991] 1 FLR 402; [1991] Fam Law 174, the youngest child was left with his mother, with whom it was preferable that he should live, due to his age, since the consultant psychiatrist in the case felt that the influence of the father, who himself had a heterosexual cohabitant whom he hoped to marry, and the existence of two other older children would be sufficient to counteract any adverse effects, besides which the mother was not a militant lesbian and was able to provide continuous child care while the father would have had to use a childminder.

25.5.7 The range of powers available to the court (CA 1989, s 1(3)(g))

The court always has power to make any suitable s 8 order(s) in a case before it, irrespective of whether any application has in fact been made for those orders. The court can, for example, by s 10(1)(b), make a residence order in favour of some non-party, such as a grandparent or other relative, if it becomes obvious that that would be preferable and the non-party is willing. The court can also bring an end to any particular saga by prohibiting any further CA 1989 applications without leave (s 91(14)). The court's powers also include the power to order investigation by the local authority (s 37(1)), which in itself may lead to any of the public law orders contained in Sections III–V inclusive of the CA 1989 being made in respect of the child or children. Clients seeking s 8 orders should be aware of the potential impact of these public law orders (see Chapter 26), especially in view of the power of the court under s 37(1) to refer a case to the local authority for investigation (see below).

25.5.8 Power of the court to order investigation by the local authority (CA 1989, s 37(1))

Such an order may be made in any 'family proceedings' as defined by s 8(3), and where the court decides to give such a direction the local authority must carry out the appropriate inquiries and consider whether it should:

- apply for a care or supervision order;
- provide any services or assistance for the child or the family; or
- take any other action in respect of the child (s 37(2)).

Where the local authority decides not to take any action, it must within eight weeks inform the court of the decision and of why that decision has been made, together with information as to any other action they have taken or propose to take in respect of that child (s 37(3)). They must also consider whether they should:

- review the decision at a later date; and
- if so, when (s 37(6)).

Unfortunately, the court can do little if the local authority decides *not* to comply with the court's direction, although the former President of the Family Division (Sir Stephen Brown P) considered the local authority would then lay itself open to judicial review. Formerly, the court could have simply made a wardship order, but could still make an interim care or supervision order (if the threshold criteria were satisfied: see Chapter 26) if the local authority co-operates; if it does not, it could simply, of course, apply for such an order to be discharged though it cannot just send the child home (CA 1989, ss 38 and 39).

THE CHILDREN ACT 1989: SECTION 8 ORDERS

THE PORTFOLIO OF ORDERS

There are four s 8 orders: orders to decide on residence, contact, specific issues and prohibited steps. Residence orders settle no more than where the child shall live and, apart from the obvious practical consequence of day to day care of the child, confer on the resident parent no greater right to decide the child's future and upbringing than in the case of the non-resident parent, who will usually have a corresponding contact order. A residence order is normally in favour of one party only, but a split residence order might be made if there is an established programme whereby the child's home life is shared equally by both parents. However, normally the courts prefer a residence order in favour of one and generous contact in favour of the other, on the basis that most children usually have only one home.

Contact orders may be defined or undefined, and provide for direct or indirect contact. There is usually a presumption of contact between a child and its biological parents, on the basis of the blood tie, but contact may be refused, regulated or postponed if there is likely to be harm to the child (eg, if there is a history of violence).

Specific issue orders determine matters outside residence and contact (eg, education and religion).

Prohibited steps orders determine whether a parent shall or shall not do any act in performance of his or her parental responsibility (eg, consent to medical treatment on behalf of the child or to remove the child from the jurisdiction).

There is an alternative to a s 8 order in the s 16 family assistance order, a temporary order designed to provide skilled social worker help for families at a time of relationship breakdown. This sometimes obviates the need for s 8 orders.

WHO MAY APPLY FOR s 8 ORDERS

A parent may apply as of right, other persons, including the child, with leave. The court decides leave applications in accordance with specific criteria, including the motive for applying for the order in question.

CHANGE OF SURNAME AND REMOVAL FROM THE JURISDICTION

These are discrete issues which are regulated by s 13(1) of the Act.

In principle, it is now thought inappropriate in practice to *change* a child's existing surname without the consent of the child's other parent or leave of the court, possibly even regardless of whether the single mother alone has sole parental responsibility for the child. In other words, there is a burden on the parent wishing to change the name to justify doing so and the presumption in favour of the status quo is very strong.

No parent may remove a child from the jurisdiction without consent of the other parent or leave of the court.

THE STATUTORY CHECKLIST (CA 1989, s 1(3))

Use of the checklist is mandatory in all contested s 8 applications. It is also used in practice in other applications in connection with children. The checklist is not new but encapsulates the existing pre-1989 case law, on the basis of which judges had been deciding pre-CA 1989 cases, but it does serve the useful purpose of formalising good practice. An important addition made to that practice by the CA 1989 was s 1(3)(g) (the range of powers at the court's disposal), since the modernisation of the law to replace parents' rights and custody, care and control and access with parental responsibility and the less emotive portfolio of s 8 orders does mean that the court has a greater chance of making orders which will reduce rather than exacerbate acrimony and ultimately be more likely to secure the welfare of the child and its upbringing in its own family even if that is no longer an intact one.

CHAPTER 26

THE CHILDREN ACT 1989: PUBLIC LAW ORDERS

26.1 THE NEW APPROACH OF PTS III–V OF THE CHILDREN ACT 1989

This is an area of law and practice where the Children Act (CA) 1989 has effected major changes. Instead of (as formerly) simply taking into care every child who is not being properly looked after (and usually resisting the return of that child to its inadequate parents), the local authority is now statutorily compelled to safeguard and promote the welfare of children within its area who are in need, and (so far as it is consistent with that duty) to promote the upbringing of children by their families, by providing a range and level of services appropriate to those children's needs (s 17(1)). This range of services includes a duty under s 20 of the Act to provide temporary accommodation, as an alternative to the former duty of provision of care or supervision under a formal order. This significant shift of emphasis underlines the change in the character of the local authority, which is thus transformed by the CA 1989, in theory at least, from ogre to fairy godmother.

It should be noted that a child is 'in need' if the child is unlikely to achieve or maintain, or to have the opportunity to achieve or maintain, a reasonable standard of health or development 'without the provision for that child of services by the local authority' (s 17(10)). 'Development' includes physical, intellectual, emotional, social or behavioural development (s 17(22)) and 'health' includes both mental and physical health (s 17(11)).

This is obviously overall a significant change. However, if all the authority's help and assistance does not work in practical terms, and it does not look as though there will be any improvement before the child suffers actual *harm*, inadequate parents can still expect either to lose control of the child through formal care proceedings under s 31, or possibly initially through an emergency protection order under s 44. Alternatively, they may at least suffer the imposition of a supervision order, which while not bestowing parental responsibility on the local authority (and therefore perhaps less interventionist than a care order and for that reason often chosen in preference to a care order by the court) will still usually enable the local authority to help the child effectively by placing the limits around decisions in relation to the child which the parents have manifestly failed to do.

To facilitate decisions in this respect, the Act created a new child assessment order available under s 43 which enables the local authority to obtain possession of the child for assessment purposes where the parents will not co-operate. However, the philosophy of the Act is that these stages should only be reached after other methods have failed. Parents whose families excite the interest of the local authority are generally therefore always advised to co-operate, since the authority's powers are in theory subject to its obligations and if the parents can demonstrate that any inadequacies in their child care are not deliberate, but as a result of ignorance or poor resources, and above all that they were unaware of the actual or potential harm caused, care orders at least should be able to be avoided and the onus thrown on to the local authority to carry out its obligations to help!

26.2 THE LOCAL AUTHORITY'S DUTY TO ACCOMMODATE (CA 1989, s 20)

This new duty is significantly different from formal 'care' and arises where:

(a) there is no person with formal parental responsibility for a child;

(b) the child is lost or abandoned; and/or

(c) the person who has been caring for the child is prevented (whether or not permanently and for whatever reason) from providing the child with suitable accommodation or care.

A child so accommodated can be removed by any person with parental responsibility at any time without formality (s 20(8)).

There are two exceptions:

(1) where a person with a residence order or with an old style care and control order made in the exercise of the High Court's inherent jurisdiction (ie, what is technically called in the Act 'an existing order') agrees to the child being looked after by the local authority (s 20(9)), though if there is more than one such person all must agree (s 20(10)); and

(2) where a child over age 16 agrees personally (s 20(11)).

26.2.1 Retaining an 'accommodated' child

If the local authority wants to object to removal of a child informally accommodated it has two choices, and must apply to the court for:

• a formal care order (it must then satisfy the statutory grounds under s 31); or

• an emergency protection order, which is for where the case is urgent (s 44(1)).

The local authority must consider the child's wishes (or such wishes as they are able to ascertain, having regard to the child's age and understanding) wherever possible before providing him or her with accommodation (s 20(6)).

If the child is over 16, any decision as to accepting accommodation from the local authority lies with the child:

• regardless of the child's parents' wishes (s 20(11)); and

• regardless of whether the local authority can accommodate the child (s 20(4)).

There are thus now two distinct categories of children:

• those with a formal care order; and

• those voluntarily in local authority accommodation for more than 24 hours.

The local authority must act as a good parent, by s 22 taking account of the child's wishes, as well as those of his or her parents and anyone else with parental responsibility, *before* taking any decisions about the child, as well as taking account of his or her religion, racial origin and cultural and linguistic background. By s 24(1), it also has a duty to 'advise, assist and befriend' the child, with a view to promoting his or her welfare when he or she ceases to be looked after by it. There is a statutory presumption that it must make arrangements to enable the child to live with one of the following:

(a) a parent;

(b) any person with parental responsibility, or who had it immediately before a formal care order was made; or

(c) a relative, friend or person connected with the child,

unless none of these solutions would be reasonably practical or consistent with his or her welfare (s 23(6)).

26.2.2 The authority's duties: welfare, reviews and contact

It should also be noted that there is a general duty on the authority to safeguard and promote the child's welfare and to make such use of services available for children cared for by their own parents as appears to the authority reasonable in any particular child's case.

Moreover, the Act requires the authority to conduct a general review at regular intervals of the progress of each child, so that the whole emphasis is on keeping children in their own families wherever possible.

If this is impossible, there is a duty to promote contact, so far as is practicable, and consistent with the child's welfare, between the child and his or her parents, or those with parental responsibility for him or her, or with any person with whom he or she is 'connected' (see Scheds 4 and 2 respectively). By s 34(1), where the child is subject to a care order, there is a presumption that the child should have contact with such persons, though other persons (eg, grandparents, and brothers and sisters) must obtain leave to apply to be named in a contact order, which can be made at the same time as the making of a full care order or later (s 34(10)).

Obviously, sometimes contact will be inadvisable (eg, in cases of sexual abuse), in which case either contact can be on conditions (s 34(7)) or the authority (but only the authority) can apply for such contact to be prohibited (s 34(4)). Contact can also be refused altogether as a matter of urgency and for no more than seven days (s 34(1)). All such orders would of course be discharged when the formal care order was discharged, whereupon an ordinary s 8 order might be made instead (s 10).

Where the child is *not* subject to a care order the local authority has limited powers to restrict contact (CA 1989, s 3(5) may be its only source of assistance).

26.2.3 Challenging the authority's accommodation decisions

The local authority's duty 'to accommodate' under this section does not normally extend as far as rehousing a family, but in a recent judicial review case the authority's decision simply to adapt the existing accommodation of a severely disabled child rather than to rehouse him together with his mother and brother was criticised for asking the wrong questions and not obtaining enough information to reach a reasonable decision (*Re C* (1999) unreported, 30 November).

It was held in *Re T* [1995] 1 FLR 159 that a decision not to accommodate could be challenged by judicial review.

In *R v Thameside Borough Council ex p H* (1999) *The Times*, 22 October, it was held that the authority should not have moved a severely disabled 13 year old from accommodation near her parents to a foster home much further away, despite their objections, as this 'trespassed into the area of parental responsibility'.

26.3 FORMAL CARE ORDER (CA 1989, s 31)

Where a formal care order is applied for, the local authority must satisfy the statutory criteria in s 31 and the court must be satisfied that both:

(a) the child is suffering, or is likely to suffer, significant harm; and

(b) the harm, or the likelihood of harm, is attributable to:

- the care being given to the child, or likely to be given to the child if the order is not made;
- not being what it would be reasonable to expect a parent to give the child; or
- the child's being beyond parental control.

These criteria are cumulative and must both be satisfied.

'Harm' means ill treatment or impairment of health and development and 'ill treatment' includes sexual abuse and non-physical ill treatment. The harm is that which is suffered immediately before the authority was involved, so that an abandoned newborn baby who is rescued is likely to have suffered significant harm within the meaning of the section immediately before rescue (*Re MM* [1996] 1 FLR 746).

It does not matter if it cannot be established which of two parents is responsible for harm if that cannot be decided, provided the court is satisfied that both parents are a danger to the child. In *Re B and W* [1992] 2 FLR 833, B, a seven month old, was twice in hospital with shaking injuries which could have been caused by either parent or by the childminder. At first instance the judge could not decide who had caused the injuries, but on appeal the court decided it was not necessary to decide which part of the care network had broken down but since unsatisfactory care was established on the part of B's parents, this was sufficient for s 31. However, a care order for the childminder's child, W, was refused as there was insufficient causal connection between the facts of B's case and the likelihood of harm to W, since it was uncertain whether W's mother had injured B or not.

The court must then consider:

- s 1(1) welfare;
- s 1(3) checklist;
- s 1(2) delay; and
- s 1(5) non-interventionist policy.

It will thus be seen that obtaining a new style care order is a demanding task for the local authority, although if the basis for an order is there, hairs will not be split, for example, over whether a truanting child is beyond parental control or the victim of parents who did not give 'him or her' reasonable care (*Re O* [1992] 1 WLR 912). The standard of proof of the threshold criteria is not as high as on a balance of probabilities because the court is dealing with predictions (ie, a significant likelihood or 'real possibility', and not mere suspicion) – this is the suggested yardstick since the court is dealing with the protection of a child (*Re H (Minors) (Child Abuse: Threshold Conditions)* [1996] AC 563, HL).

Nevertheless, satisfying the threshold criteria is not enough. Once s 31(2) is satisfied, the local authority must also satisfy the other four sections listed above – particularly the welfare principle and the checklist which includes as the final head 'the range of the court's powers' (see Chapters 24 and 25 and *Re FS* [1996] 2 FLR 158, where the judge weighed the risk of further sexual abuse in a case where the father's conduct had already satisfied the s 31 criteria against the emotional harm to the other children if the father were removed. The judge originally therefore made a supervision order but this was replaced on appeal by a sole residence order in favour of the mother coupled with an undertaking by the father not to visit the home without the mother's written consent). If necessary, an interim order will be made pending investigation or further consideration. Conditions under s 38(6) and (7) may be imposed on an interim order including imposing duties on a local authority to fund a residential assessment of the parents and child, thus compelling the authority to allocate the resources where an assessment has been identified by the local authority as being useful in the particular case (*Re C (Interim Care Order)* [1997] AC 489).

An alternative to a care order is a supervision order under s 35. This requires the same statutory grounds to be made out and will usually last for a year, unless extended. An extension can be made by the court but cannot prolong the order so that it lasts beyond three years from the date it was first made; a fresh application will need to be made if such an order is to continue. The supervising officer does not acquire parental responsibility and the purpose of the order is to provide a degree of supervision, including specifying living arrangements and activities to be engaged in, and some positive help in the form of the requirement to 'advise, assist and befriend' (s 35(1)).

26.4 SUPERVISION ORDER AS AN ALTERNATIVE TO CARE

The same criteria must be satisfied for the imposition of both care and supervision orders. Further, the local authority will have to justify the imposition of the more draconian care order where a supervision order would suffice (see *Re B (Care or Supervision Order)* [1996] 2 FLR 693). The court can decide which is appropriate regardless of which was applied for (*Re C (Care or Supervision Order)* [1999] 2 FLR 621), and is most likely to be influenced by the crucial differences (eg, whether it is necessary for the local authority to have parental responsibility for the child), since supervision, while sitting well with the non-interventionist principle of the Act, will not carry parental responsibility. The court must also decide whether it is necessary for the order to last for the child's remaining minority, since a supervision order has a limited life even with renewal of three years after which there would have to be another application (see *per* Hale LJ in *Oxfordshire County Council v L* [1998] 1 FLR 70). Proportionality is usually the key to the decision. For example, in *Re O (Supervision Order)* [2001] 1 FLR 923, CA, the court ordered the children to remain at home under a supervision order rather than the care order made at first instance, and said the order must be proportionate to the legitimate aim. In *Re C and Re B (Care Order: Future Harm)* [2001] 1 FLR 611, the court balanced the risks of future harm to two of the four children involved against the local authority's duty to support and attempt to reunite the family unless the risks were so high that there was no alternative to a care order, especially as Art 8 of the European Convention on Human Rights emphasises that intervention must be proportionate to a legitimate aim. A supervision order cannot have conditions imposed (*Re V* [1996] 1 FLR 776) because they do not fit into the supervision order framework, but a supervision order may nevertheless be more appropriate in a case where there is a need to develop a working relationship with the parents and that is already going well (*Re O* [1996] 2 FLR 755).

26.5 EMERGENCY ORDERS (CA 1989, ss 43 AND 44)

The principal orders in this category are the child assessment order under s 43 and the emergency protection order under s 44.

26.5.1 Child assessment order (CA 1989, s 43)

The child assessment order (CAO) is designed to enable the authority to obtain physical access to the child whom it suspects is being abused or neglected, in order to establish what protection steps are necessary, and is used where the parents refuse to co-operate (eg, by taking the child for a medical assessment). Application has to be on full notice and the court must be satisfied that:

(a) the applicant has reasonable cause to suspect that the child is suffering, or is likely to suffer, significant harm;

(b) an assessment of the state of the child's health or development, or of the way in which he or she is being treated, is required to enable the applicant to establish whether or not he or she is suffering, or is likely to suffer, significant harm; and

(c) it is unlikely that the assessment will be made, or be satisfactory, without a CAO.

As usual the court must have regard to s 1(1)–(3) and (5).

The maximum time for assessment is seven days (s 43(5)) and the order has no effect on parental responsibility. It merely requires production of the child for assessment and requires the person in a position to produce the child to comply with any other terms of the order. The order makes provision for contact between the child and the persons connected with the child (s 43(9) and (10)).

It should be noted that if the child is of an age to do so, he or she personally may refuse to consent. Both the child and the parents or those with parental responsibility may always apply for the order to be varied or discharged.

26.5.2 Emergency protection order (CA 1989, s 44)

The emergency protection order (EPO) is for really serious urgent circumstances where the local authority and/or the NSPCC is investigating a child's significantly worrying circumstances, their enquiries are being frustrated and they believe that access to the child is needed as a matter of urgency. The court can direct any person in a position to do so to comply with any request to *produce* the child to the applicant (s 44(4)(a)), and can authorise *removal* of him or her from any hospital or other place where he or she is being accommodated immediately prior to the order (s 44(4)(b)).

Anyone having this order has parental responsibility, but contact can be directed by the court and the applicant is under the general duty to allow contact with the usual person(s) acting on their behalf. The maximum duration of the order is eight days (s 45(1)). However, the order can be challenged by the child or his or her parents or those with parental responsibility (s 45(8)), but not before the expiry of 72 hours from the time the order was made, nor if the challenger had notice of the hearing and was present at it (s 45(11)).

Other than this, there is no appeal against the grant or refusal of an EPO (s 45(10)) and if the applicant returns the child because it appears to be safe to do so and then suffers a change of mind, the child may be removed again as long as the original order is still running (ie, within the initial eight days or the permissible seven days of extension) (s 44(10) and (12) and s 45(1) and (6)). A court can make an immediate care order when the EPO comes to an end, if the 'cogency of the evidence [is] commensurate with the gravity of the allegations' (*Re P* [1996] 1 FLR 482).

This account is of necessity brief, providing an outline only of the principles involved: besides a wealth of case law in this subject area, which is often the province of specialist practitioners on the Law Society Child Panels and specialist counsel at the Family Bar, there are other orders such as the police protection order under s 46 or the recovery order under s 50. These respectively permit the police to take *ad hoc* charge of a child for a limited period in appropriate circumstances, in which they have an obligation to notify the local authority and the parents (s 46); and under s 50 enable the retrieval of a child who has been unlawfully removed from police protection or from a place where the child should be pursuant to an EPO. Further detail of these orders may be obtained from a specialist practitioner text. The above outline account of the impact of the public law sections of the Act which sometimes affect private law provisions is offered merely to flag the potential problems parents may face if they do *not* co-operate with the local authority in appropriate circumstances.

In general terms, especially if parents were *not aware* of any ill treatment (eg, by a relative acting as childminder who *appeared* to be treating the child well), it is highly unlikely that any steps would be taken other than gentle informal supervision, *provided that* the parents then co-operated fully and took swift and decisive action to prevent the situation continuing once it had been brought to the parents' notice. However, as precedent strictly has no application in family law other than as a guide to previous decisions in similar cases, it is always open to the court to make its own decision as to whether the local authority's view should be biased towards its duty to care and provide services for children and their families or towards its protective role. One disadvantage of the legislation is that there is no power in the court to require the local authority to apply for orders, but only to direct it to investigate the child's circumstances under s 37 of the Act, a duty of which s 47 which formally sets out the local authority's duty to investigate already makes it aware. (Section 37 sets out similarly the formal power of the court to direct an investigation: the two sections are complementary in effect.)

26.6 CHILDREN ACT PROCEDURE

This is so different from that prior to the CA 1989 that it is worth detailing, since it reinforces the ethos of the Act, the philosophical impact of which cannot be exaggerated. At least a minimal overview of procedure is also important in order fully to understand how the substantive law works, and how the private and public law aspects of a case can impact on each other. It is only when this is appreciated that the full sophistication of the legislation is understood.

26.6.1 The courts

Procedure is broadly the same in both private and public law cases, and the two types of case generally proceed separately, although there are obviously cases where, due to the facts, one area of law will impact on the other.

Thus, it is convenient to have the unified structure of High Court, county court and magistrates' courts for children cases which has been created by the Act. Not every judge in each tier is able to deal with such cases, which are therefore usually assigned:

(a) in the High Court to the Family Division judges;

(b) in the county court to selected circuit judges sitting at designated trial centres; and

(c) in the magistrates' courts (formerly the Domestic Court, and now called the Family Proceedings Court) to those magistrates who are designated for the work.

It should be remembered that there are three classes of county court:

- divorce county courts (not all county courts qualify);
- family hearing centres (not all divorce county courts qualify); and
- care centres.

So, where a s 8 order is to be obtained in divorce proceedings, clearly the petition should be filed in a divorce county court which is a family hearing centre (FHC), or it will have to be transferred, and if there is a likely public law impact a centre which is a care centre as well could be a practical way of keeping the entire case under one roof, sometimes with significant benefit to the parties. It cannot be overemphasised that the various parts of the CA 1989 do not exist in a vacuum and neither do the practical implications of resolving problems. The CA 1989 was conceived as a whole, after much work at the Law Commission involving specialist Family Law Commissioners, and the resulting statutory code contains far fewer flaws of conception or realisation than most. The Act, the rules made under it and the courts in which they are both applied can therefore be most effectively used to advantage by the courts and by knowledgeable practitioners to achieve results which respect the conceptual spirit as well as the letter of the legislation.

The Children (Allocation of Proceedings) Order 1991 SI 1991/1677 contains decisive criteria on the choice of venue and allocation of business between the courts. The principle that delay is prejudicial dictates the factors to be taken into account. Relevant factors will be the:

- length, importance and complexity of the case;
- urgency of the case; and
- need to consolidate the case with other pending proceedings.

This flexibility of allocation enables, for example, a case that would otherwise go to the magistrates for several days (which would be logistically difficult to arrange as all magistrates do not sit on consecutive days) to be transferred to a district judge.

Private law proceedings are usually self-allocating, therefore they will be allocated, for example:

(a) to the divorce county court where the proceedings have been started, provided it is an FHC; or

(b) another court where existing child proceedings are on foot with which such s 8 proceedings can be consolidated; or

(c) where the application is 'freestanding', to whichever court the applicant prefers; or

(d) where the applicant is on legal aid, to the magistrates' court as this is the cheapest venue and will therefore usually be the court specified in the certificate.

It should be noted that if divorce proceedings are dismissed, a s 8 order can still be made unless the court determines that the matter would better be dealt with outside England and Wales (Family Law Act (FLA) 1986, s 2(4)).

26.6.2 A form based application

Unlike the pre-CA 1989 affidavit based procedure, proceedings begin on prescribed forms, with which no affidavit is filed, and evidence, which is strictly controlled, is given in the form of statements. The reason behind this was said to be because of the unification of the triple tier of family courts, since the magistrates in the Family Proceedings Court would not be used to affidavits. Irrespective of their type or the person applying, all applications are now made on Form C1 in all cases (Family Proceedings (Amendment) (No 4) Rules 1994).

It should also be remembered (see Chapter 11) that in *divorce proceedings*, if an application has been or is definitely to be made for a s 8 order at the time of filing the petition, this will have been stated on the Statement of Arrangements and the district judge will have been relieved of the obligation to consider the arrangements for the children and to issue the s 41 certificate, and the s 8 application will go straight to the FHC judge for hearing.

Where the application is *outside divorce proceedings*, the applicant has a choice, but if on public funding is likely to be restricted to the Family Proceedings Court for resource reasons.

Parties to be made respondents to the application are set out in Appendix 1 of the Family Proceedings Rules (FPR) 1991 SI 1991/1247 and Sched 2 to the Family Proceedings Courts (Children Act 1989) Rules (FPC(CA89)R) 1991 SI 1991/1395, and they are:

(a) every person with parental responsibility for the child;

(b) every person with parental responsibility prior to a care order, if such an order is in place; and

(c) where the application is to extend, vary or discharge an order, the parties to the order in respect of which the application is made.

Practitioners therefore need to consult r 4.7 and Appendix 3 to the FPR 1991 and r 7 and Sched 2 to the FPC(CA89)R 1991 for detailed rules about parties and notice to be given.

However, any person may make a written request to be joined as a party or that that person cease to be a party, and anyone with parental responsibility is entitled as of right to be joined (FPR 1991, r 47(4); FPC(CA89)R 1991, r 9).

The form then needs to be served. This is achieved by serving a copy with a further form setting out the date, time and place for the hearing or directions appointment on each respondent at least 14 days before the hearing or directions appointment (Family Proceedings Courts (Amendment No 2) Rules 1992; Family Proceedings Courts (Miscellaneous Amendments) Rules 1992, rr 8 and 9; and as to the rules of service FPR 1991, r 4.8; FPC(CA89)R 1991, r 8). After effective service the applicant must lodge the Form C9 statement of service at court.

The respondent must lodge an acknowledgment Form C7 within 14 days (FPR 1991, r 4.9; FPC(CA89)R 1991, r 9).

Unlike in former custody proceedings, CA 1989 applications cannot be 'settled' by a consent order or even withdrawn without leave (FPR 1991, r 4.5(1); FPC(CA89)R 1991, r 5(1)), although court conciliation may attempt to persuade the parents or other parties to agree on the child's future and to observe the spirit and philosophy of the Act by having no order, in which case the application may be withdrawn with leave.

26.6.3 Directions (and the impact of the 'no delay' principle)

The no delay principle will require a directions appointment to be held forthwith, and either this may be the only one or the first of several. Two days' notice is normally required for a directions hearing, which may be on request of the parties or one of them or of the court's own motion, though there is provision for oral application without notice to be made with leave (FPR 1991, r 4.14(4); FPC(CA89)R 1991, r 4(6)).

At the directions hearing there will be a thorough stocktaking of the case. First, a timetable will be drawn up, and adhered to, for the proceedings (CA 1989, s 11(1)). The following will also be considered:

(a) variation of time limits, which is only permitted by direction of the court or justices clerk (FPR 1991, r 4.15; FPC(CA89)R 1991, r 15(4));

(b) service of documents (only those served may be relied on and none may be served without leave of the court, a provision designed to prevent written statements potentially inflaming the situation);

(c) joinder of parties;

(d) preparation of welfare reports and attendance of the court welfare officer preparing them to give evidence;

(e) service of written evidence, in advance, including any experts' reports (no experts' or assessors' reports are allowed without written leave of the court under FPR 1991, r 4.18; FPC(CA89)R 1991, r 18);

(f) attendance of the child, unless excused;

(g) transfer of the case to another court either horizontally or vertically; and

(h) consolidation of the case with other proceedings.

All persons who have notice of a directions appointment must attend, *including* the child if of appropriate age, unless the court directs otherwise (FPR 1991, r 4.16; FPC(CA89)R 1991, r 16), though the court can decide that the proceedings can take place in the child's absence if that is in the child's interests (eg, due to the nature of the evidence to be given, or if the child is represented by a solicitor).

The respondent who does not appear may find that the court has proceeded despite his or her absence. However, they are more likely to refuse the application in such a situation unless they have sufficient evidence to dispense with the respondent's presence.

Obviously if neither party appears the court will refuse the application.

The no delay principle also requires that any adjournment of such directions appointments must include a new date for resumption of the appointment (FPR 1991, r 4.15(2); FPC(CA89)R 1991, r 15(5)). This is the legacy of the 1969 case of *J v C* [1969] 12 WLR 540; [1969] 2 All ER 788!

Alternatively, proceedings can be and commonly are transferred horizontally or vertically, for example, not only to avoid delay but if there is complex evidence and a higher court is needed. Some applications must go to the High Court (eg, an application made by the child personally).

Technically, a s 8 order can only be made in 'family proceedings' as defined in s 8(3) and (4), but this covers all the types of proceedings one would expect, and the court may also make an order of its own motion despite no application actually having been made for that order (s 10(1)(b)). Directions appointments are in chambers in the High Court and county court and in private in the Family Proceedings Court.

26.7 EVIDENCE

A major change brought about by the CA 1989 is the restriction on evidence that can be given and how it should be presented. Affidavits have in fact not entirely disappeared, except in the Family Proceedings Court where they never were beforehand, as a judge, in the High Court or county court, can order them (and some older judges do, since they feel affidavits 'tell the story' in a way in which the form based procedure does not). However, the statements which have supplanted the traditional affidavit, although not sworn, must contain a statement that the maker believes in their truth and understands that the statement will be placed before the court.

26.7.1 Evidence generally

Advance disclosure is the other principal innovation, as without leave of the court *nothing* may be adduced in evidence, not even orally, which has not been written down and served on the other side (FPR 1991, r 4.17; FPC(CA89)R 1991, r 17). By the same rules *nothing* but the *prescribed* documents (ie, as required or authorised by the rules) is allowed to be served without leave of the court. For the careful drafting required of statements, especially the parties' witness statements, see 26.7.4, below.

Evidence will be needed from any persons who will have much to do with the care of the child (eg, nannies, childminders, grandparents and other relatives). If no advance notice has been given in the case of someone new or who has been missed out in the advance disclosure stage, such evidence can always be the subject of an oral application with leave of the court at the hearing. However, it is prudent to beware of the witness who is reluctant, as their evidence may be more damaging than helpful. Limited hearsay evidence is permitted.

26.7.2 Welfare reports

These are normally prepared by the court welfare officers who work for the court welfare service, now called the Children and Family Court Advisory and Support Service (CAFCASS). The welfare officers are now officially called Child and Family Reporters, although the former term is likely to persist, not least for its comparative brevity and accuracy of description. By s 7 of the CA 1989, the court has an extended power to call for such reports, and these may be provided by the local authority (s 7(5)) or by someone delegated to do so by them (s 7(1)). Normally a welfare report is ordered automatically at the directions hearing, either requested by one of the parties or ordered of the court's own motion, as it is quite impossible to deal satisfactorily with either public law or s 8 applications without. Parents are therefore usually warned of the necessity to make a good impression on the welfare officer, since although the court is not bound by their recommendations, it is unusual that their very experienced views are not taken significantly into account and in practice they are generally followed. The report should be filed at least 14 days before the hearing unless a different time limit has been prescribed, and of course all parties will have a copy so as to be able to deal with the contents (Family Proceedings Court (Amendment No 2) Rules 1992, r 12; Family Proceedings Court (Miscellaneous Amendments) Rules 1992, para 3).

Welfare officers' reports are therefore incredibly tactful since the welfare officer is too professional to 'take sides' if this can be avoided and will not want to be seen as biased by any party, but yet will manage to convey the recommendation in the most palatable terms for the party whose aspirations and hopes are to be dashed.

26.7.3 Expert evidence

Any expert reports need leave of the court and any obtained *without* such leave in the first place will need leave of the court to be used. This embargo covers *every type* of such reports, even educational psychologists' reports, although a routine ISCO (Independent Schools Career Organisation) type test done automatically at secondary school level (eg, at most public schools in the fifth form, or Year 11) is probably acceptable if not prepared *specifically* for the proceedings.

26.7.4 The statement in support of a s 8 application

In the absence of affidavits, and with both the new constraints on evidence to be given at s 8 hearings and the increasing specialism in child work by practitioners, drafting of the witness statements, particularly those of the parties, is skilled work, and is generally now allocated to counsel who will usually conduct the application. Just as counsel used to draft old style custody, care and control and access affidavits, it is now often thought that counsel should draft these witness statements, if counsel is to conduct the hearing, since they are as much an exercise in advocacy, in which counsel is a recognised specialist as in drafting. The idea originally was that the statement acts as notice to the other side and to the court of what is to be given orally in evidence, but the mere replacement of an affidavit by an apparently more informal 'statement' has not changed the reality that even a statement also affords an opportunity to get the court's attention and sympathy for the client's side of the story. As child applications have become a highly specialised business both at the Bar and for family solicitors, this opportunity is not usually thrown away in case the position cannot be recovered at the actual hearing – since the experienced practitioner is well aware that it often cannot, and at the very least will give the advocate at the hearing a more uphill task than necessary. For this reason, anything complex normally goes straight to specialist counsel, and little has been achieved by the so called informalisation of the procedure.

Moreover, while leave will be required to withdraw a CA 1989 application once made, obviously there will usually be attempts to settle the matter without a hearing, if necessary with the aid of the court conciliation process or that of other mediators. In this connection the sight of strong witness statements which are not in one side's favour may be instrumental in reducing that party's recalcitrance, which is often all that has stood between one side and the other. This may quickly crumble once the relative hopelessness of a particular approach is spelled out in the opponent's formal statement and a trained mediator is involved who might be able to halt what is obviously going to be a painful disaster for the loser.

Such statements usually cover the following matters, cross-referenced to the s 1(3)(a) criteria:

(1) *Background information.* This should be a *brief* history of the marriage, beginning with the date of the ceremony and detailing the births of the children, with dates, and some indication of when and how the marriage went wrong, but not a blow by blow account, which is neither required nor advisable, however aggrieved the applicant feels.

(2) *The present dispute,* for which the post-CA 1989 style calls for dispassionate, good written advocacy setting out the facts.

(3) *Present living arrangements.* This should include any new relationship into which the applicant has entered, similar to the Statement of Arrangements which is filed with a divorce petition, and convey the same sort of stability and concern for the child's welfare.

(4) *Any health matters to be noted in connection with the child.* This should also include any reports mentioned and filed. If there are any such reports which have not been mentioned or filed, the court can order their disclosure if they come to their notice, despite legal professional privilege and despite any unwillingness on the part of the commissioning party to agree (*Oxfordshire County Council v M* [1994] 1 FLR 175). This is because in theory child proceedings are not seen as adversarial and it is the best result for the child which is being sought.

It is almost too obvious to mention that any parent with sub-standard accommodation is even more at risk in a s 8 application than at the Statement of Arrangements stage, and strenuous efforts are generally ideally made to remedy any such problem *before* filing the s 8 statement. If this cannot be done for some reason, clear arrangements for the foreseeable future are usually detailed and supported by evidence (eg, a council letter indicating when suitable accommodation will be available). It is much better, however, if accommodation is in place (and perhaps already being used by the child for regular contact) so that the court welfare officer may visit and report on it, preferably with the child *in situ*.

(5) *Applicant's concerns*. This will be any *genuine, non-trivial* worries about the other party's care of the child or children, but not an opportunity to enter again into the history of the unhappy marriage or a lengthy disquisition on the other party's manifold sins and wickedness. Such an approach is categorised by the court as *mud slinging*, is deprecated and discouraged and usually invites worse in return.

(6) *Proposals*. These should include the child's wishes, if they have actually been expressed, plus attitudes to contact and comments on the other party's statement if it has already been served.

The statement should end with the statement of truth as now required in all post-Woolf reforms proceedings.

26.7.5 The hearing

Procedure at CA 1989 hearings is governed by r 4.21 of the FPR 1991 and by the FPC(CA89)R 1991, and is deliberately on the informal side. Unless the court directs otherwise, the applicant's evidence will be first, then the main respondent, and any other party with parental responsibility for the child, then other respondents, and finally the guardian (ie, former guardian *ad litem*) if there is one and the child if the child is a party and there is no guardian.

A note is kept of oral evidence by the clerk (FPR 1991, r 4.20; FPC(CA89)R 1991, r 20). While hearsay evidence is admissible, the weight to be given to it will be in the discretion of the judge.

The no delay principle requires that the decision must be made 'as soon as practicable' (FPR 1991, r 4.21(3); FPC(CA89)R 1991, r 21(4)) and any finding of fact and the reasons for the court's decision must be stated (FPR 1991, r 4.21(4); FPC(CA89)R 1991, r 21(6)). If a s 8 order is made it must be entered on the appropriate form for the purpose and a copy served as soon as possible on the parties and any person with whom the child is living (FPR 1991, r 4.21(5); FPC(CA89)R 1991, r 21(7)).

A hearing may be only for an interim application, since by s 11(3) the court is empowered to grant such an order at any time when it is not yet in a position to dispose of the matter finally. This may be a tactical move, since the operation of the status quo rule means that the longer the client is out of touch with the child or children, the worse the client's chances are of retrieving the situation, provided of course that the other parent does not make any mistakes and invoke the operation of some other rule against that parent's interests. It is therefore advisable for any parent seeking, for example, a residence order to obtain an interim contact order and to make the fullest possible use of it in the time it takes to set up the substantive hearing for the residence order which is really desired.

Appeals are possible against all such orders from:

(a) the Family Proceedings Court to the High Court (CA 1989, s 94(1)) heard by a High Court judge usually sitting in open court (*President's Practice Direction (31 January 1991) [1992] 2 FLR 140*);

(b) a district judge of the FHC county court to the judge of the FHC county court in question (FPR 1991, r 8.1) – this is not by way of rehearing;

(c) a judge of the FHC county court or High Court to the Court of Appeal.

The procedure for appeals is set out in r 4.22 of the FPR 1991, and the time limit is normally 14 days or such other period as the court may direct.

THE CHILDREN ACT 1989: PUBLIC LAW ORDERS

A MAJOR SHIFT OF EMPHASIS

The CA 1989 effected a significant change of approach in child protection. There is now a duty on the authority both to protect children in need in its area and if possible to promote the upbringing of children in their home and family (s 17), by providing a range and level of services appropriate to children's needs. This includes a duty to accommodate children temporarily where necessary, either because their parents cannot do so for the time being for whatever reason, or because a child is abandoned or without anyone with parental responsibility, and to do this without seeking a formal care order unless the criteria for such an order are met (ss 20 and 31(2)). The relevant definitions are contained in s 17. There remain formal protection orders for use in appropriate circumstances, either care or supervision orders, or emergency protection (s 44) and a child assessment order created by the Act (s 43), by which the authority may obtain possession of a child where parents will not co-operate, in order to assess whether a protective order is necessary.

CARE AND SUPERVISION ORDERS

A care order gives the local authority parental responsibility to be shared with the parent, although the order limits the extent to which parents may exercise their concurrent parental responsibility. The local authority has a duty to promote contact with the child's parents or those with parental responsibility (s 34) and must act as a good parent while the child is in care. The court takes a restrictive view towards the draconian nature of a care order where a supervision order would suffice, and decides which order is appropriate in accordance with the characteristics of the orders and in relation to the demands of the case (eg, whether it is essential that the local authority should have parental responsibility for the child or whether the order should last until the child is an adult, as supervision orders are limited in time to a maximum of three years after which fresh application must be made).

OTHER ORDERS

Child assessment orders (s 43), emergency protection orders (s 44), police protection orders (s 46) and recovery orders (s 50) also support the local authority in their work.

PROCEDURE AND EVIDENCE

Procedure has changed under the CA 1989. All three tiers of the family courts can make public as well as private law orders under the Act, and the procedure has been developed to be uniform in all courts. It is now form based, supported by carefully controlled evidence, usually in the form of statements rather than affidavits and excluding any evidence not directed to be filed by the court or adduced with leave, including expert reports which are prohibited without the court's consent. Limited hearsay is admitted. The object is to informalise the procedure while carefully controlling any tendency on the parties to use evidence which may inflame the dispute and reduce the chances of settlement. The no delay principle is strictly enforced with a timetable for hearings and directions, and cases may not be settled and withdrawn without leave of the court.

The court welfare service has been renamed the Child and Family Court Advisory and Support Service and its staff are correctly known as Child and Family Court Reporters. By whatever name, their reports remain crucial to the resolution of most disputes.

CHAPTER 27

WARDSHIP AND THE INHERENT JURISDICTION

27.1 THE RELATIONSHIP OF WARDSHIP AND THE INHERENT JURISDICTION TO THE CHILDREN ACT 1989

Wardship and the inherent jurisdiction are like two layers of a Russian doll: wardship is the inner layer which fits inside the larger shell of the inherent jurisdiction, and the two sit side by side with the Children Act (CA) 1989 which has largely reduced the need for the other two jurisdictions by providing a flexible statutory framework for resolving issues about the upbringing of children, based on the wardship concept. In consequence where there is a statutory vehicle for achieving the desired result, neither wardship nor the inherent jurisdiction should be used, and this is also true where other statutes provide a regime to regulate other fields in which children may be involved, for example, immigration, where the High Court has refused to hear applications for wardship in cases where this would impact upon the powers of the Secretary of State under the Immigration Act (see *Re F (A Minor) (Immigration: Wardship)* [1990] Fam 125; *R v Secretary of State for the Home Department ex p T* [1995] 1 FLR 293).

Confusingly, wardship is now itself based in statute (the Supreme Court Act 1981), although it was originally of ancient origin and stems from the fact that the King's court was seen as an umbrella jurisdiction in which to protect children, the King having originally been perceived in feudal times as the *parens patriae*, or the father of the nation and protector of the weak. Thus wardship is a means of making the court, the modern representative of the medieval King, *in loco parentis* to the child. On the other hand, the inherent jurisdiction (of which wardship was once only one specialised part, albeit that it is now in statutory form) is as the name suggests not regulated by statute but comes directly from the (inherent) power of the courts of common law, which means that when the inherent jurisdiction is invoked the court has all its hereditary powers plus those created by statute. Thus, as wardship is 'family proceedings' within the meaning of the CA 1989, the court can therefore use any CA 1989 orders except for those it is prohibited from making by the Act, such as using wardship to send children into care.

Only an outline knowledge of wardship is therefore likely to be required in practice since the CA 1989 is likely to be the more common procedure. Nevertheless, the subject area remains of interest to academics since it is the watershed from which the CA 1989 concepts sprang and is sometimes still of unique practical use for cases which are not conveniently settled through the CA 1989 jurisdiction (eg, any case which requires urgent action and ongoing supervision, which are not well catered for by the CA 1989's s 8 orders).

As wardship is only one specialised part of the court's inherent jurisdiction, with special suitability for certain cases such as emergencies and those requiring supervision, it is the inherent jurisdiction which is used to decide complex cases referred to the High Court, where a decision is required either to investigate overriding that of a *Gillick* competent child (see Chapter 24) who has vetoed life saving medical treatment, or to decide disputes between parents and other interested parties about the proper clinical treatment of a child. Some such cases are therefore brought not technically in wardship as such (eg, where there is no ongoing supervisory element required which would need that feature), but under the inherent jurisdiction of the court, which will then be used to make a one-off decision (eg, whether there should be treatment of a life threatening condition, when such treatment has been refused by the minor or there is disagreement as to whether it should be carried out between responsible parties having an interest in the welfare of the minor, eg, parents and the local authority, doctor or other care professional).

The real distinction between wardship and the inherent jurisdiction is that wardship confers not only parental responsibility on the court, which a decision under the inherent jurisdiction does not, but that the court's parental responsibility is wider than the common sort enjoyed by natural persons, since unlike their parental responsibility which is generated by the birth of children to them, the court's version derives from the Crown which assumed the corporate mantle of the King when his personal attendance at his courts of justice became delegated to his judges and he no longer personally participated. This has not stopped modern judges referring back to the origin of wardship and stressing the parental role of the court – see *per* Lord Scarman in *Re E(SA) (A Minor)* [1984] 1 All ER 289, p 290, where he expressly refers to the court becoming the child's parent; *per* Cross J in *Re S (Infants)* [1967] 1 All ER 202, where the judge refers to the fact that every major decision must be taken by the court; and *per* Dunn LJ in *Re D (A Minor) (Justices' Decision: Review)* [1977] Fam 158, where he speaks of wardship as the 'golden thread' in complex child disputes for which wardship may be regarded as an appropriate forum, as in the recent case of the conjoined twins, *Re A (Children)* [2001] Fam 147, CA.

27.2 WARDSHIP OR CHILDREN ACT 1989?

It was suggested at the time of the drafting of the CA 1989 that wardship should be abolished. However, the valuable High Court remedy was ultimately expressly preserved, alongside the new range of s 8 orders, because it was appreciated that wardship could sometimes achieve results which the Act could not, although it is fair to say that in taking the decision to retain wardship it was anticipated that the flexibility of the orders which the court can now grant under the CA 1989, and in particular specific issue and prohibited steps orders (PSOs), would mean that s 8 orders would be applied for in preference to wardship, and this has mostly proved to be the case. Yet it is clear that the remedy of wardship can still add to the range of s 8 orders, as there are occasionally reasons for the preference of wardship which have justified its separate existence, in other words where:

(a) it is convenient to bypass the CA 1989, for example, because an applicant does not have status under the Act, though the Family Proceedings Rules 1991 SI 1991/1247 now require an interest to be shown by an applicant in bringing proceedings under the inherent jurisdiction;

(b) there is a genuine need for the court's continuing supervision (which, once s 8 orders have been granted, the court cannot achieve under the CA 1989, and which is the special feature of wardship which makes it so expensive a remedy).

An example of the supervisory use of wardship in protecting children may be seen in *Re W (Wardship: Discharge: Publicity)* [1995] 2 FLR 466, where the supervising role of parental care was the essential element of the order: the case concerned two boys, aged 10 and 15, who became wards when their parents' marriage broke down: the boys grew hostile towards their mother and care and control was eventually awarded to the father. Litigation continued over a variety of matters in dispute between the parents and the boys became identifiable in stories in the press in which they spoke of their dislike of their mother and of their dissatisfaction with being represented by the Official Solicitor. An injunction was issued prohibiting the father from giving the press any further information about the issues in the wardship proceedings: he applied to have the wardship discharged, but the court held that it should be continued, since wardship offered protection for the children which could not be achieved by orders under the CA 1989 where a PSO could not be framed to anticipate every possible way in which the father might act. The father had shown that he was not able to consider the boys' best interests objectively, which the court in wardship could do on an ongoing basis.

There are some essential restrictions to the use of wardship. A local authority cannot use wardship either to take children into care or to determine questions of parental responsibility (CA 1989, s 100(2)). Equally parents may not use it to remove a child from local authority care where there is a care order. What s 100 does permit is an application for leave to use the inherent jurisdiction if the local authority can demonstrate that the steps it wishes to take cannot be achieved by using any order already available under the CA 1989, eg, where a care order is needed to protect a 17 year old (which is not permitted under the CA 1989 for a child of that age).

Moreover, wardship cannot be used to stop abortions because a foetus *in utero* is not a child so cannot be made a ward of court (*Re F (In Utero)* [1988] 2 WLR 1297; [1988] Fam 112). However, wardship can be used to deal with:

- kidnapping;
- medical treatment cases;
- adoptions;
- undesirable associations.

Thus, for example, a liberal construction of s 100 *does* permit a local authority to use wardship where a care order would not be appropriate and where a supervision order would not achieve the desired end, as in *Devon County Council v S* [1995] 1 All ER 243, where the object was to protect the younger children in a family where the eldest was married to a person convicted of sexual offences. Wardship permitted supervision of his visits to the family without interfering in the mother's otherwise unobjectionable care of the younger children.

27.2.1 Kidnapping

The use of wardship to prevent kidnapping has to some extent been reduced in importance because of the Child Abduction Act 1984 and the Port Alert System. Nevertheless, given that the police and immigration services need to be involved to activate the latter, their aid is much more easily invoked if there is an order in force and wardship is an obvious candidate for such an emergency where the CA 1989's lengthier procedures would be useless.

Section 1(1) of the 1984 Act makes it an offence for a 'connected person' (ie, a child's parent, guardian or person with a residence order or custody of the child) to take or send a child out of the country without the appropriate consent (which correspondingly means the other parent, guardian or person having custody or parental responsibility or the court). However, under s 1(5), the offence is not committed if it is believed:

(a) that the child was at least age 16; or

(b) it was done technically without consent if that is in the belief that the consent has been given or would have been if all the relevant circumstances had been known; or

(c) all reasonable attempts to communicate to obtain it have been unsuccessful; or

(d) consent has been unreasonably withheld,

unless *inter alia* the departure is in breach of a court order. Sometimes a wardship order, in assisting in activating the Port Alert System, can make the difference between preventing a child being abducted or not (for child abduction, see Chapter 28).

It is easy to see why wardship orders have such a useful role in this respect. The Port Alert System is the subject of *Practice Direction* [1986] 1 WLR 475; [1986] 1 All ER 983 and is a 24 hour service operated in conjunction with immigration officers at all ports including airports. To use it you must show that there is real and imminent danger of removal of a child. Help cannot be sought as 'insurance', so 'real' means there must be some evidence and 'imminent' is interpreted as meaning within the next 24–48 hours. Application should in theory be made to the *local police station*, but in emergency to any police station. This will result in the child's name being entered on the 'stop' list at all ports for four weeks, after which it will be removed, unless fresh application is made.

Details are required for effective help:

(a) a photograph of the child or at least a very good description, including of any accompanying person(s) who will probably be more easily recognised than the child, especially if the child is young;

(b) the likely port of departure and destination;

(c) details of the proposed route as departures of this type are seldom direct.

So while strictly there is no need to have any order in force, in practice this will usually assist in engaging the police's attention in order to invoke the system, and a wardship order in particular not only commands respect but can be quickly obtained.

27.2.2 Medical treatment cases

These are subject to *Practice Note* [1990] Fam Law 375. Sterilisation and other disputed surgical procedure cases are particularly well dealt with by wardship as in *Re D* [1976] 1 All ER 326; [1976] Fam 185, concerning a mentally and physically handicapped girl where the parents wanted her sterilised at the age of 11, as they were worried about the likelihood of her getting pregnant and being unable to look after either herself or a child in view of her obvious disabilities, but where the local authority's child psychologist opposed the operation and applied to the court for wardship; in that particular case the wardship was continued and the operation was *not* carried out, although in a similar case a 17 year old was sterilised. In *Re B* [1981] 1 WLR 1421, the local authority wanted a life saving operation for a Down's syndrome child which the parents did not want as they wanted the child left to die; in that case the court *authorised* the operation. Also if the issue to be decided is purely a medical decision the authority could, and perhaps should, be using the s 8 specific issue/prohibited steps order route or a declaration under the inherent jurisdiction rather than wardship.

27.2.3 Adoption

The most usual role for wardship in this type of case is that the court can investigate fully where there is some issue such as a condition to be attached to the adoption, for example, where there is a dispute as to whether the natural mother will continue to see or care for the child as in *Re O* [1978] 2 All ER 27; [1978] Fam 196, where this was initially agreed and then the adopter tried to back out. The court held the matter must be fully investigated within the wardship procedure. In *Re E* [1963] 3 All ER 874, the adopters whose application to adopt had failed tried to retain care of the child in its best interests. In this type of case, the court will follow only the child's best interests, so if the application is a last ditch attempt to prevent a page turning in the child's life, the application will be dismissed immediately, but if there is an issue which requires investigation the court can look into it fully. Similarly, as in *Re K* [1997] FCR 387, if the court revokes or declines to make an adoption order, it can allow wardship to continue and leave the child with the proposed adopters rather than make a residence order.

27.2.4 Undesirable associations

The court can prevent unsuitable marriages, homosexual associations, or joining an undesirable religious sect.

27.2.5 Wardship procedure

No particular relationship is required to take out an application, which is one of the great advantages of wardship as a remedy, though a genuine interest in bringing the proceedings must now be shown. The child can apply by a litigation friend. However, this flexibility must not be abused, as it was in *Re Dunhill* (1967) 111 SJ 113, where a night club owner warded a 20 year old model for publicity purposes, and the application was struck out as frivolous, vexatious, and an abuse of the process of the court, on top of which the applicant had to pay all the costs! (This is, of course, an old case preceding the change of the age of majority from 21 to 18.)

The application is made by originating summons in the High Court. Public funding is available in appropriate cases. Applications can be made *ex parte*.

Wardship is immediately effective (which is why it is so useful in kidnapping cases) but lapses if not pursued by obtaining a hearing date within 21 days. The defendant must acknowledge service and furnish an address and also the address of the minor, noting any changes.

The first appointment will be before the district judge for directions. The full hearing will not be for many months, and will be before a High Court judge in chambers. There is power to adjourn applications to open court (eg, where the ward is missing and publicity is desired). The court will then confirm or discharge the wardship. If confirmed, 'care and control' (ie, similar to a residence order) will be entrusted to an individual, and a wardship application can if desired be coupled with any s 8 applications; the court can then make those orders instead if the wardship is not granted.

Once a wardship order is made, no important step can be taken in the child's life without the consent of the court. For example, leave will be needed even for a short holiday outside the jurisdiction – technically in wardship even to go to Scotland, which is not within the jurisdiction of England and Wales – but a certificate can be issued to show to immigration officials to obviate the need to apply every time. Leave will also be required to marry or to emigrate, in which case the wardship is likely to be discontinued as the court may not want to supervise the ward at a distance. Alternatively, the applicant can be required to give an undertaking to return the ward to the jurisdiction if ever asked to do so. What the court considers here is whether the ward will in fact be returned if return is ever asked for and therefore whether it is in the ward's interests to go at all (*Re F* [1988] 2 FLR 116).

27.3 THE INHERENT JURISDICTION

This is the jurisdiction often used by local authorities to settle an issue about a child in care as they cannot usually use wardship, since s 100 of the CA 1989 prohibits a child in care being made a ward of court, because care and wardship orders are mutually exclusive.

Since the well known cases of *Re W (A Minor: Medical Treatment: Court's Jurisdiction)* [1992] 4 All ER 627, CA; [1993] Fam 64; and *Re R (A Minor) (Blood Transfusion)* [1993] 2 FLR 757, it has been established that complex medical cases are usually best dealt with through the expertise of the High Court in its inherent jurisdiction. As a result, there have been a number of high profile cases since, which have examined the principle that a *Gillick* competent minor who has power to consent to treatment, pursuant to s 8 of the Family Law Reform Act 1969, does not also have the right to refuse it, and why there is such a distinction.

The inherent jurisdiction is particularly useful for decisions of this sort in respect of 'troubled teenagers', a topic which has already been mentioned in connection with children's rights (see Chapter 24). The approach of the English court, fairly pragmatically, is that the child should not really have the burden of such 'rights', especially in respect of acute decisions on medical treatment when they may either: (i) not fully understand the matter in detail; and/or (ii) not actually be well enough to make an informed decision which is long term in their interests, but that in so far as it can any court will attempt to see the matter from the point of view of a *Gillick* competent child and only in the case of likelihood of serious harm, such as death or long term damage, overrule the child in question. For discussion of this topic, in which it has been suggested that the law is uncertain, and the explanation of Johnson J of the court's balancing act, see 24.5.2, above.

In practice the issue appears not to be that the law is uncertain, because it is clear that the court can, and does, overrule a child's refusal of medical intervention, and for good reason. The question is surely whether this is compatible with the concept of 'children's rights', which it is fair to say do not have much articulated existence in English law, despite international conventions to which the UK is a signatory and some obligations imposed on others to consider the child's ascertainable wishes and feelings, as in s 1(3)(a) of the CA 1989.

The short point would appear to be that due to the rights and duties of parental responsibility (and, in theory, assuming a competent medical practitioner was willing to act as a matter of clinical judgment), a valid consent to medical intervention could probably be given by a parent notwithstanding the opposition of a *Gillick* competent child, but it is clear that in practice the jurisdiction of the court should be invoked, when the best interests tests would be applied and the wishes of the child given appropriate weight.

In practice, most of the reported cases on adolescents involve authorising treatment in situations which are life threatening, and where it has been possible in one way or another to hold that the child is not competent. Thus Johnson J's explanation of the 'balancing act' is tactfully illuminating. It should further be noted that, in accordance with contemporary practice, efforts should be made to resolve this sort of conflict between parent and child by means which do not exacerbate conflict or damage their long term relationship, and that parents simply going along with a child's decision, if that might not be in the child's best interests, might be grounds for the local authority to seek a care order as the s 31 criteria would probably be satisfied. For a case where a child wanted an abortion and the parent opposed it, see *Re B (Wardship: Abortion)* [1991] 2 FLR 426.

It is due to the inherent jurisdiction, therefore, that there are, for example, no reported decisions in England and Wales in which the court has allowed a Jehovah's Witness child to refuse a blood transfusion, or where parents have been allowed to do so on the child's behalf. This has also attracted the attention of academic commentators, for example, McCafferty's 'Won't consent? Can't consent! Refusal of medical treatment' [1999] Fam Law 335. In this McCafferty examined *Re L (Medical Treatment: Gillick Competency)* [1998] 2 FLR 810, which concerned a 14 year old who had signed a 'No blood' card, but needed a blood transfusion following serious burns and refused it: due to the sheltered life led by L, the surgeons had not thought it right to explain the full consequences of the failure to agree to a transfusion, as it would have been too distressing for her; as a result she had not been *Gillick* competent to take such a decision.

A more recent case is *Re M (Medical Treatment: Consent)* [1999] Fam Law 753, concerning a 15 year old girl suffering from heart failure (decided by Johnson J and actually inspiring his explanation of the court's 'balancing act', mentioned above). Her mother consented to a transplant operation but the girl refused. The court authorised the operation based on the authority of *Re W*, above, which allows them to exercise the inherent jurisdiction to override a minor's refusal whether or not there is *Gillick* competence, and even in the case where there were to be long term medical consequences since the girl would require anti-rejection drugs for the rest of her life.

WARDSHIP AND THE INHERENT JURISDICTION

WARDSHIP, THE INHERENT JURISDICTION AND THE CHILDREN ACT 1989

These three jurisdictions co-exist conveniently and remain useful in practical terms for their respective purposes despite the consolidation of most child law in the CA 1989. The Act provides a flexible framework for most orders, and was inspired by the wardship jurisdiction, but delivers its remedies at a more cost effective level, since orders may be obtained in the triple tier of family courts. Wardship is but a sub-division of the non-statutory inherent jurisdiction of High Court derived from the common law, and both wardship and the latter's more general powers may be used when there is no convenient statutory framework under which to make application. Wardship, although derived from the inherent jurisdiction, is now in fact statutory pursuant to the Supreme Court Act 1981.

WARDSHIP OR THE CHILDREN ACT 1989?

Normally the CA 1989 will be used, but some cases are more suitable to wardship, such as kidnapping, adoption, preventing undesirable associations, emergency, and where ongoing supervision is required. Local authorities can use wardship if they cannot obtain a care order and require the supervisory aspect of wardship.

THE INHERENT JURISDICTION

This is very suitable for medical cases, especially those which are urgent or complex (eg, the case of the conjoined twins, Re A (Children) [2001] Fam 147, CA). It is also used by the local authority when wardship is not available pursuant to s 100 of the CA 1989.

CHAPTER 28

CHILD ABDUCTION

28.1 INTRODUCTION

Child abduction is now a major international problem, generated by the high incidence of divorce and the increasing impact of mixed marriages and greater international mobility. It is not included in all family law syllabuses but some working knowledge is now essential for a proper understanding of cross-border contact and residence problems, and applications to remove children from the jurisdiction. This is a specialist area of law which is still developing and is not much understood in the legal profession outside its niche area of practice, but it is of increasing importance in view of the number of mixed marriages and cross-border divorces.

Attempts to address the abduction syndrome have been made: nationally, in the Child Abduction Act 1984, which makes abduction a crime; and internationally, by the Hague Convention on International Child Abduction (the Hague Convention) and the European Convention on the Recognition and Enforcement of Decisions Concerning Custody of Children (the European Convention). The UK is a signatory to both Conventions which are incorporated into English law by the Child Abduction and Custody Act 1985. The European harmonisation instrument 'Brussels II', already mentioned in connection with jurisdiction in divorce (see Chapter 7), also makes child orders enforceable internationally within the EU.

Further assistance in the case of domestic child abduction is afforded by the Family Law Act (FLA) 1986, which not only made child orders in one part of the UK enforceable in others (eg, Scottish orders in England and Wales), but also facilitates the child's discovery and return. By s 33, the court has an express power to require information as to a child's whereabouts from any person in s 8 proceedings, and publicity is permitted where necessary, enabling the judge to lift reporting restrictions (including the publication of a photograph or other identifying information (see *Re R(N) (A Minor)* [1975] 2 All ER 749; [1975] Fam 89; and *Practice Note* [1980] 2 All ER 806)).

Internationally, the operation of the Conventions depends on the concept of judicial comity, and the concept that the child's future is best served by allowing the judges of the child's habitual residence to determine disputes abut upbringing. This works in slightly different ways under each of the two Conventions. The Hague Convention provides a summary remedy to return the child to the jurisdiction of habitual residence for further proceedings, and not to impose English ideas of welfare or to judge or interfere in the merits of the case. The European Convention enforces and engages respect for existing orders, although there is more scope under this Convention for introducing English concepts because it permits settlement in England to be taken into account as a welfare issue in a way that seldom applies in the case of Hague Convention defences to repatriation overseas.

It is therefore important to distinguish (1) the welfare aspects of applications to remove children from the jurisdiction under s 13 of the Children Act (CA) 1989; and (2) resisting the summary Hague Convention remedy seeking their return overseas – two completely different types of proceedings – although it is a fact that losing either s 8 or s 13 proceedings sometimes generates a desperation which leads a dissatisfied and frustrated parent to abduct. See, for example, the recent case of *Re C (Leave to Remove from Jurisdiction)* [2000] 2 FLR 457, where Thorpe LJ, dissenting, commented adversely on the failure of his brethren and of the judge below to reflect on the consequences for the child (C) of the decision to prevent the mother taking C to Singapore where her new husband had relocated to work. In this case the mother had clearly said that this would be likely to break up her marriage as she would not leave the child in the UK to follow her husband, precisely the sort of situation which creates intolerable pressures leading to abduction. For the operation of s 13, see Chapter 25.

It is probably important therefore not to rely on retrieval of a child abducted from England and Wales, especially in cases where feelings of frustration may run high, but to attempt to prevent abduction, since in practice neither the criminal sanction of the 1984 Act nor the summary remedy of the Conventions may be 100% successful – prevention is much easier than cure. Sometimes the courts will grant leave to remove, whether temporarily or more permanently if sanctions are in place, for example, deposit of a substantial sum of money (*Re S* [1999] 1 FLR 850), swearing a solemn oath on a holy book (eg, on the Koran before a Sharia court in *Re A* [1999] 2 FLR 1), or a mirror order applied for in foreign courts (the purpose of the deposit in *Re S* was to secure such an order): such applications where a mirror order may be needed can be heard orally in the High Court so as to assess the reliability of witnesses.

Prevention of the issue of a passport, or deposit of an existing one, obtaining an order (such as a s 8 residence, specific issue or prohibited steps order or wardship if more urgent) and use of the Port Alert System are the next stages, as in practice the child may also have a foreign passport which cannot realistically be confiscated, even though there is technically jurisdiction (see *Re A (Return of Passport)* [1997] 2 FLR 137) or it may lead to an international incident. Any court – even the Family Proceedings Court – can order the surrender of a British passport or order that such a passport be not issued (FLA 1986, s 37; *Practice Direction* [1986] 1 WLR 475; [1986] 1 All ER 983). Section 33 of the FLA 1986, which enables a court to require information to be disclosed about a child's whereabouts, now also has an equivalent in international proceedings under the two Conventions, and orders can be made for disclosure against any person having knowledge (see *Re H (Abduction: Whereabouts Order to Solicitors)* [2000] 1 FLR 766).

An unmarried father should of course urgently obtain parental responsibility for his child if abduction is suspected (possibly also with a specific issue or prohibited steps order), or seek a residence order quickly which by s 12(1) will also confer parental responsibility (see *Richardson v Richardson* [1989] Fam 85). These s 8 orders can be made even if the child is already abducted, but if the child is already outside the country the court may be unwilling to make them because of concerns about enforcement. Alternatively, a wardship order may be obtained very quickly *ex parte* in the emergency and a ward will of course automatically be restricted from leaving the country (see Chapter 27).

28.2 CHILD ABDUCTION ACT 1984

This Act was a pre-CA 1989 attempt to regulate the removal of children from the jurisdiction without having to have recourse to wardship or kidnapping under the common law, for which the consent of the DPP is required for a prosecution. The Act tends to be of little practical importance since a parent who is determined to remove a child is unlikely to be deterred by any statute, even one imposing criminal liability, despite the fact that the sanction for breach is six months' imprisonment or a fine if convicted by the magistrates, or seven years' imprisonment on indictment.

By s 1(1), it is an offence for a person 'connected' with a child to take or send the child out of the UK without the appropriate consent. Connected persons are:

(a) a parent;

(b) where the parents are not married, a person who has reasonable grounds for believing he is the father;

(c) a guardian;

(d) a person with a residence order in respect of the child; or

(e) a person with custody of the child.

Consent in this case is needed from one of the following:

- the court;

- the child's other parent;

- any guardian;

- any person having parental responsibility; or

- any person having custody.

The offence is *not* committed by any person having a residence order who takes or sends the child out of the country for less than one month for a holiday unless done in breach of an order under the CA 1989 (s 1(4)).

By s 1(5)(a), the offence is not committed if done technically without consent if there is a belief that:

(a) consent has been given; or

(b) consent would be given if the person in question were aware of all the relevant circumstances; or

(c) all reasonable steps have been taken to communicate with the other person; or

(d) consent has been unreasonably refused.

The above defence does *not* apply if the person who refused consent is a person:

- who has a residence order; or

- who has custody of the child; or

- the departure is in breach of a UK court order.

By s 2, the same connected persons are prohibited from taking or detaining a child under 16 so as to:

(a) remove him or her from the lawful control of a person having lawful control of him or her; and

(b) keep him or her out of such control,

and it is also an offence for a person 'unconnected' with the child (ie, someone who is not a parent or guardian and has no residence or contact order in his or her favour) to take or detain, without lawful authority or reasonable excuse, a child under the age of 16 out of the lawful control of any person having or entitled to lawful control of him or her.

It is a defence to show that the person believed:

• the child was at least 16; and/or

• in the case of an illegitimate child, on reasonable grounds that he was the child's father.

As the statute, and the Hague Convention, only applies to under 16s, it should be noted that it is still possible to fall back on the common law offence of kidnapping for over 16s.

28.3 DEALING WITH ABDUCTION IF PREVENTION FAILS

The prime remedy is found in the Hague Convention, which establishes a network of international support for the recovery of abducted children, administered through the 'Central Authority' in each signatory country. By Art 7, such authorities must co-operate with one another to find the child, return him or her promptly (and, if possible, voluntarily), eliminate any obstacles to the proper working of the Convention and meanwhile protect the child from harm by taking provisional measures, which include the provision of all necessary judicial or administrative procedures. In order to invoke this protection the child must be habitually resident in the contracting State requesting his or her return. The Central Authority for England and Wales is the Lord Chancellor's Department. Public funding is available (Art 26), and the service is comprehensive. The Department takes over the entire task of instructing lawyers and paying them, and it must act expeditiously (Art 11). The process is one entailing summary proceedings, so that there will be no automatic right to give oral evidence. Normally evidence is given on affidavit and in any case consists largely of legal argument (*Re E (A Minor) (Abduction)* [1989] 1 FLR 135). In England, applications are heard by the High Court and the court is also empowered to make a declaration of wrongful retention or removal in contravention of Art 3. If the child is already 16, the case can still be considered under the High Court's inherent jurisdiction rather than the Act or Convention (*Re H (Abduction: Child of 16)* [2000] 2 FLR 51).

28.3.1 The Hague Convention

The objects of the Convention are to:

(a) secure the prompt return of children wrongfully removed; and

(b) ensure that rights of custody and of access under the law of one contracting State are effectively respected in the other contracting States (Art 1).

Contracting States are required to take all appropriate measures to secure within their territories the implementation of the object of the Convention, and (in an echo of the no delay principle of the CA 1989 – see 24.3, above) are to use the most expeditious procedures available for the purpose (Art 2).

Removal or retention of a child is wrongful where:

(1) it is a breach of 'rights of custody' (which does not mean the same as the old style pre-CA 1989 'custody' in English law but has a wider meaning). Those rights of custody may be attributed to any person, institution or other body, jointly or alone, under the law of the State in which the child was habitually resident immediately before the removal or retention. Thus the court can have a right of custody in respect of a ward and abduction can be in breach of it as the court is an institution (*Re J* [1990] 1 FLR 276). The same is true of any court whenever an application is served in respect of the child, so this right is not restricted to wards (*Re H (Abduction: Rights of Custody)* [2000] 1 FLR 374); and

(2) at the time of removal or retention those rights were actually being exercised, either jointly or alone, or would have been so exercised but for the removal or retention (Art 3).

Rights of custody in this sense may arise either by operation of law or from a judicial or administrative decision, or through an agreement with legal effect under the law of the relevant State. Rights of custody include:

(a) rights relating to the care of the person of the child, and in particular the right to determine the child's place of residence. *Re B (A Minor) (Abduction)* [1994] 2 FLR 249 shows that '*de facto*' custody is also included in this definition (the unmarried father in that case had no legal rights at all but used to care for the child and was therefore held to have such *de facto* rights within the meaning of the Convention); and

(b) 'rights of access', which broadly means the right to take the child for a limited time to a place other than the child's habitual residence (ie, this term does equate with our understanding of old style pre-1989 'access', now called 'contact', and is confusingly a species of 'rights of custody' under the Convention).

The Convention applies to any child under 16 who was habitually resident in a contracting State immediately before any breach of custody or access rights (Art 4).

The burden of proof is always on the applicant to prove that the removal or retention was wrongful, but there is a heavy burden on the central authority of the contracting States involved to make the Convention work. By Art 10, it is mandatory for the requested State to return the child during the first 12 months after abduction or retention, unless a defence applies, and although this duty becomes discretionary after 12 months have passed, Art 11 obliges judges in contracting States to act expeditiously.

28.3.2 Habitual residence

This term is not defined in the Act and is regarded as primarily a question of fact determined by all the circumstances of the case (see *per* Lord Brandon in *Re J (A Minor) (Abduction: Custody Rights)* [1990] 2 AC 562; *sub nom C v S (A Minor) (Abduction: Illegitimate Child)* [1990] 2 All ER 961). It is an important jurisdictional point, without which the child will not be within the Convention (Art 4), and so there can be no wrongful retention or removal without this point being decided in the applicant's favour.

Re J was a case where the unmarried mother of the child left Australia, thus giving up her habitual residence and that of the child, and came with the child to live in the UK. The Australian courts promptly gave the father sole custody and guardianship of the child, but the English court would not order the child's return as the father had no rights of custody at the time the mother and child left, ie, when they gave up their habitual residence. This case should be contrasted with *Re B*, above, where the father had *de facto* custody rights. The father in this case was unlucky since in *Re C (A Minor) (Abduction)* [1989] 1 FLR 403, the court treated the father's right of objection to the removal of his child, again from Australia, as giving him the necessary custody rights and held that Art 5 (defining custody rights) had to be read into Art 3 so that the court could extend the meaning of 'custody rights' beyond our domestic understanding of the term. Surely the father in *Re J* could not have cared for the child as he did without some *de facto* right to do so, so that the removal of mother and child thus giving up their habitual residence should not have made any difference. Moreover, although the mother had given up her habitual residence in a single day, as she was held to be entitled to do, it has been held in many subsequent cases that it usually takes a period of time to establish a new habitual residence (eg, not a three week holiday in Greece – see *Re A* [1998] 1 FLR 497), although this was *per* Stuart White J, *obiter*, and Waite J in *Re B (Minors) (No 2)* [1993] 1 FLR 993 at 995 was not sure about that. Lord Slynn, also *obiter* in *Re S (Custody: Habitual Residence)* [1998] 1 FLR 122 at 127, would apparently also not agree with Stuart White J.

Nevertheless, fathers still sometimes have a hard time proving their custody rights when it seems they logically have them: see *S v H (Abduction: Access Rights)* [1998] Fam 49; [1997] 1 FLR 971, where Hale J refused to return a child to Italy where the father had only access rights and a right to watch over the child's education, which seem not unlike the rights in *Re B* and *Re C*. However, here the judge said there was a clear distinction between what the Italian father had and 'custody rights'.

28.3.3 'Wrongful' removal or retention

Some common sense needs to be applied here. Clearly the removal of a ward is wrong as the court is *in loco parentis* (*Re J (A Minor) (Abduction)* (1989) unreported, 19 June, Fam Div). A removal or retention can be wrong even if there is no order, provided the general law of the country prohibits removal (*C v C (Minors)* (1991) *The Independent*, 8 January), and the cases above are further illustration of this. There is a Practice Direction ([1998] Fam Law 224) on the point.

Wrongful removal and wrongful retention are of course mutually exclusive, since one means taking the child without consent and the other failing to return the child at the end of an agreed period of contact (see *Re S (Minors) (Child Abduction: Wrongful Retention)* [1994] 1 FLR 82; and *Re H (Minors) (Abduction)* [1991] 2 FLR 262; [1991] Fam Law 177). There remains the query as to whether there can be wrongful retention before the end of a period of agreed contact, when the wrongful retention is already decided upon.

If there is any doubt about the matter of whether there has been a wrongful removal, a declaration that the removal was wrongful may be required, by the requested State, to be obtained in the requesting State, before a child is returned (Art 15).

28.3.4 Exercising rights of access

By Art 7, rights of access may also be enforced. Article 7(f) requires central authorities to facilitate this, by receiving an application for rights of access to be enforced in the same way as an application for return of a child (Art 21, and see *B v B (Minors: Enforcement of Access Abroad)* [1988] 1 WLR 526). There is a *Practice Note (Child Abduction Unit: Lord Chancellor's Department)* [1993] 1 FLR 804. Clearly, in view of decisions such as *S v H* (see 28.3.2, above), the query remains as to whether rights of access can amount to rights of custody and enforcing access may be an alternative remedy.

28.4 DEFENCES

By Art 12, the court is mandatorily obliged to return the child 'forthwith' if the application is brought within one year of removal. The child should still be returned if more than one year has elapsed, unless it is demonstrated that the child is now settled in its environment, but this is then within the court's discretion. This therefore begins the exceptions to the usual rule that the merits of the case will not be explored since the Hague Convention presents a summary remedy to enable the child to be returned for determination of his or her future in the courts of his or her habitual residence. This basic ethos of the Convention is based on the theory that all courts are equally competent to determine a child's future and that the merits are therefore not to be explored as to do so would drive a coach and horses through the central concept (*Re N (Minors) (Abduction)* [1991] 1 FLR 413).

By Art 13, return of a child can be refused if:

(a) a person, institution or body having the care of the person of the child was not actually exercising the custody rights at the time of removal or retention, or had consented or subsequently acquiesced in the removal or retention; or

(b) there is a grave risk that the child's return would expose the him or her to physical or psychological harm or otherwise place him or her in an intolerable situation.

Quite separately from these two situations, the judicial or administrative authority may also refuse under Art 13 if the child objects to being returned and has attained an age and degree of maturity at which it is appropriate to take account of his or her views.

In considering the circumstances referred to in this article, the judicial and administrative authorities shall take account of the information relating to the social background of the child provided by the central authority or other competent authority of the child's habitual residence.

28.4.1 Grave risk of harm

It is extremely difficult to come within the Art 13(b) defence, since this undermines the whole concept of the Convention (see *Re M (Abduction: Undertakings)* [1995] 1 FLR 1021) and the combination of mirror orders, State benefits and the presumption of judicial competence overseas combine to reinforce the presumption that a child should normally be returned. See, for example, *Re F (Abduction: Child's Right to Family Life)*, where Cazalet J said that respect must be accorded to the Portuguese court's arrangements for siblings to have contact with one another and ordered the child's return. See also *Re D (Abduction: Discretionary Return)* [2000] 1 FLR 24, where Wilson J ordered a child's return to France although the children were settled in England, as the French court was seised of the case and it was a better forum to decide their future.

If the defence is made out, the court has a discretion not to return the child, but generally a child will be returned unless a very high degree of intolerability is established; and even if the required level is made out, the child may still be returned. See, for example, *N v N (Abduction: Article 13 Defence)* [1995] 1 FLR 107, where the parents of three children lived in Australia and the father suffered from depression. There was possible sexual interference with the eight year old daughter. The mother brought the children to England for an extended holiday with the father's consent, but then changed her address and prevented telephone contact. The father then issued a summons under the Hague Convention which the mother resisted, saying there would be grave psychological harm to the children and that she would not be able to return with them. The children were still returned, Thorpe J saying that parents could not be allowed to manipulate the Convention. On the other hand, in *Re G (Abduction: Psychological Harm)* [1995] 1 FLR 64, the mother, in similar circumstances, succeeded, and three children under the age of four were not returned, as it was held that serious deterioration in the mother if she was forced to return would impact on the children. There was a similar result in *Re F (Child Abduction: Risk if Returned)* [1995] 2 FLR 31, because the child had been present at acts of violence where the father had threatened to kill the mother.

28.4.2 Where the child objects

The situation is different where it is the child who objects to being returned. This is a question of fact, and while the court still retains a discretion and will not hear oral evidence, it will inquire, through the court welfare officer, into why the child objects. No child over about the age of seven is too young to be listened to here. Children are often still returned despite their wishes. However, see, for example, *Re HB* [1998] 1 FLR 422, where an 11 year old, ordered to return to Denmark, refused to get on the plane and was subsequently allowed to stay, and *S v S (Child Abduction) (Child's Views)* [1993] Fam 242, where a 10 year old succeeded in not returning to France where she suffered from a stammer and exhibited behavioural problems which disappeared when she was in

England. In *Re M* [1994] 1 FLR 390, Butler-Sloss LJ said it was important to find out why a child objected, but in *Re K* [1997] 1 FLR 997, the children were returned to the USA despite the seven year old saying she was terrified of going, and despite the judge, Waite J, inviting the welfare officer to report on her, though he thought her at the bottom end of the age range for consultation. Perhaps this is why in *Re R* [1995] 1 FLR 717 the court decided to return the children, including a seven year old (also to the USA), despite supporting psychiatric evidence.

28.4.3 Consent (ie, no breach of Art 3) and acquiescence (Art 13(a))

This is a question of fact in each case and is sometimes complicated by the fact that negotiations at the start of a separation are encouraged.

Consent must be real, positive and clear but can be inferred from conduct. This is a defence commonly argued but seldom successful, and even if it is established the court retains a discretion to return. The effect of alleging consent is that there is no breach of Art 3 as there has been no wrongful removal or retention. Sometimes a parent will say consent is vitiated by duress or deceit.

Acquiescence is slightly different in that it is a defence to an admitted breach, although the same principles apply to disposal of the case. The leading case is *Re H* [1998] AC 72, HL, involving Israeli Jews. Lord Browne-Wilkinson gave the leading judgment. The mother brought the children to England and the Beth Din religious court told the father, who had objected to the abduction, not to take part in English proceedings, though they later changed their minds. As the father had done nothing earlier, the mother pleaded acquiescence and the Court of Appeal found for her, on the basis that objectively the father had acquiesced, though they allowed his subjective position a minor role in their largely objective test. The House of Lords overruled this, and laid down a subjective test. If the court finds as a fact that the wronged parent has not acquiesced, the children will be returned, except in the sole case where the abducting parent has as a matter of fact been led to believe that the other parent has consented, in which case the children will not be returned.

28.5 THE EUROPEAN CONVENTION

The European Convention is a Council of Europe Convention, and like the Hague Convention is given force in English law by the Child Abduction and Custody Act 1985. By Art 7, it makes the orders of one signatory State enforceable within the jurisdiction of the others.

The European Convention has the same central authority structure as the Hague Convention, but operates on the basis of 'wrongful removal' of a child, which under Art 4 triggers the right of a person holding a custody order in one State to apply for enforcement in another to which the child has been taken. By Art 12, it does not matter when the order was made (ie, whether before or after movement of the child across a qualifying international border). The approach to qualification of an application to use the

Convention is similar to the 'rights of custody' under the Hague Convention, and includes rights of access and rights to determine the child's place of residence (Art 1(c)). Enforcement involving access can involve the same problems as the Hague Convention as access rights may not always qualify as custody rights. Nevertheless, access rights can also be enforced as such, as an alternative to their being recognised as a right of custody, in which case the State addressed can decide to what extent to afford access, taking all the circumstances into account (eg, undertakings: see Art 11).

Also, if enforcement of a custody order is refused, the central authority of the refusing State can ask its own courts to decide about access at the request of the applicant (see Art 11(a) and *Re A (Foreign Access Order: Enforcement)* [1996] 1 FLR 561, where a French access order was recognised and enforced in England and Wales). In contemporary UK society, with mobility via the Channel Tunnel and Channel ports making northern France closer for many in the south of England than the border with Scotland, this obviously has great practical importance.

In England and Wales, any custody order to be enforced under the Convention must first be registered (Child Abduction and Custody Act 1985, s 16). Application is to the High Court, which can refuse on certain grounds (see below) or where there is a Hague Convention application pending, but cannot review the substance of the order.

Refusal of recognition and enforcement is covered by Arts 9 and 10. Broadly, Art 9 addresses situations where there has been no legal representation or a lack of natural justice in providing an opportunity for a fair hearing involving the applicant or his or her lawyer, or where the decision does not involve the habitual residence of the family or is incompatible with a decision of the requested State. Article 10 additionally permits the requested State to review whether the decision is still in the interests of the child's welfare due to a change of circumstances other than the simple removal to the territory of that State, a substantial difference from the Hague Convention. See *Re L (Abduction: European Convention: Access)* [1999] 2 FLR 1089, where grandparents did not succeed in enforcing a French order in England as there had been a change of circumstances. Further, by Art 15, the child's wishes can be taken into account.

28.6 NON-CONVENTION CASES

Non-Convention country abductions pose more difficulties. It used to be the policy that the Hague Convention principles, including the Art 13 defences, should apply to these cases as if the countries concerned were signatories to the Convention, since the same summary return and reliance on judicial comity was thought to be appropriate. However, it was then realised that the paramountcy of the child's welfare should be at the forefront of the court's duty, thus displacing any strict application of Hague principles.

Nevertheless, in practice it is still regarded as usually best for a child to go back to the country of his or her habitual residence for any decision about his or her upbringing unless there are any indications to the contrary such as would make out a defence under Art 13. See, for example, *Re M (Abduction: Peremptory Return Order)* [1996] 1 FLR 478, where two brothers were returned to Dubai and Waite LJ said that it must be assumed that there would be a fair hearing there so that very exceptional circumstances were required to depart from the principle of international judicial comity and the principle of return to the forum of habitual residence. However, compare *Re P (A Minor) (Abduction: Custody Rights)* [1997] 1 FLR 780, where the Court of Appeal, in allowing an appeal by the mother who had abducted the child from Bombay to London, said that the overall consideration was the child's welfare. It remains to be seen what the House of Lords will make of this change of attitude if it ever gets the chance to consider it.

The problem remains that many countries are not signatories to the Hague Convention, and although there has been a House of Commons working party on international child abduction (set up in 1990) which has made some recommendations, including appointing a Children's Commissioner to take up cases with foreign governments, and a consultation paper from the Lord Chancellor's Department (1996), it is really only the 'rapid accession to the rule of law by all nations', as suggested by Balcombe LJ in *Re F (Minor: Abduction: Jurisdiction)* [1991] Fam 25, which is likely to solve the ongoing problem. A recent concern has been an epidemic of abductions of British born teenagers from the UK with the intention of compelling them to contract forced marriages in their country of ethnic origin, a syndrome which is currently being addressed by the Home and Foreign and Colonial Offices. Abduction in these circumstances is as difficult to combat as other abductions for the rather different reason that it is not always one parent alone who effects the abduction, and it is usually resisted by younger Westernised siblings, rather than the other parent.

28.7 WHICH CONVENTION?

This is a decision which is not often necessary to take, since for the European Convention to apply there must already be a decision or order to enforce. In the absence of a decision or order, it will not be possible to access the sometimes superior benefit of the European Convention, which permits change of circumstances to be taken into account, and the Hague Convention will apply, under which peremptory return is more likely. In the exceptional case of there being qualification under both Conventions, clearly the tactical advantages must be weighed up, in which case the European Convention may afford a better chance of keeping a child in the requested jurisdiction, and equally will be a worse choice for an applicant wishing to secure the return of the child.

CHILD ABDUCTION

RESOURCES TO ADDRESS CHILD ABDUCTION

The Child Abduction Act 1984, FLA 1986 and Hague and European Conventions all combine to discourage domestic and international child abduction. These provisions apply to children under 16, above which age abduction will still fall under the common law offence of kidnapping.

The 1984 Act makes child abduction a criminal offence, and the FLA 1986 enables custody orders obtained in one part of the UK to be enforced in others, and also increases the chances of finding lost children, with the assistance of publicity and a judicial power to require information. The two Conventions set up a regime by which central authorities in signatory countries co-operate to secure the return of children under 16 for decisions about their future to be determined by the courts of their habitual residence. This doctrine depends on a theory of judicial comity which assumes a fair trial of the issues in jurisdictions other than our own.

THE HAGUE CONVENTION

This provides a summary remedy in which the merits of the case are not examined and the child is mandatorily returned, unless one of the defences to an application (under Art 13) is exceptionally made out. The remedy operates on the basis of a wrongful removal of a child from his or her habitual residence, or his or her wrongful retention outside that jurisdiction after a period of lawful contact elsewhere. An applicant must show that he or she was exercising 'custody rights', which may be less than the formal status of parental responsibility or a residence order which we associate with the concept of physical 'custody'. A right to contact which is exercised can be sufficient for *de facto* custody rights, commonly claimed by unmarried fathers. The defences under Art 13 are that the applicant was not exercising custody rights as required for jurisdiction, that the child objects to returning, that the applicant has acquiesced in the removal or retention, or that the child risks suffering grave harm (including psychological harm). Similarly, if the applicant has allegedly consented beforehand (rather than acquiesced afterwards) to the removal or retention, there will be no wrongful removal or retention in the first place.

THE EUROPEAN CONVENTION

This Convention is slightly different, in that the removal of a child across an international border of signatories to the Convention must be in contravention of an actual decision or order in relation to the child's custody or access to the child.

CHAPTER 29

ADOPTION

29.1 INTRODUCTION

English adoption law is entirely statutory and is now in a transitional stage, still being currently based on the Adoption Act (AA) 1976, which came into force in 1988, since the Adoption and Children Act (ACA) 2002 received the royal assent in November 2002 and is not intended to come into force until 2004. Meanwhile the 1976 Act will remain of interest to students when the new Act finally comes into effect. So far immediately in force are only the usual enabling sections, ss 140–50 (facilitating subordinate legislation, interpretation and funding, etc) and ss 116 and 136 (making some minor preparatory amendments to the detail of the Children Act (CA) 1989, s 17 and s 93 of the Local Government Act 1988, in connection respectively with the local authority duty to provide accommodation for children in need, and with the provision of welfare grants).

The AA 1976 repealed the previous adoption provisions of the Adoption Act 1958 and the Children Act 1975. The Adoption Rules 1984 SI 1984/265 currently govern procedure, the Adoption Agencies Regulations 1983 SI 1983/1964 and various government circulars regulate practice, and the new Act makes a variety of changes which have been suggested by various reform groups, including making a significant change to the welfare test in adoption (which has not reflected that introduced in the Children Act 1989).

The concept of adoption was introduced in 1926, and since then family law and the social context which influences it have moved on apace. This is particularly true in the period since 1976, and even since 1988, and reform was now seriously overdue: during the past 25 years the role of adoption in England has dramatically changed. Some childless parents now seek children to adopt from overseas due to restrictive adoption practices at home, others adopt from Third World and Eastern European countries out of compassion, while yet others, such as same sex couples, have resorted to surrogacy to obtain children with whom they have a genetic link. In the same period, step families have proliferated and new attitudes have developed towards what at one stage appeared the desirable norm of stepparental adoption.

Both these matters are addressed by the new Act. Sections 83–91 deal with adoption with a foreign element, restricting movement into and out of the country (ss 83 and 85), giving parental responsibility (PR) prior to adoption abroad (s 84) and giving power to make further controlling regulations by subordinate legislation. Section 112 provides for acquisition of PR by a stepparent.

The first step in proposed reforms was an interdepartmental working party on the review of adoption law, which published a consultation document in October 1992. This was followed by a White Paper in November 1993 (Cm 2288) and a second consultation document, *Placement for Adoption – A Consultation Document* (Department of Health, 1994).

In March 1996, there was yet another consultation paper, *Adoption: A Service for Children*, which contained the draft Adoption Bill which was the forerunner of the new

Act. This introduced a 'placement order', new grounds for dispensing with consent of the natural parent(s) and a new welfare test, which have subsequently been refined over the period in which the initial draft Bill went through at least two separate incarnations. The ultimate influences on the new legislation were the *Prime Minister's Review: Adoption*, from the Performance and Innovation Unit, in July 2000, and the December 2000 White Paper *Adoption – A New Approach*, Cm 5017, from the Department of Health, which set out the government's plan to promote greater use of adoption, to improve the performance of the adoption service and to make it child centred.

There are in fact fewer adoptions now than in previous decades: for example, the figure for 1974 was 22,500; this dropped to 6,326 over the 20 years to 1994. Many more older and foreign children are now adopted, and a Hague Convention on Intercountry Adoption was produced in 1993 in an attempt to regulate this latter, potentially dangerous, development. Open adoption with both direct and indirect contact between the child and his or her birth family has also developed, a practice which would have been unthinkable 30 years ago, and it is accepted that same sex couples can now adopt. In *Re W (Homosexual Adopter)* [1997] 2 FLR 406, it was held that s 15 of the AA 1976, which refers to the 'application of one person', did not stop the court making an order in favour of a homosexual woman living with her partner, as the Act need not be interpreted 'in a narrow or discriminatory way'. Although that other contemporary family unit, the unmarried couple, cannot at present adopt as such, an order can be made under the 1976 Act in favour of one partner, with a joint residence order in favour of both. In *Re AB (Joint Residence Order)* [1996] 1 FLR 27, an application was made by an unmarried couple whose stable relationship had lasted for 20 years – the adoption order was made in favour of the man with the joint residence order being made in favour of both, thus achieving the practical result they desired. The new Act permits adoption by unmarried couples: ss 49 and 50. A definition of unmarried couples (restricted to the Act) appears in s 144 and includes same sex couples.

29.2 GENERAL PROVISIONS OF ADOPTION LAW

An adoption order gives parental responsibility for the child to the adopters and the child ceases to be a member of its birth family (AA 1976, s 12(1) as amended by the CA 1989, Sched 10). This extinguishes any CA 1989 order in force (s 12(3)) and differs from some other systems, such as Islamic law, where there is no such severance but adoption provides an alternative care mechanism.

The domicile of the child is highly relevant: s 55 of the AA 1976 permits adoption of children abroad under foreign law, and this will give parental responsibility to adopters in England. The new Act in providing additional restrictions on bringing children into the UK in connection with adoption aims to ensure that British residents follow the appropriate procedures whether they adopt overseas or bring a child to the UK for adoption (see 29.1, above). Adoption in England (or overseas by British citizens) will confer both parental responsibility and British citizenship, although a British child adopted by a foreigner will not lose British citizenship. Any adoption will extinguish the parental responsibility of any person who had it previously in respect of the child in question.

Adoptions are 'family proceedings', so orders under s 8 of the CA 1989 can be made of the court's own volition where appropriate. Such an order may be better than an adoption order in some cases (eg, where a stepparent is the applicant), since the s 8 order will not cut the child off from the former family as an adoption order inevitably will, but this alternative may now be overtaken by the new power to give PR to a stepparent as mentioned at 29.1, above (see also further below).

The welfare test in adoption law under the AA 1976 is not the same as that in s 1(1) of the CA 1989. Thus, the two Acts have been out of step with one another for the past decade. There has been ongoing argument as to whether harmonisation was necessary or desirable, since different considerations apply in adoption from those affecting children generally, ie, there are the interests of the birth parents to consider, as well as the impact on the child of cutting biological ties.

Section 6 of the AA 1976 provides:

> In reaching any decision relating to the adoption of a child a court or adoption agency shall have regard to all the circumstances, first consideration being given to the need to safeguard and promote the welfare of the child throughout his childhood, and shall so far as is practical ascertain the wishes and feelings of the child regarding the decision and give due consideration to them, having regard to his age and understanding.

Section 1(2) of the ACA 2002 provides:

> The paramount consideration of the court or adoption agency must be the child's welfare throughout his life.

Thus, the matter is now settled whenever the ACA 2002 is brought into force.

29.3 WHO CAN ADOPT AND BE ADOPTED

Either a single person or a married couple over the age of 21 can adopt under the AA 1976, but, as mentioned above, under the ACA 2002 unmarried couples will in future be able to adopt too. If one partner is a parent of the child it will be sufficient if that parent is at least 18 and the other 21 (see AA 1976, ss 14(1) and 15(1)) and this is retained by s 50 of the ACA 2002. If an applicant is married it will not be possible for that person to adopt as a single person unless the spouse cannot be found, or is incapable due to physical or mental ill health, or the parties are separated permanently (AA 1976, s 15(1)). This too is retained by s 51(3) of the ACA 2002.

Stepparent adoptions were discouraged by the Houghton Committee in 1972 (although they still constituted half the adoptions in 1994) and the draft Adoption Bill of 1996 sought to introduce instead a parental responsibility agreement for stepparents that would result in shared parental responsibility with both the natural parents and as this provision has finally arrived on the statute book in s 112 of the ACA 2002 it would seem that stepparent adoptions are still likely to be discouraged, despite, or perhaps because of, the increasing numbers of step families. See, for example, *Re G (Adoption Order)* [1999] 1 FLR 400, where the mother remarried and the new couple applied to adopt the mother's child of an earlier unmarried relationship where the father had had contact, which terminated on the mother's remarriage. The guardian *ad litem*, ie, the person now called the children's guardian, supported the adoption on the basis that the family needed the order for their sense of security as a family, but on appeal the adoption order was made with limited contact for the father. The judge said that such an order should not be made simply to give the new step family identity and 'the sense of security it craves'. The judge added that in this case the father should undoubtedly have obtained parental responsibility and should therefore have had a right to have his agreement to the adoption sought. Basically, this approach reinforces the court's long held view in change of name applications that the father has some role to play in most children's lives and that links with him, even if tenuous, should usually be maintained if he wants them and they would benefit the child.

It is not possible to adopt a child who is or has been married (AA 1976, s 12(5)), though a child may be adopted more than once (AA 1976, s 12(7)).

The definition section of the 1976 Act is s 72(1) and of the ACA 2002 that providing 'basic definitions' is s 2, 'general interpretation' s 144 and a 'glossary' s 147 and Sched 6. A child is a person under the age of 18 for both Acts.

29.4 ARRANGING ADOPTIONS

Generally, adoptions are arranged through local authority agencies (AA 1976, s 1; ACA 2002, s 3), unless the child is a relative of the adopters (AA 1976, s 11). Sections 92 and 93 of the ACA 2002 continue this restriction. There is no bar, however, on a relative of the child, other than the mother, making arrangements with an agency, especially where the mother is unable to do it herself (*Re W (Arrangements to Place for Adoption)* [1995] 1 FLR 163). The ACA 2002 does not change the scope for non-agency adoptions. Section 44 requires notice of intended adoption to be given to the local authority, not more than two years nor less than three months prior to the application. The local authority must then carry out all the usual investigations as if the adoption had been arranged through them.

Sections 123 and 124 of the 2002 Act provide new restrictions on advertising children for adoption or for children to be adopted and create a criminal sanction for breach. However, by s 125 *et seq*, there is to be an official register to match children and adopters.

Every local authority must establish and run an agency, setting up an Adoption Panel to screen adopters and supervise placements. Adopters must be in good health and, under the AA 1976 process, within certain age limits. The result has been that although adoption is seen as a service to children, many children remain unadopted because of the criteria, but this is intended to change under the ACA 2002 which provides a new right to an assessment of needs for adoption support services (s 4) in respect of which detailed regulations will be made, local authorities have to prepare plans (s 5) and s 12 provides a new right to ministerial review of any determination under the new arrangements. No second time applications are entertained under either Act unless there has been a change of circumstances. No payments may be made or received, other than for certain adoption agency and medical expenses and fees (see ACA 2002, s 11; and AA 1976, s 57). In *Re Adoption Application (Surrogacy)* [1987] 2 All ER 826, £10,000 for loss of earnings of a surrogate mother was acceptable and presumably this will remain possible. Nevertheless, sometimes orders are still made where there has been a payment and/or a private placement. In *Re MW (Adoption: Surrogacy)* [1995] 2 FLR 759, there was a surrogacy arrangement and the commissioning parents applied to adopt when the mother ultimately withheld her consent: the court simply dispensed with her consent (see below).

29.4.1 Adoption agencies

The local authority agency is an 'adoption service' (AA 1976, ss 1(4); and 72(1), ACA 2002, s 2). These sections define agencies further. Such agencies must operate within the welfare test, which under the 1976 Act puts the child's welfare 'first' and does *not* make it 'paramount' as in the CA 1989, but s 1(2) of the 2002 Act will align the test with the CA 1989. This means that some regard can be paid to the interests of adult family members. This will end long confusion. For example, in *Re W (A Minor) (Adoption)* [1984] FLR 402, Cumming-Bruce J decided that it was not in the interests of the child's welfare to be adopted by the stepfather applicant, where the father had paid maintenance and had contact. At first instance the judge had decided that 'fairness' to the natural parents was irrelevant. In *Re D (An Infant) (Adoption: Parents' Consent)* [1977] AC 602, HL, p 638, this was defined as 'first' but 'not paramount' over the interests of the child's parents, though in this case the adoption was allowed as the natural father was a practising homosexual and the mother and stepfather could offer an environment which protected the child from homosexual contacts. The draft 1996 Bill would also have brought the welfare test into line with that of s 1(1) of the CA 1989 and despite debate up to the time the 2002 Act was passed, that Act now ends the long running argument.

By s 7 of the AA 1976, the child's religion may be ordered to be preserved by the adopters, but in the 2002 Act the agency only has to 'give due consideration' to the child's religion. The ACA 2002 includes in the welfare test in s 1(2) consideration of the value to the child of any relationship with relatives and the likelihood of any continuing contribution they could make to the child's life.

29.4.2 Procedure for making orders

This is governed by s 13 of the AA 1976. Whether the child is placed by an agency or with relatives, the child must be at least 19 weeks old and have spent at least 13 weeks with the prospective adopters, or alternatively be at least 12 months old and have lived the preceding 12 months with them. Under the ACA 2002 the child must have spent at least 10 weeks if placed by an agency or the court with the prospective adopters (or for longer periods of six to 12 months if the application is by a partner of a parent of the child or by foster parents) or three years in any other case unless the court abridges these periods.

The court will appoint a children's guardian in a contested case, or an independent social worker where the application is not opposed.

29.4.3 Adoption by relatives

A relative is defined by the AA 1976, s 72(1) as including the following:

> ... grandparent, brother, sister, uncle and aunt whether of the full blood or half blood or by affinity and includes, where the child is illegitimate, the father of the child and any person who could be a relative within the meaning of this definition if the child were the legitimate child of his mother and father.

Great uncles and aunts are not relatives for this purpose. The 2002 Act adopts a similar list.

It was often within the relative context that the relevance of s 8 orders under the CA 1989 was seen, as, for example, in adoption applications by grandparents to which it has usually been thought a s 8 order might be preferable (see *Re W (A Minor) (Adoption by Grandparents)* [1980] 2 FLR 161).

The approach of the ACA 2002 has built on this attitude by making no special provisions for adoption by relatives and instead introducing the new PR provision for stepparents mentioned at 29.1, above, which is intended to cater for the most common relative adoption applications of the past. The Act also creates a new status of 'special guardian' to cater for those children for whom adoption is not appropriate, and children being cared for by the wider family were thought to be the core beneficiaries of such a concept, since there were many in this category who could not return to their parents but who would benefit from greater security without losing their legal relationship with their parents. Some ethnic or religious groups also prefer such a solution and s 115 now provides for the special guardianship status. It is curious to reflect that this contemporary provision now gives legal force to a status commonly found in practice in both history and literature (where 'guardians' appear in many 18th and 19th century classics) and yet it has taken 30 years of clumsy attempts to address the fallout from the disintegration of the traditional nuclear and extended family to reach the obvious conclusion that adoption is not the solution in every case.

A special guardian takes all the day to day decisions about a child and although the birth parents cannot exercise it in an unrestricted manner, they do not completely lose their parental responsibility but remain legally the child's parents. Moreover the special guardianship order is not finite: it can be discharged, unlike adoption.

29.4.4 Notice to local authority in non-agency placements

This makes a child a 'protected child' under the AA 1976 (ss 22(1) and 32). The child must wait at least three months in such cases to be adopted. By s 36, certain information must be given in relation to a protected child. By the ACA 2002 the s 44 notice to adopt triggers an investigation at least as thorough an investigation as the local authority's own adoption agency would have conducted had it arranged the adoption itself, and s 44 also requires such a local authority to give notice to any other local authority in whose area the applicant(s) resided immediately beforehand, thus maximising the chances that all factors relating to the suitability of the proposed adopter(s) will come to light.

29.5 PARENTAL AGREEMENT TO ADOPTION

Agreement cannot be given within the first six weeks after the birth (AA 1976, s 16; ACA 2002, s 52(3)). An order can be made 'freeing the child for adoption', which gives the agency parental responsibility (AA 1976, s 18) and in effect gives the child to an agency at an early stage so that the parents cannot then change their minds so easily. But if the child is not then adopted after 12 months have elapsed, the order can be revoked. The ACA 2002 provides a new system of placement by consent and placement orders (ss 18–29) Consent to a placement may now include advance consent to adoption, so as to take this fundamental decision earlier in the adoption process.

29.5.1 Dispensing with parental consent

A parent is defined by s 72 of the AA 1976 as any person who has parental responsibility for the child under the CA 1989 and the definition is repeated by s 52(6) of the ACA 2002 subject to two minor exceptions under s 52(9) and (10). An unmarried father, therefore, does not fall into this category unless he has a parental responsibility agreement with the mother or a parental responsibility order from the court. In *Re L (A Minor) (Adoption: Procedure)* [1991] 1 FLR 171, it was held that such a father does not need to be named on the application or interviewed, as a father normally would be, by the local authority social worker in charge of the case.

The child's agreement is not required.

29.5.2 Grounds for dispensing with parental agreement

The present grounds are listed in s 16(2) of the AA 1976. These are:

(1) By s 16(2)(a), 'that the parent or guardian cannot be found or is incapable of giving agreement'. This is taken literally, so all possible steps must be taken to look for the missing parent. In *Re F(R) (An Infant)* [1970] 1 QB 385, no steps had been taken to contact the child's maternal grandfather with whom the mother was still in touch, so he had not been effectively searched for.

(2) By s 16(2)(b), 'that the parent or guardian is withholding consent unreasonably'. This is a question of fact. The welfare test does not have to be applied in considering whether the consent is unreasonably withheld. See *Re P (An Infant) (Adoption: Parental Agreement)* [1977] 1 All ER 182, CA; [1977] Fam 25, where Lord Simon questioned whether it was in fact correct that the welfare test should have no application to the issue of dispensing with parental agreement. This was a case where a 16 year old changed her mind after nine months, and this was held to be unreasonable because it was an emotionally based decision.

Re W (An Infant) [1971] AC 682 was a similar case where the change of mind was after 27 months and the mother was said to be warm hearted but motivated by guilt.

In *O'Connor v A and B* [1971] 2 All ER 1230, HL, *per* Lord Reid, where previously unmarried parents married and then divorced, the husband then remarried and wanted to take the child, then three years old, into the new marriage. It was held that strong reasons had to be shown to withdraw consent to the child's adoption: while the father was married and had accommodation, it was held that the lapse of time and instability of the union meant that withholding consent at that stage was unreasonable.

Re H (Infants) (Adoption: Parental Consent) [1977] 1 WLR 471, CA, *per* Ormrod LJ was another case of parental vacillation, which was held to be unreasonable.

Re PA (An Infant) [1971] 3 All ER 522, CA was a case of a young mother who changed her mind after consenting under pressure, but whose consent was held not to be unreasonably withheld when she withdrew it after a year.

In *Re HB (An Infant) and W(N) (An Infant)* [1983] 4 FLR 614, it was held that it is the welfare of the child that really counts, so that there is room for reasonable withholding of consent even where social workers think that adoption is best. In this case there were children aged 10 and 11 with a good chance of reintegration with their natural parents whose faults were past rather than present. This was despite the existence of good foster parents who were waiting to adopt and with whom the children were well settled.

Same sex couples are now accepted as *de facto* adopters. See, for example, *AMT (Known as AC) (Petitioners for Authority to Adopt SR)* Inner House, Court of Session, 26 July 1996, where an adoption order was made even though the mother was not unreasonably withholding her consent when the proposed adopter was planning to bring the child up jointly with a cohabiting homosexual. It should be noted that the 1976 Act permits an adoption order to be made in favour of a single person, whether he or she at the relevant time lives alone or cohabits in a heterosexual, homosexual or even asexual relationship with another person whom it is proposed should fulfil a quasi-parental role towards the child, because the first consideration is the child. In *Re W (Adoption: Homosexual Adopter)* [1997] 2 FLR 406, Singer J said that it was wholly inappropriate that judges should impose on the plain words of the statute any public policy restrictions preventing applications by homosexual persons applying to adopt, commenting 'how unruly is the horse of public policy which I am asked to mount'.

In any case, this is a classic example of a change of social attitudes affecting the law over time. For example, *Re D (An Infant)* (see 29.4.1, above), the 1977 case of the practising homosexual father, might be decided quite differently today.

It should be noted that dispensing with parental consent to the adoption of a child who is in care is perfectly possible, and even likely.

(3) By s 16(2)(c), 'that the parent or guardian has persistently failed without reasonable cause to discharge his parental responsibility for the child'. See *Re P (Infants)* [1962] 1 WLR 1296, where a mother left two illegitimate children with the local authority and took no further interest in them. Her consent was dispensed with because it was held that parental duty includes an obligation to show some affection, care and interest.

(4) By s 16(2)(d), 'that the parent or guardian has abandoned or neglected the child'. See *Watson v Nickolaisen* [1955] 2 WLR 1187, where the child was left with good people who wanted to adopt but the mother later changed her mind. She was held not to have abandoned the child in such a way that a criminal offence had been committed (such as that of neglect under s 1 of the Children and Young Persons Act 1933, which provides a yardstick by which to measure such abandonment or neglect).

(5) By s 16(2)(e), 'that the parent or guardian has persistently ill treated the child'. See *Re A (A Minor) (Adoption: Dispensing with Agreement)* [1981] 2 FLR 173, where there were severe and repeated assaults on the child over three weeks which were held to be sufficient to dispense with parental agreement.

(6) By s 16(2)(f), 'that the parent or guardian has seriously ill treated the child', a similar basis to s 16(2)(e), above, where the conduct in question is of a more serious degree but possibly without the persistent element.

By s 52 of the ACA 2002, the court must be satisfied that it should dispense with parental consent on one of two grounds: (a) that the parent or guardian cannot be found or is incapable of giving consent; or (b) that the welfare of the child requires consent to be dispensed with. The whole process of consent to *adoption* has been accelerated by the new *placement for adoption* process which has replaced 'freeing for adoption': see 29.6, below, so hat placement will, under the 2002 Act, in effect be the stage at which parental consent vill be often given to *adoption* as well. While s 52 still permits a parent to indulge in a hange of mind with all the attendant problems set out in the cases at 29.5.2, under the ew welfare test in s 1(2) of the ACA 2002, the likelihood is that adoption order hearings vill be less protracted because it will almost always be likely that the adoption is for the hild's welfare.

29.6 FREEING FOR ADOPTION

·y s 18(2) of the AA 1976, the parent(s) must consent to the application or the child must lready be in the agency's care under a formal care order. If this is not the case, the agency annot apply to free the child for adoption. By s 18(1), the court must be satisfied that the ·arents have freely and with understanding consented to the freeing for adoption, or that 1e consent is dispensed with on a s 16(2) ground, but the court cannot dispense with greement unless the child is already placed or a placement is likely. If parents disagree 1e agency can seek to dispense with their consent. If the order is made the parents lose ·arental responsibility and the agency acquires it. By s 18(7), the court must be satisfied 1at an unmarried father has not applied for parental responsibility and is not likely to. here is provision in s 20 for revocation of s 18 orders, but this is a discretionary order (*Re ; (Adoption: Freeing Order)* [1996] 2 FLR 398). Unmarried fathers have rights: their views 1ust be sought if they plan to seek PR.

See also *Re D (A Minor) (Adoption: Freeing Order)* [1991] 1 FLR 48, which shows how he freeing for adoption order works in practice. Freeing orders can be revoked under the nherent jurisdiction of the court if an application under s 20 is for some reason 1appropriate (*Re J (Adoption: Freeing Order)* (2000) *The Times*, 26 May).

By s 18 of the ACA 2002, an agency may place a child for adoption when it considers hat that is appropriate for the child, but needs either parental consent or a placement ·rder to do so, unless there is a care order in place or in process (s 19). By s 20 a parent nay also give advance consent to an adoption order, which may be revoked under s .0(3). While a placement order may also be contested and revoked 'on the application of ny person' (s 24(1)) only the child or the local authority will not have to show change of ircumstances to obtain leave to do so (s 24(3)). Various organisations, including the ·amily Rights Group and the Women's Interest Group of the Society of Labour Lawyers, 1ave been concerned about how these provisions will work in practice, and in particular vhat will happen if parents precipitately give their consent to a placement, and then hange their minds, when commentators have queried, to what extent the court will be ·repared to give leave, and the Community Legal Service to fund hearings especially 1ow such funding is provided under the secondary legislation of the Funding Code. No loubt there will be extensive further commentary before 2004.

29.7 ADOPTION ORDERS WITH CONDITIONS

3y s 12(6) of the AA 1976, an adoption order can contain 'such terms as the court sees fit', ncluding, for example, contact. In *Re C (A Minor) (Adoption: Conditions)* [1988] 1 All ER '05, the contact order was to enable a girl to see her brother. This type of sibling contact order is more common than such conditions allowing contact to a mother: see, for example, *Re O (Transracial Adoption)* [1995] 2 FLR 597, where a contact order was made in favour of the birth mother although her consent to the adoption had been dispensed with.

29.8 EFFECTS OF ADOPTION

Adopters obtain parental responsibility, and anyone who had it before the adoption order will lose it (AA 1976, s 12(2)). Natural parents will have no right to keep in touch (unless contact order has been made which is possible under the CA 1989, s 8) and have no obligation to maintain the child. An adopted child is never illegitimate, even if adopted by a natural parent (AA 1976, s 39(4)).

There is a separate adopted children's register which is not open to the general public except by court order (AA 1976, s 50). This is continued by ss 77–79 of the ACA 2002.

Children who are adopted can discover their origins once they are 18 years old (AA 1976, s 51). The ACA 2002 continues this (ss 80–81). There is an adoption contact register through which relatives can make contact subject to safeguards: their enquiries are transmitted to the adopted person.

There has been much criticism during the long period of proposals for reform of the apparent lack of support for disadvantaged natural parents in a framework which was thought to be meant to balance the interests of both children who might benefit from fresh start and of their birth families. However, the government appears to have always seen adoption more as a service to children and childless families: see the White Paper on *Adoption: The Future*, Cm 2288, 1993, introduced into the House of Commons in 1993 by the then Secretary of State for Health; the comment in [1994] Fam Law 1 by Debora Cullen, Secretary to the Legal Group, British Agencies for Adoption and Fostering; and in the same issue the article by Jolly and Sandiland of Nottingham University, 'Political correctness and the Adoption White Paper' (p 30).

The ACA 2002 attempts to address some longstanding criticisms, changing the law to make the welfare of the child the paramount consideration in all adoption decisions. It also aims to bring adoption law more closely into line with the CA 1989, for example, in allowing courts to set timetables to cut delays, improving the adoption process itself including establishing a review process for prospective adopters turned down for adoption, and providing better post-adoption support. In the summer of 2001, the Lord Chancellor's Department also issued new guidance to courts on speeding up the adoption process and making the process more efficient. There is the new special guardian order for cases where adoption is not suitable. Many regulations remain to be made under the 2002 Act and the detailed working of provisions which appear to be likely to disadvantage the birth parents remains to be assessed in practical terms. However, adoption is probably an area of the law where it is impossible to serve two mutually exclusive sets of interests, and the Act has apparently come down on the side of the presumed interests of the child to find a non-institutional home in secure circumstances. Whatever the controversy, the special guardianship seems to be an inspired idea for the older child who has always faced most difficulties in finding an exit from care.

ADOPTION

BACKGROUND TO ADOPTION

Adoption law is entirely statutory and has long been in need of reform after several abortive attempts to update it since 1976. This has now been effected by a new ACA 2002 but will not immediately be implemented.

EFFECT OF ADOPTION

The effect of an adoption is to transfer parental responsibility from the birth family to the adoptive family. An adoption made abroad under foreign law will be recognised in the UK. The welfare test in adoption law under the AA 1976 is not the same as under the CA 1989, though s 1(1) of the 2002 Act has been drafted to bring adoption and the CA 1989 closer together in respect of the welfare test. The current AA 1976 test permits some regard to be had to the interests of the parents and family of the child to be adopted but this will be much weakened under the 2002 Act where regard to the ongoing link with the birth family is seen only in the context of the child's interests.

THE ADOPTION PROCESS

Either a single person or a married couple can adopt at present, provided the applicant(s) are over age 21, or 18 if one of a couple is the parent of the child and the other at least age 21. Stepparent adoptions are discouraged, but same sex adopters, or adopters in partnership with others of the same sex, are acceptable and the new Act permits unmarried couples to adopt. Adoptions are arranged through local authority agencies, which provide a service to children; no payments may be made or received except for expenses. Private placements are outlawed except between relatives. A child must be at least 19 weeks old and have been placed for a qualifying period with the adopters. There will be a court appointed children's guardian in a contested case. Parents must agree to an adoption but consent may be dispensed with on various grounds, basically under the 1976 Act if the mother or parents have ill treated, neglected or abandoned the child, or withheld consent unreasonably. The 2002 Act reduces the grounds for dispensing with consent of a parent as a principle welfare decision which should streamline such hearings, especially because of the introduction of a new placement order system which attempts to frontload consent to adoption to an earlier stage. An unmarried father who is not applying for parental responsibility does not need to have his consent sought. Conditions may be attached to orders, including for post-adoption contact, but this is more usual for siblings than parents, unless the adopters agree. There is an adoption contact register for adopted children to contact parents if they wish when they are 18.

CHAPTER 30

HUMAN ASSISTED REPRODUCTION

30.1 INTRODUCTION

Human assisted reproduction is a relatively new area of law, since the underlying techniques are also relatively new. The term, commonly abbreviated to HAR, covers artificial insemination by a donor (AID) or by the mother's husband (AIH), also *in vitro* fertilisation (IVF), gamete intra-fallopian transfer (GIFT), egg and embryo donation and surrogacy. Surrogacy, whereby a woman carries a foetus for commissioning parents to whom she means to hand the baby when born, may be full (ie, involving both egg and sperm donation by the commissioning parents and IVF) or partial surrogacy (more common) where the surrogate is fertilised with the commissioning father's sperm. This inevitably involved questions of legal parentage when the practice became established and the legal issues were given detailed consideration by the Warnock Committee (see below).

The topic is not yet by any means regularly included in the academic syllabus, but an awareness of this area of law is important to the family law student because of its impact on other developing areas of family law, such as cohabitation, adoption, and social parenting of children through residence orders, particularly in a homosexual context, where despite the fact that homosexuals can now adopt, surrogacy enables such couples to parent children who have some genetic relationship to either or both of them. See, for example, Professor Chris Barton's article 'One dad good, two dads better?' (1999) *The Times*, 9 November.

In view of the limited relevance of this area of law to most university syllabuses, this chapter only offers an outline of the various issues involved, which must be supplemented by those who are interested in gaining greater depth and detail by further reading.

30.2 WHO IS THE MOTHER?

The answer to this may be found *per* Lord Simon in *The Ampthill Peerage Case* [1977] AC 547: 'Motherhood, although also a legal relationship, is based on a fact, being provided demonstrably by parturition.' Historically this has always been so, for example, the witnessing of births to prevent substitution, such as after the suspicious birth of the son of James II and his second wife, Mary of Modena, and the Roman practice of examining women who claimed to be pregnant as recorded by Justinian.

Surrogate parents can now obtain a parental order in order to become legal as well as social parents, but when the practice first became common (with the birth of Baby Cotton in the mid-1980s: see *Re C (A Minor) (Ward: Surrogacy)* [1985] FLR 846), problems arose unless the husband's sperm had been used. This was so because the Adoption Act 1976 makes private placements with non-relatives illegal. The parental order regime had, therefore, to be hurriedly created by the Human Fertilisation and Embryology Act (HFEA) 1990, and this enables such commissioning parents to become legal parents (see *Re W (Minors) (Surrogacy)* [1991] 1 FLR 385, in which it was realised that without parental orders the commissioning parents could only become parents by adoption and complying with the law in that respect). The Warnock Committee on Human Fertilisation recommended that the birth mother, and not the commissioning mother, should be the legal mother, since surrogacy was not recognised in the UK or USA (save in California, which gives the legal rights to the commissioning mother, since she had given her tissue and intended to be a parent), although the Family Law Reform Act of 1987 around the same time recognised genetic parentage by testing. This report led to a White Paper, *Human Fertilisation and Embryology: A Framework for Legislation*, in 1987 (Cmnd 259), in which the government accepted the Warnock recommendations but provided that, where a married couple commissioned a baby with egg/embryo donation, the baby would be 'theirs' for succession purposes except in cases involving hereditary titles (HFEA 1990, s 29(4)).

By s 27(1) of the 1990 Act, 'the woman who is carrying or has carried a child as a result of the placing in her of an embryo or of sperm and eggs, and no other woman, is to be treated as the mother of the child', and is the mother for all purposes. This is so whether the treatment is in the UK or not (s 27(3)), and s 29(3) and (4) make the commissioning married couple mentioned above the parents for all purposes except where the child is adopted, as then the child will be the child of the adopters (s 27(2)).

The HFEA 1990 now regulates all treatment and research, and has a code of practice which is issued to licensed clinics.

30.3 WHO IS THE FATHER?

This point was considered by the Law Commission in its *Working Paper on Illegitimacy* in 1979.

The Family Law Reform Act 1987 makes the donor in AID (artificial insemination by a donor) the father provided he consents (unless, of course, the donor is anonymous).

By s 28(2) of the HFEA 1990, where a married woman is carrying or has carried a child as a result of the placing in her of an embryo, or sperm and eggs, or as a result of her artificial insemination, then notwithstanding that the sperm was not donated by her husband, he and no other person is treated as the father of the child unless it is shown that he did not consent to his wife's treatment. This is subject to s 28(5)(a), which will not treat the donor as the father of the child if the rules of common law mean that the child is otherwise legitimate, in other words, is born to a woman in wedlock and her husband accepts the child as his or if the child is adopted (when it will of course be the adopters' child). By s 28(3), a man is also treated as the father of an unmarried woman's child if she and he receive treatment together – which pursuant to s 29 will make them the parents for the purposes of any will or deed, except for titles and entailed estates. See *Re CH (Contact) Parentage* [1996] 1 FLR 569, where the husband of the mother could not genetically be the child's father as he had had a vasectomy. Later, when the marriage broke down, the mother tried to prevent contact on the grounds that he was not the child's biological father, but the judge held that s 28 made him so.

On the other hand, if the woman is unmarried and receives donated sperm under a licensed clinic arrangement, there is no father (s 28(6)). See *Re Q (Parental Order)* [1996] 1 FLR 369, where in such a case Johnson J held there was no person other than the mother whose consent was required for a parental order under s 30 (see 30.4.1, below).

By s 28(6), some children are fatherless in law even though everybody knows precisely who the biological father is, because, if he died before the child's conception and had not consented to the use of his sperm, he cannot be treated as the child's father. This is the situation in the case of Diane Blood, who used her husband's sperm to give birth to two posthumous children, but he had not been able to give written consent to the fertilisation procedure as he was already unconscious when at her request the sperm used had been taken and stored. This remains so despite the fact that the couple had been trying to conceive a child so that his consent might in reality have been implied. See *R v Human Fertilisation and Embryology Authority ex p Blood* [1996] Fam Law 785; [1997] 2 FLR 742, CA.

30.4 SURROGACY

This practice is governed by the Surrogacy Arrangements Act 1985. By s 1(2), 'surrogate mother' means a woman who carries a child in pursuance of an arrangement made:

(a) before she began to carry the child; and

(b) with a view to any child carried in pursuance of it being handed over to, and parental responsibility being met (so far as practicable) by, another person or other persons.

Treatment in a licensed clinic is highly desirable because then the clinic can ensure that any man who goes for treatment with the woman, but does not contribute sperm, can be the father pursuant to s 28(3).

By s 2(1), it is an offence to negotiate surrogacy arrangements on a commercial basis. However, by s 2(2), it is not an offence for a woman, with a view to becoming a surrogate mother herself, to do any act mentioned in sub-s (1), and similarly it is not an offence for any man, with a view to a surrogate mother carrying a child for him, to do such an act. Advertising is not permitted in the news media in the UK (including on TV or radio) and no surrogacy arrangement is enforceable either by or against either party, even if not illegal.

These essentially practical provisions were generated by the experience of the 'Baby Cotton' case, where the local authority had obtained a place of safety order (similar to an emergency protection order under the pre-CA 1989 law) and made the child a ward of court when the commissioning parents wanted to take the child over, although they were subsequently allowed to take the baby to the USA.

30.4.1 Parental orders

By s 30 of the Act, a parental order will be made in favour of the commissioning parents provided that they are both over 18, they apply within six months of the birth, one of them at least is domiciled in the UK, and the court is satisfied that no money or other benefit has passed in consideration of handing over the child or of making arrangements for the order (s 30(7)). The genetic parents must agree (s 30(5)).

No agreement is required, however, where such persons cannot be found (s 30(6)).

Alternatively, if these conditions cannot be complied with, a s 8 residence order could always be made, or an adoption order.

30.5 ABORTION

For the sake of completeness in the field of managed reproduction, lawful abortion should be noted, although the criminal law of abortion is outside the scope of this book.

The legal background to abortion prior to the Abortion Act 1967 lies in the criminal law, including ss 58 and 59 of the Offences Against the Person Act (OAPA) 1861 and in the common law crime of murder, for which Coke's definition is that:

> ... murder is when a man of sound memory, and of the age of discretion, unlawfully killeth within any county of the realm any reasonable creature *in rerum natura* under the king's peace, with malice aforethought, either expressed by the party or implied by law, so as the party wounded, or hurt etc die of the wound or hurt, etc ...

Abortion is not of course murder or any kind of unlawful killing if the 1967 Act is complied with; otherwise such an act will be either murder or an offence under s 58 or 59 of the OAPA 1861. Nor is it murder to kill a child in the womb or in the process of being born. It used to be a misdemeanour to kill a child in the womb after quickening (ie, when the foetus became animated, in that the mother perceived foetal movement), but the present law in all respects is now statutory. On the other hand, the unborn foetus is part of the mother, so acting with an intention to kill or seriously injure the mother will be murder if it causes her death or the death of the child if it dies after having a separate existence – this is because of the doctrine of transferred malice. If the mother or child is killed by someone with a lesser intent than death or serious injury, the killer will be guilty of manslaughter.

The Abortion Act 1967 modified ss 58 and 59 of the OAPA 1861. By s 1 of the 1967 Act, as amended by the HFEA 1990, a pregnancy of less than 24 weeks may be terminated on social grounds if to continue with it would endanger the physical or mental health of the mother or her other children. Termination is still possible after 24 weeks if the child would be likely to be born seriously abnormal or handicapped. These terminations are lawful provided that two registered medical practitioners agree that the conditions are met, and the abortion is undertaken by a registered medical practitioner (who need not be the same as the previous two and can be a nurse, not a doctor: see *Royal College of Nursing v DHSS* [1981] AC 800; [1981] 1 All ER 545, HL). By s 2, it is permitted to take account of the woman's actual or foreseeable environment in taking these decisions. By s 3, multiple pregnancies can be reduced.

The good faith of the medical practitioners involved must be certified, but good faith is essentially a question for the jury if challenged. Normally a medical practitioner is acting in good faith if he or she believes that to be the case, and any finding of bad faith would be likely to be appealable unless there was supporting professional opinion.

The question therefore arises as to whether there may still be a defence of necessity where a termination is procured outside the provisions of the Abortion Act 1967, as to procure a miscarriage otherwise than in accordance with the Act is unlawful. In *R v Bourne* [1939] 1 KB 687, a leading Harley Street practitioner terminated a pregnancy for good medical reasons (so as to preserve the mother's life). Lord McNaghten took the view that there was not only a right for Bourne to act as he did, but also a duty to save life, so that where a doctor refuses to operate he or she could be considered no better than someone who failed to call a doctor to his or her sick child. Lord McNaghten presumably regarded such an omission resulting in the death of the patient as manslaughter, although he did not address the situation of the patient suffering only injury. Note, however, s 4 of the Abortion Act 1967 recognises that a doctor may conscientiously object to performing such an operation.

There have been numerous criticisms of the Act by academic writers, in particular in relation to the euthanasia debate.

HUMAN ASSISTED REPRODUCTION

REGULATION OF HUMAN ASSISTED REPRODUCTION TECHNIQUES

All the various forms of HAR are regulated by statute (the HFEA 1990 and the Surrogacy Arrangements Act 1985). These define who is the mother and who is the father of children conceived by HAR. This regulation was generated by the Warnock Committee and in response to the case of the surrogate 'Baby Cotton' in the mid-1980s. Commissioning parents are able to become legal as well as social parents by means of a parental order under s 30 of the HFEA 1990. Previously, the only means was adoption, which sometimes still has to be resorted to by those who do not qualify for the s 30 order.

SURROGACY

Such arrangements are not enforceable by either party, and may not be entered into commercially or advertised. Parental orders to transfer legal parentage to commissioning parents require the genetic parents' consent, either the mother's alone or both parents' depending on whether the child has a 'father' in law.

ABORTION

Abortion used to be a criminal offence but is now legal if effected in accordance with the Abortion Act 1967. It is uncertain whether the common law defence of necessity remains valid where abortion is effected outside the provisions of the Act as the Act makes any termination unlawful unless in compliance with it.

FURTHER READING

CHAPTER 1: INTRODUCTION

Bainham, A, 'Changing families and changing concepts – reforming the language of family law' [1998] CFLQ 1

Barton, C and Hibbs, M, *Questions and Answers on Family Law*, 2nd edn, 1998, London: Blackstone, Chapter 2, Question 1, 'In which members of the family is family law interested?'

Bradney, A, 'The family in family law' [1979] Fam Law 244

Bromley, PM, Katz, S, Eekelaar, J and Maclean, M, *Cross Currents: Family Law and Policy in the US and England*, 2000, Oxford: OUP

Bromley, PM, Lowe, N and Douglas, G, *Bromley's Family Law*, 9th edn, 1998, London: Butterworths, Chapter 1

Burton, F *et al*, *Teaching Family Law*, 1999, University of Warwick: NCLE

Cretney, S and Masson, J, *Principles of Family Law*, 6th edn, 1997, London: Sweet & Maxwell, 'Introduction'

Cretney, SM, *Family Law*, 3rd edn, 1997, London: Sweet & Maxwell

Coll, B, 'Tackling the issues, and facing the facts', in *Family Affairs*, Newsletter of the Family Law Bar Association, Winter 1999/2000

Curzon, L, *Lecture Notes on Family Law*, 2nd edn, 1997, London: Cavendish Publishing

Diduck, A and Kaganas, F, *Family Law, Gender and the State: Text, Cases and Materials*, 1999, Oxford: Hart, Chapter 1, 'Law and the family'

Eekelaar, J and Maclean, M (eds), *A Reader on Family Law*, 1994, Oxford: OUP, Pt I, 'The Social and Conceptual Context'

Eekelaar, J and Nhlapo, T (eds) *The Changing Family, Family Forms and Family Law*, 1998, Oxford: Hart, especially Pts I and VI

Hale, B *et al*, 'The family and marriage', in Hoggett *et al*, *The Family, Law and Society: Cases and Materials*, 5th edn, 2002, London: Butterworths, Chapter 1

Hayes, M and William, C, *Family Law*, 2nd edn, 1999, London: Butterworths, 'Preface'

Henderson, A, 'The big chill' (2000) 144 SJ 32

Herring, J (ed), *Family Law: Issues, Debates, Policy*, 2001, Cullompton: Willan

Maclean, M (ed), *Making Law for Families*, 1999, Oxford: Hart

Maine, HS, *Ancient Law*, 2001, New York: Transaction

Piper, C, 'How do you define a family lawyer?' (1999) 19 LS 93

Standley, K, *Family Law*, 3rd edn, 2001, Basingstoke: Palgrave Law Masters, Pt I

Standley, K, *Cases and Materials on Family Law*, 1997, London: Blackstone, 'Introduction'

Wragg, T, *Family Law*, 1998, London: Financial Times Pitman, 'Introduction'

Websites

www.open.gov.uk/lcd (Lord Chancellor's Department, including Family Law reform)

www.familylaw.co.uk (Family Law Journal, Jordan Publishing Ltd, regular commentary on family law topics, recent cases, links to other websites)

www.jrf.org.uk (Rowntree Foundation)

Family Law

CHAPTER 2: MARRIAGE

Cretney, S and Masson, J, *Principles of Family Law*, 6th edn, 1997, London: Sweet & Maxwell, Chapter 2, p 51

Diduck, A and Kaganas, F, *Family Law, Gender and the State: Text, Cases and Materials*, 1999, Oxford: Hart, Chapter 2, 'Love and marriage'

Hale, B *et al*, 'The family and marriage', in Hoggett *et al*, *The Family, Law and Society: Cases and Materials*, 5th edn, 2002, London: Butterworths, Chapter 1

Lowe, N and Douglas, G, *Bromley's Family Law*, 9th edn, 1998, London: Butterworths, Chapter 2

Standley, K, *Cases and Materials in Family Law*, 1997, London: Blackstone, Chapter 2, 'Marriage and cohabitation', and articles listed therein

CHAPTER 3: NULLITY

Bromley, PM, Lowe, N and Douglas, F, *Bromley's Family Law*, 9th edn, 1998, London: Butterworths, Chapter 3

Centre for Child and Family Law Reform, City University, *The Problem of Forced Marriages – Proposals for Law Reform*, unpublished report, August 2001

Cretney, S, *Family Law*, 3rd edn, 1997, London: Sweet & Maxwell, Chapter 2

Diduck, A and Kaganas, F, *Family Law, Gender and the State: Text, Cases and Materials*, 1999, Oxford: Hart, Chapter 2, 'Love and marriage'

CHAPTER 4: LEGAL CONSEQUENCES OF MARRIAGE AND COHABITATION

Allardice, M, *Middle Class Cohabitants: s 15 and Schedule 1 of the Children Act 1989*, Family *Affairs*, Newsletter of the Family Law Bar Association, Spring 2002

Barlow, A and Josiah-Lake, D, *Cohabitants and the Law*, 3rd edn, 2001, London: Butterworths

Barton, C and Hibbs, M, *Questions and Answers on Family Law*, 2nd edn, 1998, London: Blackstone, Chapter 2, Question 3, 'Do you approve of the legal differences between marriage and cohabitation?' and Chapter 15, 'Domestic partnership contracts'

Clive, E, Eekelaar, J and Maclean, M (eds), *A Reader on Family Law*, 1994, Oxford: OUP, Chapter 3.1, 'Marriage: an unnecessary legal concept?'

Cretney, S, *Family Law*, 3rd edn, 1997, London: Sweet & Maxwell, 'Introduction'

Cretney, S and Masson, J, *Principles of Family Law*, 6th edn, 1997, London: Sweet & Maxwell, Chapter 3

Davies, C, 'Cohabitation contracts' (2001) SFLA Review, Issue 87

Deech, R, *Divorce Dissent, Dangers in Divorce Reform*, 1994, Policy Study No 136, London: Centre for Policy Studies

Diduck, A and Kaganas, F, *Family Law, Gender and the State: Text, Cases and Materials*, 1999, Oxford: Hart, Chapter 1.VII, 'Marriage as contract?' and Chapter 2.VIII, 'Alternatives to formal marriage: marriage versus cohabitation?'

Dyson, H, 'Autres temps, autres moeurs' (2000) 144 SJ 25

Gouriet, M, 'Cohabitants' rights: an update' (2001) SFLA Review, Issue 87

Griffiths, J, 'Grown up laws for the 21st century – opting for partnership recognition' (2002) SFLA Review, Issue 92

Hale, B *et al*, 'The legal structure of marriage', in Hoggett *et al*, *The Family, Law and Society: Cases and Materials*, 5th edn, 2002, London: Butterworths, Chapter 2

Karsten, I, 'Atypical families and the Human Rights Act: the rights of unmarried fathers, same sex couples and transsexuals' [1999] EHRLR 195

Levy, D, 'Cohabitation and the law: an overview' (2000) 144 SJ 26

Lowe, N and Douglas, G, *Bromley's Family Law*, 1998, London: Butterworths, Chapter 1, 'Section B. Trends in family law'

Mansfield, P, 'Brides and grooms – an endangered species?' (2002) SFLA Review, Issue 92

Mee, J, *The Property Rights of Cohabitees*, 1999, Oxford: Hart

Parker, S and Dewar, J, *Cohabitants*, 4th edn, 1995, London: Sweet & Maxwell

Parry, M, *The Law Relating to Cohabitants*, 3rd edn, 1993, London: Sweet & Maxwell

Roberts, C, 'Cohabitation, some reflections on developments' (2002) SFLA Review, Issue 92

Rodgers, H, 'Fairness for families, making the case for change, proposals for reform of the law on cohabitation, Mrs Burns revisited' (2001) SFLA Review, Issue 87

Rodgers, H, 'Cohabitation debate moves to Westminster' (2002) SFLA Review, Issue 92

Standley, K, *Family Law*, 3rd edn, 2001, Basingstoke: Palgrave Law Masters, Chapter 3

Wardle, L, 'Cohabitation and registered partnership in Scandinavia – the legal position of homosexuals', in Eekelaar, J and Nhlapo, T (eds), *The Changing Family*, 1998, Oxford: Hart, Chapter 24

Wood, H, Lush, D and Bishop, D, *Cohabitation, Law, Practice and Precedent*, 2001, Bristol: Jordan

CHAPTER 5: THE UNMARRIED FAMILY

Bailey-Harris, R, *Dividing the Assets on Family Breakdown*, 1998, Bristol: Jordan

Bailey-Harris, R (ed), *The Family Lawyers Handbook,* 1997, London: Law Society, Chapter 6, 'The unmarried family: property rights'

Barlow, A, *Cohabitants and the Law*, 2nd edn, 1997, London: Butterworths

Craig, J (ed), *Cohabitation, Law and Precedents*, 2001, London: Sweet & Maxwell

Parry, M, *The Law Relating to Cohabitants*, 3rd edn, 1993, London: Sweet & Maxwell

Diduck, A and Kaganas, F, *Family Law, Gender and the State: Text, Cases and Materials*, 1999, Oxford: Hart, Chapter 13, 'Making ends meet' and Chapter 15, 'Children in non-marital relationships'

Wood, H, Lush, D and Bishop, D, *Cohabitation, Law, Practice and Precedent*, 2001, Bristol: Jordan

CHAPTER 6: HISTORICAL INTRODUCTION TO DIVORCE

Bird, R and Cretney, S, *Divorce: The New Law*, 1996, Bristol: Jordan

Bromley, PM, Lowe, N and Douglas, G, *Bromley's Family Law*, 9th edn, 1998, London: Butterworths, Chapter 7, 'Divorce'

Cretney, S and Masson, J, *Principles of Family Law*, 6th edn, 1997, London: Sweet & Maxwell, Chapter 12, 'Divorce'

Hale, B *et al*, 'Divorce', in Hoggett *et al*, *The Family, Law and Society: Cases and Materials*, 5th edn, 2002, London: Butterworths, Chapter 6

Hale, B *et al*, 'Adjudication and mediation', in Hoggett *et al*, *The Family, Law and Society: Cases and Materials*, 5th edn, 2002, London: Butterworths, Chapter 7

Sclater, S and Piper, C, *Undercurrents of Divorce*, 1999, Aldershot: Ashgate

Standley, K, *Family Law*, 3rd edn, 2001, Basingstoke: Palgrave Law Masters, Chapter 7, 'The development of divorce law', and articles cited therein

Standley, K, *Cases and Materials on Family Law*, 1997, London: Blackstone, Chapter 4, 'Divorce'

CHAPTER 7: THE MODERN LAW OF DIVORCE

Clout, I, *The Matrimonial Lawyer: A Survival Guide*, 2001, Bristol: Jordan

Hayes, M and Williams, C, *Family Law, Principles, Policy and Practice*, 2nd edn, 1999, London: Butterworths, Chapter 7, 'Ending a marriage'

Hodson, D and Green, M, 'Brussels II: the new divorce forms' (2001) SFLA Review, Issue 90

Inns of Court School of Law, *Family Law in Practice*, 2002, Oxford: OUP

Parker, D, Sax, R, Ray, P and Franklin, J (eds), *Know-How for Family Lawyers*, 1993, London: Sweet & Maxwell

Rayden, W and Jackson, J, *Divorce and Family Matters*, 17th edn, plus looseleaf supplement, 1997, London: Butterworths

Robins, J, 'Totally divorced from reason' (2001) 15 The Lawyer 14

Standley, K, *Family Law*, 3rd edn, 2001, Basingstoke: Palgrave Law Masters, Chapter 8, 'Obtaining a divorce'

CHAPTER 8: THE GROUND FOR DIVORCE, ADULTERY AND BEHAVIOUR

Burgoyne, J, Ormrod, R and Richards, M, *Divorce Matters*, 1987, Harmondsworth: Penguin

See further references for Chapter 7

CHAPTER 9: DESERTION AND CONSTRUCTIVE DESERTION

See further references for Chapter 8

CHAPTER 10: THE SEPARATION DECREES

Salter, D, *Pensions and Marriage Breakdown*, 2nd edn, 2000, Bristol: Jordan

See further references for Chapters 7 and 8

CHAPTER 11: DIVORCE PROCEDURE

Bond, T, Black, J and Bridge, J, *Legal Practice Course Guides: Family Law*, 8th edn, 2002, London: Blackstone

Clout, I, *The Matrimonial Lawyer: A Survival Guide*, 2001, Bristol: Jordan

Deech, R, 'Divorce law and empirical studies' (1990) 106 LQR 229

Inns of Court School of Law, *Family Law in Practice*, 2002, Oxford: OUP, Chapter 4, 'The divorce process'

Parker, D, Sax, R, Ray, P and Franklin, J (eds), *Know-How for Family Lawyers*, 1993, London: Sweet & Maxwell

CHAPTER 12: ANCILLARY RELIEF: THE BASIC LAW

Bailey-Harris, R, *Dividing the Assets on Family Breakdown*, 1998, Bristol: Jordan

Bailey-Harris, R (ed), *The Family Lawyer's Handbook*, 1999, London: The Law Society, Chapter 2, 'Ancillary relief'

Diduck, A and Kaganas, F, *Family Law, Gender and the State: Text, Cases and Materials*, 1999, Oxford: Hart, Chapter 5, 'Household economics' and Chapter 6, 'Equality: dividing the family assets'

Duckworth, P, *Matrimonial Property and Finance*, 2001, Bristol: Jordan

Duckworth, P and Reads, G, *The Family Finance Toolkit*, 2001, Bristol: Jordan

Hale, B *et al*, 'Family economics – income', in Hoggett *et al*, *The Family, Law and Society*, 5th edn, 2002, London: Butterworths, Chapter 3

Inns of Court School of Law, *Family Law in Practice*, 2002, Oxford: OUP, Chapter 5, 'Financial provision on divorce'

Wildblood, S and Eaton, D, *Financial Provision in Family Matters*, 2000, London: Sweet & Maxwell

CHAPTER 13: QUANTUM, VARIATION AND APPEALS OUT OF TIME

Mostyn, N and Rae, M, *Quantum Skip*, 2001, London: Family Law Bar Association, Class Publishing

Mostyn, N and Singer, P, *Capitalise*, 2001, London: Family Law Bar Association, Class Publishing

Mostyn, N *et al*, *At A Glance, 2001–02*, 2001, London: Family Law Bar Association, Class Publishing

Mostyn, N *et al*, *At A Glance, 2002–03*, 2002, London: Family Law Bar Association, Class Publishing

See further references for Chapter 12

CHAPTER 14: ANCILLARY RELIEF PROCEDURE

Bird, R, *Ancillary Relief Handbook*, 3rd edn, 2002, Bristol: Jordan

Clout, I, *The Matrimonial Lawyer: A Survival Guide*, 2001, Bristol: Jordan

See further references for Chapters 12 and 13

CHAPTER 15: CHILD SUPPORT

Hale, B *et al*, 'Family economics – income', in Hoggett *et al*, *The Family, Law and Society: Cases and Materials*, 2002, London: Butterworths, Chapter 3

Hershman, D and McFarlane, A, *Children Law and Practice*, 1991, Bristol: Jordan

Hershamn, D and McFarlane, A, *Children Act Handbook*, 2001, Bristol: Jordan

Inns of Court School of Law, *Family Law in Practice*, 2002, Oxford: OUP, Chapter 6, 'Financial provision for children'

Mostyn, N, *Child's Pay and Child's Pay Bulletin*, 2001 and annual update, London: Family Law Bar Association, Class Publishing

CHAPTER 16: THE MATRIMONIAL HOME

Duffield, N and Theobald, J, *Family Law and Practice*, 2001/02, Bristol: Jordan

Inns of Court School of Law, *Family Law in Practice*, 2002, Oxford: OUP, Chapter 5, 'Financial provision on divorce'

Reekie, P and Tuddeham, R, *Family Law and Practice*, 2nd edn, 1990, London: Sweet & Maxwell, Chapter 11.21, 'Specimen orders'

See further references for Chapters 12–14

CHAPTER 17: PREVENTING EVASION OF LIABILITY OR ENFORCEMENT OF ORDERS

Bromley, PM, Lowe, N and Douglas, G, *Bromley's Family Law*, 9th edn, 1998, London: Butterworths, Chapter 18.F, 'Enforcement'

CHAPTER 18: WELFARE BENEFITS AND TAX

Duffield, N and Theobald, J, *Family Law and Practice*, 2001/02, Bristol: Jordan, Chapter 5, 'Tax' and Chapter 6, 'Welfare and housing'

Inns of Court School of Law, *Family Law in Practice*, 2002, Oxford: OUP, Chapter 7, 'Relevant principles of taxation'

CHAPTER 19: FINANCIAL PROVISION WITHOUT A DECREE OF DIVORCE, NULLITY OR JUDICIAL SEPARATION

Bromley, PM, Lowe, N and Douglas, G, *Bromley's Family Law*, 9th edn, 1998, London: Butterworths, Chapter 17, 'Financial support for members of the family'

Inns of Court School of Law, *Family Law in Practice*, 2002, Oxford: OUP, Chapter 3, 'Applications for financial provision where no divorce is sought'

Jackson, J, *Splitting Up Precedents*, 1999, London: Sweet & Maxwell

Solicitors Family Law Association, *Agreements Between Husband and Wife*, 1993, Orpington: SFLA

CHAPTER 20: PROTECTING THE HOME AND CONTENTS ON MARRIAGE BREAKDOWN

Bond, T, Black, J and Bridge, J, *Legal Practice Course Guides: Family Law*, 8th edn, 2002, London: Blackstone, Chapter 21, 'The home: preventing a sale or a mortgage'

Duckworth, P, *Matrimonial Property and Finance*, 2001, Bristol: Jordan

Pawlowski, M and Brown, J, *Undue Influence and the Family Home*, 2002, London: Cavendish Publishing

Price, L, Schmitz, D and Nield, S, *Undue Influence after Royal Bank of Scotland v Etridge*, Seminar, University of Southampton, 6 December 2001

CHAPTER 21: OWNERSHIP OF THE HOME AND CONTENTS OUTSIDE DIVORCE PROCEEDINGS

Cretney, S and Masson, J, *Principles of Family Law*, 1997, London: Sweet & Maxwell, Pt II, 'Family Property', Chapters 4–6

Hayes, M and Williams, C, *Family Law, Principles, Policy and Practice*, 2nd edn, 1999, London: Butterworths, Chapter 9, 'Money and property for unmarried partners'

Herring, J (ed), *Family Law: Issues, Debates, Policy*, 2001, Cullompton: Willan, Chapter 2, 'Division of property upon relationship breakdown'

Solicitors Family Law Association Training Committee, *Training Committee Roadshow 2001, Do I Get Half? Section 25 After White*, 2001, Orpington: SFLA

CHAPTER 22: DOMESTIC PARTNERSHIP BREAKDOWN IN THE 21ST CENTURY

Bird, R and Cretney, S, *Divorce: The New Law, The Family Law Act 1996*, 1996, Bristol: Jordan

Bradley, D, *Family Law and Political Culture*, 1996, London: Sweet & Maxwell

Bromley, PM, Katz, S, Eekelaar, J and Maclean, M, *Cross Currents: Family Law and Policy in the US and England*, 2000, Oxford: OUP

Burton, F, *Guide to the Family Law Act 1996*, 1996, London: Cavendish Publishing

Davis, G and Murch, M, *Grounds for Divorce*, 1988, Oxford: Clarendon

Deech, R, *Divorce Dissent, Dangers in Divorce Reform*, 1994, London: Centre for Policy Studies

Eekelaar, J and Maclean, M, *Family Lawyers, The Divorce Work of Solicitors*, 2000, Oxford: Hart

Eekelaar, J and Maclean, M, *A Reader on Family Law*, 1994, Oxford: OUP, Chapter 6.2, 'Alternative dispute resolution and divorce: natural experimentation in family law'

Freeman, M (ed), *Divorce: Where Next*, 1996, Aldershot: Dartmouth

Hale, B, *Choice and Regulation in Private Life*, 1996, London: Sweet & Maxwell

Herring, J (ed), *Family Law: Issues, Debates, Policy*, 2001, Cullompton: Willan, Chapter 1, 'Marriage and divorce: the regulation of intimacy'

Sclater, S and Piper, C, *Undercurrents of Divorce*, 1999, Aldershot: Ashgate

CHAPTER 23: DOMESTIC VIOLENCE

Bird, R, *Domestic Violence, The New Law, Part IV of the Family Law Act 1996*, 1996, Bristol: Jordan

Burton, F, *Guide to the Family Law Act 1996*, 1996, London: Cavendish Publishing

Herring, J (ed), *Family Law: Issues, Debates, Policy*, 2001, Cullompton: Willan, Chapter 3, 'Domestic violence'

Horton, M, *Family Homes and Domestic Violence, The New Legislation*, 1996, London: Family Law and Tax (Pearson)

Lawson-Cruttenden, T, and Addison, N, *Blackstone's Guide to the Protection from Harassment Act 1997*, 1997, London: Blackstone

CHAPTER 24: THE CHILDREN ACT 1989

Barton, C and Douglas, G, *Law and Parenthood*, 1995, London: Butterworths

Bevan, H, *Child Law*, 1989, London: Butterworths

Bromley, PM, Katz, S, Eekelaar, J and Maclean, M, *Cross Currents: Family Law and Policy in the US and England*, 2000, Oxford: OUP

Cretney, S and Masson, J, *Principles of Family Law*, 1997, London: Sweet & Maxwell, Chapter 18, 'Children' and Chapter 19, 'Parents'

Herring, J (ed), *Family Law: Issues, Debates, Policy*, 2001, Cullompton: Willan, Chapter 4, 'Parents and children'

Thorpe, M and Cowton, C (eds), *Delight and Dole, The Children Act 10 Years On*, Papers from the President of the Family Division's Fourth Interdisciplinary Conference, September 2001, Jane Fortin, Plenary 2: Children's Rights and the Impact of Two International Conventions, 2002, Bristol: Jordan

Fortin, J, *Children's Rights and the Developing Law*, 1998, London: Butterworths

Hale, B, 'Parents and children', in Hoggett *et al*, *The Family, Law and Society: Cases and Materials*, 5th edn, 2002, London: Butterworths, Chapter 10

Hayes, M and Williams, C, *Family Law, Principles, Policy and Practice*, 2nd edn, 1999, London: Butterworths, Chapters 1 and 2

Lowe, N and Douglas, G, *Bromley's Family Law*, 9th edn, 1998, London: Butterworths, Chapters 8–12

CHAPTER 25: THE CHILDREN ACT 1989: THE S 8 ORDERS

Children Act Sub-Committee of the Lord Chancellor's Advisory Board on Family Law, *Making Contact Work*, Consultation Paper, March 2001

See further references for Chapter 24

CHAPTER 26: THE CHILDREN ACT 1989: THE PUBLIC LAW ORDERS

Inns of Court School of Law, *Family Law in Practice*, 2002, Oxford: OUP, Chapter 7, 'Children', especially the 7.24 case study

Herring, J (ed), *Family Law: Issues, Debate, Policy*, 2001, Cullompton: Willan, Chapter 5, 'Public law children's cases: whose decision is it anyway?'

See further references for Chapters 24 and 25

CHAPTER 27: WARDSHIP AND THE INHERENT JURISDICTION

Bainham, A, 'The Children Act 1989: the future of wardship' [1990] Fam Law 270

Law Commission Working Paper, *Wards of Court*, Law Com No 101, 1987, London: HMSO

Lowe, N, 'The role of wardship in child care cases' [1989] Fam Law 38

See further references for Chapter 24

CHAPTER 28: CHILD ABDUCTION

Beaumont, P and McEleavy, P, *Hague Convention on International Child Abduction*, 1999, Oxford: OUP

Freeman, M *et al*, *Occasional Papers*, 2001, London: Reunite

Hutchinson, A *et al*, *International Parental Child Abduction*, 1998, Bristol: Jordan

Websites

www.offsol.demon.co.uk/caunitfm.htm (Child Abduction Unit (Official Solicitor's Department of the Lord Chancellor's Department))

www.reunite.org (Reunite (National Council for Abducted Children))

CHAPTER 29: ADOPTION

Barton, C, 'Adoption – the Prime Minister's review' [2000] Fam Law 731

Department of Health and Welsh Office, *Adoption – A Service for Children: Adoption Bill – A Consultative Document*, 1996, London: HMSO

Herring, J (ed), *Family Law: Issues, Debates, Policy*, 2001, Cullompton: Willan, Chapter 6, 'Adoption law: a balance of interests'

Richards, M, *Adoption*, 1989, Bristol: Jordan

Standley, K, *Family Law*, 3rd edn, 2001, Basingstoke: Palgrave Law Masters

CHAPTER 30: HUMAN ASSISTED REPRODUCTION

Bainham, A et al, *What is a Parent? A Socio-Legal Analysis*, 1999, Oxford: Hart

Barton, C and Douglas, G, *Law and Parenthood*, 1995, London: Butterworths

Douglas, G, *Law, Fertility and Reproduction*, 1991, London: Sweet & Maxwell

Douglas, G, 'Assisted reproduction and the welfare of the child', in Freeman, M and Hepple, B (eds), *Current Legal Problems*, 1993, Oxford: OUP

Glendon, M, *Abortion and Divorce in Western Law*, 1989, Cambridge, Mass: Harvard UP

Human Fertilisation and Embryology Authority, *Code of Practice*, Second Revision, 1995, London: HFEA

Lee, R and Morgan, D, *Human Fertilisation and Embryology, Regulating the Reproductive Revolution*, 2001, London: Blackstone

Seymour, J, *Childbirth and the Law*, 2000, Oxford: OUP

Warnock Committee, *Report of the Committee of Inquiry into Human Fertilisation and Embryology*, Cmnd 9314 (the Warnock Report), 1984, London: HMSO

Williams, G, *Textbook of Criminal Law*, 2nd edn, 1983, London: Stevens

INDEX